ENCYCLOPAEDIA OF
INDIAN PHILOSOPHY

Encyclopaedia of
Indian Philosophy

Volume 2

Dr. Vraj Kumar Pandey

ANMOL PUBLICATIONS PVT. LTD.
NEW DELHI - 110 002 (INDIA)

ANMOL PUBLICATIONS PVT. LTD.
H.O.: 4374/4B, Ansari Road, Darya Ganj
New Delhi-110 002 (India)
Ph.: 23278000, 23261597

B.O.: No. 1015, Ist Main Road, BSK IIIrd Stage
IIIrd Phase, IIIrd Block
Bangalore - 560 085 (India)
Visit us at: www.anmolpublications.com

Encyclopaedia of Indian Philosophy

First Published, 2007

ISBN 81-261-3112-8 (Set)

PRINTED IN INDIA

Printed at Mehra Offset Press, Delhi.

CONTENTS

Preface

India is the home of Philosophy, Religion and Spirituality. Every age, she provides the world with her armies of spiritual masters. She uses every means to reach the people of various parts of the world to enlighten them to the grand avenues of a meaningful life.

In India, *spirituality* is basically tuning one's mind to consider one's self and others as different from the gross physical body and the subtle mental body, and to be beyond the limitations of space, time and causation. *Philosophy* is the theory aspect and *religion* is the practical aspect of this principle.

The beauty of the Indian philosophy is the grand unification of a *Metaphysical God* who is the Absolute Reality and the substratum of all existence, and a *Personal God* who is the basis of all morality, ethics and the inspiration to lead a meaningful life. This grand unification makes the Indian religious temper one of the most tolerant and all consuming of the religions, and also the mother of many religions of the world today.

The Indian view is to see all religions as various ways to reach the same goal of manifesting the intrinsic divinity in man. So a follower of the Indian spiritual tradition accepts all religions to be true and suited for people with various mental structures, if followed in the right spirit. This was explicitly demonstrated by Sri Ramakrishna (1836-1886) in his life. He took up various religions and spiritual paths like Vaishnavism, Shaaktha, Advaitism, Christianity and Islam, one after the other, one at a time, followed them in full ernest and showed that they all lead to the same goal

This extensive survey of topics in modern philosophy presents the ideas, theses, and arguments themselves; and the latter is a study guide that elucidates details, suggests topics for discussion, and names readings that expand the main text. The book is clearly written and well proportioned.

Dr. Vraj Kumar Pandey

1

BHAKTI PHILOSOPHY

The Bhakti Movement was essentially founded in South India and later spread to the North during the late medieval period. The notion of 'Bhakti' (loosely translated as devotional love to God) is of antiquity. A nascent consciousness of what 'Bhakti' constitutes is already to be found in the earliest Vedas, especially in relation to deities such as Varuna. A clearer expression of Bhakti began to be formed during the so-called Epic Period and the Puranic periods of Hindu history. Texts such as the Bhagavad Gita and the BhagavatQurana PuFrana clearly explore Bhakti Yoga or the Path of Devotion as a means to salvation.

The Bhakti Movement itself is a historical-spiritual phenomenon that crystallized in South India during Late Antiquity. It was spearheaded by devotional mystics (later revered as Hindu saints) who extolled devotion and love to God as the chief means of spiritual perfection. The Bhakti movement in South India was spearheaded by the sixty-three Nayanars (Shaivite devotees) and the twelve Alvars (Vaishnavaite devotees).

Among the earliest Shaivite mystics was Karaikkal Amaiyar, who probably lived around the late 5th century AD or perhaps the early 6th century. She was said to be a contemporary of the Vaishnavaite saints Bhuttalwar and Peialwar. Kannapa Nayanar was also an early Shaiva Bhakti saint. But most famous among the Shaiva Bhakti saints were the 'Nalvar' (The Four Eminent Ones), namely Sundarar, Appar, Sambandar and Manikkavasagar. Their devotional hymns are ecstatic, lyrical and moving.

The Vaishnavaite Bhakti movement was contemporaneous with the Shaiva Bhakti movement. The hymns of the twelve alvars are held together as the 'Nalayira Divya Prabandham' and recited (as are the Shaiva texts) in temple rituals. Whilst all the saints are held in great reverence, Andal (or Goda-devi) in particular holds a special place among the Vaishnava saints. Not only is she the only female Vaishnava saint but also her hymns are among the best expressions of bridal mysticism in the Hindu religion.

The twelve Alvars and the sixty-three Nayanars nurtured the incipient bhakti movement in South India under the Pallavas and Pandyas in the fifth to seventh centuries AD. They constitute [South India's 75 Apostles of Bhakti] and were greatly influential in determining the expression of faith in South India. The path of devotion as expounded by these mystics would later be incorporated into Ramanuja and Madhva philosophical systems.

During the 12th and 13th centuries A.D., the Virashaiva movement and, during the rule of the Vijayanagar Empire in South India, the Haridasa movement spread from present-day Karnataka. The Virashaiva movement spread the philosophy of Basavanna, a Hindu reformer. The seeds of Carnatic music were sown, and the philosophy of Madhvacharya was propogated by the Kannada Haridasas. The Haridasa movement presented, like the Virashaiva movement, another strong current of Bhakti, pervading the lives of millions. The Haridasas presented two groups – Vyasakuta and Dasakuta. The former were required to be proficient in the Vedas, Upanishads and other Darshanas, while the Dasakuta merely conveyed the message of Madhvacharya through the Kannada language to the people. The philosophy of Madhvacharya was preserved and perpetuated by his eminent disciples like Vyasatirtha or Vyasaraja Naraharitirtha, Vadirajatirtha, Sripadaraya, Jayathirtha and others. In the fifteenth century, the Haridasa movement took shape under Sripadaraya of Mulbagal; but his disciple Vyasatirtha provided it a strong organizational base. He was intimately associated with the Vijayanagar Empire, where he became a great moral and spiritual force. His eminent disciples were Purandaradasa and Kanakadasa.

The late Bhakti movement led to the proliferation of regional poetic literature in the various vernacular languages of India. The Bhakti movement in what is now Karnataka resulted in a burst of poetic Kannada literature in praise of Lord Vishnu. Some of its leaders include Purandara Dasa and Kanaka Dasa, whose contributions were essential to Carnatic music. The later Carnatic Trinity is also no doubt a product of this long Bhakti Movement.

The Bhakti movement began to spread to the North during the late medieval ages when North India was under Muslim domination. There was no grouping of the mystics into Shaiva and Vaishnava devotees as it was in the South. The movement was spontaneous and the various mystics had their own version of devotional expression. Unlike in the South where devotion was centered on both Shiva and Vishnu (in all his forms), the Northern devotional movement was more or less centered on Rama and Krishna, both of whom were incarnations of Vishnu. Though this did not mean that the cult of Shiva or of the Devi went into decline. In fact for all of its history the Bhakti movement co-existed peacefully with the other movements in Hinduism. It was initially considered unorthodox as it rebelled against caste distinctions and made disregarded Brahmanic rituals which according to Bhakti saints not necessary for salvation. In the course of time however, owing to its immense popularity among the masses (and even royal patronage) it became 'orthodox' and continues to be one of the most important modes of religious expression in modern India.

In the period between the 14-17th centuries, a great bhakti movement swept through Northern India initiated by a loosely associated group of teachers or 'Sants'. Chaitanya, Vallabha, Meera Bai, Kabir, Tulsi Das, Tukaram and other mystics spearheaded the Bhakti movement in the North. Their teachings were that people could cast aside the heavy burdens of ritual and caste and the subtle complexities of philosophy and simply express their overwhelming love for God. This period was also characterised by a spate of devotional literature in vernacular prose and poetry in the ethnic languages of the various Indian states or provinces.

As aforementioned whilst many of the Bhakti mystics focused their attention on Krishna or Rama, it did not necessarily mean that the cult of Shiva was marginalised. The growth of the Vira-Shaiva and the older Shaiva Siddhanta schools in this period, which incorporated Bhakti into their teachings are testimony to the growth of the Shaiva faith in this period. In the thirteenth century Basava founded the Vira-Shaiva school or Virashaivism. He rejected the caste system, denied the supremacy of the Brahmins, condemned ritual sacrifice and insisted on bhakti and the worship of the one God, Shiva. His followers were called Vira-Shaivas, meaning "stalwart Shiva-worshippers".

The Saiva-Siddhanta school is a form of Shaivism (Shiva worship) found in the south and is of hoary antiquity. It incorporates the teachings of the erstwhile Shaiva nayanars and espouses the belief that Shiva is Brahman and his infinite love is revealed in the divine acts of the creation, preservation and destruction of the universe, and in the liberation of the soul.

Seminal Bhakti works in Bengali include the many songs of Ramprasad Sen. His pieces (known as Shyama Sangeet, or Songs of the Dark Mother) are still actively sung today in West Bengal. Coming from the 17th century, they cover an astonishing range of emotional responses to Ma Kali, detailing complex philosophical statements based on Vedanta teachings and more visceral pronouncements of his love of Devi. Using inventive allegory, Ramprasad had 'dialogues' with the Mother Goddess through his poetry, at times chiding her, adoring her, celebrating her as the Divine Mother, reckless consort of Shiva and capricious Shakti, the universal female creative energy, of the cosmos.

Rama Bhakti

The leader of the bhakti movement focusing on the Lord as Rama was Ramananda. Very little is known about him, but he is believed to have lived in the first half of the 15th century. He taught that Lord Rama is the supreme Lord, and that salvation could be attained only through love for and devotion to him, and through the repetition of his sacred name.

Ramananda's ashram in Varanasi became a powerful centre of religious influence, from which his ideas spread far and wide among all classes of Indians. One of the reasons for his great popularity was that he renounced Sanskrit and used the language of the people for the composition of his hymns. This paved the way for the modern tendency in northern India to write literary texts in local languages.

Devotees of Krishna worship Him in different mellows, known as rasas. Two major systems of Krishna worship developed, each with its own philosophical system. These two moods as called aishwaryamaya bhakti and madhuryamaya bhakti. Aishwaryamaya bhakti is revealed in the abode of queens and kingdom of Krishna in Dwaraka. Madhuryamaya Bhakti is revealed in the abode of braja.

Thus krishna is variously worshipped according to the development of devotee's taste in worshipping the Supreme Personality of Godhead, Sri Krishna, as father, friend, master, beloved and many different varieties which are all extraordinary. Krishna is famous as Makhanchor, or butterthief. He loved to eat butter and is the beloved of his little village in Gokul. These are all transcendental descriptions. Thus they are revealed to the sincere devotees in proportion to the development in their love of Godhead.

Shri Madhvacharya (1238-1317) identified God with Vishnu. His view of reality is purely dualistic in that he understood a fundamental differentiation between the ultimate Godhead and the individual soul, and the system is therefore called Dvaita (dualistic) Vedanta. Madhva is considered one of the influential theologians in Hindu history. His influence was profound, and he is one of the fathers of the Vaishnava Bhakti movement. Great leaders of the Vaishnava Bhakti movement in Karnataka like Purandara Dasa, Kanaka Dasa, Raghavendra Swami and many others were influenced by Dvaita traditions.

Vallabhacharya (1479-1531) called his system of thought Shuddhadvaita (pure monism). According to him, it is by God's grace alone that one can obtain release from bondage and attain Krishna's heaven. This heaven is far above the "heavens" of Brahma, Vishnu and Shiva, for Krishna is himself the eternal Brahman.

Chaitanya Mahaprabhu (1486-1534) defined his system of philosophy as Achintya Bheda-Bheda (inconceivable and simultaneous oneness and difference). It synthesizes elements of monism and dualism into a single system. Chaitanya's philosophy is taught by the contemporary International Society for Krishna Consciousness, better known as the *Hare Krishna* movement.

Srimanta Sankardeva (1449-1568) named his religion *ek sarana naam dharma* and propagated it in Assam. An example of *dasa bhakti*, in this form there was no place for Radha. The most important symbol of this religion is the *naamghor* or prayer hall, which dot Assam's landscape. This form of worship is very strong in Assam today, and much of the traditions are maintained by the monastries called *Satras*.

Vaishnava Bhakti

Prominent historical personalities include:

- Ramanuja
- Nimbarka
- Madhva
- Vallabha
- Chaitanya

Influences: Beyond the confines of such formal schools and movements, however, the development of bhakti as a major form of Hindu practice has left an indelible stamp on the faith. Philosophical speculation was concern for the minority, and even the great Advaitist scholar Adi Shankaracharya, when questioned as to the way to God, said that chanting the name of the lord, was essential. The philosophical schools changed the way people thought, but Bhakti was immediately accessible to all, calling to the instinct emotion of love and redirecting it to the highest pursuit of God and self-realization. In general a liberal movement, its denouncement of caste offered recourse for Hindus from the orthodox Brahaminical systems. Of course, however, Bhakti's message of tolerance and love was not often heeded by those ensconced in the societal construct of caste. Altogether, Bhakti resulted in a mass of devotional literature, music and art that has enriched the world and gave India renewed spiritual impetus, one eschewing unnecessary ritual and artificial social boundaries.

Sri Ramanuja Acharya: (traditionally dated 1017–1137 CE) was an Indian philosopher and is recognized as the most important saint of Sri Vaishnavism. He held the Vishishtadvaita or qualified Nondualist belief that the world and Brahman were united, like a soul and a body are. His version of Indian Nondualism differed from Adi Shankara's because he acknowledged the existence of differences, and believed that the identity of an object as a part was as important as the unity of the whole. The Vaishnava Theology espoused by Ramanuja posits that Brahman is not devoid of attributes but is expressed as a personal God, full of infinite good qualities, as Narayana. The Adishesha on whom Lord Ranganatha of Srirangam rests is believed to be Ramanuja.

Period : 1017 to 1137

Place of Birth : Sri Perumbudur, Tamil Nadu
Guru : Sri Periya Nambigal

Names : 1. Ilaya Perumal, As named by his parents 2. Lakshmana, Family name 3. Ramanuja.

Ramanuja was born Ilaya Perumal to a smartha brahmin family in the village of Perumbudur, Tamil Nadu, India in 1017 CE. His father was Keshava Somayaji Deekshitar and mother was Kanthimathi in sect of Vadama.From a young age, his intelligence and ability to comprehend highly abstract philosophical points were legendary. He took initiation from Yadavaprakasa, a renowned Advaitic scholar. Though his new guru was highly impressed with his analytical ability, he was quite concerned by how much emphasis Ramanuja placed on bhakti. After frequent clashes over interpretation, Yadavaprakasa decided the young Ramanuja was becoming too much of a threat and plotted a way to kill him. However, Ramanuja's cousin Govinda Bhatta (a favourite of Yadavaprakasa) discovered the plot and helped him escape. An alternative version is that one of Yadavaprakasa's students plotted to kill Ramanuja as a means of pleasing their teacher, but Sri Ramanuja escaped in the afore-mentioned manner. Yadavaprakasa was horrified when learnt about the conspiracy.

After renouncing the life of a house-holder, Ramanuja travelled to Srirangam to meet an aging Yamunacharya, the pre-eminent Vishishtadvaita philosopher of the time. Yamunacharya had died prior to Ramanuja's arrival, but had left three tasks for Ramanuja to carry out. Teach the doctrine of Saranagati (surrender) to God as the means to moksha. A Visishtadvaita Bhashya should be written for the Brahma Sutras of Vyasa which had previously been taught orally to the disciples of the Visishtadvaita philosophy. That the names of Parauara, the author of Vishnu Puraoa, and saint Uahakopa should be perpetuated.

Ramanuja pledged to God to do as he had been requested and accepted Yamunacharya as his *Manasika Acharya*. All three tasks were successfully completed.

Five Acharyas: Swami Ramanuja incorporated teachings from 5 different people who he considered to be his acharyas:

1. Peria Nambigal who performed his samasrayana
2. Thirukkotiyur Nambigal : who revealed the meaning of Charama slokam to swami on his 18th trip

3. Thirumalai Nambigal : Ramayana
4. Tirumalai Aandaan : Bhagavad Vishayam
5. Thirukachchi Nambigal : The 6 sentences or Perarulalan

Visishtadvaita Philosophy: Ramanuja's philosophy is referred to as Vishishtadvaita because it combines Advaita (oneness of God) with Vishesha (attributes). The philosophy is monotheistic.

Differences with Sankara: Adi Sankara had argued that all qualities or manifestations that can be perceived are unreal and temporary. They are a result of ignorance. Ramanuja believed them to be real and permanent and under the control of the Brahman. God can be one despite the existence of attributes, because they cannot exist alone; they are not independent entities. They are Prakaras or the modes, Sesha or the accessories, and Niyama or the controlled aspects, of the one Brahman.

In Sri Ramanuja's system of philosophy, the Lord (Narayana) has two inseparable Prakaras or modes, viz., the world and the souls. These are related to Him as the body is related to the soul. They have no existence apart from Him. They inhere in Him as attributes in a substance. Matter and souls constitute the body of the Lord. The Lord is their indweller. He is the controlling Reality. Matter and souls are the subordinate elements. They are termed Viseshanas, attributes. God is the Viseshya or that which is qualified.

History shows that the followers of Sankara are answerless till date to the strong arguments of Ramanuja (in his sri bhashya) and his followers (satadushani of desika,...). In a bid to escape strong objections raised by Ramanuja and his successors, most advaitins take a disguised route of neo vedantism, where they argue that vaishnavism is one another path to realise brahman. Ironically, the very brahman of Ramanuja and Sankara are different.

Ramanuja opines, wrong is the position of the Advaitins that understanding the Upanishads without knowing and practicing dharma can result in Brahman knowledge. The knowledge of Brahman that ends spiritual ignorance is meditational, not (as Advaitins seem to presume) testimonial or verbal.

In contrast to Sankara, Ramanuja holds, There is no knowledge source in support of the claim that there is a distinctionless (homogeneous) Brahman. All knowledge sources reveal objects as distinct from other objects. All experience reveals an object known in some way or other beyond mere existence. Testimony depends on the operation of distinct sentence parts (words with distinct meanings). Thus the claim that testimony makes known that reality is distinctionless is contradicted by the very nature of testimony as a knowledge means. Even the simplest perceptual cognition reveals something (Bessie) as qualified by something else (a broken hoof, "Bessie has a broken hoof," as known perceptually). Inference depends on perception and makes the same distinct things known as does perception.

Against the Advaita contention that perception cannot make known distinctness but only homogeneous being since distinctness cannot be defined, well, sorry, perception makes known generic characters (cowhood and the like) that differentiate things. If what you Advaitins say were true, why should not a person looking for a horse be satisfied with a buffalo? Remembering could not be distinguished from perceiving, because there would be only the one object (being). And no one would be deaf or blind. Furthermore, Brahman would be an object of perception and the other sources (prameya).

He also holds, The Advaitin argument about prior absences and no prior absence of consciousness is wrong. Similarly the Advaitin understanding of a-vidya (not-Knowledge), which is the absence of spiritual knowledge, is incorrect. "If the distinction between spiritual knowledge and spiritual ignorance is unreal, then spiritual ignorance and the self are one."

The Seven Objections to Shankara's Advaita: Ramanuja picks out what he sees as seven fundamental flaws in the Advaita philosophy for special attack: he sees them as so fundamental to the Advaita position that if he is right in identifying them as involving doctrinal contradictions, then Sankara's entire system collapses. He argues:

1. The nature of Avidya. Avidya must be either real or unreal; there is no other possibility. But neither of these is possible. If Avidya is real, non-dualism collapses into dualism. If it is unreal, we are driven to self-contradiction or infinite regress.
2. The incomprehensibility of Avidya. Advaitins claim that Avidya is neither real nor unreal but incomprehensible, {anirvacaniya.} All cognition is either of the real or the unreal: the Advaitin claim flies in the face of experience, and accepting it would call into question all cognition and render it unsafe.
3. The grounds of knowledge of Avidya. No pramana can establish Avidya in the sense the Advaitin requires. Advaita philosophy presents Avidya not as a mere lack of knowledge, as something purely negative, but as an obscuring layer which covers Brahman and is removed by true Brahma-vidya. Avidya is positive nescience not mere ignorance. Ramanuja argues that positive nescience is established neither by perception, nor by inference, nor by scriptural testimony. On the contrary, Ramanuja argues, all cognition is of the real.
4. The locus of Avidya. Where is the Avidya that gives rise to the (false) impression of the reality of the perceived world? There are two possibilities; it could be Brahman's Avidya or the individual soul's {jiva.} Neither is possible. Brahman is knowledge; Avidya cannot co-exist as an attribute with a nature utterly incompatible with it. Nor can the individual soul be the locus of Avidya: the existence of the individual soul is due to Avidya; this would lead to a vicious circle.
5. Avidya's obscuration of the nature of Brahman. Sankara would have us believe that the true nature of Brahman is somehow covered-over or obscured by Avidya. Ramanuja regards this as an absurdity: given that Advaita claims that Brahman is pure self-luminous consciousness, obscuration must mean either preventing the origination of this (impossible since Brahman is eternal) or the destruction of it-equally absurd.
6. The removal of Avidya by Brahma-vidya. Advaita claims that Avidya has no beginning, but it is terminated and removed by Brahma-vidya, the intuition of the reality of Brahman as pure, undifferentiated consciousness. But Ramanuja denies the existence of undifferentiated {nirguna} Brahman, arguing that whatever exists has attributes: Brahman has infinite auspicious attributes. Liberation is a matter of Divine Grace: no amount of learning or wisdom will deliver us.
7. The removal of Avidya. For the Advaitin, the bondage in which we dwell before the attainment of Moksa is caused by Maya and Avidya; knowledge of reality (Brahma-vidya) releases us. Ramanuja, however, asserts that bondage is real. No kind of knowledge can remove what is real. On the contrary, knowledge discloses the real; it does not destroy it. And what exactly is the saving knowledge that delivers us from bondage to Maya? If it is real then non-duality

collapses into duality; if it is unreal, then we face an utter absurdity.

He was critical of the caste system. He said, "Does the wearing of a sacred thread make one a Brahmin? One who is devoted to God (Narayana) alone is a Brahmin."

His Sarangati philosophy emphasises that anyone, irrespective of colour, creed, caste, sex and religion can surrender their mind, body and soul to the Lotus foot of Lord Narayana and the God would accept him/her.

Cited from Sri Ramanuja, His Life, Religion, and Philosophy, published by Sri Ramakrishna Math, Chennai, India.

Writings: Ramanuja's most famous work is known as the Sri Bhasya. It is a commentary on the Brahma Sutras. Gadhya Thrayam (three compositions)-Vaikunta, Sriranga and Saranagati Gadhyam are great works in Vaishnava philosophy.

His other works are:

- Vedanta Sara (essence of Vedanta)
- Vedanta Sangraha (a resume of Vedanta)
- Vedanta Deepa (the light of Vedanta).

An interesting point in Ramanuja's works is that, He happens to have composed all his works only in the Sanskrit language.

Brindavan: Ramanuja's thiruvarasu (tomb) is located in Srirangam, Tamil Nadu within the temple complex, where he attained his Acharyan Thiruvadi (the lotus foot of his Acharya). His Thirumeni is covered with chandan (sandalwood paste) and saffron, is open to the public.

Nimbarka: *Nimbarka,* is known for propagating the Vaishnava Theology of Dvaitaadvaita, duality in unity. He lived in the 13th Century and hailed from the present-day Andhra Pradesh.

Nimbarka's philosophical position is known as Dvaita-advaita or Bhedabheda. The categories of existence, according to him, are three, i.e., cit, acit, and Isvara. Cit and acit are different from Isvara, in the sense that they have attributes and capacities, which are different from those of Isvara. Isvara is independent and exists by Himself, while cit and acit have existence dependent upon Him. At the same time cit and acit are not different from Isvara, because they cannot exist independently of Him. Difference means a kind of existence which is separate but dependent, (para-tantra-satta-bhava) while non-difference means impossibility of independent existence.

Thus Nimbarka equally emphasises both difference and non-difference, as against Ramanuja, who makes difference subordinate to non-difference, in as much as, for him cit and acit do not exist separately from Brahman, but its body or attributes. Thus, according to Nimbarka, the relation between Brahman, on the one hand, and the souls (cit) and universe (acit) on the other, is a relation of natural difference-non-difference (svabhavika-bhedabheda), just like between snake and coil, or between sun and its rays. Just as the coil is nothing nut the snake, yet different from it, just as the different kinds of stones, though nothing but earth, are yet different from it, so the souls and the universe, though nothing but Brahman (brahmatmaka), are different from Him because of their own peculiar natures and attributes.

Thus, according to Nimbarka, there are three equally real and co-eternal realities, viz. Brahman, the cit and the acit. Brahman is the Controller (niyantr), the cit the enjoyer (bhoktr) and the acit the object enjoyed (bhogya).

Nimbarka accepts parinamavada to explain the cause of animate and inanimate world, which he says exist in a subtle form in the various capacities (saktis) which belong to Brahman in its natural condition. Brahman is the material cause of the universe in the sense that Brahman brings the subtle rudiments into the gross form by manifesting these capacities.

For Nimbarka the highest object of worship is Krishna and his consort Radha, attended by thousands of gopis, or cowherdesses, of the celestial Vrindavana. Devotion according to Nimbarka, consists in prapatti, or self-surrender.

1. *Brahman:* The Highest Reality, according to Nimbarka, is Brahman, Krishna or Hari, a personal God. There is nothing that is equal to Him, nothing that is superior. He is the Lord of all, and Controller of all. He is called Brahman because of the unsurpassed greatness of His nature and qualities, because He is beyond any limit of any kind of space, time or thing.

   Brahman is the sole cause of creation, maintenance and destruction of the Universe. All beings arise from Him, nothing that is superior to Him. The Lord alone is the first cause, the manifestos of all names and forms, and none else.

   This Brahman is both the upadana (material cause) and the Nimitta (efficient cause). It is the material cause in the sense that it enables its natural saktis, viz. the cit and the acit in their subtle forms, to be manifested in gross forms; and it is the efficient cause in the sense that it unites the individual souls with their respective fruits of actions and means of enjoyments.

   Nimbarka discusses two aspects of Brahman. On one hand, Brahman is eternal and great, the greatest of the great, the highest of the high, the creator, etc. of the Universe, high above the individual soul, of which He is the Lord and the ruler. But, on the other aspect He is the abode of infinite beauty, bliss and tenderness, and in intimate connection with the soul. He is the abode of supreme peace, supreme grace, and the ocean of all sweetness and charms. Thus, Brahman possessed of attributes and adorable by all, has four forms or vyuhas (ie., Vasudeva, Sankarsana, Pradyumna, and Aniruddha) and appears under various incarnation as Matsya, Kurma etc.

2. *Jiva (cit):* The cit or individual soul is of the nature of knowledge (jnana-svarupa); it is able to know without the help of the sense-organs and it is in this sense that words like prajnana-ghanah svayamjyotih jnanamayah etc. as applied to jiva are to be end erstood. The jiva is the knower also; and he can be both knowledge and the possessor of knowledge at the same time, just as the sun is both light and the source of light. Thus the soul, who is knowledge, and his attribute, knowledge, though they are both identical as knowledge, can be at the same time different and related as the qualified (dharmin) and the quality (dharma), just as the sun and his light, though identical as light (taijasa), are still different from each other. Thus there is both a difference and a non-difference between the dharmin and dharma; and the extreme similarity between them implies, not necessarily their absolute identity, but only a non-perception of their difference.

   The jiva is also ego (ahamarthah). This ego continues to persist not only in the state of deep sleep, (because our consciousness immediately after getting up from sleep has the form slept happily or knew nothing) but also in the state of liberation. It even belongs to the Parabrahman. Hence it is that Krishna refers to Himself so frequently in the first person in the Gita, of which the chief object is thus Purusottama, who is omniscient and at the same time non-different from the ego or asmadartha.

The jiva also essentially active (kartr). This quality belongs to it in all its conditions, even after release. But the kartrtva is not independent. The jiva is also enjoyer (bhoktr) essentially in all its conditions.

For his knowledge and activity, however, the jiva depends on Hari; thus, though resembling Him in being intelligent and knower, he is at the same time distinguished from him by his dependence. This quality of dependence or of being controlled (niyamyatva) is the very nature of jiva even in the state of release, just as niyamyatva or the quality of being the controller, forms the eternal nature of Isvara.

The jiva is atomic in size; at the same time his attribute, knowledge, is omni-present, which makes it possible that he can experience pleasure and pain in any part of the body, just as, for instance,. the light of a lamp can spread far and wide and illum ine objects away from the lamp. The Jivas are different and in different bodies, and so are infinite in number.

3. *Acit (the jagat):* The acit is of three different kinds: viz. prakrta, aprakrta, and kala. Prakrta, or what is derived from Prakrti, the primal matter, aprakrta is defined negatively as that which is not the product of prakrti, but its real nature is not clearly by ought out. These three categories in their subtle forms are as eternal as the cit or the individual souls.

   Prakrti, or the primal matter-the stuff of the entire universe is real and eternal like the individual souls, and like them, though eternal and unborn, has yet Brahman for its cause. It consists of the three qualities of sattva, rajas and tamas, such as prakrit, mahat, ahankara etc. (just similar to 24 principles of the Sankhyas).

4. *Bondage:* The jiva has his true form distorted and obscured owing to his contact with karma resulting from ignorance, which is beginningless, but which can come to an end, by the grace of God, when its true nature is fully manifested.

5. *Mukti:* To attain deliverance, the jiva has to commence with a complete submission to the Paramatman, or prapatti, whose six constituents are:-
   (a) a resolution to yield (anukulasya samkalpah)
   (b) the avoidance of opposition (pratikulasya varjanam)
   (c) faith that God will protect (raksisyati ity visvasah)
   (d) acceptance of him as saviour (goptrtva-varanam)
   (e) throwing one's whole soul upon him (atmaniksepah), and
   (f) a sense of helplessness (karpanya).

God's grace extends itself to those who are possessed of these 6 constituents of prapatti, who are prapanna; and by that grace is generated bhakti consisting of special live for him, which ultimately ends in the realisation of the Paramatman. For a devotee knowledge of the following 5 things is quite necessary:

(a) The nature of the supreme soul

(b) The nature of the individual soul

(c) the fruit of God s grace or moksa, (which is an uninterrupted realisation of the nature and attributes of Brahman, following from the absolute destruction of all action and the consequent extinction of all nescience)

(d) the feeling of enjoyment consequent on bhakti, and

(e) the nature of the obstacles in the way of the attainment of God, such as regarding the body and the mind as the soul, depending on someone who is neither God nor the preceptor, neglecting their commands, and considering God as nothing more than an ordinary being.

Sri Nimbarka also refers to 4 other methods of sadhanas:

(i) karma (performed conscientiously in a proper spirit, with one's varna and asrama thereby giving rise to knowledge which is a means to salvation),

(ii) vidya or knowledge (not as a subordinate factor of karma but as independent means),

(iii) upasana or dhyana (3 kinds):

(a) meditation on the Lord as one s self, i.e. meditation on the Lord as the Inner Controller of the sentient,

(b) meditation on the Lord as the Inner Controller of the nonsentient,

(c) meditation on Lord Himself, as different from the sentient and non-sentient.

Sri Nimvarkacharya made the first "Bhasya" of the Bramhasutra on His Dvaitadvaita Vedanta (Principle of Dualism-Nondualism) in his famous book "Vedanta Parijata Sourabha" and was born 5000 years ago. He was born even before Sri Sankaracharya. In the Bhasya of Nimbarkacharya he had not given any arguments to other bhasya. It is the enough to proof for the ancientness of his Bhasya. Now-a-days the one sect of disciples of Sri Nimvarka which is flown after Sri Swabhuram Devacharya known as Kathia Baba.

Madhva

- Madhvacharya, Vaishnavite saint and founder of Dvaita school of thought, at Pajaka, Udupi
- A person belonging to the Dvaita school of thought
- Madhvacharya, Vaishnavite saint and founder of Dvaita school of thought, at Pajaka, Udupi
- A person belonging to the Dvaita school of thought.

Vallabhacharya: (1479-1531) was the founder of the Vallabha sect in Indian philosophy. He called his system of thought Shuddhadvaita (pure monism). He was from a region that is currently in the Indian state of Andhra Pradesh, though the bulk of his fame lies in the region that is currently in the state of Gujarat.

Everything is Krishna's Leela: According to the version of Vaishnava Theology he espoused; the glorious Krishna in His sat-chid-ananda form is the Absolute Brahman. He is permanently playing out His sport (leela) from His seat in the goloka which is even beyond the divine Vaikuntha, the abode of Vishnu and Satya-loka, the abode of Brahma the Creator, and Kailas, the abode of Shiva. Creation is His sport.

Grace, the only Path in Kali Yuga: To obtain the Bliss given out by Krishna the only path is

Bhakti. But in this age of Kali, the scripture-sanctioned bhakti is impossible to practise. So what is recommended is pushti bhakti –which we can all get from the natural Grace of God just like that, for no reason whatsoever. This path is called 'pushti-maarg'.

Atma-nivedana: It is that bhakti which gives itself up body, heart and soul to the cause of God. It is considered to be the fullest expression of what is known as Atma-nivedana (= giving-up of oneself) among the nine forms of bhakti. It is the bhakti of the devotee who worships God not for any reward or presents but for His own sake. Such a devotee goes to Goloka after leaving this body and lives in eternal bliss enjoying the sports of the Lord. The classical example of this complete self-effacement is that of the cow-headesses towards Krishna. They spoke no word except prayer and they moved no step except towards Krishna. Their supreme-most meditation was on the lotus-feet of Krishna.Thus it is by God's grace alone that one can obtain release from bondage and attain Krishna's heaven, Goloka.

Ashta-chaap: Eight disciples of Vallabhacharya are called the ashta-chaap (eight reprints). Foremost among them was Surdas, the blind poet of Agra. These are Surdas, Krushnadas, Paramanand, Kumbhandas, Chaturbhuj, Nanddas, Chhitswami, Govinddas.

Chaitanya's Life: According to Chaitanya Charitamrita, Chaitanya was born as Visvambhar Mishra in 1486 as the second son of Jagannath Mishra and Sachi Devi in the town of Navadvipa in Nadiya, West Bengal, India. In his youth, Chaitanya was an erudite scholar, whose learning and skills in argumentation were next to none. Though religious at heart, Chaitanya did not display an active interest in the Vaishnava religion in his younger years.

A significant change in Chaitanya's life came about as he traveled to Gaya to perform the shraddha ceremony for his departed father. There he met his guru, the ascetic Ishvara Puri, from whom he received initiation with the Gopala Krishna mantra. Upon his return to Bengal, the local Vaishnavas, headed by Advaita Acharya, were stunned at his sudden change and soon recognized Chaitanya as the eminent leader of the Vaishnavas of the land of Nadiya.

After leaving his homeland in Bengal and becoming an ascetic, Chaitanya journeyed throughout the length and breadth of India for several years, chanting the names of Krishna constantly.

He spent the last 24 years of his life in Puri, Orissa, the great temple city of Jagannath. The king of Orissa, Maharaja Prataparudra, regarded him as Krishna incarnate and was an enthusiastic patron and devotee of the religion of Sri Chaitanya. It was during these years that Chaitanya sank deep into various meditational trances and performed pastimes of divine ecstasy.

Chaitanya's Tradition: Deities of Chaitanya Mahaprabhu (right) and Nityananda (left) at Radha-Krishna temple in Radhadesh, Belgium.

Despite having been initiated in the Madhvacharya tradition, Chaitanya founded a tradition of his own, having some marked differences with the practices and the theology of the followers of Madhvacharya. He is not known to have composed anything but a series of verses known as the Siksastaka, "eight verses of instruction".

He requested a select few among his followers, who later came to be known as the Six Gosvamis of Vrindavan, to systematically present the theology of bhakti he had taught in their writings. The six saints and theologians were Rupa Gosvami, Sanatana Gosvami, Gopala Bhatta Gosvami, Raghunatha

Bhatta Gosvami, Raghunatha Dasa Gosvami and Jiva Gosvami, a nephew of brothers Rupa and Sanatana. These individuals were responsible for systematizing Gaudiya Vaishnava Theology.

Narottama Dasa Thakur, Srinivasa Acarya and Syamananda Pandit were among the stalwarts of the second generation of Gaudiya Vaishnavism. Having studied under Jiva, they were instrumental in propagating the teachings of the Gosvamis throughout Bengal, Orissa and other regions of Eastern India. Many among their associates, such as Ramacandra Kaviraja and Ganga-narayana Cakravarti, were also eminent teachers in their own right.

The famous festival of Kheturi, presided over by Jahnava Thakurani, the wife of Nityananda Prabhu, was the first time the leaders of the various branches of Chaitanya's followers assembled together. Through such festivals, members of the loosely organized tradition became acquainted with other branches along with their respective theological and practical nuances. That notwithstanding, the tradition has maintained its plural nature, having no central authority to preside over its matters.

Around these times, the disciples and descendants of Nityananda and Advaita, headed by Virabhadra and Krishna Mishra respectively, started their family lineages (vamsa) to maintain the tradition. The vamsa descending from Nityananda through his son Virabhadra forms the most prominent branch of the modern Gaudiya tradition, though descendants of Advaita, along with the descendants of many other associates of Chaitanya, maintain their following especially in the rural areas of Bengal.

Gopala Guru Gosvami, a young associate of Chaitanya and a follower of Vakresvara Pandit, founded another branch based in Orissa. The writings of Gopala, along with those of his disciple Dhyanacandra Gosvami, have had a substantial influence on the methods of internal worship in the tradition.

In the 20th century the teachings of Chaitanya were brought to the West by A.C. Bhaktivedanta Swami Prabhupada, a representative of the Saraswata (i.e. disciples of Bhaktisiddhanta Sarasvati Thakura) branch of Chaitanya's tradition. Also, in the 21st century this representation of Vaishnava bhakti has been studied through the academic medium of Krishnology.

Saraswata gurus and acharyas, members of the Goswami lineages and several other Hindu sects which revere Chaitanya Mahaprabhu, including devotees from the major Vaishnava holy places in Mathura District, West Bengal and Orissa, also established temples dedicated to Krishna and Chaitanya outside India in the closing decades of the 20th century.

Cultural Legacy: In addition to his deep influences on Hinduism (some contend that Hinduism in Bengal might have been eradicated but for him), his cultural legacy in Bengal remains deep. Some attribute to him a Renaissance in Bengal, different from the more well know 19th century Bengal Renaissance. Salimullah Khan, a noted linguist, maintains, *"Sixteenth century is the time of Chaitanya Dev, and it is the beginning of Modernism in Bengal. The concept of 'humanity' that came into fruition is contemporaneous with that of Europe"*. Chaitanya also (at least indirectly) influenced the Baul movement of Bengal. The son of Nityananda, Chaitanya's most famous disciple and friend, is often attributed with the establishment of the Baul movement.

Avatar: In Hindu philosophy, an avatar, avatara or avatarim most commonly refers to the incarnation (bodily manifestation) of a higher being (deva), or the Supreme Being (God) onto planet Earth. The Sanskrit word *avatara*-literally means "descent" and usually implies a deliberate descent into lower realms of existence for special purposes. The term is used primarily in Hinduism, for incarnations of Vishnu whom many Hindus worship as God. The *Dasavatara* (see below) are ten particular "great" incarnations of Vishnu.

The word has also been used by extension to refer to the incarnations of God in other religions, especially by adherents to dharmic traditions when explaining figures from other religions such as Jesus.

Teachings and Significance: The philosophy reflected in the Hindu epics is the doctrine of the avatar (incarnation of Vishnu as an animal or a human form). The two main avatars of Vishnu that appear in the epics are Rama, the hero of the Ramayana, and Krishna, the advisor of the Pandavas in the Mahabharata. Unlike the superhuman devas (gods) of the Vedic Samhitas and the abstract Upanishadic concept of the all-pervading Brahman, the avatars in these epics are intermediaries between the Supreme Being represented as either Saguna Brahman or Nirguna Brahman and mere mortals.

This doctrine has had a great impact on Hindu religious life, for to many it means that God has manifested Himself in a form that could be appreciated even by the least sophisticated. Rama and Krishna have remained prominent as beloved and adored manifestations of the Divine for thousands of years among Hindus. The Upanishadic concept of the underlying unity of Brahman is revered by many to be the pinnacle of Hindu thought, and the concept of the avatars has purveyed this concept to the ordinary Hindu as an expression of the manifestation of the Hindu's highest single divinity as an aid to humanity in difficult times. The Hindu cycle of creation, evolution, and destruction contains the essence of the idea of "avatars" and indeed relies on a final avatar of Vishnu, that of Kalki, as the final evolutionary avatar before destruction at the end of the world.

Aside from Rama and Krishna there are many other human or animal forms which appeared on earth or elsewhere in the universe. Scriptures do not describe any appearance as an avatar by Brahma or Shiva (they are themselves listed as guna avatars) of nirguna Brahman, but zay of Vishnu have appeared a number of times. Some Hindus, based on the Ramayana, aver that Shiva incarnated once as the monkey-god Hanuman. Hanuman is more well-known as the son of Vayu, the deva of wind or his emanation. (Hanuman lived in a jungle in Treta Yuga and is called vanara, which means people having characteristics of monkey, and was one of the greatest devotees of Vishnu).

The Ten Avatars of Vishnu, or Dasavatara: The Maha Avatara (Great Avatars) of Vishnu are usually said to be ten and this is popularly known as the Dasavatara (dasa (dasha) in Sanskrit means ten). The first four of the ten avatars have appeared in the Satya Yuga (the first of the four Yugas or epochs that comprise one Mahayuga-for more details please read the section above on Lord Brahma). The next three avatars appeared in the Treta Yuga, the eighth incarnation in the Dwapara Yuga and the ninth in the Kali Yuga. The tenth is expected to appear at the end of the Kali Yuga.

1. Matsya, the fish, appeared in the Satya Yuga.
2. Kurma, the tortoise, appeared in the Satya Yuga.
3. Varaha, the boar, appeared in the Satya Yuga.
4. Narasimha, the Man-Lion (Nara = man, simha = lion), appeared in the Satya Yuga.
5. Vamana, the Dwarf, appeared in the Treta Yuga.
6. Parashurama, Rama with the axe, appeared in the Treta Yuga.
7. Rama, Sri Ramachandra, the prince and king of Ayodhya, appeared in the Treta Yuga.

8. Krishna (meaning 'dark coloured' or 'all attractive') appeared in the Dwapara Yuga along with his brother Balarama. According to the Bhagavata Purana Balarama is said to have appeared in the Dwapara Yuga (along with Krishna) as an incarnation of Ananta Shesha. He is also counted as an avatar Vishnu by a number of Vaishnava movements.
9. Buddha (meaning 'the enlightened one') appeared in the Kali Yuga (specifically as Siddhartha Gautama).
10. Kalki ("Eternity", or "time", or "The Destroyer of foulness"), who is expected to appear at the end of Kali Yuga, the time period in which we currently exist, which will end in the year 428899 CE.

The 25 Avatars of the Puranas: The Puranas list twenty-five avataras of Vishnu. A description of these is found in the Bhagavata Purana, Canto 1.

1. Catursana (the four Kumaras, sons of Lord Brahma)
2. Narada
3. Varaha (the boar)
4. Matsya (the fish)
5. Yajna
6. Nara-Narayana
7. Kapila
8. Dattatreya
9. Hayasirsa (Hayagriva)
10. Hamsa (the swan)
11. Prsnigarbha
12. Rishabha
13. Prithu
14. Narasimha (The Man-Lion)
15. Kurma (The Tortoise)
16. Dhanvantari
17. Mohini
18. Vamana (the Dwarf)
19. Parasurama (Rama with the axe)
20. Raghavendra (Sri Rama or Ramachandra, king of Ayodhya)
21. Vyasa (Vyasadeva)
22. Balarama
23. Krishna
24. The Buddha (Siddhartha Gautama)
25. Kalki

Types of Avatars: Avatars (as believed) of Madhvacharya. From top (in order of occurrence): Hanuman, Bhima and Shri Madhvacharya.

- According to Madhvacharya, all avatars of Vishnu are alike in potency and every other quality. There is no gradation among them, and perceiving or claiming any differences among avatars is a cause of eternal damnation. (See Madhva's commentary on the Katha Upanishad, or his Mahabharata-Tatparya-Nirnaya.)
- According to Vaishnava doctrine, there are two type of avatars, primary avatars and secondary avatars. The most common type of primary avatars are called Svarupavatars, in which He manifests Himself in His Sat-cid-ananda form. In the primary avatars, such as Narasimha, Rama, Krishna], Vishnu directly descends. The Svarupavatars are subdivided into Amsarupavatars and Purna avatars. In Amsarupavatars, Vishnu is fully present in the body but He is manifest in the person only partially. Such avatars include the first five avatars from Matsya to Vamana except for Narasimha. Narasimha, Rama and Krishna, on the other hand, are types of Purna avatars, in which all the qualities and powers of the Lord are expressed. Narasimha and Rama are also additionally considered to be Lila avatars. See Krishnology.
- Other avatars are secondary avatars, such as Parashurama in which Vishnu does not directly descend. Parashurama is the only one of the traditional ten avatars that is not a direct descent of Vishnu. There are two types of secondary avatars: 1) Vishnu enters a soul with His form. (e.g., Parashurama) or 2) Vishnu does not enter a soul with His own form, but gives him extraordinary divine powers. (e.g., Veda Vyasa.) The secondary avatar class is sometimes called Saktyamsavatar, Saktyaveshavatar or avesha avatar.
- A number of people in more recent times have been considered to be avatars by themselves or others. See List of other people considered to be avatars.

The Ninth Avatar: Balarama is the ninth avatar according to Puranic tradition. According to Puranas, Buddha, by some scholars, is never considered as a part of Dasa Avatar. However, as of the early centuries AD, many consider Buddha to be the Ninth Avatar, and Balarama and Krishna Share the Eighth spot.

Symbolism: Many claim that the ten avatars represent the evolution of life and of mankind on earth. Matsya, the fish, represents life in water. Kurma, the tortoise, represents the next stage, amphibianism. The third animal, the boar Varaha, symbolizes life on land. Narasimha, the Man-Lion, symbolizes the commencement development of mammals. Vamana, the dwarf, symbolizes this incomplete development of human. Then, Parashurama, the forest-dwelling hermit armed with an axe, connotes completion of the basic development of humankind. The King Rama signals man's ability to govern nations. Krishna, an expert in the sixty-four fields of science and art according to Hinduism, indicates man's advancement in culture and civilization. Balarama, whose weapon was a plough could stand for the development of agriculture. Buddha, the enlightened one, symbolizes social advancement of man.

Note that the time of the avatars also has some significance: Thus, kings rule reached its ideal state in Treta Yuga with Rama Avatar and social justice and Dharma were protected in Dwapar Yuga with the avatar of Krishna. Thus the avatars represent the evolution of life and society with changing epoch from Krita Yuga to Kali yuga. The animal evolution and development connotations also bear striking resemblances to the modern scientific theory of Evolution.

The avatars described above are of Vishnu, which in a sense a symbol of the "current state" of the society. The wife of Vishnu is "Laxmi" the goddess of Wealth. The Wealth is generated by the society, and is required to keep it going. This is symbolized by keeping Laxmi at the feet of Vishnu and basically taking care of him. Brahma, the "Creator" god, is the god of Knowledge. He is supposed have created knowledge. Again this symbolizes the generation of knowledge by the society, (as it is settled and growing and backed by wealth).

The four Yugas are again the symbolically represented. The description of each Yuga is given as follows: Krita Yuga is represented by a man carrying a small piece of pot (kamandalu). Treta Yuga is represented by a man carrying a Cow and an Anchor. Dwapar Yuga is represented by a man carrying a Bow and Parashu (Axe). Kali Yuga is represented by a man who is ugly, without clothes and making offensive gestures holding in his hand his genitals (sex organ).

If the above descriptions are seen carefully, one realizes that this also represents several technological advancements of the human society. In the first yuga there is a development of pottery, language and yagna (yadnya) rituals etc. The second yuga shows the mastering of agricultural techniques. The third yuga tells the development of weapons technology whereby the agricultural society (now staying in groups) and their generated wealth needs to be protected. The last yuga represents the complete anarchy of the values developed so far and is basically the last phase in the development of any society. The symbolic gesture of holding the sex-organ in hand shows the importance given to the materialistic pleasures of life and finally destroying the peace of mind.

List of Other People Considered to be Avatars: Besides the ten traditional avatars of Hinduism, some other Indian Hindus are considered to be avatars by themselves or by others. Some of these include:

With vedic evidences:

- Chaitanya (1486-1534) is claimed to be an avatar of Krishna by the Gaudiya Vaishnavism sect. He is also known as the 'Golden Avatar'. His appearance, by his followers, is said to be predicted in the latter texts of the Srimad Bhagavatam and to be hinted at in the Mahabharata. For more information, see Gaudiya Vaishnava Theology.

Without Vedic Evidences:

- Mahavatar Babaji described by Paramahansa Yogananda in his Autobiography of a Yogi as an Avatar
- Sri Ramakrishna (1836–1886) and Sri Sarada Devi (1853–1920). Ramakrishna is reported to have said to Swami Vivekananda, "He who was Rama and Krishna is now, in this body, Ramakrishna." Sarada Devi, who was married to Ramakrishna in a traditional Indian child marriage, is likewise considered by many to be an incarnation of Kali. This pairing of contemporaneous avatars is rare if not unique in Hindu history. Ramakrishna, Sarada Devi, and Vivekananda are worshipped by devotees worldwide as a holy trinity, the latter not as an avatar but as someone who is eternally free nityasiddha or ishwarakoti, born on earth to assist avatar in His mission, possessor of total enlightenment and liberation from his very birth.
- Jagadguru Kripaluji Maharaj (1922-present) is claimed to be an avatar of Krishna and Chaitanya Mahaprabhu by his followers. He is also known as 'Bhaktiyog-Ras-Avtar and 'Jagadgurottam' (Supreme among all previous Jagadgurus), these titles were given to him by Kashi Vidvat

Parishat while declaring him 5th Jagadguru in last 2500 years and first in last 700 years (after Jagadguru Madhvachrya) on 14th January, 1957.

- Shirdi Sai Baba some of his followers believed him to be an avatar of Dattatreya and Shiva
- Sathya Sai Baba claims and is believed by his devotees to be an avatar of Shiva, Shakti and Krishna. His followers say his ádvent was predicted in the book Bihar-al-anvar containing the preachings of Mohammad, in the Bible-especially in the Book of Revelation, in Hindu scriptures (Naadi), by Hindu saints like Sri Aurobindo (argued through a misleading association of Sai Baba's birthdate with "the descent of the overmind") and several other ones by Pope John XXIII as well as by the prophet Nostradamus.
- Meher Baba (1894-1969) said he was the last avatar of the Kali Yuga or White Horse avatar.
- Hans Ji Maharaj (1900–1966) Declared that the Satguru is an avatar with the 64 kalas
- Mother Meera (1960-present) claims and is believed to be an Avatar of Adipara-Shakti
- Narayani Amma (1976-present) claimed as the real Narayani Avatar

Some Hindus with a universalist outlook view the central figures of various non-Hindu religions as avatars. Many other Hindus reject the idea of avatars outside of traditional Hinduism. Some of these religious figures include:

- Zoroaster (Zarathustra) the prophet of Zoroastrianism.
- Mahavira (599 BC-527 BC) originator of the tenets of Jainism.
- Gautama Buddha (563-483BC-543BC) the key figure in Buddhism. See Sarvepalli Radhakrishnan and Vaishnava Theology.
- Jesus (4 BC-36) whose teachings inspired Christianity.
- Baha'u'llah (1817–1892) the founder-prophet of the Baha'í Faith, believed to be Kalki Avatar.

The label of avatar has been used by others outside of the Indian subcontinent and the umbrella of mainstream religions. Some of these are:

- Samael Aun Weor (1917-1977) claimed to be the real Kalki Avatar and Buddha Maitreya.
- Patrizia Norelli-Bachelet (1938-present) claims to be the "Third", an avatar of the "solar line", and the successor to Sri Aurobindo and The Mother.
- Adi Da (1939-present) states he is the Avatar of " The Bright " incarnate, and uses the title Avatar Adi Da Samraj

Orientalised Western Conceptions

Theosophy: The avatar concept was adapted by orientalising Western occultism, specifically Theosophy and Neo-Theosophy. In a series of four lectures delivered at the Theosophical Society at Adyar, Madras, in December 1899, Annie Besant, the president of the society, combines Theosophical concepts with classic Vaishvanite ideas. A decade later, her co-worker the clairvoyant Charles Webster Leadbeater would claim that his young protege Jiddu Krishnamurti was actually the avatar of a Cosmic Christ-like being called the Maitreya. The resulting Star of the East debacle almost destroyed the Theosophical Society.

The New Age: Many New Age teachings have been strongly influenced by Neo-Theosophical ideas (primarily through Alice Bailey, and feature a celestial hierarchy of ascended masters. At the head of the hierarchy is the same being, the Maitreya, that Leadbeater claimed to see in Krishnamurti. Some New Age teachings speak of the coming return of Christ, or the coming of the Maitreya, which will usher in a new cosmic Era. According to Benjamin Creme, the Maitreya has already incarnated, and will soon reveal himself.

Patrizia Norelli-Bachelet: Cosmologist Patrizia Norelli-Bachelet contends that the Hindu Line of Ten is a parable of evolution that is best understood with esoteric knowledge of astrology. She holds that Vishnu, the Preserver, corresponds to the fixed (preserving) signs of the Zodiac (Scorpio, Leo, Taurus and Aquarius), and that his 10 incarnations appear only during Astrological Ages ruled by fixed signs. To support this controversial claim, Norelli-Bachelet cites the famous three Steps of Vishnu mentioned in the Rig Veda (1.154) which likens Vishnu to the Lion [Leo], the Bull [Taurus] and the Man [Aquarius]. This view implies that an ancient zodiacal knowledge is embedded in the Ten Avatars of Vishnu. (see History of Astrology). She considers Sri Aurobindo rather than the Buddha to be the ninth Avatar of Vishnu, on the grounds that he supposedly wrote that he "came to correct the error of the Buddha".

Criticism of Contemporary Avatars: Many new religious movements related to Hinduism, some of which are viewed as cults, have more contentious views, including a tendency in modern times to place their guru as ishta-deva. Swami Tapasyananda of Ramakrishna Mission, on commentating about this phenomenon, said:

> *The avatar doctrine has been excessively abused by many Hindus today and we have the strange phenomenon of every disciple of a sectarian Guru claiming him to be an avatar. Christianity has therefore limited the Divine Incarnation as an one-time phenomenon. The theory has strong points and equally strong defects but it surmounts the gross abuse of the doctrine indulged in by many Hindus.*

Thus, if followers respect and revere the guru, it is only proper if they are using him as a conduit to God, and respect him as a teacher.

However, Swami Sivananda has said that a guru can be likened to God if he himself has attained realization and is a link between the individual and the Absolute. Such a guru, according to his definition and interpretation, should have actually attained union with God, inspire devotion in others, and have a presence that purifies all. Such a case is limited in contemporary times.

As early as the 17th century, the great Vaishnavite saint, Raghavendra Swami, in his last speech before departing from the mortal world, warned about the dangers of fraudulent gurus by saying:

> *The search for knowledge is never easy. As the Upanishads say it is like walking on the razor's edge. But for those who have strong faith and put in sustained effort and have the blessings of Shi Hari and guru this is not difficult. Always keep away from people who merely perform miracles without following the shastras and yet call themselves God or guru. I have performed miracles, and so have great persons like Shrimadacharya. These are based on yoga siddhi and the shastras. There is no fraud or trickery at all. These miracles were performed only to show the greatness of God and the wonderful powers that one can attain with His grace. Right knowledge (jnana) is greater than any miracle. Without this no real miracle can take place. Any miracle performed without this right knowledge is only witchcraft. No good will*

come to those who perform such miracles and also those who believe in them.

Atman (Hinduism): According to Advaita Vedanta, a philosophical branch of Hinduism, *atman* is the all-pervading soul of the universe. Synonymous with *Brahman*, Atman is the universal life-principle, the animator of all organisms, and the world-soul. This view is of a sort of pantheism (not pantheism) and thus is sometimes not equated with the single creator God of monotheism. Dvaita Vedanta calls the all-pervading aspect of Brahman *Paramatman*, quantitatively different from individual Atman.

Identification of individual souls, or jiva-atmas, with the 'One Atman' is the monistic Advaita Vedanta position, which is critiqued by dualistic/theistic Dvaita Vedanta (which claims reality for both a God functioning as the ultimate metaphorical "soul" of the universe, and for actual individual "souls" as such) and compromise schools like Vishishtadvaita Vedanta. The 'dvaita' (or dualist) schools, therefore, in contrast to Advaita, advocate an exclusive monotheistic position wherein Brahman is made synonymous with Vishnu. By contrast, Jiva is the psychological or phenomenological self, the "I" which appears as the subject of verbs. The jiva is typically regarded as having its freedom limited by the triple bond of anava (ego), karma (action) and maya (illusion). Adherents to Jainism also believe in the *atman*.

Brahman: Brahman in the Vedantic (and subsequently Yogic) schools of Hindu philosophy, is the signifying name given to the concept of the unchanging, infinite, immanent and transcendent reality that is the Divine Ground of all being in this universe.

Conceptualization: This Supreme Cosmic Spirit is regarded to be eternal, genderless, omnipotent, omniscient, and omnipresent, yet indescribable. It can be at best described as infinite Being, infinite Consciousness and infinite Bliss. It is regarded as the source and sum of the cosmos, that constricted by time, space, and causation, as pure being, the "world soul" which also can take many forms or manifestations of the thousands of gods. It was deemed a singular substrate from which all that is arises, and debuts with this verse:

"Great indeed are the devas who have sprung out of Brahman." — Atharva Veda

Originally, in the earliest mantras of the Vedic Samhitas, the word Brahman probably meant pious effigies coming out of the prayers in their fire-sacrifices, and hence the actual power behind the rituals. However, as the centuries passed and the first Upanishads (the primary Vedantic scriptures that putatively serve as commentaries on the original liturgical books of the Vedas) were written, the concept of **Brahman** fittingly grew in scope and complexity. Soon, the ancient writers of the Upanishads insisted that Brahman, in addition to being material, efficient, formal and final causes of the cosmos, was also utterly *beyond* all four senses of origin. Essentially, it is also beyond being and non-being alike, and thus does not quite fit with the usual connotations of the word *God* and even the concept of monism. For this reason, some authors use the word 'Godhead' for Brahman, to distinguish it from the usual usage of the word 'God'. It is said that Brahman cannot be known by material means, that we cannot be made conscious *of* it, because Brahman *is* our very consciousness. Brahman is also not restricted to the usual dimensional perspectives of being, and thus enlightenment, moksha, yoga, samadhi, nirvana, etc. do not merely mean to know Brahman, but to realise one's 'brahman-hood', to actually realise that one is and always was of Brahman nature. Indeed, closely related to the Self concept of Brahman is the idea that it is synonymous with jiva-atma, or individual souls, our atman (or soul) being readily identifiable with the greater soul of Brahman.

The Advaitic tradition rejects the above notion of an evolving definition of Brahman. It considers the Vedas to be eternal, timeless and contemporaneous with Brahman. In this tradition, the Vedas were handed down generations by vocal memorizations. Written texts of the Vedas are a relatively recent phenomenon.

Connected with the ritual of pre-Vedantic Hinduism, *Brahman* signified the power to grow, the expansive and self-altering process of ritual and sacrifice, often visually realised in the sputtering of flames as they received the all important ghee (clarified butter) and rose in concert with the mantras of the Vedas. *Brahmin* came to refer to the highest of the four castes, the Brahmins, who by virtue of their purity and priesthood are held to have such powers.

Etymology: Brahman or brahma, and similar words, have various meanings, mostly related to Hinduism. In the correct Indian pronunciation, the first *a* is long or short as indicated, and the *h* is pronounced as a voiced consonant.

These words come from a Sanskrit root *b°h* = " to swell, grow, enlarge", cognate with English "bulge". Some, including Georges Dumzil, say that the Latin word *flamen* (= "priest") may be cognate to *brahman*. The Latin verb *flare* = "to blow" may come from the same root. There is a possible connection with the Semitic root by' aø "create, opening", but refuted by most linguists.

Semantics and Pronunciation: Here the underlined vowels carry the Vedic Sanskrit udatta pitch accent. It is usual to use an acute accent symbol for this purpose.

In later Sanskrit usage:

- *Brahma* (nominative singular), *brahman* (stem) (neuter gender) means the concept of the Supreme transcendent and immanent Reality or the One Godhead or Cosmic Spirit in Hinduism; this is discussed below. Also note that the word Brahman in this sense is exceptionally treated as masculine (see the *Merrill-Webster Sanskrit Dictionary*). It is called "the Brahman" in English.
- *Brahmaoa,* meaning one of the Hindu priestly caste; in this usage the word is usually rendered in English as "Brahmin". This usage is also found in the Atharva Veda.
- *Ishvara*, or the Supreme God (lit., Supreme Lord), which may be completely identified with the Supreme Truth Brahman, as by the Dvaita philosophy, or partially as a worldly manifestation of the Brahman having (positive) attributes.
- *Devas,* the celestial beings of Hinduism, which maybe regarded as deities, demi-gods, spirits or angels. In Vedic Hinduism, there were 33 devas, which later became exaggerated to 330 million devas. In fact, all the devas are themselves regarded as more mundane manifestations of the One and the Supreme Brahman, for devotional worship. The Hindus do not literally worship 330 million separate gods. The Sanskrit word for "ten million" also means "group", and "330 million devas" originally meant "33 types of divine manifestation".

Brahm is sometimes found as a variant form of Brahma or Brahman. In Hindi, one might find Brahma as being pronounced as and consequently Brahmana as /brahm.

Brahman and Atman: Philosopher mystics of the Upanishads identify Brahman, the world soul, with atman, the inner essence of the human being, or the human soul. The Ultimate Truth is expressed as Nirguna Brahman, or Godhead. While Advaita philosophy considers Brahman to be without any form, qualities, or attributes, Dvaita philosophy understands nirguna as without *material* form or without bad qualities.

In Dvaita, Vishnu is Brahman since the followers stress a personal God. Advaita, on the other hand, considers all personal forms of God including Vishnu and Shiva as different aspects of God in personal form or God with attributes, Saguna Brahman.

According to some, God's energy is personified as Devi, the Divine Mother. For Vaishnavites who follow Ramunjacharaya's philosophy, Devi is Lakshmi, who is the Mother of all and who pleads with Vishnu for mankind who is entrenched in sin. For Gaudiya Vaishnavas she is Radha. For Shaivites, Devi is Parvati. For Shaktas, who worship Devi, Devi is the personal form of God to attain the impersonal Absolute, God. For them, Shiva is personified as God without attributes. See this Hinduism Today article. The phrase that is seen to be the only possible (and still thoroughly inadequate) description of Brahman that humans, with limited minds and being, can entertain is the Sanskrit word *Sacchidananda*, which is combined from *sat-chit-ananda*, meaning "being-consciousness-bliss".

Enlightenment and Brahman: While Brahman lies behind the sum total of the objective universe, some human minds boggle at any attempt to explain it with only the tools provided by reason. Brahman is beyond the senses, beyond the mind, beyond intelligence, beyond imagination. Indeed, the highest idea is that Brahman is beyond both existence and non-existence, transcending and including time, causation and space, and thus can never be *known* in the same material sense as one traditionally 'understands' a given concept or object.

Imagine a person who is blind from birth and has not seen anything. Is it possible for us to explain to him the meaning of the colour red. Is any amount of thinking or reasoning on his part ever going to make him understand the sensation of the colour red? In a similar fashion the idea of Brahman cannot be explained or understood through material reasoning or any form of human communication. Brahman is like the colour red; those who can sense it cannot explain or argue with those who have never sensed it.

Brahman is considered the all pervading consciousness which is the basis of all the animate and inanimate entities and material.

Advaita Concept: The universe is not just conscious, but it *is* consciousness, and this consciousness is Brahman. Human consciousness has forgotten its identity, that of Brahman, as if a drop of water from a vast ocean thought itself separate, and that the only path to merge back into that Brahman or supreme consciousness is through the paths of devotion, moral living, following the eight-fold path of Ashtanga Yoga meditation, often expressed in various systems of spiritual practices known as yogas.

If one seeks Brahman via true knowledge, Atman seeks truth and accepts it no matter what it is. Atman accepts all truths of the self/ego, and thus is able to accept the fact that it is not separate from its surroundings. Then Atman is permanently absorbed into Brahman and become one and the same with it. This is how one forever escapes rebirth.

In Advaita Vedanta, Brahman is without attributes and strictly impersonal. It can be best described as *infinite Being, infinite Consciousness and infinite Bliss*. It is pure knowledge itself, similar to a source of infinite radiance. Since the Advaitins regard Brahman to be the Ultimate Truth, so in comparison to Brahman, every other thing, including the material world, its distinctness, the individuality of the living creatures and even Ishvara (the Supreme Lord) itself are all untrue.

When man tries to know the attributeless Brahman with his mind, under the influence of an illusionary power of Brahman called Maya, Brahman becomes God (Ishvara). God is Brahman under Maya. The material world also appears as such due to Maya. God is Saguna Brahman, or Brahman with attributes. He is omniscient, omnipresent, incorporeal, independent, Creator of the world, its ruler and also destroyer. He is eternal and unchangeable. He is both immanent and transcedent, as well as full of love and justice. He may be even regarded to have a personality. He is the subject of worship. He is the basis of morality and giver of the fruits of one's Karma. He rules the world with his Maya. However, while God is the Lord of Maya and she (ie, Maya) is always under his control, living beings (jiva, in the sense of humans) are the servants of Maya (in the form of ignorance). This ignorance is the cause of all material experiences in the mortal world. While God is Infinite Bliss, humans, under the influence of Maya consider themselves limited by the body and the material, observable world. This misperception of Brahman as the observed Universe results in human emotions such as happiness, sadness, anger and fear. The Ulimate reality remains Brahman and nothing else. The Advaita equation is simple. It is due to Maya that the one single Atman (the individial soul) appears to the people as many Atmans, each in a single body. Once the curtain of maya is lifted, the Atman is **exactly equal** to the Brahman. Thus, due to true knowledge, an individual loses the sense of ego (Aham-kara) and achieves liberation, or Moksha. Also see Advaita Vedanta.

Dvaita (Vaishnava) Concept: Vedanta Sutra 3.2.23 states, "The form of Brahman is unmanifest, so the scriptures say" (*tat avyaktam aha*). The next sutra adds, "But even the form of Brahman becomes directly visible to one who worships devoutly-so teach the scriptures" (*api samradhane pratyaksa anumanabhyam*).

Dvaita schools argue against the Advaita idea that upon attaining liberation one realizes that God is formless since this idea is contradicted by Vedanta Sutra 3.2.16: "The scriptures declare that the form of the Supreme consists of the very essence of His Self" (*aha ca tanmatram*). And furthermore Vedanta Sutra 3.3.36 asserts that within the realm of Brahman the devotees see other divine manifestations which appear even as physical objects in a city (*antara bhuta gramavat svatmanah*).

They identify the personal form of God indicated here as the transcendental form of Vishnu or Krishna (see Vaishnavism). The brahma-pura (city within Brahman) is identified as the divine realm of Vishnu known as Vaikuntha. This conclusion is corroborated by the Bhagavata Purana, written by Vyasa as his own "natural commentary" on Vedanta-sutra. The first verse of Bhagavata Purana begins with the phrase "I offer my respectful obeisances to Bhagavan Vasudeva, the source of everything" (*om namo bhagavate vasudevaya janmadyasya yatah*). Vyasa employs the words "janmadyasya yatah", which comprise the second sutra of the Vedanta Sutra, in the first verse of the Bhagavata Purana to establish that Krishna is Brahman, the Absolute Truth. This is clear testimony of the author's own conclusion about the ultimate goal of all Vedic knowledge.

Kosas: Kosas or Koshas are five cases or sheaths which cover the Atman in Hinduism. The five Koshas are:

1. Annamaya kosha, the food-body
2. Pranamaya kosha, the breath (*prana*)
3. Manomaya kosha, or "mind-sheath" (*Manas*)
4. Vijnanamaya kosha, that which discriminates, determines or wills (*Vijnana*)
5. Anandamaya kosha, or bliss (*Ananda*)

Corporal Bodies: In the consequence of acts performed in former states of being through the actions of the fivefold elements, corporal bodies (which become the dwelling place of pleasure and pain) are formed. The soul is wrapped in five investing sheaths and seems formed of these, and is darkened like crystals on coloured cloth. As winnowed rice is purified from husk, the soul burdened with its sheaths is purified by the force of meditation. To remove his bondage the wise man should discriminate between the self and the non-self. By that alone he comes to know his own self and existence-through knowledge and bliss absolute, he becomes happy. He is free indeed who discriminates all sense-objects and the indwelling, unattached and inactive self as one separates a stalk from its enveloping sheath. Always merging every thing in it, he remains in a state of identity with that self.

Covered by the five sheaths, the material one and the rest, which are the products of its own power, the self ceases to appear, like the water of the tank by accumulation of sludge. When all the five sheaths have been eliminated by the reasoning on Shruthi passages, what remains as the culminating point of the process is the witness, the knowledge absolute-the Atman. This self – effulgent Atman is distinct from the five sheaths, as witness of the three states, the real, the changeless, and the unattained everlasting bliss is to be realized by a wise man as his own self.

Five Sheaths: The five sheaths (pancha-kosas) are alluded to in the fourteen verse of the Atmabodha. It must be noted that the individualised soul, when separated from the Supreme soul, is regarded in the Vedanta as enclosed in a succession of cases (kosa) which envelope it and, as it were, folded one over the other, 'like the coats of an onion'. The five sheaths are said to cover the self. The true self or the Atman, is none of these, nor can it's true nature be known as long as it is identified with them. All the five sheaths have been eliminated in the self of man. It appears pure, of the essence of everlasting and an alloyed bliss, indwelling, supreme, and self-effulgent.

Annamaya Kosa: The physical body is said to be made of food or matter. It is Annamaya. The Atman is described as enclosed in a series of sheaths. First there is the Annamaya, the food-body. This is the sheath of the physical self, named from the fact that it is nourished by the food. Further it says that the food identifies himself with a mass of skin, flesh, fat, bones, and filth, while the man of discrimination knows his own self, the only reality that there is, as distinct from the body. A materialist thinks he is the body, a religious student identifies himself with the mixture of body and Soul, while a Sage who has attained realization due to discrimination looks upon the eternal Atman as his self, and thinks "I am Brahman".

Pranamaya Kosa: There is another and subtle sheath, which is pranamaya, different from the body of food. Pranamaya means composed of prana. Prana is the vital principle, the force that vitalizes and holds together the body and the mind. It pervades the whole organism, its physical manifestation is the breath. As long as this vital principle exists in the organisms, life continues. The prana, with which we are all familiar, coupled with the five organs of action, forms the vital sheath, permeated by which the mate ial sheath engages itself in all activities as if it were living. This is the sheath composed of breath and the other vital airs associated with the organs of action. In the Vivekachoodamani it is a modification of vayu, and like the air, it enters into and comes out of the body, and because it never knows in the least either it's own weal and woo, nor those of others, being eternally dependent on the Self.

Manomaya Kosa: Manomaya means composed of manas or mind. It is called the manomaya or sheath composed of mere intellect, associated with the organs of action. This gives the individual soul its power of thought and judgement. The manomaya kosa, for instance or "mind-sheath" is said more truly to approximate to personhood than 'annamaya kosa' or the food sheath. The vital sheath knowledge together with the mind from the mental sheath the cause of the diversity of things such as 'I' and 'mine'. It is powerful and endowed with the faculty of creating categorical differentiation, such as names. It manifests itself as permeating the preceding.

Sankara uses the example of clouds that are brought in by the wind and again driven away by the same agency. Similarly man's bondage is caused by the mind, and liberation too is caused by that alone. Attaining purity through a preponderance of discrimination and renunciation, the mind makes for liberation. Hence the wise seeker after liberation must first strengthen these two.

The mind (manas) along with the five sensory organs is said to constitute the manomaya kosa.

Vijnanamaya Koša: Vijnanamaya means composed of vijnana, or intellect, and refers to the faculty which discriminates, determines or wills. Chattampi Swamikal defines vijnanamaya as the combination of intellect and the five sense organs. It is the sheath composed of more intellection, associated with the organs of perception. This gives the personal soul its first conception of individuality. The sheath of buddhi or vijnanamaya kosha together with the pranamaya kosa compose the body. Sankara holds that the buddhi, with it's modifications and the organs of knowledge, form the vijnanamaya kosa or knowledge sheath, of the agent, having the characteristics which are the cause of man's transmigration. This knowledge sheath, which seems to be followed by a reflection of the power of the cit, is a modification of prakrti. It is endowed by the function of knowledge, and it always wholly identifies itself with the body, organs etc. Owing to its connection with superimpositions, the supreme self, even though naturally, perfect and eternally unchanging, assumes the qualities of the superimpositions and appears to act just like the changeless fire assuming the modifications of the iron which it turns red-hot.

This knowledge sheath cannot be the supreme self for the following reasons:

- It is subject to change.
- It is insentient.
- It is a limited thing.
- It is not constantly present.

Anandamaya Kosa: Anandamaya means composed of ananda (bliss), and it's sheath refers to the ego. In the Upanishads the sheath is known also as the 'causal body'. In deep sleep, when the mind and senses cease functioning, there still stands the causal body between the finite world and the blissful self. As the fifth sheath is nearest of all to the blissful self it's name in the Upanishads is anandamaya. Anandamaya or that which is composed of Supreme bliss, is also named, although not admitted, by all. It is regarded as the innermost of all, and therefore, when the five sheaths are enumerated, it is to be placed before the vijnanamaya. The blissful sheath has its fullest play during deep sleep, while in the dreaming and wakeful states it has only a partial manifestation. The blissful sheath (anandamaya kosha) is that modification nescience which manifests itself by catching a reflection of the Atman which is bliss absolute, whose attributes are pleasure and rest, and which comes into view when some object agreeable to oneself presents itself. It makes itself spontaneously felt by the fortunate during the fruition of their virtuous deeds, from which every corporeal being derives great joy without effort.

Dharma: Dharma or Dhamma (Pali) means Natural Law or Reality, and with respect to its significance for spirituality and religion might be considered the Way of the Higher Truths. Dharma forms the basis for philosophies, beliefs and practices originating in India. The four main ones are Hinduism (Sanatana Dharma), Buddhism, Jainism, and Sikhism all retain the centrality of Dharma. In these traditions, beings that live in harmony with Dharma proceed more quickly toward Dharma Yukam, Moksha, Nirvana (personal liberation). Dharma also refers to the teachings and doctrines of the various founders of the traditions, such as Gautama Buddha in Buddhism and Mahavira in Jainism. As the religious and moral doctrine of the rights and duties of each individual, Dharma can refer generally to religious duty, and also mean social order, right conduct, or simply virtue.

Meanings and Origins of the Word Dharma: In the Rigveda, the word appears as an *n*-stem, *dharman-*, with a range of meanings encompassing "something established or firm" (in the literal sense of prods or poles), figuratively "sustainer, supporter" (of deities), and in the abstract, similar to the semantics of Greek ethos, "fixed decree, statute, law".

From the Atharvaveda and in Classical Sanskrit, the stem is thematic, *dharma* it takes the form *dhamma*. Monier-Williams attempts to gesture at the semantic field of the spiritual and religious meanings of the term with "virtue, morality, religion, religious merit". It being used in most or all philosophies and religions of Indian origin, the "dharmic faiths" including Hinduism (Sanatana Dharma), Buddhism, Jainism and Sikhism, it is difficult to provide a single concise definition for Dharma. The word has a long and varied history and straddles a complex set of meanings and interpretations. Dharma also is practiced in the Surat Shabda Yoga traditions.

Rene Guenon, father of the 20th century school of perennial philosophy, said:

> *It [dharma] is, so to speak, the essential nature of a being, comprising the sum of its particular qualities or characteristics, and determining, by virtue of the tendencies or dispositions it implies, the manner in which this being will conduct itself, either in a general way or in relation to each particular circumstance. The same idea may be applied, not only to a single being, but also to an organized collectivity, to a species, to all the beings included in a cosmic cycle or state of existence, or even to the whole order of the Universe; it then, at one level or another, signifies conformity with the essential nature of beings... (from Guenon's "Introduction to the Study of Hindu Doctrines")*

David Frawley, an expert on Hindu philosophy and religion, comments on Dharma as follows:

A universal tradition has room for all faiths and all religious and spiritual practices regardless of the time or country of their origin. Yet it places religious and spiritual teachings in their appropriate place relative to the ultimate goal of Self-realization, to which secondary practices are subordinated. Sanatan Dharma also recognizes that the greater portion of human religious aspirations has always been unknown, undefined and outside of any institutionalized belief. Sanatan Dharma thereby gives reverence to individual spiritual experience over any formal religious doctrine. Wherever the Universal Truth is manifest; there is Sanatan Dharma—whether it is in a field of religion, art or science, or in the life of a person or community. Wherever the Universal Truth is not recognized, or is scaled down or limited to a particular group, book or person, even if done so in the name of God, there Sanatan Dharma ceases to function, whatever the activity is called.

According to the Natchintanai Scripture: By the laws of Dharma that govern body and mind, you must fear sin and act righteously. Wise men by thinking and behaving in this way become worthy to gain bliss both here and hereafter.

Yama, the lord of death, is also known as *Dharma*, since he works within the laws of karma and morality, regulated by divine principles. More familiar is the embodiment of Dharma in Lord Rama, an avatar of Vishnu. The eldest Pandava, Yudhishthira was referred to as *DharmaRaj* (Most pious One) owing to his steadfastness to Truth & Dharma.

In ancient Vedic tradition, the Dharma was decided by the holy Kings or Dharma Raja. Dharma rajas include Manu who by tradition saves the Vedas before the flood, Rama, Yudhisthira, and Buddha.

The teachings, doctrines, philosophies and practices associated with furthering *Dharma* are also referred to as such. Sometimes, specific qualifiers are used-viz. *Buddha-Dharma* and *Jain-Dharma* to distinguish them from Hindu Dharma.

For many Buddhists, the Dharma most often means the body of teachings expounded by the Buddha. The word is also used in Buddhist phenomenology as a term roughly equivalent to phenomenon, a basic unit of existence and/or experience.

In scripture translations *dharma* is often best left untranslated, as it has acquired a lively life of its own in English that is more expressive than any simplistic translation. Common translations and glosses include "right way of living," Divine Law, Path of Righteousness, order, faith, "natural harmony," rule, fundamental teachings, and duty. *Dharma* may be used to refer to rules of the operation of the mind or universe in a metaphysical system, or to rules of comportment in an ethical system.

Origin and Development in Hinduism

A common manner of describing Hinduism among its adherents is as a *way of life*, as "Dharma." It defies dogma and thus seeks to instead align the human body, mind, and soul in harmony with nature.

Our very limitation is guided under and over a universal understanding, that of Dharma. The Atharva Veda, the last of the four books of the Vedas, utilizes symbolism to describe *dharma's* role. Thus we are bound by the laws of time, space and causation according to finite reality, which itself is a limitation imposed by the self-projection of the infinite Brahman as the cosmos. Dharma is the foundation of this causal existence, the one step below the infinite. Indeed, dharma is the projection of divine order from Brahman, and as such:

"Prithivim Dharmana Dhritam"

"This world is upheld by Dharma" — *(Atharva Veda)*

Proto-dharma: Rta in the Vedas: To assess a concept whose explication is bewildering in range, it is useful to trace its nascence and subsequent development in Vedic culture. In the Vedas, which span back to 2000 BCE (and much further in oral tradition), the first concept that is strikingly *dharmic* is that of rta.

Rta literally means the "course of things." At first, the early Hindus (or followers of the "Sanatan Dharma") were notably inquisitive as to the inscrutable order of nature, how the heavenly bodies, the rushing winds and flowing waters, the consistent cycling of the seasons, were regulated. Thenceforth sprang rta, whose all-purpose role it was to signify this order, the path that was always followed. Through all the metamorphoses and permutations of nature, of life in general, there was one unchangeable fact: rta.

Soon it transcended its passive role as a mere signifier and took on a greater one, that of an active imposition of order. Not only the natural principles, but the gods and goddesses themselves, were obliged to abide by rta. Rta became the father, the law of justice and righteousness, unyielding but eminently fair. It grew, as Radhakrishnan states, from "physical" to "divine" in its purvey.

The world's seeming mess of altercating fortune, the caprice of the divinities, was now intelligible. Indeed, there was a single, unchanging harmony working 'behind the scenes.' A right path existed, ready to be taken by the righteous ones. Rta signifies the way life ought to be, shifting from physical to divine, from natural to moral order. Rta was morality, the equitable law of the universe. The conception of this all-transcending, supramental force that is, practically, the same concept as later understandings of dharma, is captured in this early Vedic prayer, preempting the liturgical strains of classical Hindu mantras involving *dharma*:

"O Indra, lead us on the path of Rta, on the right path over all evils."

—(Rig Veda Book X, Chapter CXXXIII, Verse 6)

Thus we see the logical progression of an early 'course of things' into an all-encompassing moral order, a path and way of righteousness, an all-encompassing harmony of the universe, in the Vedic idea of Rta.

Developing Conceptions: An earlier and insightful demonstration of the continuity of thought from rta to dharma is a brief but "pregnant definition" of dharma given in the Brihadaranyaka Upanishad, a part of the Veda. Founded upon the Hindu ideas of, as R. H. Hume's "intelligent monism," with Brahman the monad, the Upanishads saw dharma as the universal principle of law, order, harmony, all in all truth, that sprang first from Brahman. It acts as the regulatory moral principle of the universe. It is *sat*, truth, a major tenet of Hinduism. This hearkens back to the conception of the Rig Veda that "Ekam Sat," (Truth Is One), of the idea that Brahman is *"Sacchidananda"* (Truth-Consciousness-Bliss). Dharma has imbibed the highest principles of Truth, and as such is the central guiding principle in the Hindu conception of existence. Dharma is not just law, or harmony, it is pure Reality. In the Brihadaranyaka's own words:

" Verily, that which is Dharma is truth.

Therefore they say of a man who speaks truth, 'He speaks the Dharma,'

or of a man who speaks the Dharma, 'He speaks the Truth.'

Verily, both these things are the same."

Dharma as a Purushartha: In moving through the four stages of life, viz. Brahmacharya, Grihastha, Vaanprastha, Sanyaasa, a person also seeks to fulfill the four essentials (purushaartha) of Dharma, Artha (worldly gain}, Kama (sensual pleasures), and Moksha (liberation from reincarnation or rebirth). Moksha, although the ultimate goal, is emphasized more in the last two stages of life, while Artha and Kama are primary only during Grihasthaashram. Dharma, however is essential in all four stages.

Kane's View: According to Dr. Pandurang Vaman Kane, the word "Dharma" acquired a sense of "the privileges, duties and obligations of a man, his standard of conduct as a member of the Aryan community, as a member of the caste and as a person in a particular state of life."

Buddhism

Buddha's Teachings: For practicing Buddhists, references to "dharma" or *dhamma* in the singular, particularly as "the" Dharma, is used to mean the teachings of the Buddha, and is sometimes referred to as the Buddha-Dharma. This latter signification has nothing to do with the personality of the spiritual teacher Siddhartha Gautama but rather signifies the importance of the attitude of mind that enables an adept or practitioner to re-harmonies his personal nature with the underlying principle (Dharma) behind natural phenomena (an attitude known in theistic religion as 'surrendering to the Will of the Lord') leading towards the undoing of all egoistic falsehood and ultimately release in nirvana-the peace of liberation (moksha).

The status of the Dharma is regarded variably by different traditions. Some regard it as an ultimate and transcendent truth which is utterly beyond worldly things, somewhat like the Christian logos. Others, who regard the Buddha as simply an enlightened human being, see the Dharma as the 84,000 different teachings (the Kanjur) that the Buddha gave to various types of people based on their needs.

"Dharma" usually refers inclusively not just to the sayings of the Buddha but to the later traditions of interpretation and addition that the various schools of Buddhism have developed to help explain and expand upon the Buddha's teachings. For others still, they see the dharma as referring to the "truth" or ultimate reality or "the way things are" (Tib. Cho).

The Dharma is one of the Three Jewels of buddhism of which practitioners of Buddhism seek refuge in (what one relies on for his/her lasting happiness). The three jewels of Buddhism are the Buddha (mind's perfection of enlightenment), the Dharma (teachings and methods), and the Sangha (awakened beings who provide guidance and support).

Qualities of Buddha Dharma: The Teaching of the Buddha also has six supreme qualities:

1. (Svakkhato) The Dhamma is not a speculative philosophy, but is the Universal Law found through enlightenment and is preached precisely. Therefore it is Excellent in the beginning (Sila ... Moral principles), Excellent in the middle (Samadhi. . . Concentration) and Excellent in the end (Pan na . . . Wisdom),
2. (Samditthiko) The Dhamma can be tested by practice and therefore he who follows it will see the result by himself through his own experience.

3. (Akaliko) The Dhamma is able to bestow timeless and immediate results here and now, for which there is no need to wait until the future or next existence.
4. (Ehipassiko) The Dhamma welcomes all beings to put it to the test and come see for themselves.
5. (Opaneyiko) The Dhamma is capable of being entered upon and therefore it is worthy to be followed as a part of one's life.
6. (Paccattam veditàbbo vinnunhi) The Dhamma can be perfectly realized only by the noble disciples (Ariyas) who have matured and enlightened enough in supreme wisdom.

Knowing these attributes, Buddhists believe that they will attain the greatest peace and happiness through the practice of the Dhamma. Each person is therefore fully responsible for himself to put it in the real practice. Here the Buddha is compared to an experienced and skilful doctor, and the Dhamma to proper medicine. However efficient the doctor or wonderful the medicine may be, the patients cannot be cured unless they take the medicine properly. So the practice of the Dhamma is the only way to attain the final deliverance of Nibbana.

These teachings ranged from understanding karma (cause and effect) and developing good impressions in one's mind, to how to reach full enlightenment by recognizing the nature of mind.

Dharmas in Buddhist Phenomenology: Other uses include *dharma,* normally spelled with a small "d" (to differentiate), which refers to a *phenomenon* or *constituent factor* of human experience. This was gradually expanded into a classification of constituents of the entire material and mental world. Rejecting the substantial existence of permanent entities which are qualified by possibly changing qualities, Buddhist Abhidharma philosophy, which enumerated seventy-five dharmas, came to propound that these "constituent factors" are the only type of entity that truly exists. This notion is of particular importance for the analysis of human experience: Rather than assuming that mental states inhere in a cognizing subject, or a soul-substance, Buddhist philosophers largely propose that mental states alone exist as "momentary elements of consciousness", and that a subjective perceiver is assumed.

One of the central tenets of Buddhism, is the denial of a separate permanent "I", and is outlined in the three marks of existence. The three signs: 1. Dukkha-Suffering (Pali: Dukkha), 2. Anitya-Change/ Impermanence (Pali: Anicca), 3. Anatman-No-I (Pali: Annatta). At the heart of Buddhism, is the denial of an "I" (and hence the delusion) as a separate self-existing entity.

Later, Buddhist philosophers like Nagrjuna would question whether the dharmas (momentary elements of consciousness) truly have a separate existence of their own. (ie Do they exist apart from anything else?) Rejecting any inherent reality to the dharmas.

When all dharmas are empty, what is endless? What has an end?

What is endless and with an end? What is not endless and not with an end?

What is *it*? What is *other*? What is permanent? What is impermanent?

What is impermanent and permanent? What is neither?

Dharma as Righteousness: According to S. N. Goenka, teacher of Vipassana Meditation, the original meaning of dhamma is "dhareti ti dhamma', or "that which is contained". Dharma in the Buddhist scriptures has a variety of meanings, including "phenomenon", and "nature" or "characteristic". Dharma also means 'mental contents', and is paired with citta, which means heart/mind. The pairing is paralleled with the pairing of kaya (body) and vedana (feelings or sensations, that which arise within the body but experienced through the mind), in major sutras such as the Mahasatipatthana sutra. Dharma is also used to refer to the teachings of the Buddha, not in the context of the words of one man, even an enlightened man, but as a reflection of natural law which was re-discovered by this man and shared with the world. A person who lives their life with an understanding of this natural law, is a "dhammic" person, which is often translated as "righteous".

Jainism: Dharma is natural. Jain Acharya Samantabhadra writes: "Vatthu sahavo dhammo" the dharma is the nature of an object. It is the nature of the soul to be free, thus for the soul, the dharma is paralaukika, beyond worldly. However the nature of the body is to seek self-preservation and be engaged in pleasures.

Thus there are two dharmas.

The two Dharmas: Acharya Haribhadra (approx. 6-7th cent.) discusses dharma in Dharma-Bindu. he writes (Translation by Y. Malaiya):

soayam-anushhThaatRi-bhedat dvi-vidho

Grihastha-dharmo yati-dharmash-cha.

Because of the difference in practice, Dharma is of two kinds, for the householders and for the monks.

tatra Grihastha-dharmoapi dvi-vidhah

saamanyato visheshhatash-cha

Of the householder's dharma, there are two kinds," ordinary" and "special" tatra saamnayato Grihastha-dharmah kula-krama-agatam-anindyam

vibhavady-apekshayaa nyaato. Anushh´Thaanam |

The ordinary Grihastha-dharma should be carried out according to tradition, such that it is not objectionable, according to ones abilities such as wealth, in accordance with nyaya (everyone treated fairly and according to laws).

Somadeva suri (10th c.) terms the "ordinary" and "special" dharmas laukika and the paralukika dharmas respectively:

dvau hi dharamau Griahastha Nam, laukikaH, paàrlaukikaH |

lokaashrayo bhavedaadyah, parah syaad-aagama-Ashrayah ||

A householder follows both laukika and the paralukika dharmas at the same time.

References in Pop Culture: Dharma is a frequent allusion on ABC's hit show Lost. The DHARMA Initiative is the name of the corporation that controls apparently much of what happens on the island. It is responsible for the food and medicine supplies and the bunkers where some of the survivors have taken shelter (also known as hatches). It allegedly conducted (or is conducting) experiments in many fields. Any clear relation to Dharma and its philosophies are yet to be elucidated. As well, the show's producers have confirmed that DHARMA, in Lost, is an acronym, but will not yet reveal its meaning.

In the Dragon Quest video game series, *Dharma Shrine* serves as a place for players to change their job classes.

In the 1968 Jethro Tull album, *This was*, there is a song called "Dharma for One", which played two years later at the 1970 Isle of Wight Festival. In the video game Suikoden III, The main antagonist's (Luc's) motivations are based on concept of Dharma.

The female lead character in *Dharma and Greg* is named *Dharma*. She was raised by hippie parents, is a practitioner of yoga and an adherent of Eastern spiritualities.

Karma in Hinduism: *Karma* is a concept in Hinduism, based on the Vedas and Upanishads, which explains causality through a system where beneficial events are derived from past beneficial actions and harmful events from past harmful actions, creating a system of actions and reactions throughout a person's reincarnated lives. Karma in Hinduism is used to explain the problem of evil that persists in spite of an omniscient, omnipotent, benevolent God; it is thus related to theodicy. "Karma" may also mean a Hindu religious vow or ritual.

The Mahabharata is sometimes analysed as a Karma story, a story where people received the reward of their actions, good and bad. The original Hindu concept of karma was later elaborated on by several other movements within the religion, most notably Vedanta, Yoga, and Tantra. The concept was adopted by other religions such as Buddhism and Jainism, whose views differ from Hinduism as the concept of Karma does not involve a personal supreme God. Karma has had a major influence on worldwide philosophy and spirituality.

Definition: "Karma" literally means "deed" or "act", and more broadly names the universal principle of cause and effect, action and reaction, which Hindus believe governs all life. Karma is not fate; humans are believed to act with free will, creating their own destinies. According to the Vedas, if an individual sows goodness, he or she will reap goodness; if one sows evil, he or she will reap evil. Karma refers to the totality of mankind's actions and their concomitant reactions in current and previous lives, all of which determine the future. However, many karmas do not have an immediate effect; some accumulate and return unexpectedly in an individual's later lives. The conquest of karma is believed to lie in intelligent action and dispassionate reaction.

Unkindness yields spoiled fruits, called *papa*, and good deeds bring forth sweet fruits, called *punya*. As one acts, so does he become: one becomes virtuous by virtuous action, and evil by evil action.

There are three types of karma in Hinduism:

1. sanchita karma, the sum total of past karmas yet to be resolved;
2. prarabdha karma, that portion of sanchita karma that is to be experienced in this life; and
3. kriyamana karma, the karma that humans are currently creating, which will bear fruit in future.

Karma as Practised Actions: Karma may also mean a Hindu religious vow or ritual. In the Hindu tradition, emphasis is placed on performing certain *karmas* or actions; these include:

- *Nitya-karma*
- *Kaamya-karma*

Nitya-karma are those actions which have to be performed daily by Hindus; for example

Sandhyavandanam is an important *nitya-karma*. Certain *nitya-karmas*, such as *darsha-purna-maseshti*, are performed once in a fortnight, and are therefore called *naimittika karma*.

Kaamya-karma are those *karmas* performed with a certain objective, such as *putrakameshti*.

The Role of God: While the action of karma has often been compared with the Western notions of sin and judgment by God, karma instead has been commonly perceived by Westerners to operate as a law of nature without the intervention of any supernatural being. That notion is not accurate with regard to Hinduism, though it holds true for Buddhism and Jainism.

Karma in Hinduism does involve the role of God. Unlike Buddhists and Jains who believe that karma on its own joins the soul when it reincarnates, Hindus believe in the role of God in linking karma to an individual.

Hindu scriptures on mitigation of karma by God: Some non-Hindu theologians interpret the concept of the relationship between God and karma to indicate that God is neutral and detached towards all, and thus He has no power in controlling karma. It is admitted that God is free of cruelty and is hence not partial to anyone, but it is also held that those who seek Him will find His grace. However, Hindus believe that God is all-merciful, and His grace can overcome or mitigate the karma of man in many cases. It is still important to remember that man has free will and must seek Him. The nature of God is explained further in the Brahma Sutras.

Two Examples from the Puranas: The story of Markandeya, who was saved from death by Siva, illustrates that God's grace can overcome karma and death for His beloved devotee.

The story of Ajamila in the Bhagavata Purana also illustrates the same point. Ajamila had committed many evil deeds during his life such as stealing, abandoning his wife and children, and marrying a prostitute. But at the moment of death, he involuntarily chanted the name of Narayana and therefore received moksha or union with God, and was saved from the messengers of Yama. Ajamila was actually thinking of his youngest son, whose name was also Narayana. But the name of God has powerful effects, and Ajamila was forgiven for his great sins and attained salvation, despite his bad karma.

Views of Hindu Traditions on Karma: Advaita Vedanta: Swami Sivananda, an Advaita scholar, reiterates the same views in his commentary synthesizing Vedanta views on the Brahma Sutras, a Vedantic text. In his commentary on Chapter 3 of the Brahma Sutras, Sivananda notes that karma is insentient and short-lived, and ceases to exist as soon as a deed is executed. Hence, karma cannot bestow the fruits of actions at a future date according to one's merit. Furthermore, one cannot argue that karma generates apurva or punya, which gives fruit. Since apurva is non-sentient, it cannot act unless moved by an intelligent being such as God. It cannot independently bestow reward or punishment.

There is a passage from Swami Sivananda's translation of the Svetasvatara Upanishad (4:6) illustrating this concept:

Two birds of beautiful plumage — inseparable friends — live on the same tree. Of these two one eats the sweet fruit while the other looks on without eating.

In his commentary, the first bird represents the individual soul, while the second represents Brahman or God. The soul is essentially a reflection of Brahman. The tree represents the body. The soul identifies itself with the body, reaps the fruits of its actions, and undergoes rebirth. The Lord alone stands as an eternal witness, ever contented, and does not eat, for he is the director of both the eater and the eaten.

Swami Sivananda also notes that God is free from charges of partiality and cruelty which are brought against him because of social inequality, fate, and universal suffering in the world. According to the Brahma Sutras, individual souls are responsible for their own fate; God is merely the dispenser and witness with reference to the merit and demerit of souls.

In his commentary on Chapter 2 of the Brahma Sutras, Sivananda further notes that the position of God with respect to karma can be explained through the analogy of rain. Although rain can be said to bring about the growth of rice, barley and other plants, the differences in various species is due to the diverse potentialities lying hidden in the respective seeds. Thus, Sivananda explains that differences between classes of beings are due to different merits belonging to individual souls. He concludes that God metes rewards and punishments only in consideration of the specific actions of beings.

Shaivism

Thirugnana Sambanthar writes about karma in his outline of Saivism. He explains the concept of karma in Hinduism by distinguishing it from that of Buddhism and Jainism, which do not require the existence of an external being like God. In their beliefs, just as a calf among a large number of cows can find its mother at suckling time, so also does karma find the specific individual it needs to attach to and come to fruition. However Hindus posit that karma, unlike the calf, is an unintelligent entity. Hence, karma cannot locate the appropriate person by itself. Shri Sambantha concludes that an intelligent Supreme Being with perfect wisdom and power (Shiva, for example) is necessary to make karma attach to the appropriate individual. In such sense, God is the Divine Accountant.

Appaya Dikshita, a Saivite theologian and proponent of Siva Advaita, states that Siva (God) only awards happiness and misery in accordance with the law of karma. Thus persons themselves perform good or evil actions according to their own inclinations as acquired in past creations, and in accordance with those deeds, a new creation is made for the fulfillment of the law of karma. Shaivas believe that there are cycles of creations in which souls gravitate to specific bodies in accordance with karma, which as an unintelligent object depends on the will of Siva alone. Thus, many interpret the caste system in accordance with karma, as those with good deeds are born into a highly spiritual family (probably the *brahmana* caste).

Srikantha, another Saivite theologian, believes that individual souls themselves do things which may be regarded as the cause of their particular actions, or desisting from particular actions, in accordance with the nature of the fruition of their past deeds. Srikantha further believes that Siva only helps a person when he wishes to act in a particular way or to desist from a particular action.

Satguru Sivaya Subramuniyaswami explains in the lexicon section of his book, *Dancing with Siva*, that karma literally means "deed or act" and more broadly names the universal principle of cause and effect, action and reaction which governs all life. As he explains it, karma is not fate, for man acts with free will creating his own destiny. The Vedas tell us that if we sow goodness, we will reap goodness; if we sow evil, we will reap evil. Satguru Sivaya Subramuniyaswami further notes that karma refers to the totality of our actions and their concomitant reactions in this and previous lives, all of which determine our future. The conquest of karma lies in intelligent action and dispassionate reaction. Not all karmas rebound immediately. Some accumulate and return unexpectedly in this or other births.

Vaishnavism

Ramanuja attempts to fashion a solution to the problem of evil by attributing all evil things in life to the accumulation of evil karma of jivas (human souls), and maintains that God is amala or without any stain of evil.

Madhva, the founder of the Dvaita school, on the other hand, believes that there must be a root cause for variations in karma even if karma is accepted as having no beginning and being the cause of the problem of evil. Since jivas have different kinds of karma, from good to bad, all must not have started with same type of karma from the beginning of time. Thus, Madhva concludes that the jivas are not God's creation as in the Christian doctrine, but are rather entities co-existent with Vishnu, although under His absolute control. Souls are thus dependent on Him in their pristine nature and in all transformations that they may undergo.

According to Madhva, God, although He has control, does not interfere with Man's free will; although He is omnipotent, that does not mean that He engages in extraordinary feats. Rather, God enforces a rule of law and, in accordance with the just deserts of jivas, gives them freedom to follow their own nature. Thus, God functions as the sanctioner or as the divine accountant, and accordingly jivas are free to work according to their innate nature and their accumulated karma, good and bad. Since God acts as the sanctioner, the ultimate power for everything comes from God and the jiva only utilizes that power, according to his/her innate nature.

Swami Tapasyananda further explains the Madhva view by illustrating the doctrine with this analogy: the power in a factory comes from the powerhouse (God), but the various cogs (*jivas*) move in a direction in which they are set. Thus he concludes that no charge of partiality and cruelty can be brought against God. The jiva is the actor and also the enjoyer of the fruits of his/her own actions.

Madhva differed significantly from traditional Hindu beliefs, owing to his concept of eternal damnation. For example, he divides souls into three classes: one class of souls which qualify for liberation (Mukti-yogyas), another subject to eternal rebirth or eternal transmigration (Nitya-samsarins), and a third class that is eventually condemned to eternal hell or Andhatamas (Tamo-yogyas). No other Hindu philosopher or school of Hinduism holds such beliefs. In contrast, most Hindus believe in universal salvation: that all souls will eventually obtain moksha, even if it is after millions of rebirths.

Caste and Karma: As stated earlier, there are cycles of creations in which souls gravitate to specific bodies in accordance with karma, which as an unintelligent object depends on the will of God alone. Thus, many interpret the caste system in accordance with karma, as those with good deeds are born into a spiritual family, which is synonymous with the *brahmana* caste. However, Krishna said in the Gita that characteristics of a brahmin are determined by behavior, not by birth. A verse from the Gita illustrates this point:

"The duties of Brahmins, Kshatriyas, Vaishyas as also of Sudras, O scorcher of foes, are distributed according to the gunas (behavior) born of their own nature."

(Chapter 18, verse 41)

Maya (illusion)

Maya (Sanskrit *maya*, from *ma* "not" and *ya* "this"), in Hinduism, is many things. Maya is the illusion that the phenomenal world of separate objects and people is the only reality. For the mystics this manifestation is real, but it is a fleeting reality; it is a mistake, although a natural one, to believe that maya represents a fundamental reality. Each person, each physical object, from the perspective of eternity is like a brief, disturbed drop of water from an unbounded ocean. The goal of enlightenment is to understand this—more precisely, to experience this: to see intuitively that the distinction between the self and the universe is a false dichotomy. The distinction between consciousness and physical matter, between mind and body, is the result of an unenlightened perspective.

Maya in Hinduism: In Hinduism, Maya must be seen through in order to achieve moksha (liberation of the soul from the cycle of death and rebirth)-ahamkar (ego-consciousness) and karma are seen as part of the binding forces of Maya. Maya is seen as the phenomenal universe, a lesser reality-lens superimposed on the one Brahman that leads us to think of the phenomenal cosmos as real. Maya is also visualized as part of the Divine Mother (Devi) concept of Hinduism. In the Hindu scripture 'Devi Mahatmyam,' Mahamaya (Great Maya) is said to cover Vishnu's eyes in Yoganidra (Divine Sleep) during cycles of existence when all is resolved into one. By exhorting Mahamaya to release Her illusory hold on Vishnu, Brahma is able to bring Vishnu to aid him in killing two demons, Madhu and Kaitabh, who have manifested from Vishnu's sleeping form. Shri Ramakrishna often spoke of Mother Maya and combined deep Hindu allegory with the idea that Maya is a lesser reality that must be overcome so that one is able to realize his or her true Self.

Maya in Hindu Philosophy: In Advaita Vedanta philosophy, *maya* is the limited, purely physical and mental reality in which our everyday consciousness has become entangled. Maya is believed to be an illusion, a veiling of the true, unitary Self—the Cosmic Spirit also known as Brahman. Maya originated in the Hindu scriptures known as the Upanishads. Many philosophies or religions seek to "pierce the veil" in order to glimpse the transcendent truth, from which the illusion of a physical reality springs, drawing from the idea that first came to life in the Hindu stream of Vedanta. Maya is neither true nor untrue. Since Brahman is the only truth, Maya cannot be true. Since Maya causes the material world to be seen, it cannot be untrue. Hence Maya is described as indescribable. She (sic) has two principle functions—one is to cover up Brahman and hide it from our mind. The other is to present the material world instead of Brahman. She is destructible. Consider an illusion of a rope being confused as a snake in the darkness. Just as this illusion gets destroyed when true knowledge of the rope is perceived, similarly, Maya gets destroyed for a person when he perceives Brahman with the transcendental knowledge. A metaphor is also given—when the reflection of Brahman falls on Maya, Brahman appears as God (the Supreme Lord). In the pragmatic level, where the world is regarded as true, Maya becomes the divine magical power of the Supreme Lord, to create and rule the world. But Maya is God's servant—he can leave her any time he wishes. He is not affected by the impiety of Maya, just as a magician is not cheated by his own magic. Hence God is Bliss. However, the individuals are the servants of Maya, hence they are in misery.

In Hinduism, Maya must be seen through in order to achieve moksha (liberation of the soul from the cycle of death and rebirth)—ahamkar (ego-consciousness) and karma are seen as part of the binding forces of Maya. Maya is seen as the phenomenal universe, a lesser reality-lens superimposed on the one Brahman that leads us to think of the phenomenal cosmos as real.

By Sri Sankaracharya:

1. The Supreme Self (or Ultimate Reality) who is Pure Consciousness perceived Himself by Selfhood (i.e. Existence with "I"-Consciousness). He became endowed with the name "I". From that arose the basis of difference.
2. He exists verily in two parts, on account of which, the two could become husband and wife. Therefore, this space is ever filled up completely by the woman (or the feminine principle) surely.
3. And He, this Supreme Self thought (or reflected). Thence, human beings were born. Thus say the Upanishads through the statement of sage Yajnavalkya to his wife.
4. From the experience of bliss for a long time, there arose in the Supreme Self a certain state like deep sleep. From that (state) Maya (or the illusive power of the Supreme Self) was born just as a dream arises in sleep.
5. This Maya is without the characteristics of (or different from) Reality or unreality, without beginning and dependent on the Reality that is the Supreme Self. She, who is of the form of the THREE GUNAS (qualities or energies of Nature) brings forth the Universe with movable and immovable (objects).
6. As for Maya, it is invisible (or not experienced by the senses). How can it produce a thing that is visible (or experienced by the senses)? How is a visible piece of cloth produced here by threads of invisible nature?
7. As there is the emission of the generative fluid on to a good garment on account of the experience of copulation in a dream, the pollution of the garment is seen as real on waking while the copulation was not true, the man in the dream was real (while) the woman was unreal and the union of the two was false (but), the emission of the generative fluid was real, so does it occur even in the matter in hand.
8. Thus Maya is invisible (or beyond sense-perception). (But) this universe which is its effect, is visible (or perceived by the senses). This would be Maya which, on its part, becomes the producer of joy by its own destruction.
9. Like night (or darkness) Maya is extremely insurmountable (or extremely difficult to be understood). Its nature is not perceived here. Even as it is being observed carefully (or being investigated) by sages, it vanishes like lightning.
10. Maya (the illusive power) is what is obtained in Brahman (or the Ultimate Reality). Avidya

(or nescience or spiritual ignorance) is said to be dependent on Jiva (the individual soul or individualised consciousness). Mind is the knot which joins Consciousness and matter. That mind is to be as imperishable until liberation.

11. Space enclosed by a pot, or a jar or a hut or a wall has their several appellations (eg. pot space, jar space etc.). Like that, Consciousness (or the Self) covered here by Avidya (or nescience) is spoken of as jiva (the individual soul).
12. Objection: How indeed could ignorance become a covering (or an obscure factor) for Brahman (or the Supreme Spirit) who is Pure Consciousness, as if the darkness arising from the night (could become a concealing factor) for the sun which is self-luminous?
13. As the sun is hidden by clouds produced by the solar rays but surely, the character of the day is not hidden by those modified dense collection of clouds, so the Self, though pure, (or undefiled) is veiled for a long time by ignorance. But its power of Consciousness in living beings, which is established in this world, is not veiled.

Understanding Maya through Bhagavad Gita Verses

Bhagavad Gita, Ch. 13, Verse 3. "My womb is the great Nature (Prakriti or MAYA). In that I place the germ (embryo of life). Thence is the birth of all beings".

Bhagavad Gita, Ch. 14, Verse 4 "Whatever forms are born, O Arjuna, in any womb whatsoever, the great Brahma (Nature) is their womb and I am the seed-giving father."

Explanation: Prakriti (Nature), made up of the three qualities (Sattwa, Rajas and Tamas), is the material cause of all beings.

In the great Prakriti, I place the seed for the birth of Brahma (the creator, also known as Hiranyagarbha, or Ishwar, or the conditioned Brahman); and the seed gives birth to all beings. The birth of Brahma (the creator) gives rise to the birth of beings.

The primordial Nature (prakriti) gives birth to Brahma, who creates all beings.

(I am the father; the primordial Nature is the mother).

Bhagavad Gita, Ch. 13, verse 26. "Wherever a being is born, whether unmoving or moving, know thou Arjuna, that it is from the union between the field and the knower of the field". (Purusha is the knower of the field; Prakriti is the field; Shiva is another name for the knower of the field and Shakti is the field; Spirit is another name for the knower of the field and Matter (Prakriti) is the field).

Bhagavad Gita, Ch. 7, Verse 4. "I am endowed with two Shaktis, namely the superior and the inferior natures; the field and its knower (spirit is the knower of the field; matter is the field.) I unite these two".

Bhagavad Gita Ch. 9, Verse 6. "Know these two-my higher and lower natures-as the womb of all beings. Therefore, I am the source and dissolution of the whole universe".

Bhagavad Gita, Ch. 13, Verse 29. "He sees, who sees that all actions are performed by nature alone, and that the Self is action less". (The Self is the silent witness).

Bhagavad Gita, Ch. 9, Verse 17. "I am the father of this world, the mother, the dispenser of the fruits of actions and the grandfather; the one thing to be known, the purifier, the sacred monosyllable (AUM), and also the Rig, the Sama and the Yajur Vedas".

Maya in Hindu Mythology: Maya is also the name of an Asura, who was the father-in-law of the Lord of Lanka, Ravana and the father of Mandodari. He is the archenemies of Vishwakarma, the celestial architect of the Gods. His knowledge and skills are compatible with Vishwakarma. When Lanka was destroyed by Hanuman, it was the King of Demons, Maya, who had re-installed the beauty of that Island Kingdom.

Maya as the Goddess: In Hinduism, Maya is also seen as the illusory form of Devi, the Divine Goddess. Her most famous explication is seen in the Devi Mahamaya, also known as Chandi or Abhaya, which is said to spring from the Devi Sukta passage of the Vedas.

Essentially, Mahamaya (great Maya) both blinds us in delusion (moha) and has the power to free us from it. Maya, superimposed on Brahman, the one divine ground and essence of monist Hinduism, is envisioned as one with Kali, Durga, etc. A great modern (19th century) Hindu sage who often spoke of Maya as being the same as the Shakti principle of Hinduism was Shri Ramakrishna.

In the Hindu scripture 'Devi Mahatmyam,' Mahamaya (Great Maya) is said to cover Vishnu's eyes in Yoganidra (Divine Sleep) during cycles of existence when all is resolved into one. By exhorting Mahamaya to release Her illusory hold on Vishnu, Brahma is able to bring Vishnu to aid him in killing two demons, Madhu and Kaitabh, who have manifested from Vishnu's sleeping form. Sri Ramakrishna Paramahamsa often spoke of Mother Maya and combined deep Hindu allegory with the idea that Maya is a lesser reality that must be overcome so that one is able to realize his or her true Self.

Maya in Sikhism: In Sikhism, maya (the world as you normally perceive it) is said to be no more manifest than a dream. The Sikh concept is in line with Vedanta. Sikhism, as well as many other paths of spirituality, state that the world is like a dream, and there is nothing in it which is yours. (This last sentence has been translated right from the Guru Granth Sahib). An example of this is when our dreams feel so solid and real, but how will we know if we're dreaming if we do not wake up the next morning? What can a person actually call "MINE" in the temporary existence of a life spanning three-quarters of a century?

However, maya is not said to be an unimportant aspect of life. Both 'miri' (temporal) and 'piri' (spiritual) are said to be of equal importance to human beings. The key to a happy life, according to Sikkhism, is knowing how to live the right balance between these two realms of existence.

Concepts Analogous to Maya in Popular Culture: A modern concept that illustrates Maya / Illusion is the science-fiction movie "The Matrix". Everything in The Matrix is believed to be real, until the character Neo wakes up, and sees that it's just a dream world. The movie points out that one never knows he is asleep until he wakes up.

Ishta-deva

In Smartism, a denomination of Hinduism, an Ishta-deva or Ishta devata or Ishta-devatha is a term meaning "the god one prays most." It is derived from the Sanskrit roots for *good* and *god*. Traditionally it alludes to the particular form of God (from among five forms of God) as believed by Smarta Hindus. In such a concept held by Smartas, different aspects of God are held to be equivalent.

According to some commentaries on the Bhagavad Gita, the devotee will receive deliverance from ignorance and divine wisdom from their deity and come to perfection by practicing bhakti yoga regardless of the form worshiped. Vaishnavites however, disagree and believe that Krishna himself stated that worship of deities other than Supreme Lord, Vishnu, are incorrect as such worship would only lead to temporal benefits, rather than mukti, which Vaishnavites believe that only Vishnu can grant. For example, Krishna said: "Whatever deity or form a devotee worships, I make his faith steady. However, their wishes are only granted by Me." (Gita: 7:21-22) Another quote in the Gita states: "O Arjuna, even those devotees who worship other lesser deities (e.g., Devas, for example) with faith, they also worship Me, but in an improper way because I am the Supreme Being. I alone am the enjoyer of all sacrificial services (Seva, Yajna) and Lord of the universe." (Gita: 9:23)

In another example cited by Swaminarayan Vaishnavites, Swaminarayan, founder of the Hindu Swaminarayan sect, according to this site, said in verse 115 of their scripture, Shikshapatri said, "Shree Krishna Bhagwan and Shree Krishna Bhagwan's incarnations alone are worthy of meditation. Similarly, Shree Krishna Bhagwan's images are worthy. And men or devas, even if they are devotees of Shree Krishna Bhagwan or brahmavettaa (knower of divinity), they are still not worthy of meditation-and thus one should not meditate upon them." But he also recognized a Smarta view, in verses 47, 84, "And the oneness of Narayana and Shiva should be understood, as the Vedas have described both to be brahmaroopa, or form of Brahman, i.e., Saguna Brahman, indicating that Vishnu and Shiva are different forms of the one and same God. He concludes in verse 108, "And that Ishvara is Shree Krishna Bhagwan (Shree Swaminarayan Bhagwan), who is supreme Parabrahm Purushottam, our Ishta-deva (principal deity), worthy of worship, and the cause of all incarnations."

Murti: The chosen deity is typically seen as a murti — an icon or representation of a deity such as Krishna, Ganesha, or Shiva. Usually a person worships this ishta-deva, prays to it, or dedicates their actions to it. It is believed that the human mind needs a concrete form to understand the divine that ultimately can never be defined. Just as one can understand the abstract concept of a color only after one has seen a concrete form, one can only realize the deity through a form of murti.

Misunderstanding from Outsiders: The ishta-deva concept has confused outsiders, and made Hinduism to be misunderstood as polytheistic. This view is only a view of Smartism, the only denomination of Hinduism that holds this view strictly. Only a Smartist would have no problem worshiping Shiva or Vishnu together as he views the different aspects of God as leading to the same One God. It is the Smarta view that dominates the view of Hinduism in the West. After all, Swami Vivekananda, a follower of Ramakrishna, along with many others, who brought Hindu beliefs to the West, were all Smarta in belief. Adherents of Smartism (*e.g.* Smartas) are monists, and conceive of multiple manifestations of a single God or source of being. Hindu monists see a unity, with the personal deities being equally valid to worship. Accordingly, this Smarta concept is a specialized type of monotheism, termed monistic theism. Additionally, Smarta Hinduism is an inclusive monotheistic faith, which accordingly holds that the different deities are simply different manifestations of the One God. Vaishnavism and Shaivism, the other major denominations of Hinduism, on the other hand, however, conform to a Western perception of what a monotheistic faith is. For example, a Vaishnavite considers Vishnu as the one true God, worthy of worship and other forms as subordinate. See for example, an illustration of the Vaishnavite view of Vishnu as the one true God, at this link. Accordingly, many Vaishnavites, for example, believe that only Vishnu can grant the ultimate aim for mankind, moksha. See for example, this link. Similarly, many Shaivites also hold similar beliefs, as illustrated at this link and at this link. These faiths, on the other hand, are pantheistic monotheism, for the most part.

Disagreement within Hinduism: Other denominations as well as sects of Hinduism don't strictly hold this belief. For example, Arya Samaj worships only the formless Brahman, in particular, Nirguna Brahman. Other denominations, such as the monotheistic faiths of Saivism and Vaishnavism, respectively hold Shiva and Vishnu to be the only ultimate reality, although those faiths recognize other manifestations of the singular god as emanations or lesser deities subordinate to this one supreme being. For example, Shaivities may recognize Vishnu to be a manifestation of Shiva but accord Shiva the status of being the only ultimate reality. A Smarta, on the other hand, would consider Vishnu and Shiva to be the same but different aspects of only one supreme being. (See Adi Sankara's commentary on Vishnu sahasranama.) Vaishnavites may hold the same belief of other manifestations as Shaivites, thus viewing Shiva as a manifestation of Vishnu but hold that Vishnu is the only ultimate reality. The distinction is a subtle difference but noteworthy.

However, the monotheistic nature of *Saivism* does not necessarily contradict the concept of *ishta-devata*. It is the view of Saivites, like most Hindus, that Shiva can be approached and experienced through many paths. A certain deity or aspect is seen to choose and be chosen by the devotee, embracing them in life-style and vibrations, subtly guiding them to the ultimate reality. A devotee moving towards Shiva through the worship of Ganesa, Shiva's son, supposedly receives blessings and guidance of a much slower and kind nature than a devotee of the more destructive aspect of Rudra.

ISKCON and New Religious Movements: The Hare Krishna/ISKCON, organization, which is part of the traditional Gaudiya Vaishnavism denomination would accord Shiva the status of a demigod rather than another equivalent aspect of Krishna. ISKCON considers Krishna to be the Supreme Personality of Godhead. They consider Sri Chaitanya Mahaprabhu to be an avatar of Krishna but worship Krishna, like many traditional Hindu adherents, as their preferred Ishta-Deva.

Other new religious movements related to Hinduism (see Contemporary Hindu movements), many of them cults, have more contentious views, including a tendency in modern times to place their guru as ishta-deva. This is of course an unpopular view both in the minds of orthodox Hindus, as well with outsiders who often misunderstand this phenomenon as a tendency common within Hinduism.

Swami Tapasyananda of Ramakrishna Mission, in his book, *Bhakti Schools of Vedanta,* pg. 50, on commentating about this phenomenon, said:

> *The avatar doctrine has been excessively abused by many Hindus today and we have the strange phenomenon of every disciple of a sectarian Guru claiming him to be an avatar. Christianity has therefore limited the Divine Incarnation as a one-time phenomenon. The theory has strong points and equally strong defects but it surmounts the gross abuse of the doctrine indulged in by many Hindus.*

Thus, if followers respect and revere the guru, it is only proper if they are using him as a conduit to Krishna, and respect him as a teacher.

However, Swami Sivananda has said that a guru can be likened to God if he himself has attained realization and is a link between the individual and the Absolute. Such a guru, according to his definition and interpretation, should have actually attained union with God, inspire devotion in others, and have a presence that purifies all. Such a case is limited in contemporary times.

As early as the seventeenth century, the great Vaishnavite saint, Raghavendra Swami, in his last speech before departing from the mortal world, warned about the dangers of fraudulent gurus by saying:

"The search for knowledge is never easy. As the Upanishads say it is like walking on the razor's edge. But for those who have strong faith and put in sustained effort and have the blessings of Shi Hari and guru this is not difficult. Always keep away from people who merely perform miracles without following the shastras and yet call themselves God or guru. I have performed miracles, and so have great persons like Shrimadacharya. These are based on yoga siddhi and the shastras. There is no fraud or trickery at all. These miracles were performed only to show the greatness of God and the wonderful powers that one can attain with His grace. Right knowledge (jnana) is greater than any miracle. Without this no real miracle can take place. Any miracle performed without this right knowledge is only witchcraft. No good will come to those who perform such miracles and also those who believe in them."

Smarta View

Smarta Hinduism is inclusive monotheistic, hence a follower of Smarta Hinduism may worship one God over another depending on preference. The most widely worshipped among forms of God are Shiva and Vishnu. The Goddesses Kali, Durga and Amba are also widely worshipped. Ganapati is worshipped throughout India, while Murugan is worshipped more in the Southern India.

The system prevalent in Hinduism is defined by the Smartha philosophy; this theory allows for the veneration of numberless deities, but on the understanding that all of them are but manifestation of the ONE divine power. That ultimate power is termed Brahman or Atman, and is believed to have no specific form, name or attribute.

Only a Smartha, or follower of the Advaita philosophy, would have no problem worshiping every imaginable deity with equal veneration; he views these different deities as being manifestations of the same God. Other (somewhat peripheral) Hindu denominations, such as Vaishnavism and Shaivism conform more closely to a Western understanding of what a monotheistic faith is. For instance, a Vaishnavite considers Vishnu as being the one and only true God, an attitude that resonates with that of the Semitic religions. However, the Smartha philosophy defines the mainstream of Hinduism, and imparts to Indic spiritual and religious traditions their renowned liberalism.

Murti: A *murti* (also spelled *murthi* or *murthy*) typically refers to an image in which the Divine Spirit is 'murta', or expressed. A murti becomes worshippable after the Divine is invoked in it for the purpose of offering worship. Thus the murti is treated as the Deity of the Divine and regarded by Hindus and also by some Mahayana Buddhists during worship as points of devotional and meditational focus.

Murtis are sometimes abstract, but more often representations of God in a personal form like Shiva or Ganesh, Rama or Krishna, Saraswati or Kali. Murtis are made according to the prescriptions of the Silpasastra (typically of the alloy Panchaloga) and then installed by priests through the prana pratishtha ('establishing the life') ceremony. Afterward the divine personality is present in the murti but in cases of serious discrepancies in worship may leave the form.

Devotional (Bhakti) practices centered on cultivating a deep and personal bond of love with God often include veneration of murtis. Some Hindu denominations like Arya Samaj, however, reject image-worship.

Critics of murti worship equate the practice with idolatry. Hindus argue that murti worship consists of veneration of the image or statue as the representative of the Divine, or as the "manifest presence" of the transcendent God, while idolatry objectifies divinity as the material object itself.

Reincarnation: According to Hinduism, every living being is an eternally existing spirit (the soul or the self). Upon physical death, this soul passes from one body to another in accordance with the laws of Karma and reincarnation.

Reincarnation, literally "to be made flesh again", as a doctrine or mystical belief, holds the notion that some essential part of a living being (or in some variations, only human beings) can survive death in some form, with its integrity partly or wholly retained, to be reborn in a new body. This part is often referred to as the Spirit or Soul, the 'Higher or True Self', 'Divine Spark', 'I' or the 'Ego' (not to be confused with the ego as defined by psychology).

In such beliefs, a new personality is developed during each life in the physical world, based upon past integrated experience and new acquired experiences, but some part of the being remains constantly present throughout these successive lives as well. It is usually believed that there is interaction between predeterminism of certain experiences, or lessons intended to happen during the physical life, and the free-will action of the individual as they live that life.

This doctrine is a central tenet within the majority of Indian religious traditions such as Yoga, Vaishnavism, Jainism and Sikhism. Buddhist concept of Rebirth, a major part of Buddhist philosophy, differs from the Vedic based traditions, teaches that our "self" (soul) does not reincarnate (see below). Many modern Pagans also believe in reincarnation as do some new Age movements, along with followers of Spiritism, practitioners of certain African traditions, and students of esoteric philosophies.

Beliefs in reincarnation or transmigration are widespread amongst religions and beliefs, some seeing it as part of the religion, others seeing in it an answer to many common moral and existential dilemmas, such as "why are we here" and "why do bad things sometimes appear to happen to good people". Reincarnation is therefore a claim that a person has been or will be on this earth again in a different body. It suggests that there is a connection between apparently disparate human lifetimes, and (in most cases) that there may even be covert evidence of continuity between different people's lifetimes, if looked for. Proponents claim this is indeed the case, whilst critics tend to reject the notion due to its metaphysical implications or non-acceptance by science due to other possible explanations of the phenomenon not yet eliminated from consideration. Such evidence tends to be of three kinds:

- Tradition commonly holds that certain people (such as the Dalai or Panchen Lamas in Buddhism) can be identified by looking for a child born at the time of their death, and by certain signs and knowledge that such a child has of their predecessor life beyond the norm. In the case of Buddhism there are well defined tests of such a child.

- In Western culture, regression or near death experience has at times provided what are claimed to be past life memories, some of which can in theory be verified, and some of which might be tested for fraudulentlaims. Some aspects of these tend to be quite consistent in some ways (beings of light, messages of love and peace, etc.), a factor which to some people lends credence to the idea, and to others supports that "something" is going on but without certainty what that might be.
- Last, for many people, the evidence is internal and empirical, personal belief or experience. This may not be proof as such, but to them, qualifies as sufficient evidence to believe it.

Though some claims to recall past lives have been documented and tested in a scientific manner, mainstream science does not accept reincarnation as a proven phenomenon.

Reincarnation in Various Religions, Traditions and Philosophies: Philosophical and religious beliefs regarding the existence or non-existence of an enduring 'self' have a direct bearing on how reincarnation is viewed within a given tradition. There are large differences in philosophical beliefs regarding the nature of the soul (also known as the jiva or atma) amongst the Dharmic Religions such as Hinduism and Buddhism. Some schools deny the existence of a 'self', while others claim the existence of an eternal, personal self, and still others say there is neither self or no-self, as both are false.

Each of these beliefs has a direct bearing on the possible nature of reincarnation, including such concepts of samsara, moksha, nirvana and bhakti.

Eastern Religions and Traditions

Hinduism: In India the idea of reincarnation is first introduced in the Upanishads (c. 800 BCE-), which are philosophical and religious texts composed in Sanskrit. The doctrine of reincarnation is absent in the Vedas, which are generally considered the oldest of the Hindu scriptures.

The idea that the soul (of any living being-including animals, humans and plants) reincarnates is intricately linked to karma, another concept first introduced in the Upanishads. Karma (literally: action) is the sum of one's actions, and the force that determines one's next reincarnation.

The cycle of death and rebirth, governed by karma, is referred to as samsara. The ideas of reincarnation, karma, and samsara are found both in Hinduism, Buddhism, Jainism and Sikhism. In all these religious traditions, ultimate salvation is liberation, moksha or mukti from the cycle of death and rebirth. In Buddhism, this liberation is often referred to as nirvana. Other Bhakti traditions regard liberation from samsara as the beginning of true spiritual life, which continues beyond nirvana freed from the worldly nature.

The notion of nirvana was further promoted (see Advaita Vedanta) following the advent of the great Hindu sage Adi Shankaracharya. In some schools of Hinduism, the idea that stilling one's *karmas* (actions) and becoming at one, harmonious, with all would free one, ultimately, from reincarnation, became a central tenet. For Hinduism this state both exists and does not exist so that it may be likened to a dream-state, unreal in every sense. Thus from both perspectives, reincarnation cannot be likened to the re-appearance of the spirit or person within a physical body which inhabits an objective physical world rather, the perception of the world alone exists as a manifestation, around the conscious being, and this is maintained as an act of mind only. To be trapped in Samsara then is to be held by ignorance of the true nature of being, in a self-created world of error. As such, this is really nothing other than a dream.

Many paths are offered toward this state of liberation or "heaven" and most are generally initiated by proposing this life to be "real". This of course means that past-lives are also to be seen as real. However, significant progression on any such path soon causes this initial, every-day concept of "reality" to wither away. As unity with the god-head is approached, the essence of being is recalled with the result that the previously perceived "reality" vanishes as unity is achieved.

Buddhism: Since according to Buddhism there is no permanent and unchanging self (identify) there can be no metempsychosis in the strict sense. However, the Buddha himself referred to his past-lives. It can be inferred that these existed only in the world of the mind and that this is furthermore exactly the same state as is perceived by the one experiencing (or immersed in) the cyclic manifestation of Samsara.

Buddhism never rejected samsara, the process of rebirth; however, there are debates over what is reborn.

In addition to the anatta, Tibetan Buddhists, also believe that a new-born child may be the rebirth of some important departed lama. In Tibetan Buddhism, the substance that make up the impermanent "self" (skandha) of an important lama (like the Dalai Lama) is said to be reborn into an infant born nine months after his decease. This belief, however, does not contradict with Buddha's teaching on the impermanent nature of the self.

The Buddha has this to say on rebirth. Kutadanta continued: "Thou believest, O Master, that beings are reborn; at they migrate in the evolution of life; and that subject to the law of karma we must reap what we sow. Yet thou teaches the non-existence of the soul! Thy disciples praise utter self-extinction as the highest bliss of Nirvana. If I am merely a combination of the sankharas, my existence will cease when I die. If I am merely a compound of sensations and ideas and desires, whether can I go at the dissolution of the body?" Said the Blessed One: "O Brahman, thou art religious and earnest. Thou art seriously concerned about thy soul. Yet is thy work in vain because thou art lacking in the one thing that is needful. "There is rebirth of character, but no transmigration of a self. Thy thought-forms reappear, but there is no egoentity transferred. The stanza uttered by a teacher is reborn in the scholar who repeats the word.

Jainism: In Jainism, particular reference is given to how devas (gods) also reincarnate after they die. A Jainist, who accumulates enough good karma, may becom deva; but, this is generally seen as undesirable since devas eventually die and one might then come back as a lesser being. This belief is also commonplace in a number of other schools of Hinduism.

Western Religions and Traditions

Classical Greek Philosophy: Some ancient Greek philosophers believed in reincarnation; see for example Plato's *Phaedo* and *The Republic*. Pythagoras was probably the first Greek philosopher to advance the idea. We do not know exactly how the doctrine of metempsychosis arose in Greece; most scholars do not believe it was borrowed from Egypt or that it somehow was transmitted from ancient Hindu thinkers of India. It is easiest to assume that earlier ideas which had never been extinguished were utilized for religious and philosophic purposes. The Orphic religion, which held it, first appeared in Thrash upon the semi-barbarous north-eastern frontier. Orpheus, its legendary founder, is said to have taught that soul and body are united by a compact unequally binding on either; the soul is divine, immortal and aspires to freedom, while the body holds it in fetters as a prisoner. Death dissolves this compact, but only to re-imprison the liberated soul after a short time: for the wheel of birth revolves inexorably. Thus the soul continues its journey, alternating between a separate unrestrained existence and fresh reincarnation, round the wide circle of necessity, as the companion of many bodies of men and animals." To these unfortunate prisoners Orpheus proclaims the message of liberation, that they stand in need of the grace of redeeming gods and of Dionysus in particular, and calls them to turn to God by ascetic piety of life and self-purification: the purer their lives the higher will be their next reincarnation, until the soul has completed the spiral ascent of destiny to live for ever as God from whom it comes. Such was the teaching of Orphism which appeared in Greece about the 6th century BC, organized itself into private and public mysteries at Eleusis and elsewhere, and produced a copious literature.

The earliest Greek thinker with whom metempsychosis is connected is Pherecydes; but Pythagoras, who is said to have been his pupil, is its first famous philosophic exponent. Pythagoras probably neither invented the doctrine nor imported it from Egypt, but made his reputation by bringing Orphic doctrine from North-Eastern Hellas to Magna Graecia and by instituting societies for its diffusion.

The real weight and importance of metempsychosis in Western tradition is due to its adoption by Plato. Had he not embodied it in some of his greatest works it would be merely a matter of curious investigation for the Western anthropologist and student of folk-lore. In the eschatological myth which closes the Republic he tells the story how Er, the son of Armenius, miraculously returned to life on the twelfth day after death and recounted the secrets of the other world. After death, he said, he went with others to the place of Judgment and saw the souls returning from heaven and from purgatory, and proceeded with them to a place where they chose new lives, human and animal. He saw the soul of Orpheus changing into a swan, Thamyras becoming a nightingale, musical birds choosing to be men, the soul of Atalanta choosing the honours of an athlete. Men were seen passing into animals and wild and tame animals changing into each other. After their choice the souls drank of Let the and then shot away like stars to their birth. There are myths and theories to the same effect in other dialogues, the Phaedrus, Meno, Phaedo, Timeous and Laws. In Plato's view the number of souls was fixed; birth therefore is never the creation of a soul, but only a transmigration from one body to another. Plato's acceptance of the doctrine is characteristic of his sympathy with popular beliefs and desire to incorporate them in a purified form into his system. Aristotle, a far less emotional and sympathetic mind, has a doctrine of immortality totally inconsistent with it.

In later Greek literature the doctrine appears from time to time; it is mentioned in a fragment of Menander (the Inspired Woman) and satirized by Lucian (Gallus 18 seq.). In Roman literature it is found as early as Ennuis, who in his Calabrian home must have been familiar with the Greek teachings which had descended to his times from the cities of Magna Graecia. In a lost passage of his Annals, a Roman history in verse, Ennuis told how he had seen Homer in a dream, who had assured him that the same soul which had animated both the poets had once belonged to a peacock. Perseus in one of his satires (vi. 9) laughs at Ennuis for this: it is referred to also by Lucretius (i. 124) and by Horace (Epist. II. i. 52). Virgil works the idea into his account of, the Underworld in the sixth book of the Aeneid (vv. 724 sqq.). It persists in antiquity down to the latest classic thinkers, Plotinus and the other Neoplatonists.

Judaism and Kabbalah: Classic works of the Kabbalah, *Shaar ha Gilgulim* ("Gate of Reincarnations") of Arizal or *Isaac Luria*, describes complex laws of reincarnation *gilgul* and impregnation *ibbur* of 5 different parts of the soul. It shows many references of reincarnation in the Hebrew Bible (the Tanach).

The notion of reincarnation is not openly mentioned in the Hebrew Bible. The classical rabbinic works (midrash, Mishna and Talmud) also are silent on this topic.

The concept was elucidated in an influential mystical work called the *Bahir* (Illumination) (one of the most ancient books of Jewish mysticism) which was composed by the first century mystic Nehunia been Kana, and gained widespread recognition around 1150. After the publication of the *Zohar* in the late 13th century, the idea of reincarnation spread to most of the general Jewish community.

While ancient Greek philosophers like Plato and Socrates attempted to prove the existence of reincarnation through philosophical proofs, Jewish mystics who accepted this idea did not. Rather, they offered explanations of why reincarnation would solve otherwise intractable problems of theodicy (how to reconcile the existence of evil with the premise of a good God.)

Rabbis who accepted the idea of reincarnation include the founder of Chassidism, the Baal Shem Tov, Levi ibn Habib (the Ralbah), Nahmanides (the Ramban), Rabbenu Bahya ben Asher, Rabbi Shelomoh Alkabez and Rabbi Hayyim Vital. The argument made was that even the most righteous of Jews sometimes would suffer or be murdered unjustly. Further, children would sometimes suffer or be murdered, yet they were obviously too young for them to have committed sins that God would presumably punish them for. Jewish supporters of reincarnation said that this idea would remove the theodicy: Good people were not suffering; rather, they were reincarnations of people who had sinned in previous lifetimes. Therefore any suffering which was observed could be assumed to be from a just God. Yitzchak Blua writes "Unlike some other areas of philosophy where the philosophic battleground revolves around the truth or falsehood of a given assertion, the *gilgul* debate at points focuses on the psychological needs of the people."

Martin Buber's collection of *Legend of the Baal-Shem* (*Die Chassidischen Bücher*) includes several of the Baal Shem Tov's stories that explicitly discuss concrete cases of reincarnating souls.

Rabbis who rejected the idea of reincarnation include Saadia Gaon, Hasdai Crescas, Yedayah Bedershi (early 14th century), Joseph Albo, Abraham ibn Daud and Leon de Modena. Saddia, in Emunoth ve-Deoth, concludes Section vi with a refutation of the doctrine of metempsychosis. Crescas writes that if reincarnation was real, people should remember details of their previous lives. Bedershi offers three reasons why the entire concept is dangerous:

1. There is no reason for people to try and do good in this life, if they fear that they will nonetheless be punished for some unknown sin committed in a past life.
2. Some people may assume that they did not sin in their past life, and so can coast on their success; thus there is no need to try hard to live a good life. In Bedershi's view, the only psychologically tenable world view for a healthy life is to deal with the here-and-now.

3. The idea presents a conundrum for those who believe that at the end of days, God will resurrect the souls and physical bodies of the dead. If a person has lived multiple lives, which body will God resurrect?

Joseph Albo writes that in theory the idea of gil'gulim is compatible with Jewish theology. However, Albo argues that there is a purpose for a soul to enter the body, creating a being with free will. However, a return of the soul to another body, again and again, has no point. Leon De Moden thinks that the idea of reincarnation make a mockery of God's plans for humans; why does God need to send the soul back over and over? If God requires an individual to achieve some perfection or atone for some sin, then God can just extend that person's life until they have time to do what is necessary. De Modena's second argument against reincarnation is that the entire concept is absent from the entire Bible and corpus of classical rabbinic literature.

The idea of reincarnation, called *gilgul*, became popular in folk belief, and is found in much Yiddish literature among Ashkenazi Jews. Among a few kabbalists, it was posited that some human souls could end up being reincarnated into non-human bodies. These ideas can be found in a number of Kabbalistic works from the 1200s, and also among many mystics in the late 1500s. A distinction was made, however, between actual Transmigration and this form of reincarnation; the non-human subject had its own soul already, the human soul simply 'rode along with' the rock, or tree, or giraffe waiting to be 'elevated,' that is, to be raised to a higher level and to gradually approach the level of human again. The cow eats the grass, elevating the soul within it, the soul rides with the cow a while until a person eats the cow, and then the soul is elevated to the max. Rabbi Chaim Vidal, when asked how he came to be the foremost disciple and sole transmitter of the teachings of his teacher, the great Issac Luria, credits, not study or mitzvot, but his diligence in blessing his food: "For this way I elevate the souls therein. These souls then become my witnesses in the Heavenly Realm, and empower me to receive even greater revelations."

"Over time however, the philosophical teaching limiting reincarnation to human bodies emerged as the dominant view. Nonetheless, the idea that one can reborn as an animal was never completely eliminated from Jewish thought, and appears centuries later in the Eastern European folk tradition".

While many Jews today do not believe in reincarnation, the belief is common amongst Orthodox Jews, particularly amongst Hasidim; some Hasidic siddurim (prayerbooks) have a prayer asking for forgiveness for one's sins that one may have committed in this *gilgul* or a previous one.

Gnosticism: Many Gnostic groups believed in reincarnation. For them, reincarnation was a negative concept: Gnostics believed that the material body was evil, and that they would be better off if they could eventually avoid having their 'good' souls reincarnated in 'evil' bodies.

The Gnostic Gospel of the Nazirenes-Chapter 69:

1. As Yeshua sat by the west of the temple with his disciples, behold there passed some carrying one that was dead, to burial, and a certain one said to Him, "Master, if a man die, shall he live again?"
2. He answered and said, "I am the resurrection and the life, I am the good, the beautiful, the true; if a man believe in me he shall not die, but live eternally. As in Adam all (1997 = are bound to cycles of rebirth) die, so in the Messiah shall all be made alive. Blessed are the dead who die in me, and are made perfect in my image and likeness, for they rest from their

labors and their works do follow them. They have overcome evil, and are made pillars in the temple of my God, and they go out no more, for they rest in the eternal."

3. "For them that persist in evil there is no rest, but they go out and in, and suffer correction for ages, till they are made perfect. But for them that have done good and attained to perfection, there is endless rest and they go into life everlasting. They rest in the eternal."
4. "Over them the repeated death and birth have no power, for them the wheel of the eternal revolves no more, for they have attained to the center, where is eternal rest, and the center of all things is God."

The texts contains several parallels to the Gospels, which are, though, traditionally interpreted differently in their context:

"I am the resurrection and the life; he who believes in me, though he die, yet shall he live, and whoever lives and believes in me shall never die.

Him who overcomes I will make a pillar in the temple of my God. Never again will he leave it.

2

PHILOSOPHY OF RELIGIOUS CULTS

Vaishnavism

Vaishnavism is one of the principal divisions of Hinduism. Its adherents worship Vishnu as the supreme God or one of his avatars and are principally monotheistic whilst also incorporating elements which could be described as pantheistic in nature. Bhaktas, or worshipers of Vishnu are called Vaishnavites, an English term that originated from *Vaishnava* in Sanskrit, which is the Vriddhi form of *Vishnu*). The Hare Krishna movement is a modern example of a Vaishnavite organisation.

Schools of Vaishnavism: Major Vaishnava schools of thought include:

- Vishishtadvaita ("qualified nondualism"), espoused by Ramanuja; i.e., Srivaishnavism.
- Dvaita ("dualism"), espoused by Madhvacharya
- Achintya Bheda-Abheda, espoused by Sri Chaitanya adhered by Gaudiya Vaishnavism. ISKCON ("Hare Krishnas") is the most well known branch of this school.
- Shuddhaadvaita, espoused by Vallabhacharya

- Dvaitaadvaita, espoused by Nimbarka
- Ek Saran Naam Dharma, espoused by Sankardeva

The Major Schools: Vaishnavas believe that Vishnu-Narayana is the one supreme God (Parabrahman) and all other living entities (including devas such as Surya and Durga) are subservient to Him. Shiva is also viewed as subservient to lord Vishnu, although it is still understood that he is above the category of an ordinary jiva.

While many schools like Smartism and Advaitism encourage people to interpret the Vedas philosophically and metaphorically and not too literally, Vaishnavism stresses the literal meaning (*mukhya v[itti*) as primary and indirect meaning (gauga vsitti) as secondary: *skchd upadesas tu shrutih-* "The instructions of the shruti-shstra should be accepted literally, without so-called *fanciful or allegorical interpretations*." (Jiva Gosvami, *Krishna Sandarbha* 29.26-27). Thus according to Vaishnava theology, atman is not Brahman and Moksha doesn't mean "union with God" but "eternal life in heaven".

The Supreme Godhead: The heroes of both the great Indian epics are believed to be incarnations of Lord Vishnu. These epics, the *Ramayana* and the *Mahabharata*, concern Rama and Krishna, respectively. Rama with His Shakti named Sita, brother Lakshmana and devotee Hanuman are central characters of Ramayana. Rama and Lakshman are always shown to be ready for battle (with bow and arrow) as it is their Kshatriya *dharma* to fight.

History of Vaishnavism: With the help of Alvars, a set of twelve people who with their devotional hymns spread the sect to the common people, Vaishnavism flourished in south India. Some of the prominent *azhvars* are *Poigaiyazhvar*, *Peyazhvar*, *Periyazhvar*, *Nammazhvar* and *Andal*. Vaishnavism grew in later years due to the influence of sages like Ramanuja, Surdas, Tulsidas, Tyagaraja, etc.

With the entry of other religions into the Indian subcontinent, Hindus became more united and the discriminations of Vaishnavism and Saivism turned more into intellectual arguments rather than mutually exclusive philosophies.

Vaishnava Upanishads: Of the 108 Upanishads of the Muktika, 13 are considered Vaishnava Upanishads. They are listed with their associated Veda:

1. Nisibhatapani
2. Mahanarayana
3. Ramarahasya
4. Ramatapani
5. Vasudeva
6. Avyakta
7. Tarasara
8. Gopalatapani
9. Kisna
10. Hayagriva
11. Dattatreya
12. Garua
13. Kali-Sanmarana (Kali)

Shaivism

Shaivism is a form of nondual spiritual practice and philosophy originating in India. Shaivites believe that the entire creation is both an expression of conscious divinity and is non-different from that divinity which they call "Shiva". Because he is simultaneously the created and the creator, Shiva is both immanent and transcendent. This concept contrasts with many semitic religious traditions in which God is seen as fundamentally different from the creation and transcendent, or "higher" than the creation. As in all Hindu denominations, Shaivism acknowledges the existence of many other deities. These deities are expressions of the Supreme One. This type of spiritual view is called Monistic Theism: the cosmos is a "monad" or single consciousness that expresses itself dualistically, but is fundamentally one. This philosophy is known in Sanskrit as Advaita Ishvaravada. Shaivism is a very deep, devotional and mystical denomination of Hinduism. As a very broad religion, Shaivism encompasses philosophical systems, devotional rituals, legends, mysticism and varied yogic practices. It contains monistic, and dualistic traditions.

Shaivites believe God transcends form, and devotees often worship Shiva in the form of a lingam, symbolizing the entire universe. God Shiva is also revered in Shaivism as the anthropomorphic manifestation of Shiva Nataraja, the Divine Dancer who animates the universe. He is also Dakshinamurti, the silent teacher; Hari-Hara, half-Shiva half-Vishnu; and Bhairava, who wields the trishula, the trident of desire, action and wisdom. In some traditions, Hanuman is also a form of Lord Siva.

History: Originated in India, Shaivism has appeal all over India. Some traditions credit the spreading of Shaivism into southern India by the great sage, Agastya, who is said to have brought Vedic traditions as well as the Tamil language. There can be found almost innumerable Shaivite temples and shrines, with many shrines accompanied as well by murtis dedicated to Ganesa, Lord of the Ganas, followers of Shiva, and son of iva and akti. The twelve Jyotirling, or "golden Iingam", shrines are among the most esteemed in Shaivism.

Features of Shaivism: The salient features of Shaivism as it is today are:

1. Siva is the supreme God among the Hindu god-trinity-Brahma, Vishnu and Siva.
2. He is worshipped in two forms. One as a lingam and the other as human form. The human form has several varieties. The most important of them are Nataraja-the dancing posture and Dakshinamoorthy-the teacher instructing the four sages on the absolute truth.
3. His consort Parvati, his sons Ganapati and Murugan are also worshipped in the temples.
4. There are many temples in Tamil Nadu dedicated to Siva. Their architecture, layout, the location of various idols, methods of worship, are all prescribed by books called Agamas and no deviation is allowed.
5. People also worship Siva at home. They have idols of natural lingam-shaped stones to which they perform ablution flower-worship and Nivedhanam. (food offering)
6. Certain portions of the Vedas such as Rudram and Chamakam are adoratory to Siva.
7. The sacred ash forms an important part of worship. Siva is bathed in it. This is distributed to the devotees who wear it on their forehead and other parts of the body with reverence.
8. The sacred syllable Om is used during the worship profusely.
9. The five syllabled word Na-ma-si-va-ya is considered holy and devotees consider it their duty to repeat it several times.

10. The priests of the Siva temples are called Sivacharyas(Saiva Brahmins).
11. Chidambaram, a town in Tamilnadu houses the famous Nataraja temple. This place is considered the holiest of siva shrines.
12. Thirugnana Sambandar, Thirunavukkarasar, Sundaramurthy and Manicka vachakar are considered the Gurus of Shaivism. The hymns sung by the first three are collected into a book called Thevaram. The work of Manickavachakar is called Thiruvachakam. These books are reverentially worshipped and recited by the devotees. The first three form part of the 63 Nayanmars, staunch devotees of Siva.

Benares is considered the holiest city of all Hindus and Shaivites. A very revered Shaivite temple is the ancient Chidambaram, in South India.

One of the most famous hymns to Shiva in the Vedas is Shri Rudram. The foremost Shaivite Vedic Mantra is Aum Namah Sivaya.

Major theological schools of Shaivism include Kashmir Shaivism, aiva Siddhanta and Virasaivism.

It is believed that the greatest author on the Shaiva religion writing in Sanskrit was Abhinavagupta, from Srinagar, Kashmir, c. 1000 CE.

Nayanars (or Nayanmars), saints from Southern India, were mostly responsible for development of Shaivism in the Middle Ages.

Within Hinduism: The presence of the different schools within Hinduism should not be viewed as a schism. On the contrary, there is no animosity between the schools. Instead there is a healthy cross-pollination of ideas and logical debate that serves to refine each school's understanding of Hinduism. It is not uncommon, or disallowed, for an individual to follow one school but take the point of view of another school for a certain issue.

Shaiva Upanishads: Of the 108 Upanishads of the Muktika canon, 14 are associated with Shaivaism[*citation needed*]. They are listed with their associated Veda:

1. Kaivalya
2. Shira
3. Atharvasikha
4. Bhajjabala
5. Kalagnirudra
6. Dakcinamurti
7. Sharabha
8. Akcamalika (Malika)
9. Rudrahdaya
10. Bhasma
11. Rudrakca
12. Ganapati
13. Panchabrahma
14. Jabala (Samaveda)

Shaktism

Shaktism is a denomination of Hinduism that worships Shakti, or Devi Mata — the Hindu name for the Great Divine Mother — in all of her forms whilst not rejecting the importance of masculine and neuter divinity (which are however deemed to be inactive in the absence of the Shakti). In pure Shaktism, the Great Goddess, or Mahadevi, is worshiped as nothing less than the highest divinity, Supreme Brahman Itself, the "one without a second," with all other forms of Divinity, female or male, considered to be merely her diverse manifestations.

Philosophy: In his seminal *History of the Shakta Religion*, N. N. Bhattacharyya explained that "[those] who worship the Supreme Deity exclusively as a Female Principle are called Shakta. The Shaktas conceive their Great Goddess as the personification of primordial energy and the source of all divine and cosmic evolution. She is identified with the Supreme Being, conceived as the Source and the Spring as well as the Controller of all the forces and potentialities of Nature. Nowhere in the religious history of the world do we come across such a completely female-oriented system."

Alternative interpretations of Shaktism, however — primarily those of Shaivite scholars, such as Satguru Sivaya Subramuniyaswami — argue that the feminine manifest is ultimately only the vehicle through which the masculine Un-manifest Parasiva is ultimately reached. In this interpretation, the Divine Mother becomes something of a mediatrix, who bestows advaitic moksha on those who worship Her. Thus, these Shaivite views often conclude that Shaktism is effectively a sub-denomination of Shaivism, arguing that Devi is worshipped in order to attain union with Siva, who in Shaktism is the impersonal unmanifest Absolute. This remains a minority view in Shaktism proper, which considers Siva as an equal and inseparable aspect of Devi.

Origin and History: Shaktism as we know it today developed between the 4th and the 7th centuries CE in India. It was during this development that the many religious texts, known as the Tantras, were written. In a certain sense, one could consider oneself a Shakta (a devotee of Shakti), a Shaiva (a devotee of Shiva), and a Vaishnava (a devotee of Vishnu) all at the same time.

Roots in Hinduism: This form of Hinduism is strongly associated with Vedanta, Samkhya and Tantra Hindu philosophies and is ultimately monist, though there is a rich tradition of Bhakti yoga associated with it. The feminine energy (Shakti) is considered to be the motive force behind all action and existence in the phenomenal cosmos in Hinduism. The cosmos itself is Brahman, the concept of the unchanging, infinite, immanent and transcendent reality that is the Divine Ground of all being, the "world soul". Masculine potentiality is actualized by feminine dynamism, embodied in multitudinous goddesses who are ultimately reconciled in one.

The keystone text is the Devi Mahatmya which combines earlier Vedic theologies, emergent Upanishadic philosophies and developing tantric cultures in a laudatory exegesis of Shakti religion. Demons of ego, ignorance and desire bind the soul in maya (illusion) (also alternately ethereal or embodied) and it is Mother Maya, shakti, herself, who can free the bonded individual. The immanent Mother, Devi, is for this reason focused on with intensity, love, and self-dissolving concentration in an effort to focus the *shakta* (as a Shakti worshipper is sometimes known) on the true reality underlying time, space and causation, thus freeing one from karmic cyclism. A common hymn describing the 1000 names of Devi is the Lalita sahasranama.

Worship: Among the manifestations of Devi most favoured for worship by Shaktas are Kali, Durga, and Parvati. Durga is an epithet of Mahadevi, or "Great Goddess," who is celebrated in the Devi Mahatmya. Kali is the goddess of destruction and transformation, as well as the devourer of time, as her name implies (*kala* means "time," and also means "black"). Parvati is the gentle wife of Shiva, one of the most popular gods of modern Hinduism, and is strongly associated with Kali and other goddesses.

Shakta worship takes many forms, but is heavily influenced by Tantra. Shakti is worshipped in several ways in the course of a puja (worship ceremony), including offerings of sweets and flowers, chanting mantras, using mudras, and typically offering some sort of sacrifice. She is most powerfully worshipped by chanting her bija mantra, which is different for each goddess.

Animal sacrifice is performed in some places in India, including such major sites as Kalighat in Calcutta, West Bengal, where goats are sacrificed daily, but especially on Kali's holy days of Tuesdays and Saturdays, and Kamakhya in Guwahati, Assam. Black male goats are typically sacrificed, as well as male buffalo during Durga Puja, and this practice is a controversial one. Animal rights groups have clashed with those who support the sacrifices, and though Indian law forbids the public slaughter of animals, the rule is rarely, if ever, enforced. There are rules surrounding the sacrifice, however: the brahmin performing the sacrifice is not allowed to cause pain to the animal, and must wait for the animal to surrender before cutting off the head with a single stroke, the least painful method. In addition, according to various traditions, the animal is said to achieve a higher level of rebirth, or in some cases, ultimate liberation. The head is offered to the goddess, the blood is used to bless icons and worshippers, and the meat cooked and served to the worshippers and poor as prasad. Those who are averse to animal sacrifice will use a pumpkin or melon instead, which has become a popular and acceptable substitute.

Shaktism is also fused with local beliefs in villages throughout India. In Tamil Nadu, Kerala and Andhra Pradesh, she is known as Amma (mother). Rural Bengalis know her as Tushu. The Brahmanical idea of Shakti has become fused with local beliefs in protective village goddesses who punish evil, cure diseases and bring boons and blessings to the people of the village. Major annual festivals throughout India include Durga Puja (October, national), Diwali (November, national), Kali Puja (October/November, national), Minakshi Kalyanam (April/May in Madurai, Tamil Nadu) and Ambubachi Mela (June/July in Guwahati, Assam), which is the most important festival to Shakta Tantriks.

Shakta Upanishads: Of the 108 Upanishads of the Muktika, 9 are considered Shakta Upanishads. They are listed with their associated Veda:

1. Sita
2. Annapurna
3. Devi
4. Tripuratapani
5. Tripura
6. Bhavana
7. Saubhagya
8. Sarasvatirahasya
9. Bahivsca

One of the best explanations of how Shakti religion views the aspects of the Great Goddess comes from the Introduction to the poems of the Shakti poet, Ramprasad Sen, entitled "Grace and Mercy in Her Wild Hair" by Leonard Nathan and Clinton Seely :

Smartism

Smartism (or Smarta Sampradaya, *Smarta Tradition*, as termed in Sanskrit), is a denomination of the Hindu religion. The term Smarta refers to adherents who follow the Vedas and Shastras. They mainly follow the Advaita Vedanta philosophy of Adi Shankara. But there have been instances when they have advocated or followed other philosophies.

In Sanskrit, *Smarta* means "relating to memory, recorded in or based on the *Smrti*, based on tradition, prescribed or sanctioned by traditional law or usage, (etc.)", from the root *smr* ("remember"). *Smarta* is a vriddhi derivation of Smriti just as *Srauta* is a *vriddhi* derivation of Sruti.

Salient Features of Smartism: Smartas are followers and propagators of *Smriti* or religious texts derived from Vedic scriptures. It is from this that the name *smarta* is derived. This term is used with respect to a certain specialized category of Brahmins. It was Adi Shankaracharya who brought all the Vedic communities together. He removed the un-Vedic aspects that had crept into them. He said that any of the different Hindu gods could be worshipped, according to the prescriptions given in the smriti texts. He established that worship of various deities are compatible with Vedas and is not contradictory, since all are different manifestations of *Brahman*. His ideas were accepted as he succeeding in convincing brahmins of his day, that this is exactly what was indicated by the Vedas.

Advaita Vedanta: God, according to Smartas who happen to follow Advaita philosophy, is both Saguna and Nirguna. As a Nirguna he is pure consciousness dissociated from matter. He (the gender itself is meaningless here) has no attributes, and has no form. As a saguna, there is quality that can be attributed. He is infinite and thus can have a multitude of attributes. Accordingly, the scriptures hold that Vishnu and Shiva are ultimately the same. The Smarta theologians have cited many references to support this point. For example, they interpret verses in both the Shri Rudram, the most sacred mantra in Shaivism, and the Vishnu Sahasranama, one of the most sacred prayers in Vaishnavism, to show this unity. Vishnu Purana carries a story about how Maha Vishnu becomes Brahma, Vishnu and Shiva. In other words, these forms and names are just different manifestations of Nirguna Brahman-the Ultimate Reality.

One great advaita scholar, Sri Chandrasekhara Bharati (1892-1954), commentating on this, said. "you cannot see the feet of the Lord, why do you waste your time debating about the nature of His face?"

It is most essential for Smarta Brahmins to specialize in the Karma Kanda of the Vedas and associated rituals diligently, and to teach the subsequent generations. This is the only reason that these families continue to be called Smartas.

Shanmata and Influence on Contemporary Hinduism: Adi Shankara propagated the tradition of *Shanmata* (Sanskrit, meaning Six Opinions). In this six major deities are worshipped. This is based on the belief in the essential sameness of all deities, the unity of Godhead, and their conceptualization of the myriad deities of India as various manifestations of the one divine power, Brahman. Smartas accept and worship the six manifestations of God, (Ganesha, Shiva, Shakti, Vishnu, Surya and Skanda) and the choice of the nature of God is up to the individual worshipper since different manifestations of God are held to be equivalent.

Many Hindus, who may not understand or follow Advaita philosophy, in contemporary Hinduism, invariably follow the Shanmata belief worshiping many forms of God. One commentator, noting the influence of the Smarta tradition, remarked that although many Hindus may not strictly identify themselves as Smartas but, by adhering to Advaita Vedanta as a foundation for non-sectarianism, are indirect followers. Additionally, most of the Hindu teachers of the modern era such as Ramakrishna, with the notable exception of A.C. Bhaktivedanta Swami Prabhupada, the founder of the Hare Krishna movement, all adhered to this tradition. The Smarta view dominates the view of Hinduism in the West. Smartas believe that Brahman is essentially attribute-less (nirguna), all attributes (gunas) equally belong to It, within empirical reality.

Comparison with other Beliefs: By contrast, a Vaishnavite considers Vishnu to be the true God who is worthy of worship and other forms as his subordinates. See for example, an illustration of the Vaishnavite view of Vishnu as the one true God, at this link. Accordingly, Vaishnavites, for example, believe that only Vishnu can grant the ultimate salvation for mankind, moksha. See for example, this link. Similarly, many Shaivites also hold similar beliefs about Lord Shiva, as illustrated here and here.

Notably, Shakti is worshipped to reach Shiva, whom for Shaktas is the impersonal Absolute. In Shaktism, emphasis is given to the feminine manifest through which the male unmanifested, Lord Shiva, is realized. Additionally, Shaivites and Vaishnavites often regard Surya as an aspect of Shiva and Vishnu, respectively. For example, the sun is called Surya Narayana by Vaishnavites. In Saivite theology, the sun is said to be one of eight forms of Shiva, the Astamurti. Additionally, Ganesh and Skanda for them, would be aspects of Shiva and Shakti. According to smartism, most Hindus worship Saguna Brahman as Vishnu or Shiva.

Smarta Practices: The Smartas hold practice of Dharma more important than beliefs. This is a distinct feature of the Dharmic religions. The practices include mainly Yajnas. The daily routine includes performing

- Snana (bathing)
- Sandhyavandanam
- Japa
- Puja (see Panchayatana Puja, below)
- Aupasana
- Agnihotra

The last two named Yajnas are performed in only a few households today.

Panchayatana Puja: Most Smartas worship at least one of the following Gods: Shiva, Vishnu, Ganesha, Surya, Durga and Skanda.

Adi Shankaracharya recommended the Smartas to follow Panchayatana worship. This puja or worship includes the worship of the first five deities mentioned above. (In Tamil Nadu Skanda is also worshipped). In this form of worship, the favorite family deity is placed in the center. All other Gods were placed around this central God and worshipped.

There are different sets of rules for each stage of an individual's life. The stages of life prescribed in the Vedic scriptures are Brahmacharya Ashrama, Grihastha Ashrama, Vanaprastha Ashrama and Sannyasa Ashrama.

Other Practices: All Smartas who take up the Brahmacharya Ashrama by undergoing Upanayana, are expected to learn the Vedas and Shastras besides leading a celibate Life. They are expected to eat satvik food and adhere to other rules of the Smriti tradition of their respective families.

Smartas are recommended to follow the *Brahma* form of Vedic marriage (a type of arranged marriage). The marriage ceremony is based on Vedic prescriptions. Women acquire the traditions of her husband's family.

The Shrauta Tradition: Traditionally the Smartas also follow the Shrauta tradition. The Shrauta tradition emphasises on performance of Yajnas which are described in the Vedas. The number of Smartas who follow Shrauta tradition is quite less today. However in the southern states the Shrauta tradition is held to be strong.

Religious Institutions: The few of the traditional Smarta religious institutions are:

- Sharada Pitha
- Jyotirmapha Pitha
- Govardhana Pitha
- Dwaraka Pitha
- Kanchi Kamakoti Pitha

Some modern Hindu missions that can be said to follow Smarta tradition are:

- Chinmaya Mission
- Divine Life Society

Advaita Vedanta: The Smarta world view is influenced by Advaita philosophy. Adi Shankaracharya, who founded the Advaita Mathas in Sringeri (Sharada Ptha), Dvaraka (Dwaraka Pitha), Puri (Govardhana Ptha) and Badrinath (Jyotirmapha Ptha), is considered to be the fountainhead of the Smarta tradition as it stands today. All the *Jagadgurus* (heads) of the Advaita Mathas (also known as *Shankara Mathas*) are Smartas.

Some of the prominent Smarta advaitins are:

- Adi Shankaracharya and his four disciples,
- Hastamalakacharya
- Sureshwaracharya
- Padmapadacharya
- Totakacharya

Some of the later advaitins include:

- Madhusudana Saraswati
- Appaiah Dikshitar
- Vachaspati Mishra

Other Philosophies

- Sreekanta was the founder of Siva Advaita.
- Tyagaraja, a Smarta, was a Bhakti Saint and musical genius who inspired Hindus of many different sects. Deeply immersed in Bhakti, this devotee of Lord Rama, was acceptable to even non Smartas. In his compositions, the Saint is a simple and humble Bhakta. In one of his compositions he asks which one is better "Dvaita or Advaita?". He leaves the question open. He belonged to that category of saints who believe in Bhakti as the path to God. In this sense his teachings were suitable to people of all the three major south Indian sects-Smartas, Sri Vaishanavas and Madhvas. His music was said to be so enchanting that even people of all sects, castes and creeds flocked to listen to him.
- The modern philosopher Jiddu Krishnamurti, who was born in a Smarta Muluknadu family, refused to be tied down by his own tradition. Initially influenced by theosophy, he later moved away from even this. He believed in independently evaluating all spiritual questions and refusing to be tied down by any sect or tradition.
- Besides these there were a number of other Non Advaitic Scholars among Smartas prior to Shankaracharya. Ramanujacharya, Madhavacharya, Vallabhacharya were only some of the Smartas who broke away from the parent group and founded their own sects. The philosophy of the new sects was directed against the teachings of Advaita philosophy. The new sects distinguished themselves and separated from Smartas. These new groups followed different philosophies like Dvaita (dualism) and Vishishtadvaita (qualified monism) and also changed their rituals. Appaiah Deekshita, a Smarta Iyer, followed Sreekanta's Sivadvaita philosophy in his early days. This philosophy was similar to Vishishtadvaita of the Sri Vaishnavas. Siva Advaita, however, considers Shiva to be the supreme God. Communities like the *Sri Vaishnavas*, *Madhvas* and *Veera Saivas* are some of the other Hindu sects which have branched/broken away from the Smarta stream. A distinctive feature of these communities is the fact that none of them subscribe to Advaita. Some of these sects have also accepted people who came from outside the Smarta Brahmin fold; indeed, the Veera Saiva community includes non-Brahmins. Another feature of these sects is that they follow rituals recommended by their lineage of Gurus, which are different from the rituals of the Smartas.

Smartas follow the Hindu scriptures. These include:

1. The Vedas (Rig Veda, Yajur Veda, Sama Veda and Atharva Veda). These are considered primary spiritual resources; every Brahmin family is affiliated to one or more of the Vedas. The Upanishads, which are part of the Vedas, are often mentioned separately, given their especial importance as products of past intellectual ferment.
2. The *Smritis"* are religious books based on Vedas and are written by important Sages/Rishis of the past. Each of them contains recommendations and practices unique to itself. The Book an individual followed depended on his family. Thus, ritual practices sometimes varied from family to family, depending on family tradition. Some of the more common religious law books were the Manu Smriti, the Apastamba Smriti and the Bodhyayana Smriti.
3. The Puranas contain the lore and explanations of the theology of the Vedas. They are basically

a collection of sacred historical events that were passed from one generation to the next in the form of mythological stories. Smarta philosophers use the puranas to get a better understanding of Vedas, but do not consider them as completely authentic texts. However, the eighteen Puranas are revered by Smartas, just like any other Hindus. Today the Puranas are the main inspiration for many Smartas.

4. Smartas also recite Shlokas or Stotras (devotional hymns) composed by various Hindu saints and poets.

Hindu Reform Movements

Hinduism is going through a phase of regeneration and reform through the vehicle of several contemporary movements, collectively termed as contemporary Hindu movements. Although these movements are very individual in their exact philosophies they generally stress the spiritual, secular and logical/scientific aspects of the Vedic traditions, creating a form that is egalitarian that does not discriminate based on Jati (ethnic group), gender, or race.

Active Hindu communities are to be found in all parts of the world. In particular, the former Soviet Union countries and Poland have thriving Hindu communities due to the missionary work of the Hare Krishnas. It is notable that most of the Hindu movements, with the exception of Hare Krishna movement, reflect a more Smarta-like ideology.

There are groups in India that are actively engaged in getting women and those from socially disadvantaged jatis to become priests of Vedic ritual.

The new movements look up to Swami Vivekananda; Rabindranath Tagore; Ramana Maharshi; Shri Aurobindo (for his *Integral Yoga*); A.C. Bhaktivedanta Swami Prabhupada (founder of the modern Hare Krishna movement); Swami Sivananda, Swami Ramatirtha; Narayana Guru, Paramhansa Yogananda; Shrii Shrii Anandamurti and for inspiration. More recently, the work of Maharishi Mahesh Yogi, Sathya Sai Baba, Shirdi Sai Baba who has many Muslim followers, Swami Muktananda, Swami Chinmayananda, Dayananda Saraswati, Sri Sri Ravi Shankar, and Ammachi has inspired millions to create new centers of spiritual development. In the intellectual field, the writings of Ananda Coomaraswamy, Ram Swarup, Stephen Knapp, Sita Ram Goel, Subhash Kak and David Frawley have been influential.

In social work, Mahatma Gandhi, Vinoba Bhave, Pandurang Shastri Athavale, Baba Amte and Shrii Shrii Anandamurti have been most important. Sundarlal Bahuguna created the *chipko* movement for the preservation of forestlands according to the Hindu ecological ideas.

The increasing popularity of yoga and meditation has helped Hindus to re-discover their roots such as practised in the Brahma Kumaris World Spiritual Organisation and the Ananda Marga Pracaraka Samgha. The revival of Indian classical arts like dance and sculpture have been influential in instilling pride.

A socio-cultural organisation called the Rashtriya Swayamsevak Sangh (RSS) was formed by Dr. Keshav Baliram Hegdewar in 1925. The motto was to unite Hindus, make them rise over their caste differences and work for the glory of the Hindu Rashtra (Bharat). However, the group has a subset that believes sikhs should convert to hinduism due to sikhism "not being its own religion." Something that offends many sikhs.

In Indonesia there are several movements in favour of return to Hinduism in Java, Sumatra, Kalimantan, and Sulawesi. Balinese Hinduism, known as Agama Hindu Dharma, has witnessed great resurgence in recent years.

Shri Prabhat Rainjan Sarkar (founder of Ananda Marga) composed 5018 songs called Prabhat Samgeet from 1982-1990 and initiated a new renaissance in Indian world of samgeet.

The Hindu Renaissance: Since the late 1970's, Hinduism has been going through what the Hindu community calls a "Hindu Renaissance". British rule in India and western cultural influence had weakened the faith, but the popularity of Hinduism in the West and activism of certain influential leaders, such as Satguru Sivaya Subramuniyaswami, reversed this trend. New developments regarding what some view as possible fallacies regarding the Indo-Aryan migration, coupled with the consistent economic growth throughout the country are both given as important factors in the recent growth period. Hinduism has also experienced much growth internationally through a number of enthusiastic preaching movements and the migration of native Indian people to other countries.

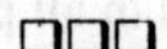

3

SUFI PHILOSOPHY

Sufi Cosmology

Although there is no consensus with regard to Sufi cosmology, one can disentangle various threads that led to the crystallization of more or less coherent cosmological doctrines. Reading various authoritative texts, one can see that practitioners of Sufism were not much bothered with inconsistencies and contradictions that have arisen due to juxtaposition and superposition of at least three different cosmographies:

The Ishraqi visionary universe as expounded by Suhrawardi Maqtul, Neoplatonic view of cosmos cherished by Islamic philosophers like Ibn Sina/Avicenna and Sufis like Ibn Arabi and Hermetic-Ptolemaic spherical geocentric world. All these doctrines (and each one of them claiming to be impeccably orthodox) were freely mixed and juxtaposed, frequently with confusing results - a situation one encounters in other esoteric doctrines, from Hebrew Kabbalah and Christian Gnosticism to Vajrayana Buddhism and Trika Shaivism. The following cosmological plan is usually found in various Sufi texts:

Alam-e-Hahoot (Realm of He-ness): It can also be thought of as the Realm of preexistence, i.e. the condition of the universe before its formation. It is equated with unknowable God's essence and named Alam-e-Hahut (the world of "He-ness"). Etymologically, the Arabic root word for God with attributes (or Manifest Absolute) is Al-Lah or "the Divinity", and Hu ("He") is the root word for Unmanifest Absolute, the naked essence of Godhead that nothing can be said about. Alam-e-Hahoot has similarities to the Christian concept of Deus absconditus, and the Hindu notion of Nirguna Brahma.

Alam-e-Lahoot (Realm of Divinity): Realm of Divinity is that region where incalculable unseen tiny dots emerge and expand to such large circles that they engulf the entire universe. This Realm is also known as Tajalliat (The Beatific Vision, or the Circle of the Beatific Vision). These countless circles are the bases of all the root causes of the universe. These very circles give rise to the species (or kinds of non living) of the universe. This whole circle is known as the Ghaib-ul-ghaib (Unseen of the Unseen). It is that ascent for which the human perception could train itself for the cognition of the Extolled Veil and Beatific Visions of the attributes of God that are operative in there. Alam-e-Lahoot has similarities to the Christian concept of Deus revelatus and the Hindu notion of Saguna Brahma.

The final boundary of the human knowledge and understanding is called *Hijab-e-Mehmood* (The Extolled Veil), which is the extreme height of the Arsh (Supreme Empyrean). *Nehr-e-tasweed (The* Channel of Black Drought/Darkness) whose last limit is in the Realm of Divinity, is the basis of the Unseen & feeds Rooh-e-Azam (The Great Soul).

Alam-e-Jabaroot (Realm of Omnipotency): The stage when the universe is constituted into features is known as the Realm of Omnipotency. *Hijab-e-Kibria* (The Grand Veil) is the last limit of this realm. *Nehr-e-tajreed (Channel of Abstraction)*, whose last limit is The Realm of Omnipotency, feeds Rooh-e-Insani (Human Soul) with its information.

Alam-e-Malakoot (Angelic Realm): When the characteristics of the species and their individuals descend from the Realm of Omnipotency, separate consciousness comes into being, this stage is called the Angelic Realm. Its last limit is called *Hijab-e-Azmat* (The Great Veil). *Nehr-e-Tasheed* (Channel of Evidence) whose last limit is Angelic Realm, feeds Latifa-e-Qalbi.

Alam-e-Nasoot (Realm of Humans): When the features further descend and come out of the limits of the angelic realm, foundations of the tangible world of matter are being laid, which is known as Alam-e-Nasoot. It includes the material realm (most of which humans can see), and all the normally visible cosmos is included in it. *Nehr-e-Tazheer* (Channel of Manifestation) whose last limit is Alam-e-Nasoot, feeds Latifa-e-Nafsi. Human Realm is categorized as under:

One Kitab-al-Mubeen, that controls

300 million Loh-e-Mehfooz, each one controlling

80 thousand Hazeere (Galaxies), each one containing

13 billion Solar systems, out of which

1 billion solar systems have life on one of their planets.

Each Star has 9, 12 or 13 planets around it.

On every planet with life on it, life exists in three different planes of existence. These include Plane of Angels, Plane of Jinns, & Plane of Humans. On the other hand, it is surrounded by another realm known as *Alam-e-Araf* or *Barzakh* (Astral plane), where humans stay after they die (when the connection of soul breaks with the physical body). Humans can also visit astral realm during sleep (in dream state) or during meditation.

Neoplatonist-Hermetic scheme

Ghayb-al-Ghaib

Aql-e-Kulli

Nafs-e-Kulliya

Lataif-e-sitta: Drawing from Quranic verses, virtually all Sufis distinguish Lataif-e-Sitta ("the six subtleties"): Nafs, Qalb, Sirr, Ruh, Khafi, and Akhfa. These lataif (singular: latifa) designate various psychospiritual "organs" or, sometimes, faculties of sensory and suprasensory perception. They are thought to be parts of the self in a similar manner to the way glands and organs are part of the body. Similar concepts in other belief systems include Chinese traditional or vedic chakras.

In general, sufic development involves the awakening in a certain order these spiritual centers of perception that lie dormant in every person. Each center is associated with a particular color and general area of the body, as well as oft times with a particular prophet, and varies from Order to Order. The help of a guide is considered necessary to help activate these centers. The activation of all these "centers" is part of the inner methodology of the sufi way or "Work". After undergoing this process, the dervish is said to reach a certain type of "completion" or becomes a Complete Man.

These six "organs" or faculties, and the purificative activities applied to them, contain the basic orthodox Sufi philosophy. The purification of elementary passionate nature (Tazkiya-I-Nafs), followed by cleansing of the spiritual heart so that it may acquire a mirrorlike purity of reflection (Tazkiya-I-Qalb) and become the receptacle of God's love (Ishq), illumination of the spirit (Tajjali-I-Ruh), fortified by emptying of egoic drives (Taqliyya-I-Sirr) and remembrance of God's attributes (Dhikr), and completion of journey with purification of the last two faculties, Khafi and Akhfa. Through these "organs" or faculties the transformative results from their activation, the basic Sufi psychology is outlined and bears some resemblance to the schemata known as the kabbalah or to some the Indian chakra system.

Latifa-e-Nafsi: This is technically not a bonafide latifa but is recognized as a location, namely slightly below the navel. This "center" is not associated with any color.

The word nafs is usually translated as self or psyche. Its etymology is rooted in "breath" (similar to Biblical or Kabbalistic nefesh) and is common to virtually all archaic psychologies where the act of breathing was connected with life, animating otherwise lifeless object. In this respect, ancient notions of "Atman" in Hinduism (cf. German noun "Atem", breath, respiration) or Greek "pneuma" (as well as Latin "spiritus")-all equate the basic visible process of breathing with energizing principle that confers existence to an individual human being. Some Sufis consider under the term "Nafs" the entirety of psychological processes, encompassing whole mental, emotional and volitional life; however, the majority of Quranic-based Sufis are of the opinion that Nafs is a "lower", egotistical and passionate human nature which, along with Tab (literally, physical nature), comprises vegetative and animal aspects of human life. Synonyms for Nafs are devil, passion, greed, avarice, ego-centeredness etc. The central aim of the Sufi path is transformation of Nafs (technical term is "Tazkiya-I-Nafs"' or "purgation of the soul'") from its deplorable state of ego-centredness through various psycho-spiritual stages to the purity and submission to the will of God. Although the majority of the Sufi orders have adopted convenient 7 maqams (maqams are permanent stages on the voyage towards spiritual transformation), and some still operate with 3 stages, the picture is clear: the Sufi's journey begins with Nafs-e-Ammara (commanding soul), Nafs-e-lawwama (self-accusing soul), and ends in Nafs-e-Mutmainna (satisfied soul)-although some Sufis's final stage is, in their technical vocabulary, Nafs-I-Safiya wa Kamila (soul restful and perfected in God's presence). In essence, this is almost identical to Christian paradigm of "vita purgativa" and various stages the spiritual aspirant traverses in the journey towards God.

Latifa-e-Qalbi: The first real center is located in the left of Chest and is associated with the color yellow. In Latifa-e-Qalbi man witnesses his deeds. By awakening it man also gets the knowledge of the realm of Jins.

The word Qalb, stands for heart. In Sufi terminology, this spiritual heart (not to be confused with the blood pumping organ) is again variously described. For some, it is the seat of beatific vision. Others consider it the gate of Ishq or Divine love. Yet, for the majority, it is the battleground of two warring armies: those of Nafs and Ruh or spirit. Here, one again encounters terminological confusion: for the Sufis influenced by Neoplatonism, a "higher" part of Nafs is equated to the Aql or intellect (called Nafs-I-Natiqa) or "rational soul" and is the central active agent in spiritual battle: Ruh or spirit, notwithstanding its name, is rather passive in this stage. In short, cleansing of the Qalb or heart is a necessary spiritual discipline for travellers on the Sufi path. The term for this process is Tazkiah-I-Qalb and the aim is the erasure of everything that stands in the way of purifying God's love or Ishq.

Qalb and Nafs form the "Rooh-e-haivani" (Animal Soul). This part of the soul has the record of every activity of life. It is also termed as Joviya (Confluence).

Latifa-e-Ruhi: The second faculty is ruh, located in the right side of the chest and its color is red. After its activation the human gets acquainted with Alam-e-Aaraf (the place where man resides after death). This center is associated with the idea of "spirit."

Ruh or spirit is the second contender in the battle for human life. Again, opinions on Ruh differ among Sufis. Some deem it coeternal with God; others consider it a created entity. Be that as it may, Ruh is the plateau of consensus for the majority of Sufis, especially the early ones (before 11th/12th century C.E.). For those Sufis with Gnostic leanings (which can be found in Bektashi or Mevlevi orders), Ruh is a soul-spark, immortal entity and transegoic "true self", similar to the Christian concepts of "synteresis" or "Imago Dei", or Vedantist notion of "jiva", as well as Tibetan Buddhist "shes-pa", principle of consciousness and Taoist "shen" or spirit. But, the majority of the Sufis would consider this an unnecessarily extravagant speculation and would stick to the more orthodox notion of dormant spiritual faculty that needs to be worked upon by constant vigil and prayer in order to achieve the Tajliyya-I-Ruh, or Illumination of the spirit. Ironically, this spiritual faculty is frequently referred to in terms one encounters in connection with Nafs- "blind" life force or life current that needs to be purified by strict religious observances in order to achieve illumination.

Latifa-e-Sirri: The third faculty is Sirr, located in the solar plexus and is associated with the color white. It records the orders of Allah for the individual in similitude to that which is originally present in Loh-e-mehfooz (Preserved Scriptorum). After its activation, human being gets acquainted with Aalam-e-Misal (The Allegorical realm-Reflection of knowledge of the preserved Scriptorum.) This center is associated with consciousness.

Sirr, literally means "the secret". Emptying of the Sirr (Taqliyya-I-Sirr) is basically focusing on God's names and attributes in perpetual remembrance or Dhikr, hence diverting one's attention from the mundane aspects of human life and fixing it on the spiritual realm. The "emptying" signifies negation and obliteration of ego-centred human propensities.

Sirr and Rooh form "Rooh-e-Insani (Human soul) or Ayan. This part of the soul is inscribed with commands characterizing the life. It is also termed as Ayan. When a human being gets acquainted with it, he can witness the record and scheme of "all that exists", written on loh-e-mahfooz.

Latifa-e-Khafi: It is located in the middle of the forehead (between the eyes or third eye position) and is associated with black. It's the equivalent of Kitab-e-Marqoom (the written book).

The term Khafi means mysterious, arcane or Latent Subtlety. It represents intuition.

Latifa-e-Akhfa: The term Akhfa or ikhfa means most arcane, deeply mysterious or obscure Subtlety. Its location alternates between deep inside the brain and the center of the chest. The color of this center is green. It's the Nuqta-e-wahida (point of unity) in every human where the Tajalliat (Beatific visions) of Allah are directly revealed. It has got recorded information about the hidden knowledge of universe. By entering into this point, the human being enters the system of universe and laws governing the universe and he understands the meaning of " for you we (allah) have revealed whatever is in the earth and the heavens ". This center is associated with deep perception.

The last center or subtlety is "accessible only to those who have developed the others, and belongs to the real sage."

Akhfa and khafa form "Rooh-e-azam" (the great soul), also called sabita. It is a bright ring of light in which all the information pertaining to the unseen and seen cosmos are inscribed. The Attributes of God that have been transferred to the existents and have become parts of the mechanism of the universe are collectively known as the Incumbent Knowledge (Ilm-e-wajib). The knowledge of Incumbent means that knowledge that has been transferred to the existents, that is, it refers to those Attributes of God with which existents enjoy an affinity and correlation. The Knowledge of Incumbent is also known as the Knowledge of the Pen (Ilm-e-Qalum).

First Descent is that state when God exhibited the program present in His Mind as He Willed. The creative formulae of the cosmos are the secrets of the First Descent. Why did God opt to create the universe and what is the Will of God, which He intends to accomplish? Reflection of all these things is found in the Great Soul; The Firmly Affixed Inscription. One side of Great Soul is the Obscure Subtlety (akhfa) and the other side is the Latent Subtlety (khafi) Great Soul is the storehouse of eleven thousand Beatific Visions of God. The person, who manages to have the acquaintance of these two subtleties, can observe these eleven thousand Beatific Visions. It will not be out of place to remind that these two subtleties of akhfa and khafi are found in every human being irrespective of the fact that who he is, what he is or to where does he belong.

It is important to mention that "Great Soul", "Human Soul", and "Animal Soul" are actually "levels of functioning" of the same soul and not three different souls. These three parts of soul are like three rings of light infused in one another and are collectively called the soul, the indivisible entity, Lord's edict of simply the man. Man gets acquainted with them one by one by Muraqaba (Sufi Meditation), Dhikr (Remembrance of God) and purification of one's psyche/life from negative thinking patterns (fear, depression), negative emotions (hate, contempt, anger, lust) and negative practices (hurting others psychologically or physically). Loving God and loving/helping every human being irrespective of his race, religion or nationality, and without consideration for any possible reward, is the key to ascension according to Sufis.

Fanaa (Sufism)

Fanaa is the Sufi term for extinction. It means to annihilate the self, while remaining physically alive. Persons having entered this state are said to have no existence outside of and unity with Allah. Fanaa is equivalent to the concept of nirvana in Buddhism or moksha in Hinduism which also aims for annihilation of the self.

Fana may be attained by constant meditation and by contemplation on the attributes of God, coupled with the denunciation of human attributes. It is a sort of mental, yet real, death. The man of the "Way" experiences it freely; it is the final passage which leads to the summit of the Stages. It liberates man from all contingency outside of his spiritual quest; his ultimate aim is the Truth. Three degrees may be distinguished here: fanâ' of acts, attributes and essence.

The Sufi fanâ' in its triple manifestation does not have an exclusively negative effect or action; it is the annihilation of everything contingent, whether this be in the form of action, attribute or essence; more precisely, it is the annihilation of everything that is not God, and God is the supreme object of all good, all beauty. Fanâ' thus conceived is an internal state which requires from the Sufi a sustained and permanent effort of concentration to break his fetters and take on the demands and calls of truth, by his acts, his moral virtues, his whole being. That implies perfect control of himself: in words, deeds and thoughts. It is at this price that he attains an interior spiritual state where he becomes the pure and clear mirror in which the lights of Truth are reflected in all their splendor.

There are three ways in man's journey towards God. The first is the way of ignorance, through which each must travel. It is like a person walking for miles in the sun while carrying a heavy load on his shoulder, who, when fatigued, throws away the load and falls asleep under the shade of a tree. Such is the condition of the average person, who spends his life blindly under the influence of his senses and gathers the load of his evil actions; the agonies of his earthly longings creating a hell through which he must pass to reach the destination of his journey. With regard to him the Quran says, 'He who is blind in life, shall also be blind in the hereafter.'

The next way is that of devotion, which is for true lovers. Rumi says, 'Man may be the lover of man or the lover of God; after his perfection in either he is taken before the King of love.' Devotion is the heavenly wine, which intoxicates the devotee until his heart becomes purified from all infirmities and there remains the happy vision of the Beloved, which lasts to the end of the journey. 'Death is a bridge, which unites friend to friend' (Sayings of Mohammed).

The third is the way of wisdom, accomplished only by the few. The disciple disregards life's momentary comforts, unties himself from all earthly bondages and turns his eyes toward God, inspired with divine wisdom. He gains command over his body, his thoughts and feelings, and is thereby enabled to create his own heaven within himself, that he may rejoice until merged into the eternal goal. 'We have stripped the veil from thine eyes, and thy sight today is keen', says the Quran. All must journey along one of these three paths, but in the end they arrive at one and the same goal. As it is said in the Quran, 'It is He who multiplied you on the earth, and to Him you shall be gathered.'

Baqaa

Baqaa, with literal meaning of permanency, is a term which describes a particular state of life with God, through God, in God, and for God. It is the summit of the mystical manazil, that is, the destination or the abode. Baqaa comprises of three degrees, each one referring to a particular aspect of the divine thiophenes as principle of existence and its qualitative evolution, comprising of faith, knowledge, and grace.

First Aspect: the Level of Acts: The first aspect of the Sufi permanency is situated at the level of acts. The action of the Sufi is here united with the divine action acquiring its order, harmony and durability. This specific degree of Sufi ''baqa''' is the result of the shooting forth of the divine theophany as existential principle and the lights of nature as source of knowledge.

Second Aspect: the Level of Qualities and Attributes: The second aspect of permanency is situated at the level of qualities and attributes. Here human virtues are raised to the level of the divine Attributes, acquiring their perfection, dignity and durability: such that the man's heart attains to a spiritual abode where it is the pure and clear mirror on which the characteristics of the supreme Creator are engraved. In its turn, the power of acts in the abode of permanence becomes a docile instrument by which the divine plans in the world and within the living person are realized. This particular form of ''baqa''' is a reflection of the divine existential thiophenes at the level of the Attributes and Qualities, and the effect of the lights of the intellect as principle of knowledge.

Third Aspect: the Level of the Essence: The last degree of 'baqa' is permanency of the essence. In this domain the essence of the servant is raised to the height of the divine Essence in its Unity, Sublimity and Universality. He is totally absorbed by the divine Life. It is through God that he sees, through Him that he hears, through Him that he expresses his will, through Him that he contemplates. This is the most perfect form of Sufi 'baqa', the final stage of the hero's quest. This particular abode is in its turn acquired by the effect of the thiophenes of the Essence on the existential plane and by the effect of the thiophenes of Light at the gnostic level.

Yaqeen

Yaqeen is generally translated as "certainty", and is considered the summit of the many stations by which the path of *walaya* (sometimes translated as Sainthood) is fully completed. This is the repository of liberating experience in Islam. In relation to the exoteric religious life Certainty is the sister of religious life in its perfection (*ehsn*), that is to say the adoration of Allah according to the visionary way; through this channel it is the pillar of Islam in the accomplishment of its external practices, as it is the foundation of faith (*imn*) in its internal dogma. It is in fact *ihsan* which gives the external religion its true meaning and the domain of faith its real values. Certainty (*al-yaqin*), comprises three degrees.

Stages

Ilm al-yaqin (the knowledge of Certainty): The first degree is referred to by the name *'ilm al-yaqin* (the knowledge of Certainty), which means that Certainty is the result of knowledge. At this degree the object of Certainty is knowledge just as the aim of knowledge is Certainty. Both together are in the soul uniquely, such that Certainty is the first degree of spiritual life and the last of speculative experience. This particular degree of mystical *yaqin* is the result of divine thiophenes in Act at the level of existence and also the result of thiophenes of lights of nature at the gnostic level.

Ayn al-yaqin (the Eye of Certainty): The second degree of *yaqin* is what one calls in Sufi terms *ayn al-yaqin* (the Eye of Certainty), that is, Certainty as a consequence of contemplation and vision.

At this level, the object of Certainty is present in front of the gnostic and is not only a speculative concept. Here knowledge becomes what one calls 'ilm-e-huzuri" (Presence of knowledge), and that is the second aspect of Certainty in the spiritual way and in liberating experience. By this kind of knowledge, the man of the Way is distinguished from philosophers and learned men. This particular degree of spiritual Certainty is the result of divine thiophenes of Attributes at the level of existence, just as it is the result of thiophenes of lights of the intellect at the level of gnosis.

Haqq al-yaqin (the total reality of Certainty): Finally, the last degree of *yaqin* is called *haqq al-yaqin* (the total reality of Certainty), that is, Certainty as supreme truth. Here, Certainty has a particular coloring: it is the fruit of an all-embracing experience because the object of Certainty is identical to the one who is experiencing it, knowledge being transformed into actual experience and actual experience into knowledge. At this stage, in fact, knowledge is not limited to the intellect, nor to the vision of the one who is contemplating it, it becomes one with the human being. This is the final phase of *yaqin*, the apotheosis of the spiritual and intellectual journey. This high degree of Sufi Certainty is the effect of the Emanation of the divine. Thiophenes in Essence at its existential level and that of the diffusion of the Light of lights (Dazzling Irradiations) at the level of the theophanies of the gnostic.

Ihsan

Ihsan (or Ehsan or Ahsan) is an Arabic term meaning "perfection" or "excellence." In Islam, Ihsan is the Muslim responsibility to obtain perfection, or excellence, in worship, such that Muslims try to worship God (Arabic Allah) as if they see Him, and although they cannot see Him, they undoubtedly believe he is constantly watching over them. That definition comes from the hadith in which Muhammad states, It (Ihsan) is to worship Allah as if you see Him, and if you cannot achieve this state then you must remember that He is seeing you." (Al-Bukhari and Al-Muslim).

The concept of Ihsan has been understood differently by various Islamic scholars. For example, some scholars explain Ihsan as being the "inner-dimension" of Islam whereas shariah is often described as the "outer-dimension". Ihsan is excellence in worship, work, and in social interactions. For example, ihsan includes sincerity during Muslim prayers and being grateful to parents, family, and God.

Sufis have divided Ihsan into two parts

- Muraqaba i.e. to worship with the thought that The God is seeing us.
- Mushahada i.e. to worship The God as if we see him

Tajalli

Tajalliat (plural of tajalli) or theophanies in the realm of being are manifestations of the divine Truth with regard to infinite perfection and eternal glory. The divine theophanies are essentially the outpouring of His Beauty, His Perfection and His Love which are expressed in the immense theatre of the universe. The Existential Theophanies taken as a whole comprise three levels which the Ibn Arabi calls *hadarât* (Presences or Dignities).

First Level: Pure Essence: These are called existential theophanies of the Essence. They are the determinations of God in Himself, for Himself in His Essence transcending all manifestation and form. The world from which these theophanies and their radiance spring is called Unity *alam al-ahadiyya*

(Realm of Unity). In this universe, the divine Essence appears as beyond all description, name or qualification. It is the world of pure Essence considered as Mystery of Mysteries and Secret of Secrets from which the theophanies of the Essence originate, the mirror in which the absolute existential Reality is reflected.

Second Level: the Attributes: These are the existential theophanies of divine qualities. The existential theophanies of divine Attributes are the determinations of God in Himself for Himself under the aspect of His intrinsic Names and Attributes. The world specified for this type of theophany is *alam al-wahda* (*Realm of Unicity* of the Essence with Its Attributes). God-Truth manifests both in His Essence and in His intrinsic Perfection after his concealment as "Hidden Treasure. This appearance arises by the mediation of what Ibn Arabi calls the most holy emanation *(al-fayd al-aqdas)*. In this particular world of theophanies the beings destined to incarnate appear in the form of immutable realities.

Third Level: Acts: These are the active existential theophanies since the nature of God or the divinity as such is Essence, Attributes and Action, personified by His Divine Names. The existential theophanies of divine Action are the extrinsic effects of divine Power in the manifest world. The world where these theophanies are exercised and revealed is called *alam al-Wahdâniyya, The Unification* in its three aspects: Essence-Attribute-Action. It appears by the way of the holy emanation (al-fayd al-Muqaddas): a universe where God manifests Himself in the form of eternal realities encompassing species and individuals, sensible forms and abstractions.

Noor

Noor or Nur may refer to:

- An Arabic name, common among royalty
- The Arabic term for light
- Queen Noor of Jordan
- Noor Jahan, a Mughal Empress
- Noor Jehan, Pakistani actress/singer
- Noor Actress, actress
- Princess Noor Inyat Khan, secret agent and a descendant of Tipu Sultan
- Noor, Iran a city in northern Iran
- Noor, a champion racehorse in the 1950s
- Noor a concept in Sufism
- Surah of Wilaya and Nurayn
- *Dhun Nurayn* or the "Possessor of Two Lights", a Sunni nickname for Uthman, the third Sunni Caliph

Maqaam: Maqaam (the station) is one's spiritual station or developmental level, as distinct from one's hal, or state of consciousness. This is seen as the outcome of one's effort to transform oneself, whereas the haal is a gift. "Maqam" is also terms for "scale". These are the topmost foundations of "walaya:" the moral distinctions and spiritual degrees accorded to the men of the Way. They constitute the stabilizing element of liberating experience. According to Ibn 'Arabi, "al-yaqn " (certainty) the apex of the maqamaat.

Haal: Haal (Lit, "state" or "condition.", plural *ahwal*) is a special-purpose, temporary state of consciousness, generally a product of spiritual practices, recognised in Sufism.

A *haal* is by nature gratuitous and one should not attempt to prolong it. It results from psychological or spiritual influences which effect the man of the Way during his progress towards the God-King. Related concepts are Ecstasy *(wajad)*, Annihilation *(istilam)*, Happiness *(bast)*, Despondency *(qabd)*, Awakening *(sahû)* Drunkenness *(sukr)*, etc. They arise like flashes on the horizon, blinding flashes of lightning which disappear immediately. However, these stages are necessary for the liberating experience of Man; thanks to them He may distinguish the contingent from the consciousness anything except that which is destined to endure. According to Ibn Arabi, ''al-fan'' (extinction) is the apex of the *ahwal*.

Manzil: Manzil (plural manazil) is the Arabic name for one of seven parts of roughly equal length into which the Quran is divided for the purpose of reciting the entire text in one week.

Another meaning is parts of the Quran which help in curing or preventing jadoo (witchcraft).

Dhikr

Dhikr, (zikr in Urdu and Persian) (Arabic "pronouncement", "invocation" or "remembrance") is the remembrance of God commanded in the Quran for all Muslims. To engage in dhikr is to have awareness of God according to Islam. Dhikr as a devotional act includes the repetition of divine names, supplications and aphorisms from hadith literature, and sections of the Quran. More generally, any activity in which the Muslim maintains awareness of God is considered dhikr. Dhikr is also spelled zikr based on its pronunciation in Turkish, Persian, and Urdu.

Dhikr Beads: Known also as tasbih are usually beads upon a string, 99 or 100 in number, which corresponds to the 99 names of Allah and other recitations. The beads are used to keep track of the number of recitations that make up the dhikr. A popular dhikr (Subhanallah (33x) al Hamduallah (33x) Laa ilaaha illa Allah (33x) Allahu Akbar) was prescribed by the Prophet and is still practiced by many muslims worldwide after each of the daily five prayers. Even muslim inmates are allowed to utilize their beads for therapeutic effects see, [1] This is a successful action brought pursuant to 28 USC @ 1983 (by Imam Hamzah S. Alameen in the State of New York against Thomas A. Coughlin III, the Deparment of Corrections) arguing that prisoners have a First Amendment Constitutional right to use dhikr beads. Many islamic clerics argue that using the beads are fobidden, however the practice is contiguous with approved islamic traditions. It should be said that use of the fingers instead of the beads is better, since it was the practice of the Prophet. Nevertheless the beads are allowed, as long as no extra religious significance is placed upon the beads themselves, and that they are not viewed as articles of worship. At best the beads are a crude form of calculator. The Prophet's companion Abu Hurayrah had a string with 1,000 knots that he used to dhikr with before bead; one of the Prophet's wives used to count her dihkr with date palm shells (see Sunan Abu Dawud, Kitabul Dhikr) and the we have nothing from the Prophet that forbids the use of the beads and therefore dhikr beads are "halal" or "allowed" in most Islamic religious traditions. Many of the Muslim scholars of the past 1400 years, whom muslims consider foremost in knowledge, used dhikr beads.

The Sufi orders engage in ritualized dhikr ceremonies. Each order or lineage within an order has one or more forms for group dhikr, the liturgy of which may include recitation, singing, instrumental music, dance, costumes, incense, meditation, ecstasy, and trance (Touma 1996, p.162). Dhikr in a group is most often done on Thursday and/or Sunday nights as part of the institutional practice of the orders.

A group dhikr ceremony in Arabic countries is usually called the hadrah ("presence", referring not to God's presence but to that of the spirit of the Prophet Muhammad and to the awareness of each participant). The hadrah marks the climax of the Sufi's gathering regardless of any teaching or formal structure. Musically this structure includes several secular Arab genres and can last for hours. (Ibid, p.165)

The hadrah section consists of the ostinato-like repetition of the name of God over which the soloist performs a richly ornamented song. Often the climax is reached through cries of "Allah! Allah!" or "hu hu" ("He! He!"), with the participants bending forward while exhaling and stand straight while inhaling. The articulation of the name of God progresses as follows, with upward beams indicating inhalation and downward beams indicating exhalation:

The hadrah is directed by a shaykh of the tariqa or one of his representatives; monitoring the intensity, depth and duration of the phases of the hadrah, the shaykh aims to draw the circle into deep awareness of God. Dhikr ceremonies may have a ritually determined length or may last as long as the shaykh deems his murids require.

Modes of Dhikr: Depending upon the mode of Dhikr, it has been divided into 3 kinds

- Dhikr-e-Jalli—Dhikr with tongue loudly
- Dhikr-e-Khaffi—Dhikr in heart (hidden dhikr-i.e. not from tongue)

Sufis further divide the mode of meditative Dhikr according to the Latifa in which they are done. These include

- Dhikr-e-nafsi
- Dhikr-e-Qalbi
- Dhikr-e-Ruhi
- Dhikr-e-Sirri
- Dhikr-e-Khafi
- Dhikr-e-Akfha

Forms of Dhikr: Different Sufi Orders have different syllabus of dhikr. Most common ones are as follows:

- Ya-Hayyu-Ya-Qayyum (O Living & Giver of life)
- La illaha illallah (There is no god but God)
- Allah Hu (He is God)
- 99 Names of God [2]
- Verses from Quran
- Darud Sharif (Asking God to send peace & blessings upon Prophet Muhammad)
- Istaghfar (Asking forgiveness from God)

Muraqaba

Muraqaba is the Sufi word for meditation. Literally it means "to watch over", "to take care of", or "to keep an eye". Metaphorically, it implies that with meditation, a person watches over or takes care of his spiritual heart (or soul), and acquires knowledge about it, its surroundings, and its creator.

Stages of Muraqaba: Following are the *maqamat* (stages) in which sufis have broadly categorised their journey of ascension. This categorization is an arbitrary one, and each level is generally further divided into several sub-levels. During the process of enlightenment, some stages can merge or overlap each other.

Gnosis of self

Ghanood (Somnolence): This is the starting level of meditation. When a person starts meditation, he enters into a somnolent or sleep state often. With the passage of time, the person goes into a state between sleep and wakefulness. So the person can remember that he saw something, but not specifically what it is.

Adraak (experience): With continuous practice of meditation, the sleepiness from meditation decreases. When the conscious mind is not suppressed by sleep and is able to focus, the person can receive the spiritual knowledge from his subconscious mind. At this stage, the person is unable to see or hear anything, but he is able to experience or perceive it.

Warood (coming, beginning): When *adraak* (experience) becomes deep, it is exhibited as sight. The stage of *warood* starts when mental concentration is sustained and somnolence is at its minimum. As soon as the mind is focused, the spiritual eye is activated. The conscious mind is not used to see through the spiritual eye, so concentration comes and goes. Gradually, the mind gets used to this kind of visions and the mental focus is sustained. With practice, the visions/experience becomes so deep that the person starts considering himself a part of the experience rather than considering himself an observer.

Gnosis of the Universe

Kashaf/Ilhaam (unveiling of arcane knowledge): *Kashaf*, or *Ilhaam* is the stage where man starts getting information that most people are unable to observe. In the beginning, this condition occurs suddenly without personal control. With practice, the mind gets so energized that it can get this knowledge by will.

Shahood (evidence): When a person can get any information about any event/person with his will, this condition is called Shahood. This stage is broadly categorized according to activation of the senses:

1. The person can see things anywhere in the universe
2. The person can hear things anywhere in the universe
3. The person can smell things anywhere in the universe
4. The person can touch things anywhere in the universe (hadith)

Fatah (opening, victory): The peak of Shahood is called Fatah. At this stage, the person doesn't need to close his eyes for meditation. Here the person is freed from both space and time. He can see/hear/taste/touch anything that are present anywhere in time and space.

Gnosis of the Creator

Fanaa (extinction, annihilation): Through a series of stages (*maqamat*) and subjective experiences (*ahwal*), this process of absorbation develops until complete annihilation of the self (*fana*) takes place and the person becomes *al-insanul-kamil*, the "perfect man". It is the disintegration of a person's narrow self-concept, social self- and limited intellect (feeling like a drop of water aware of being part of the ocean). The stage is also called *Fana fit tawheed* ("extinction with the unity"), and *Fana fil Haq* (Extinction in the reality). This stage may be equated with the concept of nirvana in Buddhism, which aims for the same goal using a similar practice.

Sair Illallah (journey towards the God): Here the person starts his spiritual journey towards the ultimate reality of the universe, i.e. God. Also called *Safr-e-Urooji.*

Fana Fillah (Extinction of the self in God): One of the important phases of mystical experience which is attained by the grace of God by a traveller on the mystical path is the state of *fana fi Allah*, "extinction of the self in God". This is the state where the person becomes extinct in the will of God. It is important to mention that this is not incarnation or union. Most Sufis, while passing through this experience, have preferred to live in the greatest depth of silence which transcends all forms and sounds, and enjoy their union with the beloved.

- The highest stage of *fana* is reached when even the consciousness of having attained *fana* disappears. This is what the Sufis call "the passing-away of passing-away" (*fana al-fana*). The mystic is now wrapped in contemplation of the divine essence.
- Since it is a state of complete annihilation of carnal self, absorbation or intoxication in God, the pilgrim is unable to participate in worldly affairs, he is made to pass into another state known as *Fana-al-Fana* (forgetfulness of annihilation). It is a sort of oblivion of unconsciousness. Since two negatives make one positive, the pilgrim at this stage regains his individuality as he was when he started the journey. The only difference is that in the beginning he was self-conscious, but after having reposed in the Divine Being, he regains that sort of individuality which is God-consciousness or absorbation in God. This state is known as ***Baqa-bi-Allah*** — living or subsisting with God. (Alhaj W.B.S. Rabbani, *Gems of Sufi Gnosticism) [1]*

This stage has sometimes been equated with realization of Brahman of the Hindus.

Sair Min Allah (journey from the God): Here the person comes back to his existence. Also called *Safr-e-Nuzooli.*

Baqaa Billah (eternal life in union with God): This is the state where man comes back to his existence and God appoints him to guide the humans. This is a state in which the individual is part of the world, but unconcerned about his or her rewards or position in it. This doctrine is further explained in an authentic tradition of the prophet which states that God said:

And the most beloved things with which My slave comes nearer to Me, is what I have enjoined upon him; and My slave keeps on coming closer to Me through performing Nawafil (praying or doing extra deeds besides what is obligatory) till I love him, so I become his sense of hearing with which he hears, and his sense of sight with which he sees, and his hand with which he grips, and his leg with which he walks.

There is another verse from Quran, that is used to explain this concept.

We (Allah) are nearer to him (man) than his jugular vein.(50:6)

When Sufis have come out of the *Fana fillah* state and enter *Baqa billah*, many of them have produced works of unsurpassed glory, especially in the fields of philosophy, literature, and music. These works have crowned the culture of the entire Islamic world and inspired Sufis and non-Sufis for generations. As the great Persian Sufi poet, Hafiz of Shiraz, who is fondly remembered as the "tongue of the unseen", said centuries ago: "He whose heart is alive with love, never dies.". Allah says about these people in the *Quran*:

"Lo, indeed, the friends of God have no fear, nor are they grieved."

There are many different kinds of *muraqaba* that are practiced in various Sufi schools in different parts of the world. Following is a list of the ones commonly practiced.

Beginner Level Muraqabas

1. *Muraqaba of light*

These are usually used for beginners, or for cure of various diseases.

- Violet
- Indigo
- Blue
- Torquise
- Green
- Yellow
- Orange
- Pink
- Red

1. Ehsan
2. Noor (Invisible Light)
3. Haatif-e-Ghabi (Unhearable sound of Cosmos)
4. Names of God — For getting acquaintance with attributes of God
5. Allah (Proper name of God) — Final level of Muraqaba of names of God

Middle Level Muraqabas

1. Moat (Death) — Forgetting acquaintance with life after Death
2. Qalb (Heart) — Forgetting acquaintance with Spiritual Heart
3. Wahdat (Unity) — Forgetting acquaintance with the reason behind cosmic unity i.e. God's will
4. La (Nothingness) — Forgetting acquaintance with material lessness, or non-material universe
   Adam (Preexistence) — Next level of Muraqaba of Nothingness.
5. Fana (Annihilation) — Annihilation of Self, getting acquaintance with the alpha and omega of universe.

High Level Muraqabas

1. Tasawwur-e-Sheikh (Focussing mind on master) — To facilate the transfer of spiritual knowledge from master to student.
2. Tasawwur-e-Rasool (Focussing mind on prophet) — To facilate the transfer of Faiz (arcane spiritual knowledge) from prophet to student. For Muslims, this focussing of mind is done on Muhammad. For people following other religions, their particular holy figures are used to focus mind upon.
3. Tasawwur-e-zat-e-Ilaahi (Focussing Mind on God) — With the help of this Muraqaba, the student experiences the Tajalli-e-Zaat of God.

Sama

- Sama, a character of the Mahabharata.
- Shamash, the Assyrian and Babylonian sun god.
- Sema, form of Sufi ritual ceremony
- SAMA, the Saudi Arabian Monetary Agency
- *Sama* (Øi) in Japanese is an honorific suffix. See also: Japanese titles

Sufi Whirling

The practice of Sufi whirling (or Sufi spinning) is a twirling meditation that originated among the Turkish Sufis, which is still practiced by the Dervishes of the Mevlevi order.

Following a recommended fast of several hours, Sufi whirlers begin with hands crossed onto shoulders and may return their hands to this position if they feel dizzy. They rotate on their left feet in short twists, using the right foot to drive their bodies around the left foot. The left foot is like an anchor to the ground, so that if the whirler loses his or her balance, he or she can think of their left foot, direct attention towards it and regain balance.

The whirling is done on the spot in an anticlockwise direction, with the right arm held high, palm upwards, and the left arm held low, palm downwards. People who feel discomfort from whirling anti-clockwise can change to clockwise. The body of the whirler is meant to be soft with eyes open, but unfocused so that images become blurred and flowing. A 15 minute period of slow rotation is followed by a gradual build up of speed over the next 30 minutes. Then the whirling takes over.

When the whirler is whirling so fast that he or she cannot remain upright, his or her body will fall by itself. The whirler does not consciously make the fall a decision or attempt to arrange the landing in advance; if his or her body is soft he or she should land softly—and the earth will absorb the energy. If the idea of letting oneself fall is too much for the practitioner then the whirler should allow his or herself to slow down very slowly. If the whirler has been whirling for an hour then the process of slowing down might take some time—even 10 minutes or more.

Once the whirler has fallen, the second part of the meditation starts—the unwhirling. The whirler rolls onto his or her stomach immediately so that his or her bare navel is in contact with the earth. If anybody feels strong discomfort lying this way, he should lie on his back. The practitioner feels his or her body blending into the earth, like a small child pressed to his mother's breasts. Eyes remain closed and the whirler remains passive and silent for at least 15 minutes. After the meditation whirlers try to be as quiet and inactive as possible.

Hadhra: Hadhra is the term given to a sacred dance performed by Sufi Muslims accompanied by dhikr recitations invoking the name of Allah. The term in Arabic literally means "presence". It is practiced primarily in the Arab world, but can also be found in some non-Arab Muslim countries such as Indonesia.

Chishti Order

The Chishti Order was founded by Khawaja Abu Ishaq Shami ("the Syrian") (d. 941) who brought sufism to the town of Chisht, some 95 miles east of Herat in present-day Afghanistan. Before returning to the Levant, Shami initiated, trained, and deputized the son of the local Amir, Khwaja Abu Ahmad Abdal (d. 966). Under the leadership of Khwaja Abu Ahmad's descendants, the *Chishtiyya* as they are also known flourished as a regional mystical order. Sema or Kawali is devotional music to enhance the remembrance of Allah and is not part of Worship or prayer. At its founding, the Chishti Order was known for its renunciation of worldly power, but this would change later when Chishti saints would ally with emperors, most notably the Mughale Emperor Akbar.

The most famous of the Chishti saints is Hazrat Khawaja Moinuddin Chishti (R.A) (also known as Khwaja Baba) who settled in Ajmer, India. Khwaja Baba (R.A) oversaw the growth of the order in the 13th century as religious laws were canonized. He saw the Prophet in a dream and then set off on a journey of discovery.

Other famous saints of the Chishti Order are Nizamuddin Auliya (R.A) of Delhi, Fariduddin Ganjshakar (R.A) of Pak Pattan, and Qutubuddin Bakhtiar Kaki (R.A). Hazrat Inayat Khan was the first to bring the Chishtia Order to North America. The Saint Kabir is also thought to have been part of the Chishti order.

The Chishti Order is famous for its emphasis on love, tolerance, openness, and ecstasy. The Order traces its origins through various saints all the way to the Prophet's Companion 'Hazrat Ali and to the Prophet Muhammad (PBUH).

The Chishti Order is also known for its nine principles. These include: Obedience to shaykh or pir, Renunciation of material world, Distance from worldly powers, Sama (or musical assemblies), Extreme prayers and fasting, Dependence on voluntary offerings, Disapproval of miraculous feats, Service to humanity and Respect for other devotional traditions.

The Golden Chain (Shijrah) Chistiya-Mujarradiya

1. Prophet Mohammad
2. Hazrat Ali ibn Abu Talib
3. Hazrat Hasan al-Basri
4. Hazrat Abdul Wahid ibn Zaid
5. Hazrat Fuzail ibn Ayaz
6. Hazrat Ibrahim ibn Adam of Balaq
7. Hazrat Khawaja Sadiyuddin Muraishi
8. Hazrat Khawaja Aminuddin Basri
9. Hazrat Khawaja Khawaja Karimuddin Mumshaad
10. Hazrat Khawaja Khawaja Abul Ishak Shami

11. Hazrat Khawaja Abu Ahmed Abdaal
12. Hazrat Khawaja Mohammad Abi Ahmed
13. Hazrat Khawaja Nasihuddin Abu Mohammad
14. Hazrat Khawaja Abu Yusuf Jamal
15. Hazrat Khawaja Nasiruddin Moudud Chisti
16. Hazrat Khawaja Haji Sharif Zindana
17. Hazrat Khawaja Usmaan Haruni
18. Hazrat Khawaja Moinuddin Chisti
19. Hazrat Khawaja Kutubuddin Baktiyaar Kaki
20. Hazrat Khawaja Kalimuddin Chisti
21. Hazrat Khawaja Sirajuddin
22. Hazrat Khawaja Alimuddin
23. Hazrat Khawaja Mehmood Chisti
24. Hazrat Khawaja Jamaluddin Chisti
25. Hazrat Khawaja Mohammad Hassan
26. Hazrat Khawaja Mohammad Sani
27. Hazrat Khawaja Yuhaiya Madni
28. Hazrat Khawaja Kalimullah
29. Hazrat Khawaja Nizamuddin Auliya
30. Hazrat Khawaja Fakruddin
31. Hazrat Khawaja Noor Mohammad
32. Hazrat Khawaja Suleiman Bande Nawaz
33. Hazrat Khawaja Allah Baksh
34. Hazrat Khawaja Shah Khairuddin Mujjarrad
35. Hazrat Khawaja Al-Haaj Abdul Rehman Sailani
36. Hazrat Mohammad Masoom Armaan
37. Hazrat Shah Sharfuddin Abdul Gafoor Abdaal
38. Hazrat Mohammed Aainuddin Arif Ali
39. Hazrat Mohammad Sadique Armani
40. Hazrat Mohammad Malang Masoom Naqshbandi

Jerrahi

The Jerrahi are a Sufi order (Tarika) derived from the Halveti (Khalwati) order. Their founder is Pir Nureddin al-Jerrahi, who died in Istanbul and is buried at the site of his tekke in Istanbul. During the late Ottoman period, the tarika was widespread throughout the Balkans, particularly Macedonia and southern Greece (Morea).

Founded in the 17th century by Hadrat Pir Muhammed Nureddin Al-Jerrahi, the Halveti-Jerrahi Order of Dervishes is an Islamic Sufi path of Love: Worship the Creator with Love and serve His

Creation with Love. Halveti-Jerrahi Order of Dervishes is a cultural, educational, and social relief organization with diverse professional, ethnic and national backgrounds.

Besides the material connection, established by the fact that Hadrat Pir Muhammed Nureddin Al-Jerrahi is a direct descendant of Prophet Muhammed both from his mother and father, the path he has founded is dedicated to the teachings and traditions through an unbroken chain of spiritual transmission that goes directly back to the Prophet Muhammed.

The head dergah (sufi convention) of the Halveti-Jerrahi Dervishes is in Istanbul. It has branches in most of the European Countries, Australia, South Africa, South America and North America including Chicago.

The Branch of the Halveti Jerrahi Order of Dervishes in Chicago conduct mountly gatherings where the dervishes perform sufi remembrance ceremony (zikrullah), practise sufi music, serve dinner, pray together and listen to the discourse of Sheikh Ilhan Al-Jerrahi, the sufi guide.

One prominent member of the tarika was Muzaffer Ozak (also known as *Muzaffer Efendi*), the 19th Sheikh, who died in 1985. He brought the Jerrahi order into the western countries.

Mevlevi

The Mevlevi Order or the Mevleviye are a Sufi order founded by the followers of Jalal al-Din Muhammad Rumi in 1273 in Konya, in present day Turkey. They are also known as the Whirling Dervishes due to their famous practice of whirling as a form of dhikr (remembrance of Allah). Dervishes are members of Sufi ascetic religious Tarika or "confraternities", known for their extreme poverty and austerity.

The Mevlevi, or Mevleviye, one of the most well-known of the Sufi orders, was founded in 1273 by Rumi's followers after his death, particularly his son, Sultan Veled Celebi (or C*elebi*, *Chelebi*). The Mevlevi, or "The Whirling Dervishes", believe in performing their dhikr in the form of a "dance" and music ceremony called the sema.

The Sema represents a mystical journey of man's spiritual ascent through mind and love to "Perfect." Turning towards the truth, the follower grows through love, deserts his ego, finds the truth and arrives to the "Perfect." He then returns from this spiritual journey as a man who has reached maturity and a greater perfection, so as to love and to be of service to the whole of creation.

The Mevlevi were a well established Sufi Order in the Ottoman Empire, and many of the members of the order served in various official positions of the Caliphate. The centre for the Mevlevi order was in Konya, where Rumi is buried. There is also a Mevlevi monastery or *dergah* in Istanbul, near the Galata Tower, where the sema ceremony is performed and accessible to the public.

During Ottoman Empire era, the Mevlevi order produced a number of famous poets and musicians such as Sheikh Ghalib, Ismail Ankaravi (both buried at the Galata Mevlevi-Hane) and Abdullah Sari. Music, especially the ney, play an important part in the Mevelevi order and thus much of the traditional "oriental" music that Westerners associate with Turkey originates with the Mevlevi order. Indeed, if one buys a CD of Turkish Sufi music, chances are it will be Mevlevi religious music.

During the Ottoman period, the Mevlevi order spread into the Balkans, Syria, and Egypt (and is still practiced in both countries where they are known as the *Mawlawi order*). The Bosnian writer Mesa Selimoviæ wrote the book *Death and the Dervish* about a Mevlevi *dergah* in Sarajevo.

The Mevlevi Order is also linked to other Dervish orders such as the Qadiri (founded in 1165), the Rifa'i (founded in 1182), and the Kalenderis.

The Mevlevi Order was outlawed in Turkey at the dawn of the secular revolution by Kemal Atatürk in 1923. In the 1950s, the Turkish government, realizing that The Whirling Dervishes had value as a tourist attraction, began allowing the Whirling Dervishes to perform annually in Konya on the *Urs of Mevlana*, December 17, the anniversary of Rumi's death. In 1974, they were allowed to come to the West. They performed in France, for Pope Paul VI, and at the Brooklyn Academy of Music and other venues in the United States and Canada-under the direction of the late Mevlevi Shaikh Suleyman Hayati Dede.

Naqshbandi

Naqshbandi (Naqshbandiyya) is one of four major Sufi orders (tariqa) of Islam. Formed in 1380, the order is considered by some to be a "sober" order which believes in silent dhikr (remembrance of God) and suhbat (an intimate relationship between student and master).

The order began with Abu Bakr a constant companion of Prophet Muhammad and father-in-law, whereas most other turuq (Chishtia, Suhrawardiyya and Qadiriyyah) trace their lineage from the Prophet Muhammad through Ali ibn Abu Talib.

The word *Naqshbandi* aÞÔEaÌÎ is Persian, taken from the name of the founder of the order, Baha-ud-Din Naqshband Bukhari. Some have said that the translation means "related to the image-maker," some also consider it to mean "Pattern Maker" rather than "image maker," and interpret "Naqshbandi" to mean "Reformer of Patterns", and others consider it to mean "Way of the Chain" or "Golden Chain."

Naqshbandi Hijazi Sufi Order

1. The Beloved of Allah, Prophet Muhammad (saws)
2. Hazrat Abu Bakr Siddiqi (ra)
3. Hazrat Salman al-Farsi (ra)
4. Hazrat Qassim ibn Abu Bakr (ra)
5. Hazrat Jafar as-Saddiq (ra)
6. Hazrat Bayazid al-Bistami (ra)
7. Hazrat Abul Hassan Ali al-Harqani (ra)
8. Hazrat Bue Ali al-Farmadi
9. Hazrat Yaqub Yusaf al-Hamadani (ra)
10. Hazrat Khawaja Abdul Khaliq Ajdwani (ra)
11. Hazrat Abul Abbas al-Khadr (ra)
12. Hazrat Arif al-Rewgani (ra)
13. Hazrat Khawaja Mahmood al-Injir al-Faghnawi (ra)
14. Hazrat Azizan Ali- Ar-Ramitani (ra)
15. Hazrat Muhammad Baba as-Samasi (ra)
16. Hazrat Sayyid Amir Kulal (ra)

17. Hazrat Mohammad Bahauddin Naqshband (ra)
18. Hazrat Alauddin al-Bukhari al-Attar (ra)
19. Hazrat Yaqub al-Charkhi (ra)
20. Hazrat Ubaydullah al-Ahrar (ra)
21. Hazrat Muhammad Az-Zahid Wali (ra)
22. Hazrat Mohammad Darwish (ra)
23. Hazrat Khawaja al-Akmangi (ra)
24. Hazrat Muhammad al-Baqi Billah (ra)
25. Hazrat Ahmad al-Faruqi as-Sirhindi, mujadid alf-at'thani (ra)
26. Hazrat Khawaja Muhammad Masoom (ra)
27. Hazrat Khawaja Saifuddin (ra)
28. Hazrat Syed Noor Muhammad Badayoori (ra)
29. Hazrat Mirza Jaane Janaan (ra)
30. Hazrat Shah Ghulam Ali Dehlvi (ra)
31. Hazrat Muhammmad Abdul Rasool Qusoori (ra)
32 Hazrat Muhâmmad Rasool Qusoori (ra)
33. Hazrat Khawaja Ghulam Dastigir (ra)
34. Munazir-e-Azam Maulana Mohammad Umar Icharvi (ra)
35. Hazrat Mujadid Abdul Wahab Siddiqi (ra)
36. Hazrat Allama Pir Shaykh Faiz-ul-Aqtab Siddiqi Hijazi

Naksi-Bendi Hakkani Golden Chain

1. Sayyidina Wa Mevlana Muhammad Mustafa (S.w.s)
2. Seyyid-ul Awliya Abu Bakr As Siddiq (R.a.)
3. Salman-i Farisi (R.a.)
4. Imam Kasim Bin Muhammed (R.a.)
5. Imam-i Jafer-i Siddiq Bin Imam Muhammed El-bakir (R.a.)
6. Sultan-ul Arifin Bayezid-i Bestami (K.s.)
7. Ebul Hasan Harkani (K.s.)
8. Ebu Ali Ahmed Farmedi (K.s.)
9. Haje Yusuf-ul Hamedani (K.s.)
10. Ebul Abbas (Hizir A.s.)
11. Imam-ul Hatim Abdul Halik Gujdevani(k.s.)
12. Haje Arif Rigveri (K.s.)
13. Haje Mahmud Injir-i Faghnevi (K.s.)
14. Haje Aziz ali Ramitani (K.s.)
15. Haje Muhammed Baba Semmasi (K.s.)
16. Haje Seyyid Emir Kulal (K.s.)

17. Imam-i Tariqa Wa Ghaus-ul Halika Haje Muhammed Bahauddin Nakshibendiy-yil Uwaysil Buhari (K.s.)
18. Haje Alauddin Muhammed-il Attar (K.s.)
19. Haje Yakub-ul Cherhi (K.s.)
20. Haje Ubeydullah-il Ahrar Semerkandi (K.s.)
21. Muhammed-uz Zahid (K.s.)
22. Dervish Muhammed-il Buhari (K.s.)
23. Hajegi-l Emkineki-l Semerkandi (K.s.)
24. Muhammed-il Bakibillah Semerkandi (K.s.)
25. Imam Rabbani Ahmed Faruki Serhendi (K.s.)
26. Muhammed Masum-urrabbani (K.s.)
27. Haje Seyfuddin-irrabbani (K.s.)
28. Nur Muhammed-il Bedvani (K.s.)
29. Habibullah Mirza Jan-u Janan-ul Mazhar (K.s.)
30. Gulam Ali Abdullah-ud Dehlevi (K.s.)
31. Ziya-uddin Halid Al Baghdadi Al-shami (K.s.)
32. Sheykh Ismail Enerani (K.s.)
33. Has Muhammed Shirvani (K.s.)
34. Sheykh Muhammed Efendi Yeraghi (K.s.)
35. Seyyid Jemaleddin Gumukiyyil Huseyni (K.s.)
36. Ebu Ahmed-is Sughuri (K.s.)
37. Ebu Muhammed-ul Medeni (K.s.)
38. Seyyid Sherafuddin Daghestan-i (K.s.)
39. Sultan-ul Awliya Abdullah Al-faizi Daghestan-i (K.s.)
40. Seyyid-ud Taife, Hatim-us Saadet, Kiblet-ul Islam, Sahib-uz Zaman, Sheykh-ul Islam, Sultan Ul Awliya, Hazreti Shah Sultan Mevlana Muhammed Nazim Adil Al-kibrisi Al-hakkani An-naksh-i bendi (K.s.)

The Golden Chain (Shijrah) of Naqshbandiya Mujaddadiya Mujarradiya

1. Prophet Huzoor Muhammad-ur-Rasoolullah s.a. (d. 12 Rabbiyul Awwal 11AH) -Medina
2. Hadhrat Abu Bakr Siddique r.a. (d. 22 Jama'dil A'lhar 13AH)-Medina
3. Hadhrat Salman al-faris r.a. (d. 10 Rajjab 35AH)-Madain
4. Hadhrat Imaam Qasim bin Muhammad bin Abu Bakr r.a. (d. 24 Jama'dil (Awwal/A'khar) 107AH)-Medina
5. Hadhrat Imaam Ja'far al-Sadiq r.a. (d. 15 Rajjab Murajjab 148AH)-Medina
6. Hadhrat Bayazid Bastami r.a. (d. 14/17 Sha'ba'n 261AH)-Bastam
7. Hadhrat Abul Hassan Khurqaani r.a. (d. 15 Ramda'n 425AH)-Khurqan
8. Hadhrat Abu Ali Farmadi r.a. (d. 4 Rabbiyul Awwal 477AH)-Mashad

9. Hadhrat Yusuf Hamdani r.a. (d. 27 Rajjab 535AH)-Turkistan
10. Hadhrat Abdul Khaliq Gajadwani r.a. (d. 12 Rabbiyul Awwal 575AH)-Bukhara
11. Hadhrat Muhammad Arif Riogri r.a. (d. 1 Shawwa'l 615AH)-Tajikistan
12. Hadhrat Mehmood Injir Faghnavi r.a. (d. 17 Rabbiyul Awwal 715AH)-Bukhara
13. Hadhrat Azizane Ali Raamitni r.a. (d. 718/721AH)-Bukhara
14. Hadhrat Muhammad Baba Samasi r.a. (d. 755AH)-Bukhara
15. Hadhrat Sayyed Amir Kulaal r.a. (d. 772AH)-Bukhara
16. Hadhrat Kwajah Bahauddin Naqshband r.a. (d. 2 Rajab al-Murajjab, 791AH)-Qasr-e-Aarifan (Bukhara)
17. Hadhrat Alaa'uddin Attaar r.a. (d. 20 Rajab 802AH)-Jafaaniyan (Mawralnahar)
18. Hadhrat Ya'qoob Charkhi r.a. (d. 5 Safar, 851AH)-Charkh (Bukhara)
19. Hadhrat Ubeydullah Ahraar r.a. (d. 20/29 Rabi al-Awwal, 895AH)-Samarqand (Mawralnahar)
20. Hadhrat Muhammad Zaahid r.a. (d. 1 Rabi al-Awwal, 936AH)-Wakhsh (Malk Hasaar)
21. Hadhrat Darwesh Muhammad r.a. (d. 19 Muharram, 970AH)-Samarqand (Mawralnahar)
22. Hadhrat Muhammad Waaqif Akangi r.a. (d. 21/22 Sha'baan, 1008AH)-Akang (Bukhara)
23. Hadhrat Khwaja Baaqi Billaah r.a. (d. 25 Jumaad al-Aakhar, 1012AH)-Delhi (India)
24. Huzoor Imam Rabbani, Mujaddid Alf Thani, Hadhrat Shaykh Ahmad Farooqui Sarhandi r.a. (d. 28 Safar, 1034AH)-Sarhand (India)
25. Hadhrat Muhammad Ma'soom Farooqui r.a. (d. 9 Rabi al-Awwal, 1079AH)-Sarhand (India)
26. Hadhrat Sayfuddeen Bin Ma'soom Farooqui r.a. (d. 19 Jumad al-Oola, 10951096AH)-Sarhand (India)
27. Hadhrat Noor Muhammad Badyooni r.a. (d. 11 Dhul Qa'dah, 1135AH)-Delhi (India)
28. Hadhrat Mirza Mazhar Jaan-I-Jaanan r.a. (d. 10 Muharram, 1195AH)-Khanqah Mazharia Dehli(India)
29. Hadhrat Abdullah Shah Naimullah r.a. (d. 22 Safar, 1240AH)-Behraich U.P.(India)
30. Hadhrat Mawla'na Muradullah r.a. (d. Dhul Qa'dah, 1248AH)-Lakhnow U.P.(India)
31. Hadhrat Sayyed Abul Hasan Saeed r.a. (d. Sha'ba'n, 1272)-Rai Bareli U.P.(India)
32. Hadhrat Niya'z Ali Shah r.a. (d. 2 Dhul Qa'dah, 1310AH)-Rai Bareli U.P.(India)
33. Hadhrat Sufi Wazeer r.a. (d. 1 Jama'dil Awwal, 1319AH)-Kasrawad Khargone M.P.(India)
34. Hadhrat Al-Haaj Abdullah r.a. (d. 6 Jama'dil Awwal, 13—AH)-Patkalyana, Samalkha, Karnaal, Haryaana, (India)
35. Hadhrat Shah Khairuddin Makhdoom Mujarrad r.a. (d. 12 Rabiyul Awwal, 1325AH)-Chopda, Jalgaon, Maharastra (India)
36. Hadhrat Al-Haaj Abdur Rehman Shah Sailaani r.a. (d. 22 Dhul Qa'dha 1326 AH)-Sailaani Gaon, 10 Miles From Chikli, Bultthana, Maharastra (India)
37. Hadhrat Mohd. Masoom Armaan r.a. (d. 5 Dhul Qa'dha 1378 AH)-Kasar Kheda, Balapur, Akola, Maharastra (India)
38. Hadhrat Shah Sharfuddin Abdul Gafoor Abda'l r.a. (d. 22 Safar 13— AH)-Kasali Muhalla,

Motipura, Amalner, Maharastra (India)

39. Hadhrat Mohd. Ainuddin Arif Ali r.a. (d. 16 Sawwa'l 1410 AH)-Kasar Kheda, Balapur, Akola, Maharastra (India)
40. Hadhrat Salimuddin/Mohd. Sa'dique Armaani (Present Sajjadah Nashin)-Near Fort, Balapur, Akola, Maharastra (India)
41. Hadhrat Muhammad Malang Masoom Naqshbandi (Present Jaanashin & Sajjadah Nashin, Founder of D N F. 12, S.K. KAPADIA CHAWL, CHIRAG NAGAR, GHATKOPAR (W) MUMBAI-400 086. E-MAIL mmmnaqshbandi@gmail.com)
42. Hadhrat Nuseyreddin Rustem Fazilahovich Kovachi Mrahorovich Naqshbandi (Present Goranchich & Bretolich Gjakova, Founder of U C K)
43. Hazrat Allama Mufasir-Quran Mufaker-e-Islam PEER SYED RIAZ HUSSAIN SHAH Sahib Damat barakatum aalia (GENERAL SECTARY JAMAT-E-AHLE SUNNAT PAKISTAN)

Mujaddidiya Branch

1. The mercy for the worlds Rasulullah [Holy City of Madinah Munawwarah].
2. Sayyedina Hadrat Abu Bakr Siddiq (radiallahu anhu) [Holy City of Madinah Munawwarah].
3. Hadrat Salman Farsi (radiallahu anhu) [Madain].
4. Hadrat Qasim bin Muhammad bin Abi Bakr (rahmatullahi alaihi) [Holy City of Madinah Munawwarah].
5. Hadrat Imam Jafar Sadiq (rahmatullahi alaihi) [Holy City of Madinah Munawwarah].
6. Hadrat Khuwaja Bayazeed Bustami (rahmatullahi alaihi) [Bastam].
7. Hadrat Khuwaja Abul Hasan Kharkani (rahmatullahi alaihi) [Kharkhan].
8. Hadrat Khuwaja Abul Qasim Gorgani (rahmatullahi alaihi) [Jarjan].
9. Hadrat Khuwaja Abu Ali Farmadi (rahmatullahi alaihi) [Mashad].
10. Hadrat Khuwaja Yusuf Hamdani (rahmatullahi alaihi) [Turkistan].
11. Hadrat Khuwaja Abdul Khaliq Gajadwani (rahmatullahi alaihi) [Bukhara].
12. Hadrat Khuwaja Muhammad Arif Riogri (rahmatullahi alaihi) [Tajikistan].
13. Hadrat Khuwaja Mehmood Injir Faghnavi (rahmatullahi alaihi) [Bukhara].
14. Hadrat Khuwaja Azizane Ali Raamitni (rahmatullahi alaihi) [Bukhara].
15. Hadrat Khuwaja Muhammad Baba Samasi (rahmatullahi alaihi) [Bukhara].
16. Hadrat Khuwaja Sayyed Amir Kalal (rahmatullahi alaihi) [Bukhara].
17. Hadrat Khuwaja Bahauddin Naqshband Bukhari (rahmatullahi alaihi) [Bukhara].
18. Hadrat Khuwaja Ala'uddin Attar (rahmatullahi alaihi) [Hassar].
19. Hadrat Khuwaja Yaqoob Charkhi (rahmatullahi alaihi) [Dushanbe].
20. Hadrat Khuwaja Ubaidullah Ahrar (rahmatullahi alaihi) [Samarqand].
21. Hadrat Khuwaja Maulana Muhammad Zahid (rahmatullahi alaihi) [Hassar].
22. Hadrat Khuwaja Darvish Muhammad (rahmatullahi alaihi) [Sher Sabz].
23. Hadrat Khuwaja Muhammad Amkangi (rahmatullahi alaihi) [Bukhara].

24. Hadrat Khuwaja Muhammad Baqibillah (rahmatullahi alaihi) [Delhi]
25. Hadrat Khuwaja Mujaddid Alf-Thani (rahmatullahi alaihi) [Sirhind Sharif].
26. Hadrat Khuwaja Muhammad Masoom (rahmatullahi alaihi) [Sirhind Sharif].
27. Hadrat Khuwaja Saifuddin (rahmatullahi alaihi) [Sirhind Sharif].
28. Hadrat Khuwaja Hafiz Muhammad Muhsin (rahmatullahi alaihi) [Delhi].
29. Hadrat Khuwaja Sayed Nur Muhammad Badaiooni (rahmatullahi alaihi) [Delhi].
30. Hadrat Mirza Mazhar Janejana (rahmatullahi alaihi) [Delhi].
31. Hadrat Shah Ghulam Ali Mujaddidi (rahmatullahi alaihi) [Delhi].
32. Hadrat Khuwaja Shah Abu Sa'eed (rahmatullahi alaihi) [Delhi].
33. Hadrat Khuwaja Shah Ahmed Sa'eed Dehlvi (rahmatullahi alaihi) [Holy City of Madinah Munawwarah].
34. Hadrat Haji Dost Muhammad Kandhari (rahmatullahi alaihi) [Musazai Sharif].
35. Hadrat Khuwaja Muhammad Usman Damani (rahmatullahi alaihi) [Musazai Sharif].
36. Hadrat Khuwaja Sirajuddin (rahmatullahi alaihi) [Musazai Sharif].
37. Hadrat Khuwaja Muhammad Fazal Ali Qureshi (rahmatullahi alaihi) [Miskeenpur Sharif].
38. Hadrat Khuwaja Muhammad Abdul Malik Siddiqui (rahmatullahi alaihi) [Khanewal].
39. Murshid-e-Alam Hadrat Khuwaja Ghulam Habib (rahmatullahi alaihi) [Chakwal].
40. Hadrat Maulana Hafiz Zulfiqar Ahmad Naqshbandi Mujaddidi (damat barakatuhu) [Jhang Sharif].

Owaisiya Branch

Naqshbandi Order has another famous branch called Naqshbandia Owaisiah Order. The method of spiritual instruction is quite close to Mujaddidya branch. However there are two main differences. First Naqshbandia Owaisiah order uses the "Pas Infas" method of zikr. Secondly, the method of spiritual instruction is "Owaisee", which means that the Shaikh can impart spiritual instruction regardless of physical distance and even difference of time period. Seekers of Naqshbandia Owaisiah can obtain spiritual blessing from their Shaikh regardless of their location in the world. Owaisiah connection is also useful in obtaining spiritual blessings from Sufies of the Past. Naqshbandia Owaisiah Order is based in Pakistan and its modern founder was Shaikh Allah Yar Khan (R.A). Current shaikhs are Hazrat Muhammad Ahsan Baig and Hazarat Syed Buniad Hussain Shah.

Owaisiya Chain of Transmission

1. Hazrat Muhammad S.A.W
2. Hazrat Abu Bakr Siddique Razi Allah Anho
3. Hazrat Imam Hasan Basri R.A
4. Hazrat Daud Tai R.A
5. Hazrat Junaid Baghdadi R.A
6. Hazrat Khwaja Ubaid Ullah Ahraar R.A
7. Hazrat Abdul Rahman Jami R.A

8. Hazrat Abu Ayub Muhammad Saleh R.A
9. Hazrat Khwaja Allah Din Madni R.A
10. Hazrat Maulana Abdul Raheem R.A
11. Hazrat Maulana Allah Yar Khan R.A
12. Hazrat Maulana Muhammad Akram Awan (Present)

Some Famous Naqshbandis

- Imam Rabbani,Mujaddid Alf Thani, Hadhrat Shaykh Ahmad Farooqui Sarhandi
- Bayazid Bastami
- Khwaja Mir Dard
- Imam Shamil
- Jami
- Shaykh Nazim al-Qubrusi
- Professor Sibghatullah Mojaddedi
- Huseyin Hilmi bin Said-i lstanboli
- Verdaro Krakov Muhamad Fihmi-Effendi bin Abu-Abdurehhmani al-Albani
- Ameer-e-Millat Pir Sayed Jamat Ali Shah
- Wali Muhammad Shah Chadar walli Sarkar
- Haji Soofi Masood Ahmad Siddiqui Lasani Sarkar
- Ahmet Kayhan Dede

Qadiriyyah

Qadiriyyah (also transliterated Qadiri), is one of the oldest Sufi tariqas, derives its name from bdul Qadir Jilani (also transliterated as Gilani) (1077-1166), a native of the Iranian province of Gilan. In 1134 he was made principal of a Hanbalite school in Baghdad.

The order is one of the most widespread of the Sufi orders in the Islamic world and can be found in India, Pakistan, Turkey and the Balkans and much of East and West Africa. Some famous Qadiri Sheikhs include Sheikh Abd al-Qadir al-Jaza'iri who led the Algerian resistance to French colonialism and Sheikh Usman dan Fodio whose followers Islamized much of West Africa and established the Caliphate of Sokoto in Northern Nigeria. The Chechen people are also mostly followers of the Qadiri Sufi order as was the famous traveller and writer Isabelle Eberhardt.

The Qadiriyyah has not developed any distinctive doctrines or teachings outside of mainstream Islam. They believe in the fundamental principles of Islam, but interpreted through mystical experience. As a result, even opponents to Sufism such as the Hanbali Sheikhs Ibn Taymiya, his student ibn al-Qayyim and ibn Rajb al-Hanbali were all followers of the Qadiri Sufi order and spoke highly of Sheikh Abdul Qadir Jilani.

Spiritual Chain

This is the spiritual chain (*silsila*) of the Qadiriyyah:

- The Prophet Muhammad
- The Caliph Ali ibn Abi Talib
- Imam Husain
- Imam Ali Zayn al-Abidin
- Imam Muhammad Baqir
- Imam Ja'far as-Sadiq
- Imam Musa al-Kazim
- Imam Ali Musa Rida
- Ma'ruf Karkhi
- Sari Saqati
- Junayd al-Baghdadi
- Sheikh Abu Bakr Shibli
- Sheikh Abdul Aziz al-Tamimi
- Abu al-Fadl Abu al-Wahid al-Tamimi
- Abu al-Farah Tartusi
- Abu al-Hasan Farshi
- Abu Said al-Mubarak Mukharrami
- Sheikh Abdul Qadir Jilani

Suhrawardiyya

Suhrawardiyya is the name of a Sufi order founded by Diya al-din Abu 'n-Najib as-Suhrawardi (1097 – 1168).

Many Sufis from all over the islamic world joined the order under the founder's nephew Shihab ad-din Abu Hafs 'Umar (1145 – 1234). Later the Order spread into India.

A well known member of the order was Shihabuddin Yahya as-Suhrawardi (1153-1191).

Shadhili

The Tariqa ash Shadhiliya is the Sufi order founded by Abu-l-Hassan ash-Shadhili. Followers, or *murids* (Arabic: seekers), of the Shadhiliya, are often known as Shadhilis.

It is the most popular Sufi order in North Africa and many of its followers have made great contributions to Arab and Islamic literature, most notably Sheikh Ibn 'Ata Allah, author of the 'Hikam' amongst other works, Sheikh Ahmed Zarruq, who died in Libya, who was the author of a commentary upon the Risala of al-Qayrawani (a standard work in Maliki Islamic jurisprudence) and a commentary upon the Hikam, he also wrote extensively on religion (Sufism) and law. Sheikh ibn Ajibah who wrote a commentary upon the Quran. Many of the sheikhs of al-Azhar University in Egypt have also been followers of the Shadhili tariqa.

The Swedish impressionist painter and Sufi scholar Sheikh Abd Al-Hadi Aqhili (1869-1917) was the first official Moqaddam (representative) of the Shadhili Order in Western Europe.

The Hamadiyya Shadhili branch is most popular. The Darqawi Shadhili branch is found mostly in Morocco and the Alawiyya (no connection to the Turkish or Syrian Alawi or Alevi groups) is found mostly in Algeria but now also in Syria, Jordan, and France amongst French North-Africans. The British Muslim convert Martin Lings wrote an extensive biography of the founding Sheikh of this branch, Sheikh Ahmad al-Alawi, entitled 'A Sufi Saint of the 20th century'.

Famous Sufis

Hasan al-Basri: Hasan al-Basri (Abu Sa'id al-Hasan ibn Abi-l-Hasan Yasar al-Basri), (642-728 or 737), was a well-known Arab theologian and scholar of Islam who was born at Medina.

His father was a freedman of Zayd ibn Thabit, one of the Ansar (Helpers of the Prophet), his mother a client of Umm Salama, a wife of the Prophet Muhammad (d.632). Tradition says that Umm Salama often nursed Hasan in his infancy. He was thus one of the *Tabi'een* (i.e. of the generation that succeeded the *Sahabah*). He became a teacher of Basra (Iraq) and founded a *madrasa* (school) there. Among his many pupils were Amr Ibn Ubayd (d.761) and Wasil ibn Ata (d.749), the founder of the Mu'tazilites.

He himself was a great supporter of orthodoxy and the most important representative of asceticism in the time of its first development. According to him, fear is the basis of morality, and sadness the characteristic of his religion. Life is only a pilgrimage, and comfort must be denied to subdue the passions. Al-Basri is also held in high regard by the Sufis, for his asceticism and subtle directions relating to the science of practical religion (*ilm-i mu'amalat*).

Many writers testify to the purity of his life and to his excelling in the virtues of Muhammad's own companions. He was "as if he were in the other world." In politics, too, he adhered to the earliest principles of Islam, being strictly opposed to the inherited caliphate of the Umayyads (r.661-750) and a believer in the election of the caliph. However, despite his critical position concerning the Umayyads, he did not approve of rebellion against tyrannical rule. His sermons contain some of the earliest and best examples of Arabic linguistic prose style.

Rabia: Rabia al-Adawiyya (717-801 C.E.) was a female Sufi saint from Basra in modern-day Iraq, who first set forth the doctrine of mystical love and who is widely considered to be the most important of the early Sufi poets. The defining work on her life and writing was written over 50 years ago by Margaret Smith, a small treatise written as a Master's Thesis.

Also known as Rabia al-Qaysiyya or Rabia of Basrah, she was born in Basra, Iraq between the years 95 A.H. and 99 A.H. (about 717 C.E.). Much of the poetry that is attributed to her is of unknown origin. After a life of hardship she became spontaneously realized. When asked by Sheikh Hasan al-Basri how she discovered the secret, she responded by stating:

You know of the how, but I know of the how-less.

One of the many myths that swirl around her life, is that she was freed from slavery because her master saw her praying while surrounded by light, realized that she was a saint and feared for his life if he continued to keep her as a slave.

One day, she was seen running through the streets of Basra carrying a torch in one hand and a bucket of water in the other. When asked what she was doing, she said:

I want to put out the fires of Hell, and burn down the rewards of Paradise. They block the way to God. I do not want to worship from fear of punishment or for the promise of reward, but simply for the love of God.

While she apparently received many marriage offers (including a proposal from Hasan al-Basri himself), she remained celibate and died of old age, an ascetic, her only care from the disciples who followed her. She was the first in a long line of female Sufi mystics.

Her name is also transliterated as *Rabia* and *Rabia al-»Adawiyya al-Quaysiyya of Basra.*

Bayazid Bastami: Bayazid Bastami also known as Abu Yazid Bistami or Tayfur Abu Yazid al-Bustami, (804-874 CE) was a Persian Sufi born in Bostam (alternate spelling: Bastam), Iran. The name Bastami means "from the city of Bastam". Bayazid Bastami had great influence on Sufi mysticism and is considered to be one of the important early teachers of Sufi Islam. Bastmi's predecessor Zu al-Nun al-Misri (d. CE 859) had formulated the doctrine of ma'rifa (gnosis), presenting a system which helped the *murid* (initiate) and the *shaykh* (guide) to communicate. Bayazid Bastami took this another step and emphasized the importance of ecstasy, referred to in his words as *drunkenness*, a means of union with God. Before him, Sufism was mainly based on piety and obedience and he played a major role in placing the concept of divine love at the core of Sufism.

Bistami was the first to speak openly of "annihilation of the self in God" (fana fi 'Allah') and "subsistence through God" (baqa' bi 'Allah). His paradoxical sayings gained a wide circulation and soon exerted a captivating influence over the minds of students who aspired to understand the meaning of the wahdat al-wujud, *Unity of Being*.

When Bayazid died, he was over seventy years old. Before he died, someone asked him his age. He said: I am four years old. For seventy years I was veiled. I got rid of my veils only four years ago."

He died in 874CE and is buried either in the city of Bistam in north central Iran, or in Semnan, Iran. Interestingly enough, there is a shrine in Chittagong, Bangladesh that local people believe to be Bastami's tomb as well. This is unlikely to be true, as Bastami was never known to have visited Bangladesh. However, Sufi teachers were greatly influential in the spread of Islam in Bengal and this might explain the belief. The Islamic scholars of Bangladesh usually regard the tomb at Chittagong attributed to him as a *jawab*, or imitation.

Bayazid lived a century before Abul Hassan Kharaqani. Attar Neishapouri has mentioned in his book Tazkiratul Awliya that Bayazid had spoken about the personality and state of Shaikh Abul Hassan Kharaqani with his disciples while passing from the village of Kharaqan, almost 100 years before the birth of Shaikh Abul Hassan.

Some of his words quoted from Tazkeratol-owlya by Attar:

- I never saw any lamp shining more brilliantly than the lamp of silence.
- I went to a wilderness, love had rained and had covered earth, as feet penetrate snow, I found my feet covered with love.
- I stood with the pious and I didn't find any progress with them. I stood with the warriors in the cause and I didn't find a single step of progress with them. Then I said, 'O Allah, what is the way to You?' and Allah said, 'Leave yourself and come.'

Al-Ghazali : Abu Hamid Muhammad ibn Muhammad al-Ghazali (born 1058 in Us, Khorasan province of Persia, modern day Iran, died 1111, Us) was a Persian Muslim theologian and philosoı her, known as Algazel to the western medieval world. Abu Hamid Al-Ghazali, or al-Ghazzali as he is written sometimes, contributed significantly to the development of a systematic view of Sufism and its integration and acceptance in mainstream Islam. Al-Ghazali was both a Sufi and a scholar of orthodox Islam, belonging to the Shafi'i school of legal thought of Sunnite Islam. Imam Ghazali received many titles: Sharaful A'emma, Zainud din (Arabic: ÒÏa ÇáÏÏa), Hujjatul Islam.

Al-Ghazali remains one of the most celebrated scholars in the history of Islamic thought. He lectured at the Nizamiyyah school of Baghdad (the highest ranked academy of the golden era of Islamic civilization) between 1091 and 1096. He was the scholar par excellence in the Islamic world. He had literally hundreds of scholars attending his lectures at the Nizamiyyah. His audience included scholars from other schools of jurisprudence. This position won him prestige, wealth and respect that even princes and viziers could not match.

After some years he distributed his wealth and left Baghdad to begin a spiritual journey that lasted over a decade. He went to Damascus, Jerusalem, Hebron, Madinah, Mecca and back to Baghdad where he stopped briefly. He then left for us to spend the next several years in seclusion. He ended his seclusion for a short lecturing period at the Nizamiyyah of Nishapur in 1106. Later he returned to Us where he remained until his death in December.

He is also viewed as the key member of the influential Asharite school of early Muslim philosophy and the most important refuter of Mutazilites. His 11th century book the *"Incoherence of the Philosophers"* marks a major turn in Islamic epistemology, as Ghazali effectively discovered philosophical skepticism that would not be commonly seen in the West until George Berkeley and David Hume in the 18th century. The encounter with skepticism led Ghazali to embrace a form of theological occasionalism, or the belief that all causal events and interactions are not the product of material conjunctions but rather the immediate and present will of God. The logical consequence of this belief in practice, and an outcome that has developed in part from it over the subsequent centuries, is a turn towards fundamentalism in many Islamic societies.

The *Incoherence* also marked a turning point in Islamic philosophy in its vehement rejections of Aristotle and Plato. The book took aim at the *falasifa*, a loosely defined group of Islamic philosophers from the 8th through the 11th centuries (most notable among them Avicenna) who drew intellectually upon the Ancient Greeks. Ghazali bitterly denounced Aristotle, Socrates and other Greek writers as non-believers and labelled those who employed their methods and ideas as corrupters of the Islamic faith.

In the next century, Averroes drafted a lengthy rebuttal of Ghazali's *Incoherence* entitled the *Incoherence of the Incoherence*; however, the epistemological course of Islamic thought had already been set.

Ghazali's influence has been compared to the works of St. Thomas Aquinas in Christian theology (he has been called the "Thomas Aquinas of Islam" by some), but the two differed greatly in methods and beliefs. Whereas Ghazali rejected non-Islamic philosophers such as Aristotle and saw it fit to discard their teachings on the basis of their "unbelief," Aquinas embraced them and incorporated ancient Greek and Latin thought into his own philosophical writings.

Ghazali wrote two of his works in Persian: Kimyayé Saadat (The Alchemy of Happiness) and Nasihatul Mulook (Counseling Kings). Abdul Qadir Jelani Sheikh.

Abdul Qadir Jelani was a noted Hanbali preacher, Sufi sheikh and the eponymous founder of the Qadiri Sufi order (*selsela*). He was born in Ramadan 470 A.H (About 1077 AD) in the Persian province of Jilan (Iran) south of the Caspian sea. His contribution and renown in the sciences of Sufism and Sharia was so immense that he became known as the spiritual pole of his time, *al-Gauth al Azam* (the "Supreme Helper" or the "Mightiest Succor"). His writings were similar to those of al-Ghazali in that they dealt with both the fundamentals of Islam and the mystical experience of Sufism.

Abdul Qadir Jilani was a Sufi master and Syed (descendant of the Prophet Muhammad) from both his father and mother. His father Abu Saleh Jangidost, was an illustrious and God-fearing man. Once while engrossed in meditation by the bank of a river he saw an apple floating down the river. He picked it up and ate it. It struck to him that he ate the apple without paying for it so he set out in search of the owner, on the bank of the river and at last reached the owner of the apple orchard "Abdullah Somai" whom he requested to tell him the price of the apple, Abdullah Somai replied that it was an expensive thing. Syed Abu Saleh replied that he had not much by way of worldly material but he, could serve him for compensation. Abdullah Somai then asked him to work for a year in the orchard. In course of time the duration was extended several times. In the end Abdullah Somai admitted that he had served him in excess of the price and desired to reward him. Abu Saleh hesitated in accepting it but when Abdullah Somai persisted, he relented. He said he had a daughter, blind of eyes, handicapped of hands and feet and wanted to give her in marriage to him. In this way Abu Saleh was married to Abdullah Somai's daughter, Syeda Fatimah. To his astonishment found her wondrously beautiful and wholesome. He complained to his father-in-law that he found her exactly the opposite to what he had described her. Abdullah Somai insisted on the truthfulness of his statement. She was blind because she had not seen any *Ghair Mehram* (a man who could marry her). She was mute because she had not uttered a word repugnant to the Shariah (Islamic law). She was deaf because she had not heard anything inconsistent with the Shariah. She was handicapped of hand and feet because she had never moved in the direction of evil.

Abdul Qadir Jilani's father died soon after and the young orphan was reared up by his mother and his grandfather, Abdullah Somai.

At the age of 18 he went to Baghdad on 488 Ah (1095 AD), where he pursued the study of Hanbalite law under several teachers. His mother sewed 40 gold coins in his quilt so that he might spend then when needed. The dacoits struck the caravan on the way, and looted all the travelers of their belongings. They asked him what he had. He replied that he had 40 gold coins. The dacoits took his reply for a joke and took him to their chief, who asked him the same question and he again replied that he had 40 gold coins. He demanded him to show, upon whom he tore away, the quilt and produced the gold coins. He was surprised and asked him why he had given the hidden gold coins when he could have kept them hidden. Young Abdul Qadir Jilani replied that he was travelling to Baghdad to receive education and his mother had instructed him to speak the truth. This left a deep effect on the chief of the dacoits and he gave up looting.

Abdul Qadir received lessons on Islamic Jurisprudence from Abu Said Ali al-Mukharrimi, Hadith from Abu-Bakra-bin-Muzaffar, and commentary (tafseer) from the renowned commentator, Abu Muhammad Jafar.

In Sufism, his spiritual instructor was Shaikh Abul-Khair Hammad. From him, he received his basic training, and with his help he set out on the spiritual journey. Abu Shuja' was also a disciple of Shaikh Hammad, once he said: "Shaikh Abdul Qadir was in the company of Shaikh Hammad, so he came and sat in front of him, observing the best of good manners, until he stood up and took his leave. I heard Shaikh Hammad say, as soon as Shaikh Abdul Qadir had left: 'This non-Arab has a foot that will be raised, when the proper time comes, and placed upon the necks of the saints of that time. He will surely be commanded to say: This foot of mine is upon the neck of every saint of Allah. He will surely say it, and the necks of all the saints of his age will surely be bent at his disposal.'" Hazrat Junayd Baghdadi (d. 910 A.D.), who died about 167 years before the birth of Shaikh Abdul Qadir Jilani, predicted about him on one occasion, when he was performing meditation & during that he said: "His foot will be over all Saints' necks." After finishing meditation, his disciples asked him about his words, he replied: "One Sufi would be born in the future, who would be greater than all saints." Thus, Shaikh Hammad proved the words of Hazrat Junayd as right. The historians says that, later Shaikh Abdul Qadir Jilani also repeated the same words on many occasion by himself.

After completion of education, Hazrat Abdul Qadir Jilani abandoned the city of Baghdad, and spent twenty-five years as a wanderer in the desert regions of Iraq as a recluse. He was over fifty years old by the time he returned to Baghdad, in 521 A.H. (1127 A.D), and began to preach in public. His hearers were profoundly affected by the style and content of his lectures, and his reputation grew and spread through all sections of society. Not only Muslims, but also Jews and Christians, not only caliphs and viziers but also farmers, merchants and traders allegedly altered their lives in response to Abdul Qadir's perorations. He moved into the school belonging to his old teacher al-Mukharrimii, there he engaged himself in teaching. Soon he became popular with his pupils. In the morning he taught *hadith* and *tafseer*, and in the afternoon held discourse on mysticism and the virtues of the Quran. The number of students increased so much that the seminary could no more contain them. He, therefore, decided to extend the premises of the seminary. The students and the people willingly came forward with their wholehearted contributions. The campus buildings were ready in 528 Hijri and thereafter it came to be known as *Madarsai-e-Qadriya.*

Hazrat Abdul Qadir Jilani was a Non-Arab (*ajami*), so he wasn't fluent in Arabic and was having some difficulties because of it. Once The Prophet Muhammad came to him in a dream, before the time of the midday prayer (Zuhr), and he said him: "O my dear son, why do you not speak out?" He replied: "O dear father, I am a Non-Arab man. How can I speak fluently in the classical Arabic language of Baghdad?" Holy Prophet said: "Just open your mouth!" He opened his mouth, and The Holy Prophet put his slavia seven times in his mouth. A few moments later, Hazrat Ali ibn Abi Talib also came & did the same to him six times. And from that time, Hazrat Abdul Qadir Jilani spoke classical Arabic language with fluency, his memory increased and he felt some great positive spiritual changes in him.

Once some one asked Shaikh Abdul Qadir Jilani about Mansur Al-Hallaj, he replied: "His claim extended too far, so the scissors of the Sacred Law (Shari'a) were empowered to clip it."

He busied himself for forty years in the service of the Islam from 521 to 561 Hijri During this period hundreds embraced Islam because of him and organized several teams to go abroad for the purpose. He arrived in Indian sub-continent in 1128 A.D., and stayed at Multan (Pakistan). He died in 561 A.H. (1166 A.D.) at the age of 91 years, and was buried in Baghdad.

Some of Abdul Qadirs major literary works include; *Al-Ghunya li-talibi tariq al-haqq* (Sufficient

Provision for Seekers of the Path of Truth), *Al-Fath ar-Rabbani* (The Sublime Revelation), *Malfuzat* (Utterances), *Futuh al-Ghaib* (Revelations of the Unseen), and *Jala' al-Khatir* (The Removal of Care) or *Jala' al-Khawatir* (The Removal of Cares). As mentioned earlier, the Sheikh was a *seyyid*, which is considered a title of high regard in both Sunni and Shia Islam. Abdul Qadir's full name is Abu Muhammad Abd al-Qadir ibn Abi Salih Musa ibn Abdullah al-Jili ibn Yahya az-Zahid ibn Muhammad ibn Daud ibn Musa ibn Abdullah ibn Musa ibn Abdullah al-Mahd ibn al-Hasan al Muthanna ibn al-Hasan ibn Ali ibn Abi Talib.

Ibn Arabi: Abu 'Abd Allah Muhammad. 'Ali b. Muhammad b. al-'Arabi al-Satimi al-lâ'i commonly known as Ibn Arabi, was an Islamic scholar. He was born 1165 in Murcia, Spain and died 1240 in Damascus.

Also known in the Islamic world by the titles of *Muhyi id-Din* ("Revivifier of religion") and *al-Shaykh al-Akbar* ("Great Master"), he is sometimes described as a mystical philosopher. Even in his lifetime he was acknowledged to be one of the most important spiritual teachers within Sufism, the mystical tradition of Islam. His name is usually confused with another scholar of Andalusia known as Ibn a-Arabi that was a master of Al-Maliki Jurisprudence.

A vastly prolific writer, Ibn Arabi is generally known as the prime exponent of the idea that would later be termed *wahdat al-wujud* ("unity of being"). His emphasis, as with any mystic, lay rather on the true potential of the human being and the path to realising that potential, which reaches its completion in the Perfect or Complete Man (al-insan al-kamil). Ibn Arabi wrote at least 300 works, ranging from minor treatises to the huge 37-volume Meccan Illuminations (al-Futuhat al-Makkiyya) and the quintessence of his teachings, The Bezels of Wisdom (Fusus al-hikam). Approximately 110 works are known to have survived in verifiable manuscripts, some 18 in Ibn Arabi's own hand. He exerted an unparalleled influence, not only upon his immediate circle of friends and disciples, many of whom were considered spiritual masters in their own right, but also on succeeding generations, affecting the whole course of subsequent spiritual thought and practice in the Arabic, Turkish and Persian-speaking worlds. In recent years his writings have also become increasingly the subject of interest and study in the West, leading to the establishment of an international academic Society in his name.

Ibn Arabi's life can be divided into three discrete phases: born in Medinat Mursiya the present day Murcia in south-eastern Spain in 560AH/1165AD, he spent the first thirty-five years of his life in the Maghreb, the western lands of Islam which stretched from al-Andalus to Tunis; then he embarked on pilgrimage and spent the next three years in or around Mecca, where a series of dramatic experiences initiated the writing of several works including his magnum opus, the Meccan Illuminations ; the final phase of his life was spent in the Levant and Anatolia, where he raised a family, and in addition to an unceasing literary output and instruction given to numerous disciples, he became adviser to kings and rulers. He settled in Damascus, where he lived for 17 years, dying in 638AH/1240AD, and his tomb is still an important place of pilgrimage.

Many Wahabis reject the notion that Ibn Arabi was a Muslim, despite the fact that he openly accepted shahadat. Reasons for Ibn Arabi being branded a heretic were some of his statements in his books such as Fusoos Al-Hikam and Al-Ahkaam. One example is where Ibn Arabi said, "Al-`Abdu Rabbun Warrabbu `Abdun" meaning The slave (human) is the Lord/God and the Lord/God is the slave (human)." Sufis claim that such statements were always considered to be the most elevated exposition of mystical thought in Islam, and therefore unsuitable for the untrained mind.

A profound visionary capacity, coupled with a remarkable intellectual insight into human experience and a thorough comprehension of all the traditional sciences, marks out Ibn Arabi from comparable figures in Islam. It has been tempting for scholars to characterise him as a mystical philosopher, a formulation which is rather at odds with his own teachings on the limitations of philosophical thinking. He was as much at home with Quran and Hadith scholarship as with medieval philology and letter symbolism, philosophy, alchemy and cosmology. He could write with equal facility in prose or poetry, and utilised the polysemous ambiguity of the Arabic language to great effect. The characteristic resonances of rhymed prose (saj), which are to be found in the Quran, abound in his works.

In recent years Western scholars such as William Chittick and Michel Chodkiewicz have begun to explore the radical way in which Ibn Arabi's thought is underpinned and inspired by the infallible revelation of the Quran. He adopts the rich vocabulary of spiritual phenomenology which previous mystics had built up, and gives it both a scriptural basis and an ontological root.

This all-inclusiveness and flexibility equally make him one of the most demanding of authors, and one whose subtlety lesser minds have often struggled to comprehend, some falling into rejection and outright opposition. He combines a detailed architecture of spiritual experience, theory and practice, with descriptions of the attainments of other masters he met as well as his own personal visions, insights and dreams. It is his propensity to recount stories from his own direct experience, primarily in order to make a teaching point, that allows readers to gain such a detailed insight into the inner world of one of the greatest mystics the world has known, and also allows us to reconstruct his life and times with some accuracy.

Mawlana Rumi: Mawlana Jalâl ad-Din Muhammad Rûmi known as Mawlana Jalal ad-Din Muhammad Balkhi but known to the world simply as Rumi, was a 13th century Persian poet, jurist, theologian and teacher of Sufism.

Rumi was born in Balkh (then a city of Khorasan, now part of Afghanistan) and died in Konya (in present-day Turkey). His birthplace and native tongue indicate a Persian heritage. He also wrote his poetry in Persian and his works are widely read in Iran and Afghanistan where the language is spoken. He lived most of his life and produced his works under the Seljuk Empire.

Rumi's importance transcends national and ethnic borders. He has had a significant influence on both Persian and Turkish literature throughout the centuries. His poems have been translated into many of the world's languages and have appeared in various formats. He was also the founder of the Mevlevi order, better known as the "Whirling Dervishes", who believe in performing their worship in the form of dance and music ceremony called the sema.

Rumi's life is fully described in Shams ud-Din Ahmad Aflaki's *"Manâkib ul-Ârifin"* (written between 1318 and 1353). He is described as a descendant of the caliph Abu Bakr, and of the Khwrizm-Shh Sultân Alâ ud-Din bin Takash (1199–1220), whose only daughter, Mâlika-e Jahân, had allegedly been married to Rumi's grandfather.

When the Mongols invaded Central Asia sometime between 1215 and 1220, his father (Bahauddin Walad, a theologian, jurist and a mystic of uncertain lineage) set out westwards with his whole family and a group of disciples. On the road to Anatolia, Rumi encountered one of the most famous mystic

Persian poets, Attar, in the city of Nishapur, located in what is now the Iranian province of Khorsn. Attar immediately recognized Rumi's spiritual eminence. He saw the father walking ahead of the son and said, "Here comes a sea followed by an ocean." He gave the boy his Asrarnama, a book about the entanglement of the soul in the material world. This meeting had a deep impact on the eighteen-year-old Rumi's thoughts, which later on became the inspiration for Rumi's works.

From Nishapur, Walad and his entourage set out for Baghdad, meeting many of the scholars and Sufis of the city. From there they went to the Hejaz and performed the pilgrimage at Mecca. It was after this journey that most likely as a result of the invitation of Allâh ud-Din Key-Qobâd, ruler of Anatolia, Bahauddin came to Asia Minor and finally settled in Konya in Anatolia within the western most territories of Seljuk Empire.

Bahauddin became the head of a madrassa (religious school) and when he died Rumi succeeded him at the age of twenty-five. One of Bahauddin's students, Syed Burhanuddin Mahaqqiq, continued to train Rumi in the religious and mystical doctrines of Rumi's father. For nine years, Rumi practiced Sufism as a disciple of Burhanuddin until the latter died in 1240-1. During this period Rumi also travelled to Damascus and is said to have spent four years there.

It was his meeting with the dervish Shams Tabriz in the late fall of 1244 that changed his life completely. Shams had traveled throughout the Middle East searching and praying for someone who could "endure my company". A voice came, "What will you give in return?" "My head!" "The one you seek is Jelaluddin of Konya." On the night of December 5, 1248, as Rumi and Shams were talking, Shams was called to the back door. He went out, never to be seen again. It is believed that he was murdered with the connivance of Rumi's son, Allaedin; if so, Shams indeed gave his head for the privilege of mystical friendship.

Rumi's love and his bereavement for the death of Shams found their expression in an outpouring of music, dance and lyric poems, *Divani Shamsi Tabrizi*. He himself went out searching for Shams and journeyed again to Damascus. There, he realized:

Why should I seek? I am the same as

He. His essence speaks through me.

I have been looking for myself!

For more than ten years after meeting Shams, Mevlana had been spontaneously composing ghazals, and these had been collected in the *Divan-i Kabir*. Rumi found another companion in Saladin Zarkub, the goldsmith. After Saladin's death, Rumi's scribe and favorite student Husam Chelebi assumed the role. One day, the two of them were wandering through the Meram vineyards outside of Konya when Husam described an idea he had to Rumi: "If you were to write a book like the Ilahiname of Sanai or the Mantik'ut-Tayr'i of Attar it would become the companion of many troubadours. They would fill their hearts from your work and compose music to accompany it."

Rumi smiled and took out a piece of paper on which were written the opening eighteen lines of his Mathnawi, beginning with:

Listen to the reed and the tale it tells,

How it sings of separation...

Husam implored Rumi to write more. Rumi spent the next twelve years of his life in Anatolia dictating the six volumes of this masterwork, the *Mathnawi* to Husam. In December 1273, Rumi fell ill; he predicted his own death and composed the well-known ghazal, which begins with the verse:

How doest thou know what sort of king I have within me as companion?

Do not cast thy glance upon my golden face, for I have iron legs.

He died on December 17, 1273 in Konya; Rumi was laid to rest beside his father, and a splendid shrine, the *Ye"il Türbe* "Green Tomb", was erected over his tomb. His epitaph reads:

"When we are dead, seek not our tomb in the earth, but find it in the hearts of men."

The general theme of his thoughts, like that of the other mystic and Sufi poets of the Persian literature, is essentially about the concept of Tawheed (unity) and union with his beloved (the primal root) from which/whom he has been cut and fallen aloof, and his longing and desire for reunity.

The "Mathnawi" weaves fables, scenes from everyday life, Qur'anic revelations and exegesis, and metaphysics, into a vast and intricate tapestry. Rumi is considered an example of *"insani kamil"* — the perfected or completed human being. In the East, it is said of him, that he was, "not a prophet — but surely, he has brought a scripture". Rumi believed passionately in the use of music, poetry and dancing as a path for reaching God. For Rumi, music helped devotees to focus their whole being on the divine, and to do this so intensely that the soul was both destroyed and resurrected. It was from these ideas that the practice of Whirling Dervishes developed into a ritual form. He founded the order of the Mevlevi, the "whirling" dervishes, and created the "Sema", their "turning", sacred dance. In the Mevlevi tradition, Sema represents a mystical journey of spiritual ascent through mind and love to "Perfect." In this journey the seeker symbolically turns towards the truth, grows through love, abandons the ego, finds the truth, and arrives at the "Perfect"; then returns from this spiritual journey with greater maturity, so as to love and to be of service to the whole of creation without discrimination against beliefs, races, classes and nations.

According to Shahram Shiva, one reason for Rumi's popularity is that "Rumi is able to verbalize the highly personal and often confusing world of personal/spiritual growth and mysticism in a very forward and direct fashion. He does not offend anyone, and he includes everyone. The world of Rumi is neither exclusively the world of a Sufi, nor the world of a Hindu, nor a Jew, nor a Christian; it is the highest state of a human being — a fully evolved human. A complete human is not bound by cultural limitations; he touches every one of us. Today Rumi's poems can be heard in churches, synagogues, Zen monasteries, as well as in the downtown New York art/performance/music scene." In Divan-i Shams, Rumi says:

What is to be done, O Muslims? for I do not recognize myself.

I am neither Christian, nor Jew, nor Gabr, nor Muslim.

I am not of the East, nor of the West, nor of the land, nor of the sea;

I am not of Nature's mint, nor of the circling heaven.

I am not of earth, nor of water, nor of air, nor of fire;

I am not of the empyrean, nor of the dust, nor of existence, nor of entity.

I am not of India, nor of China, nor of Bulgaria, nor of Saqsin

I am not of the kingdom of 'Iraqian, nor of the country of Khorasan

I am not of the this world, nor of the next, nor of Paradise, nor of Hell

I am not of Adam, nor of Eve, nor of Eden and Rizwan.

My place is the Placeless, my trace is the Traceless.

According to Professor Majid Naini, one of the foremost international Rumi scholars who travels the world trying to spread Rumi's universal message of love, Rumi's life and transformation provide true testimony and proof that people of all religions and backgrounds can live together in peace and harmony throughout the world. At Rumi's grand funeral procession Jews, Christians, Muslims, Hindus, Buddhists, and Sufis cried and mourned in a manner that one would have thought that Rumi belonged to each one of them. Rumi's visions, words, and life teach us how to reach inner peace and happiness so we can finally stop the continual stream of hostility and hatred and achieve true global peace and harmony.

In other beautiful verses in Mathnavi, Rumi describes in detail the universal message of love. For example, he states:

Love's nationality is separate from all other religions,

The lover's religion and nationality is the Beloved (God).

The lover's cause is separate from all other causes

Love is the astrolabe of God's mysteries.

Rumi's poetry is often divided into various categories: the quatrains (rubaiyat) and odes (ghazals) of the Divan, the six books of the Mathnawi, the discourses, the letters, and the almost unknown Six Sermons. Rumi's major work is Masnavi-ye Manavi (Spiritual Couplets), a six-volume poem regarded by many Sufis as second in importance only to the Quran. In fact, the Masnawi is often called the "Quran-e Parsi" (The Persian Quran). It is considered by many to be one of the greatest works of mystical poetry. Rumi's other major work is the Diwan-e Shams-e Tabriz-i (The Works of Shams of Tabriz-named in honor of Rumi's great friend and inspiration, the darvish Shams), comprising some 40,000 verses. Several reasons have been offered for Rumi's decision to name his masterpiece after Shams. Some argue that since Rumi would not have been a poet without Shams, it is apt that the collection be named after him. Others have suggested that at the end, Rumi became Shams, hence the collection is truly of Shams speaking through Rumi. Both works are among the most significant in all of Persian literature. Shams is believed to have been murdered by disciples of Rumi who were jealous of his relationship with Shams (also spelt Shems).

Fihi Ma Fih (*In It What's in It*) is composed of Rumi's speeches on different subjects. Rumi himself did not prepare or write these discourses. They were recorded by his son *Sultan Valad* or some other disciple of Rumi and put together as a book. The title may mean, "What's in the Mathnawi is in this too." Some of the discourses are addressed to *Muin al-Din Parvane*. Some portions of it are commentary on Masnavi.

Majalis-i Sab'a (seven sessions) contains seven sermons (as the name implies) given in seven different assemblies. As *Aflaki* relates, after *Sham-i Tabrizi*, Rumi gave sermons at the request of notables, especially *Salah al-Din Zarqubi*.

The Mevlevi Sufi order was founded in 1273 by Rumi's followers after his death. His first successor in the rectorship of the order was Husam Chelebi himself, after whose death in 1284 Rumi's younger and only surviving son, Sultan Walad, favorably known as author of the mystical Mathnawi Rabbnma, or the Book of the Guitar (died 1312), was installed as grand master of the order. The leadership of the order has been kept in Jalaluddin's family in Iconium uninterruptedly for the last six hundred years. The Mevlevi, or "The Whirling Dervishes", believe in performing their dhikr in the form of sema. During the time of Rumi (as attested in the "Manakib ul Arifin" of Eflaki Dede), his followers gathered for musical and "turning" practices. Mevlana himself was a notable musician, who played the rebab although his favorite instrument was the ney. The music accompanying the traditional ritual consists of settings of poems from the "Mathnawi" and "Diwan-i-Kebir" or of his son Sultan Veled's poems. The Mevlevi were a well-established Sufi Order in the Ottoman Empire, and many of the members of the order served in various official positions of the Caliphate. The centre for the Mevlevi order was in Konya. There is also a Mevlevi monastery or dergah in Istanbul, near the Galata Tower, where the sema ceremony is performed and accessible to the public. Rumi's order issues invitation to people of all backgrounds:

"*Come, come, whoever you are.*

Wanderer, idolater, worshipper of fire,

"Come even though you have broken your vows a thousand times,
Come, and come yet again.

Ours is not a caravan of despair.

During Ottoman times, the Mevlevi order produced a number of famous poets and musicians such as Sheikh Ghalib, Ismail Ankaravi (both buried at the Galata Mevlevi-Hane) and Abdullah Sari. Music, especially the ney, play an important part in the Mevlevi order and thus much of the traditional 'oriental' music that Westerners associate with Turkey originates with the Mevlevi order. Indeed, if one buys a CD of Turkish Sufi music, chances are it will be Mevlevi religious music.

The Mevlevi Order was outlawed in Turkey at the dawn of the secular revolution by Kemal Atatrk in 1923. In the 1950s, the Turkish government, realizing that The Whirling Dervishes had value as a tourist attraction, began allowing the Whirling Dervishes to perform annually in Konya on the Urs of Mevlana, December 17, the anniversary of Rumi's death. In 1974, they were allowed to come to the West. The Mevlana annual festival is held every year in Konya in December. It lasts two weeks and its culminating point is the 17th December called *Sheb-i Arus* meaning 'Nuptial Night', the night of the union of Mevlana with God.

Rumi's importance transcends national and ethnic borders. Speakers of the Persian language in Iran, Afghanistan and Tajikistan see him as one of their most significant classical poets and an influence on many poets through history. He has also had a great influence on Turkish literature throughout the centuries. His poetry forms the basis of much classical Iranian and Afghan music. Contemporary classical interpretations of his poetry are made by Muhammad Reza Shajarian (Iran), Shahram Nazeri (Iran), Davood Azad (Iran) and Ustad Mohammad Hashem Cheshti (Afghanistan). To many modern Westerners, his teachings are one of the best introductions to the philosophy and practice of Sufism. Pakistan's National Poet, Muhammad Iqbal (November 9, 1877-April 21, 1938) was also inspired by Rumi's works and considered him to be his spiritual leader and addressed him as *Pir Rumi* in his poems (*pir* literally means *old*, but in sufi/mystic context, it means *guide*, *teacher*, *master*, *guru*.)

Rumi's work has been translated into many of the world's languages including Russian, German, French, Italian and Spanish, and is appearing in a growing number of formats including concerts, workshops, readings, dance performances and other artistic creations. Coleman Barks's translations of Rumi have sold more than a 250,000 copies in the United States. Recordings of Rumi poems have made it to Billboard's Top 20 list. A collection of Deepak Chopra's translations of Rumi's love poems has been sung by Hollywood personalities such as Madonna, Goldie Hawn and Demi Moore; also Shahram Shiva's CD, *Rumi: Lovedrunk* has been very popular on the Internet's music communities such as MySpace.com. The 13th-century poet of the Seljuk Empire is one of the most widely read poets in the United States.

Data Ganj Bakhsh: Syed Abul Hassan Bin Usman Bin Ali Al-Hajweri (sometimes spelled Hujwiri), also known as Shaikh Ali Hajweri, Data Ganj Bakhsh, or Data Sahib, was a scholar of Islam and a Sufi saint, and writer of the 11th century. His contribution in spreading of Islam in South Asia is huge.

He was born in Ghazna (in present day Afghanistan) and died in Lahore (in present day Punjab, Pakistan) in 1077 CE. His most famous work is Kashf al Mahjub ("Unveiling the Veiled"), which was the first Persian language treatise on Sufism. The work debates Sufi doctrines of the past. Hujwiri said that individuals should not claim to have attained "marifat" or gnosis because it meant that one was prideful. True understanding of God should be a silent understanding.

Hujwiri is also viewed as an important intercessor for many Sufis.

His mausoleum, popularly known as Data Durbar, is located in Lahore, Punjab, Pakistan.

Amir Khusro: Abul Hasan Yaminuddin Khusro (1253-1325 CE), better known as Amir Khusro Dehlavi is one of the iconic figures in the cultural history of the Indian subcontinent. A Sufi mystic and a spiritual disciple of Nizamuddin Auliya of Delhi, Amir Khusro (or Khusrau or Khusraw) was not only one of India's greatest poets, he is also credited with being the founder of both Hindustani classical music and Qawwali (the devotional music of the Sufis). He was born of a Turkish father, Saif Ad-din, and an Indian mother, in India.

Major life events in chronological order

1. 1253 Khusro was born in Patiali near Etah in what is today the state of Uttar Pradesh in northern India. His father Amir Saifuddin came from Balkh in modern day Afghanistan and his mother hailed from Delhi.
2. 1260 After the death of his father, Khusro went to Delhi with his mother.
3. 1271 Khusro compiled his first divan of poetry, "Tuhfatus-Sighr".
4. 1272 Khusro got his first job as court poet with King Balban's nephew Malik Chhajju.
5. 1276 Khusro started working as a poet with Bughra Khan (Balban's son).
6. 1279 While writing his second divan, Wastul-Hayat, Khusrau visited Bengal.
7. 1281 Employed by Sultan Mohammad (Balban's second son) and went to Multan with him.
8. 1285 Khusro participated as a soldier in the war against the invading Mongols. He was taken prisoner, but escaped.
9. 1287 Khusro went to Awadh with Ameer Ali Hatim (another patron).
10. 1288 His first mathnavi, "Qiranus-Sa'dain" was completed.

11. 1290 When Jalal ud din Firuz Khilji came to power, Khusro's second mathnavi, "Miftahul Futooh" was ready.
12. 1294 His third divan "Ghurratul-Kamal" was complete.
13. 1295 Ala ud din Khilji (sometimes spelled "Khalji") came to power and invaded Devagiri and Gujarat.
14. 1298 Khusro completed his "Khamsa-e-Nizami".
15. 1301 Khilji attacked Ranthambhor, Chittor, Malwa and other places, and Khusro remained with the king in order to write chronicles.
16. 1310 Khusro became close to Nizamuddin Aulia, and completed Khazain-ul-Futuh.
17. 1315 Alauddin Khilji died. Khusro completed the mathnavi "Duval Rani-Khizr Khan" (a romantic poem).
18. 1316 Qutb ud din Mubarak Shah became the king, and the fourth historical mathnavi "Noh-Sepehr" was completed.
19. 1321 Mubarak Khilji (sometimes spelled "Mubarak Khalji") was murdered and Ghiyath al-Din Tughluq Ghiassuddin Tughluq (Real Name in Arabic, Farsi and Urdu Languages)came to power. Khusro started to write the Tughluqnama.
20. 1325 Sultan Muhammad bin Tughluq came to power. Nizamuddin Aulia died, and six months later so did Khusro. Khusro's tomb is next to that of his master in the Nizamuddin Dargah of Delhi.

Khusro was a prolific classical poet associated with the royal courts of more than seven rulers of the Delhi Sultanate. He is popular in much of North India and Pakistan, because of many playful riddles, songs and legends attributed to him. Through his enormous literary output and the legendary folk personality, Khusro represents one of the first (recorded) Indian personages with a true multi-cultural or pluralistic identity.

He wrote in both Persian and Hindustani. His poetry is still sung today at Sufi shrines throughout Pakistan and India.

Amir Khusro was the author of a Khamsa which emulated that of the earlier Persian-language poet Nizami Ganjavi. His work was considered to be one of the great classics of Persian poetry during the Timurid period in Transoxiana.

Amir Khusro is credited with fashioning the *tabla* as a split version of the traditional Indian drum, the *pakhawaj*.

Popular lore also credits him with inventing the *sitar*, the Indian grand lute, but it is more likely that the sitar was invented by a different Amir Khusro several centuries later. This later namesake is said to be an 18th century descendant of the son-in-law of Tansen, the celebrated classical singer in the court of the Mughal Emperor Akbar. For an article about this theory, see Origin Of Sitar

Some samples of Khusro's poetry

Agar firdaus bar roo-e zameen ast,

Hameen ast-o hameen ast-o hameen ast.

If there is paradise on face of the earth,

It is this, it is this, it is this (India)

Persian Poems

Kafir-e-ịshqam musalmani mara darkaar neest

Har rag-e mun taar gashta hajat-e zunnaar neest;

Az sar-e baaleen-e mun bar khez ay naadaan tabeeb

Dard mand-e ishq ra daroo bajuz deedaar neest;

Nakhuda dar kashti-e maagar nabashad go mubaash

Makhuda daareem mara nakhuda darkaar neest;

Khalq mi goyad ki Khusrau but parasti mi kunad

Aarey aarey mi kunam ba khalq mara kaar neest.

I am a pagan and a worshipper of love: the creed (of Muslims) I do not need;

Every vein of mine has become taut like a wire,

the (Brahman's) girdle I do not need.

Leave from my bedside, you ignorant physician!

The only cure for the patient of love is the sight of his beloved –

other than this no medicine does he need.

If there be no pilot in our boat, let there be none:

We have god in our midst: the sea we do not need.

The people of the world say that Khusrau worships idols.

So he does, so he does; the people he does not need,

the world he does not need.

Hindi Couplets

Khusrau darya prem ka, ulti wa ki dhaar,

Jo utra so doob gaya, jo dooba so paar.

Khusro says the river of love

Has a strange flow

One who jumps into it drowns,

And one who drowns, gets across.

Sej wo sooni dekh ke rovun main din raen,

Piya piya main karat hoon pehron, pal bhar sukh na chaen.

Day and night, I see an empty bed, and cry

Calling for my beloved, I remain restless for ever.

Chhap tilak sab cheeni ray mosay naina milaikay

Chhap tilak sab cheeni ray mosay naina milaikay

Prem bhat e ka madhva pilaikay

Matvali kar leeni ray mosay naina milaikay

Gori gori bayyan, hari hari churiyan

Bayyan pakar dhar leeni ray mosay naina milaikay

Bal bal jaaon mein toray rang rajwa

Apni see kar leeni ray mosay naina milaikay

Khusrau Nijaam kay bal bal jayyiye

Mohay Suhaagan keeni ray mosay naina milaikay

Chhap tilak sab cheeni ray mosay naina milaikay

You've taken away my looks, my identity, by just a glance.

By making me drink the wine of love-potion,

You've intoxicated me by just a glance;

My fair, delicate wrists with green bangles in them,

Have been held tightly by you with just a glance.

I give my life to you, Oh my cloth-dyer,

You've dyed me in yourself, by just a glance.

I give my whole life to you Oh, Nijam,

You've made me your bride, by just a glance.

Spoiler Warning: The answers to the riddles are given at the end.

1. *Nar naari kehlaati hai,*
   aur bin warsha jal jati hai;
   Purkh say aaway purkh mein jaai,
   na di kisi nay boojh bataai.

Is known by both masculine and feminine names,

And lightens up (or burns up) without rain;

Originates from a man and goes into a man,

But no one has been able to guess what it is.

2. *Pawan chalat weh dehe badhavay*
   Jal peevat weh jeev ganvavay
   Hai weh piyari sundar naar,
   Naar nahin par hai weh naar.

With the blow of wind she flares up,

And dies as soon as she drinks water;

Even though she is a pretty woman,

She's not a woman, though she's feminine.

Answers

1. Nadi (River) 2. Aag (Fire)

Works

- Tuhfa-us-Sighr (Offering of a Minor) his first divan, contains poems composed between the age of 16 and 19
- Wastul-Hayat (The Middle of Life) his second divan, contains poems composed at the peak of his poetic career
- Ghurratul-Kamaal (The Prime of Perfection) poems composed between the age of 34 and 43
- Baqia-Naqia (The Rest/The Miscellany) compiled at the age of 64
- Nihayatul-Kamaal (The Height of Wonders) compiled probably a few weeks before his death.
- Qiran-us-Sa'dain (Meeting of the Two Auspicious Stars) Mathnavi about the historic meeting of Bughra Khan and his son Kyqbad after long enmity
- Miftah-ul-Futooh (Key to the Victories) in praise of the victories of Jalauddin Khalaji
- Ishqia/Mathnavi Duval Rani-Khizr Khan (Romance of Duval Rani and Khizr Khan) a tragic love poem about Gujarat's princess Duval and Alauddin's son Khizr.
- Mathnavi Noh Sepehr (Mathnavi of the Nine Skies) Khusrau's perceptions of India and its culture
- Tughlaq Nama (Book of the Tughlaqs) in prose
- Khamsa-e-Nizami (Khamsa-e-Khusrau) five classical romances: Hasht-Bahisht, Matlaul-Anwar, Sheerin-Khusrau, Majnun-Laila and Aaina-Sikandari
- Ejaaz-e-Khusrovi (The Miracles of Khusrau) an assortment of prose compiled by himself
- Khazain-ul-Futooh (The Treasures of Victories) one of his more controversial books, in prose
- Afzal-ul-Fawaid utterances of Nizamuddin Auliya
- Khaliq-e-Bari a versified glossary of Persian and Hindvi words and phrases
- Jawahar-e- Khusrovi often dubbed as the Hindvi divan of Khusrau

Fariduddin Ganjshakar: Fariduddin Ganjshakar (Farid-ul-Din Masaud Shakar Ganj) c. 1173-c. 1266, was a respected Sufi Sheikh and noted Punjabi poet. He is also referred to as "Baba Farid" or "Shaikh Farid". He is buried near Pak Pattan in Punjab, present-day Pakistan.

Baba Farid Ganjshakar is revered by Muslims as well as the Sikhs as one of the Sikh Bhagats because the Sikh Gurus included several of his verses in the Guru Granth Sahib. Every year thousands of people gather around at his shrine at Pak Pattan to pay their respects and to take blessings. He was the spiritual master of Nizamuddin Awliya. He was also the spiritual disciple and *khalifa* (spiritual successor) of Qutbuddin Bakhtiar Kaki in the Chishtiyya sufi order.

Kabir: Kabir was an Indian mystic who preached an ideal of seeing all of humanity as one. He was known to be a weaver and later became famed for scorning religious affiliation. His philosophies and ideas of loving devotion to God are expressed in metaphor and language from both the Hindu Vedanta and Bhakti streams and Muslim Sufi ideals, using vernacular Hindi. Kabir is also considered one of the early northern India Sants. He was initiated by Ramananda.

His greatest work is the *Bijak* (that is, the *Seedling*), an idea of the fundamental one. This collection of poems demonstrates Kabir's own universal view of spirituality. His vocabulary is constantly full of ideas regarding Brahman and Hindu ideas of karma and reincarnation, and yet he also espouses ideas that are clearly Sufi as well as Hindu Bhakti understandings of God. His Hindi was a very vernacular, straightforward kind, much like his philosophies. He often advocated leaving aside the Quran and Vedas and to simply follow Shahaj path, or the Simple/Natural Way to oneness in God. He believed in the Vedantic concepts of *atman* and therefore spurned the orthodox Hindu societal caste system and worship of statues, thus showing clear belief in both bhakti and sufi ideas. The major part of Kabir's work as a Sikh Bhagat was collected by the first Sikh guru, Guru Nanak, and is published in the holy Sikh scripture "Gurû Granth Sahib".

While many ideas reign as to who his living influences were, the only Guru of whom he ever spoke was Ramananda, a Vaishnav saint whom Kabir claimed to have taken initiation from in the form of the "Rama" mantra.

His poems resonate with praise for the true guru who reveals the divine through direct experience, and denounced more usual ways of attempting god-union such as chanting, austerities etc. His verses, which being illiterate he never expressed in writing, often began with some strongly worded insult to get the attention of passers-by. Kabir has enjoyed a revival of popularity over the past half century as arguably the most acceptable and understandable of the medieval Indian 'sants', with an especial influence over spiritual traditions such as that of Sant Mat and Radha Soami. Prem Rawat ('Maharaji') also refers frequently to Kabir's songs and poems as the embodiment of deep wisdom.

It is a fruitless endeavor, indeed one that Kabir himself disliked, to classify him as Hindu or Muslim, Sufi or Bhakta. The legends surrounding his lifetime attest to his strong aversion to communalism.

In fact, Kabir always insisted on the concept of *Koi bole Ram Ram Koi Khudai...*, which means that someone may chant the Hindu name of God and someone may chant the Muslim name of God, but God is the one who made the whole world.

His birth and death are surrounded by legends. He grew up in a Muslim weaver family, but some say he was really son of a Brahmin widow who was adopted by a childless couple. When he died, his Hindu and Muslim followers started fighting about the last rites. In Maghar, his tomb or Dargah and samadhi still stand side by side.

Another legend surrounding Kabir is that shortly before death he bathed in both the river Ganges and Karmnasha to wash away both his good deeds and his sins.

One popular legend of his death, which is even taught in schools in India (although in more of a moral context than a historical one), says that after his death his Muslim and Hindu devotees were fighting over his proper burial rites. The problem arose, as Muslim customs called for the burial of their dead, whereas Hindus cremated their dead. The scene is depicted as two groups fighting around his coffin one claiming that Kabir was a Hindu, and the other claiming that Kabir was a Muslim. However when they finally open Kabir's coffin, they find the body is missing, in lieu of which is placed a set of flowers. The legend goes on to state that the fighting was resolved, and both groups looked upon the miracle as an act of divine intervention.

Kabir is revered as Satguru by the Kabirpanthi religion, based in Maghar.

Shah Waliullah: Shah Waliullah Dehlavi also known as Shah Waliullah of Delhi (1703–1762) was an important Islamic reformer who worked for the revival of Muslim rule and itellectual learning in the South Asia, hoping to restore the ulama's former power and influence. He despised the divisions and deviations within Islam and its practice in the subcontinent and hoped to 'purify' the religion and unify all Indian Muslims under the banner of the 'truth' (*Haq*).

One of his main desires was to intellectually revive Islamic learning and did so by emphasising studies in madrassas (Islamic schools), especially his own, Madrassa-i Rahimiyya. Waliullah advocated the strenuous study of the Islamic "sciences of revelation", which comprised studies of the Hadith (the oral tradition of the sayings of the Prophet) and the Quran (the Islamic holy scripture). Shah Waliullah attempted to simplify the texts in order to spread their message to Muslims of every educated class. In addition, Waliullah was a powerful advocate of the establishment of Urdu as a mainstream literary and liturgical language, citing it as the lingual link among all Indian Muslims. Shah Waliullah's approach to learning and his Muslim revivalist agenda inspired the Deobandi movement, who claim their scholastic heritage and lineage back to Shah Waliullah).

Shah Waliullah was also a key protagonist in initiating the spiritual revival of Muslims through tasawwaf and Sufism (Islamic spirituality). He spread the message of Islamic spiritualism to the Indian masses and emphasised Da'wah and Tableegh (Islamic propagation) to his students and he supported the well-established tradition of the Sufis in the South Asia, while at the same time condemning external influences and innovations (bida) in Sufi practices, advocating the idea of a pure Islam devoid of such influences on the basis that Muslims should assert an independent identity free from the influence of Hindu *polytheists*. In this respect as well as others, Shah Waliullah was a follower of the Ghazalian tradition of Imam Al-Ghazali.

It is interesting to note that Shah Waliullah is respected and revered greatly by all Muslims in the South Asia and beyond, including the Barelvi, Deobandi and Ahl-e-Hadeeth groups and movements of Pakistan, Bangladesh and India, who include both Sufis and Salafis. The Deoband movement as well as the Ahl-e-Hadeeth both claim to espouse the ideology and thought of Shah Waliullah and the Barelvi movement follow his spiritual tradition. Shah Waliullah belongs to a noble family.

Shah Waliullah was a prolific writer who wrote extensively on several Islamic topics. His works include an instrumental and one of the earliest translations of the Quran from Arabic into Urdu, as well as one into Sanskrit, contrary to the will of many of his Muslim contemporaries who opined that the Quran should be left in its original language. Later Indian Islamic scholars, however, accepted such efforts and rather than criticise this, they welcomed it. Other famous works include Hujjat al-Balagha amd Al-Tafheemat al-Ilahia.

Ahmad Sirhindi: Ahmad Sirhindi (d. in Delhi in 1624), a mujaddid who founded the Naqshbandiyya-Mujaddidiyya lineage, is known for his great impact in the Mogul empire. Sirhindi's worldview focused on the idea that ontologically, the prophethood is far greater than closeness with God. He believed that Sufi ideas which centered around spiritual growth beyond the material world, while exhibiting key concepts, fell short of encompassing Islam as a whole. Sirhindi, still accepting and using these ideas of *walayat*, or closeness with God, focused on a much more human understanding and reality by focusing on following the sunnah of Muhammad and his companions. His influence went so far as implementing jurisprudence in the Islamic world by emphasizing the Shariah and fiqh, integrating both into Indian Muslim government and society. This was accomplished through his 536 letters collectively entitled *Collected Letters* or *Maktubat*, to the Ottoman rulers conveying his ideas.

Shah Abdul Latif Bhittai: Shah Abdul Latif Bhittai (1689-1752), was a great Sufi scholar and saint, and is considered as the greatest poet of the Sindhi language. He settled in the town of Bhit Shah in Sindh, Pakistan. His most famous written work is the Shah Jo Risalo. His shrine is located in Bhit and attracts hundreds of pilgrims every day.

Shah Abdul Latif Bhitai is most famous Sindhi poet and Sufi. He was not just adored for his poetry alone. People from far and near respected and loved this man as a saint, a sufi and a spiritual guide. Not much is known about the early life of this noble son of Sindh from written records. Most of the information that has come down to us has been collected from oral traditions. A renowned Sindhi scholar, educationist, and a foremost writer of plays, dramas and stories, Mirza Kalich Beg, has rendered a yeoman service to Sindhi literature by collecting details about the early life of Shah Bhitai, from the dialogues that he has constantly held with some of the old folks, still living at that time, who knew these facts from their fathers and grandfathers for they had seen Shah Latif in person and had even spoken to him.

"The next day I sat down, and listened to the Story of the 'Vairagis.' Their salmon-coloured clothes were covered with dust. Their hair-bands were worn out. They had let their hair grow quite long. The lonely ones never talk to anyone about their being. These 'Nanga' are content and happy. They move about unmarked amongst the common folk."

Shah Latif Bhitai: He was born sometime around 1689 CE (1102 A.H.) at a small village called Bhainpur near Khatian. More properly, his birthplace was Hala Haveli (a cluster of houses to the Southeast of Bhainpur, not very far from it), of Taluka Hala in Hyderabad district of Sindh. He died, at the age of sixty three, on 14th Safar 1165 Hijra, that is, 1752 CE To commemorate his memory, every year, on 14th Safar of the Hijri Calendar, an Urs is held at Bhit Shah, where he lived the last years of his life and where his elaborate and elegant mausoleum stands.

"Beloved's separation kills me friends, At His door, many like me, their knees bend. From far and near is heard His beauty's praise, My Beloved's beauty is perfection itself."

The Urs is a grand affair in Sindh, where people from almost every village and town of Sindh-rich and poor, young and old, scholars and peasants-make a determined effort to attend. The Urs lasts for three days. Along with other features, like food fairs, open-air markets selling traditional Sindhi ware, and entertaining and competitive sports, a literary gathering is also held where papers concerning the research work done on the life, poetry, and message of Bhitai, are read, by scholars and renowned literary figures. His disciples and ascetics, singers and artists, gather around and sing passages from his Risalo. Scholarly debates and exhibitions of his work and traditional Sindhi artefacts are also organised.

"Sleeping on the river's bank, I heard of Mehar's glory, Bells aroused my consciousness, longing took its place, By God! fragrance of Mehar's love to me came, Let me go and see Mehar face to face.".....Bhitai [Sur Suhni]

Shah Abdul Latif's lineage has been traced back directly to Prophet Mohammad, through Imam Zain-ul-Abideen, son of Imam Hussain, grandson of the Prophet. His ancestors had came from Herat in Central Asia, and settled at Matiari. Shah Abdul Karim 1600 CE, whose mausoleum stands at Bulri, about 40 miles from Hyderabad, a mystic Sufi poet of considerable repute, was his great, great grand father. His verses are extant and his anniversary is still held at Bulri, in the form of an Urs.

Shah Latif's father, Syed Habib Shah, lived in Hala Haveli, a small village, at a distance of about forty miles from Matiari and not far from the village of Bhitshah. Later he left this place and moved to Kotri, where Shah Latif spent some part of his adolscent life.

Early education of the pet did not exceed what the village school curriculum could provide. His first teacher was Noor Muhammad Bhatti Waiwal. Mostly, Shah Latif was self-educated. Although he has received scanty formal education, the Risalo gives us an ample proof of the fact that he was well-versed in Arabic and Persian. The Quran, the Hadiths, the Masnawi of Maulana Jalaluddin Rumi, along with the collection of Shah Karim's poems, were his constant companions, copious references of which have been made in Shah Jo Risalo.

In appearance, Bhitai was a handsome man, of average height-like every othe son of mother Sindh. He was strongly built, had black eyes and an intelligent face, with a broad and high forehead. He grew a beard of the size of Muhammad's beard. He had a serious and thoughful look about himself and spent much time in contemplation and meditation, since he was concerned about his moral and spiritual evolution with the sole purpose of seeking proximity of the Divine. He would often seek solitude and contemplate on the burning questions running through his mind concerning man's spiritual life:

Why was man created? What is his purpose on this earth? What is his relationship with his Creator? What is his ultimate destiny?

Although he was born in favoured conditions, being the son of a well-known and very much respected Sayed family, he never used his position in an unworthy manner, nor did he show any liking for the comforts of life. He was kind, compassionate, generous and gentle in his manner of speech and behaviour which won him the veneration of all those who came across him. He had great respect for woman, which, unfortunately, the present day Sayed's and Vaderas (the landlords) do not have, and he exercised immense reserve in dealing with them, in an age when these qualities were rare. He hated cruelty and could never cause physical pain to any man or even to an animal He live a very simple life of self-restraint. His food was simple and frugal, so was his dress which was often deep yellow, the colour of the dress of sufis, jogis, and ascetics, wtitched with black thread. Till this day, his relics are preserved at Bhitsah (where his mausoleum stands), some of which include a "T"-shaped walking stick, two bowls, one made of sandal-wood and another of transparent stone, which he used for eating and drinking. His long cap and his black turban are also preserved.

Perhaps, it would be appropriate to mention here, that the Sayed's, who are called Sayed's because it is believed that they are the descendants of the Prophet, are held in great reverence, respect and awe by the common Sindhis, who would do anything at a Sayed's bidding. Most of the Sayed families in Sindh have given birth to scholars, educationists, professional-and they have served Sindh well. However, there are many unscrupulous Sayed's, who has ruthlessly and obscenely used and abused their name and power to subjugate and oppress the poor, simple and naive common Sindhi people for their own selfish, lascivious and greedy-political and economical-gains. It is these Sayeds and the Vadera's (the landlords) of Sind, who has taken away the dignity of the simple people and turned them into serfs, slaves, and subervient and servile subjects of their vast empire-like serfdom. So, you see, it is not just the Arabs, the Arghuns, the Targhuns, the Mughals, and the Mohajirs, alone to be blamed for the rape of mother Sindh. Sindhis should blame themselves first. The devil lies within us. It is we, especially, the Sayeds, the religious fanatics and bigots, the Mirs, the Vaderas, the Merchants, the Vanias, of the beuatiful land of Sindh, who have methodically and surreptitiously clawed and mauled away the august and venerable body of their mother, Sindh. Shame! What a shame!

"Cloud was commanded to prepare for rain, Rain pattered and poured, lightening flared. Grain horders, hoping for high prices, wring their hands, Five would become fifteen in their pages they had planned. From the land may perish all the profiteers, Herdsmen once again talk of abundant showers, Latif says have hope in God's blessed grace."......Bhitai [Sur Sarang]

In quest of religious truths, Shah Bhitai travelled to many parts of Sindh and also went to the bordering lands. He kept himself aloof from the political scene of favouritism and intrigues which was going on at the height of the power and rule of Kalhoras in Sindh. Instead of visiting towns and cities, in political canvassing, to serve the purpose of the rulers and elite of the land, though he was much respected by the members of the dynasty and could have benefited from it, he went to hills, valleys, the banks of river, and the fields, where he met the ordinary simple people, the sufis (mystics). He went to the Ganjo Hills in the south of Hyderabad for contemplation, and then to mountains in Las Bela in the south of Sindh and Balochistan. For three years, he travelled with these jogis and sanyasis, in search of the truth, peace, and harmony, to Hinglay, Lakhpat, Nani at the foot of the Himalays and to Sappar Sakhi. At several places in the Risalo, mention has been made of these jogis and of his visits to these wonderful, holy and peaceful places. The two surs, Ramkali and Khahori, describe them under various endearing names and a detailed account of the jogis' lifestyle is given. He also travelled to such far away places as Junagardh. Jesalmere and parts of the Thar desert.

"In deserts, wastes and Jessalmir it has rained, Clouds and lightening have come to Thar's plains; Lone, needy women are now free from care, Fragrant are the paths, happy herdsmen's wives all this share." Bhitai

By the time he was a young man of twenty one years, he began to be known for his piety, his ascetic habits and his absorption in prayers. Observation and contemplation were chief traits of his character. A number of people flocked round him adding to the already large number of his disciples. This aroused jealousy of some powerful, ruthless, tyrranical persons-landlords, Pirs, Mirs, and Rulers-who became his enemiesfor some time. Later, seeing his personal worth, and the peaceful and ascetic nature of his fame, abandoned their rivalry. At this time he was living with his father at Kotri, five miles away from the present site of Bhitshah. It was here that his marriage was solemnised in 1713 CE with Bibi Sayedah Begum, daughter of Mirza Mughul Beg. She was a very virtuous and pious lady, who was a proper companion for him. The disciples had great respect for her. They had no children.

In the true ascetic spirit, Shah Latif was now in search of a place where in solitude, he could devote all his time in prayers and meditation. Such a place he found nar Lake Karar, a mere sand hill, but an exotic place of scenic beauty, four miles away from New Hala. This place was covered by thorny bushes surrounded by many pools of water. It was simply and aptly called 'Bhit' (the Sand Hill). On the heaps of its sandstones he decide to settle down and build a village. As it was sandy, he along with his disciples dug out the hard earth from a distance and covered the sand with it to make the ground firm. After months of hard labour, carrying the earth on their heads and shoulders, the place was now fit enough for the construction of an underground room and two other rooms over it, alongwith a room for his old parents. A mosque was also built and the houses of his disciples properly marked out. In 1742, whilst he was still busy setting up a new village, Bhit, he got the sad news of the death of his dear father.. Soon after this Shah Latif shifted all his family members from Kotri to Bhitsah, as the village now began to be called. His father was burried there, in accordance to his will, where his mausoleum stands only eight paces away, from that of Shah Abdul Latif, towards its north.

For the last eight years of his remarkable life, Shah Latif lived at Bhitshah. A few days before his death, he retired to his underground room and spent all his time in prayers and fasting, eating very little.

"Laggi Laggi wa'a-u wiarra angrra latji, Pa-i kharren pasah-a pasand-a karrend-i pirin-a jay." ......Bhitai "Wind blew! The sand enveloped the body, Whatever little life left, is to see the beloved."

After 21 days in there, he came out and having bathed himself with a large quantity of water, covered himself with a white sheet and asked his disciples to sing and start the mystic music. This went on for three days continuously, when the musicians, concerned about the motionless poet, found that his soul had already left for its heavenly abode to be in the proximity of the Beloved for whome he had longed for, all his life, and only the body was there. He suffered from no sickness or pain of any kind. The date was 14th Safar 1165 Hijra corresponding to 1752 CE. He was burried at the place where his mausoleum now stands, which was built by the ruler of Sindh, Ghulam Shah Kalhoro. His name literally means, 'the servant of the Shah'. He, along with his mother, had adored and revered Shah Latif and were his devoted disciples. The work of the construction of the mausoleum was entrusted to the well-known mason, Idan from Sukkur. The mausoleum, as well as the mosque adjoining it, were later repaired and renovated by another ruler of Sindh, Mir Nasir Khan Talpur. A pair of kettle drums, that are beaten every morning and evening even till today by the fakirs, jogis and sanyasis, who frequent the mausolem, were presented by the Raja of Jesalmeer.

"Korren kan-i salam-u achio aatand-a unn-a jay." "Countless pay homage and sing peace at his abode."

"Tell me the stories, oh thorn-brush, Of the mighty merchants of the Indus, Of the nights and the days of the prosperous times, Are you in pain now, oh thorn-brush? Because they have departed: In protest, cease to flower. Oh thorn-brush, how old were you When the river was in full flood?

Have you seen any way-farers Who could be a match of the Banjaras? True, the river has gone dry, And worthless plants have begun to flourish on the brink, The elite merchants are on decline, And the tax collectors have disappeared, The river is littered with mud And the banks grow only straws The river has lost its old strength, You big fish, you did not return When the water had its flow Now it's too late, You will soon be caught For fishermen have blocked up all the ways. The white flake on the water: Its days are on the wane.". .....Bhitai [translated by Prof. D. H. Butani (1913-1989) in "The Melody and Philosophy of Shah Latif".

Shaikh Muhammad Alawi al-Maliki: Al- Sayyid Muhammad ibn Alawi ibn Abbas al-Maliki (1947-2004) was a prominent Islamic scholar from Saudi Arabia. He was born in Mecca to a family of reputed scholars who, like himself, taught in the Sacred Mosque.

Whereas Wahhabism is the official branch of Islam in Saudi Arabia, al-Maliki adhered to the Maliki traditional school of Islamic jurisprudence, and was a renowned teacher of Sufism. Because of this difference with the Wahhabi religious establishment, al-Maliki has been accused of heresy, banned from preaching at the Sacred Mosque, had his passport revoked, and has even been arrested.

Hisham Kabbani: Shaykh Muhammad Hisham Kabbani (born in Lebanon) is a prominent Sufi Muslim, and a scholar of mainstream, traditional Islam. The Shaykh has spent his life advocating an understanding of Islam as fundamentally and inviolably based on peace, tolerance, respect and love. He believes these principles to be authentically inherent to mainstream traditional Islam.

He has been a resident of the United States since [1991] and has opened thirteen Sufi Centres there and in Canada.

Shaykh Kabbani has lectured at many universities, including the University of Chicago, Columbia University, and the University of California, Berkeley, as well as at many spiritual and religious centers throughout North America, Europe, the Far East, and the Middle East.

He is on the boards of a number of organisations that promote the tolerance and moderation inherent in traditional Islam:

- Co-Chair, Council of Muslim Leadership
- Chairman, Islamic Supreme Council of America
- President, The Muslim Magazine
- U.S. Leader, Naqshbandi Haqqani Sufi Order
- Chairman, As-Sunnah Foundation of America
- Chairman, Kamilat Muslim women's organization
- Advisor, UnityOne, an organization devoted to ending gang violence.
- Advisor, Human Rights Council, U.S.A. for supporting the establishment of human rights and freedom in all nations.
- Advisor, American Islamic Association of Mental Health Providers.
- Works closely with the government and people of Muslim nations around the world to restore traditional Islamic practices and prevent the increase of religious radicalism.

- Co-founder of the Haqqani Worldwide Educational Foundation center for teaching Islamic Divine Law and spirituality in London, England, which houses over 800 students each year and more than 2,000 students per year who attend seminars, workshops and retreats for learning about the essentials of Islam.
- Speaker and advisor, Inter-Religious Organization, Singapore.
- Working at the highest political levels to support relief efforts in Bosnia, Kosova, Afghanistan, Iraq, his native Lebanon and Somalia.
- Supporting peace initiatives in the Middle East, Bosnia, Kashmir, Afghanistan and Kosova.
- Working with international organizations to establish the International Day of the Orphan as a globally-observed day for highlighting the plight of orphans, foster children and child victims of abuse.
- Chairman of the highly successful International Islamic Unity Conference, whose second conference took place in Washington, DC from August 7-9, 1998.
- Co-developer and former General Manager of the Jeddah Medical Center in Saudi Arabia.
- Was invited by Maharishi Mahesh Yogi to attend the opening of his first healing clinic in October 1998.
- Met with Devi Gowda, former PM of India, and C.M. Ibrahim, at that time Aviation Minister of India, when they were all guests at the 7th annual conference of the IMRC in San Jose, 1997.

Kabir Helminski: Kabir Helminski is a Shaikh of the Mevlevi Order and is the Co-Director of the Threshold Society, a non-profit educational foundation that has developed programs that provide a structure for practice and study within Sufism and spiritual psychology. He has translated many volumes of Sufi literature, including the works of Rumi, and is the author of two books on Sufism: *Living Presence* and *The Knowing Heart.*

From 1980 until 1999 he was the director of Threshold Books, one of the foremost publishers of Sufi literature. Between 1994 and 2000 he toured with the Whirling Dervishes of Turkey, bringing the spiritual culture of the Mevlevis to more than 100,000 people. His books have been translated into Spanish, Italian, Dutch, German, and Turkish. He has an M.A. in psychology and an (honorary) Ph.D. in literature from Selçuk University, Konya, Turkey.

For more than twenty years Kabir's focus has been developing and sharing a contemporary approach to Islamic concepts and practice both within the Islamic community and outside of it. In 2001 he was the first Muslim to deliver the prestigious Wit Lectures on spirituality at Harvard Divinity School, which will be published as a book by The Paulist Press. Living with his family in Santa Cruz, Kabir now focuses on Sufi music, writing, teaching, and developing a program of spiritual education with an international team of scholars.

Inayat Khan: Hazrat Inayat Khan (July 5, 1882 – February 5, 1927) was the founder of Universal Sufism and the Sufi Order International. He initially came to the West as a representative of several traditions of classical Indian music, having received the title Tansen from the Nizam of Hyderabad.

However, Khan's life mission was soon revealed to be the introduction and transmission of Sufi thought and practice to the West. His universal message of Divine Unity – Tawhid – focused on the themes of "Love, Harmony and Beauty" and evinced his distinctive and effective ability to transmit the highest spiritual truths of Islam to Western audiences of his day.

Although Inayat Khan was initiated into the Suhrawardiyya, Qadiriyya and Naqshbandi orders of Sufism, his primary initiation was in the Nizamiyya subbranch of the Chishti Order by Shaykh Muhammed Abu Hashim Madani, with whose encouragement he left India in 1910 to come the West. He traveled first as a touring musician and then as a teacher of Sufism, visiting over three continents. Eventually, he married Ora Ray Baker, an American woman from New Mexico, and they had had four children: Noor-un-Nisa (1913), Vilayat (1916), Hidayat (1917) and Khair-un-Nisa (1919). The family settled in Suresnes, near Paris.

Khan returned to India at the end of 1926. While there chose the site of his tomb, the Nizamuddin Dargah complex in Delhi, where the eponymous founder of the Nizami Chishtiyya, Shaykh Nizamuddin Auliya (died 1325), is buried. Khan died shortly after his decision, on February 5, 1927.

Today active branches of Inayat Khan's lineage can be found in France, England, the Netherlands, the United States and Canada. He left behind a rich legacy of English literature infused with his vision of the unity of religious ideals, which calls humanity to awaken to the "Truth of Divine Guidance and Love".

Even though Inayat Khan was a devout Muslim and followed the religious law of Islam (Sharia), he was also keenly aware of the Euro-American prejudice against Islam in his time. He therefore made the controversial decision to present Sufism without specifically focusing on its connection to Islam. In his autobiography he importantly states:

"Among the existing religions of the world Islam is the only one which can answer the demand of Western life, but owing to political reasons a prejudice against Islam has existed in the West for a long time. Also, the Christian missionaries, knowing that Islam is the only religion which can succeed their faith, have done everything within their power to prejudice the minds of Western people against it. Therefore there is little chance of Islam being accepted in the West. However, those seekers after religious ideals have more or less regard for the religions of the East and those who seek after truth show a desire to investigate Eastern thought."

Indebted to both his Sufi heritage and the philosophical Vedanta/Shankara spirituality, Khan continued the deeply-rooted Indian tradition of spirituality over creed and the renaissance Indian notion of religious tolerance and openness. In the fifteenth and sixteenth century, spiritual leaders such as Kabir, Guru Nanak Dev and the Mughal King Akbar and his Din-i-Ilahi founded a tradition in which the faithful, especially Hindus and Muslims, would crush their differences on the ideal of spiritual unity. Despite the advance of colonial English influences in the nineteenth century, Khan took this Mughal ideal on his mission to the West.

Inayat Khan's decisive downplaying of Islam in his teachings has resulted in many contemporary Westerners assuming that Islam and Sufism are ultimately unrelated, although his followers continue to perform the traditional Islamic invocations of God (Dhikr) in the original Arabic as found in the

Quran and the Prophetic traditions (Hadith). There is a historic precedent of certain Chishti masters (and masters of other orders) not requiring their non-Muslim followers to convert to Islam. The numbers of non-Muslim Sufis before the twentieth century, however, were relatively few.

Although Hazrat Inayat Khan's son, Pir Vilayat Inayat Khan did not specifically self-identify with the Islamic tradition, his grandson Pir Zia Inayat Khan is an observant Muslim, a scholar of Islam and the current head of the Sufi Order International.

Hazrat Inayat Khan set forth ten thoughts that form the foundational principles of Universal Sufism:

1. There is one God the Eternal, the Only Being, None exists save God.
2. There is one Master the Guiding Spirit of all souls, who constantly leads all followers toward the Light.
3. There is one Holy Book the Sacred Manuscript of Nature, the only Scripture that can enlighten the reader.
4. There is one Religion the unswerving progress in the right direction, toward the Ideal, which fulfills the life's purpose of every soul.
5. There is one Law the Law of Reciprocity, which can be observed by a selfless conscience together with a sense of awakened justice.
6. There is one Family the Human Family, which unites the Children of Earth indiscriminately in the Parenthood of God.
7. There is one Moral Principle the Love which springs forth from a willing heart, surrendered in service to God and Humanity, and which blooms in deeds of beneficence.
8. There is one Object of Praise the Beauty which uplifts the heart of its worshipper through all aspects, from the seen to the unseen.
9. There is one Truth the true knowledge of our being, within and without, which is the essence of Wisdom.
10. There is one Path the effacement of the limited self in the Unlimited, which raises the mortal to immortality, in which resides all Perfection.

Some of Inayat Khan's most famous sayings are:

- "Shatter your ideals on the rock of Truth."
- "There is nothing valuable except what we value in life."
- "In a small affair or in a big affair, first consult yourself and find out if there is any conflict in your own being about anything you want to do. And when you find no conflict there, then feel sure that a path is already made for you. You have but to open your eyes and take a step forward, and the other step will be led by God."
- "The difference between the divine and the human will is like the difference between the trunk of a tree and its branches. As from the boughs other twigs and branches spring, so the will of one powerful individual has branches going through the will of other individuals. So there are the powerful beings, the masters of humanity. Their will is God's will, their word is God's word, and yet they are branches, because the trunk is the will of the Almighty. Whether the

branch be large or small, every branch has the same origin and the same root as the stem."

Nuh Ha Mim Keller: Sheikh Nuh Ha Mim Keller, is an American-Muslim translator of Islamic books and specialist in Islamic Law as well as an authorised sheikh in tasawwuf in the Shadhili Sufi order. Born in 1954 in the Northwestern United States of America, he was educated in philosophy and Arabic at the University of Chicago and University of California at Los Angeles. He entered Islam in 1977 at al-Azhar in Cairo, and later studied the traditional Islamic sciences of hadith (Prophetic traditions), Shafi'i and Hanafi schools of Islamic jurisprudence, legal methodology (usul al-fiqh), and tenets of faith ('aqidah) in Syria and Jordan, where he has lived since 1980.

His English translation of 'Umdat al-Salik, *Reliance of the Traveller*, (Sunna Books, 1991) is the first Islamic legal work in a European language to receive the certification of Al-Azhar University, the Muslim world's oldest institution of higher learning. The book, which has become a modern classic, is a bestseller and has had numerous print runs. It is the best example in the English language of a complete orthodox Sunni work on the Shariah. He also possesses ijazas, or "certificates of authorisation", in Islamic jurisprudence from sheikhs in Syria and Jordan.

His other translations and works include:

- *Al-Maqasid : Imam Nawawi's Manual of Islam,* a shorter manual of Shafi'i fiqh
- *A Port in the Storm: A Fiqh Solution to the Qibla of North America*, a detailed and complex study of the most sound position on which direction North American Muslims should face to pray.
- *The Sunni Path: A Handbook of Islamic Belief*
- *Evolution Theory in Islam*
- *Tariqa Notes*, a small handbook for those following the Shadhili sufi order.

He has also written numerous articles on traditional Islam is presently a regular contributor to Islamica Magazine. He is currently translating Imam Nawawi's Kitab al-Adhkar (*The Book of Remembrance of Allah*), a compendium of some 1227 hadiths on prayers and dhikrs of the prophetic sunnah.

He was authorised as a sheikh in the Shadhili Tariqa by the late Sheikh Abd al-Rahman al-Shaghouri in Damascus. He has students throughout the world and has annual retreats (suhbas) with his students where he teaches the traditional science of tasawwuf in Canada, USA, UK, Turkey, Australia, Egypt, and Pakistan.

Martin Lings: Martin Lings (Abu Bakr Siraj Ad-Din) (January 24, 1909 – May 12, 2005) was a lifelong student and follower of Frithj of Scone and a British scholar of Sufism.

Lings was born in Burnage, Lancashire in 1909 to a Protestant family. The young Lings gained an introduction to travelling at a young age, spending significant time in the United States due to his father's employment. Lings completed his studies at Clifton College, and then studied at Oxford University, Magdalen College. At Oxford, he was a student of C. S. Lewis, who would become a close friend of his. After studying at Oxford, Lings went to Lithuania where he taught in Kaunas.

For Lings himself, however, the most important event that occurred while he was at Oxford was his discovery of the writings of the French Muslim writer and traditionalist philosopher Ren Gunon and the German spiritual authority and metaphysician Frithj of Scone. In 1938 Lings went to Basle to make Scone's acquaintance, and he remained Frithj of Scone's disciple and expositor for the rest of his life. Having found an authentic and orthodox spiritual path was for him the most important event of his life and he devoted the rest of his life to the spiritual path and serving God.

In 1939 Lings went to Cairo, Egypt in order to visit a friend of his, who was an assistant of Ren Gunon. Not long after arriving in Cairo, his friend died, and Lings began studying and learned the Arabic language. It was in Cairo that Lings studied Sufism, and converted to Islam.

Cairo became his home for over a decade; he became an English teacher at the University of Cairo and produced Shakes pearean plays annually. Lings married Lesley Smalley in 1944, and lived with his wife in a village near the pyramids. Despite having settled comfortably in Egypt, Lings was forced to leave in 1952 after anti-British disturbances.

Upon returning to the United Kingdom, he continued his education, earning a Ph.D. from SOAS. His thesis at SOAS became a well-received book on Algerian Sufi Ahmad al-Alawi.(see also: Sufi studies) After earning his Ph.D., Lings worked at the British Museum and later British Library, overseeing eastern manuscripts and other textual works.

A writer throughout this period, Lings output increased in the last quarter of his life. While his thesis work on Ahmad al-Alawi had been well-regarded, his most famous work was a biography about the Prophet Muhammad, written in 1983, that earned him acclaim in the Muslim world, and prizes from the governments of Pakistan and Egypt. He also continued travelling extensively, although he made his home in Kent.

4

PHILOSOPHIES OF MUSLIM SECTS IN INDIA

Barelvi Sect

Deobandis and Barelvis are the two major groups of Muslims in the Subcontinent apart from the Shia. Barelvi Hanafis deem Deobandis to be kaafir. Those hostile to the Barelvis deprecated them as the shrine-worshipping, the grave-worshiping, ignorant Barelvis. Much smaller sects in Pakistan include the Ahl-e-Hadees and Ahl-e-Tashee. The non-Pakhtun population of Pakistan is predominantly Barelvi. The stronghold of Barelvism remains Punjab, the largest province of Pakistan. By one estimate, in Pakistan, the Shias are 18%, ismailis 2%, Ahmediyas 2%, Barelvis 50%, Deobandis 20%, Ahle Hadith 4%, and other minorities 4%. The Ahle-e-Hadith is a small group of Sunni Muslims in India who do not consider themselves bound by any particular school of law and rely directly on the Prophet's Sunnah. By another estimate some 15 per cent of Pakistan's Sunni Muslims would consider themselves Deobandi, and some 60 per cent, are in the Barelvi tradition based mostly in the province of Punjab. But some 64 per cent of the total seminaries are run by Deobandis, 25 per cent by the Barelvis, six percent by the Ahle Hadith and three percent by various Shiite organisations.

The Muslim League was founded by the Aga Khan, leader of the Ismaili Sevener Shiites. And Jinnah was an Ismaili. The barelvis and shias and ismailis and Ahmediyas joined the Pakistan movement, while the deobandis opposed the formation of Pakistan, since they wanted to islamise all of India. But the Deobandis in Pakistan owed their allegiance to Maulana Shabbir Ahmed Usmani, who organized the Deobandi ulema who were in favour of Pakistan into the Jamiat Ulema-i-Islam. The so-called "nationalist Muslims" who opposed Partition, such as Maulana Azad and Maulana Maudoodi, were Sunnis.

The differences between these sects can be difficult to understand. For the Barelvis, (who are mostly from the Pakistan province of Punjab) the holy Prophet is a superhuman figure whose presence is all around us at all times; he is *hazir*, present; he is not *bashar*, material or flesh, but *nur*, light. The Deobandis, who also revere the Prophet, argue he was the *insan-i-kamil*, the perfect person, but still only a man, a mortal. Barelvis emphasise a love of Muhammad, a semi-divine figure with unique foreknowledge. The Deobandis reject this idea of Muhammad, emphasising Islam as a personal rather than a social religion.

The Barelvis follow many Sufi practices, including use of music (*Qawwali*) and intercession by their teacher. A key difference between Barelvi and Deobandi that Barelvi's believe in intercession between humans and Divine Grace. This consists of the intervention of an ascending, [illegible] and unbroken chain of holy personages, *pirs*, reaching ultimately to Prophet Mohammad, who intercede on their behalf with Allah. It is a more superstitious-but also a more tolerant-tradition of Indian Islam. Their critics claim that Barelvis are guilty of committing innovation (*Bidat*) and therefore, they are deviated from the true path-the path of *Sunnah*.

The Pakistan Movement got support from the Barelvis (Low Church). It had faced opposition from the National Indian Congress which was supported by the Deobandi seminaries (High Church). However, after the establishment of Pakistan as an Islamic state in 1949, Barelvi Low Church was too mixed up with mysticism to be a source of Islamic law. Ironically, Pakistan moved away from the 'spiritual pluralism' of the Barelvis, who had supported Pakistan, and relied on the more puritanical Deobandis who had opposed it.

Unlike the Deobandis, the Barelvis see the Prophet Mohammad as more than a man, a part of the divine light of Allah. This doctrine gives rise to a form of Islam that provides a space for holy men and esoteric practices and graves appear to be often more ornate than those found within Deobandi communities. The Wahhabi (Arabia), Deobandi (Pakistan and India) and Jamaat-I-Islami all are anti-sufi, and against the over devotion to Muhammad, whereas the Barelvis emphasize Muhammad's uniqueness. Indeed, nearly 85% of South Asia's Sunni Muslims are said to follow the Barelvi school, closer to Sufism. The remaining 15% of Sunnis follow the Deobandi school, more closely related to the conservative practice of Islam. Most Shiites in the subcontinent also tend to be influenced by the Sufis. Pakistan's Muslims, like other Muslims in the region, tend to follow a school of Islam which is less conservative, and hence the support for strongly and overtly religious parties has been minimal.

The Barelvis believe the Prophet is a human being made from flesh and blood. [bashar] and a *noor* [light] at the same time. This is like the example of when Gabriel, who is also noor [light], used to appear to the Prophet in the form of a man, flesh and blood. He is infallible and perfect and free from all imperfections and sinless (as are all Prophets). He is human but not like other humans. Allah has given him the ability to see the whole of Creation in detail while he is in his blessed grave as if he was looking at it in the palm of his hand. This is called being "*nazir*" ("witnessing"). Allah has given him the ability to go physically and spiritually to anywhere in the Created Universes he pleases whenever he pleases (peace be upon him) and to be in more than one place at the same time. This is what is meant by "*hazir*" (present). This is not the same as believing that he (peace be upon him) is present everywhere all the time!

Sunni Sect

There was only one madh-hab (school of fiqh) during the time of the Righly-guided Caliphs. With the emergence of the Umayyad rule, the situation changed. The Umayyad caliphs did not have the same religious authority as the previous ones. After the Umayyad (661-750 CE) came the Abbasids. In comparison to the Umayyads, they were more supportive of Islamic law. The crystallization of four major Sunni madhahib of Islamic fiqh came about by the third century of Hijrah; before this there were about twenty different madhahib.

In the Sunni world there are now Four Orthodox Schools (Schools of Fiqh) of thought [the Four Madhahib]: the Shafi'i, Hanafi, Maliki and Hanbali. With regard to legal matters, these four orthodox schools give different weight in legal opinions to prescriptions in the Quran, the hadith or sayings of the Prophet Muhammad, the consensus of legal scholars, analogy (to similar situations at the time of the Prophet), and reason or opinion. Towards the end of the first century of Islam, Imam Abu Hanifa in Kufa and Imam Malik in Madina founded mazahib (schools) or religio-legal thought, named after them as the Hanafi and the Maliki schools. In the following century, the two other great schools were founded — the Shafei school of Imam Idris al-Shafei in Egypt and the Hanbali school of Imam Ahmad ibn Hanbal in Baghdad. The differences between the four famous Jurists Imaam Abu Hanifa, Shaafee, Maaliki and Hanbaliy stem from their differences on principles. The basic principle according to Imaam Maaliki is to prefer Amal-e-Madinah, that is the practices of the people of Madina Munawwarah. However, that principle is not adopted by Imaam Ahmad ibn Hanbal.

The fanatical loyalty to a particular madh-hab among Muslims is decreasing. Now Hanafi, Shafi'i, Maliki and Hanbali and even Jafari followers pray together and work together. Most scholars hold that it is not required of the Muslim to follow a certain Fiqh School because nothing can be made required of Muslims except that made by Allah and His Prophet. When in need of Fatwa, Muslims could consult with any scholar regardless of his Madh-hab. A common Muslim is said to have no Madh-hab.

Sunni Islam does not possess clerical hierarchies and centralized institutions. The absence of a hierarchy has been a source of strength that has permitted the faith to adapt to local conditions. However, it also has been a weakness that makes it difficult for Sunni Muslims to achieve any significant degree of solidarity. Despite some very minor disputes there are many Sub-Groups in the four groups like Kharjiites, Wahabis, Deobandi, Barelvi, Ahle-Sunnat Wal Jamat, Ahle Hadith, Ghurba Ahle Hadits, Sunnis of Green Turban, Sunnis of Brown Turbans etc. etc. They declare each other wrong and seldom offer prayer behind each other.

Among Sunni Muslims, effective power and the ability to maintain order are sufficient for legitimate authority, in stark contrast to the more uncompromising Shia views of government as the sole province of religious leaders. For Sunnis, even a bad Muslim ruler is preferable to chaos and anarchy, and the Sunni religious tradition contains only a limited right to rebel. However, if a ruler commands something that is contrary to God's law, the subject's duty of obedience lapses.

Originally political, the differences between Sunni and Shia interpretations rapidly took on theological and metaphysical overtones. In principle a Sunni approaches God directly; there is no clerical hierarchy. Some duly appointed religious figures, however, exert considerable social and political power. Imams usually are men of importance in their communities but they need not have any formal training; among the beduins, for example, any tribal member may lead communal prayers. Committees of socially prominent worshipers usually run the major mosque-owned land and gifts. In many Arab countries, the administration of waqfs (religious endowments) has come under the influence of the state. Qadis (judges) and imams are appointed by the government.

Hanafi Sect

Within the Sunni Muslim tradition, Hanafi is one of four "schools of law" and considered the oldest and most liberal school of law. Hanafi is one of the four schools of thought (madhabs / Maddhab) of religious jurisprudence (fiqh) within Sunni Islam. Named for its founder, the Hanafi school of Imam Abu Hanifa, it is the major school of Iraqi Sunni Arabs. It makes considerable use of reason or opinion in legal decisions. Sunni Hanafi creed is essentially non-hierarchial and decentralized, which has made it difficult for 20th century rulers to incorporate its religious leaders into strong centralized state systems.

The Hanafi school of Islamic jurisprudence was founded by Abu Hanifa, born in Kufa, Iraq about A.D.700. He was one of the earliest Muslim scholar-interpreters to seek new ways of applying Islamic tenets to everyday life. In his lifetime Abu Hanifa was disgraced, called ignorant, inventor of new beliefs, hypocrite and kafir. He was imprisoned and poisoned. He died in 150 A.H. [circa 767-768 C.E.]. Abu Hanifa's interpretation of Muslim law was extremely tolerant of differences within Muslim communities. He also separated belief from practice, elevating belief over practice. Hanafi took Shafi as his rival and vice versa.

Most of the Hanafi school follows al-Maturidi in doctrine. Muhammad ibn Muhammad ibn Mahmud Abu Mansur al-Samarqandi al-Maturidi al-Hanafi of Maturid in Samarqand, Shaykh al-Islam, was one of the two foremost Imams of the mutakallimun of Ahl al-Sunna. He was known in his time as the Imam of Guidance (Imam al-Huda). The majority of the Taliban are Maturidis.

Broad-minded without being lax, this school appeals to reason (personal judgment) and a quest for the better. It is generally tolerant and the largest movement within Islam. The Hanafi school is known for its liberal religious orientation that elevates belief over practice and is tolerant of differences within Muslim communities.

A sectarian dispute in the United States was transformed into a mass hostage taking by Hanafi Muslims in Washington, DC in 1977. The Hanafi Movement in the United States was founded by Hamas Abdul Khaalis in 1968. Khaalis, formerly Ernest X McGee, had been the Nation of Islam's first National Secretary and a friend of Malcolm X. He had converted to orthodox Islam and founded the Hanafi Movement with money donated by Kareem Abdul-Jabar. On 09 March 1977, Khaalis and about a dozen of his followers armed with shotguns and machetes seized control of seized the District Building [city hall], the Banai Brith building, and the Islamic Center, in the District of Columbia. Khaalis said they were seeking revenge for the murders of Khaalis' family members by Black Muslims in 1973. They held 134 hostages for more than 39 hours, they shot Washington DC city councilman Marion Barry in the chest, and they shot a radio reporter dead. The standoff ended and the hostages were freed after ambassadors from three Islamic nations joined the negotiations. The Hanafis were convicted and sentenced to long terms in prison.

Hanafi scholars refuse to control a human religious or spiritual destiny, and refuse to give that right to any human institution. Among the Hudud crimes, those crimes against God, blasphemy is not listed by the Hanafis. Hanafis concluded that blasphemy could not be punished by the state. The state should not be involved in deciding God-human relationships. Rather, the state should be concerned only with the violation of human rights within the jurisdiction of the human affairs and human relationships.

Notwithstanding their common heritage from Imam Abu Hanifah, the scholars belonging to the Hanafi madhhab are divided in the Barelvi and the Deobandi school, and these two schools have different attitude toward Wahhabism.

The Sunni Hanafi school is dominant in the Arab Middle East, India, Pakistan and Afghanistan. The followers of Imam Abu Hanifa (d. 767) are found in Pakistan, India, Afghanistan, Turkey, Iraq, Syria, China, North Africa, Egypt, and in the Malay Archipelago. The school is followed by the majority of the Muslim population of Turkey, Albania, the Balkans, Central Asia, Afghanistan, Pakistan, China, India and Iraq. Most of the Kyrgyz are Sunni Muslims of the Hanafi school. Ethnic Kazakhs, who constitute approximately one half of the national population, historically are Sunni Muslims of the Hanafi School. Ethnic Uzbeks, Uyghurs, and Tatars, comprising less than 10 percent of the population, also largely are Sunni Hanafi. Other Islamic groups, which account for less than 1 percent of the population of Kazakhstan, include Shafit Sunni (traditionally practiced by Chechens), Shiite, Sufi, and Akhmadi.

Sunni are found throughout Afghanistan. An estimated 84% of Afghanistan's population is Sunni, following the Hanafi school of jurisprudence; the remainder is predominantly Shi'a, mainly Hazara. In March 2003 Ayatollah Mohammad Asef Mohseni, leader of the predominantly Shia Harakat-e Islami-yi Afghanistan, proposed that, along with the Sunni Hanafi school of jurisprudence, the Shia Jafari school of jurisprudence be included in the new constitution as an official sect.

Deobandi Sect

The northern Indian Deobandi school argues that the reason Islamic societies have fallen behind the West in all spheres of endeavor is because they have been seduced by the amoral and material accoutrements of Westernization, and have deviated from the original pristine teachings of the Prophet.

Deoband is a town a hundred miles north of Delhi where a *madrasa* (religious school) was established there in 1867. The so-called 'Deobandi Tradition' itself is much older than the eponymous Dar-Ul-Ulum at Deoband. The Deoband *madrasa* brought together Muslims who were hostile to British rule and committed to a literal and austere interpretation of Islam.

For the last 200 years, Sunnis often have looked to the example of the Deoband madrassa (religious school) near Delhi, India. The Deoband school has long sought to purify Islam by discarding supposedly un-Islamic accretions to the faith and reemphasizing the models established in the Koran and the customary practices of the Prophet Mohammed. Additionally, Deobandi scholars often have opposed what they perceive as Western influences.

Just as Sikhs originated from Hinduism, but are not Hindus, and Protestants came from Roman Catholicism, but are not Catholics, similarly, the Deobandi sect originated in the Sunni community, but are not strictly Sunnis. The tack of Darul Uloom Deoband is in accordance with the Ahlus-Sunnah wal-Jama'ah, Hanafiate practical method (Mazhab) and the disposition (Mashrab) of its holy founders,

Hazrat Maulana Mohammad Qasim Nanautavi (Allah's mercy be on him!) and Hazrat Maulana Rasheed Ahmed Gangohi (may his secret be sanctified).

The Deobandi interpretation holds that a Muslim's first loyalty is to his religion and only then to the country of which he is a citizen or a resident; secondly, that Muslims recognise only the religious frontiers of their Ummah and not the national frontiers; thirdly,that they have a sacred right and obligation to go to any country to wage jihad to protect the Muslims of that country.

The Deobandi interpretation of Islamic teachings is widely practiced in Pakistan. The Deobandi movement in Sunni Islam, was founded in response to British colonial rule in India and later hardened in Pakistan into bitter opposition to what its members views as the country's neo-colonial elite. The Islamic Deobandi militants share the Taliban's restrictive view of women, and regard Pakistan's minority Shiia as non-Muslim. They seek a pure leader, or amir, to recreate Pakistani society according to the egalitarian model of Islam's early days under the Prophet Mohammed. President Musharraf himself, is a Deobandi, actually born in the city in India, where the school took it's name.

During the first half of April 2000, the Government of Pakistan permitted a 3-day conference organized by the Deobandi Muslim political party Jamiat-Ulema-Islami (JUI). Several speakers at the conference made anti-Western political declarations. Deobandi and Barelvi sects struggled, sometimes violently, for control over local mosques in Lahore neighborhoods.

The fundamentalist Deoband Dar-ul-Uloom brand of Islam inspired the Taliban movement and had widespread appeal for Muslim fundamentalists. Most of the Taliban leadership attended Deobandi-influenced seminaries in Pakistan. The Taliban was propped up initially by the civil government of Benazir Bhutto, then in coalition with the Deobandi Jama'at-ulema Islam (JUI) led by Maulana Fazlur Rehman [who by 2003 was the elected opposition leader at the Center in Islamabad and whose protégé is now the chief Minister in the NWFP]. Traditionally, Sunni Islam of the Hanafi school of jurisprudence was the dominant religion of Afganistan. The Taliban also adhered to the Hanafi school of Sunni Islam, making it the dominant religion in the country for most of 2001. For the last 200 years, Sunnis often have looked to the example of the Deoband madrassah (religious school) near Delhi, India. Most of the Taliban leadership attended Deobandi-influenced seminaries in Pakistan. The Deoband school has long sought to purify Islam by discarding supposedly un-Islamic accretions to the faith and reemphasizing the models established in the Koran and the customary practices of the Prophet Mohammed. Additionally, Deobandi scholars often have opposed what they perceive as Western influences. Much of the population adheres to Deobandi-influenced Hanafi Sunnism, but a sizable minority adheres to a more mystical version of Sunnism generally known as Sufism. Sufism centers on orders or brotherhoods that follow charismatic religious leaders.

Although the majority of the Islamic population (Sunni) in Afghanistan and Pakistan, belong to the Hanafi sect, the theologians who have pushed Pakistan towards Islamic Radicalism for decades, as well as the ones who were the founders of the Taliban, espoused Wahabi rhetoric and ideals. This sect took its inspiration from Saudi Hanbali theologians who immigrated there in the 18th century, to help their Indian Muslim brothers with Hanbali theological inspiration against the British colonialists. Propelled by oil-generated wealth, the Wahhabi worldview increasingly co-opted the Deobandi movement in South Asia.

Hanbali Sect

Imam Ahmad ibn Hanbal was kept in prison for 28 months, with a heavy chain around his feet. He was publicly humiliated, slapped and spat upon. Every evening he used to be flogged. All this was because of the controversy regarding whether the Quran was 'uncreated'.

The Shafi school is considered the easiest school and the Hanbali is considered the hardest in terms of social and personal rules.

The government of Saudi Arabia vigorously enforces its prohibition against all forms of public religious expression other than that of those who follow the government's interpretation and presentation of the Hanbali school of Sunni Islam. This is despite the fact that there are large communities of non-Muslims and Muslims from a variety of doctrinal schools of Islam residing in Saudi Arabia. Under the Hanbali interpretation of Shari'a law, judges may discount the testimony of people who are not practicing Muslims or who do not have the correct faith. Legal sources report that testimony by Shia is often ignored in Saudi courts of law or is deemed to have less weight than testimony by Sunnis. The explanation of Saudi officials is that their Hanbali school of Islam religiously mandates that they deny other religions the right to function openly on the Arabian Peninsula-a right that is clearly protected in international law.

Wahhabi Sect

This branch of Islam is often referred to as "Wahhabi," a term that many adherents to this tradition do not use. Members of this form of Islam call themselves *Muwahhidun* ("Unitarians", or "unifiers of Islamic practice"). They use the *Salafi Da'wa* or *Ahlul Sunna wal Jama'a*. The teachings of the reformer Abd Al-Wahhab are more often referred to by adherents as *Salafi*, that is, "following the forefathers of Islam."

The basic text of this form of Islam is the Kitab at-tawhid (Arabic, "Book of Unity"). Central to Muhammad ibn Abd al Wahhab's message was the essential oneness of God (*tawhid*). The movement is therefore known by its adherents as *ad dawa lil tawhid* (the call to unity), and those who follow the call are known as *ahl at tawhid* (the people of unity) or *muwahhidun* (unitarians). The word Wahhabi was originally used derogatorily by opponents, but has today become commonplace and is even used by some Najdi scholars of the movement. Most Wahhabi people live in Saudi Arabia. Almost all people in Mecca and Medina belong to this school.

The Caliphate was brought into being by the implementation of Islam for about three decades. They called this shortlived experiment *Khilafat Rashidah*, the rightly-guided Caliphate, implying thereby that the rulers that followed were misguided. Fundamentalists seek the restoration of the Islamic State i.e. the Khilafah, and by electing a Khaleefah and taking a bayah on him that he will rule by the Word of Allah (Subhaanahu Wa Ta'Ala) i.e. he will implement Islamic laws in the country where the Khilafah has been established.

Wahhabism [Wahabism] is a reform movement that began 200 years ago to rid Islamic societies of cultural practices and interpretation that had been acquired over the centuries. The followers of Abdul Wahab (1703-1792) began as a movement to cleanse the Arab bedouin from the influence of Sufism. Wahhabis are the followers of Ibn 'Abd ul-Wahhab, who instituted a great reform in the religion of Islam in Arabia in the 18th century. Mahommed ibn 'Abd ul-Wahhab was born in 1691 (or 1703) at al-Hauta of the Nejd in central Arabia, and was of the tribe of the Bani Tamim. He studied literature and jurisprudence of the Hanifite school. After making the pilgrimage with his father, he spent some further time in the study of law at Medina, and resided for a while at Isfahan, whence he returned to the Nejd to undertake the work of a teacher.

Aroused by his studies and his observation of the luxury in dress and habits, the superstitious pilgrimages to shrines, the use of omens and the worship given to Mahomet and Mahommedan saints rather than to God, he began a mission to proclaim the simplicity of the early religion founded on the Koran and Sunna (i.e. the manner of life of Mahomet).

To understand the significance of Muhammad ibn Abd al Wahhab's ideas, they must be considered in the context of Islamic practice. There was a difference between the established rituals clearly defined in religious texts that all Muslims perform and popular Islam. The latter refers to local practice that is not universal. The Shia practice of visiting shrines is an example of a popular practice. The Shia continued to revere the Imams even after their death and so visited their graves to ask favors of the Imams buried there. Over time, Shia scholars rationalized the practice and it became established. Some of the Arabian tribes came to attribute the same sort of power that the Shia recognized in the tomb of an Imam to natural objects such as trees and rocks.

Muhammad ibn Abd al Wahhab was concerned with the way the people of Najd engaged in practices he considered polytheistic, such as praying to saints; making pilgrimages to tombs and special mosques; venerating trees, caves, and stones; and using votive and sacrificial offerings. He was also concerned by what he viewed as a laxity in adhering to Islamic law and in performing religious devotions, such as indifference to the plight of widows and orphans, adultery, lack of attention to obligatory prayers, and failure to allocate shares of inheritance fairly to women. When Muhammad ibn Abd al Wahhab began to preach against these breaches of Islamic laws, he characterized customary practices as jahiliya, the same term used to describe the ignorance of Arabians before the Prophet.

Muhammad ibn Abd al Wahhab focused on the Muslim principle that there is only one God, and that God does not share his power with anyone — not Imams, and certainly not trees or rocks. From this unitarian principle, his students began to refer to themselves as muwahhidun (unitarians). Their detractors referred to them as "Wahhabis"—or "followers of Muhammad ibn Abd al Wahhab," which had a pejorative connotation. The idea of a unitary god was not new. Muhammad ibn Abd al Wahhab, however, attached political importance to it. He directed his attack against the Shia.

Muhammad ibn Abd al Wahhab's emphasis on the oneness of God was asserted in contradistinction to shirk, or polytheism, defined as the act of associating any person or object with powers that should be attributed only to God. He condemned specific acts that he viewed as leading to shirk, such as votive offerings, praying at saints' tombs and at graves, and any prayer ritual in which the suppliant appeals to a third party for intercession with God. Particularly objectionable were certain religious festivals, including celebrations of the Prophet's birthday, Shia mourning ceremonies, and Sufi mysticism. Consequently, the Wahhabis forbid grave markers or tombs in burial sites and the building of any shrines that could become a locus of shirk.

His instructions in the matter of extending his religious teaching by force were strict. All unbelievers (i.e. Moslems who did not accept his teaching, as well as Christians, &c.) were to be put to death. Immediate entrance into Paradise was promised to his soldiers who fell in battle, and it is said that each soldier was provided with a written order from Ibn 'Abd ul-Wahhab to the gate-keeper of heaven to admit him forthwith. In this way the new teaching was established in the greater part of Arabia until its power was broken by Mehemet Ali. Ibn'Abd ul-Wahhab is said to have died in 1791.

The teaching of ul-Wahhab was founded on that of Ibn Taimiyya (1263-1328), who was of the school of Ahmad ibn Hanbal. Copies of some of Ibn Taimiyya's works made by ul-Wahhab are now extant in Europe, and show a close study of the writer. Ibn Taimiyya, although a Hanbalite by training, refused to be bound by any of the four schools, and claimed the power of a mujtahid, i.e. of one who can give independent decisions. These decisions were based on the Koran, which, like Ibn Hazm, he accepted in a literal sense, on the Sunna and Qiyds (analogy). He protested strongly against all the innovations of later times, and denounced as idolatry the visiting of the sacred shrines and the invocation of the saints or of Mahomet himself. He was also a bitter opponent of the Sufis of his day.

The Wahhabites also believe in the literal sense of the Koran and the necessity of deducing one's duty from it apart from the decisions of the four schools. They also pointed to the abuses current in their times as a reason for rejecting the doctrines and practices founded on Ijma, i.e. the universal consent of the believer or their teachers. They forbid the pilgrimage to tombs and the invocation of saints. The severe simplicity of the Wahhabis has been remarked by travellers in central Arabia. They attack all luxury, loose administration of justice, all laxity against infidels, addiction to wine, impurity and treachery.

Muhammad ibn Abd al Wahhab's mission in his own district was not attended by success, and for long he wandered with his family through Arabia. Realizing that he needed political support and authority to effectively reverse the status quo, Ibn Abdul-Wahhab presented his program of reform to the governors of the central Arabian city-states. He began by approaching Othman ibn Mu'amar, the governor of Uyayna, his home state. Ibn Mu'amar was receptive to Abdul-Wahhab's ideas and allowed him to preach within the city. As word of the movement spread, however, strong pressure to silence Ibn Abdul-Wahhab came from powerful tribes in the region who viewed change as a threat to their decadent lifestyle. Fearing invasion, Othman ibn Mu'amar felt compelled to ask the reformer to leave Uyayna.

At last he settled in Dara'iyya, or Deraiya (in the Nejd), where he succeeded in converting the greatest notable, Mahommed ibn Saud, who married his daugther, and so became the founder of an hereditary Wahhabite dynasty. This gave the missionary the opportunity of following the example of Mahomet himself.

This association between the Al Saud and the Al ash Shaykh, as Muhammad ibn Abd al Wahhab and his descendants came to be known, effectively converted political loyalty into a religious obligation. According to Muhammad ibn Abd al Wahhab's teachings, a Muslim must present a bayah, or oath of allegiance, to a Muslim ruler during his lifetime to ensure his redemption after death. The ruler, conversely, is owed unquestioned allegiance from his people so long as he leads the community according to the laws of God. The whole purpose of the Muslim community is to become the living embodiment of God's laws, and it is the responsibility of the legitimate ruler to ensure that people know God's laws and live in conformity to them.

Under 'Abd ul-Azlz they instituted a form of Bedouin (Bedawi) commonwealth, insisting on the observance of law, the payment of tribute, militaiy conscription for war against the infidel, internal peace and the rigid administration of justice in courts established for the purpose. Wahhabis consider Wahhabism to be the only true form of Islam. They do not regard Shi'as as true Muslims are particularly hostile to Sufism.

It is clear that the claim of the Wahhabis to have returned to the earliest form of Islam is largely justified. The difference between ul-Wahhab's sect and others is that the Wahabis rigidly follow the same laws which the others neglect or have ceased altogether to observe. Even orthodox doctors of Islam have confessed that in Ibn 'Abd ul-Wahhab's writings there is nothing but what they themselves hold. At the same time the fact that so many of his followers were rough and unthinking Bedouins has led to the over-emphasis of minor points of practice, so that they often appear to observers to be characterized chiefly by a strictness (real or feigned) in such matters as the prohibition of silk for dress, or the use of tobacco, or of the rosary in prayer.

Imam Muhammad bin Abdul Wahhab died in 1792.

The Wahhabi ulama reject reinterpretation of Quran and sunna in regard to issues clearly settled by the early jurists. By rejecting the validity of reinterpretation, Wahhabi doctrine is at odds with the Muslim reformation movement of the late nineteenth and twentieth centuries. This movement seeks to reinterpret parts of the Quran and sunna to conform with standards set by the West, most notably standards relating to gender relations, family law, and participatory democracy. However, ample scope for reinterpretation remains for Wahhabi jurists in areas not decided by the early jurists.

The 1920s marked the beginnings of modern Arabia. 'Abd al-Aziz understood the potential advantages Western technology offered; the importation of a fleet of automobiles and, later, the building of airstrips gave him the means of reaching distant parts of his territory in a fraction of the time required previously. He also ordered the creation of an extensive information network based on the wireless telegraph, through which he was able to extend his "eyes and ears" across the country. However, some of his followers were less than enthusiastic, and their leader spent much time and effort explaining personally the value of the telephone in particular. 'Abd al-Aziz finally overcame their opposition by inviting skeptics to listen to recitations from the Qur'an being read down the phone line. Aware that the fledgling nation would be ill-equipped to function in the 20th century without industrial modernization, 'Abd al-Aziz was eager to embrace technology; however, he was no less aware that change had to be selective and gradual if it was to be accepted by the citizenry. Arabist and historian Leslie McLoughlin pointed out that "it was the insight of Ibn Saud that slow change without disabling disputes was better than speed of change with great disruption."

Under Al Saud rule, governments, especially during the Wahhabi revival in the 1920s, have shown their capacity and readiness to enforce compliance with Islamic laws and interpretations of Islamic values on themselves and others. The literal interpretations of what constitutes right behavior according to the Quran and hadith have given the Wahhabis the sobriquet of "Muslim Calvinists." To the Wahhabis, for example, performance of prayer that is punctual, ritually correct, and communally performed not only is urged but publicly required of men. Consumption of wine is forbidden to the believer because wine is literally forbidden in the Quran. Under the Wahhabis, however, the ban extended to all intoxicating drinks and other stimulants, including tobacco. Modest dress is prescribed for both men and women in accordance with the Quran, but the Wahhabis specify the type of clothing that should be worn, especially by women, and forbid the wearing of silk and gold, although the latter ban has been enforced only sporadically. Music and dancing have also been forbidden by the Wahhabis at times, as have loud laughter and demonstrative weeping, particularly at funerals.

The Wahhabi emphasis on conformity makes of external appearance and behavior a visible expression of inward faith. Therefore, whether one conforms in dress, in prayer, or in a host of other activities becomes a public statement of whether one is a true Muslim. Because adherence to the true faith is demonstrable in tangible ways, the Muslim community can visibly judge the quality of a person's faith by observing that person's actions. In this sense, public opinion becomes a regulator of individual behavior. Therefore, within the Wahhabi community, which is striving to be the collective embodiment of God's laws, it is the responsibility of each Muslim to look after the behavior of his neighbor and to admonish him if he goes astray.

In the 1990s, Saudi leadership did not emphasize its identity as inheritor of the Wahhabi legacy as such, nor did the descendants of Muhammad ibn Abd al Wahhab, the Al ash Shaykh, continue to hold the highest posts in the religious bureaucracy. Wahhabi influence in Saudi Arabia, however, remained tangible in the physical conformity in dress, in public deportment, and in public prayer. Most significantly, the Wahhabi legacy was manifest in the social ethos that presumed government responsibility for the collective moral ordering of society, from the behavior of individuals, to institutions, to businesses, to the government itself. King Fahd ibn Abd al Aziz Al Saud repeatedly called for scholars to engage in ijtihad to deal with new situations confronting the modernizing kingdom.

Maliki Sect

Maliki is one of the four schools of Fiqh or religious law within Sunni Islam, named for Malik ibn Anas (ca. 710-95), a leading jurist from Medina. This school recorded the Medina consensus of opinion, and uses hadith (tradition) as a guide. The Maleki is predominant in north, central and west Africa and Egypt. Following the tradition of Imam Malik, this school appeals to "common utility...the idea of the common good."

Malik did not record the fundamental principles on which he based his school and on whose basis he derived his judgements and to which he limited himself in the derivation of his rulings. In that respect he resembled his contemporary, Abu Hanifa, but not his student, ash-Shafi'i, who did record the principles he used in derivation and defined them precisely, specifying the motives which moved him to consider them and their position in deduction. Malik only transmitted from people in whose mursal and balaghat hadith he had absolute confidence. That is why his great concern was with the choice of transmitter. When he had confidence in the character, intelligence and knowledge of the transmitter he dispensed with the chain of narration. Malik clearly stated that he took the practice of the people of Madina as a source. He never wore shoes whilst in Medinatul Munawwarah [Medina]. He never sat on a horse or used the toilets in this blessed city. He always went out of the city to relieve himself.

Maliki is practiced in North Africa and parts of West Africa. It is the second-largest of the four schools, followed by approximately 25% of Muslims. Arabia, North and West Africa, Upper Egypt and the Sudan is the location. The colonial legal system influenced development of Morocco's legal system while sharia courts continued to apply Maliki fiqh to matters of family law. Also local tribunals applying customary law. Following independence in 1956, a Code of Personal Status (al-Mudawwana) was issued, based on dominant Maliki doctrine.

Shafii Sect

The Shaf'i school is predominant in east Africa, Indonesia and southeast Asia. Al Shafii's (d. 855) thought influenced Indonesia, Southern Arabia, Lower Egypt, parts of Syria, Palestine, Eastern Africa, India and South Africa. The school remains predominant in Southern Arabia, Bahrain, the Malay Archipelago, East Africa and several parts of Central Asia. Shafii is practiced in Indonesia, Malaysia and the Philippines. It is followed by approximately 15% of Muslims world-wide.

The Shaf'i school is considered the easiest school and the Hanbali is considered the hardest in terms of social and personal rules. Hanafi took Shafi as his rival and vice versa. Tradition, the consensus of the Muslim community and reasoning by analogy are characteristics of this school.

Most Kurds in Iraq follow the Shafii school of Sunni Islam. A minority of Kurds, concentrated in parts of the Kifri and Klar areas of Kirkuk, follow the Hanafi school.

The Shafi'iyyah school of Islamic law was named after Muhammad ibn Idris al-Shafii [Shafi, Shaafiee] (767-819). The school of Imam Abu Abd Allah Muhammad Shafii of the Quraysh tribe of the Prophet, brought up in Mecca. He later taught in both Baghdad and Cairo and followed a somewhat eclectic legal path, laying down the rules for analogy that were later adopted by other legal schools. He was a descendant of the Prophet's uncle, Abu Talib, and came to Egypt in the 9th century. Saladin who founded the first madrasa, dedicated to the Shafii rite near the tomb of its founder, Imam al-Shafii. Al-Shafii was known for his peculiar strength in Arabic language, poetry, and philology. Imam Shafi'i was called devil and imprisoned. Prayers were said for his death. He was taken in captivity from Yemen to Baghdad, in a condition of humiliation and degradation.

Then at the time of Al-Shafi'i, the Prophet's ahadith were gathered from different countries, and the disagreements among the scholars increased until Al-Shafi'i wrote his famous book, Al-Risalah, which is considered the foundation of Islamic jurisprudence. The Shafi'i tradition is particularly accessible to English speaking Muslims due to the availability of high quality translations of the Reliance of the Traveler.

Shiia Sect

Shi'a Islam (also called Shiite, or Shi'i) is the second largest division of Islam, constituting about 10-15% of all Muslims. The Sunni Muslims recognise the Four Caliphs as 'rightly guided', while Shi'a Muslims recognise Ali as the First Caliph and his descendants. Shias differ on how many Imams there have been. Some talk of Twelve and others of Fourteen. They also differ on who is the las. Imam (Mahdi). Imamites say it was the Twelfth Imam, Muhammad Al Mahdi, the Zaydites say the Fifth, Zayd, and, the Ismailites say the Seventh Imam, Ismail. However, Shi'as agree that the Last Imam went into hiding and will return to bring in the end of the world.

Shia Beliefs

The Five Shia Principles of Religion (Usul ad Din) are: belief in divide unity (tawhid); prophecy (nubuwwah); resurrection (maad); divine justice (adl); and the belief in the Imams as successors of the Prophet (imamah). The latter principle is not accepted by Sunnis.

Most Sunnis believe the Sharia (religious law of Islam) was codified and closed by the 10th century.

Shia followers believe the Sharia is always open, subject to fresh reformulations of Sunna, hadith, (traditions of what Muhammad and his companions said and did) and Qur'an interpretations.

Like Sunni Islam, Shia Islam has developed several sects. Because of their belief that the leader of the Muslim community must be a blood relative of the prophet, disputes arose when two sons of an Imam (the title given to the Shia leader) both claimed to be the rightful successor. These disputes caused the Shia sect to further divide into three groups: Zaids, Ismai'ilis, and Ithna Asharis. The Twelver or Ithna-Ashari sect is the most important of these, as it predominates not only in Iraq but in the Shia world generally. Broadly speaking, the Twelvers are considered political quietists as opposed to the Zaydis who favor political activism, and the Ismailis who are identified with esoteric and gnostic religious doctrines.

Canonical schools in Islam, are called "Fiqh's"; the only Fiqh's in Shia Islam, are Usuli, Akhbari, and Shaykhi. These 3 all belong to the Ithna-Ashari or mainstream Shia Islam, which believes in the 12 Shia Imams; hence the name which means "Twelver's". The dominant Shia legal school is sometimes termed the Jafari Fiqh, after lmam Jaafar Sadiq (a.s.), the Sixth Infallible Imam of the world of Shiism. The term "Jaafari" is something of a pejorative term, just like "Wahhabiyyah" is; and one that is not used by Shias themselves. It is used by Sunnis, to derided Shias, just as "Wahhabiyyah" is used by Westerners and Shias, to deride Sunnis, but neither term is correct in and of itself.

A student assimilates from very early the ijtihad methodology as he assumes religious ranks: preacher, then mujtahid, hujjat Al-Islam [Proof of Islam], and then hujjat Al-Islam wa Al-Muslimeen until he becomes a Source or ayatollah, and thereafter the great ayatollah or ayatollah al-uzma.

The 1964 Afghan Constitution, which was the basis of new 2003 constitution, stated: "Islam is the sacred religion of Afghanistan. Religious rites performed by the state shall be according to the provisions of the Hanafi school of jurisprudence." This stipulation left Afghan Shia without proper representation. Thus in March 2003, Ayatollah Mohammad Asef Mohseni, leader of the predominantly Shia Harakat-e Islami-yi Afghanistan, proposed that, along with the Sunni Hanafi school of jurisprudence, the Shia Jafari school of jurisprudence be included in the new constitution as an official sect. Mohseni said he proposed two additional formulas if his proposal is not accepted: mentioning "Islam and the Islamic sects," or just mentioning Islam without any mention of sects to ensure that Afghan Shia have their jurisprudence recognized and are allowed to "perform their religious duties according to it."

The Jafari [Hafari] fiqh of the Imami Shias is in most cases indistinguishable from one or more of the four Sunni madhahib, except that "Muta'h" or temporary marriage is considered lawful by the Fiqh Jafari, whereas it is prohibited in all the Sunni schools. But the Shia are still viewed with great caution by the Ulema of the Sunni world. Although Sunni and Shia Muslims are historically ambivalent, this traditional enmity was dampened in Central Asia due to shared resistance to Russian and Soviet rule. Indeed, both Sunni and Shia delegations to the 1905 Third Congress of Muslims in Russia declared Ja'farite Shi'ism as a fifth legal school, equivalent to the Hanafi, Maliki, Hanbali, and Shafi'i madrasehs.

Shi'as do not believe in predestination. They accept the teachings of the *Mu'tazilities*, a group of Sunni scholars who were later declared heretical. The Mu'tazilities believed that God cannot be responsible for evil, and therefore, humans must have freewill and be independent of God's authority in this life. A further belief of Shia Muslims concerns divine justice and the individual's responsibility for his acts, which are judged by a just God. This contrasts with the Sunni view that God's creation of man allows minimal possibility for the exercise of free will.

Two distinctive and frequently misunderstood Shia practices are mutah, temporary marriage, and taqiyah, religious dissimulation.

Mutah, that is, marriage with a fixed termination contract subject to renewal, was practiced by Muslims as early as the formation of the first Muslim community at Medina. Banned by the second caliph, it has since been unacceptable to Sunnis, but Shias insist that if it were against Islamic law it would not have been practiced in early Islam. Mutah differs from permanent marriage because it does not require divorce proceedings for termination because the contractual parties have agreed on its span, which can be as short as an evening or as long as a lifetime. By making the mutah, a couple places the sexual act within the context of sharia; the act then is not considered adulterous and offspring are considered legitimate heirs of the man.

Taqiyah is another practice condemned by the Sunni as cowardly and irreligious but encouraged by Shia Islam and also practiced by Alawis and Ismailis. A person resorts to taqiyah when he either hides his religion or disavows certain religious practices to escape danger from opponents of his beliefs. Taqiyah can also be practiced when not to do so would bring danger to the honor of the female members of a household or when a man could be made destitute as a result of his beliefs. Because of the persecution frequently experienced by Shia imams, particularly during the period of the Umayyad and Abbasid caliphates, taqiyah has been continually reinforced.

Shia practice differs from that of the Sunnis concerning both divorce and inheritance in that it is more favorable to women. The reason for this reputedly is the high esteem in which Fatima, the wife of Ali and the daughter of the Prophet, was held.

The Imamate: Among Shias the term imam traditionally has been used only for Ali and his eleven descendants. None of the twelve Imams, with the exception of Ali, ever ruled an Islamic government. During their lifetimes, their followers hoped that they would assume the rulership of the Islamic community, a rule that was believed to have been wrongfully usurped. Because the Sunni caliphs were cognizant of this hope, the Imams generally were persecuted during the Umayyad and Abbasid dynasties. Therefore, the Imams tried to be as unobtrusive as possible and to live as far as was reasonable from the successive capitals of the Islamic empire.

The Imamate began with Ali, who is also accepted by Sunni Muslims as the fourth of the "rightly guided caliphs" to succeed the Prophet. Shias revere Ali as the First Imam, and his descendants, beginning with his sons Hasan and Husayn, continue the line of the Imams until the twelfth, who is believed to have ascended into a supernatural state to return to earth on Judgment Day. Shias point to the close lifetime association of the Prophet with Ali. When Ali was six years old, he was invited by the Prophet to live with him, and Shias believe Ali was the first person to make the declaration of faith in Islam. Ali also slept in the Prophet's bed on the night of the hijra or migration from Mecca to Medina when it was feared that the house would be attacked by unbelievers and the Prophet stabbed to death. He fought in all the battles the Prophet did except one, and the Prophet chose him to be the husband of his favorite daughter, Fatima.

The Sunni-Shia division of Islam originated as a succession dispute shortly after the death of the prophet Muhammad in 632 A.D. Shia believe that the proper successor of Muhammad was Ali. The word "Shia" means partisan or faction of Ali. Ali was elected to be the fourth Muslim ruler or caliph, but was later overthrown and assassinated. Shia Muslims believe that the first three caliphs Abu Bakr, Umar and Uthman were usurpers, and that Ali was the first true Imam.

Shia venerate Ali only second to Muhammad, considering him the first Imam and the true caliph. Ali was buried in the Iraqi city of Najaf, which established an early connection between Iraq and Shiism and became a shrine city that continues to be a destination for Shia pilgrims.

In 661 A.D. Mu'awiya, the governor of Syria, named himself caliph and made the caliphate hereditary in his own family, the Umayyads, who the Shia rejected as usurpers of Ali and his sons' rights to the caliphate. In the year AD 661, Imam Ali, Muhammad's son-in-law and the fourth caliph of Islam, was assassinated in southern Iraq in a struggle over who would rule the faithful. Ali was buried in Najaf, and his tomb is housed in a mosque in the city's center.

Nineteen years after Ali's death, his two sons were killed in battle and subsequently buried in nearby Karbala. Their battlefield deaths made martyrdom one of the most important tenets of Shiism. Shia attempts to challenge the Umayyad leaders resulted in the death of Ali's son and the third Shia Imam, Husayn, at the Battle of Karbala in 680. The city of Karbala has become a Shia shrine city.

Husayn's death is commemorated annually in the Ashura ceremony, and is seen as a symbol of the persecution and oppression experienced by the Shia community. Celebration of Ashura can also be a form of Shia political dissent. Male participants in the Ashura rituals beat their chests and chant in an action called lahtom. Some use swords to lacerate their heads to symbolize the beheading of Husayn, or use chains to beat their backs to evoke the suffering of Husayn.

Shia may place a piece of stone or clay, known as a turba, from the shrine of an Imam or other Shia figure on the ground so that their forehead touches the stone when they prostrate themselves in prayer. The possession of such a disc is a sign of Shia identity.

Jaafari [Jafari] Faith means the Religion according to Imam Jaafar Sadiq (a.s.), the Sixth Infallible Imam of the world of Shiism. Ascription of the Shiite Religion to Imam Jaafar ben Muhammad Al-Sadiq (a.s.) was due to the fact that this noble Imam lived longer than all other Infallible Imams and, thus, he has had more time and opportunity for action. Because of the conditions of his time, the role of imam Sadeq (a.s.) in reviving true, genuine Islamic teachings, formation of numerous education centers and training of faithful men was exceptional to the point that the Shiite religion by ascription to him has been named the "Jaafari Faith". The infirmity and confusion of the Caliphate due to the clashes between the Abbasid, and the Omayyad dynasties, in particular, afforded wider opportunities to the Imam to teach, instruct, discuss and train the faithful and sincere forces and to establish lbeologic Centers and promulgate the Islamic truths.

During the eighth century the Caliph Mamun, son and successor to Harun ar Rashid, was favorably disposed toward the descendants of Ali and their followers. He invited the Eighth Imam, Reza (A.D. 765-816), to come from Medina (in the Arabian Peninsula) to his court at Marv (Mary in the present-day Soviet Union). While Reza was residing at Marv, Mamun designated him as his successor in an apparent effort to avoid conflict among Muslims. Reza's sister Fatima journeyed from Medina to be with her brother, but took ill and died at Qom, in present-day Iran. A major shrine developed around her tomb and over the centuries Qom has become a major Shia pilgrimage and theological center.

Mamun took Reza on his military campaign to retake Baghdad from political rivals. On this trip Reza died unexpectedly in Khorasan. Reza was the only Imam to reside or die in what in now Iran. A major shrine, and eventually the city of Mashhad, grew up around his tomb, which has become the most important pilgrimage center in Iran. Several important theological schools are located in Mashhad, associated with the shrine to the Eighth Imam.

Reza's sudden death was a shock to his followers, many of whom believed that Mamun, out of jealousy for Reza's increasing popularity, had the Imam poisoned. Mamun's suspected treachery against Imam Reza and his family tended to reinforce a feeling already prevalent among his followers that the Sunni rulers were untrustworthy.

The Twelfth Imam is believed to have been only five years old when the Imamate descended upon him in A.D.874 at the death of his father. Because his followers feared he might be assassinated, the Twelfth Imam was hidden from public view and was seen only by a few of his closest deputies. Sunnis claim that he never existed or that he died while still a child. Shias believe that the Twelfth Imam never died, but disappeared from earth in about A.D. 939. Since that time, the greater occultation of the Twelfth Imam has been in force and will last until God commands the Twelfth Imam to manifest himself on earth again as the Mahdi or Messiah. Shias believe that during the occultation of the Twelfth Imam, he is spiritually present—some believe that he is materially present as well—and he is besought to reappear in various invocations and prayers. His name is mentioned in wedding invitations, and his birthday is one of the most jubilant of all Shia religious observances.

The Shia doctrine of the Imamate was not fully elaborated until the tenth century. Other dogmas were developed still later. A characteristic of Shia Islam is the continual exposition and reinterpretation of doctrine.

Shia Muslims hold the fundamental beliefs of other Muslims. But, in addition to these tenets, the distinctive institution of Shia Islam is the Imamate — a much more exalted position than the Sunni imam, who is primarily a prayer leader. In contrast to Sunni Muslims, who view the caliph only as a temporal leader and who lack a hereditary view of Muslim leadership, Shia Muslims believe the Prophet Muhammad designated Ali to be his successor as Imam, exercising both spiritual and temporal leadership. Such an Imam must have knowledge, both in a general and a religious sense, and spiritual guidance or walayat, the ability to interpret the inner mysteries of the Quran and the sharia. Only those who have walayat are free from error and sin and have been chosen by God through the Prophet. Each Imam in turn designated his successor—through twelve Imams—each holding the same powers. Implied in the Shia principle of the imamah is that imams, are imbued with a redemptive quality as a result of their sufferings and martyrdoms. And, although imams are not divine, they are sinless and infallible in matters of faith and morals, principle very similar to the notion of papal infallibility in the Roman Catholic Church. That man needs an intermediary with God is an Iranian idea that long predates Islam, as is the idea of a savior or messiah (Mahdi) who will come to redeem man and cleanse the world. To expect that the Mahdi, who is the last (twelfth) Imam, really will one is a religious virtue (intizar).

Twelvers/Ithna Ashari Sect

The Twelvers are by far the largest group of Shiite Muslims, because the Iranians are Twelvers. Perhaps eighty percent of the Shiis are Twelvers. Twelvers constitute ninety percent of the modern population of Iran and fifty-five to sixty percent of the population of Iraq. Twelver Shiites are the majority in Iran, Iraq, Azerbaijan and also have substantial populations in Turkey, Pakistan, Lebanon, Syria, India, Afghanistan and Bahrain.

The following of Jafar Sadik bifurcated into two branches-the Ismailis, the followers of Ismail, and the Musawite, the supporters of Musa Kazim, who later on came to be known as Twelvers, or Ithna Asharites. Canonical schools in Islam are called "Fiqh's". the only Fiqh's in Shia Islam, are Usuli, Akhbari, and Shaykhi. These 3 all belong to the Ithna-Ashari or mainstream Shia Islam, which believes in the 12 Shia Imams; hence the name which means "Twelver's".

Those who believe that the third son was the rightful ruler of Islam are called the "Twelvers", because they believe that there were 12 Imams. The last one is still alive, according to the Twelvers, and has been hiding in a cave for the last more than one thousand years. They hold that the twelfth Imam (Muhammad) who disappeared about 874 is still living. He will come out and resume his rule soon, the Twelvers say.

Modern Twelvers believe that, for his own protection, Mohammad al-Mahdi went into "occultation" (hiding). He is reported to have communicated to the faithful via intermediaries called Babs (Gates), the first of whom was Uthman al-Amri. When the last of the four gates died in 941 CE, the lesser occultation ended and the greater occultation began. The line of Twelver Imams came to an end.

About the time the lesser Occultation came to an end the Twelvers came to believe that the Twelfth Imam would return to earth in the last days as the Mahdi, and would establish a reign of justice and peace on earth. After his coming, they believe, Christ will return. Some from Iran claimed when Imam Khomeini was alive that he was in fact the "Disappearing Imam" who had come back to rule. Others said that he was the Mehdi or "Promised Messiah".

The Twelvers are the largest Shiite group today, but they are not the only one, and historically they were often a very small, weak group. They emerged as a distinct Shii group mostly in the third Muslim century (the eighth century C.E.) after the death of the twelfth Imam. Twelver Shiism appears to have grown in size partly because it did not have a living Imam; many other descendants or alleged descendants of the Prophet called themselves the Imam, formented militarty revolt, and were killed. By not having a living Imam, Twelver Shiism was able to survive and grow, and other Shiis often were absorbed into it when their revolts were crushed and their Imams executed.

In law, the Twelvers do not accept hadiths, transmitted by enemies of the Imans such as 'A'isha, and make use also of the sayings of the Imams. In addition to the Shi'i regulations for the prayer call and ablutions, they admit the doctrine of taqiya or katman, the prophecy or even necessity of hiding one's true beliefs among non-Shi'is...and they retain the peculiar institution of legal temporary marriage between a free man and woman for mut'a (pleasure).

An integral part of the Shii doctrine of the Imam is that he is the legitimate political leader of Islam; just as the caliphs usurped Ali's authority, modern governments, in the absence of the authority of the Imam, are not legitimate. Most Imams of the Twelver line, after Hossein's martydom, did not make a claim to political leadership; rather, they acknowledged the authority of the caliphs, and urged their followers to do the same. Thus political quietism was a common option pursued by Twelver Shiis. Early Shii thinkers living after the occultation of the Imam felt leaderless. They felt a profound alienation from the world and generally adopted a quietest political policy.

Within Twelver Shia Islam there are three major legal schools, the Usuli, the Akhbari and the Shayki. Akhbaris constitute a very small group and are found primarily around Basra and in southern Iraq as well as around Khorramshahr in Iran. The dominant Usuli school is more liberal in its legal outlook and allows greater use of interpretation (ijtihad) in reaching legal decisions, and considers that one must obey a mujtahid (learned interpreter of the law) as well as an Imam.

Twelvers / Ithna Ashari Islamic Schools of Thought

The 17th Century Akhbari/Usuli controversy was directed towards establishing the 'Ulama' as regents of the Imam in social and political matters. Usuli [variants: Usooli] was a religious movement by Persian Shiite Muslims in 17th century Iran that was opposed to the Akhbari. The Usuli-Akhbari controversy resulted in the victory of rationalism and upheld the role of the ulama, but it would be wrong to assumed that all Akhbari `ulama' were reactionary and all Usuli `ulama' were progressive.

The dominant Usuli (from "*usul-i-fiqh*," principles of jurisprudence) school is more liberal in its legal outlook than the Akhbari. It allows greater use of interpretation (*ijtihad*) in reaching legal decisions, and considers that one must obey a *mujtahid* (learned interpreter of the law) as well as an Imam. The Iranian religious center at Qom was the focal point of Usuli Shiism, and from the 1760s, the Usuli school began to win out in the strategic Shi`ite shrine centers of Najaf and Karbala in Iraq. By the establishment of the Qajar dynasty in 1785 (CE) the Usuli ulama had emerged as a force to be reckoned with across Iran, with it's leadership emanating from the Atabat (Karbila and Najaf in Iraq).

Usuli Shiism produced the politically active caste of priests that is a distinctive feature of Iranian Shiism. Usuli rationalists insisted that the consensus of scholars and independent reasoning (ijtihad) can be a basis for activism. Usuli Shiism provided the religious legitimacy for Ayatollah Ruhollah Khomeini's Islamic revolution of 1979 and the subsequent theocratic state. But the *na'ib-i-amm* concept — that the ulama acted in "general deputyship" in the absence of the Hidden Imam-expanded only slowly over time. Most ulama were politically inactive. The concept was developed to its logical conclusion in Ayat'ullah Khumayni's construct that that government is rightfully administered by Islamic jurists in the absence of the Imam.

In mainstream Usuli Shiite jurisprudence it is illegitimate to continue following the controversial rulings of a dead jurisprudent. Laypersons must adopt a new, living jurisprudent in such circumstances. The practice of *taqlid al-mayyit* is permited in the Akhbari school.

Akhbari (or communicators of tradition, *akhbar* being the Shi'i term for the Traditions) was a religious movement by Arab Shiite Muslims in 17th century Iraq that was opposed to the Usuli. Akhbari Shiism did not promote political control, and held that clerics should advise political leaders but not govern themselves. The shrine cities of Ottoman Iraq — Najaf (tomb of 'Ali) and Karbala (tomb of Husayn) — were the center of Akhbari scholars. The Akhbari school restricted to the Quran and oral reports of the Prophet and the Imams. They held that, during the *ghaiba* (occultation) of the Twelfth Imam, religious scholars were not permitted to use reason (*ijtihad*) to apply law to a specific situation. They also insisted that laymen can equally emulate the 12 Imams — that is, Akhbaris supported in the ability of all believers to interpret the Traditions of the Imams.

This school crystallised into a separate movement following the writings of Mulla Muhammad Amin Astaraabadi (d. 1033/1623). Shaykh Yusuf al-Bahrani, a refugee from Afghan slaughter in Iran in 1724, rejected the legitimacy of holy war (jihad) during the occultation of the Imam. The school achieved its greatest influence during the late and post-Safavid periods but was crushed by the Usuli Mujtahidin at the end of the Qajar era. Shaykh Murtada bin Muhammad Amin Ansari established conclusively the dominance of the Usuli position against the neo-Akhbari Traditionism.

There is some confusion as to the present adherence to the Akhbari school. Many sources claims that Iraqi Shi'ism is Akhbari while Iranian Shi'ism is Usuli. Other reports characterized Abdul Majid al-Khoei, who was killed by a rampaging mob soon after he returned to Iraq from emigration in London, and as Akhbari. This may overstate matters, though "some residual influence of the Akhbari position still persists not only in Iran but to a much greater degree among the Shii ulama of Iraq, India, Pakistan and Bahrain and among their followers."

Other sources report that both Iraqi and Iranian are Shia are Usulis, and that Iraq is fully part of the marja' (source or religious leader) system. Thus, Grand Ayatullah as-Sayyid Ali al-Hussaini as-Seestani is Marja Taghlid (source of emulation). Sharia is updated, interpreted and relayed by a Mojtahed (supreme religious leader) or a Marja Taghlid (source of emulation). According to this view, Akhbaris are today a small group which only survives in any numbers in Bahrain, where the majority of Shiites are Akhbaris. They are also found around Basra in southern Iraq as well as around Khorramshahr in Iran. Akhbari Shi'ism also has a few adherents in other Gulf regions.

After the defeat of the Akhbaris, the primary doctrinal challenge to Usuli jurisprudecne came from the Shaykhi school. This movement was founded on the teachings of Shaykh Ahmad-i-Ahsa'i (d. 1825 C.E.) and his successor Siyyid Kazim-i-Rashti (d. 1844 C.E.). Whereas the Akhbari school differed from the 'Usulis principally in matters of furu', the Shaykhi School, founded by Shaykh Ahmad ibn Zaynu'd-Din al-Ahsa'i (d. 1241/1826), differed principally in usul. There is evidence that Shaykh Najafi made attempts to marginalize their role. There remains a strong Shaykhi movement in Pakistan

Seveners/Ismaili Sect

Ismailis are Shia Muslims who claim that Ismail, the eldest son of Imam Jaffar, was the rightful ruler of all Muslims. They are also known as the "Seveners", because Imam Jaffar was the seventh and, according to them, the last Imam. An important Shii Muslim community, the Ismailis as an entity emerged in 765 from a disagreement over the successor to the sixth imam, Jafar al-Sadiq. According to the Ismailis, starting from Ali, the eldest son has always inherited the right to rule. Shia Twelvers, those who accept the first Twelve Imams, believe that Jafar, the Sixth Imam, passed over his eldest son, Ismail, in favor of Ismail's brother Musa al Kazim. Ismailis, however, believe that Jafar appointed Ismail to be the Seventh Imam—hence Ismailis are often called Seveners.

Ismaili Shia doctrine closely resembled Twelver Shia Islam with regard to observance of the sharia but also included a system of philosophy and science coordinated with religion that proved the divine origin of the Imamate and the rights of the Fatimids to it. Ubaid Allah al Mahdi, the founder of the Fatimid Dynasty, came to North Africa in the early tenth century and actively promoted the Ismaili faith. The Fatimid rulers proclaimed themselves true caliphs.

Little is known of the early history of the sect, but it was firmly established by the end of the ninth century. From 969 to 1171, an Ismaili dynasty, the Fatimids, ruled as caliphs in Egypt. The Fatimids, unlike the Tulinids and the Ikhshidids, wanted independence, not autonomy, from Baghdad.

In addition, as heads of a great religious movement, the Ismaili Shia Islam, they also challenged the Sunni Abbasids for the caliphate itself. The name of the dynasty is derived from Fatima, the daughter of the Prophet Muhammad and the wife of Ali, the fourth caliph and the founder of Shia Islam. The leader of the movement, who first established the dynasty in Tunisia in 906, claimed descent from Fatima.

Under the Fatimids, Egypt became the center of a vast empire, which at its peak comprised North Africa, Sicily, Palestine, Syria, the Red Sea coast of Africa, Yemen, and the Hijaz in Arabia, including the holy cities of Mecca and Medina. Control of the holy cities conferred enormous prestige on a Muslim sovereign and the power to use the yearly pilgrimage to Mecca to his advantage. Cairo was the seat of the Shia caliph, who was the head of a religion as well as the sovereign of an empire. The Fatimids established Al Azhar in Cairo as an intellectual center where scholars and teachers elaborated the doctrines of the Ismaili Shia faith.

The first century of Fatimid rule represents a high point for medieval Egypt. The administration was reorganized and expanded. It functioned with admirable efficiency: tax farming was abolished, and strict probity and regularity in the assessment and collection of taxes was enforced. The revenues of Egypt were high and were then augmented by the tribute of subject provinces. This period was also an age of great commercial expansion and industrial production. The Fatimids fostered both agriculture and industry and developed an important export trade. Realizing the importance of trade both for the prosperity of Egypt and for the extension of Fatimid influence, the Fatimids developed a wide network of commercial relations, notably with Europe and India, two areas with which Egypt had previously had almost no contact.

Egyptian ships sailed to Sicily and Spain. Egyptian fleets controlled the eastern Mediterranean, and the Fatimids established close relations with the Italian city states, particularly Amalfi and Pisa. The two great harbors of Alexandria in Egypt and Tripoli in present-day Lebanon became centers of world trade. In the east, the Fatimids gradually extended their sovereignty over the ports and outlets of the Red Sea for trade with India and Southeast Asia and tried to win influence on the shores of the Indian Ocean. In lands far beyond the reach of Fatimid arms, the Ismaili missionary and the Egyptian merchant went side-by-side.

In the end, however, the Fatimid bid for world power failed. A weakened and shrunken empire was unable to resist the crusaders, who in July 1099 captured Jerusalem from the Fatimid garrison after a siege of five weeks.

Ismailis accept many Shia doctrines, such as the esoteric nature of truth and the inspiration of the Imams. Although holding their Imams to be of divine origin, as the Shia do, Ismailis have a dual Imamate. They believe the succession of visible Imams has continued to the present. There are, however, two imams, the visible and the hidden, the speaker and the silent. The identity of the hidden imam is not known to the community but it is believed he will return to lead the faithful. Ismailis generally follow the religious practice of the Shia Twelvers in prayers, fasts, and Quranic prescriptions, but in their conservatism they resemble Sunnis on some points. For example, they do not observe the tenth of Muharram in the impassioned way of the Shia.

Ismaili beliefs are complex and syncretic, combining elements from the philosophies of Plotinus, Pythagoras, Aristotle, gnosticism, and the Manichaeans, as well as components of Judaism, Christianity, and Eastern religions. Ismaili conceptions of the Imamat differ greatly from those of other Muslims and their tenets are unique. Their beliefs about the creation of the world are idiosyncratic, as is their historical ecumenism, tolerance of religious differences, and religious hierarchy. There is a division of theology into exoteric (including the conservative Shariah) and esoteric (including the mystical exegesis of the Quran which leads to haqiqa, the ultimate realty). These beliefs and practices are veiled in secrecy and Ismaili place particular emphasis on taqiya meaning to shield or guard, the practice that permits the believer to deny publicly his Shia membership for self-protection, as long as he continues to believe and worship in private. Taqiya is permissible in most Shia, and some Sunni, sects.

The Ismailis who number 15 million, are divided into several main branches. One, who call themselves Bohras, have their headquarters in Mumbai (formerly Bombay), India. Another branch — known as Khojas — are headed by the Agha Khan and concentrated in Gujarat State, India.

Alawi Sect

There are an estimated 5 to 12 million Alevis in Turkey. They are followers of a belief system that incorporates aspects of both Shia and Sunni Islam and draws on the traditions of other religions found in Anatolia as well. The Turkish Government considers Alevism a heterodox Muslim sect; however, some Turkish Alevis and radical Sunnis maintained Alevis were not Muslims. Many Alevis alleged discrimination in the Turkish Government's failure to include any of their doctrines or beliefs in religious instruction classes. Alevis also charged that there was a Sunni bias in the Diyanet since the directorate viewed Alevis as a cultural rather than a religious group and did not fund their activities. During a September 2003 visit to Germany, Turkish Prime Minister Erdogan told reporters that "Alevism is not a religion" and said Alevi Cem houses are "culture houses" rather than "temples."

The Alawis, who number about 1,350,000 in Syria and Lebanon, constitute Syria's largest religious minority. Historically they have been called Nusayris, Nusairis, Namiriya or Ansariyya. They live chiefly along the coast in Al Ladhiqiyah Province, where they form over 60 percent of the rural population; the city of Latakia itself is largely Sunni.

The Alawi sect, which integrates doctrines from other religions — in particular from Christianity— arose from a split within the Ismailite sect. The Alawis appear to be descendants of people who lived in this region at the time of Alexander the Great. When Christianity flourished in the Fertile Crescent, the Alawis, isolated in their little communities, clung to their own preIslamic religion. After hundreds of years of Ismaili influence, the Alawis moved closer to Islam. However, contacts with the Byzantines and the Crusaders added Christian elements to the Alawis' new creeds and practices. For example, Alawis celebrate Christmas, Easter, and Epiphany.

For several centuries, the Alawis enjoyed autonomy within the Ottoman Empire, but, in the mid-nineteenth century, the Ottomans imposed direct rule. Regarding the Alawis as infidels, the Ottomans consistently persecuted them and imposed heavy taxation. During the French Mandate, the Alawis briefly gained territorial autonomy, but direct rule was reimposed in 1936.

For centuries, the Alawis constituted Syria's most repressed and exploited minority. Most were indentured servants and tenant farmers or sharecroppers working for Sunni landowners. However, after Alawi President Assad and his retinue came to power in 1970, the well being of the Alawis improved considerably.

Split by sectional rivalries, the Alawis have no single, powerful ruling family, but since independence many individual Alawis have attained power and prestige as military officers. Although they are settled cultivators, Alawis gather into kin groups much like those of pastoral nomads. The four Alawi confederations, each divided into tribes, are Kalbiyah, Khaiyatin, Haddadin, and Matawirah.

Alawis claim they are Muslims, but conservative Sunnis do not always recognize them as such. Like Ismaili Shias, Alawis believe in a system of divine incarnation. Unlike Ismailis, Alawis regard Ali as the incarnation of the deity in the divine triad. As such, Ali is the "Meaning;" Muhammad, whom Ali created of his own light, is the "Name;" and Salman the Persian is the "Gate." Alawi catechesis is expressed in the formula: "I turn to the Gate; I bow before the Name; I adore the Meaning." An Alawi prays in a manner patterned after the shahada: "I testify that there is no God but Ali."

According to Alawi belief, all persons at first were stars in the world of light but fell from the firmament through disobedience. Faithful Alawis believe they must be transformed seven times before returning to take a place among the stars, where Ali is the prince. If blameworthy, they are sometimes reborn as Christians, among whom they remain until atonement is complete. Infidels are reborn as animals.

Because many of the tenets of the faith are secret, Alawis have refused to discuss their faith with outsiders. Only an elect few learn the religion after a lengthy process of initiation; youths are initiated into the secrets of the faith in stages. Their prayer book, the source of religious instruction, is the Kitab al Majmu, believed to be derived from Ismaili writings. Alawis study the Quran and recognize the five pillars of Islam, which they interpret in a wholly allegorical sense to fit community tenets.

Alawis do not set aside a particular building for worship. In the past, Sunni government officials forced them to build mosques, but these were invariably abandoned. Only the men take part in worship.

Alawis are sometimes pejoratively referred to as Mutazila, but they are distinct from this early Islamic sect. The Mu'tazilites were people following the Mu'tazila religious sect that emerged at the last period of the Ummayad dynasty. It became popular in the reign of the Abbasids. The name, Mutazila or Mutazalite means the Withdrawers or Secessionists. The Mutazila come from the Khawarij, who make takfir of the main body of believers. Some then split from their original allegiance and set up a further correctness — Mutazili "those who decided to go alone". The Khawariji were the very first sect to split away from the main body of the Muslims. The mutazila allowed for civil disobedience, but not for open rebellion as had the Kharijites. The Mutazila argued for the metaphorical nature of the Koran and the supremacy of reason over the text.

Musta'lis [Bohras or Bohri] with Tayyibi Ismailism

Among the Shias of India the Ithna-Asharis are in the majority while the Khojas and Bohras of Western and Central India belong to the two internal divisions of the Isma'ili group of Muslims-the Nizaris [Khojas] with Satpanth Ismailism and the the Musta'lis [Bohras or Bohri] with Tayyibi Ismailism.

Most bohras are Daudi [Dawoodi] Ismailis. The Bohras have their headquarters in Mumbai (formerly Bombay), India. The bohras are am ethnic group in India and Pakistan, originally a hindu caste — Bohri Muslims were originally Brahmins. They are under the leadership of a Da'i Mutlaq, or "Absolute Preacher." The bohras believe their leader is a reincarnation of the previous leader, who was initially a reincarnation of Ali(ra). The sect was formed in the 11th Century C.E. The Mustalis accepted the caliphate of al-Mustali. They remained in Egypt until the fall of the Fatimid dynasty in 1171. From there the sect moved to Yemen where it split, with some remaining in Yemen and others moving to India where they became known as Bohras.

A community of up to one million devout Shia, the Daudi Bohras shatter stereotypes about traditionalist Islam. Bohras accept most aspects of modernity, and support the concept of a pluralist civil society. The Bohras have used modernity as a tool to reinvigorate their core traditions. The Bohra clergy has succeeded in establishing a communal identity that is both universally Islamic and unique to the denomination.

Though highly Islamised as compared to the Isma'ili sects like the Khojas, the Bohras have retained much from the native Indian culture. The Dawoodi Bohras are a Shia Isma'ili sect numbering over a million today. The breeding ground for this dissident sect was non-Arab territories of what was once Babylonia, Assyria and a few areas of Persia, besides Yemen in the south of Arabian peninsula. The Bohras are of Indian origin, conversion in India having taken place in twelfth and thirteen centuries.

Maliki Sect

Maliki is one of the four schools of Fiqh or religious law within Sunni Islam, named for Malik ibn Anas (ca. 710-95), a leading jurist from Medina. This school recorded the Medina consensus of opinion, and uses hadith (tradition) as a guide. The Maleki is predominant in north, central and west Africa and Egypt. Following the tradition of Imam Malik, this school appeals to "common utility...the idea of the common good."

Malik did not record the fundamental principles on which he based his school and on whose basis he derived his judgements and to which he limited himself in the derivation of his rulings. In that respect he resembled his contemporary, Abu Hanifa, but not his student, ash-Shafi'i, who did record the principles he used in derivation and defined them precisely, specifying the motives which moved him to consider them and their position in deduction. Malik only transmitted from people in whose mursal and balaghat hadith he had absolute confidence. That is why his great concern was with the choice of transmitter. When he had confidence in the character, intelligence and knowledge of the transmitter he dispensed with the chain of narration. Malik clearly stated that he took the practice of the people of Madina as a source. He never wore shoes whilst in Medinatul Munawwarah [Medina]. He never sat on a horse or used the toilets in this blessed city. He always went out of the city to relieve himself.

Maliki is practiced in North Africa and parts of West Africa. It is the second-largest of the four schools, followed by approximately 25% of Muslims. Arabia, North and West Africa, Upper Egypt and the Sudan is the location. The colonial legal system influenced development of Morocco's legal system while shari'a courts continued to apply Maliki fiqh to matters of family law. Also local tribunals applying customary law. Following independence in 1956, a Code of Personal Status (al-Mudawwana) was issued, based on dominant Maliki doctrine.

Druze Sect

The Druze religion is a tenth-century offshoot of Islam, but Muslims view Druzes as heretical for accepting the divinity of Hakim, the third Fatimid caliph of Egypt. The group takes its names from Muhammad Bin Ismail ad Darazi, an Iranian mystic. Druzes regard Jethro, father-in-law of Moses, as their chief prophet and make annual pilgrimages to his tomb in lower Galilee. They also revere Moses, Jesus, and Muhammad, the three most important prophets of Islam.

The Druze have always kept their doctrine and ritual of secret to avoid persecution. Only those who demonstrate extreme piety and devotion and the correct demeanor are initiated into the mysteries. The initiated (uqqal; sing., aqil) are a very small minority and may include women. Most Druzes are juhhal, ignorant ones. Apparently the religion is complex, involving neo-Platonic thought, Sufi mysticism, and Iranian religious traditions.

Endogamy and monogamy are the rule among the Druzes. Until recently, most girls were married between the ages of 12 and 15, and most men at the age of 16 or 17. Women are veiled in public, but, in contrast to Muslim Arab custom, they can and do participate in the councils of elders. The Druze community, at 3 percent of the population Syria's third largest religious minority, is the overwhelming majority in the Jabal al Arab, a rugged and mountainous region in southwestern Syria.

Khoja [Nizaris] Satpanth Ismailism

Among the Shias of India the Ithna-Asharis are in the majority while the Khojas and Bohras of Western and Central India belong to the two internal divisions of the Isma'ili group of Muslims-the Nizaris [Khojas] with Satpanth Ismailism and the the Musta'lis [Bohras or Bohri] with Tayyibi Ismailism.

The Khojas are headed by the Agha Khan, who has followers in Pakistan, India, Iran, Yemen, and East Africa. The present Aga Khan, Prince Karim, is the 49th direct descendant in a male line down from Ali. His great-grandfather, Hasan Ali Shah, was given the title of Aga Khan by the Sultan of Persia. The Ismaili followers of the Aga Khan professedly believe that the Quran was time bound and was not meant to be a Universal message for all times. The Aga Khan has officially declared himself, before his followers, as the "Mazhar of Allah on earth". The word "mazhar" means "copy" or "manifest".

The followers of the Agha Khan maintain Allah made the Caliphate hereditary office and not an office "by election" or "nomination". They note that Allah promised Hazrat Ibrahim that his progeny would rule the nations, and the Prophet Muhammad was descended from Prophet Ibrahim's elder son Ismail's line. The Quran outlined the inheritance laws in detail and the legacy passes to the children, related by blood, and not outsiders. Hazrat Ali a.s. was Prophet Muhammad's cousin, Abdul Muttalib was the shared Grandfather to both Prophet Muhammad and Hazrat Ali, and moreover, Prophet Muhammad gave his daughter Fatima a.s., to his favorite and chosen, Hazrat Ali in marriage. Their children, Hazrat Hassan and Hazrat Hussein carried the pure blood of Prophet Muhammad in their veins. The present Living Imam, Imam e Zaman, Prince of Peace for Islam, Mowlana Shah Karim Aga Khan (prayers of peace), is the 49th in the direct line.

The Khojas are concentrated in Gujarat State, India. Khojas were originally Hindus of the trading class converted by Pir Sadruddin [Pir Sadr Al-Dine] in Sind in the later 14th Century (CE). From Sind, the conversion spread into Kutch, then into Kathiawar and through Gujarat to Bombay. Pir Sadr Al-Dine is credited with the conversion of the Khojas from the Hindu caste of the Lohanas. He laid the foundation of the communal organization, built the first assembly and prayer halls (Jamaat Khanahs) and appointed the community leaders (Mukhis). Khojas live chiefly in lower Sind, Cutch, Gujarat,

Bombay and in wide diaspora, particularly in East and South Africa, Arabia, Sri Lanka and Myanmar (Burma).

The Khojas appeared in Eastern Turkestan in the 16th century as leaders of two sects of Nakshbandiye Sufi order-the White mountaineers and the Black mountaineers. The khojas soon assumed informal temporal power. Any political decision in the Mogol khanate of the 17th century could not be accepted without approval of the khojas. China seized Eastern Turkestan in 1759.

Zanzibar attracted Indians from Kutch and Kathiawad, and Khojas emigrated in hundreds by dhows in the 19th century.

Satpanth, really Sat Panth, i.e. the "True Path (to Salvation)", is the name of a sect of Islam, forming a kind of transition from ordinary Islamic doctrine of the Shi 'ite type, to Hinduism. The majority of the Khoja community gives preponderance to Islamic elements at the expense of the Hinduistic, while in the Imam-shahi branches certain groups may pursue just the opposite course of drifting back to Hinduism.

The Nizari sect began when Hasan Ibn al-Sabbah refused to recognize al-Musta'li as the new caliph in 1094. He support al-Musta'li's brother Nizar, who soon disappeared under obscure circumstances in 1095. Musta'liyah Isma'ilis were centered in Cairo while the Nizaris, consolidated their positions in Iran and Syria. Hasan-i Sabbah established his mountains stronghold at Alamut, intending to to destroy the Abbasid Caliphate by murdering its most powerful members. The group followed in the steps of the Kharijites, elaborating an ideology directed against Muslim rulers that they regarded as impious usurpers. The Nizaris [Misaris] gained prominence during the Crusades when a society of Misaris, called Assassins, harassed both the Crusaders and Saladin (Salah ad Din al Ayyubi) at the time of the crusades of the eleventh century. They became famous in the 12th Century for their seizing of Crusader forts and assassinating Christian leaders. The sect was thought to be active possibly continued through the 14th century as a group of bandits on the Afghanistan Silk Road.

Accoring to one account, the Hashshashin (Assassins) received their name from their use of hashish. Other writers suggest that assassin simply means 'followers of Al-Hassan' (or Hasan-i Sabbah, the Sheikh of Alamut, known as "The Old Man of the Mountain"). Their own name for the sect was *ad-dawa al-jadida* which means "the new doctrine" and they called themselves *fedayeen* from the Arabic *fida'i* which means "one who is ready to sacrifice his life for the cause."

Zaydi Sect

Zaydis (also: Zaidi, Zaiddiyah, or in the West Fivers) are the most moderate of the Shia groups and the nearest to the Sunnis in their theology. They say that they are a "fifth school" of Islam (in addition to the four Sunni orthodox schools). This Shi`ite sect is named after Zayd b. Ali, grandson of Husayn. The Zaydi sect was formed by the followers of Zayd b. Ali, who led an unsuccessful rebellion against the Umayyad caliph Hisham in 740.

According to Zaydi political theory, Ali, Hasan and Husayn are the first three rightful Imams; after them, the imamate is open to whomever of their descendants establishes himself through armed rebellion. Shia regard Imam Ali Zayn al-Abidin as the fourth imam. While most shias take Muhammed Al-Baqir to be the next Imam, Zayadis take Al-Baqir's brother Zayd as imam.

Zaidi see Zayd as the fifth Imam because of the rebellion he led against the Umayyad dynasty, which he believed was corrupt. Muhammad al-Baqir did not engage in political action, whereas Zayd preached that a true Imam must fight against corrupt rulers.

Not all Zaidis believe that Zaid is the true Imam. Zaidis known as Wastis believes in Twelver Imams. They are part of Shia Ithna Ashiri. Most of them settled in India, Pakistan. The biggest group of Zaidis having their belive on Twelve Shia Imams is known as Saadat-e-Bahra. Saadat means descendents of Imam Husayn bin Ali and Bahra means twelve in Hindi and Urdu Languages.

The first Zaydi state was established in Tabaristan (northern Iran) in 864; it lasted until the death of its leader at the hand of the Samanids in 928. Forty years later the state was revived in Gilan (north-western Iran) and survived under Hasanid leaders until the 12th century.

In Yemen, a Zaydi state was established in 893 by a Hasanid who had originally been invited to mediate between quarrelling Yemeni tribes. A succession of occupations by foreign dynasties beginning in the tenth century occasionally forced the Zaydi imamate to retreat northwards; however, the imamate survived until the death of its last imam in 1962.

Yemen is a country with deep Muslim traditions, but is often most mentioned for its relatively large Zaydi Shi'i group, even if this represents a minority in the country as a total. The Zaydi order of Shi'a Islam represents approximately 25 percent of the total population. Yemen's north is the center of Zaydism. Zaydism is known for putting less importance on the position of the Imam, than among the Twelver (Iran), perhaps because the Zaydis have enjoyed far more political and religious freedom than the other.

In the rugged mountains of northern Yemen live some four hundred Zaydi tribes with a total of some five million members. For over one thousand years they have been the dominant community in the Yemen, often fighting against the Sunni Shafi'i tribes and the smaller Isma'ili and Twelver Shi'a communities.

Zaidi beliefs are moderate compared to other Shia sects. The Zaidis do not believe in the infallibility of the Imams, nor that they receive divine guidance. Zaidis also do not believe that the Imamate must pass from father to son, but believe it can be held by any descendant of Ali. They also reject the Twelver notion of a hidden Imam, and like the Ismailis believe in a living imam, or even imams.

In matters of law or fiqh, the Zaidis are actually closest to the Sunni Shafie school.

Kharijite Sect

The Kharijites [Kharidjites, in Arabic Khawarij, singular Khariji, meaning "those that seceded"] were members of the earliest sect in Islam that left the followers of Ali [cousin and son-in-law of Muhammad]. The third Caliph, Uthman, was killed by mutineers in 656 AD, and a struggle for succession ensued between Ali, and Mu'awiya, governor of Damascus. The Kharijites left the followers of Ali [the Shia] because of Shia willingness to allow human arbitration of Ali's dispute with Mu'awiya in 657, rather than divine judgment. The Kharijites believed that the Imam should be elected for his moral qualities. The Kharijites considered that Ali made a mistake in looking for a compromise with Mu'awiya. For this reason they are not considered as properly Shiite by some commentators. Ali defeated their rebellion, but the Kharijites survived and an adherent of the movement murdered Ali in 661.

Kharijites rejected primogeniture succession of the Quraysh, the tribe of Muhammad, and assert that leadership of Islam, the caliphate, should be designated by an imam elected by the community from candidates who possess spiritual and personal qualities.

The Kharijite theology was a radical fundamentalism, with uncompromised observance of the Quran in defiance of corrupt authorities. Kharijites considered moderate Muslims to be "hypocrites" and "unbelievers" who could be killed with impunity. The Khawarij made *takfir* — declaring a person to be Kafir — of the main body of believers. The Kharijite held that only the most pious members of the community could be entrusted with political power.

The most prominent quality of the Kharijite movement was opposition to the caliph's representatives and particularly to Muawiyah, who became caliph after Ali. Although the Kharijites were known to some Muslims as bandits and assassins, they developed certain ideal notions of justice and piety. The Prophet Muhammad had been sent to bring righteousness to the world and to teach the Arabs to pray and to distribute their wealth and power fairly. According to the Kharijites, whoever was lax in following the Prophet's directives should be opposed, ostracized, or killed.

The Kharijites Islamic sect in late 7th and early 8th century AD was concentrated in today's southern Iraq. Kharijite uprisings continued under the Umayyads in Iraq, Iran, and Arabia. The apogee of Kharijites influence came between 690 and 730, when their main city, Basra, emerged as a center of Islamic learning. Finally, under the Abbasids, Kharijism was suppressed in Iraq.

Modern Kharijites are sometimes called Ibadites after Abu Allah ibn Ibad (ca. 660-ca. 715), a moderate Kharijite who spent considerable time in Basra, Iraq. Ibad's followers founded communities in parts of Africa and southern Arabia.

In the eighth century, some Kharijites began to moderate their position. Leaders arose who suppressed the fanatical political element in Kharijite belief and discouraged their followers from taking up arms against Islam's official leader. Kharijite leaders emphasized instead the special benefits that Kharijites might receive from living in a small community that held high standards for personal conduct and spiritual values.

The Kharijite movement continued to be significant on the Persian Gulf coast in the ninth through the eleventh century. It continued to play an important political role in eastern Arabia, North Africa, and eastern Africa. Over time the views of the movement moderated and adherents became less antagonistic to the rest of Islam. Eventually, the Kharijite insistence on the primacy of religion in political life moved into the mainstream of Islamic thought.

The Kharijites Islamic sect survived into the twentieth century in the more moderate form of Ibadi Islam. Ibadites refer themselves back to the Kharijites but reject their aggressive methods. There is a Kharidjite majority in Oman and, there are significant Kharidjite minorities in Algeria (in the Mzab, more than 100,000). Some 40,000 Berber-speaking Ibadi people living on Jerba [Djerba] Island in Tunisia still kept to austere Kharidjite beliefs in the mid-1980s.

Ibadi leadership is vested in an imam, who is regarded as the sole legitimate leader and combines religious and political authority. The imam is elected by a council of prominent laymen or shaykhs. Adherence to Ibadism accounts in part for Oman's historical isolation. Considered a heretical form of Islam by the majority Sunni Muslims, Ibadis were not inclined to integrate with their neighbors.

The term Kharijites became a designation for Muslims who refused to compromise with those who differed from them. The uncompromising fanaticism of the original Kharijites was indicative of the fervor with which the tribal Arabs had accepted the missionary ideology of Islam. It was this fervor that made it possible for Arab armies to conquer so much territory in the seventh century. This same spirit helped the Al Saud succeed at the end of the eighteenth century and again at the beginning of the twentieth. Some observers compare today's radical Salafis with the ancient Khawarij terrorist sect, since they pioneered the political killing of Muslims considered heretic.

Ahmadiyya Sect

Ahmadis are followers of 77 (1839-1908), who founded a religious community in the late nineteenth century in what was then British India. He began to publish his Barahin-i Ahmadiyya in 1880. He declared himself a mujaddid (a renewer of faith) in 1882 and set about spreading his message. In 1889, he announced he had received divine revelation authorizing him to accept the baya, the allegiance of the faithful. Then in 1891 he declared himself the Mahdi, the promised Messiah (masih) of Islam, and the last avatara of Vishnu. He ruled out jihad against the kuffar who occupied the Islamic lands.

When he died the Ahmadiyyahs split into two sects, the Qadianis and the Lahorites. The Qadianis claimed that Ghulam was a prophet, and accused all muslims who did not accept him, as being kuffar (non-muslims),

After his death, the community elected a series of Khalifas (successors). The current and Fourth Successor (Khalifatul Masih IV), to the Promised Messiah was chosen in the person of Hazrat Mirza Tahir Ahmad on 10 June 1982.

Although Ahmadis consider themselves to be Muslim, some Muslims in Pakistan hold the opposite view because of the Ahmadis' claim that their founder was a recipient of divine revelation and a prophet of God. This claim is believed by some Muslims to violate a basic Islamic tenet regarding the finality of the prophet Muhammad. This religious difference has been used in the past by certain Pakistani governments to justify a number of legal restrictions on the Ahmadis' practice of their faith.

The Ahmadiyya belief as professed and practiced for the last 100 years is a Movement within the broad spectrum of Islam. According to Ahmadiyya perception it is a movement for spiritual revival. According to its followers, the Movement does not depart from Islam in the very least, nor does it add one iota to the doctrine and teachings of Islam. Yet, it is a fresh presentation of Islam and more particularly of the wisdom and the philosophy that underlies its teachings based upon and deriving entirely from the Holy Quran and pronouncements and practices of the Holy Prophet of Islam.

The Ahmadiyya community has its presence in 166 countries of the world, and everywhere, they are identified as Muslims. It is in Pakistan alone that they have been denied that right of self-identification. The Ahmadis are subject to specific restrictions under law. Discriminatory laws, including the blasphemy and anti-Ahmadi laws, have been used to imprison individuals for the peaceful practice of their faith and also help to create an atmosphere of religious intolerance that contributes to violence. Many of Pakistan's Islamic religious schools continue to provide ideological training and motivation to those who take part in violence targeting religious minorities in Pakistan and elsewhere.

The constitutional amendment of 1974 denuded the Ahmadiyya community of their religious identity. Nothing is left of the Ahmadiyya faith if they are not allowed to profess their faith in Islam, which they consider to be their faith. This constitutional amendment declared Ahmadis to be a non-Muslim minority because, according to the Government, they do not accept Mohammed as the last prophet of Islam. However, Ahmadis regard themselves as Muslims and observe Islamic practices. In May the Government announced the restoration of a voter registration form designed to single out Ahmadis. The section, which required Muslims to swear they believe in the "finality of Mohammed's prophethood," singled out members of the Ahmadis sect who are less categorical about this tenet of Islam. The Government and anti-Ahmadi religious groups have used this provision extensively to harass Ahmadis.

Barred by law from "posing" as Muslims, Ahmadis may not call their places of worship "mosques," worship in non-Ahmadi mosques or public prayer rooms (otherwise open to all Muslims), perform the Muslim call to prayer, use the traditional Islamic greeting in public, publicly quote from the Quran, or display the basic affirmation of the Muslim faith. These acts are punishable by imprisonment of up to three years. It is illegal for Ahmadis to preach in public, to seek converts, or to produce, publish, and disseminate their religious materials. These acts are also punishable by imprisonment of up to three years.

Ahmadis suffer from various restrictions of religious freedom and widespread societal discrimination, including violation of their places of worship, being barred from burial in Muslim graveyards, denial of freedom of religion, speech, and assembly, and restrictions on their press. Several Ahmadi mosques remained closed. Ahmadis have been prohibited from holding conferences or gatherings. Ahmadis are prohibited from taking part in the Hajj (the annual Muslim pilgrimage to Mecca). Some popular newspapers publish anti-Ahmadi "conspiracy" stories, which contribute to anti-Ahmadi sentiments in society.

Ahmadi individuals and institutions often are targets of religious intolerance, much of which is instigated by organized religious extremists. Ahmadi leaders charge that militant Sunni mullahs and their followers sometimes stage marches through the streets of Rabwah, a predominantly Ahmadi town and spiritual center in central Punjab. Backed by crowds of 100 to 200 persons, the mullahs purportedly denounce Ahmadis and their founder, a situation that sometimes leads to violence. The Ahmadis claim that police generally are present during these marches but do not intervene to prevent trouble. For example, in January Ghulam Mustafa Mohsin was killed in his home in District Toba Tek Sing, after receiving a series of death threats.

Ahmadis suffer from harassment and discrimination and have limited chances for advancement into management levels in government service. In the past few years Ahmadis claim that even the rumor that someone may be an Ahmadi or have Ahmadi relatives can stifle opportunities for employment or promotion. Ahmadi students in public schools are subject to abuse by their non-Ahmadi classmates, and the quality of teachers assigned to predominantly Ahmadi schools by the Government generally is poor. However, most Ahmadis are home-schooled or go to private Ahmadi-run schools. Young Ahmadis complain of difficulty in gaining admittance to good colleges and consequently having to go abroad for higher education. Certain sections of the Penal Code discriminate against Ahmadis, particularly the provision that forbids Ahmadis from "directly or indirectly" posing as Muslims. Armed with this vague wording, mullahs have brought charges against Ahmadis for using standard Muslim salutations and for naming their children Mohammed.

Sufi Sect

The term "Sufi" derives from three Arabic letters sa, wa and fa. There have been many opinions on the reason for its origin from sa wa fa. The most frequently cited in Western dictionnaries suggests the Arabic word "suf" meaning "wool" in the sense of "cloak", referring to the simple cloaks the original Sufis wore. Some initiates are given a specially designed, colored wool vest which is symbolic of the woolen robes of poverty worn by ancient dervishes, and signifies the loving commitment of the dervish to serve humanity. The Sufis use letters of words to express hidden meanings, and so the word could also be understood as "enlightenment". According to some the word is derived from safa which means purity. According to another view it is derived from the Arabic verb safwe which means "those who are selected"-a meaning quoted frequently in Sufi literature.

The problem with understanding Sufism, is thus illustrated by the diversity of possible derivations of the word itself. There are many different Sufi movements, and many dimensions of Sufism. Although frequently characterized as the mystical component of Islam, there are also "Folklorist" Sufis, and the "Traditional" Sufis.

Sufis are "movements", within, and in a few extreme cases outside of mainstream Islam. Sufis in general, are complex, and cover many different "stripes" of Islam. Sufism started out as a Shia movement, but over the past several hundred years, has almost disappeared from Shia Islam, and is now, mainly a Sunni movement. Hanbalis, Shafis, Malikis and Hanafis can all belong to different Sufi "tariqas" or "brotherhoods, as they are called. In fact, the Islamic brotherhood in Egypt, and Al Qaeda, are both Sufi based movements.

The Traditional Sufis, are actually people like the Wahhabiyyah and Al Qaeda, who eschew that type of thing as apostasy, and instead, insist that Sufism is all an Internal (internal to an individual) movement/spiritualism, that should never adopt external/folkloric elements, like the Dervishes, etc.

Sufi Brotherhoods: Sufism is a movement of organized brotherhoods, who are grouped around a spiritual leader or *sheik*. There are no Islamic states which regard themselves as officially Sufi. Sufism is characterized by the veneration of local saints and by brotherhoods that practice their own rituals. Sufis organize themselves into "orders" or groups, called Tariqas. These groups are headed by a leader called a Shaykh who is considered the most spiritual man with the most Taqwa among them.

These orders emerged in the Middle East in the twelfth century in connection with the development of Sufism, a mystical current reacting to the strongly legalistic orientation of orthodox Islam. The orders first came to Sudan in the sixteenth century and became significant in the eighteenth. Sufism seeks for its adherents a closer personal relationship with God through special spiritual disciplines. The exercises (dhikr) include reciting prayers and passages of the Quran and repeating the names, or attributes, of God while performing physical movements according to the formula established by the founder of the particular order. Singing and dancing may be introduced. The outcome of an exercise, which lasts much longer than the usual daily prayer, is often a state of ecstatic abandon.

A mystical or devotional way (sing., tariqa; pl., turuq) is the basis for the formation of particular orders, each of which is also called a tariqa. The specialists in religious law and learning initially looked askance at Sufism and the Sufi orders, but the leaders of Sufi orders in Sudan have won acceptance by acknowledging the significance of the sharia and not claiming that Sufism replaces it.

The principal turuq vary considerably in their practice and internal organization. Some orders are tightly organized in hierarchical fashion; others have allowed their local branches considerable autonomy. Some are restricted to that country; others are widespread in Africa or the Middle East. Several turuq, for all practical purposes independent, are offshoots of older orders and were established by men who altered in major or minor ways the tariqa of the orders to which they had formerly been attached.

The four main Sufi orders are the Chishtiyya, the Naqshbandiyya, the Qadiriyya [Quaddiri] and the Mujaddiyya. Other orders include the Mevlevi, Bektashi, Halveti, Jerrahi, Nimatalahi, Rufi, and Noori. The Mawlawis, the whirling dervishes, are famous for their dancing ritual, an organized variation of earlier practices which were confined to music and poetry.

Three Sufi orders are prominent: the Naqshbandiya founded in Bokhara, the Qadiriya founded in Baghdad, and the Cheshtiya located at Chesht-i-Sharif east of Herat.

Among the Naqshbani, Ahmad al Faruqi Kabuli, born north of Kabul, acquired renown for his teachings in India during the reign of the Moghul Emperor Akbar in the sixteenth century. Sometime during the nineteenth century members of this family moved back to Kabul where they established a madrassa and a khanaqah in Shor Bazar which became a center of religious and political influence.

The Cheshtiya order was founded by Mawdid al-Cheshti who was born in the twelfth century and later taught in India. The Cheshtiya brotherhood, concentrated in the Hari Rud valley around Obe, Karukh and Chehst-i-Sharif, is very strong locally and maintains madrasas with fine libraries. Traditionally the Cheshtiya have kept aloof from politics, although they were effectively active during the resistance within their own organizations and in their own areas.

Many Iraqi Sunni Kurds belong to Sufi orders, of which the Qadiri and Naqshbandi are the largest. Both orders have followers across the Middle East, Central, and South Asia. A Qadiri Sufi shrine in Baghdad attracts annual transnational pilgrimages. While Sufi Islam has broad acceptance in Iraqi society, Sufism has frequently been viewed by orthodox Sunni Muslim theologians with some degree of suspicion because of its strong mystical components. Shia Muslims tend to be hostile towards Sufism because they believe it is heretical. Sufi orders serve to both strengthen and divide Kurdish society. Kurds of the same order feel a common bond, regardless of tribe. There is, however, tension between rival orders. Jalal Talabani, the leader of the Patriotic Union of Kurdistan (PUK), follows the Qadiri order. The Massoud Barzani, leader of the Kurdish Democratic Party (KDP), and the influential Barzani family are Naqshbandi Sufis.

The Tijaniyah (Tijaniyya) Order, founded in Morocco by Ahmad at-Tijani in 1781, extended the borders of Islam toward Senegal and Nigeria, and their representatives founded large kingdoms in West Africa. The Tijaniyah Order is strongly associated with the Muslim Brotherhood, which began in Egypt in the late 1920s and later spread throughout the Arab world. Hasan al-Banna, who founded the Muslim Brotherhood in 1928 in Egypt, called for radical measures to bring about a return of Islamic government. The goal of the Muslim Brotherhood was the establishment of an Islamic state based on Shariah. It transcended the narrower sectarianism of the more traditional political parties. Moreover, the Brotherhood's superior organization made it a political force far stronger than its numbers might suggest. Many of the methods which made Sufism a succesfull occult underground helped the Muslim Brotherhood function effectively.

After World War II, the Muslim Brotherhood acquired a reputation as a radical group prepared to use violence to achieve its religious goals. The group was implicated in several assassinations, including the murder of one prime minister. The Brotherhood had contacts with the Free Officers in Egypt before the 1952 Revolution and supported most of their initial policies. The Brotherhood, however, soon came into conflict with Nasser. The government accused the Brotherhood of complicity in an alleged 1954 plot to assassinate the president and imprisoned many of the group's leaders. In the 1940s and early 1950s, the Muslim Brotherhood had appealed primarily to urban civil servants and white-and blue-collar workers. After the early 1970s, the Islamic revival attracted followers from a broad spectrum of social classes. In the 1970s, Anwar as Sadat amnestied the leaders and permitted them to resume some of their activities. But by that time, the Brotherhood was divided into at least three factions. The more militant faction was committed to a policy of political opposition to the government. A second faction advocated peaceful withdrawal from society and the creation, to the extent possible, of a separate, parallel society based upon Islamic values and law. The dominant moderate group advocated cooperation with the regime.

Bayat ("taking hand") is sanctioned by "Verily, those who give thee their allegiance, they give it but to Allah Himself" Quran 48:10. It is the initiation ceremony specific to many Sufi Orders. The Prophet Muhammad established this ceremony when he allowed his trusted companions to take his hand and commit themselves to vastly increase their love and loyalty to Allah and the Messenger: this is directly referred to in the Qur'an. Most Sufi Orders still practices some form of this sacred ceremony as a sacramental reenactment of the initiation offered by Prophet Muhammad to his companions. During the "taking hand" ceremony, the new dervish receives the blessings of the lineage, and a promise of spiritual protection along their life's journey.

Members of al-Qaeda take bayat [an oath of allegiance] to their sheik, Bin Laden, as an act of initiation. Al-Qaeda is a secret society without acclamation or public bayat to him. Bayat, the Arabic word for an oath of loyalty, means religious fealty or the submission more than personal allegiance. It means the link between the one making bayat, the shaykh and Prophet Muhammad (saws) is unbroken. This makes a Sufi connection possible during the solemn moment of taking bayat (pact) with the shaykh, who is the link in the chain-it connects to the chain and you become a recipient of the light of Muhammad (saws). Bayat is the ritual of accepting the shaykh as guide and coming under the protection of the lineage of the order. The number of actual members pledging bayat is unknown, but al-Qaida is said to have trained as many as 5000 militants in camps in Afghanistan and perhaps Indonesia.

Sufi Mysticism: Because of Islam's austere rational and intellectual qualities, many people have felt drawn toward the more emotional and personal ways of knowing God practiced by mystical Islam, or Sufism. Found in many parts of the Muslim world, Sufism endeavored to produce a personal experience of the divine through mystic and ascetic discipline.

Sufi adherents gathered into brotherhoods, and Sufi cults became extremely popular, particularly in rural areas. Sufi brotherhoods exercised great influence and ultimately played an important part in the religious revival that swept through North Africa during the eighteenth and nineteenth centuries.

Sufi followers understand Islam in a mystic way. Sufi doesn't differ from Islam in the theological point of view, to use a Western term. The Sufi interpretation is a different way to look at Islam. Ardor is the medium to get in touch with God. Sufi followers use a variety of techniques to move toward God, like singing, circular dances, etc.

The fundamental nature of Sufi is that the person who has chosen this path can reach an individual contact with God. Sufi followers have a teacher who acts as an intermediary between God and the person. The teacher gives the precepts according to which people should behave. Usually Sufi followers respect these rules. A *wali Allah* is a Sufi who has reached the end of the Journey to Allah.

Sufism has come to mean those who are interested in finding a way or practice toward inner awakening and enlightenment. This movement developed as a protest against corrupt rulers who did not embody Islam and against the legalism and formalism of worship which paid more attention to the form rather than content of the faith. Many of the sufis became ascetics, began to gather disciples around themselves and developed into religious orders, known as dervishers. Others forsook the orders and became mendicants, traveling around the country side, living off the charity of others. Many sufis were outstanding men of saintly stature. Not all sufis were accepted by the more conservative elements of Islam due to their unorthodox habits and beliefs. Sufi influence has grown over the centuries and today there are literally hundreds of mystic orders with millions of adherents. They are most prevalent in Egypt, Syria, Iraq, Turkey and Arabia.

Islam's mystical tradition emphasizes the direct knowledge, personal experience, and spiritual sovereignty of God, is at odds with the official Sunni establishment and its dedication to enforcing the legal and political sovereignty of Allah. Sufism, which makes use of paradigms and concepts derived from Greek, Hindu, and other non-Islamic sources, is generally less concerned with reinforcing and defending religious boundaries. The Sufi doctrine of "the unity of being," moreover, has inclined Sufis to emphasize interiority and the oneness of humanity, often at the expense of militant Islam's insistence on the conformity of the external world of state and society to Sharia.

To the Sufi, perhaps the greatest absurdity in life is the way in which people strive for things— such as knowledge — without the basic equipment for acquiring them. They have assumed that all they need is "two eyes and a mouth," as Nasrudin says. In Sufism, a person cannot learn until he is in a state in which he can perceive what he is learning, and what it means ... This is why Sufis do not speak about profound things to people who are not prepared to cultivate the power of learning— something which can only be taught by a teacher to someone who is sufficiently enlightened to say: "Teach me how to learn." There is a Sufi saying: "Ignorance is pride, and pride is ignorance. The man who says 'I don't have to be taught how to learn' is proud and ignorant."

Sufi Syncretism-Folklorist Sufis: Sufism follows the basic tenets of Islam but does not follow all of the orthodox practices of Sunni or Shi'ah Islam. In many Muslim areas, a mystical version of Hanafi Sunnism provided the means by which pagan and Christian practices were accommodated within Islam. Sufism centers on orders or brotherhoods that follow charismatic religious leaders.

There is a distinction between official and folk religion. Official religion stresses religious texts, the sharia (Islamic law), the literal interpretation of religious teachings, and worship at mosques. Folk religion, reflecting Arabic and Kurdish nomadic heritages, emphasizes sacred forces, the symbolic interpretation of texts, and worship at shrines. Folk religion continues to flourish in rural areas. Sufi orders, like folk religion, focus on the allegorical interpretation of texts and have historically been organized around a pious founder or saint.

The Folklorist Sufis, have been under attack, and discriminated against, for centuries. The Folklorists Sufis, have incorporated "un-Islamic" beliefs into their practices, such as celebrating the

Birthday of Mohammed, visiting the shrines of "Islamic saints", dancing during prayer (the whirling dervishes), etc.

The followers of Salafist Islam, such as Wahhabis, oppose all practices not sanctioned by the Koran. Wahabbism is named after Abdul Wahab, a religious thinker who two centuries earlier had fought the influence of Sufism in Sunni Islam. Wahhabis look at Sufi Islam as a deviation from the original Islamic rules. This view of Islam rejects "magical rituals," pilgrimages to saint shrines, or recitations of the Koran in cemeteries — all activities that had become commonplace among the Sufi orders. Wahhabis deny the role of the teacher, which for the Sufi is very important. They also deny the cult of the saints and pilgrimages to the saint shrines that are widespread among the followers of Sufi Islam. The inner link with God, typical for the Sufi followers, is denied by the Wahhabis. Wahhabis follow the old concept of jihad, meaning the holy war to convert the infidels. The Sufis have another interpretation of jihad. They see it not as a war against the infidels, but as a war that a Muslim has to fight against his own defects to try to reach perfection.

Islam was introduced into Chechnya over a period of centuries, gaining a number of converts by the 15th and 16th centuries but not taking firm root until well into the 18th and mid-19th centuries. The Chechens were converted to the Sunni branch of Islam, with particular emphasis on its mystic Sufi form. The Chechens practice the mystical version of Islam known as Sufism. This wins the Chechens little sympathy from the Sunni and Shia establishments in most Muslim states. The prevalent form of Islam as practiced in the north Caucasus is Nakshbandi Sufism, which is not favored in Saudi Arabia — which is a Wahhabi regime — and is not favored in Shia Iran, either. The Chechens, through a combination of Islam which is popular in their homeland, combined with economic issues, have dropped below the level of Islamic solidarity that one might expect from other Islamic countries. *Zikr*, which means "remembrance of God," is the central ritual practice of most Caucasian Sufi orders. This mystical ceremony, designed to lead participants into an ecstatic union with God, involves the group repetition of a special prayer.

Albania is the world center of the Bektashi school (a particularly liberal form of Shia Sufism), which moved from Turkey to Albania in 1925 after the revolution of Ataturk. Bektashis are concentrated mainly in central and southern regions of the country and claim that 45 percent of the country's Muslims belong to their school.

Alawiya is an underground movement that appeared in the third century on the Hijri calendar. The group followers do prayers different from that of Muslims and allow many practices prohibited under Islam. Turkish Alawiya Muslims' number vary from 5 to 25 million, mostly inhabited in impoverished central areas of the country. The situation of the Shadhiliya/'Alawiya Sufi order of Sanaa is a typical case of the problems facing Sufi orders in Yemen, where covert but commanding devotion to the saints and Sufi shaykhs of Yemen can still be found.

The vast majority of Muslims in Chad are adherents of a moderate branch of Sufism known locally as Tidjani, which originated in 1727 under Sheik Ahmat Tidjani in what is now Morocco and Algeria. Tidjani Islam, as practiced in the country, incorporates some local African religious elements. Of the total population, 54 percent are Muslim, approximately one-third are Christian, and the remainder practice traditional indigenous religions or no religion at all. Most northerners practice Islam and most southerners practice Christianity or a traditional indigenous religion.

Mouridism is one of four Sufi movements in Senegal, and one of the most distinctive aspects of contemporary Senegalese social life. Sheikh Amadou Bamba (1853-1927), the spiritual leader of four million Muslims in Senegal and thousands more around the globe, was a Sufi who resisted French colonial oppression through pacifism. The influential Senegalese Sufi movement called the Mouride Way is grounded in his teachings about the dignity and sanctity of work. The abundant images of Bamba convey the saint's blessings to his followers.

The Black Muslim Movement (BMM) is a largely black urban movement in the US that has many of the attributes of a syncretic Sufi movement. One driving force was a rejection of Christianity as the religion of the historically oppressing white race.

The Moorish Science Temple of America was organized in 1913 in Newark, New Jersey by Timothy Drew. His followers believed he had been ordained Prophet Noble Drew Ali by Allah. Although the truth is difficult to know, He is reported to have been born in North Carolina in 1886 the son of a Moroccan Muslim father and a Native American mother. It is said that at age sixteen Drew began his wanderings as a circus magician, which eventually took him to Egypt where he learned about Islam. Drew advocated a "return" to Islam, teaching was that blacks were of Moorish, and thus Muslim, origins. His followers refused to fight in World War I. In 1940 and FBI investigation was conducted to determine if the Moorish Science Temple of America was committing subversive activities by adhering to and spreading Japanese propaganda. The investigation failed to substantiate that members were pro-Japanese in their attitude. The Temple was investigated in 1953 for violation of the Selective Service Act of 1948 and sedition. In September of 1953, the Department of Justice, concluded that prosecution for violation of the Selective Service Act was not warranted.

The Nation of Islam was started by Wallace Fard, who built the first temple in Detroit. Fard was an immigrant from New Zealand, born to Pakistani parents. He had joined Noble Drew Ali's Moorish Science Temple in the late 1920s, and gradually made his way to the group's leadership when Drew died under obscure circumstances in 1929.

Elijah Muhammad (born Elijah Poole) established a second temple in Chicago and later supervised the creation of temples in most large cities with significant black populations. Fard disappeared in 1931, and Elijah Muhammad assumed the leadership of The Lost Found Nation of Islam-known in the news media as the "Black Muslims". They taught that blacks were racially superior to whites and that a racial war is inevitable. The charismatic Malcolm X was perhaps their most famous spokesperson; he played an important role in reversing the BMM's anti-white beliefs. In its earlier years, the movement deviated significantly from traditional Islamic beliefs (particularly over matters of racial tolerance and the status of the BMM leaders as prophets).

After the death of Elijah Muhammad in 1975, there were unsuccessful attempts to shed the idiosyncratic elements of belief by Wallace Muhammad, Elijah's seventh (legitimate) child, who formed the Muslim American Society. He shed the Nation's core beliefs that Elijah Muhammad was a divine messenger and that W. Fard Muhammad, was God incarnate. Mainstream Sunni Islam teaches that the prophet Muhammad was God's final messenger, and rejects the idea of human divinity. The Nation of Islam was opened to those of the white race and members were encouraged to participate in the civic and political life of the country. The Nation of Islam became the World Community of Islam in the west and then the American Muslim Mission.

Minister Louis Farrakhan, long regarded as a race-baiter and Jew-hater, heads spin-off movement from the old Nation of that continued espousing the movements idiosynratic views. Under the leadership of minister Louis Farrakhan a group of Blacks broke with the American Muslim Mission and returned to the original teaching and ideals of Elijah Muhammad and readopted the old name, Nation of Islam. Black Muslims are to live by a strict ethical code that excludes alcohol, drugs, tobacco, sports, movies, and cosmetics. Pork is not to be eaten. Orthodox Islam rejects Nation of Islam as heretical because its doctrines are contrary to the Islamic Quran.

Salafi Sect

Salafi is a term often used to describe fundamentalist islamic thought.

The teachings of the reformer Abd Al-Wahhab are more often referred to by adherents as *Salafi*, that is, "following the forefathers of Islam." This branch of Islam is often referred to as "Wahhabi," a term that many adherents to this tradition do not use. Members of this form of Islam call themselves *Muwahhidun* ("Unitarians", or "unifiers of Islamic practice"). They use the *Salafi Dawa* or *Ahlul Sunna wal Jama'a*. Wahhabism is a particular orientation within Salafism. Most puritanical groups in the Muslim world are Salafi in orientation, but not necessarily Wahhabi.

The Salafiyyah are a movement, and like the Sufis, can come from the Maliki, the Shafi, the Hanbali, or the Hanafi. But, that said, the Salafiyyah movement, is primarily confirmed to the Hanbali, and in particular the Wahhabiyyah, and their theological equivalents. The Salafiyyah movement to return Islam to it's purest roots (like the Islamic Amish!) has taken as reference points the teachings of Imam Ahmad bin Hanbal, Al Barbahaaree, or Al Laalikaaee, or Ash-Shaatibee, or Adh-Dhahabee, or Al Layth ibn Sad, or Abu Haneefah, and other scholars who adhered to the methodology of the salaf.

As-Salaf us-Salih (or briefly: the Salaf) refers to the first and best three generations of Muslims. They are the Companions (Sahabah) of the Prophet (s), their immediate followers (Tabiun), and the followers of the Tabi'in. The meaning in the Arabic language is "Those who precede, have gone before". It is a word used by the earliest scholars for "The first three generations of Muslims" and those who are upon their way in accordance with the Ahaadeeth of the Messenger Muhammad (sallallaahu alayhi wa sallam) which is reported in Saheeh al-Bukhaaree: The best of people/mankind is my generation, then those that follow them, then those that follow them.

The description "Salafi" is the name of a group of Muslims who try as hard as they can to imitate the Blessed Prophet in every aspect of life. Sometimes it may seem that the Salafis emphasize the laws and punishments of Islam so much that they make you feel there is no Islamic love and mercy. This is because they are sometimes very zealous in their views. A true Salafi values Tawhid, singling out Allah in all acts of worship: in supplication, in seeking aid, in seeking refuge in times of ease and hardship, in sacrifice, in making vows, in fearing and hoping and total reliance, and so on. A true Salafi actively seeks to remove shirk (polytheism) with all his capacity. They tend to be conservative on women's issues. The Salafi Da'wah is that of the Quran and the Sunnah. It is claimed to be the Religion of Islam-pure and free from any additions, deletions or alterations.

In the United States, Salafism has been equated by some with radicalism and terrorism in some newspaper articles, books, and public discourse. However, "Salafism" is not inherently synonymous with violence, terrorism, or radicalism. Many Salafis throughout the world are doctrinally rigid, but peaceful.

It is important to distinguish between the following groups, thought of (perhaps) as concentric circles:

1. "Jihadist Salafis"-such as the followers of al-Qaeda and like-minded local groups;
2. "Salafis"-those who believe that the imitation of the behavior of the Prophet's closest companions should be the basis of the social order;
3. "Islamists"-a still broader category, which includes anyone who thinks that the precepts of Islam-however interpreted-should be fundamental to the political and social order; and
4. "Discontented Muslims"-people who identify themselves as Muslims,and who are unhappy with their life prospects, with the justice of their societies and/or with the state of the wider world.

The Salafi jihadist movement has attracted rootless and or committed internationalist militants. They fight for the jihad, seeking to re-create the Muslim ummah and shariat to build an Islamic community. Simultaneously conservatives and radical, they form a global network that has attracted Muslims from around the world to fight jihad in Kashmir, Bosnia, Chechnya, Afghanistan, and the Philippines. The salafi-jihadist movement in Central Asia and the Caucuses is more localized — an expression of identity in areas such as Ferghana, villages in Daghestan, and upper Gharm valley. In Central Asia, the term "Wahabi" refers to fundamentalists who come from Pakistan or Afghanistan, but they are not necessarily a political movement. For example, Wahabis in Tajikistan do not recognize themselves as a political alignment. However, most Central Asian regimes use the term Wahabi more broadly to describe Islamic religious movements outside the states control.

❑❑❑

5

PHILOSOPHY OF SIKHISM

Over twenty million Sikhs follow a revealed, distinct, and unique religion born five centuries ago in the Punjab region of northern India. Between 1469 and 1708, ten Gurus preached a simple message of truth, devotion to God, and universal equality. Often mistaken as a combination of Hinduism and Islam, the Sikh religion can be characterized as a completely independent faith:

Sikhism rejects idolatry, the caste system, ritualism, and asceticism. It recognizes the equality between both genders and all religions, prohibits the intake of any intoxicants, and encourages an honest, truthful living. Sikhs have their own holy scripture, Guru Granth Sahib. Written, composed, and compiled by the Sikh Gurus themselves, the Guru Granth Sahib serves as the ultimate source of spiritual guidance for Sikhs. While the Sikhs hold their Gurus in high reverence, they are not to be worshipped; Sikhs may only worship God.

Members of the Sikh community are mainly concentrated in their homeland, Punjab; however, substantial Sikh populations exist throughout the rest of India and the world. Punjabi, a variant of the Hindi language with some Persian influence, is the spoken and written language of the Sikh people.

Male members of the Sikh religion use the name, Singh (lion), as their middle or last name, while females use the name, Kaur (princess). Sikhs tend to be industrious and pioneering; this accounts for their general success wherever they live and settle. The hard-working nature of the Sikhs is derived from their religion, which can be best characterized as a faith of unlimited optimism.

Basics of Sikhism

1. Sikhism is the youngest of the World religions. Its history dates back to 1469.
2. Its founder Guru Nanak Dev was born in a village called Talwandi, now known as Nankana Sahib in Pakistan, in 1469.
3. The Sikhs have ten Gurus. It is believed that they all had same soul though they had different bodies, and that it was Guru Nanak Dev's spirit which passed on into his nine successors.
4. The Sikhs call God as 'Waheguru', meaning that God is great. Their common salutation is Sat Siri Akal (God is supreme and is immortal).

"Waheguru Ji Ka Khalsa, Waheguru Ji Ki Fateh"

has a two fold meaning. It denotes a special relationship between God and those who dedicate their lives to His love and service. Also it is the expression of a devotee's faith in the ultimate triumph of Truth over Falsehood. This Sikh salutation means "Khalsa belongs to God and to God alone belongs the Victory".

5. Guru Granth Sahib is the holy book of the Sikhs. It is believed that the tenth Guru, Guru Gobind Singh bestowed upon the Granth the title of the Guru.
6. The Sikhs worship only one Almighty God in his abstract form. They are not allowed to worship any idols, images or photographs.
7. According to the Sikh belief, God is the eternal truth; he is beyond fear, enmity and death. He is unborn and is self illuminated. He himself is the creator, preserver and destroyer.
8. The Sikhs believe that all existence is controlled by one omnipotent, omnipresent and omniscient Lord called by different names: Ishwar, Jehovah, Allah and Waheguru.

Who is a Sikh: A Sikh is any person whose faith consists of belief in One God, the ten Sikh Gurus, the Guru Granth Sahib and other scriptures and teachings of the Sikh Gurus. Additionally, he or she must believe in the necessity and importance of 'Amrit', the Sikh baptism.

God and the Sikhs: According to the Sikh belief, God is all omnipotent, omnipresent and omniscient. The sun, moon/s, wind, fire, water, vegetation and all other things which exist are His witnesses. A Sikh must worship only the abstract form of God. The worship of images or any other object is strictly forbidden.

God is both the creator and the destroyer. He is beyond birth and death. He is both merciful and compassionate. He is beyond fear and enmity. He is self illuminated. He is the Master of all the treasures. All our possessions are a result of His grace. The Sikhs call God as Waheguru, meaning the most wonderful Master.

The belief of the Sikhs in Waheguru is similar to that of Judaism, Christianity and Islam i.e., God is the greatest power, He is supreme, He is the king of kings, He pervades everywhere, He knows the inner thoughts of everyone, He is the giver, He existed before the start of the time, He existed when the time was started, He exists now and He will exist forever.

Relationship with God: The Sikh Gurus called Waheguru as Master and themselves as his servants. In some hymns they called Him as Father, Mother, Friend and Brother as well1. Like Jesus Christ, Guru Gobind Singh, the tenth Guru of the Sikhs, in one of his hymns, called himself as God's son2.

Universality: Sikhism does not believe in asceticism, celibacy or living alone at mountains or in caves or in forests in the search of Truth and God. It also rejects the orders of monasteries. For a Sikh the true life is the life of a householder. Living in a family environment and by serving the community both Truth and God can be realised. Thus it rejects the order of monks (Buddhism and Jainism) and nuns (Christianity).

The Sikh teachings are based on the principles of Fatherhood of God and brotherhood of humankind.

Sikhism rejects the concept of chosen people (as in Judaism) and caste system (as in Hinduism); it also rejects the concept of entering 'Nirvana' without the blessings of God (as in Buddhism and Jainism).

In a Sikh temple people of all the faiths are welcome. The Sikh holy book, Guru Granth Sahib also has in it the hymns composed by both Hindu and Muslim saints of various denominations.

The first five baptised Sikhs, called the beloved ones, were also from both lower and upper Hindu castes. They were the first Khalsa, the pure ones:

Bhai Daya Singh, aged 30, a Khatri from Lahore (Punjab)

Bhai Dharam Singh, aged 33, a Jat from Delhi

Bhai Mohkam Singh, aged 36, a washerman from Dwarka (Gujrat)

Bhai Sahib Singh, aged 37, a barber from Bidar (Karnatak)

Bhai Himmat Singh, aged 39, a water carrier from Puri (Orissa)

Guru Gobind Singh, the tenth prophet of the Sikhs, urged his followers to drop caste symbols after their names and instead write a common surname: Singh, meaning lion, for men and Kaur, meaning princess for women.

The Khalsa

A baptised Sikh is called Khalsa, who must observe and follow strict code of conduct:

1. worship only one Almighty God,
2. recite five prescribed banis (hymns) everyday
3. learn Punjabi language and read Guru Granth Sahib,
4. wear and observe the significance of five Ks: kesh -uncut hair, kanga-a small comb, kara-a stainless steel bracelet, kirpan - a sword and kuchcha - an underwear.
5. live a truthful life and treat all humans as equal

He must not:

1. cut body hair
2. eat kosher meat,

3. smoke, take drugs or intoxicants,
4. have faith in black magic, superstitions, charms and rituals

Rules, Concepts and Commandments: A Sikh lives by the rules made for him by the ten Gurus. The fundamental rules, concepts and the commandments are as follows:

Worship of God

1. Worship only God and no one else.
2. Make worship and prayer a part of your daily life.
3. Do not make images of God, worship him in his abstract form.

Fatherhood of God and Brotherhood of man

1. Believe that everyone is the child of God.
2. Believe that all human-beings are equal.
3. Do not discriminate on the basis of colour, religion, cast and creed.

Rituals and Superstitions

1. Do not believe in any rituals and superstitions.
2. Do not believe in the worship of images, tombs and graves.

Social and Family Guidelines

1. Do not take alcohol, tobacco and drugs.
2. Do not eat halal meat.
3. Do not eat any food which inflames the passions.
4. Be true to your parents and children.
5. Do not steal.
6. Do not gamble.
7. Love and respect your guests.

The belief

1. Believe in the oneness of the ten Gurus.
2. Believe in the sovereignty of Guru Granth Sahib
3. Believe in the spiritual authority of the five takhats.

The Nitnem (Daily prayers): The banis which must be recited everyday are:

The bani	***The author***	***Where is it recorded***
Japji Sahib	Guru Nanak Dev	pages 1-8 Guru Granth Sahib
Jap Sahib	Guru Gobind Singh	pages 1-10 Dasam Granth
Swayas	Guru Gobind Singh	pages 13-15Dasam Granth
Rehras	Guru Nanak	pages 8-12 Guru Granth Sahib
	Guru Amardas	
	Guru Amardas	

	Guru Arjan	
Kirtan Sohila	Guru Nanak	pages 12-13 Guru Granth Sahib
	Guru Ramdas	
	Guru Arjan	

The Sikh prayers and their timings: The prayers are classified as: Individual and Collective prayers. The Individual prayers are Morning prayers: Jap ji, Jap Sahib and Sudha Swayas Evening prayer: Rehras Sahib Night time prayer: Kirtan Sohila

The Congregational prayer is: Morning prayer: Asa di var(composed by Guru Nanak Dev)

In addition to the above prayers a Sikh normally reads the following: At the end of every service or prayer: Anand Sahib (composed by Guru Amardas) At any special occasion or otherwise: Sukhmani Sahib (composed by Guru Arjan) At the time of marriage: Lavan (composed by Guru Ramdas) At the time of cremation: Kirtan Sohila

The main sources of Sikh material to understand the religion in depth are:

1. Guru Granth Sahib, the Sikh holy book
2. Dasm Granth, the holy book of the Tenth Guru Gobind Singh
3. Janam Sakhis, the life stories of the Sikh Gurus
4. Hukamnama, the letter written by the Sikh Gurus
5. Varan Bhai Gurdas, the hymns composed by Bhai Gurdas I & II, contemporaries of Guru Arjan and Guru Gobind Singh Ji respectively.

The Sikh Festivals: The Sikhs celebrate both religious and social festivals. The religious festivals are however called Gurbpurbs

The important Sikh festival calendar is as follows:

Month	***Gurpurb***	***Other festivals***
Jan-Feb	Birthday Guru Harrai	Maghi, Basant
Feb-March	xxxxxxxxx	Hola Mohalla
March-April	Birthday Guru Angad	Baisakhi
April-May	Birthday Guru Arjan	
	Birthday Guru Tegh Bahadur	
May-June	Birthday Guru Amardas	
	Martyrdom day Guru Arjan	
June-July	Birthday Guru Hargobind	
July-August	Birthday Guru Harkrishen	
August-September	xxxxxxxxxxx	Rakhsha Bandan
September-October	Birthday Guru Ramdas	
	Installation Guru Granth Sahib	
October-November	Birthday Guru Nanak	Diwali
November-December	Martyrdom of Guru Tegh Bahadur	
December-January	Birthday Guru Gobind Singh	Lohri

The Sikh Shrine:Gurudwara:

1. A Sikh shrine is called a Gurdwara, meaning the doorway to the house of God.

2. The first Gurdwara was built by Guru Nanak Dev at Kartarpur.
3. The Sikh Gurdwaras must have a religious flag, called Nishan Sahib in the front of the Gurdwara.
4. Guru Granth is placed on the far side centre of the hall.
5. There should be no photographs of the Gurus or others in the hall where Guru Granth Sahib is installed.
6. Gurdwaras normally have two halls/rooms. The main hall where Guru Granth Sahib is placed and the second hall where the community kitchen is served.
7. All entrants must take off their shoes, wash their feet and cover their heads before entering the main hall.
8. All Sikh services end with the distribution of parshad (sweet pudding) and langar (dinner/lunch).

Five historical Sikh gurdwaras have been declared as the Sikh Takhats (thrones). These gurdwaras are vested with the power and authority to regulate the religious life of the Sikh nation. The head priests of these shrines constitute a Sikh parliament and they are empowered with executive, legislative and judicial powers regarding the Sikh religious issues. All Sikhs are under the authority of the five takhats. The takhats are as follows:

The name of the Shrine

The names of the Guru its relates to:

Takhat Akal Takhat: Founded by Guru Hargobind

Takhat Patna Sahib: The birth place of Guru Gobind Singh

Takhat Hazoor Sahib: The place where Guru Gobind Singh breathed his last.

Takhat Kesgarh Sahib: The birth place of the Khalsa

Takhat Damdama Sahib: The place where Guru Gobind Singh composed the second version of Guru Granth Sahib.

All the five takhats relate to the two Gurus who were Saint-soldiers.

The ten Gurus

Sri Guru Nanak Dev Ji

Sri Guru Angad Dev Ji

Guru Amar Das Ji

Sri Guru Ram Das Sahib Ji

Sri Guru Arjan Dev Ji

Sri Guru HarGobind Sahib Ji

Sri Guru Har Rai Sahib Ji

Sri Guru HarKishan Sahib ji

Sri Guru Tegh Bhadur Sahib Ji

Guru Gobind Singh Ji

Skhism and the Sikh Gurus

Guru Nanak Dev Ji (1469-1539): The Sikhs had ten prophets called the Gurus. The time-period of the history of the Gurus ranged from 1469 A.D , when Guru Nanak, the founder of the Sikhism was born, to 1708 A.D, when the last prophet, Guru Gobind Singh left this mortal world for his heavenly abode (239 years).*Guru Nanak,* the founder of the Sikh religion was born in a Hindu family of Kshatriya caste. He revolted against that order when he was only 13 years old. God spoke to him when he was 38. He was taken to God's abode where God gave him two Commandments known as 'Moolmantar' and 'Sloak'.

Moolmantar: *There is only one God He is the Truth (permanent being) He is the Creator, He is devoid of fear He is devoid of enmity He is beyond death He is not born He is self-illuminated He is the master of all the gifts.*

God existed before the start of the time God existed when the time started. God exists now and, God will always exist. Guru Nanak was appointed as God's latest prophet and was asked to spread the name of God and the rules of both divinity and morality.Guru Nanak travelled as far as Tibet in the north, Sri Lanka in the south, Mecca in the west and Dhaka in the east to deliver God's message. He was welcomed wherever he went. He met both kings and robbers, gave them the message of God and reformed them. He is the only prophet in the world who did not meet any violent opposition and was not harmed by the enemies. In fact he had no enemies. (compare him with: Moses and the Pharaos; Jesus and the Jewish clergy and the Romans; Ram and Ravan; Krishen and Kans; Mohammed and the Meccan pagans).Guru Nanak was revered by both the Hindus and the Muslims. He was received with respect and folded hands by Babar, the Muslim Emperor of India and Shivnabh, the Hindu King of Sri Lanka; he was honoured by the clergy of both the Hindus and the Muslims. Guru Nanak was a family man, was married and had two sons. While living with his father he looked after the family fields and the cattle; staying with his sister, Babe Nanki, he worked as a store keeper with the local ruler; and for the last 17 years of his life, he tilled his own fields at Kartarpur, a town founded by him. There are 41 Sikh shrines founded in his memory.For 14 years, from 1507-1510 he travelled around the then known world and spread the message of God. In history, he is the most travelled of all the known prophets. (Jesus travelled in the central plains of Palestine; Mohammed travlled from Mecca to Medina and back to Mecca; Moses travelled from Egypt to outskirts of Palestine; Ram travelled from Ayodhaya to Sri Lanka; Krishna travelled from Mathura to Dwarka).Guru Nanak died at the age of 70. His 974 hymns are recorded in the Sikh holy book.

The Prophets

2nd Guru - 10th Guru

Guru Angad (1504-1552): was the second Guru of the Sikhs. He was a disciple of Guru Nanak and was chosen as his successor after being put to a great many tests. He became Guru at the age of 35 and his pontificate lasted for 13 years. He rationalised the Panjabi language and gave to it a new grammar. He also encouraged his followers to look after their health. He gave them instructions to have a balanced diet and regular exercises. He built many wrestling arenas and encouraged his followers to participate in wrestling competitions Like Guru Nanak, he founded a new town and named it Khadur. There are 2 Gudwaras built in his memory, and there are in Guru Granth Sahib, 65 hymns composed by him. He died at the age of 48.

Guru Amardas (1479 - 1574): Became the third Guru at the age of 73. For twelve years he personally served Guru Angad. He walked daily for 5 miles to fetch water for the Guru's bath. He was chosen from amongst many by Guru Angad as his successor. His pontificate lasted for 17 years. He inculcated amongst his followers, the spirit of Service to humankind and to God Like both Guru Nanak and Guru Angad he was a very simple man. There are 4 Gurdwaras related to his memory and there are, in Guru Granth Sahib, 907 hymns composed by him. He died at the age of 90.

Guru Ramdas (1534-1581): Became Guru when he was 40. His pontificate lasted for only 7 years. He was a son-in-law of Guru Amardas. He re-organised the Sikh Church and founded the city of Amritsar.He died at the age of 47. There are 3 Gurdwaras built in his memory and there are 679 of his hymns recorded in Guru Granth Sahib.

Guru Arjan (1563-1606): became Guru at the young age of 18. He was the youngest son of Guru Ramdas, He built the Golden Temple and compiled the Sikh holy book. He also founded the city of Taran Taran. He is the first martyr of the Sikh history. He died at the age of 43, There are 12 Gurdwaras built in his memory and there are 2,218 of his hymns recorded in Guru Granth Sahib.

Guru Hargobind (1595-1644): Became Guru at the age of 11. He was the only son of Guru Arjan. His pontificate was longest amongst all the Gurus, it lasted for 38 years. He was the first Guru to fight with the Mughals against their injustice and tyranny. . He wore two swords, symbolising Miri and Piri, royalty and saintliness. He organised early morning Sikh choirs. He founded the city of Kiratpur3. There are 16 Gudwaras built in his memory. He travelled upto Kashmir in the north to spread the message of the house of Nanak. He died at the age of 49. He did not write any hymns.

Guru Harrai (1630-1661): was a grandson of Guru Hargobind. He became Guru at the age of 14 and remained Guru for 17 years. He built many clinics for both sick human beings and animals/ birds. He was expert in Aryuvedic medicine. Most of the time he lived in Nahan and preached the divine message over there. There are 3 Gurdwaras dedicated to his memory. He died at the age of . He did not write any hymns.

Guru Harkrishen (1656 - 1664): was the youngest son of Guru Harrai. He became Guru at the tender age of 5 and died at the age of 8. Thus his pontificate lasted for only 3 years. He took over the sufferings of the people of Delhi over himself and saved them from effects of smallpox epidemic (compare this sacrifice with the Christian saying, "Jesus died for our sins"). He instructed his followers to build schools for religious education. There are 4 Gurdwaras related to him. He did not write any hymns. Most of the modern Sikh Schools are named after him.

Guru Tegh Bahadur (1621-1675): was a grand uncle of Guru Harkrishan. He became Guru at the age of 43 and remained Guru until the age of 54. He travelled towards east of India up to Dhaka to spread the message of the house of Nanak. He offered himself for martyrdom for saving the Hindu religion. He gave his life but saved the annihilation of Hindu religion by the then Mughal Emperor, Aurangzeb. He was beheaded in Delhi at a place known as 'Chandni Chowk' He founded the city of Anandpur. There are 16 Gurdwaras built in his memory and there are 115 hymns recorded under his name in Guru Granth Sahib.

Guru Gobind Singh (1666 - 1708): became Guru at the age of 9. He was the only son of Guru Tegh Bahadur. Like his grand-father Guru Hargobind, he also had to resort to sword to protect the young Sikh nation from an onslaught of the Mughals. He initiated a new baptism and called it 'Amrit'

He created the order of Khalsa (Saint-soldiers) and prescribed the compulsion of wearing the 5 Ks. He wrote hymns which were later collected by one of his followers, Bhai Mani Singh, at the orders of his widow Mata Sundri. He declared the mission of Guru Nanak completed. He passed on the spiritual authority of the Sikhs to the Sikh holy book, and called it Guru Granth Sahib. He passed on the temporal authority of the Sikh to the Khalsa. He died at the age of 42. His hymns are preserved in the Granth called Dasam Granth. He was the last prophet (Guru) of the Sikhs.

The Theory of one Sprit: The Sikhs believe that all the ten Gurus had the same spirit. This is one of the fundamental beliefs of the Sikhs. Guru Gobind Singh had recorded in one of his hymns that though after Nanak came Angad and then Amardas and then Ramdas, Arjan, Hargobind, Harrai, Harkrishen and Tegh Bahadur, but they all had the same spirit. They looked different for they had different bodies but their spirit, the inner self, was the same. (Compare it with Christian belief of Holy Spirit).

1. Guru Granth Sahib - Guru Arjan Dev: "Tu mera pita tu hai mera mata, tu mera bandhu tu mera bharata".
2. Dasam Granth - Bachitar Natak: "Tu nae apna sut mujae niwaja".
3. *It is at this place that the Sikhs immerse the ashes of their dead. The Gurdwara is called 'Patal Ṛuri'.*

Political Philosophy of the Sikh Gurus

The Sikhs and their polity have attracted good deal of attention as a result of recent developments in Punjab and some of the basic formulations are being questioned. The author, who has based his work on original sources such as the *Adi Granth*, *Dasam Granth*, *Varan Bhai Gurdas* and other contemporary sources, has developed answers to some of the problems relating to Sikh polity by quoting the authority of the Gurus themselves.

The major focus of the present work is on the political philosophy of the Sikh Gurus as conceived by Guru Nanak and developed by the successive Gurus. The author asserts that Guru Nanak clearly understood the political milieu and reacted to the politics of oppression whether it was from the ruling elite or vested priestly interests. The Guru had clearly laid the foundation of a viable political alternative by giving a distinct political ideology and creating a model society, in which there were neither the suppressors nor the oppressed. In the present context it will be relevant to point out that while the Gurus clearly condemned political oppression they also emphasised the use of moral force as a major weapon to fight political opponents. Paradoxical as it may sound, Guru Gobind Singh suggested a code of ethics even in the conduct of wars

'Religion' is derived from the Latin religare, which means to tie back. But in its institutionalised form, religion refers to an institution with a recognised body of communicants who gather together regularly for worship and accept a set of doctrines offering some means of relating the individual to what is taken to be the ultimate nature of reality.Sikhism is also a religion, which aims at reunion of the individual with the Ultimate Reality. But in this process of reunion Sikhism does not negate the world, which, though, impermanent, yet holds some meaning. According to Sikhism living in this world in a rightful manner is a part of the path leading to reunion with the Ultimate Reality. To achieve the goal the Sikh Gurus did not advocate seclusion from the society. Thus the Sikh view of life is active participation in various spheres of activities of life in a rightful manner. One comes across many evils of society but Sikhism advises not to close one's eyes to these but to attempt boldly to face. and eradicate worldly evils.

The Fifth Guru Arjan Dev Writes: O righteous man, speak up: Why are you silent so?For, you have seen with your eyes the treacherous ways of Maya ! Contrary to the prevalent practice of denouncing the world in order to realise the Truth or to become a true Yogi, the Sikh Gurus believed that the world was worth living and it was possible to live pure among the impurities of life.

Guru Nanak says:Yoga is not abiding at the tombs or the crematoriums, or in entering into a pseudo-trance.Yoga consists not in roaming the world, nor in bathing at the pilgrim-stations.Only in remaining Detached in the midst of attachments, one attains to the (True) state of Yoga.

Guru Nanak and his all the nine successors were householders and advocated that it was possible to attain spiritual bliss while enjoying worldly comforts provided one does not for-get the Lord. The fourth Guru, Ramdas, makes it clear when he says:Blessed are the eats, wears and riches of those ho are imbued with the Lord's Name.Blessed are their homes, temples, palaces and rest houses, dedicated to the Devotees and mendicants of God.Blessed are their horses, saddles and horse-cloths, which are yoked to the Service of the Saints.Pure are all their deeds who utter ever the Lord's True Name. Rather than advocating and supporting the traditional living of a yogi the Gurus emphasised Raj-Yoga. In this context a dialogue between the Sixth Guru, Hargobind, and a con-temporary Maratha Saint Ramdas, the preceptor of Shivaji, is worth quoting here:Once the Guru was staying in Kashmir. There came a Sadhu to see him. He was a Deccani, Ramdas by name.

Riding a horse, the Guru bad returned from a hunt. Many Sikhs were there with him. He asked him, I had heard you occupied the gaddi of Guru Nanak. Guru Nanak was a tyagi Sadhu-a saint who had renounced the world. You are wearing arms and keeping an army and horses. You have yourself called Sacha Padshah-A true King. What sort of a Sadhu are you? Guru Hargobind said,Internally a hermit, and externally a prince; arms mean protection for the poor and destruction for the tyrant. Baba Nanak had not renounced the world but had renoun-ced Maya, the self and ego. Ramdas was pleased (to hear this) and said, This appealeth to my mind.(Sakhi 39, Pothi Panjah Sakhian)So the Sikh Gurus did not discard any positive aspect of life but forcefully denounced the evils of life. The political situation of their times was no exception to it. They denoun-ced evils of the contemporary politics and taught us the clean and the pure one.That is why the Sikh Gurus responded to the social as well as political situation of their times. They did not turn a deaf ear to these happenings of their times. They boldly pointed out the weaknesses of society as well as political set-up. Their response finds expression in the scriptures in direct or latent form. Though, primarily, Sikh Gurus were religious thinkers and did not give us any systematic political treatise as such unlike those of Plato and others yet we can infer their politi-cal ideology from their references to the prevalent political system and metaphorical usage of the contemporary political phraseology. So it is unfair to contend that the Sikh Gurus did not give any political thought or the Sikh scriptures con-tains no distinct political ideology, simply on the pretext that the term 'politics' and 'political' have not been used as such.To infer political theory of the Sikh Gurus we have to study the milieu in which they lived and the situations they responded to.Guru Nanak, the founder, was a contemporary of five monarchs-Bahlul Lodi (1469-89), Sikandar Lodi (1489-1517) and Ibrahim Lodi (1517-1526) and Mughal rulers-Babur (1526-1530) and Humayun (1530-1539). But Guru Nanak does not mention the name of any of these rulers except Babur while attacking their unrighteous policies. Whenever he points out or criticises some policy he attributes it to the general term 'ruler'.

The most important event that took place during the days of Guru Nanak was the invasions of Babur and subsequent establishment of Mughal rule in India. In Guru Nanak's reaction to the political events of his time Babur's invasion of India figures prominently. His compositions pointing to this event are known as Babar-Vani. 'In 1520 AD Babur crossed river Chenab and occupied Sialkot without much resistance. Then he marched on Sayyidpur (Eminabad) which was taken by assault and put to the sword3.Guru Nanak reacted against the atrocities committed by the armies of Babur. He condemned excesses committed by his soldiers. Guru Nanak says while addressing Lalo:Bringing a bridal procession of sin (Babur) hath hasted from Kabul and demandeth wealth as his bride, O Lalo.Modesty and Religion have vanished; falsehood marcheth in the van, O Lalo.The occupation of the Qazis and the Brahmans is gone; the devil readeth the marriage service, O Lalo. Musalman women read the Quran, and in suffering call upon God, O Lalo.Hindu women whether of high or low caste, meet the same fate as they, O Lalo

They sing the paean of murder, O Nanak, and smear them-selves with the saffron of blood.Nanak singeth the praises of the Lord in the city of corpses, and uttereth this commonplace. In the Babar Vani Guru Nanak gives a vivid description of the havoc brought by the armies of invaders led by Babur and describes how the soldiers dishonoured the innocent women. Further while the Guru made a scathing attack on Babur and his army of sinners but in keeping with the higher spiritual values he believed that everything happened accord-ing to Lord's will.The Guru was equally opposed to the idea of either the invaders imposing their culture on the subjugated populace or the people copying the culture of the ruling elite. With the advent of Muslim rule the Hindu culture started acquiring the Islamic tinge because of the pressures of the ruling elite. To quote Guru Nanak:Now that the turn of Sheikhs has come, the Primal Lard is called AllahAnd the (Hindu) gods and temples have been taxed: such is the current wayThe ablution pot, the prayer, the prayer-mat, the call to prayer, have all assumed the Muslim garbeven God is now robed in blue (like the Muslims did)And men have changed their tongue and the Muslim wayof greetings prevails. It becomes clear that Guru Nanak did not like the imposition of elite culture on the subjects and equally the acceptance of alien culture or language under pressure. This he indicates clearly in Asa ki Var when he says:In the time of Atharva Veda, or the Kali-age, Allah became the name of God.The Hindus wear the (Islamic dress) blues and follow the suits of the Turks or Pathans.

Another comment on the situation of his time is:The kings are like whores, the courtiers like dogs:For, they awaken those that asleep in God's Peace.The king's servants tear (the docile subjects) with their nails.And, like curs, lick up all the blood that they spill. This clearly indicates the type of rulers and administrative machinery of his time. Kabir also refers to the low ebb of morality of the administrative officials of his time. Though he uses the terms as metaphors yet the latent meaning is clearly discernible when he says:The nine Assessors and the ten Judges leave no one (subjects) in Peace;For, they measure not the Farms honestly, and want their palms to be greased.

Guru Nanak makes another general statement about the poli-tical situation of his times:Kings are butchers, cruelty their knife,Sense of duty has taken wings and vanished.Falsity prevails like the darkness of darkest night,The moon of truth is visible nowhere.I have tired myself in Search, but,In the darkness of the Age, No path (of righteousness) is visible. Guru Nanak makes many indirect references to the con-temporary political situation. This may be inferred from the metaphorical use of the prevalent political terminology. It has been remarked recently that Guru Nanak had a first hand knowledge of the condition of the people under the Lodis and of the behaviour of the ruling class towards the subject people.4 The number of passages often quoted by writers in illustration of Guru Nanak's political concerns is not more than ten. But there are other verses, which have a bearing on the subject and the number of such verses is by no means small. Altogether, they suggest Guru Nanak's familiarity with contemporary politics and bureaucratic set up. This may be inferred from the occurrence, in these verses, of such phrases as sultan, patshah, shah-i-alam, takht, taj, hukm, amr, pathani-aml, wazir, diwan, naib, lashkar, umara, khan, malik, shiqdar, qazi, chaudhari, muqaddam, raiyat, for instance. Also, there are references to the court and palaces, royal canopy, elephants, armour, cavalry, trumpets, treasury, coins, mint, salary (wajh), taxes and even to revenue-free land.5Bhai Gurdas is another important contemporary source.

He mentions the political milieu of Guru Nanak's times. He tells us that at the times of Guru Nanak the kings were un-righteous and did not look after their subjects rather harassed them. For Bhai Gurdas it was just like the fence, which is meant to protect the fields, eating the crop. The subjects were also blind or lacking proper knowledge and wisdom. This expression of the situation finds confirmation in the Bani of Guru Nanak:Avarice and Sin are the king and the minister, and False-hood is their chief:And Lust is the adviser, and so they all confabulate.Their subjects too are blind, without wisdom; and like the dead, they dance to their tune. Bhai Gurdas also mentions the religious discrimination during the Muslim rule. He tells that the Hindu temples were razed to the ground and Muslim mosques were built at those places and all over there was injustice-Var, 1:24. On the whole, Guru Nanak saw in his contemplation that the entire world was in agony-Var, 1:24. The second Guru, Angad Dev had similar opinion. He comments:The beggar is called the king; the fool is termed wise;The blind man is called the seer; yea, so are the words bandied about.The mischievous ones and those addicted to falsehood secure the first place in life.This is what the Guru teaches that in the Kali-age men dis-criminate but indiscriminately. This was his general statement about the Kali-age and not that particular short period. The following hymn of the third Guru, Amardas, aptly describes the agony of the contemporary world:The world is on fire: O God, Save it Thou in Thy Mercy, Through whichever Door it comes unto Thee, Save it that wise, pray.

Similarly the fifth Guru, Arjan Dev, refers to the rulers indulged in lustful pleasures and pastimes:He (the king) rules in ten directionsAnd with numerous females indulges in pleasure and merry-making. From the martyrdom of the fifth Guru, Arjan Dev, the situation changed. The Gurus themselves were actively invol-ved in the contemporary political situation. This is evident from the Sixth Guru wearing two swords and thereby clearly indicating the combination of religion and politics but with a vital difference that politics was to be subservient to religion. This also shows that the Guru was introducing a new type of politics based on ethics.There was no confrontation between the fifth Guru, Arjan Dev and the emperor Jehangir as such. Actually the emperor tried to placate the Muslim orthodoxy which led to his order-ing persecution and ultimately death of Guru Arjan Dev. But a careful perusal of the later period of Jehangir's reign shows that he was wearing the cloak of fanaticism as a political expediency in order to gain support of the Muslim orthodoxy. But later as a result of the reversal of Emperor's policy cordial relations between Jehangir and Guru Hargobind were established.Guru Hargobind maintained a regular army, of which he himself was the supreme commander. He had his own source of income through the system of Daswand-one tenth of the income to be donated by every Sikh. He acted as Chief Justice for the Sikhs.

He used to hold courts at Akal Takhat. His followers called him Sacha Patshah-the true king. With this almost 'a state within the state' came into existence, which can never be tolerated by any government and is treated as a rebellion in the legal sense.After the demise of Jehangir, his son Shahjehan ascended the throne. Relations between the new ruler and Guru Har-gobind developed strains after some time. There was open confrontation also. Four battles were fought. According to the Sikh chronicles the Guru fought all the battles decisively and was victorious. However Mohsin Fani, a contemporary Persian writer differs regarding the first battle at least. But Sikh chroniclers' claim of success of the Guru in the battles to an extent cannot be discounted6. Macauliffe stands by the view of Sikh chroniclers.From the detailed account of the battles fought by the Guru we can easily infer his fighting tactics and war strategy and also the code of ethics to be followed during the battle, i.e. the laws of war. Detailed accounts of battles are available from various sources such as Gurbilas Patshahi 6 written by Kavi Sohan in about 1718 AD, the famous Suraj Prakash Granth written by Kavi Santokh Singh, Panth Prakash of Giani Gian Singh etc.

After Guru Hargobind's battles, the next important historical event, which took place was the martyrdom of Guru Tegh Bahadur, the ninth Guru. His son, Guru Gobind Singh, the tenth and last Sikh Guru took to sword. He himself has written about his mission on this earth in his autobiography, the Bachitra Natak:The divine Guru sent me for religion's sakeOn this account I have come into the world'Extend the faith everywhere,Seize and destroy the evil and the sinful'.Understand this, ye holy men, in your souls.I assumed birth for the purpose of spreading the faith, saving the saints,And extirpating all tyrants.

During the time of Guru Gobind Singh, Aurangzeb was the ruler who was very fanatic. He was following policy of persecution of non-Muslims. His was the age of utmost hatred, religious intolerance, bigotry and discrimination. All this was against the principles of justice and humanity. The Guru faced the challenge militarily. Firstly he fought some battles with the Hindu hill-chiefs, which were puppets of the central ruler. Then he fought battles with the royal armies. The Guru gives a vivid description of his battles in his auto-biography, the Bachitra Natak, and the Zafarnama-his epistle of victory written to Aurangzeb. These two are the most dependable sources to understand Guru's philosophy relating to war and politics. He was of the firm opinion that moral principles must be followed even during war. One more thing we can understand from his philosophy is that his enemy was not any individual but the element of the unrighteousness. This is borne out from the incident of Bhai Kanahiya as told in Sikh chronicles. Some of the Guru's soldiers complained that while serving water Bhai Kanahiya made no distinction between the soldiers of the army of the Guru and those of the enemy. When asked to explain his conduct Kanahiya replied that he saw the Guru's image in every being. The Guru was so impressed by the altruistic spirit of Kanahiya's thought that he gave him a small box of ointments saying that the latter could apply these also to the wounds of the soldiers in both the camps while serving water. This incident can be called a precursor to the modern concept of Red Cross.

Rights of the Ruler: We have no authentic information as to how the State was born. Through inferences and generalization regarding the dim past on the basis of the slender evidence at our disposal, we can deduce that state existed in some form or the other wherever human beings lived together in large numbers. Various theories regarding its origin have been propounded from time to time such as 'The Divine Origin Theory', 'The Social Contract Theory', and 'The Force Theory'. 'The Patriarchal Theory', and 'The Matriarchal Theory'.The oldest theory is the Divine Origin Theory.

According to it the State is established and governed by God Himself or through His special representatives. The chief exponents of this theory in early times were the Jews. In the Old Testament there are many references supporting this fact.

The Greeks and Romans regarded the State as only indirectly divine. This very theory later on made the rulers dictators. Man had to suffer much at their hands. However, all these theories are specula-tive in nature.Almost the first type of State, which emerged from primitive conditions, was the Imperial State. The plateaus of Mexico and Peru produced the earliest form of the State. Then arose many more vast empires such as the Sumerian, the Assyrian, the Persian, the Egyptian, the Chinese etc. For the most part these were merely tax collecting and recruit-raising agencies. As soon as the ruling dynasty became weak, the powerful rivals establi-shed the authority. No individual liberty or true political progress was possible. The second important stage was reached in Greece in the form of city-states. The Sparta city-state alone remained con-servative and maintained a steady tradition of unbroken conti-nuity in its government. In the other city-states the normal political evolution was from monarchy to aristocracy, from aristocracy to tyranny and from tyranny to democracy. It was in Greece where Plato, the great political philosopher, took birth in 427 BC. He was the first to have prescribed some qualifications for the rulers of those city-states. He did not think everyone to be fit to rule. For Plato the individual mind is divided into three elements-Reason, Spirit and Appetite. The lowest is 'Appetite' and the highest is 'Reason'.

Reason is the rational element with its main function 'to think and to know'. For him the ruler must be from this category of mind. Plato was the first person to dream of the Philosopher King. According to Plato the foremost task of such a king was to deliver justice. He must be over and above the selfish interests. He must have the capacity to think reasonably and take right decisions. For this he must be properly educated.In ancient India also such qualifications and duties of the ruler existed in some form or the other. Several terms like Rajadharma, Rajyasastra, Dandaniti, Nitisastra etc. indicate this. The terms like Rajadharma used by Manu, 'Duties of the Kings' and Rajyasastra-'Science of the State' require no expla-nation. Monarchy was the normal form of government. The term Dandaniti is also self-explanatory.

These terms have occurred in the epic Mahabharta. Kautilya goes to the extent of declaring Danda as the real king, the real leader and the real protector-Arthasastra VII 17. The rules about the functions and duties of the king and welfare of the state were, therefore, naturally, called Dandaniti. In the Arthasastra of Kautilya it is written that the king must regard his own happiness as indis-solubly connected with that of his subjects-I.19. Just as an expectant mother sacrifices her own desires and pleasures, lest they should be harmful to the child to be born, the king must sacrifice his own conveniences, inclinations and pleasures in order to be of the maximum help and service to his people-Agni Purana, 222.8. The body of the king is not meant for enjoyment and pleasures; he has to put up with great troubles and worries while carrying out the royal duty of protecting the subjects and fulfilling the dharma-Markandya Purana, 130-33. Happiness, it was believed, depended upon virtue and piety, and these could prosper only if the king himself set a proper example and standard. Under a good king, prosperity will prevail-Rg Veda, V.10.From time to time in almost all the parts of the world various scholars and spiritual leaders put forward many valu-able theories so that the State can become truly a welfare state. But very often the rulers have misused the state power. The rulers in history have often forgotten all such teach-ings of our great scholars and leaders.While giving the ideas on Politics the Sikh Gurus had welfare state in their mind. They did not commend any parti-cular form of the state unlike other political philosophers.

They were more concerned with the qualifications and duties of the ruler. They took ruler as a general term for the premier of a state. The were not concerned with the prevailing forms such as monarchy, aristocracy or democracy etc. At the most what the Sikh Gurus talked of is the Ideocracy which is called Halemi Raj by the fifth Guru. Keeping the Ideocracy in their mind the Gurus prescribed certain qualifications and duties of the rulers.In Sikhism the main goal of the human being is to be one with the Supreme Being. The fifth Guru says:Thou hast obtained from God a human's bodyNow alone is the time to Attain to thy Lord. A.G. p. 12Each and every action of man should be such that takes him more and more near to this Goal. He should not do anything, which may lead him astray. The principal means to achieve this Goal is Nam-Simran and good actions. 'The Fifth Guru says in Sukhmani:Of all religions, this one is the superbThat one Meditates on the Lord's Name and does what is pure. A.G. p. 266So the ruler, in Sikhism, should be one who creates such con-ditions for his subjects as well as for himself so that this goal is achieved easily. Not only that he should not become an obstacle in the path but also he should be helpful by creating a good and peaceful atmosphere in his kingdom so that his subjects find it easier to achieve their Goal.Only such a person who has become one with God, who has conquered all weaknesses can be able to lead his subjects to the Goal. Only such a person is fit to be the ruler and deserves respect from the subjects because he, automatically, will be the just ruler. Guru Nanak himself prescribes such qualifications:Only he should sit on the throne who is worthy of itAnd who has realised the Guru's Word and Silenced the Five desires. Such a king gets full respect everywhere.

Nanak again writes: To such throne everyone pays his obeisance, night and day.This is the true glory that one earns, by attuning to the Guru's Word.

The third Guru also says: That king alone must sit on the throne, who is worthy of it, Yea, he, who Realises the (God's) Truth, he (alone) is the worthy king. In Adi Granth, Janak has been used as a simile to an ideal ruler, Janak mean Jnani-one who has the true knowledge, as Bhatt Kal has explained in the Adi Granth:He alone is Janaka, who hitches the chariot (of his mind)to the state of Ever blessedness.And gathers the Contentment, and fills the Empty Vessel (of the heart).Unutterable is the Story of the 'Eternal Abode' and he alone is Blest with it, whom God Blesses,O Blessed Guru Ram Das! such a kingship, like Janaka's, becomes only Thee.

According to Mahankosh (the Sikh encyclopaedia) edited by Kahan Singh Nabha, Janak was the king of Mithila. He was son of 'Mith', who in turn was son of 'Nim'. From this Janak, this name has been given to the descendent genealogy. The name of father-in-law of Lord Rama was Sirdhwaj who was the twentieth descendent of Raja Janak. According to Valmik Raja Janak was a great king. Raja Sirdhwaj, the twenty-first Janak, was a great saint-king. It is this Janak referred to in the Adi Granth. The fourth Guru says about Janak:Janak too was attuned to the Lord's Name, Blest by the Guru. Both these qualities of Janak are a rare combination. It is because of these two qualities (of being saint and king) he is used as a model for an ideal king. Bhatt Kalsahar writes in the Adi Granth while addressing to the fourth Guru:Through Thee, the benign rule of Janak has again come to the world, the age of truth has dawned. The fourth Guru writes about Janak:And Janak, seated on his kingly throne, anointed his fore-head with the Dust of the Feet of nine seers.

Keeping this idea of an ideal ruler in mind, some qualifica-tions and duties of the ruler can be deduced from Gurbani. The foremost quality of a ruler is that he/she should be a realised soul. Guru Nanak writes about it:Only he should sit on the throne, who is worthy of itAnd who has realised the Guru's word and silenced the five desires. Further:They should sit on the throne who contemplate the Guru's Word; And find the Essence of God. O, such is the True Glory of those who are associated with the Name of God. The third Guru writes:That king alone must sit on the throne, who is worthy of it Yea, he, who Realises the (God's) Truth, he (alone) is the worthy king.

According to the Sikh Gurus, only such a person who has realised the Truth is qualified to be a ruler. He must have conquered the Five evils-lust, anger, greed, attachment and ego. Only such a ruler can become selfless. Only a realised soul can truly understand the meaning of 'fatherhood of God and brotherhood of man'. For this he has to renounce worldly passions. The king should first subdue himself, and then seek to subdue his foes. The conquest of these, viz., the aggregate of five is regarded as the conquest of self. The king who has succeeded in subduing his senses is competent to resist his foes.-The Mahabharta (Anusasna Parva). Only the person who has realised the Soul can be truly just.

In Sikhism, great stress is laid on Raj-yoga. Only a true Yogi can become a true ruler. Here Yogi means the person who has realised God through Nam Simran and good actions. In the Adi Granth the poet (Bhatt) Kalsahar describes the three personalities-Lord Bawan, Lord Rama and Lord Krishna-as Raja-Yogis. After that he gives this title to Guru Nanak. To quote him:In the Satyuga too, you enjoyed the state of Rajyoga, when you deceived Bali, becoming a dwarf, whose form pleased you.And in the Treta age too, when you were called Rama of the Raghu clan,And in the Duapar age too as Krishna, when you Emanci-pated Kansa.And blest Ugrasena with kingdom and thy Devotees with the state of fearlessness, In the Kali age you are called Nanak, and Angad and Amardas.Yea, eternal and moveless is thy rule, O Guru, for such was the command of the Primeval Lord. For the fourth Guru he writes that the third Guru has passed the throne of Raja Yoga to Guru Ramdas. To quote him:Throne of Raj-Yoga, he passed on the Guru Ramdas.

So both the terms 'Raj-Yoga' and 'Janak-Raj' are synony- mous in the Adi Granth. And poet Kalsahar on page 1389 in the Adi Granth also explains these in the same meaning. Both the terms indicate that the ruler must have attain-ed union with God. The person who has not conquered the weaknesses of common man is not at all fit to sit on the throne. The person who has conquered his weaknesses can never be defeated in any sphere. The ruler should consider himself as a servant to the Master and not master himself. He should take it for granted that he has to answer for his weaknesses to his Master. Guru Nanak writes:From his mind he forsakes covetousness, avarice and evil, In his fortress he proclaims the victory of his Monarch and returns not vanquished ever.He who calls himself the Lord's servant and replies to Him in defiance.He loses his wages and he is not seated on the throne. The ruler must be full of virtues.

He should transcend greed, illusion and sin. He should practise chastity, charity and self-control. He must be manned by Truth. He should always be contented. Guru Nanak indicates all these qualities when he takes his body as fortress and mind as a king.

In the strong fortress of the body with beauteous doors, abides the mind king with his special assistants. Whosoever is engrossed in falsehood and avarice, he obtains not an abode in the Lord-

Home.Through greed and sin one regrets, If the mortal seeks the Lord's protection, then in this body village of king come and abide the powerful truth, con-tentment, chastity, charity and self-control.Nanak, through the Guru's word one easily meets with Lord, the Life of the world and honour. At one place Bhagat Kabir hints at some other qualities which the ruler should possess while fighting the battle with the evil. He has put duality and the three qualities of Maya (illusion), woe and weal, worldly love, evil understanding, covetousness in the category of evil forces and the Divine love, Nam Simran (meditation), poise, truth, contentment, company of saints and grace of Lord as the forces of Godliness or Truth. Kabir has asked his king (mind) to use the forces of Godliness against the forces of evil and he will surely be victorious.

The ruler should follow the path of Truth and Compassion. Namdev said this when he was tortured by the ruler of his time and when the latter came to know about his saintli-ness, begged for his pardon. To quote Namdev:And the test there of is thatHereafter you (king) will tread the path of Truth and Compassion. Kabir asks the ruler to inculcate wisdom or Jnan and detach-ment or Vairag and he should stop his outgoing mind through meditation. He can inculcate such virtues only through Nam-Simran. Only such a person deserves to be a ruler. To quote Kabir:He alone is a Sultan, the king, who aims with the two arrows (of wisdom and Detachment), And stops the outgoings of his mind,And gathers the hosts (of virtue) abiding in the (mind's) Sky, yea, the Tenth Door, 0, that Sultan alone is canopied (by God). The ruler must consider himself as the servant to his subjects because God dwells in the subjects as well as in the ruler.

Doing all his duties he must not forget the Name of the Lord. While enjoying the facilities, which he gets due to his status, it is tendency of the man to forget His Name. In such a case all these enjoyments will take him to serpent's birth. He will have to pay for his indulgence, as the fifth Guru says:Dominion over other, vast estates and overlordship and enjoyments of myriad kinds, And beauteous gardens and the proud command that runs, And indulgence in various kinds of colourful shows (all these are vain); For, if one remembers not the Lord in the heart, one gets the life of a serpent. He must not at all indulge in enjoying the riches, which he gets. It is of no use to amass riches and live in luxury. If by the use of force one becomes the ruler and issues decrees and while indulging in all these he forgets His Name, all these things and riches are worthless. He must be careful that while enjoying all these gifts of God he does not forget the Name of the Lord. Guru Nanak elaborates this in the very first hymn of Siri Raga in the Adi Granth.

He says: If my palace were raised of jewels and inlaid with rubies, And pleasantly plastered with musk and saffron, and sandal paste, Would then I lose myself and forget the Lord's Name? Even if I were a king, a gatherer of armies, and my seat were on a throne.And I commanded people about and about,And that would be vain, If I forget thee, O my Loved Lord!

Duties of a Ruler Justice: According to Sikhism every one has to realise God sooner or later. One can only realise Him by adopting His qualities. As He is just God so the man has also to be-come just, especially the man who is ruling over others. He has to become as just as God does, only then he can find place near Him. So dispensing justice becomes the foremost duty of a ruler. If a ruler wants to purify himself he can't do so with water. For a ruler it is justice, which makes him pure as Guru Nanak says:For the monarch through justice and for the learned bydwelling on Truth (that the mind is cleansed).

The ruler should not become a thorn in the eyes of his subjects.Even his Nam-Simran is acceptable only when he delivers justice to the subjects. Like this he can become a true ruler. The third Guru says:Enjoy thou a griefless kingdom by practising Truth, through the Guru's grace, While sitting on the throne of truth administer justice and this will unite thou with the True one. Such a ruler who delivers full justice to his people needs not depend upon others for help. He becomes self-dependent.

The Fifth Guru Says: In whose court justice is ever administered. He is self-dependent and leans on none.

Only the government of such a just ruler is stable and he is respected everywhere and lives in history. Says Guru Nanak:The sovereignty of the truthful king is known in many ages to come, Only he, whosoever, obeys such lord becomes a noble in his court. But if any ruler becomes corrupt in delivering justice to his subjects, he loses his right to be a ruler. Guru Nanak even goes to the extent that if the subjects obey the orders of such corrupt ruler, who has failed to deliver justice or who takes bribe for delivering justice, it is the fault more of the subjects than that of the ruler. It is just like the habit of a dog who obeys the just or unjust orders of his master only for a piece of bread. The Guru says:If the king administers justice only when his palm is greased, Only in the name of God, none obeys. Nanak says such men are men only in shape and name, In deeds they are dogs, waiting for command at his (ruler's) door.

Guru Nanak vehemently condemned corruption in the judicial system of his time. He equally condemned the corruption in this department in the name of God or scriptures, which was in practice in those days. The priests of Islam-the Kazis- used to take bribe and do injustice. If any person objected they used to quote the verses from the Holy Scriptures and misinterpreted those to suit their own interests. Guru Nanak writes:Becoming a judge the Kazi sits to administer justice.He tells the rosary and mutters God's Name;Taking bribe, he does injustice.If someone asks him, then he quotes and reads out some aphorism.

Such a situation it becomes the duty of the ruler to ensure that there is no corruption in his department of judiciary. He himself should rise above such corrupt practices, deliver justice to his people and punish the guilty.In Western school Plato was the first to talk of justice in the state. In the Republic he tells that society is to be con-cerned as a system of services in which every member both gives and receives. Justice is the bond, which holds a. society together, a harmonious union of individuals, each of whom has found his life work in accordance with his natural fitness and his training.For St. Augustine State without justice is simply robbery writ large. Or in his words, Justice being taken away, then, what are kingdoms but great robberies.

And he cites the story of Alexander the Great and the pirate who had been captured by that, Monarch. When the ruler asked the robber how he could have so much presumption as to dominate the sea and prey upon men the pirate replied What do you yourself mean by seizing the whole earth, not merely the sea? But because I do it with petty ship, I am called a robber, whilst you who do it with a great fleet are called emperor.3In the Mahabharata Bhisma tells Yudhisthira about the latter's duty to deliver justice to his subjects, while telling him his overall duties He says, If the king fails to administer justice, he can neither have heaven nor fame. A king should, without doubt, look upon his subjects as his own children. In determining their disputes, however, he should not show com-passion.

For hearing the complaints and answers of disputants in judicial suits he should always appoint persons possessed of wisdom and knowledge of the affairs of the world, for the state really rests upon a proper administration of justice- Anusasna Parva.In the Vedic literature justice is one of the fundamental aims of the state. The king or the head of the state was to be like god Varuna, the upholder of the law and order- the dhritavrata; he was to punish the wicked and help the virtuous.

Religion was to be promoted, morality was to be encouraged and education was to be patronised- Chhandogya Upanisad, V. II. 5 Unhappiness, misery and pestilence among the subjects were attributed to failure in duty Pon the part of the king. The popular notion on this subject is well illustrated by the Jatakas. The ox of a ploughman is struck accidentally by his plough-share; for this the king is to blame; a milkman is killed by a vicious cow, the blame is assigned to the same quarter; even a frog does not spare the king when it is bitten by hungry crows.—Jatakas, Happiness, it was believed, depended upon virtue and piety and these could prosper only if the king set a proper example and standard. -Rigveda, V. 10.

Duty to Protect the Subjects: In the Mahabharata Bhisma is said to have told king Yudhisthira, Regarding those that are desirous of kingdom, there is no other eternal duty more obligatory than the protection of subjects. The protection the king grants to his subjects upholds the world. 'Manu the son of Prachetas sang these two verses respecting the duties of king. Listen to them with attention. 'These six persons should be avoided like a leaky boat on the sea, viz., a preceptor that does not speak, a priest that has not studied the scriptures, a king that does not grant protection, a wife that utters what is disagreeable, a cow-herd that likes to rove the village and a barber that is desirous of going to the wood'. Protection of the subjects, O Yudhisthira, is the very cheese of kingly duties. A divine Kavi Usanas of austere penance, the thousand eyed Indra, the Manu, the son of Prachetas, the divine Bharadwaja and the sage Gaurasivas, all devoted to Brahmanand, have composed Treatises on the duties of kings.

All of them praise the duty to protection in respect of kings.- Anusasna Parva.Yajnavalkya Smriti supports the above view. Narada regards the taxation as the king's pay for the protection of his people. No one ever makes a payment, says Apararka, without expecting a return; the taxes therefore, are paid only as a return for the protection expected from the king. In the western school of thought Bertrand Russell suggests the idea of a modified state. The state, according to him, should perform the essential functions of preserving internal law and order and affording protection against foreign aggres-sion and some other minor functions. He writes, I think that its (state's) powers ought to be very strictly limited to what is absolutely necessary.

There is no way of limiting its powers except by means of groups which are zealous of their privileges and determined to preserve their autonomy even if this should involve resistance to laws decreed by the state, when these laws interfere in the internal affairs of a group in ways not warranted by the public interest.And a good community does not spring from the glory of the state, but from the unfettered development of the individuals.4In Sikhism also it is the holy duty of the ruler to protect his subjects. It is his duty to keep the opposite elements to-gether without harming each other. The fifth Guru illustrates with the examples of water and earth, fire and wood, which are kept together and due to the Ruler's control these do not harm each other. To quote him:He has stringed the whole world with breath and has kept the fire along with the wood.He has kept the water and the earth together and no one bears enmity with (or harms) each other.

Similarly the fourth Guru illustrates: The earth and water abide in one place and the fire is locked in wood.The sheep and the lion, the Lord has kept in one place.O man! contemplate thou on God and shake thy doubt and dread. Guru Nanak says that under His rule no enemy or suffering can ever harm us. To quote him:The Rule is eternal it goes neverYea, ever lasting is Thy Rule it stays forever. .No adversary, no pain, can touch him, nor şin contaminates. As the servant of the Master has not to be afraid of anyone, similarly the subjects should not be afraid of any one. It is the ruler who has to ensure the security of his subjects.

The Fifth Guru says: To whom can Thy servant now pay obeisance When Thou, the king, Preservest his Honour. In an ideal state described by the fifth Guru, none can harm others because of the protection provided to everyone by the ruler. Everyone lives in perfect peace and enjoys life. All over there is courtesy, modesty and humbleness. He says: The Merciful Master has now given the command.No one now domineers and annoys another. All abide in peace and this now has become a benign regime. The tenth Guru says that if the ruler protects his subjects then the latter need not worry about their protection, just as if anyone gets the shelter of a lion, one does not then need to be afraid of goats etc. Guru Gobind Singh writes in the Zafarnama, the epistle of victory, addressed to Aurangzeb:And when the lion brave and bold Doth shelter one from the nasty foe, The timid goat, buffalo, dapple dear can never near his sojourn dare go.

Duty to Protect the Subjects from Exploitation: It is a common tendency among men to exploit others at any oppor-tune time. It is the rich who always exploit the poor. It is the duty of the ruler to protect his people from such exploi-tation. Guru Nanak called the rulers of his times, who exploited their subjects, as blood sucking kings and ferocious tigers who lick up the blood of the poor subjects and his courtiers dogs. When they will be called for settlement of their accounts, such rulers will be dishonoured for it. In a very scathing attack he writes:The kings are like whores; the courtiers like dogs;For they awaken those that sleep in God's peace.The king's servants tear (the docile subjects) with their nails,And, like curs, lick up all the blood that they spill.But, hark, where men are to be judged (at the Lord's Court)Their noses will be chopped off, for, God will trust them not. Amassing wealth by exploiting the subjects is bitterly con-demned by the fifth Guru also. He says that God will give such wealth away to someone else one day. Such wealth takes the man astray.

Becoming, a king, one has dominion over all, And through oppression, one gathers richesGathers he the bagful, bit by bit, But God (in His Justice) snatches it away and gives it to another. Sikhism condemns exploitation of the subjects through heavy taxation. Kabir condemns such rulers who realise more tax than is due. He says that at least he will not pay such un-due tax. He says that the officials, who come to collect the tax, measure the land unlawfully and try to extract even more. But when he reports the matter to the higher authorities and checks his accounts then there stands nothing due. So he condemns the realisation as well as payment of undue taxes. To quote him:In the fortress, the five are like the king's officials, who make ever a fresh demand for Revenue.

But I am the Tenant of no one, then why am I asked to pay? O Saints, the Tax-gatherers torture me each day and so I raise my hands to God and lo, He saves me.The nine Assessors and the ten Judges leave no one in Peace,For they measure not the Farms honestly, and want their palms to be greased. It behoves the ruler not to appoint such officials who rea-lise the amount of tax, which is not due to the concerned person. Ravidas, through metaphors, points to the Ideal State in his verses.

In such a State, be says, there is no pain or worry because there is no such tax, there is no awe, none commits error etc. He writes: 'Griefless' is the name of my state Where abide not either pain or care No anguish there of tax on goods, Neither fear, nor error, nor dread, nor decline. Guru Nanak says that if any clothe is defiled with blood then how a person who sucks the blood of the poor through exploitation can be without stain? He cannot be truthful. To quote him:If blood sticks to the clothes, the clothes become impure, Will the minds of those be pure who suck the blood of human beings? It is the duty of the ruler to see whether one's due is being paid to the same person or anyone else who has not put any labour is taking away the prize, which often happens. The person who labours with all his sweat and blood is not given the price and the 'owner' takes away the entire prize without put-ting any kind of effort.

It is just like that a poor peasant who sows the seeds, puts his labour for the crop to come up, guards it for the whole time but it is reaped by the owner of the land and that poor fellow cannot do anything except to watch help-lessly. The fifth Guru puts it like this: As is the watchman over the farm of another,And the farm remains with the master,while the watchman passes away.The watchman suffers hard to protect the farm,But for this, he goes away (in the end) with empty hands. The notion of the kingship as a trust was there in ancient India. The king was particularly enjoined to note that the treasury was not his private or personal property. In the Mahabharta it is written, If a king misappropriates public funds and diverts them to his personal use, he will be guilty of sin and be condemned to hell.

To Fulfill the Basic Needs of the Subjects: It is the duty of the ruler to fulfill the basic needs such as livelihood, of his people. Just as the King God first of all manages the liveli-hood and then he creates the creature, similarly the ruler should take the duty to provide his subjects the things of basic necessity as his foremost task. Only such a ruler can expect any respect from the public. The fifth Guru says:In every home rings the praise of this King, in every home are men Zealous of Him.He first Provides Succour andthereafter Createth He the creatures. The subjects of such a ruler are always satiated because they are fed to the full and they always enjoy life. The people need not worry about their livelihood and other basic needs. They are always happy and delightful because of such ameni-ties.

The fifth Guru addresses to the King of kings: Content is he and ever at Peaceof whom Thou art the King and Master.

According to Guru Nanak only such a person is fit to be a king or ruler who takes proper care of his subjects. It is his duty to ensure that each and every person in his dominion gets the things of bare necessities of day-to-day. Only such a government can rule successfully and is a true government. To quote Guru Nanak:Only His is the true government who nourishes the people day and night. Only such a ruler is free from any stain or stigma in whose dominion everyone is happy and gay and has no scarcity of anything of the basic necessity.

Guru Nanak commends such a ruler: O king !Thou art free from Flaw for your people are blissful. In Vedic India also the State was to secure not only moral but also material wellbeing of its citizens. The kingdom of King Parikshit, idealised in the Atharvaveda , flowed with milk and honey. All round welfare of the public was clearly regarded as the chief aim of the state during the Vedic and Upanisadic ages, i.e., down to 600 BC.In the Mahabharta Bhisma teaches Yudhisthira that the ruler must feed his subjects. He should ensure that none has slept hungry any day. To quote him,

He should feed those that have not been fed and enquire after those that have been fed.-Anusasna Parva.

To Uphold Fundamental Rights of the Citizens: It is the moral duty of the ruler to guarantee personal liberty and other fundamental rights. He is to protect the honour of his people because death is better than a life of dis-honour. The foremost freedom should be that of conscience. It was for this freedom that the ninth Guru, Tegh Bahadur, laid down his life in 1675. Aurangzeb, the then ruler, did not provide his subjects with this freedom. He was trying to impose his own religion, culture and thoughts upon his subjects.Guru Nanak in his times vociferously condemned not only such rulers who were trying to impose their culture and faith on their subjects but also condemned such people who adopt-ed the culture and faith of the ruling class under pressure. He condemned the wearing of blue (Islamic) clothes by the Hindus who had also started reading Islamic scriptures.

In Asa ki Var he writes: Who (Hindu) Decked Himself in (the Muslim) blue andassumed the attributes of a Turk and a Pathan.They seek approval of the Muslim rulers by wearing blueWithin, they worship (their idols); (outside) they read Quran and observe the codes of the Turks.Shed Thy Deceit and Hypocrisy, O Brahmin. He even condemned the adoption of the language of the other people under pressure. When the Hindus adopted the Islamic language and script in the place of Sanskrit and Devnagri, he criticised the Hindus for this.In every house all the persons say 'Mian' (Islamic lang-uage), Your language has become different, O men (Hindus). He bitterly criticised such kings who imposed their faith and culture on the subjects. He attacked their policy of repression of others' faith when the Muslim rulers levied tax on the Hindu temples and their religious rites and practices, even though the Guru himself did not believe in those beliefs, rites and practices. What he wanted to speak against was the forcible suppression of the feelings of anyone. While condem-ning such tax he says:Ah! Tax is levied on the temples of gods.

Such a practice has come into vogue. In the western school of thought Hegel regards freedom as the very essence of man. It is his distinctive quality. To remove freedom is to renounce one's humanity.While discussing the rights Herbert Spencer condemned the barbarous government, which interfere with the operation of the law of the energy of faculty. Firstly the government can efface itself for the sake of the law of equal freedom by admitting the rights of the citizens to ignore the state. State intervention, by and large, affords greater scope for the love of power, the selfishness, the injustice and untruthfulness. State intervention constitutes a proposal to improve life by breaking through the fundamental conditions to life.

Men are bound together by a common natural reason; they are at the same time strongly egoistic and always in danger of breaching peace. While on the whole and on most occasions they respect one another's natural rights, their periodic breaches of peace essentially lead them to contract for entry into the state. In his Second Treatise on Civil Government Locke clearly says that the state was contracted because the enjoyment of the freedom and security of the state of nature is very uncertain and constantly exposed to the invasion of others-Second treatise VI. Therefore, the function of the state is to redress the injuries that may happen to any member of the commonwealth-Second treatise, Harold J. Laski, the great English Political thinker of early 20th century is of the opinion, A state is known by the rights that it maintains. The state briefly does not create but recog-nizes rights. Rights are those conditions of social life without which no man can seek in general to be himself at his best.5 For him without rights there can't be any liberty. He does not want to reduce the individual to the position of a sheer member of a herd.

He describes three aspects of liberty. Firstly private liberty- .the opportunity to exercise freedom of choice in those areas of life where the results of any effort mainly affects me in that isolation by which, at least ultima-tely, I am always surrounded. Example of this liberty is, of course, religion also. Private liberty will go to stray dogs if law fails to protect an individual in the matters of access to public places on grounds of religion, caste, creed or sex or if there is discrimination in the matters of employment. Second is political liberty and the third one is economic liberty which means that the citizens should be free from the constant fear of employment and insufficiency. Bertrand Russell was very emphatic in minimising the state's powers to interfere in human rights. In his words, I think that its (state's) powers ought to be very strictly limited to what is absolutely necessary. There is no way of limiting its powers except by means of groups, which are zealous of their privileges and determined to preserve their autonomy even if this should involve resistance to laws decreed by the state, but the community, the world-wide community of all human beings, present and future, that we ought to serve. And a good community does not spring from the glory of the state, but from the unfettered development of individuals

Proper Distribution of Wealth: It is the duty of the ruler to work for the elimination of the improper difference between 'have-s' and 'have-nots'. Especially when in the modern times there is a wide gap between the two, it is the duty of the ruler to lessen this gap and bring both closer to each other. Communists call it equal distribution of wealth and that is what gave birth to communism. According to Communist philosophy modes of production should not be in the hands of capitalist class but in the hands of working class. With this the equal distribution of wealth is possible. FW Coker writes about the ideas of Karl Marx, the doctrine that wage-workers in fields, factories, and mines are the real pro-ducers of wealth, most of which is unjustly taken away from them by employers, traders, and other non-producers; and they proposed collectivist schemes-a state monopoly of the servi-ces of marketing and banking, a currency system based on time unit of labour, voluntary co-operative societies-in-order either to ensure an exchange of goods on the basis of the quantities of labour employed in producing them or to secure generally an equitable distribution of wealth among those who create it. Wayper writes The class which exercises ownership of the means of production will dominate the rest when, for instance, the most important factor in the forces of production is agricultural, land owners will be the ruling class. The dominant class alone has freedom, and to preserve this must act the part of oppressors. They, therefore, create an executive and repressive instruments by the use of which they hope to maintain their position and which is called state. 9Egalitarian concept in Sikh society is so deep rooted that this has become a part of their daily prayer, Raj Karega Khalsa Aaki Rahe Na Koye.

10 Generally, the term Aaki is misinterpreted. It is often used for the rebellious. Actually both Aaka and Aaki are Arabic words. The word Aaka is quite commonly used for Malak or owner and Aaki means Malkiat or the ownership. So the correct meaning of this couplet should be 'the Pure shall rule and none other (who is not Pure) will have the ownership'. It is somewhat like the nationalisation of the property. The persons, who are not pure at heart and mind, have tendency to hoard things to exploit others. Such persons should not get chance to accumulate the wealth. Only persons who are pure at heart and mind will never exploit anyone nor accumulate the wealth. They will always seek the welfare of all. Only such persons are fit to rule and such ruler should have the

ownership so that the hoarding and exploitation can be put to an end. Almost every devout Sikh recites this couplet twice a day as a part of his daily prayers.There can't be proper distribution of wealth where the rulers arc greedy and lustful. Guru Nanak condemns such rulers who do not maintain proper circulation of wealth and hoard it themselves. To quote

Gathers the world's riches, thou the egoistic king ! The fifth Guru says that such wealth, which is always collected through untruthful means, never helps.

He condemns the accumulation of wealth by rulers:Becoming a king, one has dominion over all.And through oppression, one gathers riches.Gathers he the bagful, bit by bit,But God, (in His Justice) snatches it away and gives it to others.

Kabir also criticises such rulers who accumulate wealth:The kings wasted their lives gathering riches and burying their treasures under the earth.my soul such a world is a blind deep pit,on all sides the death's net is thrown. If the ruler himself tries to accumulate wealth, its proper distribution cannot be possible at all. So for this the ruler should, first of all, be contented. Therefore, it is essential that the ruler himself be contented, only then he can arrange for proper distribution of wealth amongst his subjects. The fifth Guru advises the people to boycott such a ruler who runs after wealth. To quote him:I will abandon the wealth-accumulating king. Ravidas calls a state an ideal one where there is proper distribution of wealth, where there are no 'have-nots'. All the necessities of life are available to everyone in sufficient quantity; where all are rich and none poor; all live satisfied. He writes:Populated and ever famous is that city,The wealthy and the content dwell there. In such a state, he says, there is no agony, no grief, and no sorrow. He calls such a state as Begumpura or the 'griefless' state:'Griefless' is the name of my town, where abide not either pain or care.

To Keep the Subjects United: The ruler has to keep his subjects united so that they can face the enemy from within as well as from without. There can be difference of opinion but that must be taken in a healthy way. There may be living, people from various races, religions, castes and cultures etc. the ruler must behave with all as a common father, just as God treats all of us as His children. As God keeps even the opposite elements in the nature united, for example, earth and water, wood and fire etc. are kept close to each other without harming each other. The fourth Guru says:The earth and water abide in one place and the fire is locked in wood.The sheep and the lion, the Lord has kept in one place. Similarly the ruler must keep the people of different belongings united just like the different pearls of a necklace. The fifth Guru says:He has stringed the whole world with breath and has kept the fire along with the wood.He has kept the water and the earth together and no one bears enmity with (or harms) each other. This will create unity in diversity. The ruler should not have in his mind even an idea to act partially. In the Mahabharta Bhisma advises Yudhisthira, The king should always bear himself towards his subjects as a mother towards the children of her womb.-Anusasna Parva.In addition to all these duties the tenth Guru lays much stress on the unity of thought, word and deed. For him the person who does not have this unity in practice is not at all fit to be a ruler. In the Zafarnama Guru Gobind Singh reminds Aurangzeb of his promise not to harm the former while eva-cuating the Anandpur Fort. Further the Guru condemns Aurangzeb for not keeping his word and contrary to the assurances subjecting the Guru, his family and armies to un-told sufferings. The Guru tells the king that one, especially the ruler, must not go back from his promises. Otherwise the ruler is becoming unjust.

To quote him: O mortal man thyself thou do adorn with the bliss of being utter true!Stick to the position once taken up, Within and without the same be you! The Guru condemned his injustice of not keeping his promises:Aurangzeb proud lord of the world Who adoreth a monarch's high throne!Strange is the justice thou dispenses And the royal qualities by thee shown! Virtually the whole of the Zafarnama is full of such coup-lets written against this policy of the ruler of his time. Even the fifth Guru says, in general, that the man must keep the unity of thought, word and deed. To quote him:He pledges his Word but keeps it not, and all the speaks is falseYea,' False is he from within, with Illusion involved. In the Zafarnama the Guru also writes about some more qualities required of a ruler. For him, he must possess wisdom and wit to settle the matters in time and to such a ruler the Guru pays his respect. The ruler must conquer the enemies of the kingdom. He must protect the poor. The Guru gives the example of some ancient Chinese ruler who had these qualities.

Rights of the Ruler: From the preceding analysis about the duties of a ruler it should not be deduced as if a ruler has only obligations and is not entitled to any special privileges. The foremost right of a ruler is that he must have sovereignty. He must be treated as the supreme power of the state. He must have the right to order and get the things done. Otherwise he will not be able to function effectively. He must be able to exercise supreme jurisdiction. While telling about the need of inner life for a saint the fifth Guru says that a king without the above powers is just like a warrior without weapons: As a Brahmin without a saffron-mark, As a Kingship without commandAs a warrior without weapons, So is a Saint without an Inner life.

The subjects must treat a righteous ruler, as their sove-reign king Only then they can get happiness or bliss. A righteous ruler is entitled to respect from his subjects. If the subjects pay full respect to such a ruler who looks after them well, then they have not to worry at all in any matter. They will have full access to him. He will be able to listen to them carefully.

They looked upon him as a king andwere stopped not at the door of his castle. Without right to get respect what will be the status of the ruler? He must get some status, which he deserves. Guru Nanak gives the example of a cow, which does not yield milk. What is the use of such a cow? How can the vegetation sur-vive without water? Birds can't survive without wings. Similarly no ruler or king can survive or perform his duties, effectively without having some status and respect or rights.

To quote him: Without milk a cow, without wings a bird, without water the vegetation of no avail; As without obedience a king, so without the Lord's Name the mind is but a blind spot. The fifth Guru says that the ruler must have sovereignty. Only a person having this right can be the ruler. He takes canopy as the symbol of sovereignty: He is the monarch who has the royal umbrella over His head.

Another right Guru Nanak concedes to an ideal ruler is that he can levy tax for the earnings of the state. The ruler must have the right to levy the rightful taxes. It becomes the duty of the subjects to pay such rightful taxes so as to main-tain the state. He says as the goldsmith solders the gold with the help of heat, one is, soldered with the world through son, soldered with the body by taking meals and the love is soldered with sweet words, similarly the subjects are soldered with the ruler by the payment of such taxes. These are some of the privileges, which a righteous ruler must get. But with getting these rights he must remember his duties. Only such a ruler is acceptable who, getting these rights performs his duties well and actually earns these rights

Sikh Rehat Maryada (Sikh Code Of Conduct): History judges a nation by its collective character and conduct. It is believed that human life is full of problems and pains. Discipline in life is the basic tool to address and solve these problems. The ultimate aim of human being is to overcome the problems and lead a pure and pious life to attain unity with God. According to Sikhism, the remedy of pain lies within. *Dukh daroo sukh rog bhaia* Every religion has prescribed the code of conduct for its followers. The Sikh religion is not an exception. Sikh religion is a practical way of life.The Sikh Gurus prescribed comprehensive rules and a code of conduct (Reht Maryada) for the Sikhs to be followed truthfully in their day to day life. The distinctive Sikh code of conduct is feature of fundamental importance to the life of the Panth that is the Sikh religion.The Sikh code of conduct can be traced from within Sri Guru Granth Sahib, Rehtnamas and practical life of the Gurus. Guru Nanak Dev says, Reflecting on the Name, man's mind is accustomed to serve others. Stilling one's ego, one is deemed to have practised worship, penance and self mortification. When man hears the Lord's Name, he becomes emancipated in life. Through such a true way of life, he is blessed with eternal peace.

Guru Nanak Dev is the founder of Sikhism. He started the institution of *Sangat* and *Pangat* which is the first step to *Reht Maryada* ladder. According to Sikhism, the mission of human life is the attainment of God and the realization is possible by observing the principles of truth in their true spirit. It is desired of a Sikh to live upto the discipline of Bani (*Nam Simran*) and Bana (Wearing of Five Kakars and keeping piety of outlook) to attain the ultimate goal. Sikh code of conduct provides social, cultural, religious and spiritual precepts for governance of Khalsa corporate life. Sikh faith is established on observance of the principles and rules formulated by the Sikh Gurus in the true sense. Sikhism is a way of life and the game of love needs truth and commitment on that way. In micro sense, Sikhism is concerned with individual life style (Gurmat and Reht Maryada style of life) of a Sikh but in macro sense, it is concerned with his corporate style of life (Sangat, Pangat, supermacy of Akal Takht and Wand Chhakna etc)conducted and governed truely at all the times and at all the places and in every behaviour according to the Word of God.

Guru Nanak Dev says, "If you want to play the game of love, then enter my path with head on thy palm. But once you set foot on my way, find not the way out, and lay down thy head." Guru Gobind Singh says, I love Sikh but for his acceptance of my discipline". He commanded the Khalsa never to follow the rituals, rites and traditions but if still they ever follow, "he shall withdraw his support and protection. So long as Khalsa retains his distinct identity, I will give him my entire radiance and strength. But if he should take on a non-Sikh way of life, then I shall have no confidence in him and withdraw my support and protection". Jab lag Khalsa rahe niara. tab lag tej dio mai sara. jab eh gahe bipran ki reet. mai na karo in ki parteet.

There is significant truth in these words. When due to comforts and pleasures, the Sikhs slackened and sacrificed the code of conduct, the Guru withdrew his grace. The Sikhs recite daily in Ardas that: Only the Khalsa (Pure) shall rule. Those who disobey shall perish and suffer. As a result of sufferings, they shall return to the pure faith. *Raj karega khalsa Aki rahe na koe, khuar hoe sabh milainge bache sharan jo hoe* (Tankhahnama Bhai Nand Lal) According to the code of conduct for the Sikhs, Khalsa is a person who believes in one God. In whose heart the light of the Almighty God shines for ever. He who has full love, faith and confidence in God; Who meditates on the Name of

God day and night; Who believes in the teachings of the ten Gurus and Sri Guru Granth Sahib. Who believes in honest labor, sharing his earnings with the less fortunate, does selfless Seva and leads a virtuous life. He who does not have faith even by mistake in fasting, worshipping, burial places, crematoriums or places of Jogi sepulcher is recognized as a pure member of the Khalsa. Khalsa is he who adopts the concept of Bani and Bana (Five Kakars). Guru Angad Dev says, "He who both offers salutation and says 'no' to his Master, has gone wrong since the very beginning. Both of his actions are false. He obtains no place in God's court"

Meaning of Rehat: Sikhism is a way of life which believes in pure and pious living. It is a dynamic and practical religion. It has got certain principles and discipline to follow. More important than belief in the principles of the Sikh faith is the actual practice of the teachings of the Gurus. There are set rules and ways for the ideal life in Sikhism which determine Sikh beliefs and practices. Sikh Code of Conduct is called Sikh Rehat Maryada. It is a manual and code of discipline for the followers of Sikh faith for social, moral, religious, spiritual and general living. According to the Sikh code of conduct published in 1945 by Shiromani Gurdwara Parbandhak Committee Amritsar, a Sikh must practice the concept of Bani (Spiritual life) and Bana (Uniform with Five Kakars). He must live upto the Internal and External code of conduct. Internal Rehat Maryada means living a pure, pious and spiritual inner life. External Rehat Maryada means the outer code of conduct and visible living of virtuous life (Bani & Bana ie. Norm and Form) Rehat Maryada literally means "the code of conduct or way of life". Reht means mode of living or conduct and Maryada means tradition, practice of the faith or code or discipline of life. It extends its meaning to life discipline. It meets the principles for ethical, moral and spiritual life. It is a code which tells the Sikh followers how to live and how not to live. It is a manual for the Sikh which tells him to live like a Lotus which has its roots in muddy water but its flower blooms floating pure and spotless over the muddy base. Sikhism is essentially a practical religion. It gives great significance to voluntary discipline and self restraint in the physical, mental, moral and spiritual fields. Sikhism gives reverence to its sacred traditions (Maryada), heritage, culture and religious living. It does not call for blind and arrogant compliance of its way of life. Sikh Rehat is touch stone which reveals the purity and perfection of the Khalsa.

Rehat Maryada is willing discipline: Sikhism believes in willing discipline of body and mind. It aims at serving the mankind and attaining the Ultimate Reality through Naam Simran, Sachi Kirt and Wand Chhakna. There is no use of coercion in observance of the discipline. It is not punitive. The code of Sikh conduct is positive, correctional and requires the devotee to attune with the Will of God. Sikhism believes in gradual progress of Sehaj Dharis to become the Khalsa. The deviants and slow movers are to be treated with sympathy and loving care so that they learn their roots and join the main stream. Sikh Rehat Maryada has been evolved on the basic principles of God's universe, discipline of planetary system and the law of nature. Human body, mind and consciousness are gifts of the Lord leased to mankind for a pre-determined life time. Sikhism wants these gifts to be used for attainment of God through service of mankind.

Sri Guru Granth Sahib is the primary source of Sikh Code of Conduct. It is supported by Dasam Granth, Vars of Bhai Gurdas and writings of Bhai Nand Lal. The Rehat is further strengthened through the Rehat Namas of Bhai Nand Lal, Bhai Daya Singh, Bhai Desa Singh, Bhai Champa Singh and others.

Gurbani says that blessed with infinite joy, without a trace of sorrow, is the house that Guru Nanak has inherited. Sikhism wants to keep peace and tranquillity in that house. Harkh anant sog nahi biya, so ghar gur Nanak ko diaya. The doctrine of five Kakars gifted by Guru Gobind Singh helps the Sikhs to live life in full measure and with universal resources. The Guru ordained not only the Khalsa how to live but also how not to live. He gave certain do's and don'ts to the Khalsa Panth. It is very essential to point out that no individual or individual organisation has the authority to change or alter the Sikh Rehat Maryada as per personal needs and whims. Every Sikh is required to bow head before the Sikh Rehat Maryada published by Shiromani Gurdwara Parbandhak Committee. There is only one Rahit Maryada for the Khalsa Panth, it does not belong to any particular Jatha or entity, yet as Sikhs we are all obliged to follow it. It is explicit in Gurbani that the principles of Gurmat are unchangeable and of permanent standing: The Instruction of the Guru is Unshakable. None can change it. Gurmat Mat Achal Hai Chalaey Na Sakey Koey (p-548) Every Sikh must strengthen its rallying point i.e. Sri Akal Takht Sahib Amritsar failing which the Sikhs will lose their Vatican axle resulting in confusion everywhere.

Reht and discipline: How can the traveller (Sikh) who asks the experts (God-oriented) the way (of spirituality), but does not take even a step, ever reach his destination by mere asking ? How can the patient who consults the physician, but does not take the medicine or follow instructions, be rid of the disease and regain his health? How can an apparently lewd wife, who asks another woman about true love but herself is full of lust, be loved by her husband ? How can the Sikh who apparently sings Kirtan or listens to it with closed eyes and full brain (hypocritically) find spiritual fulfilment, unless he accepts the Guru's teaching and practises it faithfully. Sikhism is a religion of Bani and Bana, not for show but for practice. Guru Arjan Dev says, Man professes one thing and practises quite another. In his heart there is no love, but with his mouth he talks tall. The Omniscient Lord, Who is Inner Knower, is not pleased with the deceitful show of garment of such person.

Important principles of Sikh Reht Maryada

1. Dharam-Di- Kirt Karna (Honest earning and truthful living)
2. Vand Ke Chhakna (Sharing honest earnings with needy and less fortunate)
3. Naam Japna (Meditation on the Name of One God)
4. Puja Akal Ki (Worshipping the Almighty God)
5. Parcha Sabad Ka (Understanding and practicing Gurbani)
6. Didar Khalse Ka (Appreciation of Sikh Rehat) Attending company of holy Sangat
7. Amrit Chhakna, (Initiation of Amrit Pahul and stay away from taboos)
8. Sarbat Da Bhala (Well-being of all)
9. Seva Sambhal (Selfless service for welfare of humanity)
10. Sacha Achar (Keeping good moral character in life)
11. Bhana Manana (Surrender before Will of God)
12. Believe in One God, Sri Guru Granth Sahib and teachings of ten Gurus
13. Practicing the principles of both Bani and Bana (Norm and Form)

14. No commission of Kurehts
15. Adopt and practice compassion, honesty, generosity, patience, perseverence and humility
16. Non observance of blind rites, rituals and superstitions. No worship of idols and images.

The code of conduct is (such as rigorous socio-moral discipline for the Sikhs) prescribed so that the Sikhs must remain pure and emancipated. If a Sikh breaches the cardinal instructions of no hair cutting, no adultery, no use of intoxicants and no eating of *Kutha* meat, he is called *Patit* and the transgressor must get rebaptized. If a Sikh violates the code of conduct other than the four cardinal transgressions, he becomes *Tankhaya* and has to appear before the Panj Pyaras for undergoing *Tankhah*. The study of Sikh Rehat Maryada published by Shiromani Gurdwara Parbandhak Committee Amritsar will answer many of the questions about Sikh way of life. Views of different Sikh organizations, eminent Sikhs and Sikh bodies on Sikh Rehat Maryada were considered from 1936 to 1945. Sikh Reht Maryada was finally approved by Shiromani Gurdwara Parbandhak Committee vide its resolution No: 97 on February 3, 1945. It was published by Shiromani Gurdwara Parbandhak Committee Amritsar in 1945 after deliberations with different Sikh Individuals and representatives of different organizations.

INDIAN PHILOSOPHERS

Adi Shankara

Dates: c. 788 to 820 CE

Birth place: Kalady, Kerala, India

Philosophy: Advaita Vedanta

Teacher: Govinda Bhagavatpada

Influenced: Hinduism, Hindu philosophy

Founded: Dashanami Sampradaya, Shanmata

Adi Shankara and Bhagavatpadacarya (or, the teacher at the feet of God), c. 788 – 820 CE, was the first philosopher in the tradition of Advaita Vedanta, a sub-school of the Vedanta school of Hindu philosophy, and is recognized as the first teacher to have consolidated its doctrine. His teachings are based on unity of the soul and God, wherein the latter is viewed as simultaneously being personal and attributeless. In the Smrta tradition, he is regarded as an incarnation of Shiva.

Adi Shankara toured India with the purpose of propagating his philosophies primarily through seminal debates with other philosophers. In the process, he founded four mathas (abbeys) at the four cardinal directions, which, along with the Hindu Smartas, played a key historical role in the further development and spread of Hinduism and the Advaita Vedanta philosophy and continue to do so.

Life: The traditional source for accounts of Adi Ṣhankara's life are the Shankara Vijayams (literally *Victory of Shankara*), which are poetic works that contain biographical material written in an the epic style of legend. The most important among these biographiesz According to these texts, Adi Shankara was born in Kalady, Kerala, India, to a Namboothiri brahmin couple, Shivaguru and Aryamba and lived for thirty two years.

Birth and Childhood: The birth place of Adi Shankara at Kalady.

Adi Shankara's parents were childless for many years. They prayed at the Vadakkumnathan (Vicacala) temple in Thrissur, Kerala, for the birth of a child. Legend has it that Shiva appeared to both husband and wife in their dreams, and offered them a choice: a mediocre son who would live a long life, or an extraordinary son who would not live long. Both the parents chose the latter; thus a son was born to them. He was named Shankara (bestower of happiness), in honour of Shiva (one of whose epithets is Shankara).

His father died while Shankara was very young. Shankara's upanayanac, the initiation into student-life, was performed at the age of five. As a child, Shankara showed remarkable scholarship, mastering the four Vedas by the age of eight. Following the customs of those days, Shankara studied and lived at the home of his teacher. It was customary for students and men of learning to receive Bhikca (alms) from the laity; on one occasion, while accepting Bhikca, Shankara came upon a woman who had only a single dried amalaka fruit to eat. Rather than consuming this last bit of food herself, the pious lady gave away the fruit to Shankara as Bhikca. Moved by her piety, Shankara composed the Kanakadhara Stotram on the spot. Legend has it that on completion of the stotra, golden amalaka fruits were showered upon the woman by Lakshmi, the Goddess of wealth.

Madhvạ: From a young age, Shaṇkara was attracted to sannyasa (monastic life). His mother was against his becoming an monk, and refused him her formal permission. However, once when Shankara was bathing in the Purna River near his house, a crocodile gripped his leg and began to drag him into the water. Only his mother was nearby, and it proved impossible for her to rescue him. Shankara then told his mother that he was on the verge of death, would live only if she gave him permission to renounce the world and become a monk. At the end of her wits, his mother agreed. Shankara immediately recited the mantras that made a renunciate of him. The crocodile released him and swam away. Shankara emerged unscathed from the river.

With the permission of his mother, Shankara left Kerala and travelled towards North India in search of a Guru. On the banks of the Narmada River, he met Govinda Bhagavatpada, the disciple of Gaudapada. When Govinda Bhagavatpada asked Shankara's identity, he replied with an extempore verse that brought out the Advaita Vedanta philosophy. Govinda Bhagavatapada was impressed and took Shankara as his disciple.

Adi Shankara was commissioned by his Guru to write a commentary on the Brahma Sutras and propagate the Advaita Vedanta philosophy. The Madhaviya Shankaravijaya states that Adi Shankara calmed a flood from the Reva River by placing his *kamagalu* (water pot) in the path of the raging water, thus saving his Guru, Govinda Bhagavatpada, who was engaged in Samdhi (meditation) in a cave nearby. On his mission to spread the Advaita Vedanta philosophy, Adi Shankara travelled to Kashi, where a young man named Sanandana from Choladesha in South India, became his first disciple. In Kashi, Adi Shankara had an encounter with an untouchable-on his way to the Vishwanath Temple, he came upon an untouchable with four dogs. When asked to move aside by Shankara's disciples, the untouchable replied: "Do you wish that I move my ever lasting Atman (Self), or this body made of food?" Understanding that the untouchable was none other than god Shiva, and his dogs the four Vedas, Shankara prostrated himself before him, composing five shlokas known as Manisha Panchakam.

On reaching Badari in the Himalayas, he wrote the famous *Bhashyas* (commentaries) and *Prakarana granthas* (philosophical treatises). Afterwards he taught these commentaries to his disciples. Some, like Sanandana, were quick to grasp the essence; the other disciples thus became jealous of Sanandana. In order to convince the others of Sanandana's inherent superiority, Adi Shankara summoned Sanandana from one bank of the Ganga River, while he was on the opposite bank. Sanandana crossed the river by walking on the lotuses that were brought out wherever he placed his foot. Adi Shankara was greatly impressed by his disciple and gave him the name Padmapada (lotus-footed one). The sage, Vedavysa, visited Adi Shankara in the guise of an old brhmaGa. Adi Shankara debated with the brahmana for over eight days when at last, Vyasa revealed his real identity and blessed Adi Shankara.

Meeting with Mandana Mishra: One of the most famous debates of Adi Shankara was with the ritualist Mandana Mishra. Mandana Mishra's Guru was the famous Mimamsa philosopher, Kumarla Bhamma. Shankara sought a debate with Kumarila Bhamma and met him in Prayag where he had buried himself in a slow burning pyre to repent for sins committed against his Guru: Kumarila Bhamma had learnt Buddhist philosophy incognito from him in order to be able to refute it. This constitues a sin according to the Vedas. Kumarila Bhamma thus asked Adi Shankara to proceed to Mahicmati (known today as Maheshwar in Madhya Pradesh) to meet Mandana Mishra and debate with him instead.

Adi Shankara had a famous debate with Mandana Mishra in which the wife of Mandana Mishra, Ubhaya Bharati, was the referee. After debating for over fifteen days, Mandana Mishra accepted defeat. Ubhaya Bharati then challenged Adi Shankara to have a debate with her in order to 'complete' the victory. This debate was to be on the subject of *kmauastra* (science of sex-love). But Adi Shankara, being a sannyasi, had no knowledge of this subject; thus, after requesting for some time before entering into this fresh debate, he entered the body of a king by his yogic powers and acquired the knowledge of kamauastra. Later, however, Ubhaya Bharati declined to debate with him and allowed Mandana Mishra to accept sannyasa with the monastic name, Sureuvaracarya as per the agreed rules of the debate.

Dig-vijaya: Adi Shankara then travelled with his disciples to Maharashtra and Srisailam. In Srisailam, he composed Shivanandalahari, a devotional hymn to Shiva. The Madhaviya Shankaravijayam says that when Shankara was about to be sacrificed by a Kapalika, the god Narasimha appeared to save Shankara on Padmapada's prayer to him. So Adi Shankara composed the Laksmi-Narasimha stotra to praise Narasimha. He then travelled to Gokarna, the temple of Hari-Shankara and the Mkambika temple at Kollur. At Kollur he accepted a boy believed to be dumb by his parents, as his disciple. He gave him the name, Hastmalakcrya (one with the amalaka fruit on his palm, i.e., one who has clearly realised the Self).

After this, Adi Shankara began a *Dig-vijaya* (missionary tour) for the propagation of the Advaita philosophy by controverting all philosophies opposed to it. With King Sudhanva of Kerala as companion, Shankara passed through Tamil Nadu, Andhra Pradesh and Vidarbha. He then started towards Karnataka where he encountered a band of armed Kapalikas. King Sudhanva, with his army, resisted and defeated the kapalikas. They safely reached Gokarna where Shankara defeated in debate the Shaiva scholar, Neelakanta.

Proceeding to the west in Dwarka, Shankara defeated the Vaicnavas in debate. Bhamma Bhaskara of Ujjayini, the proponent of Bhedabeda philosophy, was humbled. All the scholars of Ujjayini (also known as Avanti) accepted Adi Shankara's philosophy. He then defeated the Jainas at a place called Bahlika. Later, he had an encounter with a tantrik, Navagupta at Kamarupa. Navagupta pretended to have become a disciple, but later çaused Adi Shankara to develop a rectal fistula. However, Adi Shankara was soon cured and Navagupta later died of the same disease.

Adi Shankara thus travelled throughout India, from the South to Kashmir and Nepal, preaching to the local populace and debating philosophy with Hindu, Buddhist and other scholars and monks along the way.

Accession to Sarvajnapitha: Adi Shankara visited *Sarvajnapimha* in Kashmir (now in Pakistan-occupied Kashmir). The Madhaviya Shankara Vijaya states this temple had four doors for scholars from the four cardinal directions. The southern door (representing South India) had never been opened, indicating that no scholar from South India had entered the Sarvajna Pitha. Adi Shankara opened the southern door by defeating in debate all the scholars there in all the various scholastic disciplines such as Mimamsa, Vedanta and other branches qf Hindu philosophy; he ascended the throne of Transcendent wisdom of that temple. The Madhaviya Shankara Vijaya states that Goddess Saraswati (goddess of knowledge and all literary arts) herself proclaimed the unquestioned scholarly triumph of Adi Shankara on this occasion.

Shankara then travelled to Kedarnath and attained *videha mukti* (final liberation) at the age of thirty two. However, there are variant traditions on the location of his last days. The Kanchi matha followers believe he achieved *videha mukti* in Kanchi. Another tradition expounded by *Keraliya Shankaravijaya* places his place of death as Vadakkunnathan temple in Thrissur, Kerala.

Philosophy and Religious Thought: The swan is an important motif in Advaita Vedanta. Its symbolic meanings are: firstly, the swan is called *hamsa* in Sanskrit (which becomes *hamso* if the first letter in the next word is /h/). Upon repeating this *hamso* indefinitely, it becomes *so-aham*, meaning, "I am That". Secondly, just as a swan lives in water but its feathers are not soiled by water, similarly a liberated Advaitin lives in this world full of maya but is untouched by its illusion. Thirdly, a Sannyasi of the Dashanami order (founded by Adi Shankara) is called a *Paramahansa* (the Supreme Swan).

Advaita (literally, *non-duality*) is often called a monistic system of thought. The word "Advaita" essentially refers to the identity of the Self (Atman) and the Whole (Brahman). The key source texts for all schools of Vedanta are the Prasthanatrayi– the canonical texts consisting of the Upanishads, the Bhagavad Gita and the Brahma Sutras. Adi Shankara was the first in its tradition to consolidate the siddhanta (system) of Advaita Vedanta. He wrote commentaries on the Prasthana Trayi. A famous quote from Vivekacmagi, one of his *prakarana granthas* (philosophical treatises) that succintly summarises his philosophy is:

Brahman is the only truth, the world is unreal, and there is ultimately no difference between Brahman and individual self.

Advaita Vedanta is based on *uastra* (scriptures), *yukti* (reason) and *anubhava* (experience), and aided by *karmas* (spiritual practices). This philosophy provides a clear-cut way of life to be followed. Starting from childhood, when learning has to start, the philosophy has to be realised in practice throughout one's life even upto death. This is the reason why this philosophy is called an experiential philosophy, the underlying tenet being "That thou art", meaning that ultimately there is no difference between the experiencer and the experienced (the world) as well as the universal spirit (Brahman). Among the followers of Advaita, as well those of other doctrines, there are believed to have appeared *Jivanmuktas*, ones liberated while alive. These individuals (commonly called *Mahatmas*, great souls, among Hindus) are those who realised the oneness of their self and the universal spirit called Brahman.

Advaita Vedanta in Summary: Adi Shankara's treatises on the Upanishads, the Bhagavad Gita and the Brahma Sutras are his principal and almost undeniably his own works. Although he mostly adhered to traditional means of commenting on the Brahma Sutra, there are a number of original ideas and arguments. He taught that it was only through direct knowledge of Brahman that one could be enlightened.

Adi Shankara's opponents accused him of teaching Buddhism in the garb of Hinduism, because his non-dualistic ideals were a bit radical to contemporary Hindu philosophy. However, it may be noted that while the Later Buddhists arrived at a changeless, deathless, absolute truth after their insightful understanding of the unreality of samsara, historically Vedantins never liked this idea. Although Advaita proposes the theory of Maya, explaining the universe as a "trick of a magician", Adi Shankara and his followers see this as a consequence of their basic premise that Brahman alone is real. Their idea of Maya emerges from their belief in the reality of Brahman, rather than the other way around.

Historical and Cultural Impact: At the time of Adi Shankara's life, Hinduism had began to decline because of the influence of Buddhism and Jainism. Hinduism had become divided into innumerable sects, each quarreling with the others. The followers of Mimamsa and Sankhya philosophy were atheists, in so much that they did not believe in God as a unified being. Besides these atheists, there were numerous theistic sects. There were those who rejected the Vedas, like the Charvakas.

Adi Shankara held debates with the leading scholars of all these sects and schools of philosophy to controvert their doctrines. He unified the theistic sects into a common framework of Shanmata system. In his works, Adi Shankara stressed the importance of the Vedas, and his efforts helped Hinduism regain strength and popularity. He travelled on foot to various parts of India to restore the study of the Vedas.

Even though he lived for only thirty-two years, his impact on India and on Hinduism was striking. He reintroduced a purer form of Vedic thought. His teachings and tradition form the basis of Smartism and have influenced Sant Mat lineages. He is the main figure in the tradition of Advaita Vedanta. He was the founder of the *Daanmi Sampradya* of Hindu monasticism and *bagmata* of Smarta tradition. He introduced the *Pacyatana* form of worship. Adi Shankara, along with Madhva and Ramanuja, was instrumental in the revival of Hinduism. These three teachers formed the doctrines that are followed by their respective sects even today. They have been the most important figures in the recent history of Hindu philosophy. In their writings and debates, they provided polemics against the non-Vedantic schools of Sankhya, Vaisheshika etc. Thus they paved the way for Vedanta to be the dominant and most widely followed tradition among the schools of Hindu philosophy. The Vedanta school stresses most on the Upanishads (which are themselves called Vedanta, *End or culmination of the Vedas*), unlike the other schools that gave importance to texts authored by their founders. The Vedanta schools have the belief that the Vedas, which include the Upanishads, are unauthored, forming a continuous tradition of wisdom transmitted orally. Thus the concept of *apaurusheyatva* (being unauthored) came to be the guiding force behind the Vedanta schools. However, along with stressing the importance of Vedic tradition, Adi Shankara gave equal importance to the personal experience of the student. Logic, grammar, Mimamsa and allied subjects form main areas of study in all the Vedanta schools.

A well known verse, recited in the Smarta tradition, in praise of Adi Shankara is:

I salute the compassionate abode of the Vedas, Smritis and Puranas known as Shankara Bhagavatpada, who makes the world auspicious.

Works: Adi Shankara's works deal with logically establishing the doctrine of Advaita Vedanta as he saw it in the Upanishads. He formulates the doctrine of Advaita Vedanta by validating his arguments on the basis of quotations from the Vedas and other Hindu scriptures. He gives a high priority to *svanubhava* (personal experience) of the student. A large portion of his works is polemical in nature. He directs his polemics mostly against the Sankhya, Bauddha, Jaina, Vaisheshika and other non-vedantic Hindu philosophies.

Traditionally, his works are classified under Bhacya (*commentary*), Prakaraga gratha (*philosophical treatise*) and Stotra (*devotional hymn*). The commentaries serve to provide a consistent interpretation of the scriptural texts from the perspective of Advaita Vedanta. The philosophical treatises provide various methodologies to the student to understand the doctrine. The devotional hymns are rich in poetry and piety, serving to highlight the helplessness of the devotee and the glory of the diety. Of his works, the authenticity of the Viveka Chudamani and a few *Bhashyas* are questioned.

Adi Shankara wrote *Bhashyas* on the ten major Upanishads, the Brahma Sutras and the Bhagavad Gita. In his works, he quotes from Shveshvatara, Kaushitakai, Mahanarayana and Jabala Upanishads, among others. *Bhashyas* on Kaushitaki, Nrisimhatapani and Shveshvatara Upanishads are extant but the authenticity is doubtful. Adi Shankara's commentary on the Brahma Sutras is the earliest one available on this topic. However Adi Shankara mentions older commentaries like those of Dravida, Bhartiprapancha and others.

In his Brahma Sutra Bhashya, Adi Shankara cites the examples of Dharmavyadha, Vidura and others who were born with the knowledge of Brahman acquired in previous births. He mentions that the effects cannot be prevented from working on account of their present birth. He states that the knowledge that arises out of the study of the Vedas could be had through the Puranas and the Itihasas. In the Taittiriya Upanishad Bhashya 2.2, he says:

It has been established that everyone has the right to the knowledge (of Brahman) and that the supreme goal is attained by that knowledge alone.

Ramanuja Acharya

Period: 1017 to 1137

Place of Birth: Sri Perumbudur, Tamil Nadu

Guru: Sri Periya Nambigal

Names: 1. Ilaya Perumal, As named by his parents 2. Lakshmana

Family Name: 1. Ramanuja, 2. Yetiraja, 3. Bhashyakarar, 6. Udeyavar, 7. Emberumanar, As named by his guru Thirukkottiyur Nambi

Avatars (believed): Adishesha

Sishyas: 1. Mudaliyandan, 2. Koorathalwan

Sri Ramanuja Acharya (traditionally dated 1017–1137 CE) was an Indian philosopher and is recognized as the most important saint of Sri Vaishnavism. He held the Vishishtadvaita or qualified Nondualist belief that the world and Brahman were united, like a soul and a body are. His version of Indian Nondualism differed from Adi Shankara's because he acknowledged the existence of differences, and believed that the identity of an object as a part was as important as the unity of the whole. The Vaishnava Theology espoused by Ramanuja posits that Brahman is not devoid of attributes but is expressed as a personal God, full of infinite good qualities, as Narayana. The Adishesha on whom Lord Ranganatha of Srirangam rests is believed to be Ramanuja.

Formative Years: Ramanuja was born Ilaya Perumal to a smartha brahmin family in the village of Perumbudur, Tamil Nadu, India in 1017 CE. His father was Keshava Somayaji Deekshitar and mother was Kanthimathi in sect of Vadama.From a young age, his intelligence and ability to comprehend highly abstract philosophical points were legendary. He took initiation from Yadavaprakasa, a renowned Advaitic scholar. Though his new guru was highly impressed with his analytical ability, he was quite concerned by how much emphasis Ramanuja placed on bhakti. After frequent clashes over interpretation, Yadavaprakasa decided the young Ramanuja was becoming too much of a threat and plotted a way to kill him. However, Ramanuja's cousin Govinda Bhatta (a favourite of Yadavaprakasa) discovered the plot and helped him escape. An alternative version is that one of Yadavaprakasa's students plotted to kill Ramanuja as a means of pleasing their teacher, but Sri Ramanuja escaped in the afore-mentioned manner. Yadavaprakasa was horrified when learnt about the conspiracy.

After renouncing the life of a house-holder, Ramanuja travelled to Srirangam to meet an aging Yamunacharya, the pre-eminent Vishishtadvaita philosopher of the time. Yamunacharya had died prior to Ramanuja's arrival, but had left three tasks for Ramanuja to carry out.

- Teach the doctrine of Saranagati (surrender) to God as the means to moksha.
- A Visishtadvaita Bhashya should be written for the Brahma Sutras of Vyasa which had previously been taught orally to the disciples of the Visishtadvaita philosophy.
- That the names of Parauara, the author of Vishnu Puraoa, and saint Uahakopa should be perpetuated.

Ramanuja pledged to God to do as he had been requested and accepted Yamunacharya as his *Manasika Acharya*. All three tasks were successfully completed.

Five Acharyas: Swami Ramanuja incorporated teachings from 5 different people who he considered to be his acharyas

1. Peria Nambigal who performed his samasrayana
2. Thirukkotiyur Nambigal : who revealed the meaning of Charama slokam to swami on his 18th trip
3. Thirumalai Nambigal : Ramayana
4. Tirumalai Aandaan : Bhagavad Vishayam
5. Thirukachchi Nambigal : The 6 sentences or Perarulalan

Visishtadvaita Philosophy: Ramanuja's philosophy is referred to as Vishishtadvaita because it combines Advaita (oneness of God) with Vishesha (attributes). The philosophy is monotheistic.

Differences with Sankara: Adi Sankara had argued that all qualities or manifestations that can be perceived are unreal and temporary. They are a result of ignorance. Ramanuja believed them to be real and permanent and under the control of the Brahman. God can be one despite the existence of attributes, because they cannot exist alone; they are not independent entities. They are Prakaras or the modes, Sesha or the accessories, and Niyama or the controlled aspects, of the one Brahman.

In Sri Ramanuja's system of philosophy, the Lord (Narayana) has two inseparable Prakaras or modes, viz., the world and the souls. These are related to Him as the body is related to the soul. They have no existence apart from Him. They inhere in Him as attributes in a substance. Matter and souls constitute the body of the Lord. The Lord is their indweller. He is the controlling Reality. Matter and souls are the subordinate elements. They are termed Viseshanas, attributes. God is the Viseshya or that which is qualified.

History shows that the followers of Sankara are answerless till date to the strong arguments of Ramanuja (in his sri bhashya) and his followers (satadushani of desika,...). In a bid to escape strong objections raised by Ramanuja and his successors, most advaitins take a disguised route of neo vedantism, where they argue that vaishnavism is one another path to realise brahman. Ironically, the very brahman of Ramanuja and Sankara are different.

Ramanuja opines, wrong is the position of the Advaitins that understanding the Upanishads without knowing and practicing dharma can result in Brahman knowledge. The knowledge of Brahman that ends spiritual ignorance is meditational, not (as Advaitins seem to presume) testimonial or verbal.

In contrast to Sankara, Ramanuja holds. There is no knowledge source in support of the claim that there is a distinctionless (homogeneous) Brahman. All knowledge sources reveal objects as distinct from other objects. All experience reveals an object known in some way or other beyond mere existence. Testimony depends on the operation of distinct sentence parts (words with distinct meanings). Thus the claim that testimony makes known that reality is distinctionless is contradicted by the very nature of testimony as a knowledge means. Even the simplest perceptual cognition reveals something (Bessie) as qualified by something else (a broken hoof, "Bessie has a broken hoof," as known perceptually). Inference depends on perception and makes the same distinct things known as does perception.

Against the Advaita contention that perception cannot make known distinctness but only homogeneous being since distinctness cannot be defined, well, sorry, perception makes known generic characters (cowhood and the like) that differentiate things. If what you Advaitins say were true, why should not a person looking for a horse be satisfied with a buffalo? Remembering could not be distinguished from perceiving, because there would be only the one object (being). And no one would be deaf or blind. Furthermore, Brahman would be an object of perception and the other sources (prameya).

He also holds, The Advaitin argument about prior absences and no prior absence of consciousness is wrong. Similarly the Advaitin understanding of a-vidya (not-Knowledge), which is the absence of spiritual knowledge, is incorrect. "If the distinction between spiritual knowledge and spiritual ignorance is unreal, then spiritual ignorance and the self are one."

The Seven Objections to Shankara's Advaita: Ramanuja picks out what he sees as seven fundamental flaws in the Advaita philosophy for special attack: he sees them as so fundamental to the Advaita position that if he is right in identifying them as involving doctrinal contradictions, then Sankara's entire system collapses. He argues:

1. The nature of Avidya. Avidya must be either real or unreal; there is no other possibility. But neither of these is possible. If Avidya is real, non-dualism collapses into dualism. If it is unreal, we are driven to self-contradiction or infinite regress.
2. The incomprehensibility of Avidya. Advaitins claim that Avidya is neither real nor unreal but incomprehensible, {anirvacaniya.} All cognition is either of the real or the unreal: the Advaitin claim flies in the face of experience, and accepting it would call into question all cognition and render it unsafe.
3. The grounds of knowledge of Avidya. No pramana can establish Avidya in the sense the Advaitin requires. Advaita philosophy presents Avidya not as a mere lack of knowledge, as something purely negative, but as an obscuring layer which covers Brahman and is removed by true Brahma-vidya. Avidya is positive nescience not mere ignorance. Ramanuja argues that positive nescience is established neither by perception, nor by inference, nor by scriptural testimony. On the contrary, Ramanuja argues, all cognition is of the real.
4. The locus of Avidya. Where is the Avidya that gives rise to the (false) impression of the reality of the perceived world? There are two possibilities; it could be Brahman's Avidya or the individual soul's {jiva.} Neither is possible. Brahman is knowledge; Avidya cannot co-exist as an attribute with a nature utterly incompatible with it. Nor can the individual soul be the locus of Avidya: the existence of the individual soul is due to Avidya; this would lead to a vicious circle.
5. Avidya's obscuration of the nature of Brahman. Sankara would have us believe that the true nature of Brahman is somehow covered-over or obscured by Avidya. Ramanuja regards this as an absurdity: given that Advaita claims that Brahman is pure self-luminous consciousness, obscuration must mean either preventing the origination of this (impossible since Brahman is eternal) or the destruction of it-equally absurd.
6. The removal of Avidya by Brahma-vidya. Advaita claims that Avidya has no beginning, but it is terminated and removed by Brahma-vidya, the intuition of the reality of Brahman as pure, undifferentiated consciousness. But Ramanuja denies the existence of undifferentiated {nirguna}

Brahman, arguing that whatever exists has attributes: Brahman has infinite auspicious attributes. Liberation is a matter of Divine Grace: no amount of learning or wisdom will deliver us.

7. The removal of Avidya. For the Advaitin, the bondage in which we dwell before the attainment of Moksa is caused by Maya and Avidya; knowledge of reality (Brahma-vidya) releases us. Ramanuja, however, asserts that bondage is real. No kind of knowledge can remove what is real. On the contrary, knowledge discloses the real; it does not destroy it. And what exactly is the saving knowledge that delivers us from bondage to Maya? If it is real then non-duality collapses into duality; if it is unreal, then we face an utter absurdity.

He was critical of the caste system. He said, "Does the wearing of a sacred thread make one a Brahmin? One who is devoted to God (Narayana) alone is a Brahmin."

His Sarangati philosophy emphasises that anyone, irrespective of colour, creed, caste, sex and religion can surrender their mind, body and soul to the Lotus foot of Lord Narayana and the God would accept him/her.

Cited from Sri Ramanuja, His Life, Religion, and Philosophy, published by Sri Ramakrishna Math, Chennai, India.

Writings: Ramanuja's most famous work is known as the Sri Bhasya. It is a commentary on the Brahma Sutras.

Gadhya Thrayam (three compositions)-Vaikunta, Sriranga and Saranagati Gadhyam are great works in Vaishnava philosophy.

His other works are:

- Vedanta Sara (essence of Vedanta)
- Vedanta Sangraha (a resume of Vedanta)
- Vedanta Deepa (the light of Vedanta).

An interesting point in Ramanuja's works is that, He happens to have composed all his works only in the Sanskrit language.

Shri Madhvacharya

Period : 1238 to 1317

Place of Birth : Pajaka, Udupi

Guru : Achyuta Prajnya

Names : 1. Vasudeva, as named by his parents 2. Poornaprajnya (One who knows everything)-named after attaining sainthood 3. Anandateertha (One who brings bliss through his preachings)-named after he succeeded his guru 4. Shri Madhvacharya. This name is not given to him by anyone but it comes from the vedas. There is a hymn in the vedas called "balitthaa sookta" where the term "madhva" has been used to refer to "mukhya praana"

Avatars: 1. Hanuman 2. Bhima Madhvaachaarya declares, in his work "Vishnu-tatva-vinirNaya:", that he was the one who took the avatars of Hanuman and Bhima. Significantly, the only other person who openly makes such a declaration about his original form is Sri Krishna, (in Bhagavad-gita).

Madhvacharya (1238-1317) was the chief proponent of Tattvavada (True Philosophy), popularly known as Dvaita or dualistic school of Hindu philosophy. It is one of the three most influential Vedanta philosophies. Madhva was one of the important philosophers during the Bhakti movement. He was a pioneer in many ways, going against standard conventions and norms. Madhvacharya is believed by his followers to be the third incarnation of Vayu, aka Mukhya Prana, after Hanuman and Bhima.

Shri Madhvacharya was born as *Vaasudeva* to Madhyageha Bhatta (father) and Vedavati (mother) at Pajaka in Udupi, Karnataka.

Madhva: The basic tenet of Madhva philosophy is the existence of two kinds of realities, namely "Independent reality" (or svatantra tatva) and "Dependent reality" (or asvatantra tatva).

- *Independent reality* (svatantra)-who/which we refer to as "God". 5 generic names are applicable to God (as per shreemad bhaagavata mahaapuraan). They are "brahman", "para brahman", "aatman", "paramaatman" and "bhagavaan". It is to be noted that by "brahman", aacharya madhva does not mean "chaturmukha brahma". The word "brahman" refers to "brihat" (meaning "big") i.e., the one who/which is the biggest in this universe which, is none other than "God".

In general, aachaarya madhva's important message is that every word, every sound in this entire universe only means God which he equated with Vishnu.

According to Madhva, only Brahman is indepedent in every sense of the word.

- *Dependent reality* (asvatantra)-plurality of Jivas and Prakriti or Nature. Both the Jivas and Nature are dependent on Brahman for their very "being" and "becoming". This dependence is expressed metaphorically as ***Bimba-pratibimba*** (source-reflection) relation. The reflection is in everyway dependent on the source that gets reflected.

Madhva's Credo: Madhva was motivated by his four convictions-

1. A determination to remain true to experience above everything.
2. A commitment to sound reasoning
3. A fervent devotion to a personal God (Vishnu) that drove all his actions
4. Fearless tenacity in expounding his vision in the most hostile environments.

Philosophy of Realism: Dvaita school belongs to the Realist school of Indian philosophy, in the same category as Samkhya, Nyaya, Vaisheshika and Purva mimamsa schools. They believe that the universe is a real creation of Brahman. The plurality of souls are bound by a "real" bondage due to beginning-less ignorance, and sadhana through Vishnu bhakti is the only way to be released from this bondage. Further, Madhva explains that Jnana or knowledge alone is not sufficient for the release from beginningless avidya or ignorance, since this bondage is sustained by the "Will" of Brahman and so needs Vishnu Prasadam to ultimately break the bonds of My.

"The difference between the jiva (soul) and Ishvara (Creator), and the difference between jada (insentient) and Ishvara; and the difference between various jivas, and the difference between jada and jiva; and the difference between various jadas, these five differences make up the universe." From the Paramopanishad a.k.a. Parama-shruti, as quoted by Ananda Tirtha in his 'Vishnu-tattva-vinirNaya'.

Another way of saying this is that these five fundamental real differences are between: Selves and Brahman; matter and Brahman; one Self and another Self; matter and Selves; and, matter and matter.

Contrary to the Idealistic schools like Yogacara, Madhyamika buddhism or Advaita, Dvaita maintains that difference is in the very nature of a substance. This is the reason why some refer to the doctrine of Tattvavada (the preferred name) as 'Dvaita'. However, 'Dvaita' is thought to be inadequately representative of the true grain of Tattvavada.

The doctrine of Tattvavada is considered to be eternal (in a flow-like sense, just as Creation is eternal); in historical times, it was revived by Ananda Tirtha, who is also known as Madhvacharya. Because of this, followers of Tattvavada are called Madhvas, meaning followers of Madhva.

Avatars(as believed) of Shri Madhvacharya. From top (in order of occurrence): Hanuman, Bhima and Shri Madhvacharya.

Souls are not Created by God

- Madhvacharya has established that souls are eternal, and are not created by God as in the Semitic religions. The souls are dependent, not generated by Vishnu but co-exist with Him eternally, supported by His will and entirely controlled by Him. The souls, however, are dependent on Him in their pristine nature and in all transformation that they may undergo.

Three Classes of Souls and Eternal Damnation

- Additionally, Madhvacharya differed significantly from traditional Hindu beliefs in his concept of eternal damnation. For example, he divides souls into three classes, one class which qualify for liberation, Mukti-yogyas, another subject to eternal rebirth or eternally transmigrating due to samsara, Nitya-samsarins, and significantly, a class that is eventually condemned to eternal hell or Andhatamas, known as Tamo-yogyas.

Madhva followers cite authorities such as Bhagavad Gita, Chapter 17, verses 2 et seq. "'There are three types of inclination, which are the self-same natures of the souls, these being satvika, rajasa, and tamasa," Chapter 16, verses 19-20, "These cruel haters, worst among men in the world, I hurl these evil-doers into the wombs of demons only. Entering into demoniacal wombs and deluded, birth after birth, not attaining me, they thus fall, Oh Arjuna, into a condition still lower than that," for their concept of eternal damnation. Madhvacharaya was the first in the recent years who revived the timeless Vaishnava tradition. There were 21 different Bashayas (commenteries) before Sri Madhvacharaya. He is the first to establish the facts of tri-patriate classification of souls. By contrast, most Hindus believe that souls will eventually obtain moksha, even after millions of rebirths.

Madhvacharya's Theology as an Answer to the Eternal Problem of Evil.

- By following the concepts of souls not being created by God and classification of the souls, Madhvacharya provides a lucid answer to the problem of evil by seeking a root cause like the intrinsic nature of the soul itself. Often, evil behaviour displayed in the world might not be just the nature of the soul but also depends upon the timeless actions (Karma) of the soul itself.

Impact of Dvaita Movement

- Madhva's Dualistic view, along with Shankara's Advaita or Nondualism and Ramanuja's

Qualified Nondualism or Vishishtadvaita form some core Indian beliefs on the nature of reality.

- Madhva is considered to be one of the influential theologians in Hindu history. He revitalized an Hindu monotheism in light of attacks, theological and physical, by foreign invasion. Great leaders of the Vaishnava Bhakti movement, in Karnataka, for example, Purandara Dasa and Kanaka Dasa were part of the Dvaita traditions. Also, the famous Hindu saint, Raghavendra Swami, was a leading figure in the Dvaita tradition.

Madhvacharaya during his time not only established dvaita philosophy, but also displayed extraordinary strength and skills to show that he is the third avatara of Vayu, who came down to earth to help people suffering from delusional philosophies and guide them in the right path. Madhvacharaya at the age of 79, year 1317, disappeared from the eyes of humans and continue to reside in Upper Badari in his continuning service to his eternal master Sri Vedavyasa.

Narayana panditAcharya captures Madhvacharaya's life in a beautiful poetic verses in his "Shri Madhva Vijaya" which is in 16 Sarga (chapters), this book is an authentic work composed during his own time. This is a very rare work, there is no evidence of anyone composing works on any major philosopher like this before or after him from other disciplines. "Shri Madhva Vijaya" is a composition which captures life history of Mahdvacharaya.

Religious Establishments: The main icon (vigraha) in Udupi of Lord Krishna was established by Madhvacharya. The 8 monasteries (ashta mathas) of Udupi have been following his philosophy since then.

Icon of Lord Krishna in Udupi installed by Shri Madhvacharya

Comparison to Mainstream Hinduism

The teachings of Sri Madhvacharya were in many ways quite radical for his times. One example is his doctrine of eternal damnation. This idea which is prevalent in Abrahamic religions, is generally not endorsed by most schools of Hindu philosophy. Many Western scholars see this and the importance given to *Mukhya Prana*-as the mediator to *Brahman*-as Christian influence. But Dvaita scholars argue that Madhva has derived these concepts from within the Vedic framework. There are many instances in the Upanishads and Gita that support Madhva's position. They also argue that since the knowledge of whether a Jiva is *Muktiyogya* (liberation-worthy) or *Tamoyogya* (damnation-worthy) is not accessible to the Jiva himself, this philosophy does not discourage *sadhana* for anyone.

Ramakrishna Paramahansa

Born: February 18, 1836 Kamarpukur, West Bengal, India

Died: 16 August, 1886 Garden House in Cossipore.

Historically, in India, emphasis is given to the teachings of saints and less attention is paid to dates and details. In the case of Ramakrishna though, we have first-hand accounts of his life and times. This was possible because many of his disciples were well-educated and had a strong desire to present only facts that could be verified from multiple sources. Some credit for collecting and recording such facts goes to Swami Saradananda, a disciple of Ramakrishna. He wrote a biography from the legends and stories which were growing around Ramakrishna. A new English translation of this by Swami Chetanananda is available.

However, the best known record of Ramakrishna's teachings is the Bengali *Kathamrita* written by Mahendranath Gupta. Swami Nikhilananda's translation of this into the English language, *The Gospel of Sri Ramakrishna*, is the most widely read. In the preface to his translation, Nikhilananda states, "I have made a literal translation, omitting only a few pages of no particular interest to English-speaking readers." Some claim that Nikhilananda's omissions have led to Western difficulties in interpreting the *Kathamrita*.

Childhood: Gadadhar was born in the village of Kamarpukur, in what is now the Hooghly district of West Bengal. Gadadhar's parents, Khudiram and Chandramani, were poor and made ends meet with great difficulty. Gadadhar was extremely popular in his village. He was considered handsome and had a natural gift for the fine arts. He, however, disliked going to school, and was not interested in the pursuit of money. He loved nature and spent his time in fields and fruit gardens outside the village with his friends. He was seen visiting monks who stopped at his village on their way to Puri. He would serve them and listen with rapt attention to the religious debates they often had.

When arrangements for Gadadhar to be invested with the sacred thread (Upanayana) were nearly complete, he declared that he would have his first alms as a Brahmin from a certain Sudra woman of the village. This was a shock in the days when tradition required that the first alms be from a brahmin, but he was adamant. He said he had given his word to the lady and if he did not keep his word, what sort of Brahmin would he be? No argument, no appeal, no amount of tears are said to have budged him from his position. Finally, Ramkumar, his eldest brother and the head of the family after the passing away of their father, gave in.

Meanwhile, the family's financial position worsened every day. Ramkumar ran a Sanskrit school in Calcutta and also served as purohit priest in some families. About this time, a rich woman of Calcutta, Rani Rashmoni, founded a temple at Dakshineswar. She approached Ramkumar to serve as priest at the temple of Kali and Ramkumar agreed. After some persuasion, Gadadhar agreed to decorate the deity. When Ramkumar retired, Gadadhar took his place as priest.

Career as Priest: When Gadadhar started worshipping the deity Bhavatarini, he began to question if he was worshipping a piece of stone or a living Goddess. If he was worshipping a living Goddess, why should she not respond to his worship? This question nagged him day and night. Then, he began to pray to Kali:

> *"Mother, you've been gracious to many devotees in the past and have revealed yourself to them. Why would you not reveal yourself to me, also? Am I not also your son?"*

He is known to have wept bitterly and sometimes even cry out loudly while worshipping. At night, he would go into a nearby jungle and spend the whole night praying. One day, the famous account goes, he was so impatient to see Mother Kali that he decided to end his life. He seized a sword hanging on the wall and was about to strike himself with it, when he is reported to have seen light issuing from the deity in waves. He is said to have been soon overwhelmed by the waves and fell unconscious on the floor.

Gadadhar, however, unsatiated, prayed to Mother Kali for more religious experiences. He especially wanted to know the truths that other religions taught. Strangely, these teachers came to him when necessary and he is said to have reached the ultimate goals of those religions with ease. Soon word spread about this remarkable man and people of all denominatiohs and all stations of life began to come to him.

Initiation: Ramakrishna was initiated in Advaita Vedanta by a wandering monk named Totapuri, in the city of Dakshineswar. Totapuri was "a teacher of masculine strength, a sterner mien, a gnarled physique, and a virile voice". Ramakrishna would soon affectionately address the monk as Nangta, the "Naked One", because as a sannyasin (renunciate) he did not wear any clothing.

After the departure of Totapuri, RamakrisHna reportedly remained for six month in a state of absolute contemplations:

> *For six months in a stretch, I [Ramakrishna] remained in that state from which ordinary men can never return; generally the body falls off, after three weeks, like a sere leaf. I was not conscious of day or night. Flies would enter my mouth and nostrils as they do a dead's body, but I did not feel them. My hair became matted with dust.*

Married Life: Rumors spread to Kamarpukur that Ramakrishna had gone mad as a result of over-taxing spiritual exercises at Dakshineswar. Alarmed, neighbours advised Ramakrishna's mother that he be persuaded to marry, so that he might be more conscious of his responsibilities to the family. Far from objecting to the marriage, he, in fact, mentioned Jayrambati, three miles to the north-west of Kamarpukur, as being the village where the bride could be found at the house of one Ramchandra Mukherjee. The bride of six-years, Sarada, was found and the marriage was duly solemnised. Sarada was Ramakrishna's first disciple. He attempted to teach her everything he learnt from his various Gurus. She is believed to have mastered every religious secret as quickly as Ramakrishna had. Impressed by her religious potential, he began to treat her as the Universal Mother Herself and performed a Puja considering Sarada as veritable Tripura Sundari Devi. He said, 'I look upon you as my own mother and the Mother who is in the temple'. Ramakrishna impressed upon Sarada Devi that she was not only the mother of his young disciples, but also of the entire humanity. Initially, Sarada Devi was shy about playing this role, but slowly, she filled it with courage.

Her r enunciation is believed by devotees to be a striking quality that she shared with her husband in a measure equal to, if not beyond, his. The true nature of their relationship and kinship was believed to be beyond the grasp of ordinary minds. Ramakrishna concluded, after close and constant association with her, that her relationship and attitude toward him were firmly based on a divine spiritual plane. Devotees believe that as they shared their lives, day and night, no other thought, other than that of the divine presence, arose in their minds. An account of such continued divine relationship between two souls of opposite gender is unique in religious records, not known in any of the past hagiographies. After the passing away of Ramakrishna, Sarada Devi became a religious teacher in her own rights.

Later Life: He soon came to be known as Ramakrishna Paramahansa, and like a magnet, is said to have begun to attract genuine seekers of God. He taught ceaselessly for fifteen years or so through parables, metaphors, songs and above all by his own life, the basic truths of religion. He had developed throat cancer and attained Mahasamadhi at a Garden House in Cassiopeia on 16 August, 1886, leaving behind a devoted band of 16 young disciples headed by the well-known saint-philosopher and orator, Swami Vivekananda and host of householder disciples. Among his contemporaries, Keshab Chandra

Sen and Pandit Ishwar Chandra Vidyasagar, who were known to be against Hindu idol-worship, were his admirers.

Teachings: Ramakrishna emphasised that God-realisation is the supreme goal of all living beings. Hence, for him, religion served as a means for the achievement of this goal. Ramakrishna's mystical realization, classified by Hindu tradition as nirvikalpa samadhi (literally, "constant meditation", thought to be absorption in the all-encompassing Consciousness), led him to believe that various religions are various ways to reach the Absolute, and that the Ultimate Reality could never be expressed in human terms. This is in agreement with the Rigvedic proclamation that "Truth is one but sages call it by many a name." As a result of this opinion, Ramakrishna actually spent periods of his life practising his own understandings of Islam, Christianity and various other Yogic and Tantric sects within Hinduism.

Devotees believe that Ramakrishna's realization of nirvikalpa samadhi also led him to an understanding of the two sides of maya (illusion), to which he referred as avidyamaya and vidyamaya: He explained that *avidyamaya* represents the dark forces of creation (eg. sensual desire, evil passions, greed, lust and cruelty), which keep the world system on lower planes of consciousness. These forces are responsibie for human entrapment in the cycle of birth and death, and they must be fought and vanquished. *Vidyamaya*, on the other hand, represents the higher forces of creation (e.g. spiritual virtues, enlightening qualities, kindness, purity, love, and devotion), which elevate human beings to the higher planes of consciousness. With the help of vidyamaya, he said that devotees could rid themselves of avidyamaya and achieve the ultimate goal of becoming mayatita-that is, free from maya.

Ramakrishna's proclamation of *jatra jiv tatra Shiv* (wherever there is a living being, there is Shiva) stemmed from his Advaitic perception of Reality. This would lead him teach his disciples," Jive *daya noy, Shiv gyane jiv seba*". (not kindness to living beings, but serving the living being as Shiva Himself). This view differs considerably from the "sentimental pantheism" of Francis of Assisi.

Ramakrishna, though not formally trained as a philosopher, had an intuitive grasp of complex philosophical concepts. According to him the visible universe and many other universes (brahmanda) are mere bubbles emerging out of the all supreme ocean of intelligence (*Brahman*).

The key concepts in Ramakrishna's teachings were:

- the oneness of existence
- the divinity of all living beings
- the unity of God and the harmony of religions
- that the primal bondage in human life is lust and greed (*kamini* and *kanchana* in Bengali)

A personal account of his life and teachings is recorded by his disciple, Mahendranath Gupta, simply known as "M", in *Kathamrita.* The account makes us aware of Ramakrishna's distinctive conversational style, his profuse employment of metaphors and parables, his characteristic wit and his frequent use of Bangla dialect words and idioms.

Like Adi Sankara had done more than a thousand years earlier, Ramakrishna Paramahansa revitalized Hinduism which had been fraught with excessive ritualism and superstition in the nineteenth century and helped it better respond to challenges from Islam, Christianity and the dawn of the modern era. However, unlike Adi Sankara Ramakrishna developed ideas about post-samadhi descent of consciousness into the phenomenal world, which he went on to term as *Vignana*. While he asserted the supreme validity of Advaita Vedanta, he also proclaimed that he accepts both the *Nitya* (Eternal Substratum) and the *Leela* (lit.play, indicating the dynamic Phenomenal Reality) as aspects of the Brahman.

The idea of the descent of consciousness shows the influence of the Bhakti movement and certain sub-schools of Shaktism on Ramakrishna's thought. The idea would later influence Aurobindo's views about the Divine Life on Earth.

Ramakrishna's Impact: Born as he was during a social upheaval in Bengal in particular and India in general, Ramakrishna and his movement was an important part of the direction that Hinduism and Indian nationalism took in the coming years.

On Hinduism: The Hindu Renaissance that India experienced in the 19th century may be said to have been spurred by his life and work. Although the Brahmo Samaj and the Arya Samaj preceded the Ramakrishna Mission, their influence was limited on a broader level. With the emergence of the Mission, however, the situation changed dramatically. The Ramakrishna Mission was founded by Ramakrishna himself when he had distributed the gerua cloth of renunciation to his direct disciples. This is corroborated by Swami Vivekananda himself when he says that without Thakur's grace all this would not have been possible. Many Ramakrishnites believe that Vivekananda acted as Ramakrishna's message-bearer to the West and hence helped in the fulfillment of their master's spiritual mission.

Hinduism faced a huge intellectual challenge in the 19th century, from Westerners and Indians alike. The Hindu practice of idol worship came under intense pressure specially in Bengal, then the center of British India, and was declared intellectually unsustainable. Response to this was varied, ranging from Young Bengal movement that denounced Hindusim and embraced Christianity or atheism, to the Brahmo movement that retained primacy of Hinduism but gave up idol worship, and to the staunch Hindu nationalism of Bankim Chandra Chattopadhyay. Ramakrishna's influence was crucial in this period for a Hindu revival of a more traditional kind, and can be compared to that of Chaitanya's contribution centuries earlier, when Hinduism in Bengal was under similar pressure from the growing power of Islam.

It would be difficult to give a comprehensive description of Ramakrishna's influence on Hinduism, being as deep as it is, but some important contributions of his can nevertheless be detected. In his worship of Mother Kali's murti, he questions the crux of idol worship-whether he is worshipping a piece of stone or a living Goddess and why she does not respond to his prayers. He is reassured several times by experiences that show him that she is present. To the many that revered him, this reinforced centuries old traditions that were in glaring spotlight at the time. Ramakrishna also touted an inclusive version of the religion, declaring *Joto mot toto path*. In Bangla, this roughly means *Every opinion yields a path*. He adopted a name that is clearly Vaishnavite (Rama and Krishna are both incarnations of Vishnu), but was a devotee of Kali, the mother Goddess, and known to have followed various other religious paths including Tantrism and even Christianity and Islam.

On Indian Nationalism: Ramakrishna's impact on the growing Indian nationalism was, if more indirect, nevertheless quite notable. A large number of intellectuals of that age had regular communication with him and respected him, though not all of them necessarily agreed with him on religious matters. Numerous members of the Brahmo Samaj respected him. Though some of them embraced his form of Hinduism, the fact that many others didn't shows that they detected in him a possibility for a strong national identity in the face of a colonial adversary that was intellectually undermining the Indian civilization. A similar statement could be made about the fact that Ishwar Chandra Vidyasagar and Ramakrishna held each other in high esteem, in spite of the fact that the first was a declared atheist.

Sarada Devi

Born: 1853

Died: 1920

The affectionate term "Holy Mother" refers to Sarada Devi (1853-1920), Ramakrishna's wife and spiritual counterpart. According to the custom then prevalent in India, she was betrothed to him while still a child. At the age of 18, she left her parental home to join her husband, who lived some sixty miles away, near Calcutta.

By that time Ramakrishna had dedicated his body and mind to the spiritual search and lived the life of a monk. Yet he received Sarada very kindly, feeling that Divine Providence had brought her. After nursing her to recovery from an illness contracted on the journey, Ramakrishna one day asked her why she had come to join him. She replied that she had come only to help him in his chosen way, which as she well knew meant the way of complete renunciation of all earthly ties for the sake of God-realization. Thus, instead of seeking conjugal fulfillment, she became his first disciple..

Sarada Devi was a spiritual and intellectual leader in her own right. She served Ramakrishna and his disciples for many years. After Ramakrishna's passing away, she carried on his religious ministry, serving as guide and inspiration of the new spiritual movement.

Although by all accounts she was a modest and self-effacing woman, the movement started by Ramakrishna continued to grow in prominence and become quite influential in the waning days of British colonial rule. Swami Vivekananda, because he was a man and because of his family background, perhaps had more of an impact politically back in Calcutta, but Sarada Devi remained the head of the religious community in Dakshineswar. Before his death, Ramakrishna encouraged his disciples to treat her as if she were their mother, paralleling the role of Kali as the mother of humanity. She nurtured them accordingly, helping with personal matters. Moreover, she was an important interpreter and teacher of Ramakrishna's thinking for all comers.

Quotes

- "I am the mother of the righteous, I am the mother of the wicked as well. Never fear. Whenever you are in distress, just say to yourself 'I have a mother.'"
- "I tell you one thing. If you want peace of mind, do not find fault with others. Rather see

your own faults. Learn to make the whole world your own. No one is a stranger, my child; the whole world is your own."

- "God is one's very own. The more intensely a person practices spiritual disciplines, the more quickly he attains to God."
- "Never fear. He is ever looking after you. Do His work and practice Sadhana. A little work daily drives away idle thoughts from the mind."
- "Call on the Lord who pervades the entire universe. He will shower His blessings upon you."
- "The mind is rendered pure as a result of much austerities. God who is purity itself cannot be attained without austerities."

Swami Vivekananda

Vivekananda, Ramakrishna's most illustrious disciple, is considered by some to be one of his most important legacies.

Please expand and improve this section as described on this article's talk page or at Requests for expansion, then remove this message.

Contemporary Influence: It could be argued that Ramakrishna's vision of Hinduism, and its popularisation by western converts like Christopher Isherwood, have largely coloured Western notions of what Hinduism is. Some, like Andrew Harvey and Ken Wilber, see the beginning of a new planetary consciousness with Ramakrishna's life.

Religious scholar Jeffrey Kripal has written a controversial psychoanalytic study of Ramakrishna entitled *Kali's Child: The Mystical and the Erotic in the Life and Teachings of Ramakrishna*. The book theorizes upon an alleged homoerotic strain in Ramakrishna's life, sadhana and philosophy. It has been criticized by the Ramakrishna Mission and other followers as being based on many mistranslations of primary sources, deceptions, and an incorrect use of psychoanalysis as a tool in forming the theory.

Historian Narasingha Sil has also written an account of Ramakrishna that acknowledges Ramnakrishna's sexuality and which contradicts the accounts endorsed by the Ramakrishna Mission.

12 January 1863 Kolkata, West Bengal, India

Died: 4 July, 1902 Belur Math near Kolkata

Swami Vivekananda (Bengali: *Shami Bibekanondo*), whose pre-monastic name was Narendranath Dutta (*Nôrendronath Dotto*) (January 12, 1863-July 4, 1902) was one of the most famous and influential spiritual leaders of the Vedanta philosophy. He was the chief disciple of Ramakrishna Paramahansa and was the founder of Ramakrishna Math and Ramakrishna Mission. Many consider him an icon for his fearless courage, his positive exhortations to the youth, his broad outlook on social problems, and countless lectures and discourses on Vedanta philosophy.

Birth and Early Life: Narendranath Dutta was born in Shimla Pally, Kolkata, West Bengal, India on January 12, 1863 as the son of Viswanath Dutta and Bhuvaneswari Devi. Even as he was young, he showed a precocious mind and keen memory. He practiced meditation from a very early age. While at school, he was good at studies, as well as games of various kinds. He organised an amateur theatrical company and a gymnasium and took lessons in fencing, wrestling, rowing and other sports. He also studied instrumental and vocal music. He was a leader among his group of friends. Even when he was young, he questioned the validity of superstitious customs and discrimination based on caste and religion.

In 1879, Narendra entered the Presidency College, Calcutta for higher studies. After one year, he joined the Scottish Church College, Calcutta and studied philosophy. During the course, he studied western logic, western philosophy and history of European nations.

Questions started to arise in young Narendra's mind about God and the presence of God. This made him associate with the Brahmo Samaj, an important religious movement of the time, led by Keshab Chandra Sen. But the Samaj's congregational prayers and devotional songs could not satisfy Narendra's zeal to realise God. He would ask leaders of Brahmo Samaj whether they have seen God. He never got a satisfying answer. It was during this time that Professor Hastie of Scottish Church College told him about Sri Ramakrishna of Dakshineswar.

With Ramakrishna: Narendra met Ramakrishna for the first time in November 1881. He asked Ramakrishna the same old question, whether he had seen God. The instantaneous answer from Ramakrishna was, *"Yes, I see God, just as I see you here, only in a much intenser sense."* Narendra was astounded and puzzled. He could feel the man's words were honest and uttered from depths of experience. He started visiting Ramakrishna frequently. Though Narendra could not accept Ramakrishna and his visions, he could not neglect him. It had always been in Narendra's nature to test something thoroughly before he could accept it. He tested Ramakrishna to the maximum, but the master was patient, forgiving, humorous, and full of love. He never asked Narendra to abandon reason, and he faced all of Narendra's arguments and examinations with infinite patience. In time, Narendra accepted Ramakrishna, and while he accepted, his acceptance was whole-hearted. While Ramakrishna predominantly taught duality and Bhakti to his other disciples, he taught Narendra the Advaita Vedanta, the philosophy of non-dualism.

During the course of five years of his training under Ramakrishna, Narendra was transformed from a restless, puzzled, impatient youth to a mature man who was ready to renounce everything for the sake of God-realization. Soon, Ramakrishna's end came in the form of throat cancer in August 1886. After this Narendra and a core group of Ramakrishna's disciples took vows to become monks and renounce everything, and started living in a supposedly haunted house in Baranagore. They took alms to satisfy their hunger and their other needs were taken care of by Ramakrishna's richer householder disciples.

Wanderings in India: Soon, the young monks of Baranagore wanted to live the life of a wandering monk with rags and a begging bowl and no other possessions. On July 1890, Vivekananda set out for a long journey, without knowing where the journey would take him. The journey that followed took him to the length and breadth of the Indian subcontinent. During these days, Vivekananda assumed various names like Vividishananda, Satchidananda, etc., It is said that he was given the name *Vivekananda* by Maharaja of Khetri for his discernment of things, good and bad.

During these wandering days, Vivekananda stayed on king's palaces, as well as the huts of the poor. He came in close contact with the culture of different regions of India and various classes of people in India. Vivekananda observed the imbalance in society and tyranny in the name of caste. He realised the need for a national rejuvenation if India was to survive at all. He reached Kanyakumari, the southernmost tip of the Indian subcontinent on 24 December, 1892. There, he swam across the sea and started meditating on a lone rock. He thus meditated for three days and said later that he meditated about the past, present and future of India. The rock went on to become the Vivekananda memorial at Kanyakumari.

Vivekananda went to Madras and spoke about his plans for India and Hinduism to the young men of Madras. They were impressed by the monk and urged him to go to the United States and represent Hinduism in the World Parliament of Religions. Thus, helped by his friends at Madras, Raja of Ramnad and Maharajas of Mysore and Khetri, Vivekananda set out on his journey to the USA.

In the West: Vivekananda was received well at the 1893 World Parliament of Religions in Chicago, Illinois, where he delivered a series of lectures. He also earned wild applause for beginning his address with the famous words, ***"Sisters and brothers of America."*** Vivekananda's arrival in the USA has been identified by many to mark the beginning of western interest in Hinduism not as merely an exotic eastern oddity, but as a vital religious and philosophical tradition that might actually have something important to teach the West. Within a few years of the Parliament, he had started Vedantic centres in New York City, New York and London, lectured at major universities and generally kindled western interest in Hinduism. His success was not without controversy, much of it from Christian missionaries of whom he was fiercely critical. After four years of constant touring, lecturing and retreats in the West, he came back to India in the year 1897.

Back in India: Admirers and devotees of Vivekananda gave him an enthusiastic reception on his return to India. In India, he delivered a series of lectures, and this set of lectures known as "Lectures from Colombo to Almora" is considered to have uplifted the morale of the then downtrodden Indian society. He founded the Ramakrishna Mission. This institution is now one of the largest monastic orders of Hindu society in India.

However, he had to bear great criticism from other orthodox Hindus for having travelled in — what they perceived to be — the impure West. His contemporaries also questioned his motives, wondering whether the fame and glory of his Hindu evangelism compromised his original monastic vows. His enthusiasm for America and Britain, and his spiritual devotion to his motherland, caused significant tension in his last years.

Death: On July 4, 1902 at Belur Math near Kolkata, he taught Vedanta philosophy to some pupils in the morning. He had a walk with Swami Premananda, a brother-disciple and gave him instructions concerning the future of the Ramakrishna Math. In the evening he went for meditation in his room facing the Ganga and died in Mahasamadhi.

Principles and Philosophy: Vivekananda was a renowned thinker in his own right. One of his most important contributions was to demonstrate how Advaitin thinking is not merely philosophically far-reaching, but how it also has social, even political, consequences. One important lesson he claimed to receive from Ramakrishna was that "Jiva is Shiva " (each individual is divinity itself). This became his Mantra, and he coined the concept of *daridra narayana seva*-the service of God in and through (poor) human beings. *If there truly is the unity of Brahman underlying all phenomena, then on what* *basis do we regard ourselves as better or worse, or even as better-off or worse-off, than others?* This was the question he posed to himself. Ultimately, he concluded that these distinctions fade into nothingness in the light of the oneness that the devotee experiences in Moksha. What arises then is compassion for those "individuals" who remain unaware of this oneness and a determination to help them.

Swami Vivekananda belonged to that branch of Vedanta that held that no one can be truly free until all of us are. Even the desire for personal salvation has to be given up, and only tireless work for the salvation of others is the true mark of the enlightened person. He founded the Sri Ramakrishna Math and Mission on the principle of Atmano Mokshartham Jagad-hitaya cha. (for one's own salvation and for the welfare of the World).

However, Vivekananda also pleaded for a strict separation between religion and government ("church and state"). Although social customs had been formed in the past with religious sanction, it was not now the business of religion to interfere with matters such as marriage, inheritance and so on. The ideal society would be a mixture of Brahmin knowledge, Kshatriya culture, Vaisya efficiency and the egalitarian Shudra ethos. Domination by any one led to different sorts of lopsided societies. Vivekananda did not feel that religion, nor, any force for that matter, should be used forcefully to bring about an ideal society, since this was something that would evolve naturally by individualistic change when the conditions were right.

Vivekanda advised his followers to be holy, unselfish and have shraddha (faith). He encouraged the practise of Brahmacharya (Celibacy). In one of the conversations with his childhood friend *Sri Priya Nath Sinha* he attributes his physical and mental strengths, eloquence to the practice of brahmacharya.

Vivekananda didn't advocate the emerging area of parapsychology, astrology (one instance can be found in his speech *Man the Maker of his Destiny, Complete-Works, Volume 8, Notes of Class Talks and Lectures*) saying that this form of curiosity doesn't help in spiritual progress but actually hinders it.

Many years after his death, Rabindranath Tagore (a prominent member of the Brahmo Samaj) had said: *If you want to know India, study Vivekananda. In him everything is positive and nothing negative.* Incidentally, in the earlier years Tagore did not have much respect for Swami Vivekananda for his idol-worshipping. On the other hand, Vivekananda was not particularly impressed by Tagore, though he had been interacting with Tagore's father Maharshi Debendra Nath. Vivekananda was a very good singer and used to sing lots of *Bhajans*, including about twelve written and composed by Tagore.

Mahatma Gandhi who strived for a lot of reform in Hinduism himself, said: *Swami Vivekananda's writings need no introduction from anybody. They make their own irresistible appeal.*

Though it may not be obvious, Swami Vivekananda inspired India's freedom struggle movement. His writings inspired a whole generation of freedom fighters, in Bengal in particular and India at large. Most prominent among them are Subhash Chandra Bose and Aurobindo Ghosh.

Sri Aurobindo, actually considered *Swamiji* as his mentor. While in Alipore Jail, Sri Aurobindo used to be visited by Swami Vivekananda in his meditation. *Swamiji* guided Sri Aurobindo's yoga.

Vivekananda was a soul of ruissance if ever there was one, a very lion among men, but the definitive work he has left behind is quite incommensurate with our impression of his creative might and energy. We perceive his influence still working gigantically, we know not well how, we know not well where, in something that is not yet formed, something leonine, grand, intutive, upheaving that has entered the soul of India and we say, "Behold, Vivekananda still lives in the soul of his Mother and in the souls of her children. —Sri Aurobindo—1915 in Vedic Magazine.

Abroad, he had some interactions with Max Mueller and Romain Rolland. The latter also wrote a book in 1930 entitled *Vie de Vivekananda (Life of Vivekananda).* Nikola Tesla was one of those influenced by the Vedic philosophy teachings of the Swami Vivekananda.

Works: His books (compiled from lectures given around the world) on the four Yogas (Raja Yoga, Karma Yoga, Bhakti Yoga, Jnana Yoga) are very influential and still seen as fundamental texts for anyone interested in the Hindu practice of Yoga. His letters are of great literary and spiritual value. He was also a very good singer and a poet. He had composed many songs including his favorite *Kali the Mother*. He used humor for his teachings and was also an excellent cook. His language is very free flowing. His own Bengali writings stand testimony to the fact that he believed that words-spoken or written should be for making things easier to understand rather than show off the speaker or writer's knowledge.

Quotes

"Each soul is potentially divine. The goal is to manifest this divinity within, by controlling nature, external and internal. Do this either by work, or worship, or psychic control, or philosophy-by one, or more, or all of these-and be free. This is the whole of religion. Doctrines, or dogmas, or rituals, or books, or temples, or forms, are but secondary details."

"The one theme of the Vedanta philosophy is the search after unity. The Hindu mind does not care for the particular; it is always after the general, nay, the universal. "what is it that by knowing which everything else is to be known." That is the one search."

"Look upon every man, woman, and everyone as God. You cannot help anyone, you can only serve: serve the children of the Lord, serve the Lord Himself, if you have the privilege."

"It may be that I shall find it good to get outside of my body — to cast it off like a disused garment. But I shall not cease to work! I shall inspire men everywhere, until the world shall know that it is one with God."

"Mankind ought to be taught that religions are but the varied expressions of THE RELIGION, which is Oneness, so that each may choose the path that suits him best."

" So long as even a single dog in my country is without food, my whole religion will be to feed it."

"This is the gist of all worship-to be pure and to do good to others. He who sees Siva (Hindu God) in the poor, in the weak, and in the diseased, really worships Siva, and if he sees Siva only in the image, his worship is but preliminary. He who has served and helped one poor man seeing Siva in him, without thinking of his caste, creed, or race, or anything, with him

Siva is more pleased than with the man who sees Him only in temples."

"Aye , who ever saw money make the man? It is man that always make money. The whole world has been made by the energy of man, by the power of enthusiasm, by the power of faith."

"It is a tremendous error to feel helpless. Do not seek help from anyone. We are our own help. If we cannot help ourselves, there is none to help us."

" All power is within you, you can do anything and everything. Believe in that, do not believe that you are weak... You can do anything and everything, without even the guidance of any one. All power is there. Stand up and express the divinity with you... Arise, awake, sleep no more. With each of you there is the power to remove all wants and all miseries. Believe in this, that power will be manifested. "

"On this basic-begin right and doing right the whole world can unite."

The turban that Vivekananda used to wear is generally believed to be suggested by Maharaja of Khetri. But some people claim that Vivekananda visited the Swamithope Pathi during his visit to Kanyakumari in December 1892 and believe that he was impressed by the principles behind rituals of this monistic faith, such as wearing a head gear during worship in temple, worshipping in front of mirror etc., and started wearing a turban from then on. Some also suggest that Vivekananda received some spiritual instructions from the disciples of Ayya Vaikundar. There is no mention of this in Vivekananda's biographies or works. It is also said that while he was a child, he was impressed by the turban of the horse cab driver, who used to ferry his father on his daily work. Subsequently when he renounced the world and took to sanyasa, he started using one himself.

Trivia

- Swami Vivekananda was the first Indian to be invited to accept the chair of Oriental Philosophy at Harvard University.
- Jamshedji Tata set up the Tata Institute or the Indian Institute of Science on the Swami's advice and he was offered the post of Director for the Institute which he declined.
- India celebrates *National Youth Day* on his birthday

Narayana Guru (1856-1928)

Narayan Guru was a great sage and social reformer of India. Born in *Ezhava/Thiyya* (Ezhavas were a middle rung caste and have to face social injustices), he revolted against the brahminical dominance and thereby transformed the social face of Kerala.

Narayana Guru is revered for his *Vedic* knowledge, poetic proficiency, openness to the views of others, non-violent philosophy and most importantly his unrelenting resolve to set aright social wrongs. Narayana Guru was instrumental in setting the spiritual foundations for social reform in the current State of Kerala (erstwhile states of Travancore, Kochi and Malabar district of British India) and was one of the most successful social reformers who tackled caste in India. He demonstrated a path to social emancipation without invoking the dualism of the opressed and the opressor.

In contrast to certain other reformers who criticized Brahmins and upper caste Hindus for the conditions of the lower castes, Narayana Guru stressed on the upliftment of a community through its own efforts by the establishment of schools and temples. In the process he brushed aside the Hindu religious conventions based upon *Chaturvarna*. His transformation of the social face of Kerala relied on emphasizing the Advaita philosophy of Sankara.

Early Life: The Guru was born at Chempazhanthi, a small village near Thiruvananthapuram, circa 1856. As the only son of his parents, who had three daughters, the young boy was named Nanu (shortname for *Narayana*). The small thatched house where Nanu was born is preserved to date as a historic monument. Nanu's father Madan Auan, of the *Valyalvarathu* joint family, was a Sanskrit teacher knowledgeable in astrology, Ayurvedic medicine and the epics of Hinduism. Nanu's uncle Krishnan Vaidyan was a reputed Ayurvedic physician and Sanskrit scholar. Nanu is said to have been initiated into traditional formal education *Ezhuthinirithal* under Chempazhanthi Pillai, a local schoolmaster and village officer. Besides schooling, young Nanu continued to be educated at home, under the guidance of his father and his uncle Krishnan Vaidyan, where he was taught basics of the Tamil and Sanskrit languages and traditional subjects such as *Siddharupam, Balaprobhodhanam* and *Amarakoœam.*

Biographical accounts talk of Nanu as a reticent and intelligent boy who was intensely drawn to devout worship at the *Manackal* temple adjacent to the *Valyalvarathu* home. The boy Nanu is also said to have many a times challenged his own relatives for social discrimination and the apartheid-like practices of segregation of children of, supposedly, lower castes in his times. He is also said to have preferred solitude, to be immersed in thought, and to have shown a strong aptitude for rhyme and reason, composing his own hymns and singing them in praise of God. Having lost his mother around the age of 15, Nanu is thought to have spent most of his teenage assisting both his father, with tutoring, and his uncle in the practice of Ayurvedic medicine whilst also self-indulging in intense devotional practices at temples nearby.

Transformation as Master, Yogi and Seeker of Truth: At the age of 21 young Nanu was sent for further education under an eminent scholar Kummampilli Raman Pillai Auan of Karunagapalli. Living as a guest in a prominent family house *Varanapallil* near Kayankulam, Nanu, along with other students, was tutored by this scholar in subjects like advanced Sanskrit Language and Poetry, Drama and Literary Criticism, and Logical Rhetoric.

Around the age of 25, Nanu returned to his village after which he was off and on involved in running a village school for children. His role as a teacher gained him the name Nanu Auan (Auan meaning a master or teacher). Whilst teaching and also experimenting with truth, through self-study and his own experiences with life, Nanu Auan moved on foot to places in the vicinity, often spending time in the confines of temples, writing poems and hymns and lecturing to village folk on philosophy and moral values.

Though married, through an initiative by his sisters, Nanu Auan was not inclined towards a married life, nor is much known about his marital life, which would have ended with the increasing intensity of his spiritual inclination and drifting as a wandering ascetic in search of truth, as did Gautama Buddha.

During his meandering days, at the house of another Sanskrit scholar and old classmate, Perunalli

Krishnan Vidayar, Nanu Auan got introduced to many learned men and peers, including Kunjan Pilla, who was destined to become his spiritual guide and soulmate Chattampi Swamikal. Kunjan Pilla, who discovered and appreciated Nanu Auan's philosophical genius and passion for Yoga, introduced Nanu Auan to a master of Yogic practices by name Thycaud Ayyavu. Under the Yogi Thycaud Ayyavu, Nanu Auan mastered various Yogic practices including Hatha Yoga. The exposure gained from this scholastic experience had a lasting impact on the later life and philosophy of Narayana Guru.

Enlightenment and its Poetic Expression: It is uncertain as to when precisely Nanu Auan moved to his hermitage deep inside the hilly forest area in Maruthwamala, where he is said to have subjected himself to the most austere life immersed in meditative thought, other rigorous yoga practices and extreme sustenance rituals. After an unpretentious life of over thirty years abounding in knowledge and harsh experiences, this epoch is considered the culmination of the meditative recluse; the point at which Narayana Guru is believed to have attained a state of Enlightenment, i.e. an absolute state of wisdom or awakening.

Narayana Guru's later literary and philosophical masterpiece *Atmopadeœa satakam (one hundred verses of self-instruction, written in Malayalam circa 1897)* is considered a fertile poetic expression, encapsulating the Guru's philosophy of egalitarianism, emanating from the author's attainment of an experienced state of primordial knowledge and quintessence of the Universe; and his ensuing ability to view the human race, from a dignified and elevated perspective, as nothing but one of a genus, in unqualified equality and without any racial, religious, caste or other discriminations whatsoever.

Consecration of Siva Lingam at Aruvippuram: During his wandering life he happened to be at Aruvippuram in 1888. In the month of March that year, because of the request from local people who had no privileges to enter into Hindu temples, he decided to build a place of worship. He picked up a stone from a nearby river (Neyyar) and used it as an idol for the proposed temple and consecrated it. This in itself was revolutionary step for according to some of the Hindu scriptures, only brahmins can consecrate a temple. To the brahmins who questioned his right to do so, he replied that what he consecrated was an *Ezhava Siva*. Those who questioned the timing of the consecration saying it was not an astrologically auspicious time, he replied: *Horoscope is to be cast after the birth of a child, not before*. He instructed to place a plaque containing a motto on the temple wall which read as:

Devoid of dividing walls

Of caste or race

Or hatred of rival faith,

We all live here

In Brotherhood,

Such, know this place to be!

This Model Foundation!

A new phase began in the Guru's life in 1904. He decided to give up his wandering life and settle down in a place to continue his Sadhana (spiritual practice) he choose Sivagiri, twenty miles to the north of Thiruvananthapuram. Goddess 'Amba' became his deity of worship.

Next, he started a Sanskrit school in Varkala. Poor boys and orphans were taken under his care. They were given education regardless of caste distinctions. Temples were built at different places-Trichur, Kannur, Anjuthengu, Tellicherry, Calicut, Mangalore. A temple was built for Sharada Devi in 1912, at Sivagiri. Worship at such temples helped to reduce to a large extent superstitious beliefs and practices.

In 1913, he founded an Ashram at Alwaye. It was called *Advaita Ashram*. This was an important event in his spiritual quest. That Ashram was dedicated to a great principle-*Om Sahodaryam Sarvatra* (all men are equal in the eyes of God). This became the motto of the new Ashram.

When Narayana Guru attained the age of sixty, his birth day was observed throughout the west-coast from Mangalore to Sri Lanka. Between the years 1918 and 1923 he visited and taught in Sri Lanka. In 1921, a Conference of Universal Brotherhood was held at Alwaye. Again in 1924, a conference of all religions was held at Alwaye. The Guru stressed the need for a *Brahma Vidyalaya* for a comparative study of different religious faiths.

Sree Narayana Guru has many followers and disciples. Nataraja Guru, a notable disciple of Sree Narayana Guru, introduced Guru's visions and ideals to the western world. He established Narayana Gurukulamin 1923 at the Nilgiris with the blessings of Narayana Guru.

Narayana Guru's Philosophy: After a span of a millennium since the time of Adi Shankara, Sree Narayana Guru was the next greatest proponent and re-evaluator of Advaita Vedanta and hailing from the same geographic region, i.e., present-day Kerala. Narayana Guru's philosophy, which is fundamentally of Advaitic and non-dual wisdom in principles, further extended Advaita concepts into practical modes of self-realisation through spiritual education, compassion and vision for peaceful co-existence of the human race, whilst promoting social equality and universal brotherhood. His philosophy of non-violence and ahimsa strongly denounced discrimination in the name of caste or religion, and emphasised focusing on education and private enterprise for the ongoing uplift of the quality of life. The Guru's philosophy emphasised the consistency between true existence of the "common reality" on Earth and one Divine behind the creation and sustenance of the Universe, dismissing any concepts of illusory worlds or any mid-way "city on high".

The Guru's philosophy is exemplified in his mystical writings that are truly interchanging warps and wefts of ethics, logic, aesthetics and metaphysics woven into masterpieces of silken rich poetry. The Guru's literary works are in Malayalam, Sanskrit and Tamil languages, and these works are of a conceptual and aesthetic quality at par with the Upanishads.

At the time of its conception, Narayana Guru's philosophy was in many respects ahead of its time and focused on a futuristic world order that could be shaped from his philosophical connotations that are underlain with transcendental aesthetics and logic embodied in knowledge and pure reason. Most of the serious scholars of Narayana Guru's philosophy have been from generations beyond his lifetime; and this list keeps growing.

Rationalism and Atheism: Although Narayana Guru had built a number of temples and composed many poems in praise of popular Hindu deities, he had many atheist followers. This shows his love for humanity as a whole which is irrespective of any faith based affiliations. Many of his atheist followers in fact considered him as an atheist1. For instance, one of his prominent disciples Sahodaran Ayyappan was a militant atheist and one of the founders of Yukthivadi, the first rationalist/atheist magazine in Malayalam. When Sahodaran Ayyappan modified Narayana Guru's famous catch phrase, *Oru Jati, Oru Matham, Oru Daivam Manushyanu* (One Caste, One Religion, One God for Humanbeing) and re-written it as *Jati Venda, Matham Venda, Daivam Venda Manushyanu* (No Caste, No Religion, No God for Humanbeing), the latter did not protest2.

Casteism prevalent amongst the Hindus even in the first half of 20th century was so rabid that uppercaste people refused to have food along with the people belonging to lower caste and "untouchable" communities. Hindu scriptures were profusely quoted by them to justify this practice. The Ezhava community in which Narayana Guru was born too was not immune to this barbaric practice even after half-a-century of Narayana Guru's work. When Sahodaran Ayyappan inspired by Narayanaguru's message of caste-less and creedless society launched what is called *"Panthibhojanam"* or community feasts participating people belonging to various castes and communities, the Ezhava lords called him *"Pulayanaiappan"* (*Pulaya* was used as a derogatory term for having feast with the *"Pulayas"*, an "untouchable" community in the caste-hierarchy of Hinduism) and tried to forcibly prevent the feast. It was in this context that Narayana Guru came out in support of Sahodaran Ayyappan and sent the message reproduced alongside. Translated into English, the message reads: ***"Whatever be one's religion, costume, language etc., since their caste is the same, there is nothing wrong in having inter-marriages and community feasts"***. It is this message of Narayanaguru which transgresses the established canons of Hindu religion (or any religion for that matter) that makes Narayanaguru a rationalist icon.

To avoid the attempts made by a section of his followers to identify him with Hinduism alone, Narayana Guru was forced to state explicitly that he did not belong to any religious sects. Through a message he sent in the year 1916, he proclaimed : ***It is years since I left castes and religions. Yet some people think that I belong to their religion. That is not correct. I do not belong to any particular caste or religion.***

Some other prominent rationalist/atheist leaders, apart from Sahodaran Ayyappan, associated with Narayana Guru were M.C. Joseph, C.V. Kunhiraman and Mithavadi Krishnan.

Works by Narayana Guru

In Malayalam: 1. Swanubavageethi , 2. Atmopadesa Satakam , 3. Advaitha Deepika, 4. Arivu, 5. Daiva Desakam, 6. Jeevakarunya Panchakam, 7. Anukamba Dasakam, 8. Jathi Nirnayam, 9. Jathi Lakshanam, 10. Sadacharam, 11. Chijanda Chinthakam, 12. Daiva Chintanam-1 & 2, 13. Athma Vilasam.

In Sanskrit: 1. Darsana Mala, 2. Brahmavidya Panchakam, 3. Nirvruthi Panchakam, 4. Slokathrayi, 5. Vedantha Suthram, 6. Homa Manthram, 7. Municharya Panchakam, 8. Asramam, 9. Dharmam, 10. Charama Slokangal, 11. Homa Mantram, 12. Chidambarashtakam, 13. Guhashtakam, 14. Bhadrakaliashtakam, 15. Vinayaka Ashtakam, 16. Sree Vasudeva Ashtakam, 17. Navamanjari.

In Tamil: 1. Thevarappathinkangal.

Translations: 1. Thirukural, 2. Isavasyo Upanishad.

Sri Aurobindo

Sri Aurobindo (Bangla: *Sri Orobindo* Sanskrit: *Sri Aravinda*) (August 15, 1872–December 5, 1950) was an Indian nationalist, scholar, poet, mystic, evolutionary philosopher, yogi and guru. His followers

further believe that he was an avatar, an incarnation of the Absolute.

Sri Aurobindo spent his life — through his vast writings and through his own development — working for the freedom of India, the path to the further evolution of life on earth, and to bring down what he called the Supermind to enable such progress. He referred to his teachings as the "integral yoga".

Early Experiences: Sri Aurobindo was born Aurobindo Akroyd Ghose (pronounced and often written as Ghosh) in Kolkata (Calcutta), India, on 15th August, 1872. His father was Dr. K. D. Ghose and his mother Swarnalata Devi. Dr. Ghose, who had lived in Britain, and had studied at Aberdeen University, was determined that his children should have a completely European upbringing, sent Aurobindo and his siblings to the *Loreto Convent School* at Darjeeling. At the age of seven Aurobindo was taken along with his two elder brothers, Manmohan and Benoybhusan, to England. There, they were placed with a clergyman and his wife, a Mr and Mrs. Drewett, at Manchester. Mr. and Mrs. Drewett tutored Aurobindo privately. Mr. Drewett, himself a capable scholar, grounded Aurobindo so well in Latin that Aurobindo was able to gain admission into St Paul's School in London. At St. Paul's Aurobindo mastered Greek and excelled at Latin. The last three years at St. Paul's were spent in reading, especially English Poetry. At St. Paul's he received the Butterworth Prize for literature, the Bedford Prize for history and a scholarship to King's College, Cambridge University. He returned to India in 1893.

During the First Partition of Bengal from 1905 to 1912, he became a leader of the group of Indian nationalists known as the Extremists for their willingness to use violence and advocate outright independence, a plank more moderate nationalists had shied away from up to that point. He was one of the founders of Jugantar party, an underground revolutionary outfit. He was the editor of a nationalist Bengali newspaper *Vande Mataram* (spelt and pronounced as *Bônde Matôrom* in the Bengali language) and came into frequent confrontation with the British Raj as a result. In 1907 attended a convention of Indian nationalists where he was seen as the new leader of the movement. But his life was beginning to take a new direction. In Baroda he met a Maharashtrian yogi called *Vishnu Bhaskar Lele* who convinced him to explore the ancient Hindu practices of yoga.

It was at this point that Rabindranath Tagore paid him a visit and wrote the now famous lines:

> *Rabindranath, O Aurobindo, bows to thee! O friend, my country's friend, O Voice incarnate, free, Of India's soul....The fiery messenger that with the lamp of God Hath come...Rabindranath, O Aurobindo, bows to thee.*

Final Conversion: His final conversion from an active nationalist into a profound sage and seer occurred while incarcerated for a year in the Alipur jail in Kolkata in the province of Bengal. While incarcerated he was inspired by his meditating on the famed Hindu scripture of the Bhagavad Gita.

While in Alipore Jail, Sri Aurobindo claimed to be visited by the renowned Swami Vivekananda, a Hindu philosopher of great importance to Advaita Vedanta, in his meditation. The swami guided Sri

Aurobindo's yoga and helped him to scale great heights. It was there Sri Aurobindo saw the convicts, jailers, policemen, the prison bars, the trees, the judge, the lawyer etc., in the experience and realization of Vasudeva, a form of Vishnu. Sri Aurobindo was even áble to see compassion, honesty and charity in the hearts of murderers.

The trial for which he was incarcerated was one of the important trials in Indian nationalism movement. There were 49 accused and 206 witnesses. 400 documents were filed and 5000 exhibits were produced including bombs, revolvers and acid. The English judge, C.B. Beechcroft, had been a student with Sri Aurobindo at Cambridge. The Chief Prosecutor Eardley Norton displayed a loaded revolver on his briefcase during the trial. The case for Sri Aurobindo was taken up by Chittaranjan Das. Chittaranjan Das, in his conclusion to the Judge, said: "... My appeal to you is this, that long after the controversy will be hushed in silence, long after this turmoil, this agitation will have ceased, long after he (Sri Aurobindo) is dead and gone, he will be looked upon as the poet of patriotism, as the prophet of nationalism and lover of humanity. Long after he is dead and gone, his words will be echoed and re-echoed, not only in India, but across distant seas and lands. Therefore, I say that the man in his position is not only standing before the bar of this Court, but before the bar of the High Court of History." The trial ("Alipore Bomb Case, 1908") lasted for one full year. Aurobindo was acquitted.

Afterwards Aurobindo started two new weeklies: the *Karmayogin* in English and the *Dharma* in Bengali. However, it appeared that the British government would not tolerate his nationalist program as Lord Minto wrote about him: *I can only repeat that he is the most dangerous man we have to reckon with.*

Sought again by the Indian police he was guided to the French settlements and on April 4, 1910 he finally found refuge with other nationalists in the French colony of Pondicherry.

In 1914 after four years of concentrated yoga at Pondicherry, Sri Aurobindo launched *Arya*, a 64 page monthly review. For the next six and a half years this became the vehicle for most of his most important writings, which appeared in serialised form. These included *The Life Divine*, *The Synthesis of Yoga, Essays on The Gita, The Secret of The Veda, Hymns to the Mystic Fire, The Upanishads, The Foundations of Indian Culture, War and Self-determination, The Human Cycle, The Ideal of Human Unity*, and *The Future Poetry*. Sri Aurobindo however revised some of these works before they were published in book form.

He also wrote a very small book entitled "THE MOTHER" which was first published in 1928. In a way, it is the "Instructions Manual" for "Sadhaka"-aspirant-the "Yogi"-of the "Integral Yoga". In this book (less then 16 full size pages), the "Seer of the Modern Age" has written about his "Seeing" the Supreme Divine Mother-The Divine Shakti; especially "Four great Aspects of the Mother, four of her leading Powers and Personalities (which) have stood in front in her guidance of the Universe and her dealings with the terrestrial play. ...". He clearly and very explicitly wrote the conditions to be fulfilled by the "Sadhaka" for receiving the Grace of the Divine Mother for the "... great transmutation". He is probably the only Spiritual Master who has very clearly and emphatically written about Money/Wealth. ".... This is indeed one of the three forces-power, wealth, sex-that have the strongest attraction for the human ego and.....".

After this prolific output, Sri Aurobindo's only literary works, apart from some poems and essays, was his epic poem *Savitri*, which he continued to revise for the rest of his life. However, following his retirement from public life in 1926, he maintained a voluminous correspondence with his disciples. His letters, most of which were written in the 1930s, numbered in the several thousands, and some of these were later published in three volumes as *Letters on Yoga*.

Although Sri Aurobindo wrote most of his material in English, his major works were later translated into a number of languages, including the Indian languages Hindi, Bengali, Oriya, Gujarati, Marathi, Sanskrit, Tamil, Telugu, Kannada, and Malayalam, as well as French, German, Italian, Dutch, Spanish, Chinese, Portuguese, Slovene and Russian. A large amount of his work in Russian translation is also available online.

The Mother: His closest collaborator in his yoga, Mirra Richard (nee Alfassa), was known as *The Mother*. She was born in Paris on February 21, 1878, to Turkish and Egyptian parents. Involved in the cultural and spiritual life of Paris, she counted among her friends Alexandra David-Neel. She went to Pondicherry on March 29, 1914, finally settling there in 1920. Sri Aurobindo considered her his equal and because of her astuteness as an organiser, left it to her to plan, run and build the growing ashram. After November 24, 1926, when Sri Aurobindo retired into seclusion, she supervised the organization of the ashram, the Sri Aurobindo International Centre of Education (which, with its pilot experiments in the field of education, very much impressed observers like Jawaharlal Nehru), and later institutes like Auroville, the international township near the town of Pondicherry. She became the leader of the community after Sri Aurobindo died; she is revered by followers of Sri Aurobindo as well. Executing the mandate she received from her Guru, she did not leave Pondicherry till her last breath on November 17, 1973. She was to play an active role in the merger of the French pockets in India and, according to Sri Aurobindo's wish, to make of Pondicherry a seat of cultural exchange between India and France.

The Mother's attempts to bring the new consciousness into life and her personal effort of physical transformation of her own body are described in the 13-volume series of books known as The Agenda.

Contribution to Indian Philosophy: One of Sri Aurobindo's main philosophical achievements was to introduce the concept of evolution into Vedantic thought. Samkhya philosophy had already proposed such a notion centuries earlier, but Aurobindo rejected the materialistic tendencies of both Darwinism and Samkhya, and proposed an evolution of spirit rather than matter.

He rejects the Mayavada of Advaita Vedanta, and solves the problem of the linkage between the ineffable Brahman or Absolute and the world of multiplicity by positing a transitional hypostasis between the two, which he called The Supermind. The super mind is the active principle present in the transcendent Satchidananda; a unitary mind of which our individual minds and bodies are minuscule subdivisions.

Sri Aurobindo rejected a traditional Indian thinking that rejecting the World as Maya and living as a renunciate was the only way to Moksha. He says that people can be enlightened while enjoying the World, by following all the main Yogas-Gyan, Bhakti, Karma, Tantra as one philosophy, which he called Purna or Integral Yoga.

Discovering the Hidden Meaning of the Vedas: One of the most significant contributions of Sri Aurobindo to Hinduism was his discovery of the Esoteric meaning of the Vedas. Rig Veda is considered by some to be a book written by barbaric culture worshipping violent Gods. Aurobindo realised that this was due to the biased view of Westerners who had some preconceived views on Hindu culture.

So Aurobindo decided to look for hidden meanings in the Vedas. He looked at the Rig Veda as a psychological book, inspiring the people to move towards God, but in hidden language.

So Indra is the God of Indriya, or the senses (Look, touch, hear, taste etc.). Varun means air, but in esoteric terms means Pran, or the Life force. So when the Rig Vedas says "Call Indra and Varun to drink Soma Rasa" they mean use the Senses and Pran to receive divine bliss(Soma means wine of Gods, but in several texts also means Divine Bliss, as in Right handed Tantra).

Agni, or God of Fire, is the hidden Divine Spark in us, which we have to fan, so it grows and engulfs our whole body. So the sacrifice of the Vedas could mean sacrificing ones ego to the internal Agni, or Divine spark.

These essays originally appeared in the Arya, but have been condensed as a book form as "The Secret of the Vedas" by Sri Aurobindo.

Sri Aurobindo's Evolutionary Philosophy: These philosophical and cosmological themes are applied to Sri Aurobindo's vision of cosmic and human evolution. He argues that mankind as an entity is not the last rung in the evolutionary scale, but can evolve spiritually beyond its current limitations, moving out of an essential Ignorance born of creation, to a future state of Supramental existence. This would be a Divine Life on Earth characterised by knowledge, truth, substance and energy of supramental consciousness.

There are interesting parallels between Sri Aurobindo's vision and that of Teilhard de Chardin.

Involution: Sri Aurobindo's cosmology (described in his opus *The Life Divine*) explains the cosmos as coming about through the Absolute dividing into Existence, i.e. it existed; Consciousness-Force, i.e. It is a force and it is conscious of its existence; and Delight, i.e. it delights in the awareness of Its existence. This triene extended to a fourth aspect, the Supramental power that enabled the Consciousness Force to divide into an essential energy at rest. This is the plane of Life. That energy/life then moved, taking shape first as matter, then animus of life, then mind (predominantly in man). In other words, the supramental is the power that organized the spirit into the forms of creation. It divides the Conscious-Force so that it could take shape as individual forms of creation. All existence is thus forms of the original Force/Energy.

Process of Creation — The process of creation of the universe is the very same process by which an individual and any collective entity in the cosmos develops, grows, and evolves.

Purpose is Delight of Being — The universe created a universe in order to extend its own delight into the details of creation. When we discover our higher nature, that discovery results in the delight for which the Absolute enabled the cosmos.

Ignorance to Knowledge Enables Delight — The universe was born of ignorant forms. In discovering the highest consciousness, one moves from Ignorance to Knowledge, experiencing the delight of being for which the universe was created.

Reason for Ignorance — All forms were born of an inconsonance, unconsciousness, and Ignorance. It was so because it allowed for the greatest multiplicity and possibility of forms, which would enable the greatest possibility for delight in discovery of its highest nature.

Evolution: The process of the universe emerging from the Absolute is referred in *The Life Divine* as involution. The subsequent process of life emerging from matter and mind from life is evolution.

Each level that emerges in the evolution (matter, then the vital, then the mind) is already involved in the previous level, including the spirit in the deepest part of each. (The planes of Spirit/Supermind, Mind, and Life emerged in the descent of the Involution from out of the Conscious-Force, and then were involved, i.e. hidden in the evolution, where they reemerge in the universe after matter is created, through the emergence of animus of life and then mind and then spirit/super mind.)

The process of the evolution is to unfold in the universe the involved planes, and do so at levels of perfection and ultimate possibility, culminating in the supramentalization, spiritualization of everything in creation. It is also to reunite the Consciousness (lost in the Involution) with the (unconscious) Force (which is there in creation) by bringing the Spiritual Being into the Becoming of life, enabling a Divine life on earth, at each point aided by the supramental unifying action.

Evolution is described as a dual movement; inward, away from the surface consciousness and into the depths, culminating in the Psychic Being (the personal evolving soul); and then upward to higher levels of spiritual mind (Higher Mind, Illumined Mind, Intuitive Mind, and Overmind), culminating in the final stage of superalimentation.

Sri Aurobindo's Integral Yoga: The metaphysical teaching is balanced by a practical method, called Integral Yoga.

Integral Yoga is so-called because it involves the synthesis of the three yogas-bhakti, karma, and jnana-of the Bhagavad Gita. It is also called "Integral" because it embodies and integrates all aspects of life.

Of these three, bhakti is central, and in keeping with the Hindu tradition of the Divine Mother, Sri Aurobindo teaches devotion to the Mother (see his short devotional book *The Mother*), personified in his co-worker *Mirra Richard*, henceforth called 'The Mother'. In his letters to his disciples, advises them to consecrates every action to the Mother, and surrender to Her and the Divine Force expressed through Her.

In his essay "The Mother" Sri Aurobindo describes the yoga as consisting of three essential movements. Aspiration for the Divine in one's life, Rejection of all wanting elements of the individual person (physical, vital, and mental), and Surrender to the Divine Spirit and Force through the Divine Mother.

Though he provided this approach to yoga, he also subscribed to the idea that all of life is an adventure of consciousness, and that there are no exact fixed approaches for a particular individual. Each person must start from where he is at, and move upward from there, through the adventure of self-discovery.

This process of transformation is three-fold. The individual moves upward (along a vertical scale) in his conciousness, centering more at the mental and then the spiritually oriented levels of mind, as well as moving inward (in the horizontal scale) to the soul. The more he moves inward, the further upward he moves, and the more each of the existing planes in the vertical scale (physical, vital, mental) are perfected.

In the final stage, the dualistic mind is replaced with the unitary super mind consciousness. Beyond that, according to the later experiences of The Mother (see *Mother's Agenda*) is the replacement of our current physical attributes (e.g. breathing, digestion, blood circulation, skeletal system, human form, etc.) with more subtler forms of substance of the body. The Mother's preoccupation was with this stage of the supramental evolution of Sri Aurobindo's Yoga. A new species of supramentalized being replacing the current human functioning is the ultimate state of the (supramental) yoga.

As a result of these process, there emerges Gnostic, Supramentalized individuals who are the forerunners of an emerging Divine Life on earth, in which all of life moves to its highest spiritual and supramental status.

Sri Aurobindo's Influence: Sri Aurobindo lived at a very crucial moment in the history of thought when Marxist materialism, Nietzschean individualism and Freudian vitalism were popular and fashionable. Besides, phenomenology and existentialism had their run along-side him. On the whole, along with the new-fangled science and Theosophy, these new philosophical formulations fermented enough confusion among the elite. In a way, the disparate positions arrived at in Western thought find their synthesis in Sri Aurobindo's philosophy. By aligning them with the ancient Indian wisdom, he comes up with an integral vision that breathes universality as well as contemporarily.

Thus, Kant's sublime, Hegel's absolute, Schopenhauer's will, Kierkegaard's passion, Marx's matter, Darwin's evolution, Nietzsche's overman, Bergson's lan vital, all find their due representation in Sri Aurobindo's grand exposition. His thought successfully overarchs cultural as well as religious chasms. S. K. Maitra and Haridas Chaudhuri are first among the academicians to discern the import of Sri Aurobindo's integral philosophy. D. P. Chattopadhyay wrote a seminal treatise juxtaposing Sri Aurobindo and Marx to examine their utopian prophecies.

Sri Aurobindo's ideas about the further evolution of human capabilities influenced the thinking of Michael Murphy (who stayed at Sri Aurobindo's Ashram in India for eighteen months) – and indirectly, the human potential movement, through Murphy's writings. The American philosopher Ken Wilber, although influenced by Aurobindo, has tried to reduce the reliance on metaphysics in Aurobindo's thought; Wilber's interpretation has been strongly criticised by Rod Hemsell. New Age writer Andrew Harvey also looks to Aurobindo as a major inspiration. Cultural historian William Irwin Thompson is also heavily influenced by Sri Aurobindo and the Mother.

Esoteric cosmologist Patrizia Norelli-Bachelet controversially claims that she is an integral part of the avataric line initiated by Sri Aurobindo and the Mother, calling herself "The Third". These claims are not taken seriously by any followers or students of Sri Aurobindo and the Mother, apart from those few students of Norelli-Bachelet herself.

Quotations

- "They proved to me by convincing reasons that God doen not exist; Afterwards I saw God, for he came and embraced me. And now what am I to believe-the reasoning of others or my own experience? Truth is what the soul has seen and experienced; the rest is appearance, prejudice and opinion."-*From the Hour of God*
- "The one aim of [my] yoga is an inner self-development by which each one who follows it can in time discover the One Self in all and evolve a higher consciousness than the mental, a spiritual and supramental consciousness which will transform and divinize human nature."
- "Threefold are those supreme births of this divine force that is in the world, they are true, they are desirable; he moves there wide–overt within the Infinite and shines pure, luminous

and fulfilling.... Of that which is in mortal in mortals, and possessed of the truth, is a God and established inwardly as an energy working out in our divine powers.... Become high uplifted, O Strength, pierce all veils, manifest in as the things of the Godhead."

- "Hidden nature is secret God" — *The Life Divine*

Ramana Maharshi

Ramana Maharshi (December 30, 1879 – April 14, 1950) was a Hindu mystic of the Advaita Vedanta stream, who lived on Arunachala hill near Tiruvannamalai. Dozens of contemporary Satsang teachers in the West claim him to be their Satguru. The core of his teachings was the practice of *atma-vichara* (self-enquiry).

Ramana Maharshi was born in a village called Tirucculi near Madurai in southern India. He was given the name Venkataraman. After his father had died when Venkataraman was twelve, he went to live with his uncle in Madurai, where he briefly attended the American Missioan experience that was to change his life:

It was in 1896, about 6 weeks before I left Madurai for good (to go to Tiruvannamalai-Arunachala) that this great change in my life took place. I was sitting alone in a room on the first floor of my uncle's house. I seldom had any sickness and on that day there was nothing wrong with my health, but a sudden violent fear of death overtook me. There was nothing in my state of health to account fr it nor was there any urge in me to find out whether there was any account for the fear. I just felt I was going to die and began thinking what to o about it. It did not occur to me to consult a doctor or any elders or friends. I felt I had to solve the problem myself then and there.

The shock of the fear of death drove my mind inwards and I said to myself mentally, without actually framing the words: "Now death has come; what does it mean? What is that called dying? This body dies." And at once I dramatised the occurrence of death. I lay with my limbs stretched out still as though rigor mortis has set in, and imitated a corpse so as to give greater reality to the enquiry. I held my breath and kept my lips tightly closed so that no sound could escape, and that neither the word "I" nor any word could be uttered. "Well then," I said to myself, this body is dead. It will be carried stiff to the burning ground and there burn and reduced to ashes. But with the death of the body, am I dead? Is the body I? It is silent and inert, but I feel the full force of my personality and even the voice of I within me, apart from it. So I am the Spirit transcending the body. The body dies but the spirit transcending it cannot be touched by death. That means I am the deathless Spirit. All this was not dull thought; it flashed through me vividly as living truths which I perceived directly almost without thought process. "I" was something real, the only real thing about my present state, and all the conscious activity connected with the body was centered on that "I". From that moment onwards, the "I" or Self focussed attention on itself by a powerful fascination. Fear of death vanished once and for all. The ego was lost in the flood of Self awareness. Absorption continued in the Self continued unbroken from that time. Other thought might come and go like the various notes of music, but the "I" continued like the fundamental shruthi [that which is heard] note which underlies and blends with all other notes.

Venkataraman stayed at the family home for two months after his 'death experience', but after his brother remarked on his intense introspection he secretly left the family home and travelled to the sacred mountain of Arunachala, at the town of Tiruvannamalai, Madras Province (now Tamil Nadu). He stayed at Arunachala for the rest of his life.

Teachings: Ramana Maharshi taught a method called "Atma-Vichara" or "self-inquiry" in which the seeker focuses continuous attention on the "I-thought" in order to find its source. In the beginning this would require effort, said Ramana, but eventually something deeper than the "small self" would take over and the mind would dissolve in what he called the "heart center". This was possible Ramana claimed, because the human personality is but a mental idea.

He is an acknowledged Hindu master of the Advaita Vedanta stream, and has followers throughout India and abroad. This system of philosophy endorses the view that the "true being" within each human is the ultimate, "sublime reality", the Brahman, the "one without a second" or simply the Self. What prevents humans from realizing this, so the teachings of Advaita, is the identification with the mind and the body. therefore, these identifications-which make up the "ego"-must be transcended in order to realize the truth. However, from the Vedanta perspective, 'realize the truth' is a bit of a misnomer, because the Self, in Vedanta thought already is the truth, already is free. One need merely remove the false veil of wrong identification with the body and mind to see this.

Ramana recommended his followers to go back to the "source from wherein all thought arises" and for example ask themselves, "to whom is this thought?" or "to whom has this anger arisen?" The answer would be obviously "to me"; after that, they were asked to enquire as to "who am I?". Ramana Maharishi would also suggest the question "whence am I?" which some of his devotees consider to be more important than "who am I?". In this way they would try to trace the "I-thought" back to the "source". The word "source" in this context is used synonymous of the words "God" or "Self". Another often used teaching of Ramana's is: "Stay in silence." Many spiritual western authors, including the American philosopher Ken Wilber, claim to have been influenced by Ramana Maharshi's nondual approach. In fact, Ken Wilber is said to have called Ramana Maharshi "the greatest sage of the 20th Century". Journalist Paul Brunton was one of the first Westerners to write about Ramana Maharshi. His book "A Search in Secret India" was written in the 1930's and has made Ramana popular in Europe and America.

Teachers in the Tradition: Several followers of Ramana Maharshi became teachers in their own right, and have subsequently spawned their own successors as well, including H. W. L. Poonja, Lakshmana Swamy, and Annamalai Swami. Western followers of Ramana Maharshi include Robert Adams, Paul Brunton, A. Ramana (AHAM), Nome (Society of Abidance in Truth), Neelam (Fire of Truth Satsanga), Gangaji, Eli Jaxon-Bear, Catherine Ingram, and Isaac Shapiro.

Swami Sivananda

Swami Sivananda Saraswati (Sep 8, 1887—Jul 14, 1963), as he is known under his monastic name, was born Kuppuswamy in Pattamadai, Tamil Nadu, India. A Hindu by birth, he is a well-known proponent of yoga and vedanta. He is reputed to have written over 300 books, on these and related subjects, during his life.

He went to medical school in Tanjore and worked as a doctor in Malaya.

In 1923 he left Malaya for India on an extensive pilgrimage. At Banaras, he had the Darshan (vision) of Lord Vishvanath. Dr. Kuppuswami next went to Rishikesh where met his guru, Swami Vishwananda Saraswati. It was Vishwananda who initiated him into the Sannyas order and gave him his monastic name. However, since Swami Sivananda spent only a few hours with Swami Vishwananda, the full Viraja Homa ceremonies were performed later by Swami Vishnudevananda, the Mahant of Sri Kailas Ashram.

Sivananda performed austerities for many years but he also continued to help the sick. With some money from his insurance policy that had matured, he started a charitable dispensary at Lakshmanjula in 1927. He later created the *Sivananda Ayurvedic Pharmacy* in 1945.

Sivananda traveled the length and breadth of India during his Parivrajaka (wandering monk) life. He visited important places of pilgrimage in the south, including Rameshvaram. He conducted sankirtian and delivered lectures. He visited the Sri Aurobindo ashram and met Maharishi Suddhananda Bharati. At the Ramana ashram, he allegedly had the darshan of Ramana Maharshi on Maharshi's birthday. He sang bhajans and danced in ecstasy with Maharshi's bhaktas. He also went on pilgrimages to Kailas-Manasarovar and Badri.

He returned to Rishikesh and in 1936 founded the new religious movement the Divine Life Society on the bank of the holy Ganges River. The free distribution of spiritual literature drew a steady flow of disciples to the Swami, including the young U.G. Krishnamurti, who studied with him for seven summers, Swami Satyananda Saraswati, founder of Satyananda Yoga.

Swami Sivananda organized the All-world Religions Federation in 1945 and established the All-world Sadhus Federation in 1947. He called his *yoga* the *Yoga of Synthesis.*

On the 14th of July 1963, the Great Soul Swami Sivananda entered Mahasamadhi (departure of a Self-realized saint from his mortal coil) in his Kutir on the bank of Ganga, in Shivanandanagar.

Sivananda Yoga

After ten years of service to his Master Swami Vishnu-devananda was sent to the West to spread the teachings of yoga and vedanta and set up the International Sivananda Yoga Vedanta Centres and Ashrams.

People are waiting were the words of his Master.

Chinmayananda

Swami Chinmayananda (May 8, 1916-Aug 3, 1993) was born Balakrishna Menon (Balan) in Ernakulam, Kerala in a devout Hindu noble family called *"Poothampilil"*. Graduating from Lucknow University, he entered the field of journalism where he felt he could influence political, economic and social reform in India. But his life was changed when he met Swami Sivananda at Rishikesh and became

interested in the Hindu spiritual path.

Balakrishna Menon took sanyas (monkhood) from Swami Sivananda to become Swami Chinmayananda-the one who is saturated in Bliss and Consciousness. Swami Shivananda saw the potential in Swami Chinmayananda and sent him to study under a guru in the Himalayas-Swami Tapovan Maharaj under whom he studied for 12 years. At the end of the education he decided to spread his teaching all over the world.

During his forty years of travelling and teaching, Gurudev opened numerous centres and ashrams worldwide, he also built many schools, hospitals, nursing homes and clinics. As well as reinvigorating India's rich cultural heritage, Swami Chinmayananda made Vedanta accessible to everybody regardless of age, nationality, or religious background.

Swami Chinmayananda died on 3 August 1993 in San Diego, California. His admirers regard him as having attained Mahasamadhi at that point. His work has resulted in the creation of an international organization called the *Chinmaya Mission*.

Satguru Sivaya Subramuniyaswami

Sivaya Subramuniyaswami (1927-2001), affectionately known as Gurudeva by his followers, was born Robert Hansen in Oakland, California on January 5, 1927. He established a Hindu monastery in Kauai, Hawaii and founded the magazine *Hinduism Today*. He also authored many books and was one of the most prominent faces of Hinduism during the last two decades of the 20th century. He was the founder and leader of the Saiva Siddhanta Church, world's first hindu church. He was one of Saivism's most orthodox and revered Gurus and a Westerner who adopted Saivism as a young man. Saivism is a Hindu denomination that considers Shiva to be the supreme God, which is a belief contrasted with Smartism, another influential Hindu denomination which considers Shiva to be one of the personal forms of God.

Satguru Sivaya Subramuniyaswami is recognized worldwide as one of Hinduism's foremost ministers. In 1947, as a young man of 20, he journeyed to India and Sri Lanka and two years later was initiated into sannyasa by the renowned siddha yogi and worshiper of Siva, Jnanaguru Yogaswami of Sri Lanka, regarded as one of the 20th century's most remarkable mystics.

For over five decades Subramuniyaswami, affectionately known as Gurudeva by followers, taught Hinduism to Hindus and seekers from all faiths. In the line of successorship, he was considered the 162nd *Jagadacharya* of the *Nandinatha Sampradaya's Kailasa Parampara* and Guru Mahasannidhanam of Kauai Aadheenam (also known as Kauai's Hindu Monastery), a 458 acre (1.9 km²) temple-monastery complex on Hawaii's Garden Island. From this verdant Polynesian ashram on a river bank near the foot of an extinct volcano, Gurudeva's successor, Satguru Bodhinatha Veylanswami, and the monastics live their cherished vision, following a contemplative and joyous existence, building a jewel-like white granite Siva temple, meditating together in the hours before dawn, then working to promote the Sanatana Dharma together through four areas of service: 'Saiva Siddhanta Church', 'Himalayan Academy', Hindu Heritage Endowment and the 'Hinduism Today' international monthly magazine.

Gurudeva was lauded as one of the strictest and most traditional gurus in the world. His Hindu church nurtures its membership and local missions on five continents. The Academy serves, personally and through its magazine, books, courses and travel/study programs, serious seekers and Hindus of all denominations. Gurudeva's mission, received from his satguru, was to protect, preserve and promote the Saivite Hindu religion as expressed through its three pillars: temples, satgurus and scripture. That mission is now carried forward by his monastic and family communities. The congregation of Saiva Siddhanta Church is a disciplined, global fellowship of family initiates, monastics and students who follow the sadhana marga, the path of inner effort, yogic striving and personal transformation. Gurudeva was the hereditary guru of 2.5 million Sri Lankan Hindus. His various institutions form a Jaffna-Tamil-based organization which has branched out from his Sri Subramuniya Ashram in Alaveddy to meet the needs of the growing Hindu diaspore of this century. He also established a seven acre (28,000 m²) monastery in Mauritius, which includes a public Spiritual Park. Gurudeva gently oversaw more than 50 independent temples worldwide. Missionaries and teachers within the family membership provide counseling and classes in Saivism for children, youth and adults.

'Hinduism Today' is an influential, award-winning, international monthly magazine founded by Gurudeva in 1979. It is a public service of his monastic order, created to strengthen all Hindu traditions by uplifting and informing followers of the Sanatana Dharma everywhere. Gurudeva was author of more than 30 books unfolding unique and practical insights on Hindu metaphysics, mysticism and yoga. His Master Course lessons on Saivism, taught in many schools, are preserving the teachings among thousands of youths. Hindu Heritage Endowment is a public service trust founded by Gurudeva in 1995. It seeks to establish and maintain permanent sources of income for Hindu institutions worldwide. In 1986, New Delhi's World Religious Parliament named Gurudeva one of five modern-day Jagadacharyas, world teachers, for his international efforts in promoting and chronicling a Hindu renaissance.

Then in 1995 the title of Dharmachakra was bestowed on him for his publications. The Global Forum of Spiritual and Parliamentary Leaders for Human Survival chose Subramuniyaswami as a Hindu representative at its conferences. Thus, at Oxford, England, in 1988, Moscow in 1990 and Rio de Janiero in 1992, he joined hundreds of religious, political and scientific leaders from all countries to discuss privately, for the first time, the future of human life on this planet. At Chicago's centenary Parliament of the World's Religions in September, 1993, Gurudeva was elected one of three presidents, along with Swami Chidananda Saraswati of the Rishikesh-based Divine Life Society and Kerala's Mata Amritanandamayi, to represent Hinduism at the prestigious Presidents' Assembly, a core group of 25 men and women voicing the needs of world faiths.

In 1996 Gurudeva upgraded the newspaper 'Hinduism Today' to a magazine, a quantum leap that placed it on newsstands everywhere, alongside Newsweek, Time and India Today. In 1997 he responded to the US President's call for religious opinions on the ethics of cloning from the Hindu point of view. Later that year, he spearheaded the 125th anniversary of Satguru Yogaswami and his golden icon's diaspore pilgrimage through many of the over 75 Sri Lanka temples and societies around the globe. In 1998, the Vishva Hindu Parishad of Kerala sent an envoy to Kauai to honor and recognize Gurudeva as the "Hindu Voice of the Century."

In the last few years of his life Gurudeva was a key member of *Vision Kauai 2020*, a small group of community leaders that includes the Mayor, former Mayor and County Council members. They met on a monthly basis to fashion the island's future for twenty years ahead, based on moral and spiritual values.

In April of 1999 Gurudeva led 45 spiritual aspirants on an Innersearch from Vancouver to Anchorage, Alaska. Their ship, the MS Narcoma, journeyed for 7 days and nights as they studied meditation and the mystical life together, explored the glaciers and redefined the cruise experience along the way. In Anchorage, Gurudeva founded the first Hindu temple in that state, calling together the native American Indian leaders to participate in the event. He also initiated a powerful series of book signings in California, Washington and Alaska, introducing his newest book, Merging with Siva, to thousands of seekers.

In August he traveled to Malaysia and Mauritius, where he met with the nation's leaders on several family-related topics, opened his Spiritual Park for 3,000 special guests, spent time with his Church members and continued the dynamic book signing, this time adding his newest book, Weaver's Wisdom, to the list.

In March and April of 2000 he led another Innersearch Travel-Study program to the Caribbean, visiting six nations with 53 of his devotees and meeting the Hindu leadership in that remote part of the world, with special events among 4,500 Hindus who came to honor him in Trinidad.

In August of 2001 Gurudeva took 72 devotees on a journey through Northern Europe, founding new Hindu temples along the way and visiting the Tamil communities in a dozen nations. Just before departing for the European Innersearch, he completed his last book, Living with Siva. Only weeks after returning from that dynamic odyssey, he died.

Gurudeva was known to the end for spending personal time with new members, island visitors who pilgrimaged to his sacred home on Kauai and new young monks who have come to the monastery to give their life in selfless service and the search for God within man. All of his work and mission, his vision and projects now go forward under the guidance of his successor, Satguru Bodhinatha Veylanswami.

Books: Gurudeva has written several books on Hinduism, Saivism, yoga and meditation; his works are highly regarded by many contemporary Hindu leaders. His **Master Course** is Gurudeva's most monumental work, a comprehensive treatise on every aspect of Saivism in three books and more than 3,000 pages, composed in what he called "talkanese"-a flowing version of written English that resembles the spoken language and evokes ancient Hindu oral traditions.

Bhagwan Swaminarayan

Bhagwan Swaminarayan (April 2, 1781-1830) was born Ghanshyam Pande to a Brahmin family in the village of Chhapaiya, Uttar Pradesh, India. His father's name was Hariprasad Pande (also known as Dharmadev) and his mother's name was Premvati (also known as Bhaktimata). He had two brothers, Rampratapji Pande, the older brother, and Icharamji Pande, the younger brother. After serving his parents, he left home at the age of 11 to travel over 8,000 miles throughout India on a holy pilgrimage

for 7 years, 1 month, and 11 days. During his travels, Ghanshyam was given the name Neelkanth, another name for Lord Shiva, for the intensive tapas, meditation, and yoga he performed. In many instances, yogis, rishis and sadhus were attracted to his figure in awe, for they had never before seen such a young renunciant who is so advanced in the art of meditation.

To dispel the perceived misinterpretation and malpractice that had befallen Hindu practice in the 19th century, he travelled across the length and breadth of India in search for an Ashram or sampradaya (following) that practiced a correct understanding of Vedanta, Samkhya, Yoga, and Pancaratra — the four primary schools of Hinduism. He would measure the various yogis' understanding of the scriptures by asking the following five questions and assessing their responses: "What is the nature of jiva? What is the nature of Ishwar? What is the nature of Maya? What is the nature of Brahman? What is the nature of Parabrahman?" His journey as a profound yogi eventually concluded in Gujarat, where Swami Muktananda, a senior monk-disciple of a highly respected Vaishnav guru Swami Ramananda, answered the five questions with astounding sophistication.

Neelkanth was pleased to see a pure understanding of the essence of Hindu thought and practice as well as an ashrama that was strict in abiding by the laws of Dharma, and so he decided to stay to get an opportunity to meet and become a disciple of Swami Ramananda.

Neelkanth's profound understanding of the metaphysical and epistemological concepts of the Pancha-Tattvas (five eternal entities as outlined above) combined with the level of his mental and physical discipline inspired even the senior sadhus of Swami Ramananda. At age 21, he was given the headship of the religious sect known as *Uddhav Sampraday* (later known as Swaminarayan Sampradaya), with the blessings of his Guru Sadguru Ramanand Swami. He later became known as *Bhagwan Swaminarayan* after the mantra he taught. Although the name that was given by his Guru Swami Ramananda at the time of initiation into the monk order was Swami Sahajananda, he become commonly known as Bhagwan Swaminarayan, or *Shreeji Maharaj* or *Shri Hari.*

The profound personality of Bhagwan Swaminarayan transformed a significant portion of Gujarat, Saurashtra, and even parts of Rajasthan into people of all castes, creeds, and ashramas developing a pure understanding of spirituality and shedding the false conceptions of the scriptures that had led to a long-standing practice of superstitions, violence, and killing of animals in Vedic yagnas. Lord Swaminarayan, as a hallmark of his philosophy of temple theism and idol worship, constructed nine magnificent menders in: Ahmedabad, Bhuj, Muli, Vadtal, Junagadh, Dholera, Dholka, Gadhpur & Jetalpur – installing images of various manifestations of God, such as NarNarayan Dev, LaxmiNarayan Dev, Radha Krishna, Radha Raman, Revti Baldevji, etc. Lord Swaminarayan made Gadhpur his home, in recognition of the exceptional devoted love from Dada Khachar, one of his most devoted disciples.

Lord Swaminarayan's philosophical, social, and practical teachings are contained in the Vachanamrut, a collection of 271 dialogues which were recorded with precision by five of his disciples verbatim to His spoken words. As a result, the Vachanamrut is shared by the entire Swaminarayan Sampradaya to be the most central scripture to attain a comprehensive knowledge of dharma (moral conduct), jnan (understanding of the nature of the atman), vairagya (mental and physical detachment from material pleasure or maya), and bhakti (pure, selfless devotion to God) — the four essentialities for a jiva to attain the state of Brahman and become a perfect disciple of God. As a commentary to the practice and understanding of Dharma, Lord Swaminarayan composed the Shikshapatri, a small booklet containing 212 Sanskrit hymns that outline the basic tenets of Dharma that all disciples should follow to live a well-disciplined and moral life.

Historically, the movement that Lord Swaminarayan started can be seen to have a significant effect in the state of affairs of Gujarat and Rajasthan, for the amount of social work He conducted can be seen as one of the major factors leading to the stabilization of Gujarat during the 19th century, a time where the British Empire and the Muslims of the north were gaining a stronger foothold. The advent of the Swaminarayan Sampradaya is arguably the strongest influence in 19th century India to provide a resurgence of Hindu philosophy and practice, defying significant outside influence and a widespread misinterpretation and malpractice of the Hindu texts, injecting a strong ideal of non-violence, religious and cultural tolerance, and simply developing a pure love for God. The abolition of the prejudice and segregation that had resulted from the caste system is another hallmark of Lord Swaminarayan's social work to reach out to all people and open the gateway of spiritual discipline and participation in the congregation (which Swaminarayan referred to as Satsang). Thus, Lord Swaminarayan, through his profoundly attractive personality, was able to transform the inherited Uddhav Sampradaya from his Guru Swami Ramananda into a massive fellowship that some historians estimate attracted up to two million followers and over 2,000 men and women by 1820 C.E. to follow the path of renunciation and celibacy to join the monk order.

The advent of almighty God in the form of Swaminarayan Bhagwan is claimed to have ben forecast in ancient Vedic scriptures by followers. Many doubts are raised as to how Swaminarayan Bhagwan can be considered Bhagwan or God.

The world's first Swaminarayan Temple was built in Ahmedabad by the instructions of Bhagwan Swaminarayan.

Bhagwan Swaminarayan was a Narayan and Krishna bhakta considered by his followers to be Narayan himself, Rama, Krishna, etc. being his avataras. Swaminarayan sampraday stems from the Ramanuja sampraday, which holds Lord Narayan to be supreme and Krishna to be an avatar.

In his main work called Shikshapatri (108) he writes:

"Sa Sri Krshnaha Param Brahma Bhagvaan Purushotamaha Upasya Ishtadevo Naha Sarvaavirbhaav Kaaranam"

That ishvara is Shi Krishna who is PraBrahma Bhagwan Purushottam and our most cherished deity (istadev). He is worthy of being worshipped by us all (upasya). He is the cause of all manifestations and incarnations.

Fundamentals of the Swaminarayan Philosophy: Shree Hari is Shree NarNarayan Dev Himself:

- Dharma (Religion): Virtuous conduct as defined in the 'Shrities' and 'Smrities' (Holy Scriptures) be known as the Dharma.

- Bhakti (Devotion): Supreme fervour of the soul combined with the consciousness of the Glories of the Supreme be known as ' Bhakti'. Nothing other then Gods devotion can guide the enlighten vision of God to great deliverance.
- Jnana (Enlightenment): Correct awareness about the forms of the Soul, illusion, and God be known as 'Jnyana'.
- Vairagya (Renunciation): Detachment of the affection for all material possessions and be absolutely attached towards the love for the Eternal God is known as Vairagya.
- Maya (Illusion): It is considered 'Tri-Gunatmika' i.e. deceptive illusion prevails in all the three qualities of minds viz. Satva, Rajas and Tamas; To be possessed by Maya is to be caught in darkness; God is the Lord of maya who acts as the power of God; It breeds ego in one for his body and for the relatives of the body too.
- Mukti-Moksha (Great Deliverances): To worship God in knowing he is the Supreme Deity and reaching ultimate salvation.
- Atman (Self): The innate physiology of the subtle Self that is imperceptible by the human senses. Recognition of the Atman, after which one experiences a transcendental bliss, is achieved through bhakti-yoga as outlined in the Bhagavad Gita, according to the teachings of Lord Swaminarayan. It is the source of energy and is the real knower; It pervades the entire body and is the essence that differentiates matter and life; in character it is inseparable, impenetrable, indestructible and immortal.
- Paramatman (The Supreme Soul): It is omnipresent within the souls, just as soul is present in the body; it is independent and is the one whom rewards the Fala (fruits) to the souls. It is the source of infinite material universes and the First Cause. It has no prior causes, and is the inherent cause of all effects (i.e. law of causality or the Hindu concept of karma). S. Radhakrishnan, a renowned Hindu scholar, writes "The Supreme is described as a kavi, a poet, an artist, a maker or creator, not a mere imitator...even as art reveals man's wealth of life, so does the world reveal the immensity of God's life," (p. 86, The Principal Upanishads). That Paramatman is believed by followers of the Swaminarayan Sampradaya to have manifested as Lord Swaminarayan.

Prior to Bhagwan Swaminarayan departing for Akshardham, Shriji Hari divided his menders into two regions and in Vadtal, he established the dual Acharyaship, in direct succession to himself. He did so by means of a legal document Desh Vibhag Lekh which is a scripture that was dictated to Shuk Swami on Maghshar Sud 15, Vikram Samvat 1883 and witnessed by elder saints and satsangis of the Sampraday. The Lekh serves two primary purposes:

1. Demarcation of the jurisdiction and responsibilities of the respective Gadis
2. Means of appointing future Acharyas.

The concept of having a householder (non-monk) as guru and that of hereditary succession are unique to the Shree Swaminarayan Sampraday. It is the uniqueness of the Swaminarayan Sampraday, that the closest a tyagi (saint) comes to leadership is being appointed the Mahant Swami (head-saint) of a Shikharbandh Temple. At all times, the true saints of the Sampraday take their instructions from the Acharya, their ultimate guru and leader.

Additionally, Swaminarayan put an emphasis on association with enlightened Sadhus (also called

"Saints" by followers). These Sadhus are viewed as spiritual guides on the path to enlightenment. The Vachanamrut details the specific attributes of an enlightened Sadhu, or Ekantik Sadhu, and explains that such a saint has his mind constantly attuned to the divine form of God, is totally detached from material pleasure (nishkami), bodily attachment (nisnehi), covetousness (nirlobhi),and ultimately ego (nirmani). Such a saint offers selfless devotion to God while desiring nothing but the spiritual, moral and social stabilization of the disciples. The devotees of BAPS Swaminarayan Sanstha believe that such a Saint Lord Swaminarayan speaks of is Pramukh Swami Maharaj, a spiritual guide who incorporates extensive social work with moral and intellectual development.

BAPS

BAPS (Bochasanwasi Shri Akshar Purushottam Swaminarayan Sanstha) is a socio-spiritual organization with its roots in the Vedas, and was revealed by Bhagwan Swaminarayan in the late 18th century and established in 1907 CE by Swami Yagnapurushdas.

BAPS split from the Vadtal temple in 1906, rejecting the householder line of succession in favour of a Guru-based line of sucession. In the words of its critics, BAPS is a split from the original Swaminarayan Sampraday which is under Ahmdavad and Vadtal Gadi, which Swaminarayan Bhagwan established himself. However, BAPS has become "one of the fastest growing religious movements in the world." [Williams, 2001] Whilst BAPS are neither confirmed nor stated in the Swaminarayan Scriptures in any form, followers are quick to point out that the underlying philosophy the group is founded on is mentioned and discussed on numerous occasions throughout the texts of the BAPS Sanstha. Followers of BAPS regard Gunatitanand Swami, a sadhu whom Swaminarayan referred to as "My divine abode" and "My ideal devotee", as his immediate spiritual successor.

He is succeeded in turn by Bhagatji Maharaj, Jaga Swami Maharaj, Shastriji Maharaj, Yogiji Maharaj and Pramukh Swami Maharaj.

Philosophy: Bhagwan Swaminarayan's philosophy, known as Navya Vishishtadvaita (Neo-qualified non-dualism), upholds the existence of the five eternal realities, namely: Jiva, Ishwar, Maya, Brahman and Parabrahman.

Jiva (Soul) is sentient (chaitanya), subtle and is the knower (jnata) and enjoyer (bhokta) of things. He is immutable, unpierceable, indivisible and eternal. Jivas are infinite in number and bound by vasana (impressions and desires from past births and present birth) according to their karmas. Ishwars transcend Jiva. Each Ishwar is a conscious spiritual being, possessing excellence involved in the creation, sustenance and destruction of the universe. They also are infinite in number and bound by Maya. Parabrahman is the inner Ruler and Controller (antaryamin) of both Jiva and Ishwar. Just as the gross, subtle and causal are the three bodies of Jiva, similarly, Virat, Sutratma and Avyakrut are the three bodies of Ishwar. Maya or Prakruti is trigunatmika-consisting of the three gunas-sattva, rajas and tamas. Its nature is of ignorance and darkness, and is also the instrument-shakti of Parabrahman. It is non-sentient primordial matter out of which the whole universe is evolved. Difficult to transcend, it is the cause of attachment of the Jivas and Ishwars to their bodies and bodily relations.

Brahman, also known as Akshar, is the highest eternal reality beyond which stands only Purushottam or Parabrahman. Akshar as-personal (sakar) is the choicest devotee, eternally in the service of Lord Purushottam, in the highest abode.

This same Akshar, also serves Lord Purushottam as His infinitely effulgent abode (Dham), wherein Lord Purushottam and innumerable released souls reside.

It is the same Akshar who, as infinite, homogeneous, all-pervading, sentient-space (Chidakash) pervades within and without an infinite number of universes and every element thereof. And, it is the same Akshar, who in the form of the Param Ekantik Sadhu, perennially manifests on earth to redeem the seekers of moksha. Akshar is also the medium who embodies Lord Purushottam fully in his person.

Parabrahman or Purushottam, is the Supreme Reality. He possesses an infinite number of kalyankari (redemptive) attributes. He transcends Jiva, Ishwar, Maya and Brahman, and is immanent in them, they being absolutely dependent on Him. He is the cause, controller, sustainer, redeemer, the support of all and dispenser of the fruits of all karmas. He alone is independent.

He is also the indwelling spirit, antaryamin, of the other four realities. He is eternally full of divine bliss and has eternally a divine form, shaped like a human being. Nothing transcends Parabrahman. He is the goal for meditational worship-of upasana, by all, including Aksharbrahman. He is one and unparalleled and is commonly known as Paramatma, Param-Purush, Parameshwar, Purna Purushottam and Narayan.

Concept of Moksha: Bhagwan Swaminarayan elaborates moksha or final emancipation, known as Atyantik Mukti in the Sampradaya, in the following manner :

> *Jiva is bound by avidya-karma (Maya). This is ignorance, a delusion of the Jiva. Therefore, in order to be rid of this ignorance, the Jiva has to develop Atmanishtha-the knowledge that he is not the body, but Atma. But to transcend Maya, this type of mere (samanya) Atmanishtha is not enough. A higher (vishesh) Atmanishtha needs to be realised-in which the Atma identifies itself with Aksharbrahman to become Akshar-rup-like Akshar. This is known as true Jnan and true Atmanishtha.*

The liberated soul, Akshar mukta, then becomes eligible to worship Parabrahman-the Lord Purushottam, in Akshardham. This is in consonance with the Taittiriya Upanishad:

'Attaining' Parabrahman does not mean merging in Him, as water merges with water, or light into light. The servitor-Master relationship-Swami-sevak bhava, always prevails.4 The individuality of the sevak-the mukta always remains.

To become Akshar-rup, the Jiva has to associate with the Satpurush who is the manifest form of Aksharbrahman, the living embodiment of Ekantik Dharma, known also as Bhagawata Dharma in the Shrimad Bhagwatam. Only then does the gateway of moksha open for the Jiva when he associates with the Satpurush.

In the Swaminarayan Sampradaya, its founder, Bhagwan Swaminarayan is worshipped as Parabrahman (Purushottam), the Supreme Reality, while Gunatitanand Swami, His ideal Bhakta, is worshipped as Aksharbrahman. Aksharbrahman occupies the same place which Shri Laxmi and Radha occupy in the Vaishnav schools of Vedanta. Therefore in spite of being a form of pure Vaishnavism, it is popularly known as Akshar Purushottam Swaminarayan Sampradaya, and its philosophy is best described as Neo-Vishishtadvaita. After incarnating on earth, Parabrahman Bhagwan Swaminarayan, manifests continuously through the Gunatit Guru, the Param Ekantik Sadhu, the living embodiment of Aksharbrahman. Today, His Divine Holiness Pramukh Swami Maharaj, is the current manifest form of Aksharbrahman.

Bhagwan Swaminarayan's Nand Santos: 'Nand Santos' are the saints of the Swaminarayan Sampraday who were initiated Paramhans by Shree Swaminarayan, and came to believe in his divinity. Here are a few nand santos' biography.

- Ramanand Swami-Guru of Bhagwan Swaminarayan Samvat Year 1795-1858 (1739-1802 AD)
- Muktanand Swami Samvat Year 1814-1887 (1758-1830 AD)
- Brahmanand Swami Samvat Year 1828-1888 (1772-1832 AD)
- Gopalanand Swami Samvat Year 1837-1908 (1781-1852 AD)
- Nityanand Swami Samvat Year 1832-1908 (1776-1852 AD)
- Shukanand Swami Samvat 1855-1925 (1799-1869 AD)
- Nishkulanand Swami Samvat 1822-1903 (1766-1847 AD)
- Shatanand Swami
- Akhandanand Swami
- Premanand Swami Samvat 1840-1911 (1784-1855 AD)
- Gunatitanand Swami Samvat 1841-1923 (1785-1867 AD)
- Devanand Swami Samvat 1859-1910 (1803-1854 AD)
- Vyapakanand Swami
- Swarupanand Swami
- Sachchidanand Swami

Swami Prabhupada

A.C. Bhaktivedanta Swami Prabhupada (September 1, 1896–November 14, 1977) was born Abhay Charan De, in Kolkata, West Bengal, India. He studied at the Scottish Churches College, Calcutta, which was then administered by the British. In his later years, as a Vaishnava sadhu, he became an influential communicator of Gaudiya Vaishnava theology to India and specifically to the West through his founding of the International Society for Krishna Consciousness (popularly called "Hare Krishna") in 1966. He has been described as a charismatic leader (in the sense used by sociologist Max Weber), and was successful in acquiring followers in the United States, Europe, and elsewhere.

Before adopting the life of a vanaprastha, or pious renunciant, in 1950, he was married with children and owned a small pharmaceutical business. He later took sannyasa (a vow of renunciation) in 1959.

Bhaktisiddhanta Sarasvati Thakura

In 1922, when Prabhupada first met his spiritual master, Sri Bhaktisiddhanta Sarasvati Thakura (1874–1937), Sri Bhaktisiddhanta requested that Prabhupada spread the message of Lord Chaitanya in the English language. In 1933 Prabhupada became a formally initiated disciple. In 1944 Prabhupada started *Back to Godhead,* an English language fortnightly, for which he acted as publisher, editor and copy editor. In 1947 the Gaudiya Vaisnava Society recognised Prabhupada's scholarship with the honorific *Bhaktivedanta,* indicating devotion (Bhakti) and conclusive knowledge (Vedanta). Beginning in 1950 he lived at the medieval temple of Radha-Damodara in the holy city of Vrindavan, where he began his translation work on the Sanskrit epic Srimad Bhagavatam. His Divine Grace Sri Bhaktisiddhanta Sarasvati Thakura had always encouraged Prabhupada, "If you have any money, print the books!", referring to Srimad Bhagavatam, Bhagavad Gita, Chaitanya Caritamrta, and other fundamental works.

Sannyasa: He took *sannyasa* (renunciant) vows in 1959 from his god brother Sri Bhakti Prajnana Keshava Maharaja at Mathura, following which he single-handedly published the first three volumes of his thirty-volume translation of the 18,000-verse Bhagavata Purana and the commentary on it. He then left India to fulfill his master's spiritual mission. In his possession were a suitcase, an umbrella, a supply of dry cereal, about seven dollars worth of Indian currency, and several boxes of books.

Mission to the West

Sri Prabhupada in the West: Prabhupada sailed to New York City in 1965. By July 1966 he had brought Hare Krishna to the West, founding the International Society for Krishna Consciousness (ISKCON) in New York City. Sri Prabhupada became well known as one who truly practiced what he preached; leading by example he expanded the movement from a small group of people in New York in 1966, to an international movement incorporating many thousands of people. By the time of his death in Vrindavan eleven years later (1977), ISKCON was a widely known expression of Hinduism in the West.

Through his mission, Prabhupada followed and communicated the teachings of Chaitanya Mahaprabhu and introduced bhakti yoga to a Western audience.

Reactions to Prabhupada's Death: Prabhupada spent much of the last decade of his life setting up the institution of ISKCON. Since he was the Society's leader, his personality and management were responsible for much of ISKCON's growth and the reach of his mission.

Upon Prabhupada's death on November 14, 1977, eleven of his disciples became initiating gurus for ISKCON. Those chosen were Tamal Krishna Goswami, Satsvarupa dasa Goswami, Jayapataka Swami, Hridayananda Goswami, Bhavananda Goswami, Hamsaduta Swami, Ramesvara Swami, Harikesa Swami, Bhagavan dasa Adhikari, Kirtanananda Swami, and Jayatirtha dasa Adhikari. Of these eleven, only the first four have stayed within ISKCON.

Since Prabhupada's death, ISKCON has been managed by the Governing Body Commission. Sri Prabhupada created this body to handle affairs in his absence concerning the daily management and spiritual standards for the organization and its members.

Views on other Religious Traditions: Prabhupada considered Moses, Jesus, and Mohammed to be empowered representatives of God. He considered them pioneers of the same essential message of dedication to God with love and devotion.

- "Actually, it doesn't matter – Krishna or Christ – the name is the same. The main point is to follow the injunctions of the Vedic scriptures that recommend chanting the name of God in this age." (from *The Science of Self-Realization,* ISBN 9171494472)

Respect in India: In 1996 the Government of India issued a commemorative postage stamp in Sri Prabhupada's honor.

In India ISKCON has become a highly respected organization. Sri Prabhupada has been honored by the Government and praised by the highest leaders of the country.

In 1996 the Government of India recognized Sri Prabhupada's accomplishments by issuing a commemorative stamp in his honor.

Speaking at the inauguration of ISKCON's cultural center in New Delhi in 1998, Sri Atal Behari Vajpayee, then India's prime minister, said:

"If the Bhagavad Gita, the holy text of the Hindu traditions, is printed in millions of copies and scores of languages and distributed in all nooks and corners of the world, the credit for this great sacred service goes chiefly to ISKCON. For this accomplishment alone, Indians should be eternally grateful to the devoted spiritual army of Swami Prabhupada, the founder of the Hare Krishna movement, and to his followers. . . .

"The arrival of Bhaktivedanta Swami Prabhupada in the United States in 1965 and the particular popularity his movement gained in a very short span of twelve years must be regarded as one of the greatest spiritual events of the century."

1. Bhagavad-gita As It Is (1968)
2. Sri Isopanisad (1969)
3. Srimad-Bhagavatam (1972-77) (multiple volumes)
4. Chaitanya-caritamrta (1974) (multiple volumes)
5. The Nectar of Instruction (1975)

Other works published within Prabhupada's lifetime

1. Beyond Illusion and Doubt (1967)
2. Easy Journey to Other Planets (1970)
3. Krishna Consciousness: The Topmost Yoga System (1970)
4. Beyond Birth and Death (1972)
5. Perfection of Yoga (1972)
6. On The Way to Krishna (1973)
7. Raja Vidya: The King of Knowledge (1973)
8. Elevation to Krishna Consciousness (1973)
9. Krishna Consciousness: The Matchless Gift (1974)
10. Perfect Questions, Perfect Answers (1977)
11. Teachings of Lord Kapila (1977)
12. The Science of Self-Realization (1977)

Published Posthumously

1. Light of the Bhagavata (1977)
2. Teachings of Queen Kunti (1978)
3. Life Comes From Life (1978)
4. Krishna, The Reservoir of Pleasure (1979?)
5. Chant and Be Happy (1982)

6. Coming Back (1983?)
7. Narada-bhakti-sutra (1989?)
8. Path of Perfction (1989?)
9. Mukunda-mala-stotra (1989)
10. A Second Chance (1991)
11. Journey of Self Discovery (1991)
12. Laws of Nature: An Infallible Justice (1991)
13. Renunciation Through Wisdom (1992)
14. Quest for Enlightenment (1993?)
15. The Path of Yoga (1995)
16. Message of Godhead (1996?)
17. Civilization and Transcendence (1998)
18. Dharma: The Way of Transcendence (1998)
19. Introduction to Bhagavad-gita (2005)

Baba Lokenath Brahmachari

Baba Lokenath Brahmachari was born on Janmastami, the birthday of Lord Krishna, in 1730 (18th Bhadra,1137 bangabda) to a Brahmin family in the village of Chaurasi Chakla, a couple of miles from Kolkata. His father Ramnarayan Ghosal's one wish in life was to dedicate a child to the path of renunciation to liberate the family. So when the fourth son was born to his wife Kamaladevi, he knew that the time had come to initiate his boy to the service of God. He pleaded with Pandit Bhagawan Ganguly of the nearby village of Kochuya to be his son's guru and teach him the wisdom of the Shastras. At the age of 11, young Lokenath left home with his guru. He visited Kalighat Temple in Kolkata and then ived in the forests for 25 years, selflessly serving his master and practising the Ashtanga Yoga of Patanjali along with the most difficult Hatha Yoga. After this he travelled to the Himalayas where he meditated in the nude for nearly five decades. Finally, the attained enlightenment at the age of ninety.

After his enlightenment he traveled extensively on foot to Afghanistan, Persia, Arabia and Israel, making three pilgrimages to Mecca. When he came to the small town Baradi near Dhaka, a wealthy family built him a small hermitage, which became his ashram. He was at the time one hundred and thirty six years old. There he accepted the sacred thread of the Brahmins and clothed himself in saffron robes. For the rest of his life he performed miracles on and gave divine wisdom to all who came to him to seek his blessings.He received the title *Baba*(Bengali for Father).

On the 19th day of Jyestha, 1297 (1890), at 11:45 am, the Baba was meditating when he went into a trance with his eyes open, and while still meditation, left his physical body forever. He was aged 160. He had said before his death:

I am eternal, I am deathless. After this body falls, do not think that everything will come to an end. I will live in the hearts of all living beings in my subtle astral form. Whoever will seek my refuge, will always receive my Grace.

Teachings: His teachings were infused with simplicity that endeared the common man. He preached love, devotion and unwavering faith in God and in one's deeper, immutable self. After attaining enlightenment he had said:

> *I have seen only My self. I am bound by my own karma. The materialistic world is bound by the tongue and the sex organ. He who can restrain these two is fit to attain enlightenment.*

Baba Lokenath is said to have been nearly seven feet tall with little flesh on him. He was an ascetic, denying him self physical pleasures. He could even negate sleep, never closing his eyes or even blinking.

Impact: Today, Lokenath Brahmachari is a household deity of millions of Bengali families on both sides of the Indo-Bangladesh border. He is regarded a saint among Hindus and is often deified as a living God.

An often repeated legend tells that Baba Lokenath was an avatar of Shiva, sent as a Messiah to redeem the world of sin.

7

PHILOSOPHICAL RELEVANCE OF SOCIAL REFORM MOVEMENT

Since the counter-culture revolution of the 1960s, there have been an increasing number of Western devotees of various Hindu lineages and practices. These have come about not only through the Hare Krishnas, but also through the Universalist teachings of such Hindu figures as Sri Ramakrishna, and the yoga teachings of B.K.S. Iyengar. The growing number of Indian immigrants relocating into the West, and the subsequent building of Hindu temples to meet the spiritual needs of these newly established Hindu communities, has also resulted in Westerns having ready access to traditional teachings.[*citation needed*] Many Western converts were introduced to Hinduism after attending the Western temples and then embracing the tradition. There can also be no doubt that the fitness revolution's ecstatic love-affair with yoga in the 1990's has helped spur on new interest in the teachings of Hinduism in the West.

More and more texts are being written by Western-born Hindu converts specifically for a new Western audience, the vast bulk of which have little to no experience with Sanskrit which renders traditional literature all but useless. Some of the more notable instructional texts are the Shaivistic teaching series of the Western-born Satguru Sivaya Subramuniyaswami's Himalayan Academy, which includes a book on how to convert to Hinduism, along with the instructional texts on beginning a mantra practice by Western-born, traditionally Vedic-trained Hindu priest, Thomas Ashley-Farrand, also known as Namadeva, and the Devi Mandir publications of the modern saint Shree Maa and Western-born sadhu Swami Satyananda Saraswati.

A new movement of Western Hindus has emerged. Coupling a deep love for the Hindu faith and a commitment to liberal values, the Western Hindu Association (now called the Progressive Hindu Association) initially reached out to Hindus who were Westerners (both born and converts.) This movement was initially called Western Hindu Association and supported many Western Values such as feminism, gay rights, and environmentalism. They later broadened their scope to aiding converts, providing spiritual direction, and the formation of a religious order of monks and nuns who hold to a progressive liberal Hindu outlook.

Along with the traditional Hindu lineages that are opening their doors to Westerners, there are also many non-traditional spiritualities that are also embracing the beliefs and practices of Hinduism to varying extents. The Universalist Unitarian Church often makes room in their schedule to host events tied to Hindu holidays and celebrations, during which non-Hindus can learn more about the tradition and begin to take part in the observances. There are also several Neopagan and Wiccan traditions, such as SHARANYA, which teaches traditional Shakta Tantra within a Western Wicca-influenced context, and Shakti Wicca, a "Western Universalist Shakta Bhakti Tradition", which seeks to provide a synergistic, syncretic spirituality based on a combination of Hindu Shaktism and eclectic Wicca's educational, ritual, and training structure.

The German Indologist Axel Michaels in his 1998 book about Hinduism distinguished *founding, proselytizing religions*, "guruism" as religious groups originating in India, but also widespread in the West, founded by charismatic persons with a corpus of esoteric writings of gurus predominantly in English: Maharishi Mahesh Yogi and Transcendental Meditation, Sathya Sai Baba and the Sathya Sai Federation, Bhaktivedanta Swami Prabhupada and ISKCON, Guru Maharaj Ji and the Divine Light Mission, Rajneesh Chandra Mohan and the Sannyasi movement in Poona, et cetera. These *founding, proselytizing religions*, "guru-ism" are according to the book one of the three subgroups of *founded religions* of Hinduism. The other two being *sectarian religions* and *syncretically founded religions*. The *founded religions* in turn are, according to the book, one of the three Hindu religions that comprise Hinduism. The other two Hindu religions that comprise Hinduism are *Brahmanic-Sanskritic Hinduism*, and *folk religions and religions of social communities* (subcastes, castes, tribes); *Hindu folk or tribal religions*.

Brahmo Samaj

Brahmo Samaj is a social and religious movement founded during the 19th century movement known as the Bengal Renaissance.

Rabindranath Tagore succinctly explains the backdrop for the movements:

"Unfortunately, when Englishmen alighted at our doorsteps with their material power, science and philosophy, our hearts were immobile. The religious asceticism, which had assisted the positioning of India as a preceptor in the world, had withered away. At that time, we were occasionally drying our ancient manuscripts in the sun, collecting them back and storing them in our houses. We were really doing nothing. The days of our glory were visible as a shadow on the horizon far behind. Even the banks of the nearby pond appeared to be more realistic and higher than those distant hill ranges."

Origin of Name: *Brahmo Samaj* literally means the society of worshippers of One True God. *Brahmo* means one who worships Brahma, or the supreme spirit of the universe, and *Samaj* means a community of men.

History and Time Line: The movement was started on 20th August 1828 by Raja Rammohun Roy and his friends when they opened a place for public worship, *Brahma Sabha* (One God Society) on Chitpore Road (now Rabindra Sarani), Kolkata, India. It was publicly inaugurated on 11th Magh or 23rd January 1830. The former date is celebrated as *Bhadrotsab* and the latter as *Maghotsab*. These are the two main festivals of Brahmo Samaj.

Roy's movement the noted physicist, Jayant Narlikar, writes:

"Roy understood that the emerging knowledge from the West could not be ignored...He was deeply appreciative of the liberal philosophical traditions of India, and he founded the Brahmo Samaj, a religious movement to popularise those enlightened ideas... Since religion played a dominant role in the public life of his times, he went on to reform religion itself... His criticism of the existing religion and its rigid practices and caste barriers was inspired by his desire to make religion consistent with the changing world of his times..."

Following the death of Raja Rammohun Roy in 1833, internal management was left entirely in the hands of Pandit Ram Chandra Vidyabagish. In 1839, Debendranath Tagore, son of Prince Dwarkanath Tagore, a friend and active supporter of Raja Rammohun Roy, joined the Sabha. On 7th Pous 1765 Shaka (1843) Debendranath Tagore and twenty others were formally initiated into what was then named Calcutta Brahmo Samaj for the first time with a signed covenant. The Pous Mela at Santiniketan starts on this day.

Keshub Chunder Sen joined the Calcutta Brahmo Samaj in 1857. This name it retained till the year of the first schism in 1866, after which it was changed to Adi (original) Brahmo Samaj. The new one was called Brahmo Samaj of India.

Although, the Brahmo Samaj movement was born in Kolkata, the idea soon spread to the rest of India. That happened to be the period when the railways were expanding and communication was becoming easier. Outside Bengal presidency some of the prominent centres of Brahmo activity were: Punjab, Sind, and Bombay and Madras presidencies. Even to this day, there are several active branches outside Bengal. Bangladesh Brahmo Samaj at Dhaka keeps the lamp burning.

Social Reform: In all fields of social reform, including abolition of the caste system and of the dowry system, emancipation of women, and improving the educational system, the Brahmo Samaj reflected the ideologies of the Bengal Renaissance. *Brahmoism*, as a means of discussing the dowry system, was a central theme of Sarat Chandra Chattopadhyay's noted 1914 Bengali language novella, *Parineeta*. The *Brahmo Samaj Marriage Act of 1872* set the age at which girls could be married to 14.

It also supported social reform movements of people not directly attached to the Samaj, such as Pandit Iswar Chandra Vidyasagar's movement which promoted widow re-marriage.

Aims of Movement: The Brahmo Samaj aimed at developing a universal religion and that has evolved over a period. Bipin Chandra Pal has succinctly summarised the evolution:

"Raja Rammohan Roy had given us a philosophy of universal religion. But philosophy was not religion. It is only when philosophy becomes organised in ethical exercises and disciplines and spiritual sacraments that it becomes a religion. Devendranath gave us a national religion, on the foundations of the Raja's philosophy of universal religion. To Keshub, however, was left the work of organising the Raja's philosophy into a real universal religion through new rituals, liturgies, sacraments and disciplines, wherein were sought to be brought together not only the theories and doctrines of the different world religions but also their outer vehicles and formularies to the extent that these were real vehicles of their religious or spiritual life, divested, however, through a process of spiritual sifting, of their imperfections and errors and superstitions."

One of the major contributions was the study of other religions and going to their roots. In 1869, Keshub Chunder Sen chose from amongst his missionaries, four persons and ordained them as *adhyapaks* or professors of four old religions of the world – Gour Govinda Ray for Hinduism, Protap Chandra Mazoomdar for Christianity, Aghore Nath Gupta for Buddhism and Giris Chandra Sen for Islam. All of them did adequate justice to the task allotted to them. The efforts of these four persons were subsequently followed up by others in the Brahmo Samaj.

The attempt to create a universal religion has been analytically explained by Deshbandhu Chittaranjan Das. Speaking in 1917 he said:

"The earlier religion of his (Keshub Chunder Sen's) life was perhaps somewhat abstract. But his religion in developed form, as we find it, in his Navavidhan, is full of concrete symbols of all religions...This brings me to another predominant note of Bengali culture. This is the note of universality... The different sects into which our country is apparently divided, all point to this universalism. The differences are deceptive. They deceive those that are strangers to our thought and culture. Every Hindu is conscious of the underlying unity of this universalism. Read the devotional poems of the Vaishnavas, read the devotional poems of the Shaktas and the other sects, you will find they were identical in this character. The life and work of Keshub Chunder Sen also point to attempt after attempt at this very universalism. The earlier attempt was abstract in its character, brought about by what is called the universal of subtractions. It was based on this, 'There is truth in every religion! Thus in discarding what it conceived to be false in every religion, and accepting what it conceived to be true build up a sort of an abstract universal religion.' From Hinduism it took the Upanishads discarding the subsequent scriptures and systems. From Christianity it took the ideal of the

son ship of man and the Fatherhood of God divorced from it scriptures and its traditions. From Mohammedanism it took the idea of equality of man without the characteristic traditions in which that idea lived and moved and had its being. Similarly, from all known systems of religion. But as the spiritual experience of Keshub Chunder Sen deepened, he could not remain satisfied with abstract ideas thus taken and formulated. He wanted flesh and blood for the life of his religion. It was then that he formulated what I regard, as one of the grandest attempts at universal religion... The result may or may not be considered satisfactory. But I refuse to judge it by the results. I rejoice in the glory of the attempt."

Divisions and Re-organization: The Brahmo Samaj split twice, once when Keshub Chunder Sen came out of the Calcutta Brahmo Samaj (or Adi Samaj as it was later known) in 1866 and formed the Brahmo Samaj of India. The second split was when Sadharan Brahmo Samaj was formed in 1878 and Keshub Chunder Sen went on to develop the *Navavidhan* or New Dispensation in 1880.

When the bitterness died down, there were efforts at reconciliation and re-understanding of all that had happened in the past. While Sadharan Brahmo Samaj and Nava Bidhan Samaj function on their own, the one in Bhowanipur is known as Sammelan Samaj. Many feel that Rabindranath Tagore contributed substantially towards synthesis in the Brahmo Samaj.

The fundamental principles of the Brahmo Samaj are that:

- There is only one God, the creator and sustainer of the world who is infinite in power, wisdom, love and holiness (see monotheism).
- The human soul is immortal, capable of eternal progress, and responsible to God for its doings.
- God manifests himself directly to the human soul, and no prophets or scriptures are mediators between God and the soul.
- All religious teachers and books are to be honored to the extent that they are in harmony with divine revelation to the soul.
- God is to be worshipped daily by loving him and doing his will.

Additionally, Brahmos do not believe in heaven and hell as eternal, unchanging conditions of reward or punishment. Instead, they see heaven as the state of being filled with divine revelation and hell as the state of being filled with sinful thoughts.

The basic religious ideology is derived to a large extent from the Isha Upanishad, a monotheistic Hindu scripture and one of the principal Upanishads, whose tentative date is assigned the 7th century BC.

This article or section may contain original research or unverified claims. Please help Wikipedia by adding references. See the talk page for details.

The splits, or schisms as they are called, occupy an important place in the history of the Brahmo Samaj. There were immediate reasons for them – the move against caste symbols in the first case and the marriage of Keshub Chunder Sen's daughter in the second, but obviously there were deeper reasons for it. First, there was a conflict of opinions amongst people in different generations. Second, there was a clash between authoritarianism and democracy. Third and more importantly, there was divergence between spirituality and rationalism.

Unlike traditional religions, which are based on authority of some divine revelation or word that cannot be questioned, Brahmo Samaj was founded on rationalism merged with spiritualism, or of intuition and reason as some have put it. Therefore, there always was a subtle conflict about the proportionate mix of the two. Such conflicts did not always surface but often remained simmering underneath. There were thorough rationalists such as Pandit Iswar Chandra Vidyasagar, who were close to the Brahmo Samaj in their approach towards social reformation but did not agree on spiritualism and hence kept away from it. Within the samaj, the question played a leading role in shaping its history. Even as late as 1886 when Bijay Krishna Goswami, a leading missionary, left the Sadharan Brahmo Samaj, the underlying note was the conflict between spiritualism and rationalism.

When Max Muller and Romain Rolland, both highly respected and knowledgeable about India, analysed the Indian religious scenario, they heaped substantial praise upon both Raja Rammohan Roy and Keshub Chunder Sen but they seem to suggest that the movement had ended with them. It was left to David Kopf who emphasized the valuable role played by Sadharan Brahmo Samaj in social reform particularly women's education and the role of Rabindranath Tagore as a great synthesiser in the Brahmo Samaj. Jayant Narlikar has viewed the entire scenario from a completely different angle. Being a scientist, he has noted with considerable apprehension the growing gap between India and the West. He feels that Raja Rammohan Roy had initiated steps for reformation of Indian society and that could assist in reducing the gap, but by and large, Indian society has remained unchanged. The point evidently is that social reformation of Indian society has to be undertaken if we are to attempt a reduction in its backwardness. Whether it is done along the lines of the Brahmo Samaj or in some other fashion is a moot point. This brings us to a question where it is being doubted whether economic development with high rates of growth, which is essential and welcome, alone would be able to assist India in emerging from its backwardness.

We are living in a world where religion itself is losing its relevance and value. In the developed countries, many people are declaring themselves as not belonging to any religion. In such a scenario the future of an organisation such as the Brahmo Samaj is doubtful, to say the least, but the sad part of the story is that the glorious task it had undertaken remains unfulfilled.

Arya Samaj

Arya Samaj (*Arya Society* or *Society of Nobles*) is a Hindu reform movement in India that was founded by Swami Dayananda in 1875. He was a sannyasin (renouncer) who believed in the infallible authority of the Vedas. Dayananda advocated the doctrine of karma and reincarnation, and emphasised the ideals of brahmacharya (chastity) and sanyasa (renunciation).

Doctrines: The doctrines of the Samaj are summed up in Ten Principles:

1. God is the primary cause of all true science and of all that can be known through it.
2. God is Existent, Intelligent and Blissful. He is Formless, Almighty, Just, Merciful, Unborn, Infinite, Unchallengeable, Beginningless, Incomparable, the Support and Lord of all, Omniscient, Imperishable, Immortal, Fearless, Eternal, Holy and the Maker of the universe. To Him alone worship is due.
3. The Vedas are scriptures of true knowledge. It is the duty of all Aryas to read them, hear them being read and recite them to others.
4. All persons should be ready to accept the truth and give up untruth.
5. All action should be performed in conformity with Dharma, that is, after due consideration

of the right and wrong.

6. The primary aim of the Arya Samaj is to do good for all, that is, promote physical, spiritual and social well-being.
7. All people should be treated with love, fairness and due regard for their merit.
8. One should aim at dispelling ignorance and promoting knowledge.
9. One should not only be content with one's own welfare, but should look for it in the welfare for others also.
10. One should regard oneself under restriction to follow altruistic rulings of society, while all should be free in following the rules of individual welfare.

Dayananda rejected all non-Vedic beliefs altogether. Hence the Arya Samaj unequivocally condemned iconolatry, animal sacrifices, ancestor worship, pilgrimages, priestcraft, offerings made in temples, the caste system, untouchability and child marriages, on the grounds that all these lacked Vedic sanction. It aimed to be a universal church based on the authority of the Vedas. Dayananda stated that he wanted 'to make the whole world Arya'. That is, he wanted to develop a *missionary* Hinduism based on the universality of the Vedas. To this end the Arya Samaj set up schools and missionary organisations, extending its activities outside India. It now has branches around the world. It has a disproportional amount of adherents among people of Indian ancestry in Suriname and the Netherlands, in comparison with India. Arya Samaj is a global organisation having about 8000 and odd Arya Samaj units popularly known as Arya Samaj Temples but not in the orthodoxies appearance. They are rather the controlling offices of the philanthropic activities undertaken by the team in the society. The apex body of Arya Samaj ie. SARVADESHIK ARYA PRATINIDHI SABHA is based at Delhi.CaptDev Ratan Arya is the President and Shri Vimal Wadhawan Arya is the Secretary of the SAPS. The latest founded Arya Samaj is at Pondicherry. SAPS has started an orphanage known as Jeewan Prabhat Vedhapuri at Pondicherry. The ancient name of Pondicherry is Vedhapuri.

Ramakrishna Mission

The Ramakrishna Mission Emblem: The Ramakrishna Mission is an association founded by Sri Ramakrishna's chief disciple and religious leader, Swami Vivekananda on May 1, 1897. The Mission carries on missionary and philanthropic work in conjunction with householders (Grihastha) disciples.

The Ramakrishna Mission acquired a legal status when it was registered in 1909 under Act XXI of 1860. Its management is vested in a Governing Body. Though the Mission with its branches is a distinct legal entity it is closely related to the Ramakrishna Math. The Trustees of the Math are simultaneously the members of the Governing Body. The administrative work of the Mission is mostly in the hands of the monks of Math. The Mission has its own separate funds, for which it keeps detailed accounts, audited annually by chartered accountants. The Math and the Mission both have their Headquarters at Belur Math.

The Motto: The Mission is a registered Society laying emphasis on rendering welfare services undertaken with a spiritual outlook. The service activities are rendered looking upon all as veritable manifestation of the Divine. The Motto of the organisation is *Atmano Mokshartham Jagad-hitaya Cha*. Translated from Sanskrit it means "For one's own salvation, and for the good of the world."

Math and Mission: The distinction between Math and Mission is ordinarily blurred to the common people who loosely associate Math with the Mission and vice versa.

Emblem of Ramakrishna Math and Mission: Designed and explained by Swami Vivekananda *given in his own words:*

> *The wavy waters in the picture are symbolic of Karma; the lotus, of Bhakti; and the rising-sun, of Jnana. The encircling serpent is indicative of Yoga and the awakened Kundalini Shakti, while the swan in the picture stands for Paramatman (Supreme Self). Therefore, the idea of the picture is that by the union of Karma, Jnana, Bhakti and Yoga, the vision of Paramatman is obtained.*

Presidents of the Ramakrishna Mission: The following is the traditionally accepted list of Presidents (spiritual heads) of the monastic order.

1. Swami Brahmananda (1901–1922)
2. Swami Shivananda (1922–1934)
3. Swami Akhandananda (1934–1937)
4. Swami Vijnanananda (1937–1938)
5. Swami Shuddhananda (1938–1939)
6. Swami Virajananda (1939–1952)
7. Swami Shankarananda (1952–1959)
8. Swami Vishuddhananda (1959–1960)
9. Swami Madhavananda (1960–1965)
10. Swami Vireshwarananda (1966–1985)
11. Swami Gambhirananda (1985–1988)
12. Swami Bhuteshananda (1988–1998)
13. Swami Ranganathananda (1998–2005)
14. Swami Gahanananda (2005– Present President of the Order)

Prominent Monks: Apart from Direct disciples of Shri Ramakrishna, some of the other great monks of the order are

1. Swami Ashokananda
2. Swami Yatishwarananda
3. Swami Prabhavananda
4. Swami Nikhilananda
5. Swami Ghanananda
6. Swami Siddheshwarananda
7. Swami Tapasyananda
8. Swami Nityaswarupananda
9. Swami Shambhavananda
10. Swami Budhananda
11. Swami Purushottamananda

□□□

8

MODERN POLITICAL PHILOSOPHERS

Mohandas Karamchand Gandhi

2 October 1869–30 January 1948

Popular Name: Mahatma Gandhi

Place of Birth: Porbandar, Gujarat, India

Place of Death: New Delhi, India

Movement: Indian independence movement

Major Organizations: Indian National Congress

An English-educated lawyer, Gandhi first employed his ideas of peaceful civil disobedience in the Indian community's struggle for civil rights in South Africa. Upon his return to India, Gandhi organised poor farmers and labourers to protest oppressive taxation and widespread discrimination. Leading the Indian National Congress, Gandhi led a nationwide campaign for the alleviation of poverty, for the liberation of Indian women, for brotherhood amongst communities of differing religions and ethnicity, for an end to untouchability and caste discrimination, and for the economic self-sufficiency of the nation, but above all for *Swaraj* — the independence of India from foreign domination. Gandhi famously led Indians in the disobedience of the salt tax through the 400 kilometer (248 miles) Dandi Salt March in 1930, and in an open call for the British to *Quit India* in 1942. He spent his final years fighting for communal peace and harmony amongst Hindus, Muslims and Sikhs.

Throughout, Gandhi remained committed to non-violence and truth even in the most extreme situations. Gandhi was a student of Hindu philosophy and lived simply, organizing an ashram that was self-sufficient in its needs. He made his own clothes — the traditional Indian dhoti and shawl, woven with a charkha — and lived on a simple vegetarian diet. He used rigorous fasts — abstaining from food and water for long periods — for self-purification as well as a means of protest. Gandhi's life and teachings inspired Dr. Martin Luther King Jr., Steve Biko and Aung San Suu Kyi and, respectively, the American civil rights movement, civil rights struggles in South Africa and Myanmar. His criticism of many aspects of western modernity (such as modern technology and industrialization) in that it harmed the poor and benefited the rich has also earned him the reputation of a development critic whose thinking has inspired many later political thinkers.

Gandhi is honoured as the *Father of the Nation* in India, a title first given him by Subhash Chandra Bose. Gandhi's birthday on October 2 is annually commemorated as Gandhi Jayanti, and is a national holiday.

Early Life: Mohandas Karamchand Gandhi was born into a Hindu Modh Vanik family in Porbandar, Gujarat, India in 1869. He was the son of Karamchand Gandhi, the *diwan* (Chief Minister) of Porbandar, and Putlibai, Karamchand's fourth wife, a Hindu of the Pranami Vaishnava order. Karamchand's first two wives, who each bore him a daughter, died from unknown reasons (rumored to be in childbirth). His third wife was deemed incapacitated and gave her permission to Karamchand for him to marry again. Growing up with a devout mother and surrounded by the Jain influences of Gujarat, Gandhi learned from an early age the tenets of non-injury to living beings, vegetarianism, fasting for self-purification, and mutual tolerance between members of various creeds and sects. He was born into the *vaishya*, or business, caste.

Gandhi and His Wife Kasturba (1902): In May 1883, at the age of 13, Gandhi was married through his parents' arrangement to Kasturba Makhanji (also spelled "Kasturbai" or known as "Ba"), who was his age. They had four sons: Harilal Gandhi, born in 1888; Manilal Gandhi, born in 1892; Ramdas Gandhi, born in 1897; and Devdas Gandhi, born in 1900. Gandhi was a mediocre student in his youth at Porbandar and later Rajkot. He barely passed the matriculation exam for the University of Bombay in 1887, where he joined Samaldas College. He was also unhappy at the college, because his family wanted him to become a barrister. He leapt at the opportunity to study in England, which he viewed as "a land of philosophers and poets, the very centre of civilization."

At the age of 18 on September 4, 1888, Gandhi went to University College London to train as a barrister. His time in London, the Imperial capital, was influenced by a vow he had made to his mother in the presence of a Jain monk Becharji, upon leaving India to observe the Hindu precepts of abstinence from meat, alcohol, and promiscuity. Although Gandhi experimented with adopting "English" customs — taking dancing lessons for example — he could not stomach his landlady's mutton and cabbage. She pointed him towards one of London's few vegetarian restaurants. Rather than simply go along with his mother's wishes, he read about, and intellectually embraced vegetarianism. He joined the Vegetarian Society, was elected to its executive committee, and founded a local chapter. He later credited this with giving him valuable experience in organizing institutions. Some of the vegetarians he met were members of the Theosophical Society, which had been founded in 1875 to further universal brotherhood and devoted to the study of Buddhist and Hindu Brahmanistic literature. They encouraged Gandhi to read the *Bhagavad Gita*. Not having shown a particular interest in religion before, he read works of and about Hinduism, Christianity, Buddhism, Islam and other religions. He returned to India after being admitted to the bar of England and Wales, but had limited success establishing a law practice in Bombay, later applying and being turned down for a part-time job as a high school teacher.

He ended up returning to Rajkot to make a modest living drafting petitions for litigants but was forced to close down that business as well when he ran afoul of a British officer. In his autobiography, he describes this incident as a kind of unsuccessful lobbying attempt on behalf of his older brother. It was in this climate that (in 1893) he accepted a year-long contract from an Indian firm to a post in Natal, South Africa.

Gandhi in South Africa (1895): At this point in his life, Gandhi was a mild-mannered, diffident and politically indifferent individual. He had read his first newspaper at the age of 18, and was prone to stage fright while speaking in court. South Africa changed him dramatically, as he faced the discrimination that was commonly directed at blacks and Indians in that country. One day in court in the city of Durban, the magistrate asked him to remove his turban. Gandhi refused to do so and stormed out of the courtroom. In another incident, he was thrown off a train at Pietermaritzburg, after refusing to move from the first class coach to a third class compartment while holding a valid first class ticket. Later, travelling further on by stagecoach, he was beaten by a driver for refusing to travel on the footboard to make room for a European passenger. He suffered other hardships on the journey as well, including being barred from many hotels on account of his race. These incidents have been acknowledged by several biographers as a turning point in his life that would serve as the catalyst for his activism later in life. It was through witnessing first-hand the racism, prejudice and injustice against Indians in South Africa that Gandhi started to question his people's status, and his own place in society. Gandhi in the uniform of a sergeant of the Indian Ambulance Corps. He served during the Boer War (1899).

At the end of his contract, Gandhi prepared to return to India. However, at a farewell party in his honour in Durban, he happened to glance at a newspaper and learned that a bill was being considered by the Natal Legislative Assembly to deny the right to vote to Indians. When he brought this up with his hosts, they lamented that they did not have the expertise necessary to oppose the bill, and implored Gandhi to stay and help them. He circulated several petitions to both the Natal Legislature and the British Government in opposition to the bill. Though unable to halt the bill's passage, his campaign was successful in drawing attention to the grievances of Indians in South Africa. Supporters convinced him to remain in Durban to continue fighting against the injustices levied against Indians in South Africa. He founded the Natal Indian Congress in 1894, with himself as the Secretary. Through this organization, he moulded the Indian community of South Africa into a homogeneous political force, publishing documents detailing Indian grievances and evidence of British discrimination in South Africa. Gandhi returned briefly to India in 1896 to bring his wife and children to live with him in South Africa.

When he returned in January 1897, a white mob attacked and tried to lynch him. In an early indication of the personal values that would shape his later campaigns, he refused to press charges on any member of the mob, stating it was one of his principles not to seek redress for a personal wrong in a court of law.

At the onset of the South African War, Gandhi argued that Indians must support the war effort in order to legitimize their claims to full citizenship, organizing a volunteer ambulance corps of 300 free Indians and 800 indentured labourers called the Indian Ambulance Corps, one of the few medical units to serve wounded black South Africans. He himself was a stretcher-bearer at the Battle of Spion Kop, and was decorated. At the conclusion of the war, however, the situation for the Indians did not improve, but continued to deteriorate. In 1906, the Transvaal government promulgated a new Act compelling registration of the colony's Indian population. At a mass protest meeting held in Johannesburg that September, Gandhi adopted his methodology of *satyagraha* (devotion to the truth), or non-violent protest, for the first time, calling on his fellow Indians to defy the new law and suffer the punishments for doing so, rather than resist through violent means. This plan was adopted, leading to a seven-year struggle in which thousands of Indians were jailed (including Gandhi himself on many occasions), flogged, or even shot, for striking, refusing to register, burning their registration cards, or engaging in other forms of non-violent resistance. While the government was successful in repressing the Indian protesters, the public outcry stemming from the harsh methods employed by the South African government in the face of peaceful Indian protesters finally forced South African General Jan Christiaan Smuts to negotiate a compromise with Gandhi. In May 1915, Gandhi founded an ashram on the outskirts of Ahmedabad, India and called it Satyagrah Ashram (also known as Sabarmati Ashram). There lodged twenty five men and women who took vows of truth, celibacy, ahimsa, nonpossession, control of the palate, and service of the Indian people.

Fighting for Indian Independence (1916–1945): As he had done in the South African War, Gandhi urged support of the British in World War I and was active in encouraging Indians to join the army. His rationale, opposed by many others, was that if he desired the full citizenship, freedoms and rights in the Empire, it would be wrong not to help in its defence. He spoke at the conventions of the Indian National Congress, but was primarily introduced to Indian issues, politics and the Indian people by Gopal Krishna Gokhale, at the time one of the most respected leaders of the Congress Party.

Champaran and Kheda: Gandhi in 1918, at the time of the Kheda and Champaran satyagrahas.

Gandhi's first major achievements came in 1918 with the Champaran agitation and *Kheda Satyagraha*, although in the latter he was involved at par with Sardar Vallabhai Patel, who acted as his right-hand and leader of the rebels. In Champaran, a district in the state of Bihar, he organized civil resistance on the part of tens of thousands of landless farmers and serfs, and poor farmers with small lands, who were forced to grow indigo and other cash crops instead of the food crops necessary for their survival. Suppressed by the militias of the landlords (mostly British), they were given measly compensation, leaving them mired in extreme poverty. The villages were kept extremely dirty and unhygienic, and alcoholism, untouchability and purdah were rampant. Now in the throes of a devastating famine, the British levied an oppressive tax which they insisted on increasing in rate. The situation was desperate. In Kheda in Gujarat, the problem was the same. Gandhi established an ashram there, organizing scores of his veteran supporters and fresh volunteers from the region. He organized a detailed study and survey of the villages, accounting the atrocities and terrible episodes of suffering, including the general state of degenerate living. Building on the confidence of villagers, he began leading the clean-up of villages, building of schools and hospitals and encouraging the village leadership to undo and condemn many social evils, as accounted above.

But his main assault came as he was arrested by police on the charge of creating unrest and was ordered to leave the province. Hundreds of thousands of people protested and rallied outside the jail, police stations and courts demanding his release, which the court unwillingly granted. Gandhi led organized protests and strikes against the landlords, who with the guidance of the British government, signed an agreement granting more compensation and control over farming for the poor farmers of the region, and cancellation of revenue hikes and collection until the famine ended. It was during this agitation, that Gandhi was addressed by the people as *Bapu* (Father) and *Mahatma* (Great Soul). In Kheda, Patel represented the farmers in negotiations with the British, who suspended revenue collection and granted relief. All prisoners were released. Gandhi's resulting fame spread all over the nation.

Non-cooperation: In Punjab, the Jallianwala Bagh massacre of civilians by British troops caused deep trauma to the nation, and increased public anger and acts of violence. Gandhi criticized both the actions of the British, and the retaliatory violence of Indians. He authored the resolution offering condolences to British civilian victims and condemning the riots, which after initial opposition in the party, was accepted after Gandhi made an emotional speech pushing forth his principle that all violence was evil and could not be justified. But it was after the massacre and violence that Gandhi's mind focused upon obtaining complete self-government and control of all Indian government institutions, maturing soon into *Swaraj* or complete individual, spiritual, political independence. Gandhi was invested with executive authority on behalf of the Indian National Congress in December 1921. Under Gandhi's leadership, the Congress was reorganized with a new constitution, with the goal of *Swaraj*. Membership in the party was opened to anyone prepared to pay a token fee. A hierarchy of committees was set up to improve discipline, transforming the party from an elite organization to one of mass national appeal. Gandhi expanded his non-violence platform to include the *swadeshi* policy – the boycott of foreign-made goods, especially British goods. Linked to this was his advocacy that *khadi* (homespun cloth) be worn by all Indians instead of British-made textiles. Gandhi exhorted Indian men and women, rich or poor, to spend time each day spinning *khadi* in support of the independence movement. This was a strategy to inculcate discipline and dedication to weed out the unwilling and ambitious, and include women in the movement at a time when many thought that such activities were not "respectable" for women. In addition to boycotting British products, Gandhi urged the people to boycott British educational institutions and law courts, to resign from government employment, and to forsake British titles and honours.

"Non-cooperation" enjoyed wide-spread appeal and success, increasing excitement and participation from all strata of Indian society, yet just as the movement reached its apex, it ended abruptly as a result of a violent clash in the town of Chauri Chaura, Uttar Pradesh, in February 1922. Fearing that the movement was about to take a turn towards violence, and convinced that this would be the undoing of all his work, Gandhi called off the campaign of mass civil disobedience. Gandhi was arrested on March 10, 1922, tried for sedition, and sentenced to six years. Beginning on March 18, 1922, he only served about two years of the sentence, being released in February 1924 after an operation for appendicitis. Without Gandhi's uniting personality, the Indian National Congress began to splinter during his years in prison, splitting into two factions, one led by Chitta Ranjan Das and Motilal Nehru favouring party participation in the legislatures, and the other led by Chakravarti Rajagopalachari and Sardar Vallabhbhai Patel, opposing this move. Furthermore, cooperation among Hindus and Muslims, which had been strong at the height of the nonviolence campaign, was breaking down. Gandhi attempted to bridge these differences through many means, including a three-week fast in the autumn of 1924, but with limited success.

Swaraj and The Salt Satyagraha: Gandhi stayed out of the limelight for most of the 1920s, preferring to resolve the wedge between the Swaraj Party and the Indian National Congress, and expanding initiatives against untouchability, alcoholism, ignorance and poverty. He returned to the fore in 1928. The year before, the British government appointed a new constitutional reform commission under Sir John Simon numbering not a single Indian in its ranks. The result was a boycott of the commission by Indian political parties. Gandhi pushed through a resolution at the Calcutta Congress in December 1928 calling on the British government to grant India dominion status or face a new campaign of non-violence with complete independence for the country as its goal. Gandhi had moderated the views of younger men like Subhas Chandra Bose and Jawaharlal Nehru, who sought a demand for immediate independence, but also modified his own call to a one year wait, instead of two. The British did not respond. On December 31, 1929, the flag of India was unfurled in Lahore. January 26, 1930 was celebrated by the Indian National Congress, meeting in Lahore as India's Independence Day. This day was commemorated by almost every other Indian organization. Making good on his word in March 1930, he launched a new satyagraha against the tax on salt, highlighted by the famous Salt March to Dandi from March 21 to April 6, 1930, marching 400 kilometres (248 miles) from Ahmedabad to Dandi, Gujarat to make his own salt. Thousands of Indians joined him on this march to the sea. This campaign was one of his most successful, resulting in the imprisonment of over 60,000 people.

The government, represented by Lord Edward Irwin, decided to negotiate with Gandhi. The Gandhi-Irwin Pact was signed in March 1931. In it, the British Government agreed to set all political prisoners free in return for the suspension of the civil disobedience movement. Furthermore, Gandhi was invited to attend the Round Table Conference in London as the sole representative of the Indian National Congress. The conference was a disappointment to Gandhi and the nationalists as it focused on the Indian princes and Indian minorities rather than the transfer of power. Furthermore, Lord Irwin's successor, Lord Willingdon, embarked on a new campaign of repression against the nationalists. Gandhi was again arrested, and the government attempted to destroy his influence by completely isolating him from his followers. This tactic was not successful. In 1932, through the campaigning of the Dalit leader B. R. Ambedkar, the government granted untouchables separate electorates under the new constitution. In protest, Gandhi embarked on a six-day fast in September 1932, successfully forcing the government to adopt a more equitable arrangement via negotiations mediated by the Dalit cricketer turned political leader Palwankar Baloo. This began a new campaign by Gandhi to improve the lives of the untouchables, whom he named Harijans, the children of God. On May 8, 1933 Gandhi began a 21-day fast of self-purification to help the Harijan movement. In the summer of 1934, three unsuccessful attempts were made on his life.

When the Congress Party chose to contest elections and accept power under the Federation scheme, Gandhi decided to resign from party membership. He did not at all disagree with the party's move, but felt that if he resigned, his popularity with Indians would cease to stifle the party's membership, that actually varied from communists, socialists, trade unionists, students, religious conservatives, to those with pro-business convictions. Gandhi also did not want to prove a target for Raj propaganda by leading a party that had temporarily accepted political accommodation with the Raj. Gandhi returned to the head in 1936, with the Nehru presidency and the Lucknow session of the Congress. Although Gandhi desired a total focus on the task of winning independence and not speculation about India's future, he did not restrain the Congress from adopting socialism as its goal. Gandhi had a clash with Subhas Bose, who had been elected to the presidency in 1938. Gandhi's main issues with Bose were his lack of commitment to democracy, and lack of faith in non-violence. Bose won his second term despite Gandhi's criticism, but left the Congress when the All-India leaders resigned en masse in protest of his abandonment of principles introduced by Gandhi.

World War II and Quit India: Mahadev Desai (left) reading out a letter to Gandhi from the viceroy at Birla House, Mumbai, April 7, 1939.

World War II broke out in 1939 when Nazi Germany invaded Poland. Initially, Gandhi had favored offering "non-violent moral support" to the British effort, but other Congress leaders were offended by the unilateral inclusion of India into the war, without consultation of the people's representatives. All Congressmen elected to office resigned en masse. After lengthy deliberations, Gandhi declared that India could not be party to a war ostensibly being fought for democratic freedom, while that freedom was denied in India herself. As the war progressed, Gandhi increased his demands for independence, drafting a resolution calling for the British to *Quit India*. This was Gandhi's and the Congress Party's most definitive revolt aimed at securing the British exit from Indian shores.

Gandhi was criticized by some Congressmen and other Indian political groups, both pro-British and anti-British. Some felt that opposing Britain in its life-death struggle was immoral, and others felt that Gandhi wasn't doing enough. *Quit India* became the most forceful movement in the history of the struggle, with mass arrests and violence on an unprecedented scale. Thousands of freedom fighters were killed or injured in police firing, and hundreds of thousands were arrested. Gandhi and his supporters made it clear they would not support the war effort unless India was granted immediate independence. He even clarified that this time the movement would not be stopped if individual acts of violence were committed, saying that the *"ordered anarchy"* around him was *"worse than real anarchy"*. He called on all Congressmen and Indians to maintain discipline in ahimsa, and *Karo Ya Maro* (*Do or Die*) in the cause of ultimate freedom. Gandhi and the entire Congress Working Committee were arrested in Bombay by the British on August 9, 1942. Gandhi was held for two years in the Aga Khan Palace in Pune. It was here that Gandhi suffered two terrible blows in his personal life — his wife Kasturba died, just a few months after Mahadev Desai, his 42-year old secretary died of a heart attack. He was released before the end of the war because of his failing health and necessary surgery; the Raj did not want him to die in prison and enrage the entire nation beyond control. Although the ruthless suppression of the movement by British forces brought relative order to India by the end of 1943, Quit India succeeded in its objective. At the end of the war, the British gave clear indications that power would be transferred to Indian hands, and Gandhi called off the struggle, and the Congress leadership and around 100,000 political prisoners were released. In February 1944 Kasturbai Gandhi died in prison and six weeks later Gandhi suffered a severe malaria attack. During this time Gandhi's health continually deteriorated to the point that the government on May 6, 1944 decided to release him.

Freedom and Partition of India: Gandhi advised the Congress to reject the proposals the British

Cabinet Mission offered in 1946, as he was deeply suspicious of the *grouping* proposed for Muslim-majority states — Gandhi viewed this as a precursor to partition. However, this became one of the few times the Congress broke from Gandhi's advice (not his leadership though), as Nehru and Patel knew that if the Congress did not approve the plan, the control of government would pass to the Muslim League. Between 1946 and 1947, over 5,000 people were killed in violence. Gandhi was vehemently opposed to any plan that partitioned India into two separate countries. Many Muslims in India lived side by side with Hindus and Sikhs, and were in favour of a united India. But Muhammad Ali Jinnah, the leader of the Muslim League, commanded widespread support in West Punjab, Sindh, NWFP and East Bengal. The partition plan was approved by the Congress leadership as the only way to prevent a wide-scale Hindu-Muslim civil war. Congress leaders knew that Gandhi would viscerally oppose partition, and it was impossible for the Congress to go ahead without his agreement, for Gandhi's support in the party and throughout India was strong. Gandhi's closest colleagues had accepted partition as the best way out, and Sardar Patel endeavoured to convince Gandhi that it was the only way to avoid civil war. A devastated Gandhi gave his assent.

On the day of the transfer of power, Gandhi did not celebrate independence with the rest of India, but was alone in Calcutta, mourning the partition and working to end the violence. After India's independence, Gandhi focused on Hindu-Muslim peace and unity. He conducted extensive dialogue with Muslim and Hindu community leaders, working to cool passions in northern India, as well as in Bengal. Despitè the Indo-Pakistani War of 1947, he was troubled when the Government decided to deny Pakistan the Rs. 55 crores due as per agreements made by the Partition Council. Leaders like Sardar Patel feared that Pakistan would use the money to bankroll the war against India. Gandhi was also devastated when demands resurged for all Muslims to be deported to Pakistan, and when Muslim and Hindu leaders expressed frustration and an inability to come to terms with one another. He launched his last fast-unto-death in Delhi, asking that all communal violence be ended once and for all, and that the payment of Rs. 55 crores be made to Pakistan. Gandhi feared that instability and insecurity in Pakistan would increase their anger against India, and violence would spread across the borders. He further feared that Hindus and Muslims would renew their enmity and precipitate into an open civil war. After emotional debates with his life-long colleagues, Gandhi refused to budge, and the Government rescinded its policy and made the payment to Pakistan. Hindu, Muslim and Sikh community leaders, including the RSS and Hindu Mahasabha assured him that they would renounce violence and call for peace. Gandhi thus broke his fast by sipping orange juice.

On January 30, 1948, on his way to a prayer meeting, Gandhi was shot dead in Birla House, New Delhi, by Nathuram Godse. Godse was a Hindu radical with links to the extremist Hindu Mahasabha, who held Gandhi responsible for weakening India by insisting upon a payment to Pakistan. Godse and his co-conspirator Narayan Apte were later tried and convicted, and on 15 November 1949, were executed. A prominent revolutionary and Hindu revivalist, the president of the Mahasabha, Vinayak Damodar Savarkar was accused of being the architect of the plot, but was acquitted due to lack of evidence. Gandhi's memorial (or *Samadhi*) at Rajghat, New Delhi, bears the epigraph,, which may be translated as "Oh God". These are widely believed to be Gandhi's last words after he was shot, though the veracity of this statement has been disputed by many. Jawaharlal Nehru addressed the nation through radio:

"Friends and comrades, the light has gone out of our lives, and there is darkness everywhe:e, and I do not quite know what to tell you or how to say it. Our beloved leader, Bapu as we called him, the father of the nation, is no more. Perhaps I am wrong to say that; nevertheless, we will not see him again, as we have seen him for these many years, we will not run to him for advice or seek solace from him, and that is a terrible blow, not only for me, but for millions and millions in this country."

Gandhi's Principles

Truth: Gandhi dedicated his life to the wider purpose of discovering truth, or *Satya.* He tried to achieve this by learning from his own mistakes and conducting experiments on himself. He named his autobiography *The Story of My Experiments with Truth.*

Gandhi said that the most important battle to fight was in overcoming his own demons, fears and insecurities. Gandhi summarized his beliefs first when he said "God is Truth," but as typical of Gandhi, he evolved, later to correct himself and state that "Truth is God." The first statement seemed insufficient to Gandhi, as the mistake could be made that Gandhi was using Truth as a description of God, rather than the summative definition of the entire essence of God. *Satya* (Truth) in Gandhi's philosophy is God. It shares all the characteristics of the Hindu concept of God, or Brahman.

Nonviolence: The concept of nonviolence (*ahinsa*) and nonresistance has a long history in Indian religious thought and has had many revivals in Hindu, Buddhist, Jain and Christian contexts. Gandhi explains his philosophy and way of life in his autobiography *The Story of My Experiments with Truth.* He was quoted as saying:

"When I despair, I remember that all through history the way of truth and love has always won. There have been tyrants and murderers and for a time they seem invincible, but in the end, they always fall — think of it, always."

"What difference does it make to the dead, the orphans, and the homeless, whether the mad destruction is wrought under the name of totalitarianism or the holy name of liberty and democracy?"

"An eye for an eye makes the whole world blind."

"There are many causes that I am prepared to die for but no causes that I am prepared to kill for."

Criticism: Throughout his life and after his death, Gandhi has evoked serious criticism. B. R. Ambedkar, the Dalit political leader condemned Gandhi's terming the untouchable community as *Harijans*, which he found condescending. Ambedkar and his allies also felt Gandhi was undermining Dalit political rights. Muhammad Ali Jinnah and contemporary Pakistanis often condemn Gandhi for undermining Muslim political rights. Vinayak Damodar Savarkar condemned Gandhi for *appeasing* Muslims politically — Savarkar and his allies blamed Gandhi for thus facilitating the creation of Pakistan and increasing the influence of the Muslim community in politics beyond proportion. Savarkar himself was implicated in the trial following Gandhi's murder, as he was the mentor of the assassin Nathuram Godse and an important Hindu Mahasabha leader. In contemporary times, historians like Ayesha Jalal blame Gandhi and the Congress for being unwilling to share power with Muslims and thus hastening partition. Hindu political activists like Pravin Togadia and Narendra Modi have been known to criticize Gandhi's leadership and actions.

Gandhi has also been criticized by various historians and commentators for his attitudes regarding Hitler and Nazism. Gandhi apparently believed that Hitler's hatred could be transformed by the application of non-violent resistance. Gandhi has come under fire in particular for statements to the effect that the Jews would win God's love if they willingly went to their deaths as martyrs. Some criticism of Gandhi has been challenged in a number of articles.

Gandhi has also been criticized by anti-communists for referring to Vladimir Lenin as a "titan in spirit" and for generally supporting the cause of the Soviet Union.

Gandhi never received the Nobel Peace Prize, though he was nominated for it five times between 1937 and 1948. Decades later, however, the Nobel Committee publicly declared its regret for the omission, and admitted to deeply divided nationalistic opinion denying the award to Gandhi. The Prize was not awarded in 1948, the year of Gandhi's death, on the grounds that "there was no suitable living candidate" that year, and when the Dalai Lama was awarded the Prize in 1989, the chairman of the committee said that this was "in part a tribute to the memory of Mahatma Gandhi". After Gandhi's death, Albert Einstein said of Gandhi: "Generations to come will scarcely believe that such a one as this walked the earth in flesh and blood." He also once said," I believe that Gandhi's views were the most enlightened of all the political men in our time. We should strive to do things in his spirit: not to use violence in fighting for our cause, but by non-participation in anything you believe is evil."

Time Magazine named Gandhi as the runner-up to Albert Einstein as "Person of the Century" at the end of 1999, and named The Dalai Lama, Lech Walsa, Dr. Martin Luther King, Jr., Cesar Chavez, Aung San Suu Kyi, Benigno Aquino Jr., Desmond Tutu, and Nelson Mandela as *Children of Gandhi* and his spiritual heirs to the tradition of non-violence. The Government of India awards the annual Mahatma Gandhi Peace Prize to distinguished social workers, world leaders and citizens. Nelson Mandela, the leader of South Africa's struggle to eradicate racial discrimination and segregation, is a prominent non-Indian recipient of this honour. In 1996, the Government of India introduced the Mahatma Gandhi series of currency notes in Rupees 5, 10, 20, 50, 100, 500 and 1000 denomination.

Mahatma: The word *Mahatma*, while often mistaken for Gandhi's given name in the West, is taken from the Sanskrit words *maha* meaning *Great* and *atma* meaning *Soul*. The title "Mahatma" was first accorded to Gandhi on January 21, 1915 by his pioneer supporter Nautamlal Bhagavanji Mehta at the Kamribai School in Jetpur, Gujarat, India (in the erstwhile princely state of Kathiawad). In his autobiography, Gandhi nevertheless explains that he never felt worthy of the honour. According to the *manpatra*, the name *Mahatma* was given in response to Gandhi's admirable sacrifice in manifesting justice and truth.

Across the world: Statue of Mahatma Gandhi in Tavistock Square Gardens, London. The centennial commemorative statue of Mahatma Gandhi in the center of downtown Pietermaritzburg, South Africa.

In the United Kingdom, there are several prominent statues of Gandhi, most notably in Tavistock Square, London (near University College London), where he studied law. January 30 is commemorated in the United Kingdom as National Gandhi Remembrance Day. In the United States, there are statues of Gandhi outside the Ferry Building in San Francisco, Union Square Park in New York City, the Martin Luther King, Jr. National Historic Site in Atlanta, the Heritage Park in Skokie (north suburb of Chicago), the hermann park in Houston and near the Indian Embassy in the Dupont Circle neighbourhood of Washington, DC. The city of Pietermaritzburg, South Africa, where Gandhi was ejected in 1893 from a first-class train, now hosts a commemorative statue. The Government of India donated a statue to the city of Winnipeg, Manitoba, Canada, to signify their support for the future Canadian Museum for Human Rights. There are wax statues of Gandhi at the Madame Tussaud's wax museums in New York and London, and other cities around the world, including Moscow, Paris, Amsterdam, Barcelona, Lisbon, Canberra, Santiago de Chile, Mexico City and Trinidad and Tobago's two cities, Port of Spain and San Fernando.

Ahimsa (Nonviolence): Ahimsa is not merely a negative state of harmlessness , but it is positive state of love , of doing good even to the evil-doer. - *Young India, August 25, 1920*

Ahimsa is a weapon of matchless potency. It is the summum bonum of life. It is an attribute of the brave, in fact, it is their all. It does not come within the reach of coward. It is no wooden or lifeless dogma, but a living and life giving force. - *Young India, Sept 6, 1926.*

Ahimsa is not the way of the timid or cowardly. It is the way of the brave ready to face death. He who perishes sword in hand is no doubt brave; but he who faces death without raising his little finger and without flinching, is braver. - *Young India, Oct. 11, 1928.*

Satya (Truth): Truth has no form. Therefore everyone one will form such an idea or image of Truth as appeals to him, and there will be as many images of Truth as there are men. These will be true as long as they last. For they enable a man to obtain everything he wants. - *Diary of Mahadevbhai, p. 120.*

Truth should be Truth in thought, Truth in speech, and Truth in action. To the man who has realised this Truth in its fulness , nothing else remains to be known, because all knowledge is necessarily included in it. What is not included in it, is not truth and so not true knowledge. - *From Yeravda Mandir, p. 2.*

Asteya (Non-stealing): Non-stealing does not mean merely not to steal. To keep or take anything which one does not is also stealing. And of course, stealing is fraught with violence.- *Bapu-ke-Aashirvad, November 24, 1944.*

We are not always aware of our real needs, and most of us improperly multiply our wants and thus , unconsciously, make thieves of ourselves. One who follows the observance of Non-stealing will bring about a progressive reduction of his own wants. Much of the distressing poverty in this world has risen out of the breaches of the principle of Non-stealing.- *From Yeravda Mandir, p. 20.*

Brahmacharya (Self Discipline): Brahamchraya means control of all the organs of sense. He who attempts to control only one organ, and allows all the others free play is bound to find his effort futile- *Bapu's Letters to Mira.*

To hear suggestive stories with the ears, to see suggestive sights with the eyes, to taste stimulating food with the tongue, to touch exciting things with the hands, and at the same time to expect to control the only remaining organ, is like putting one's hands in the fire and expecting to escape being hurt. *Bapu's letters to Mira.*

Aparigraha (Non-possession): Non possession means that we should not hoard anything that we do not need today.

The less you possess, the less you want, the better you are. And better for what ? Not for your enjoyment of this life but for enjoyment of personal service to your fellow beings ; service to which you dedicate yourself, body, soul and mind.

When you dispossess yourself of everything you have, you really possess all the treasures of the world. In other words , you really get all that is in reality necessary for you, everything . If the food is necessary, food will come to you.-

Sharirshrama (Bread Labour): Earn thy bread by the sweat of the brow- says Bible . Bread labour means that everyone is expected to perform sufficient body-labour in order to entitle him to his living. It is not ,therefore, necessary to earn one's living by bread labour, taking living' in its broader sense. But everyone must perform some useful body-labour. Young India, Nov. 5, 1925.

The economics of Bread labour are the living way of life . It means that every man has to labour with his body for his food and clothing. If I can convince the people of the value and necessity of bread-labour, there never will be any want of bread and cloth. - Harijan, Sept. 7, 1947.

The idea is that every healthy individual must labour enough for his food and his intellectual faculties must be exercised not in order to obtain a living or amass a fortune, but only in the service of mankind. If this principle is observed everywhere, all men would be equal, none would starve and world would be saved from a sin.- Harijan, Aug 3, 1935.

Aswada (Control of the Palate): Unless we are satisfied with foods that are necessary for the proper maintenance of our physical health, and unless we are prepare to rid ourselves of stimulating heating and exciting condiments that we mixed with food. We will certainly not be able to control the over-abundant, unnecessary, and exciting stimulation that we may have. If we do not do that, the result naturally is that we abuse ourselves, and become less than animals and brutes. - *Speeches & Writings of Mahatma Gandhi.*

The diet should be healthy and well-balanced. The body was never meant to be treated as a refuse-bin. Food is meant to sustain the body. - *My Philosophy of Life.*

Sarvatra Bhayavarjana (Fearlessness): Fearlessness should connote absence of all kinds of fear - fear of death, fear of bodily injury, fear of hunger, fear of insults, fear of public disapprobation, fear of ghosts and evil spirits, fear of anyone's anger. Freedom from all these and other such fears constitute fearlessness. - *Bapu - Ke Ashirwad. Nov 26, 1944*

Fearlessness does not mean arrogance and aggressiveness. That in itself is a sign of fear. Fearlessness presupposes calmness and peace of mind. For that it is necessary to have a living faith in God. - *Harijan, Nov. 3, 1946.*

Sarva Dharma Samantva (Equality of the Religions): Religions have been interwoven . One sees a special quality in every one of them . But no one religion is higher than another. All are complimentary to one another. Since this is my belief, the speciality of any one religion cannot run counter to another, cannot be at variance with universally accepted principles. - Harijanbandhu, March 19, 1933.

For I believe in the fundamental truth of all great religions of the world. I believe that they are all God-given, and I believe that they were necessary for the people to whom these religions were revealed. And I believe that, if only we could all of us read the scriptures of the different faiths from the standpoint of the followers of those faiths we should find that they were at bottom all one and were all helpful to one another.- *Harijan, Feb. 16, 1934* .

Just as men have different names and faces, these religions also are different. But just as men are all human in spite of their different names and forms, just as leaves of a tree though different as leaves are the same as the leaves of the same tree, all religions though different are the same. We must treat all religions as equals. - *Harijanbandhu, July 22, 1934.*

Swadeshi (Use Locally Made Goods): Swadeshi is that sprit in us which requires us to serve our immediate neighbours before others , and to use things produced in our neighborhood in preference to those more remote. So doing, we cannot serve humanity to the best of our capacity, we cannot serve humanity by neglecting our neigbours. - *Young India, April 20, 1919.*

It is sinful to buy and use articles made by sweated labour. It is sinful to eat American wheat &and let my neighbour, the grain dealer starve for want of custom. Similarly, it is sinful for to wear the latest finery of Regent Street when I know that if I had but worn the things woven by the neighbouring spinners and weavers, that would have clothed me, and fed and clothed them. - *Young India, Oct. 13, 1921.*

My definition of Swadeshi is well known . I must not serve my distant neighbor at the expense of the nearest. It is never vindictive or punitive. It is in no sense narrow , for I buy from every part of the world what is needed for my growth. I refuse to buy from anybody anything, however nice or beautiful, if it interferes with my growth or injures those whom Nature has made my first care. - *Young India, March 12, 1925.*

Swadeshi is that spirit in us which restricts us to the use and service of our immediate surroundings to the exclusion of the more remote & I should use only things that are produced by my immediate neighbors and serve those industries by making them efficient and complete where they might be found wanting. It is suggested that such Swadeshi, if reduced to practice, will lead to the millennium. - *Speeches and Writings of Mahatma Gandhi.*

Sparshbhavna (Untouchability): Untouchability means pollution by the touch of certain persons in reason of their birth in a particular state or family. It is an excrescence. In the guise of religion, it is always in the way, and erupts religion. - *From Yeravda Mandip.*

Removal of untouchability means love for, and service of, the whole world and thus merges into Ahimsa. Removal of untouchability spells the breaking down of barriers between man and man and between the various orders of Being. *-From Yeravda Mandir.*

I consider untouchability to be a heinous crime against humanity. It is not a sign of self-restraint, but an arrogant assumption of superiority. - *Young India, Dec. 8, 1920*

Village Development: India does not need to be industrialized in the modern sense of the term . It has 7,50,000 villages scattered over the vast area 1900 miles long 1500 broad. The people are rooted to the soil and the vast majority are living a hand to mouth life. What ever may be said to the contrary, having traveled throughout the length and breath of the land with the eyes open and having mixed with millions are living in enforced idleness for the last four month in a year. Agriculture does not need revolutionary changes. The Indians peasant requires a supplementary industry .The most natural is the introduction of the spinning wheel not the handloom. The latter cannot be included introduced in every home, whereas the farmer can, and it used to be so even a century ago. It was driven out not by economic pressure but by force deliberately used as can be proved from authentic records. The restoration therefore of the spinning wheel solves the economic problem of India at a stroke.

Medium of Education: I find daily proof of the increasing & continuing wrong being done to the millions by our false de-Indianizing education.

We seem to have come to think that no one can hope to be like a Bose unless he knows English. I cannot conceive a grosser superstition than this. No Japanese feels so helpless as we seem to do....

The medium of instruction should be alerted at once, and at any cost, the provincial languages being given their rightful place. I would prefer temporary chaos in higher education to the criminal waste that is daily accumulating.

Education through a foreign Language entails a certain degree of strain, and our boys have to pay dearly for it. To a large extent, they lose the capacity of shouldering any other burden afterwards., for they become a useless lot who are weak of body, without any zest for work and imitators of the West. They have little interest in original research or deep thinking, and the qualities of courage, perseverance. bravery and fearlessness are lacking. That is why we are unable to make new plans or carry our projects to meet our problems. In case we make them to fail to implement them. A few who do show promise usually die young......

We, the English educated people alone are unable to assess the great loss that this factor has caused. Some idea of its immensity would be had if we could estimate how little we have influenced the general mass of our people.

The school must be an extension of home there must be concordance between the impressions which a child gathers at home and at school, if the best results are to be obtained. Education through the medium of strange tongue breaks the concordance which should exist. Those who breaks this relationship are enemies of the people even though their motives may be honest. To be a voluntary victim of this system of education is as good as the betrayal of our duty towards our mothers. The harm done by this alien type of education does not stop here; it goes much further . It has produced a gulf between the educated classes and the masses. The people look on us as beings apart from them.

It is my considered opinion that English education in the manner it has been given has emasculated the English educated Indian, it has put a severe strain upon the Indian students' nervous energy and has made of us imitators. The process of displacing the vernaculars has been one of the saddest chapters in the British connection. Ram Mohan Rai would have been a greater reformer, and Lokmanya Tilak would have been a greater scholar, if they had not to start with the handicap of having to think in English and transmit their thoughts chiefly in English. Their effect on their own people, marvelous as it was, would have been greater if they would have been brought under a less unnatural system. No dought they both gained from their knowledge of the rich treasures of English literature. But these should have been accessible to them through their own vernaculars. No country can become a nation by producing a race of imitators.

English is today studied because of its commercial and so called political value. Our boys think and rightly in the present circumstances, that without English they cannot get Government service. Girls are taught English as a passport to marriage. I know several instances of women wanting to learn English so that they may be able to talk in English. I know families in which English is made a mother tongue. Hundreds of youth believe that without the Knowledge of English. freedom of India is practically impossible. The canker has so eaten into the society that in many cases the only meaning of education is Knowledge of English. All these are for me signs of our slavery and degradation. It is unbearable to me that the vernaculars should be crushed and starved as they have been. I cannot tolerate the idea of parents writing to their children, or husbands writing to their wives, not in their own vernaculars but in English.

The foreign medium has caused brains fag, put an undue strain upon the nerves of our children, made them crammers and imitators, unfitted them for original work and thought, and disabled them for filtrating their learning to the family or the masses. The foreign medium has made our children practically foreigners in their own lands. It is the greatest tragedy of the existing system. The foreign medium has prevented the growth of our vernaculars. If I had the powers of a despot, I would today stop the tuitions of our boys and girls through a foreign medium and require all the teachers and professors on pain of dismissal to introduce the change forthwith. I would not wait for the preparation of Text books. They will follow the change. It is an evil that need a summary remedy.

Among the many evils of foreign rule, this blighting imposition of a foreign medium upon the youth of the country will be counted by history as one of the greatest. It has sapped the energy of the nation, it has estranged them for the masses, it has made education unnecessarily expensive. If this process is still persisted in, it bids fair to rob the nation of its soul. The sooner, therefore educated India shakes itself free from the hypnotic spell of the foreign medium, the better it would be for them and the people.

Gandhi's Views On Religion

1. My own experience has led me to the knowledge that the fullest life is impossible without an immovable belief in a Living Law in obedience to which the whole universe moves. A man without that faith is like a drop thrown out of the ocean bound to perish. Every drop in the ocean shares its majesty and has the honour of giving us the ozone of life.
2. There is an indefinable mysterious power that pervades everything. I feel it, though I do not see it. It is this unseen power that makes itself felt and yet defies proof, because it is so unlike all that I perceive through out the existence of God to a limited extent.
3. I have made he world's faith in God my own, and as my faith is ineffaceable, I regard that to describe faith as experience is to tamper with Truth, it may perhaps be more correct to say that I have no word for characterizing my belief in God.
4. God is that indefinable something which we all feel but which we do not know. To me God is Truth and Love, God is ethics and morality. God is fearlessness, God is the source of light and life and yet. He is above and beyond all these. God is conscience. He is even the atheism of the atheist. He transcends speech and reason. He is a personal God to those who need His touch. He is purest essence. He simply Is to those who have faith. He is long suffering. He is patient but He is also terrible. He is the greatest democrat the world knows. He is the greatest tyrant ever known.
5. You have asked me why I consider that God is Truth. In my early youth I was taught to repeat what in Hindu scriptures are known as one thousand names of God. But these one thousand names of God were by no means exhaustive. We believe and I think it is the truth- that God has as many names as there are creatures and, therefore, we also say that God is nameless and since God many forms we also consider Him formless, and since He speaks to us through many tongues we consider Him to be speechless and so on.

And when I came to study Islam I found that Islam too had many for God. I would say with those who say that God is Love, God is Love. But deep down in me I used to say that thought God may be, God, God is Truth, above all. If it is possible for the human tongue to give the fullest description, I have come to the conclusion that for myself God is Truth. But two years ago, I went a step further and said Truth is God. You will see the fine distinction between the two statements, viz. That God is Truth and Truth is God. And I came to that conclusion after a continuous and relentless search after Truth which began nearly fifty years ago. I then found that the nearest approach to Truth was love. But I also found that love has many meanings in the English language at lest and that human love in the sense of passion could become a degrading also. I found, too, that love in the sense of never found a double meaning in connection with truth and not even the atheists had demurred to the necessity or power of truth. But in their passion for discovering truth the atheists have not hesitated to deny the very existence of God from their own point of view rightly. And it was because of this reasoning that I saw that rather than say God is Truth I should say Truth is God. I recall the name of Charles Brad laugh who delighted to call himself an atheist, but knowing as I do something of, I would never regard him as an atheist. I would call him a God-fearing man though I know he would reject the claim. His face would redden if I would say, "Mr. Brad laugh, you are a truth-fearing man and not a God-fearing man." I would automatically disarms his criticism by saying that Truth is God, as I have disarmed the criticism of many a young man. Add to this the difficulty that millions have taken the name of God and in His name committed nameless atrocities. Not that scientists very often do not commit cruelties in the name of truth. I know how in the name of truth and science inhuman cruelties are perpetrated on animals when men perform vivisection. There are thus a number of difficulties in the way, no matter how you describe God. But the human mind is a limited thing and you have to labour under limitations when you think of a being or entity who is beyond the power of man to grasp. And than we have another thing in Hindu philosophy, viz. God alone is and nothing else exists, and the same truth you find emphasized and exemplified in the kalema of Islam. There you find it clearly stated-that God alone is and nothing else exists. In fact the Sanskrit word for Truth is a word which literally means that which exists-Sat. For these and several other reasons that I can give you I have come to the conclusion that the definition - Truth is God-gives me the greatest satisfaction. And when you want to find Truth as God the only inevitable means is Love, i.e. non-violence, and since I believe that ultimately means and end are convertible terms, I should not hesitate to say that God is Love. At then is Truth?' A difficult question, but I have solved it for myself by saying that it is what the voice within tells you. How, then, you ask, different people think of different and contrary truths? Well, seeing that the human mind works through innumerable media and that the evolution of the human mind is not the same for all, it follows that what may be truth for one may be untruth for another, and hence those who have made experiment have come to the conclusion that there are certain conditions to be observed in making those experiments. Just as for conduction scientific experiments there is an indispensable scientific course of instruction, in the same way strict preliminary discipline is necessary to qualify a person to make experiments in the spiritual realm. Everyone should, therefore, realize his limitations before he speaks of his inner voice. Therefore, we have the belief based upon experience, that those who would make individual search after truth as God, must go through several vows, as for instance, the vow of truth, the vow of brahmacharya (purity)-for you can not possibly divide your love for Truth and God with anything else - the vow of non-violence, of poverty and non-possession Unless you impose on yourselves the five vows, may not embark on the experiment at all. There are several other conditions prescribed, but I must not take you through all of them Suffice it to say that who have made these experiments know that it is not proper for everyone to claim to hear the voice of conscience and it is because we have at the present moment everyone claiming the right of conscience without going through any discipline whatsoever that there is so much untruth being delivered to a bewildered world. All that I can in true humility present to you is that truth is not to be found by anybody who has not got an abundant sense of humility. If you would swim on the bosom of the ocean of Truth you must reduce yourselves to a zero. Further then this I cannot go along this fascinating path.

6. I do not regard God as a person. Truth for me is God, and God's Law and God are not different things or facts, in the sense that an earthly king and his law are different. Because God is an Idea, Law Himself. Therefore, it is impossible to conceive God as breaking the Law. He therefore, does not rule our actions and withdraw Himself. When we say He rules our actions, we are simply using human language and we try to limit Him. Otherwise, He and His Law abide everywhere and govern everything. Therefore, I do not think that He answers in every detail every request of ours, but there is no doubt that He rules our action. And I literally believe that not a blade of grass grows or moves without His will. The free will we enjoy is less than that of a passenger on a crowded deck." Do you feel a sense of freedom in your communion with God?" I do. I do not feel cramped as I would on a boat full of passengers. Although I know that my freedom is less than that of a passenger, I appreciate that freedom as I have imbibed through and through the central teaching of the Gita that man is the maker of his own destiny in the sense that he has freedom of choice as to the manner in which he uses that freedom. But he is no controller of results. The moment he thinks he is, he comes to grief.
7. Man was supposed to be the maker of his own destiny. It is partly true. He can make his destiny only in so far as he is allowed by the Great Power which overrides all our intentions, all our plans and carries out His Own plans. I call that Great Power not by the name of Allah, not by the name of Khuda or God but by the name of Truth. For me, Truth is God and Truth overrides all our plans. The whole truth is only embodied within the heart of that Great Power- Truth. I was taught from my early days to regard Truth as unapproachable - something that you cannot reach. A great Englishman taught me to believe that God is unknowable. He is Knowable to the extent that our limited intellect allows.
8. Truth is by nature self-evident. As soon as you remove the cobwebs of ignorance that surround it, it shines clear.
9. Every expression of truth has in it the seeds of propagation, even as the sun cannot hide its light.
10. Life is a very complex thing, and truth and non-violence present problems, which often defy analysis and judgment. One discovers truth and the method of applying the only legitimate means of vindicating it, i.e. Satyagraha or soul-force, by patient endeavour and silent prayer. I can only assure friends that I spare no pains to grope to my way to the right, and that humble but constant endeavour and silent prayer are always my two trusty companions along the weary but beautiful path that all seekers must tread.

11. You cannot realize the wider consciousness, unless you subordinate completely reason and intellect, and the body, too.
12. It is unnecessary to believe in an extra mundane Power called God in order to sustain our faith in ahimsa. But God is not a Power residing in the clouds. God is an unseen Power residing within us and nearer to us than finger-nails to the flesh. There are many powers lying hidden within us and we find this Supreme Power if we make diligent search with the fixed determination to find Him. One such way of ahimsa. It is so very necessary because God is in every one of us and, therefore, we have to identify ourselves with every human being without exception. This is called cohesion or attraction in scientific language. In the popular language it is called love. In the popular language it is called love. It binds us to one another and to God. Ahimsa and love are one and the same thing. I hope this is all clears to you.
13. I am but a poor struggling soul yearning to be wholly good-wholly truthful and wholly non-violent in thought, word and deed; but ever failing to reach the ideal which I know to be true. It is a painful climb, but the pain of it is a positive pleasure to me. Each step upward makes me feel stronger and fit for the next.
14. But I know that I have still before me a difficult path to traverse. I must reduce myself to zero. So long as one does not of his own free will put himself last among his fellow creatures, there is no salvation for him. Ahimsa is the farthest limit of humility.
15. I am impatient to realize the presence of my Maker, Who to me embodies Truth and in the early part of my career I discovered that if I was to realize Truth, I must obey, even at the cost of my life, the law of Love.
16. I have but shadowed forth my intense longing to lose myself in the Eternal and become merely a lump of clay in the Potter's divine hands so that my service may become more certain because uninterrupted by the baser self in me.
17. God as Truth has been for me a treasure beyond price; may He be so to every one of us.
18. Devotion to this Truth is the sole justification for our existence.-YM, 2.
19. But He is no God who merely satisfies the intellect, if He ever does. God to be God must rule the heart and transform it. He must express Himself in every the smallest act of His votary. This can only be done through a definite realization more real than the five senses can ever produce. Sense perceptions can be, often are false and deceptive, however real they may appear to us. Where there is realization outside the senses it is infallible. It is proved not by extraneous evidence but in the transformed conduct and character of those who have felt the real presence of God within. Such testimony is to be found in the experiences of an unbroken line of prophets and sages in all countries and climes. To reject this evidence is to deny oneself.
20. But it is impossible for us to realize perfect Truth so long as we are imprisoned in this mortal frame. We can only visualize it in our imprisoned in this mortal frame. We can only visualize it in our imagination. We cannot, through the instrumentality of this ephemeral body, see face to face Truth which is eternal. That is why in the last resort one must depend on faith.
21. No one can attain perfection while he is in the body for the simple reason that the ideal state is impossible so long as one has not completely overcome his ego, and ego cannot be wholly

got rid of so long as one is tied down by the shackles of the flesh.

22. Man will ever remain imperfect, and it will always be his part to try to be perfect. So that perfection in love or non-possession will remain an unattainable ideal as long as we are alive but towards which we must ceaselessly strive.
23. Our existence as embodied being is purely momentary; what are a hundred years in eternity? But if we shatter the chains of egotism, and melt into the ocean of humanity, we share its dignity. To feel that we are something is to set up a barrier between God and ourselves; to cease feeling that we are something is become one with God. A drop in the ocean partakes of the greatness of its parent, although it is unconscious of it. But it is dried up as soon as it enters upon an existence independent of the ocean. We do not exaggerate, when we say that life is a mere bubble.
24. No niggardly acceptance of the inevitable will appear pleasing to God. It must be a thorough change of heart.
25. I must go with God as my only guide. He is a jealous Lord. He will allow no one to appear before Him in all one's weakness, empty-handed and in a spirit of full surrender, and then He enables you to stand before a whole world and protects you from harm.
26. I have no special revelation of God's will. My firm belief is that He reveals Himself daily to every human being but we shut our ears to 'the still small voice'. We shut our eyes to the Pillar of Fire in front of us. I realize His omnipresence.
27. I do not want to foresee the future, I am concerned with taking care of the present. God has given me no control over the moment following.
28. The impenetrable darkness that surrounds us is not a curse but a blessing. He has given us power to see only the step in front of us, and it should be enough it Heavenly light reveals that step to us. We can then sing with Newman, 'One step enough for me'. And we may be sure from our past experience that the next step will always be in view. In other words, the impenetrable darkness is nothing so impenetrable as we imagine. But it seems impenetrable when, in our impatience, we want to look beyond that one step.
29. We are living in the midst of death. What is the value of 'working for our own schemes' when they might be reduced to naught in the twinkling of an eye, or when we may equally swiftly and unawares be taken away from them? But we may feel strong as a rock, if we could truthfully say 'we work for God and His schemes'. Then nothing perishes. All perishing is them only what seems. Death and destruction have them, but only then no reality about tem. For death and destruction is then but a change.
30. This led the interviewer on to a fundamental question. From a reading of Gandhiji's writings the friend had gathered that the root of all of Gandhiji's activities was the desire for moksha, emancipation. But why was not this aspect emphasized sufficiently? Gandhiji replied by taking recourse to a simile. He said the desire for moksha was indeed there, but it was not meant for anyone other than the individual himself. The world was interested in the fruits, not root. For the tree itself, however the chief concern should be not the fruit, but the root. It was in the depth of one's being that the individual had to concentrate. He had to nurse it with the water of his labour and suffering. The root was his chief concern.

31. Prayer is the very soul and essence of religion, and therefore, prayer must be the very core of the life of man, for no man can live without religion.
32. When a man is down, he prays to God to lift him up. The appalling disaster in Quetta paralyses one. It baffles all attempt at reconstruction. The whole truth about the disaster will perhaps never be known. The dead cannot be recalled to life. Human effort must be there always. Those who are left behind must have help. Such reconstruction as is possible sill no doubt undertaken. All this and much more along the same line can never be a substitute for prayer. But why pray at all? Does He stand in need of prayer to enable Him to do His duty? No, God needs no reminder. He is within everyone. Nothing happens without His permission. Our prayer is a heart search. It is a reminder to ourselves that we are helpless without His support. No effort is complete without prayer, without a definite recognition that the best human endeavour is of no effect if it has not God's blessing behind. Prayer is a call to humility. It is a call to self-purification, to inward search. It ask those who appreciate the necessity of inward purification to join in the prayer that we may read the purpose of God in such visitations, that they may humble us and prepare us to face our Maker whenever the call comes, and that we may be.
33. Prayer is not asking. It is a longing of the soul. It is daily admission of one's weakness. It is better in prayer to have a heart without words than words without a heart.
34. We are born to serve our fellowmen, and we cannot properly do so unless we are wide awake There is an eternal struggle raging in man's breast between the powers of darkness and of light, and he who has not the sheet-anchor of prayer to rely upon will be a victim to the powers of darkness. The man of prayer will be at peace with himself and with the whole world, the man who goes about the affairs of the world without a prayerful heart will be miserable and will make the world also miserable. Apart therefore from its bearing on man's condition after death, prayer has incalculable value for man in this world of the living. Prayer is the only means of bringing about orderliness and peace and repose in our daily acts. We inmates of the Ashram who came here in search of truth and for insistence on truth professed to believe in the efficacy of prayer, but had never up to now made it a matter of vital concern. We did not bestow on it the care that we did on other matters. I awoke from my slumbers one day and realizes that I had been woefully negligent of my duty in the matter. I have suggested measures of stern discipline and far from being any the worse, I hope we are the better for it. For it is so obvious. Take care of the vital thing and other things will take care of themselves. Rectify one angle of the square and the other angles will be automatically right.
35. It is easy enough to say, 'I do not believe in God.' For God permits all things to be said of Him with impunity. He looks at our acts. And any breach of His law carries with it, not its vindictive, but its purifying, compelling punishment.
36. God is the hardest taskmaster I have known on earth, and He tries you through and through. And when you find that your faith is failing or your body is failing you, and you are sinking, He comes to your assistance somehow or other and proves to you that you must not lose your fai h and that He is always at your beck and call, but on His terms, not on your terms.

The Gospel of Faith : It is faith that steers us through stormy seas, faith that moves mountains and faith that jumps across the ocean. That faith is nothing but a living, wide-awake consciousness of God within. He who has achieved that faith wants nothing. Bodily diseased, he is spiritually healthy; physically poor, he rolls in spiritual riches.

Without faith this world would come to naught in a moment. True faith is appropriation of the reasoned experience of people whom we believe to have lived a life purified by prayer and penance. Belief, therefore, in prophets or incarnations who have lived in remote ages is not an idle superstition but a satisfaction of an inmost spiritual want.

Faith is not a delicate flower, which would wither under the slightest stormy weather. Faith is like the Himalaya mountains which cannot possibly change. No storm can possibly remove the Himalaya mountains from their foundations. ... And I want every one of you to cultivate that faith in God and religion.

Limitations of Reason: Experience has humbled me enough to let me realize the specific limitations of reason. Just as matter misplaced becomes dirt, reason misused becomes lunacy.

Rationalists are admirable beings, rationalism is a hideous monster when it claims for itself omnipotence. Attribution of omnipotence to reason is as bad a piece of idolatry as is worship of stock and stone believing it to be God.

I plead not for the suppression of reason, but for a due recognition of that in us which sanctifies reason itself. (ibid)

To me it is as plain as a pikestaff that, where there is an appeal to reason pure and undefiled, there should be no appeal to authority however great it may be.

There are subjects where Reason cannot take us far and we have to accept things on faith. Faith then does not contradict Reason but transcends it. Faith is a kind of sixth sense, which works in cases, which are without the purview of Reason.

Meaning of Religion: Let me explain what I mean by religion. It is not the Hindu religion which I certainly prize above all other religions, but the religion which transcends Hinduism, which changes one's very nature, which binds one indissolubly to the truth within and which ever purifies. It is the permanent element in human nature which counts no cost too great in order to find full expression and which leaves the soul utterly restless until it has found itself, known its Maker and appreciated the true correspondence between the Maker and itself.

By religion, I do not mean formal religion, or customary religion, but that religion which underlies all religions, which brings us face to face with our Maker.

My Religion: My religion has no geographical limits. If I have a living faith in it, it will transcend my love for India herself.

Mine is not a religion of the prison-house. It has room for the least among God's creation. But it is proof against insolence, pride of race, religion or colour.

There is undoubtedly a sense in which the statement is true when I say that I hold my religion dearer than my country and that, therefore, I am a Hindu first and nationalist after. I do not become on that score a less nationalist than the best of them. I simply thereby imply that the interests of my country are identical with whose of my religion.

Similarly when I say that I prize my own salvation above everything else, above the salvation of India, it does not mean that my personal salvation requires a sacrifice of India's political or any other salvation. But it implies necessarily that the two go together.

This is the maxim of life which I have accepted, namely, that no work done by any man, no matter how great he is, will really prosper unless he has religious backing.

I have abundant faith in my cause and humanity. Indian humanity is no worse than any other; possibly it is better. Indeed, the cause presumes faith in human nature. Dark though the path appears, God will light it and guide my steps, if I have faith in His guidance and humility enough to acknowledge my helplessness without that infallible guidance.

This may be considered to be quixotic, but it is my firm faith that he who undertakes to do something in the name of God, and in full faith in Him, even at the end of his days, does not work in vain; and I am sure that the work I have undertaken is not mine, but is God's.

That is dharma, which is enjoined by the holy books, followed by the sages, interpreted by the learned, and which appealed to the heart. The first three conditions must be fulfilled before the fourth comes into operations must be fulfilled before the fourth comes into operations. Thus one has no right to follow the precepts of an ignorant man or a rascal even though they commend themselves to one. Rigorous observance of harmlessness, non-enmity and renunciation are the first requisites for a person to entitle him to lay down the law, i.e., dharma.

The Meaning of God: Go may be called by any other name so long as it connotes the living Law of Life in other words, the Law and the Law-giver rolled into one.

God Himself is both the Law and the Law-giver. The question of anyone creating Him, therefore, does not arise, least of all by an insignificant creature such as man. Man can build a dam, but it is beyond him to make the wood. He can, however, picture God in his mind in many ways. But how can man who is unable to create even a river or wood create God? That God has created man is, therefore, the pure truth. The contrary is an illusion. However, anyone may, if he likes, say that God is neither the doer nor the cause. Either is predicable of him. (ibid)

No Personal God: I do not regard God as a person. Truth for me is God, and God's Law and God are not different things or facts, in the sense that an earthly king and his law are different. Because God is an Idea, Law Himself. Therefore, it is impossible to conceive God as breaking the Law. He, therefore, does not rule our actions and withdraw Himself. When we say He rules our actions, we are simply using human language and we try to limit Him. Otherwise He and His Law abide everywhere and govern everything.

Therefore, I do not think that He answers in every detail every request of ours, but there is no doubt that He rules our action. …The free will we enjoy is less than that of a passenger on a crowded deck.

…Although I know that my freedom is less than that of a passenger, I appreciate that freedom, as I have imbibed through and through the central teaching of the Gita that man is the maker of his own destiny in the sense that he has freedom of choice as to the manner in which he uses that freedom. But he is no controller of results. The moment he thinks he is, he comes to grief.

Let this however be quite clear. The Almighty is not a person like us. He or It is the greatest living Force or Law in the world. Accordingly, He does not act by caprice, nor does that Law admit of any amendment or improvement. His will is fixed and changeless, everything else changes every second.

His Personality: I have not seen God face to face. If I had, I would have no need to be speaking to you. My thought would be potent enough to render speech and action on my part unnecessary. But I have an undying faith in the existence of God. Millions all over the world share this faith with me. The most learned cannot shake the faith of the illiterate millions.

God is wholly good. There is no evil in Him. God made man in His own image. Unfortunately for us, man has fashioned Him in his own. This arrogation has landed mankind in a sea of troubles. God is the Supreme Alchemist. In His presence all iron and dross turn into pure gold. Similarly does all evil turn into good.

Again, God lives, but not as we. His creatures live but to die. But God is life. Therefore, goodness and all it connotes is not an attribute. Goodness is God. Goodness conceived as apart from Him is a lifeless thing and exist only whilst it is a paying policy. So are all morals. If they are to live in us, they must be considered and cultivated in their relation to God. We try to become good because we want to reach and realize God. All the dry ethics of the lifeless. Coming from God, they come with life in them. They become part of us and ennoble us.

Conversely, God conceived without goodness is without life. We give Him life in our vain imagining.

There is a bit gulf between 'seeing God face to face' and 'seeing Him in the embodiment of Truth from a far distance'. In my opinion, the two statements are not only not incompatible but each explains the other. We see the Himalayas from a very great distance and when we are on the top, we have seen the Himalayas face to face. Millions can see them from hundreds of miles if they are within the range of that seeing distance, but few having arrived at the top, after years of travels, see them face to face. I have never had [the slightest doubt] about the reality that God Is and that His most graphic name is Truth.

Power of God: Everything that has a beginning must end. The sun, the moon and the earth must all perish one day, even though it might be after an incalculable number of years. God alone is immortal, imperishable. How can anyone find words to describe Him?

God cannot be realized through the intellect. Intellect can lead one to a certain extent and no further. It is a matter of faith and experience derived from faith. One might rely on the experience of one's betters or else be satisfied with nothing less than personal experience. Full faith does not feel the want of experience.

God alone knows Absolute Truth. Therefore, I have often said, Truth is God. It follows that man, a finite being, cannot know Absolute Truth.

I call that great Power not by the name of Allah, not by the name of Khuda or God, but by the name of Truth. For me Truth is God and Truth overrides all our plans. The whole truth is only embodied within the heart of that Great Power—Truth. I was taught from my early days to regard Truth as un-approachable—something that you cannot reach. A great Englishman taught me to believe that God is unknowable. He is knowable, but knowable only to the extent that our limited intellect allows.

God is all-powerful. He can change the hearts of man and bring real peace among them.

His Rule: Today, in the West, people talk of Christ, but it is really the Anti-Christ that rules their lives. Similarly, there are people who talk of Islam, but really follow the way of Satan. It is a deplorable state of affairs. If people follow the way of God, there will not be all this corruption and profiteering that we see in the world. The rich are becoming richer and the poor poorer. Hunger, nakedness and death stare one in the face. These are not the marks of the Kingdom of God, but that of Satan, Ravana or Anti-Christ. We cannot expect to bring the reign of God on earth by merely repeating His name with the lips. Our conduct must conform to His ways instead of Satan's.

Only when God reigns in men's hearts will they be able to shed their anger.

All universal rules of conduct known as God's commandments are simple and easy to understand and carry out if the will is there. They only appear to be difficult because of the inertia, which governs mankind. Man is a progressive being. There is nothing at a standstill in nature. Only God is motionless for, He was, is and will be the same yesterday, today and tomorrow, and yet is ever moving. We need not, however, worry ourselves over the attributes of God. We have to realize that we are ever progressing. Hence, I hold that if mankind is to live, it has to come growlingly under the sway of truth and non-violence. It is in view of these two fundamental rules of conduct that I and you have to work and live.

A mind not set on God is given to wandering and lacks the quality of a temple of worship. (ibid)

Genesis of Evil: Why is there evil in the world is a difficult question to answer. I can only give what I may call a villager's answer. If there is good, there must also be evil, just as where there is light there is also darkness, but it is true only so far as we human mortals are concerned. Before God there is nothing good, nothing evil. We poor villagers may talk of His dispensation in human terms, but our language is not God's.

The Vedanta says the world is maya. Even that explanation is a babbling of imperfect humanity. I, therefore, say that I am not going to bother my head about it. Even if I was allowed to peep into the innermost recesses of God's chamber I should not care to do it. For I should not know what to do there. It is enough for our spiritual growth to know that God is always with the doer of good. That again is a villager's explanation.

I cannot account for the existence of evil by any rational method. To want to do so is to be coequal with God. I am therefore humble enough to recognize evil as such. And I call God long-suffering and patient precisely because He permits evil in the world. I know that He has no evil. He is the author of it and yet untouched by it.

I know too that I shall never know God if I do not wrestle with and against evil even at the cost of life itself. I am fortified in the belief by my own humble and limited experience. The purer I try to become, the nearer I feel to be to God. How much more should I be, when my faith is not a mere apology as it is today but has become as immovable as the Himalayas and as white and bright as the snows on their peaks?

In a strictly scientific sense God is at the bottom of both good and evil. He directs the assassin's dagger no less than the surgeon's knife. But for all that good and evil are, for human purpose, from each other distinct and incompatible, being symbolical of light and darkness, God and Satan.

To say that God permits evil in this world may not be pleasing to the ear. But if His is held responsible for the good, it follows that He has to be responsible for the evil too. Did not God permit

Ravana to exhibit unparalleled strength? Perhaps, the root cause of the perplexity arises from a lack of the real understanding of what God is. God is not a person. He transcends description. He is the Law-maker, the Law and the Executor. No human being can well arrogate these powers to himself. If he did, he would be looked upon as an unadulterated dictator. They become only Him whom we worship as God. This is the reality, a clear understanding of which will answer the question ['Does God permit evil?']

There is a saying to the effect that the outer is only the reflection of the inner. If you are good, the whole world will be good to you. On the contrary, if you feel tempted to regard anybody as evil, the odds are that the evil is within you.

We must neither think evil about others nor suspect others of thinking evil about us. Proneness to lend ear to evil reports is a sign of lack of faith.

Miracles: I do [believe in miracles] and I do not. God does not work through miracles. But the divine mind is revealed in a flash and it appears like a miracle to man. We do not know God, we know Him only through the working of His law. He and His law are one. There is nothing outside His law. Even earthquakes and tempests do not occur without His will—not a blade of grass grows but He will it. Satan is here only on His sufferance, not independently of him.

Man cannot be transformed from bad to good overnight. God does not exercise magic. He too is within His own law. His law, however, is different from the law of the State. There may be mistakes in the latter, but God cannot err. If he were to go beyond the limits of His law, the world will be lost.

History provides us with a whole series of miracles of masses of people being converted to a particular view-point in the twinkling of an eye. Take the Boer War. It has given to the English language the word 'Maffeking'. People went mad on the Maffeking Day. Yet, inside of two years, the whole British nation underwent a transformation. Henry Campbell Bannerman became the Premier and practically all the gains of war were given up. The recent Labour victory at the polls is another instance in point. To me it is a sufficient miracle that, in spite of his oratory and brilliance, Churchill should cease to be the idol of the British people who till yesterday hung on his lips and listened to him in awe. All these instances are enough to sustain the faith of a believer like me that, when all other powers are gone one will remain, call it God, Nature or whatever you like.

Incarnation: All embodied life is in reality an incarnation of God, but it is not usual to consider every living being an incarnation. Future generations pay this homage to one who, in his own generation, has been extraordinarily religious in his conduct. I can see nothing wrong in this procedure; it takes nothing from God's greatness, and there is no violence done to Truth. ...

This belief in incarnation is a testimony of man's lofty spiritual ambition. Man is not at peace with himself till he has become like unto God. The endeavour to reach this state is the supreme, the only ambition worth having. And this is self-realization. And this self-realization is the subject of the Gita, as it is of all scriptures.

Belief, therefore, in prophets or incarnations who have lived in remote ages is not an idle superstition, but a satisfaction of an inmost spiritual want.

Nature's Visitations: I share the belief with the whole world—civilized and uncivilized—that calamities such as the Bihar one [earth-quake] come to mankind as chastisement for their sins. When that conviction comes from the heart, people pray, repent and purify themselves....

I have but a limited knowledge of His purpose. Such calamities are not a mere caprice of the deity or Nature. They obey fixed laws as surely as the planets move in obedience to laws governing their movements. Only me do not know the laws governing these events and, therefore, call them calamities or disturbances.

This earthly existence of ours is more brittle than the glass bangles that ladies wear. You can keep glass bangles for thousands of years if you treasure them in a chest and let them remain untouched. But this earthly existence is so fickle that it may be wiped out in the twinkling of an eye. Therefore, while we have yet breathing time, let us get rid of the distinctions of high and low, purify our hearts and be ready to face our Maker when an earthquake or some natural calamity or death in the ordinary course overtakes us.

There is a divine purpose behind every physical calamity. That perfected science will one day be able to tell us beforehand when earthquakes will occur, as it tells us today of eclipses, is quite possible. It will be another triumph of the human mind. But such triumph even indefinitely multiplied can bring about no purification of self without which nothing is of any value.

I ask those who appreciate the necessity of inward purification to join the prayer that we may read the purpose of God behind such visitations, that they may humble us and prepare us to face our Maker whenever the call comes, and that we may be ever ready to share the sufferings of our fellows whosoever they may be.

God's Names: God has a thousand names, or rather, He is Nameless. We may worship or pray to Him by whichever name that pleases us. Some call Him Rama, some Krishna, others call Him Rahim, and yet others call Him God. All worship the same spirit, but as all foods do not agree with all, all names do not appeal to all. Each chooses the name according to his associations, and He, being the In-Dweller, All-Powerful and Omniscient knows our innermost feelings and responds to us according to our deserts.

Worship or prayer, therefore, is not to be performed with the lips, but with the heart. And that is why it can be performed equally by the dumb and the stammered, by the ignorant and the stupid. And the prayers of those whose tongues are endeared but whose hearts are full of poison are never heard. He, therefore, who would pray to God, must cleanse his heart.

Rama was not only on the lips of Hanuman, He was enthroned in his heart. He gave Hanuman exhaustless strength. In His strength he lifted the mountain and crossed the ocean.

I talk of God exactly as I believe Him to be... I believe God to be creative as well as non-creative. This too is the result of my acceptance of the doctrine of the manyness of reality. From the platform of the Jains I prove the non-creative aspect of God, and from that of Ramanuja the creative aspect. As a matter of fact, we are all thinking of the Unthinkable, describing the Indescribable, seeking to know the unknown, and that why our speech falters, is inadequate and even often contradictory. That is why the Vedas describe Brahman as 'not this', 'not this'.

In my opinion, Rama, Rahaman, Ahuramazda, God or Krishna are all attempts on the part of man to name that invisible force which is the greatest of all forces. It is inherent in man, imperfect though he be, ceaselessly to strive after perfection. In the attempt he falls into reverie. And, just as a child tries to stand, falls down again and sagain and ultimately learns how to walk, even so man, with all his intelligence, is a mere infant as compared to the infinite and ageless God. This may appear to be an exaggeration but is not. Man can only describe God in his own poor language.

I claim to be a man of faith and prayer, and even if I were cut to pieces, I trust God would give me the strength not to deny Him and to assert that He is.

No act of mine is done without prayer. Man is a fallible being. He can never be sure of his steps. What he may regard as answer to prayer may be an echo of his pride. For infallible guidance man has to have a perfectly innocent heart incapable of evil. I can lay no such claim. Mine is a struggling, striving, erring, imperfect soul.

Even if I am killed, I will not give up repeating the names of Rama and Rahim, which mean to me the same God. With these names on my lips, I will die cheerfully.

God's Response: Never own defeat in a sacred cause and make up your minds henceforth that you will be pure and that you will find a response from God. But God never answers the prayers of the arrogant, nor the prayers of those who bargain with Him....

If you would ask Him to help you, you would go to Him in all your nakedness, approach Him without fear or doubts as to how He can help a fallen being like you. He who has helped millions who have approached Him, is He going to desert you? He makes no exceptions whatsoever and you will find that every one of your prayers will be answered. I am telling this out of my personal experience. I have gone through the purgatory. Seek first the Kingdom of Heaven and everything will be added unto you. Names on my lips, I will die cheerfully.

I have never found Him lacking in response. I have found Him nearest at hand when the horizon seemed darkest—in my ordeals in jails when it was not at all smooth sailing for me. I cannot recall a moment in my life when I had a sense of desertion by God.

Character of Prayer: Supplication, worship, prayer are no superstition; they are acts more real than the acts of eating, drinking, sitting or walking. It is no exaggeration to say that they alone are real, all else is unreal.

Such worship or prayer is no flight of eloquence; it is no lip-homage. It springs from the heart. If, therefore, we achieve that purity of the heart when it is 'emptied of all but love', if we keep all the chords in proper tune, they 'trembling pass in music out of sight'.

Prayer needs no speech. It is in itself independent of any sensuous effort. I have not the slightest doubt that prayer is an unfailing means of cleansing the heart of passions. But it must be combined with the utmost humility.

It is better in prayer to have a heart without words than words without a heart.

We go to the temple to worship not the stone or the metal image, but God who resides in it. The image becomes what man makes of it. It has no power independently of the sanctity with which it is invested by the worshipper. Therefore everyone, including children, should observe perfect silence at the time of prayer.

Prayer is an impossibility without a living faith in the presence of God within.

Prayer is the first and the last lesson in learning the noble and brave art or sacrificing self in the various walks of life, culminating in the defense of one's nation's liberty and honour. Undoubtedly, prayer requires a living faith in God.

Man often repeats the name of God parrot-wise and expects fruit from so doing. The true seeker must have that living faith which will not only dispel the untruth of parrot-wise repetition from within him, but also from the hearts of others.

Need for Prayer: As food is necessary for the body, prayer is necessary for the soul. A man may be able to do without food for a number of days—as Mac Swiney did for over 70 days—but, believing in God, man cannot, should not live a moment without prayer.

There are many who, whether from mental laziness or from having fallen into a bad habit, believe that God is and will help us unasked. Why, then, is it necessary to recite His name? It is true that if God is, He is irrespective of our belief. But realization of God is infinitely more than mere belief. That can come only by constant practice. This is true of all science. How much more true of the science of all sciences?

Prayer is the key of the morning and the bolt of the evening.

I am giving you a bit of my experience and that of my companions when I say that he who had experienced the magic of prayer may do without food for days together, but not a single moment without prayer. For without prayer there is no inward peace.

I agree that, if a man could practice the presence of God all the twenty-four hours, there would be no need for a separate time for prayer. But ne's own caste or community. It is all inclusive. It comprehends the whole of humanity. Its realization would thus mean the establishment of the Kingdom of Heaven on earth.

True meditation consists in closing the eyes and ears of the mind to all else except the object of one's devotion. Hence the closing of eyes during prayers is an aid to such concentration. Man's conception of God is naturally limited. Each one has, therefore, to think of Him as best appeals to him, provided that the conception is pure and uplifting.

He can truly pray who has the conviction that God is within him. He who has not need not pray. God will not be offended, but I can say from experience that he who does not pray is certainly a loser.

What matters, then, whether one man worships God as Person and another as Force? Both do right according to their lights. None knows and, perhaps, never will know what is the absolutely proper way to pray. The ideal must always remain the ideal. One need only remember that God is the Force among all the forces. All other forces are material. But God is the vital force or spirit which is all-pervading, all-embracing and, therefore, beyond human ken.

Efficacy of Silence: It has often occurred to me that a seeker after truth has to be silent. I know the wonderful efficacy of silence. I visited a Trapezist monastery in South Africa. A beautiful place it was. Most of the inmates of that place were under a vow of silence. I inquired of the Father the motive of it and he said the motive is apparent: 'We are frail human beings. We do not know very often what we say. If we want to listen to the still small voice that is always speaking within us, it will not be heard if we continually speak.' I understood that precious lesson. I know the secrete of silence.

Experience has taught me that silence is a part of the spiritual discipline of a votary of truth. Proneness to exaggerate, to suppress or modify the truth. Wittingly or unwittingly, is a natural weakness of man, and silence is necessary in order to surmount it. A man of few words will rarely be thoughtless in his speech; he will measure every word.

Silence of the sewn-up lips is no silence. One may achieve the same result by chopping off one's tongue, but that too would not be silence. He is silent who, having the capacity to speak, utters no idle word.

It [silence] has now become both a physical and spiritual necessity for me. Originally it was taken to relieve the sense of pressure. Then I wanted time for writing. After, however, I had practiced it for some time, I saw the spiritual value of it. It suddenly flashed across my mind that that was the time when I could best hold communion with God. And now I feel as though I was naturally built for silence.

Prayer is for remembering God, and for purifying the heart, and can be offered even when observing silence.

As I believe that silent prayer is often a mightier [force] than any overt act, in my helplessness I continuously pray in the faith that the prayer of a pure heart never goes unanswered.

Power of Prayer: I can give my own testimony and say that a heartfelt prayer is undoubtedly the most potent instrument that man possesses for overcoming cowardice and all other bad old habits.

Not until we have reduced ourselves to nothingness can we conquer the evil in us. God demands nothing less than complete self-surrender as the price for the only real freedom that is worth having. And when a man thus loses himself, he immediately finds himself in the service of all that lives. It becomes his delight and his recreation. He is a new man, never weary of spending himself in the service of God's creation.

There is an eternal struggle raging in man's breast between the powers of darkness and of light, and he who has not the sheet-anchor of prayer to rely upon will be a victim to the powers of darkness. The man of prayer will be at peace with himself and with the whole world; the man who goes about the affairs of the world without a prayerful heart will be miserable and will make the world also miserable....

Prayer is the only means of bringing about orderliness and peace and repose in our daily acts....Take care of the vital thing and other things will take care of themselves. Rectify one angle of a square, and the other angles will be automatically right.

Prayer is not an old woman's idle amusement. Properly understood and applied, it is the most potent instrument of action.

When the mind is completely filled with His spirit, one cannot harbour ill-will or hatred towards anyone and, reciprocally, the enemy will shed his enmity and become a friend. It is not my claim that I have succeeded in converting enemies into friends, but in numerous cases it has been my experience that, when the mind is filled with His peace, all hatred ceases. An unbroken succession of world teachers since the beginning of time have borne testimony to the same. I claim to merit for it. I know it is entirely due to God's grace.

One with a wicked heart can never be conscious of the all-purifying presence of God.

God answers prayer in His own way, not ours. His ways are different from the ways of mortals. Hence they are inscrutable. Prayer presupposes faith. No prayer goes in vain. Prayer is like any other action. It bears fruit whether we see it or not, and the fruit of heart prayer is far more potent than action so-called. (ibid, p215)

Gandhi's Views On Nonviolence: The world is weary of hate. We see the fatigue overcoming the Western nations. We see that this song of hate has not benefited humanity. Let it be the privilege of India to turn a new leaf and set a lesson to the world.

In the past, non-co-operation has been deliberately expressed in violence to the evil-doer. I am endeavoring to show to my countrymen that violent non-co-operation only multiplies evil and that as evil can only be sustained by violence, withdrawal of support of evil requires complete abstention from violence. Nonviolence implies voluntary submission to the penalty for non-co-operation with evil.

I am not a visionary. I claim to be practical idealist. The religion of nonviolence is not meant merely for the rishis and saints. It is meant for the common people as well. Nonviolence is the law of our species as violence is the law of the brute. The spirit lies dormant in the brute and he knows no law but that of physical might. The dignity of man requires obedience to a higher law-to the strength of the spirit.

I have therefore ventured to place before India the ancient law of self-sacrifice. For satyagraha and its off-shoots, non-co-operation and civil resistance, are nothing but new names for the law of suffering. The rishis, who discovered the law of non-violence in the midst of violence, were greater geniuses than Newton. They were themselves greater warriors than Wellington. Having themselves known the use of arms, they realized their uselessness and taught a weary world that its salvation lay not through violence but through nonviolence.

Nonviolence as a World-force: You might of course say that there can be no nonviolent rebellion and there has been none known to history. Well, it is my ambition to provide an instance, and it is my dream that my country may win its freedom through non-violence. And, I would like to repeat to the world times without number, that I will not purchase my country's freedom at the cost of nonviolence. My marriage to nonviolence is such an absolute thing that I would rather commit suicide than be deflected from my position. I have not mentioned truth in this connection, simply because truth cannot be expressed excepting by nonviolence.

Science of war leads one to dictatorship pure and simple. Science of nonviolence alone can lead one to pure democracy. England, France and America have to make their choice. That is the challenge of the two dictators.

Russia is out of the picture just now. Russia has a dictator who dreams of peace and thinks he will wade to it through a sea of blood. No one can say what Russian dictatorship will mean to the world.

True democracy or the Swaraj of the masses can never come through untruthful and violent means, for the simple reason that the natural corollary to their use would be to remove all opposition through the suppression or extermination of the antagonists. That does not make for individual freedom. Individual freedom can have the fullest play only under a regime of unadulterated ahimsa.

Granted that India produced sufficient arms and ammunition and men who knew the art of war, what part or lot will those who cannot bear arms have in the attainment of Swaraj? I want Swaraj in the winning of which even women and children would contribute an equal share with physically the strongest. That can be under ahimsa only. I would, therefore, stand for ahimsa as the only means for obtaining India's freedom even if I were alone.

And so I plead for non-violence and yet more nonviolence. I do so not without knowledge but with sixty years' experience behind me.

The accumulated experience of the past thirty years, fills me with the greatest hope that in the adoption of nonviolence lies the future of India and the world. It is the most harmless and yet equally effective way of dealing with the political and economic wrongs of the downtrodden portion of humanity. I have known from early youth that nonviolence is not a cloistered virtue to be practised by the individual for his peace and final salvation, but it is a rule of conduct for society if it is to live consistently with human dignity and make progress towards the attainment of peace for which it has been yearning for ages past.

War Vs. Nonviolence: A believer in nonviolence is pledged not to resort to violence or physical force either directly or indirectly in defence of anything, but he is not precluded from helping men or institutions that are themselves not based on non-violence. If the reverse were the case, I would, for instance, be precluded from helping India to attain Swaraj because the future Parliament of India under Swaraj, I know for certain, will be having some military and police forces, or to take a domestic illustration, I may not help a son to secure justice, because forsooth he is not a believer in nonviolence.

Mr. Zacharias' proposition will reduce all commerce by a believer in non-violence to an impossibility. And there are not wanting men, who do believe that complete non-violence means complete cessation of all activity.

Not such, however, is my doctrine of nonviolence. My business is to refrain from doing any violence myself, and to induce by persuasion and service as many of god's creatures as I can to join me in the belief and practice. But I would be untrue to my faith, if I refused to assist in a just cause any men or measures that did not entirely coincide with the principle of non-violence. I would be promoting violence, if finding the Mussalmans to be in the right, I did not assist them by means strictly nonviolent against those who had treacherously plotted the destruction of the dignity of Islam. Even when both parties believe in violence there is often such a thing as justice on one side or the other. A robbed man has justice on his side, even though he may be accounted as a triumph of non-violence, if the injured party could be persuaded to regain his property by methods of satyagraha, i.e. love or soul-force rather than a free fight.

My resistance to war does not carry me to the point of thwarting those who wish to take part in it. I reason with them. I put before them the better way and leave them to make the choice.

I accept broad facts of history and draw my own lessons for my conduct. I do not want to repeat it in so far as the broad facts contradict the highest laws of life. But positively refuse to judge man from the scanty material furnished to us by history. De mortuis nil nisi bonum. Kamal Pasha and De Valera too I cannot judge. But for me as a believer I nonviolence out and out they cannot be my guides in life in so far as their faith in war is concerned. I believe in Krishna perhaps more than the writer. But my Krishna is the Lord of the Universe, the creator, preserver and destroyer of us all. He may destroy because He creates. But I must not be drawn into a philosophical or religious argument with my friends. I have not the qualification for teaching my philosophy of life. I have barely qualifications for practising the philosophy I believe. I am but a poor struggling soul yearning to be wholly good-wholly truthful and wholly nonviolent in thought, word and deed, but ever failing to reach the ideal which I know to be true. I admit, and assure my revolutionary friends, that it is a painful climb, but the pain of it is a positive pleasure for me. Each step upward makes me feel stronger and fit for the next. But all that pain and pleasure are for me. The revolutionaries are at liberty to reject the whole of my philosophy. To them I merely present my own experiences as a co-worker I the same cause even as I have successfully presented them to the Ali Brothers and many other friends. They can and do applaud whole-heartedly the action of Mustafa Kamal Pasha and possibly De Valera and Lenin. But they realize with me that India is not like Turkey or Ireland or Russia and that revolutionary activity is suicidal at this stage of the country's life at any rate if not for all time, in a country so vast, so hopelessly divided and with the masses so deeply sunk in pauperism and so fearfully terror-struck.

I would say to my critics to enter with me into the sufferings, not only of the people of India but of those, whether engaged in the war or not, of the whole world. I cannot look at this butchery going on in the world with indifference. I have an unchangeable faith that it is beneath the dignity of men to resort to mutual slaughter. I have no doubt that there is a way out.

The accumulated experience of the past thirty years, the first eight of which were in South Africa, fills me with the greatest hope that in the adoption of nonviolence lies the future of India and the world. It is the most harmless and yet equally effective way of dealing with the political and economic wrongs of the downtrodden portion of humanity. I have known from early youth that nonviolence is not a cloistered virtue to be practised by the individual for peace and final salvation, but it is a rule of conduct for society if it is to live consistently with human dignity and make progress towards the attainment of peace for which it has been yearning for ages past.

Moral Equivalent of War: Up to the year 1906, I simply relied on appeal to reason. I was a very industrious reformer. I was a good draftsman, as I always had a close grip of facts which in its turn was the necessary result of my meticulous regard for truth. But I found that reason failed to produce an impression when the critical moment arrived in South Africa. My people were excited; even a worm will and does sometimes turn-and there was talk of wreaking vengeance. I had then to choose between allying myself to violence or finding out some other method of meeting the crisis and stopping the rot and it came to me that we should refuse to obey legislation that was degrading and let them put us in jail if they liked. Thus came into being the moral equivalent of war. I was then a loyalist, because, I implicitly believed that the sum total of the activities of the British empire was good for India and for humanity. Arriving in England soon after the outbreak of the war I plunged into it and later when I was forced to go to India as a result of the pleurisy that I had developed, I led a recruiting campaign at the risk of my life, and to the horror of some of my friends. The disillusionment came in 1919 after the passage of the Black Rowlatt Act and the refusal of the Government to give the simple elementary redress of proved wrongs that we had asked for. And so, in 1920, I became a rebel. Since then the conviction to the people are not secured by reason alone but have to be purchased with their suffering. Suffering is the law of human beings; war is the law of the jungle. But suffering is infinitely more powerful than the law of the jungle for converting the opponent and opening his ears, which are otherwise shut, to the voice of reason. Nobody has probably drawn up more petitions or espoused more forlorn causes than I and I have come to this fundamental conclusion that if you want something really important to be done you must not merely satisfy the reason, you must move the heart also. The appeal of reason is more to the head but the penetration of the heart comes from suffering. It opens up the inner understanding in man. Suffering is the badge of the human race, not the sword.

The Essence of Nonviolence: Nonviolence affords the fullest protection to one's self-respect and sense of honour, but not always to possession of land or movable property, though its habitual practice does prove a better bulwark than the possession of armed men to defend them. Nonviolence in the very nature of things is of no assistance I the defence of ill-gotten gains and immoral acts.

Individuals and nations who would practise nonviolence must be prepared to sacrifice (nations to the last man) their all except honour. It is therefore inconsistent with the possession of other people's countries, i.e. modern imperialism which is frankly based on force for its defence.

Nonviolence is a power which can be wielded equally by all-children, young men and women or grown up people, provided they have a living faith in the God of Love and have therefore equal love for all mankind. When non-violence is accepted as the law of life it must pervade the whole being and not be applied to isolated acts.

It is a profound error to suppose that whilst the law is good enough for individuals it is not for masses of mankind.

Perfect nonviolence is impossible so long as we exist physically, for we would want some space at least to occupy. Perfect non-violence whilst you are inhabiting the body is only a theory like Euclid's point or straight line, but we have to endeavour every moment of our lives.

Let us now examine the root of ahimsa. It is uttermost selflessness. Selflessness means complete freedom from a regard for one's body. If man desired to realize himself i.e. Truth, he could do so only by completely detached from the body i.e. by making all other beings feel safe from him. That is the way of ahimsa.

Ahimsa does not simply mean non-killing. Himsa means causing pain to or killing any life out of anger, or from a selfish purpose. Or with the intention of injuring it. Refraining from so doing is ahimsa.

Violence will be violence for all time, and all violence is sinful. But what is inevitable, is not only declared the inevitable violence involved in killing for sacrifice as permissible but even regarded it as meritorious.

It is no easy thing to walk on the sharp sword-edge of ahimsa in this world which is full of himsa. Wealth does not help; anger is the enemy of ahimsa; and pride is a monster that swallows it up. In this strait and narrow observance of this religion of ahimsa one has often to know so-called himsa as the truest form of ahimsa.

The sin of himsa consists not in merely taking life, but in taking life for the sake of one's perishable body. All destruction therefore involved in the process of eating, drinking etc. is selfish and therefore himsa. But man regards it to be unavoidable and puts up with it. But the destruction of bodies of tortured creatures being for their own peace cannot be regarded as himsa, or the unavoidable destruction caused for the purpose of protecting one's wards cannot be regarded as himsa.

It is impossible to sustain one's body without the destruction of other bodies to some extent.

All have to destroy some life,

for sustaining their own bodies,

for protecting those under their care, or

Something for the sake of those whose life is taken.

A progressive ahimsaist will, therefore, commit the himsa contained in (a) and (b) as little as possible, only when it is unavoidable, and after full and mature deliberation and having exhausted all remedies to avoid it.

Taking life may be a duty. We do destroy as much life as we think necessary for sustaining our body. Thus for food we take life, vegetable and other, and for health we destroy mosquitoes and the like by the use of disinfectants etc. and we do not think that we are guilty of irreligion in doing so...for the benefit of the species, we kill carnivorous beasts...Even man-slaughter may be necessary in certain cases. Suppose a man runs amuck and goes furiously about sword in hand, and killing anyone that comes in his way, and no one dares to capture him alive. Any one who dispatches this lunatic, will earn the gratitude of the community and be regarded as a benevolent man.

I see that there is an instinctive horror of killing living beings under any circumstances whatever. For instance, an alternative has been suggested in the shape of confining even rabid dogs in a certain place and allowing them to die a slow death. Now my idea of compassion makes this thing impossible for me. I cannot for a moment bear to see a dog, or for that matter any other living being, helplessly suffering the torture of a slow death. I do not kill a human being thus circumstanced because I have more hopeful remedies. I should kill a dog similarly situated, because in its case I am without a remedy. Should my child be attacked with rabies and there was no helpful remedy to relieve his agony, I should consider it my duty to take his life. Fatalism has its limits. We leave things to Fate after exhausting all the remedies. One of the remedies and the final one to relieve the agony of a tortured child is to take his life.

Absence of Hatred: I hold myself to be incapable of hating any being on earth. By a long course of prayerful discipline, I have ceased for over forty years to hate anybody. I know this is a big claim. Nevertheless, I make it in all humility. But I can and do hate evil wherever it exists. I hate the system of government that he British people have set up in India. I hate the ruthless exploitation of India even as I hate from the bottom of my heart the hideous system of untouchability for which millions of Hindus have made themselves responsible. But I do not hate the domineering Hindus. I seek to reform them in all the loving ways that are open to me. My non-co-operation has its roots not in hatred, but in love. My personal religion peremptorily forbids me to hate anybody.

We can only win over the opponent by love, never by hate. Hate is the subtlest form of violence. We cannot be really nonviolent and yet have hate in us.

Truth in Speech and Nonviolence: To say or write a distasteful word is surely not violent especially when the speaker or writer believes it to be true. The essence of violence is that there must be a violent intention behind a thought, word or act, i.e. an intention to do harm to the opponent so-called.

False notions of propriety or fear of wounding susceptibilities often deter people from saying what they mean and ultimately land them on the shores of hypocrisy. But if non-violence of thought is to be evolved in individuals or societies or nations, truth has to be told, however harsh or unpopular it may appear to be for the moment.

Satyam bruyat, Priyam bruyat na bruyat Satyam apriyam

In my opinion the Sanskrit text means that one should speak the truth in gentle language. One had better not speak it, if one cannot do so in a gentle way; meaning thereby that there is no truth in a man who cannot control his tongue.

Positive Aspects of Ahimsa: Love and Patience

In its positive form, ahimsa means the largest love, greatest charity. If I am a follower of ahimsa, I must love my enemy. I must apply the same rules to the wrong-doer who is my enemy or a stranger to me, as I would to my wrong-doing father or son. This active necessarily includes truth and fearlessness. As man cannot deceive the love one, he does not fear or frighten him or her. Gift of life is the greatest of all gifts; a man who gives it in realty,, disarms all hostility. He has paved the way for an honourable understanding. And none who is himself subject to fear can bestow that gift, He must therefore be himself fearless. A man cannot practise ahimsa and be a coward at the same time. The practice of ahimsa calls forth the greatest courage.

Having flung aside the sword, there is nothing except the cup of love which I can offer to those who oppose me. It is by offering that cup that I expect to draw them close to me. I cannot think of permanent enmity between man and man, and believing as I do in the theory of rebirth, I live in the hope that if not in this birth, in some other birth, I shall be able to hug all humanity in friendly embrace.

Love is the strongest force the world possesses and yet it is the humblest imaginable. .

The hardest heart and the grossest ignorance must disappear before the rising sun of suffering without anger and without malice.

Love has special quality of attracting abundance of love in return.

Nonviolent Resistance: Nonviolence is 'not a resignation from all real fighting against wickedness'. On the contrary, the non-violence of my conception is a more active and real fight against wickedness than retaliation whose very nature is to increase wickedness. I contemplate, a mental and therefore a moral opposition to immoralities. I seek entirely to blunt the edge of the tyrant's sword, not by putting up against it a sharper-edged weapon, but by disappointing his expectation that I would be offering physical resistance. The resistance of the soul that I should offer would elude him. It would at first dazzle him and at last compel recognition from him, which recognition would not humiliate him but would uplift him. It may be urged that this is an ideal state. And so it is.

Nonviolence in its dynamic condition means conscious suffering. It does not mean meek submission to the will of the evil-doer, but it means the putting of one' whole soul against the will of the tyrant. Working under this law of our beings, it is possible for a single individual to defy the whole might of an unjust empire to save his honour, his religion, his soul and lay the foundation for that empire's fall or its regeneration.

Yours should not merely be a passive spirituality that spends itself in idle meditation, but it should be an active thing which will carry war into the enemy's camp.

Never has anything been done on this earth without direct action. I reject the word 'passive resistance', because of its insufficiency and its being interpreted as a weapon of the weak.

What was the larger 'symbiosis' that Buddha and Christ preached? Gentleness and love. Buddha fearlessly carried the war into the enemy's camp and brought down on its knees an arrogant priesthood. Christ drove out the money-changers from the temple of Jerusalem and drew down curses from heaven upon the hypocrites and the Pharisees. Both were for intensely direct action. But even as Buddha and Christ chastized, they showed unmistakable love and gentleness behind every act of theirs.

Our aim is not merely to arouse the best in the Englishman but to do so whilst we are prosecuting our cause. If we cease to pursue our course, we do not evoke the best in him. The best must not be confounded with good temper. When we are dealing with any evil, we may have to ruffle the evil-doer. We have to run the risk, if we are to bring the best out of him. I have likened nonviolence to aseptic and violence to antiseptic treatment. Both are intended to ward off the evil, and therefore cause a kind of disturbance which is often inevitable. The first never harms the evil-doer.

True and False Non-violence: Non-violence presupposes ability to strike. It is a conscious, deliberate restraint put upon one's desire for vengeance. But vengeance is any day superior to passive, effeminate and helpless submission. Forgiveness is higher still. Vengeance too is weakness. The desire for vengeance comes out of fear of harm, imaginary or real. A man who fears no one on earth would consider it troublesome even to summon up anger against one who is vainly trying to injure him.

Ahimsa is the extreme limit of forgiveness. But forgiveness is the quality of the brave. Ahimsa is impossible without fearlessness.

My creed of non-violence is an extremely active force. It has no room for cowardice or even weakness. There is hope for a violent man to be some day nonviolent but there is none for a coward. I have therefore said more than once in these pages that if we do not know how to defend ourselves, our women and our places of worship by the force of suffering, i.e. nonviolence, we must, if we are men, be at least able to defend all these by fighting.

There are two ways of defence. The best and the most effective is not to defend at all, but to remain at one's post risking every danger. The next best but equally honourable method is to strike bravely in self-defence and put one's life in the most dangerous positions.

The strength to kill is not essential for self-defence; one ought to have the strength to die. When a man is fully ready to die, he will not even desire to offer violence. Indeed I may put it down as a self-evident proposition that the desire to kill is in inverse proportion to the desire to die. And history is replete with instances of men who by dying with courage and compassion on their lips converted the hearts of their violent opponents.

Non-violence and cowardice go ill together. I can imagine a fully armed man to be at heart a coward. Possession of arms implies an element of fear, if not cowardice. But true non-violence is an impossibility without the possession of unadulterated fearlessness.

Violence, rather than Cowardice: I do believe that, where there is only a choice between cowardice and violence, I would advise violence. I would rather have India resort to arms in order to defend her honour than that she should, in a cowardly manner, become or remain a helpless witness to her own dishonour.

But I believe that non-violence is infinitely superior to violence, forgiveness is more manly than punishment. Forgiveness adorns the soldier. But abstinence is forgiveness only when there is the power to punish; it is meaningless when it pretends to proceed from a helpless creature. But I do not believe India to be helpless. I do not believe myself to be a helpless creature. Strength does not come from physical capacity. It comes from an indomitable will.

The people of a village near Bettiah told me that they had run away whilst the police were looting their houses and molesting their womenfolk. When they said that they had run away because I had told them to be nonviolent, I hung my head in shame. I assured them that such was not the meaning of my nonviolence. I expected them to intercept the mightiest power that might be in the act of harming those who were under their protection, and draw without retaliation all harm upon their own heads even to the point of death, but never to run away from the storm centre. It was manly enough to defend one's property, honour religion at the point of the sword. It was manlier and nobler to defend them without seeking to injure the wrongdoer. But it was unmanly, unnatural and dishonourable to forsake the post of duty and, in order to save one's skin, to leave property, honour or religion to the mercy of the wrongdoer. I could see my way of delivering the message of ahimsa to those who knew how to die, not to those who were afraid of death.

The weakest of us physically must be taught the art of facing dangers and giving a good account of ourselves. I want both the Hindus and the Mussalmans to cultivate the cool courage, to die without killing. But if one has not that courage, I want him to cultivate the art of killing and being killed, rather than in a cowardly manner flee from danger. For the latter in spite of his flight does commit mental himsa. He fleas because he has not the courage to be killed in the act of killing.

Self-defence is the only honourable course where there is unreadiness for self-immolation.

I would risk violence a thousand times than the emasculation of a whole race.

The Hindus think that they are physically weaker than the Mussalmans. The latter consider themselves weak in educational and earthly equipment. They are now doing what all weak bodies have done hitherto. This fighting, therefore, however unfortunate it may be, is a sign of growth. It is like the Wars of the Roses. Out of it will rise a mighty nation.

Limitations of Violence: Hitherto I have given historical instances of bloodless non-co-operation. I will not Insult the intelligence of the reader by citing historical instances on non-co-operation combined with violence, but I am free to confess that there are on record as many successes as failúres in violent non-co-operation.

Revolutionary crime is intended to exert pressure. But it is the insane pressure of anger and ill-will. I contend that non-violent acts exert pressure far more effective than violent acts, for that pressure comes from goodwill and gentleness.

I do not blame the British. If we were weak in numbers as they are, we too would perhaps have resorted to the same methods as they are now employing. Terrorism and deception are weapons not of the strong but of the weak. The British are weak in numbers, we are weak in spite of our numbers. The result is that each is dragging the other down. It is common experience that Englishmen lose in character after residence in India and that Indians lose in courage and manliness by contact with Englishmen. This process of weakening is good neither for us two nations, nor for the world.

I object to violence because when it appears to do good, the good is only temporary; the evil it does is permanent. I do not believe that the killing of even every Englishman can do the slightest good to India. The millions will be just as badly off as they are today, if someone made it possible to kill of every Englishman tomorrow. The responsibility is more ours than that of the English for the present state of things. The English will be powerless to do evil if we will but be good. Hence my incessant emphasis reform from within.

Good brought through force destroyed individuality. Only when the change was effected through the persuasive power of nonviolent non-co-operation, i.e. love, could the foundation of individuality be preserved, and real, abiding progress be assured for the world.

History teaches one that those who have, no doubt with honest motives, ousted the greedy by using brute force against them, have in their turn become a prey to the disease of the conquered..

To The Revolutionary: Those whom you seek to depose are better armed and infinitely better organized than you are. You may not care for your own loves, but you dare not disregard those of your countrymen who have no desire to die a martyr's death.

Form violence done to the foreign ruler, violence to our own people whom we may consider to be obstructing the country's progress is an easy natural step. Whatever may have been the result of violent activities in other countries and without reference to the philosophy of non-violence, it does not require much intellectual effort to see that if we resort to violence for ridding society of the many abuses which impede our progress, we shall add to our difficulties and postpone the day of freedom. The people unprepared for reform because unconvinced of their necessity will be maddened with rage over their coercion, and will seek the assistance of the assistance of the foreigner in order to retaliate. Has not this been happening before our eyes for the past many years of which we have still painfully vivid recollections?

I hold that the world is sick of armed rebellions. I hold too that whatever may be true of other countries, a bloody revolution will not succeed in India. The masses have no active part can do no good to them. A successful bloody revolution can only mean further misery for the masses. For it would be still foreign rule for them. The non-violence I teach is active non-violence of the strongest. But the weakest can partake in it without becoming weaker. They can only be the stronger for having been in it. The masses are far bolder today than ever were. A non-violent struggle necessarily involves construction on a mass scale. It cannot therefore lead to tamas or darkness or inertia. It means a quickening of the national life. That movement is still going on silently almost imperceptibly, but none the less surely.

I do not deny the revolutionary's heroism and sacrifice. But heroism and sacrifice in a bad cause are so much waste of splendid energy and hurt the good cause by drawing away attention from it by the glamour of the misused heroism and sacrifice in a bad cause.

I am not ashamed to stand erect before the heroic and self-sacrificing revolutionary because I am able to pit an equal measure of non-violent men's heroism and sacrifice untarnished by the blood of the innocent. Self-sacrifice of one innocent man is a million times more potent than the sacrifice of million men who die in the act of killing others. The willing sacrifice of the innocent is the most powerful retort to insolent tyranny that has yet been conceived by God or man.

Nonviolence, the Swifter Way: The spiritual weapon of self-purification, intangible as it seems, is the most potent means of revolutionizing one's environment and loosening external shackles. It works subtly and invisibly; it is an intense process though it might often seem a weary and long-drawn process, it is the struggliest way to liberation. The surest and quickest and no effort can be too great for it. What it requires is faith-an unshakable mountain-like faith that flinches from nothing.

You need not be afraid that the method of nonviolence is a slow long-drawn out process. It is the swiftest the world has seen, for it is the surest.

India's freedom is assured if she has patience. That way will be found to be the shortest even though it may appear to be the longest to our impatient nature. The way of peace insures internal growth and stability.

Non-violence also the Noble Way: I am more concerned in preventing the brutalization of human nature than in the prevention of the sufferings of my own people. I know that people who voluntarily undergo a course of suffering raise themselves and the whole of humanity; but I also know that people who become brutalized in their desperate efforts to get victory over their opponents or to exploit weaker nations or weaker men, not only drag down themselves but mankind also. And it cannot be a matter of pleasure to me or anyone else to see human nature dragged to the mire. If we are all sons of the same God and partake of the same divine essence, we must partake of the sin of every person whether he belongs to us or to another race. You can understand how repugnant it must be to invoke the beast in any human being, how mush more so in Englishmen, among whom I count numerous friends. I invite you all to give all the help that you can in the endeavour that I am making.

The doctrine of violence has reference only to the doing of injury by one to another. Suffering injury in one's own person is on the contrary of the essence of non-violence and is the chosen substitute for violence to others. It is not because I value life low that I can countenance with joy thousands voluntarily losing their lives for satyagraha, but because I know that it results in the long run in the least loss of life and what is more, it ennobles those who lose their lives and morally enriches the world for their sacrifice.

The method of passive resistance is the clearest and safest, because, if the cause is not true, it is the resisters, and they alone, who suffer.

Passive resistance is an all-sided sword; it can be used anyhow; it blesses him who uses it and him against whom it is used.

The beauty of satyagraha, of which non-co-operation is but a chapter, is that it is available to either side in a fight; that it has checks that automatically work for the vindication of truth and justice for that side, whichever it may be, that has truth and justice in preponderating measure. It is as powerful and faithful a weapon in the hand of the capitalist as in that of the labourer. It is as powerful in the hands of the government, as in that of the people, and will bring victory to the government, if people are misguided or unjust, as it will win the battle for the people if the government be in the wrong. Quick disorganization and defeat are bound to be the fate of bolstered up cases and artificial agitations, if the battle is fought with satyagraha weapons. Suppose the people are unfit to rule themselves, or are unwilling to sacrifice for a cause, then, no amount of noise will bring them victory in non-co-operation.

Criminal Assaults: The main thing, however, is for women to know how to be fearless. It is my firm conviction; that a fearless woman who knows that her purity is her best shield can never be dishonoured. However beastly the man, he will bow in shame before the flame of her dazzling purity. There are examples even in modern times of women who have thus defended themselves. I can, as I write, recall two such instances. I therefore recommend women who read this article to try to cultivate this courage. They will become wholly fearless, if they can and cease to tremble as they do today at the mere thought of assaults. It is not, however, necessary for a woman to go through a bitter; experience for the sake of passing a test of courage. These experiences mercifully do not come in the way of lakhs or even thousands. Every soldier is not a beast. It is a minority that loses all sense of decency. Only twenty per cent of snakes are poisonous, and out of these a few only bite. They do not attack unless trodden on. But this knowledge does not help those who are full of fear and tremble at the sight of a snake. Parents and husbands should, therefore, instruct women in the art of becoming fearless. It can best be learnt from a living faith in God. Though He is invisible, He is one's unfailing protector. He who has this faith is the most fearless of all.

But such faith or courage cannot be acquired in a day. Meantime we must try to explore other means. When a woman is assaulted she may not stop to think in terms of himsa or ahimsa. Her primary duty is self-protection. She is at liberty to employ every method or means that come to her mind in order to defend her honour. God has given her nails and teeth. She must use them with all her strength and, if need be, die in the effort. The man or woman who has shed all fear of death will be able not only to protect himself or herself but others also through laying down his life. In truth we fear death most, and hence we ultimately submit to superior physical force. Some will bend the knee to the invader, some will resort to bribery, some will crawl on their bellies or submit to other forms of humiliation, and some women will even give their bodies rather than die. I have not written this in a carping spirit. I am only illustrating human nature. Whether we crawl on our belies or whether a woman yields to the lust of man it is symbolic of that same love of life which makes us stoop to anything. Therefore only he who loses his life shall save it; (tena tyaktena bhunjithah). Every reader should commit this matchless shloka to memory. But mere lip loyalty to it will be of no avail. It must penetrate deep down to the innermost recesses of his heart. To enjoy life one should give up the lure of life. That; should be part of our nature.

So much for what a woman should do. But what about a man who is witness to such crimes? The answer is implied in the foregoing. He must not be a passive onlooker. He must protect the woman. He must not run for police help; he must not rest satisfied by pulling the alarm chain in the train. If he is able to practise non-violence, he will die in doing so and thus save the woman in jeopardy. If he does not believe in non-violence or cannot practise it, he must try to save her by using all the force he may have. In either way there must be readiness on his part to lay down his life.

Prayer In Gandhi's Ashram: "Worshipping God is singing the praise of God. Prayer is a confession of one's unworthiness and weakness. God has a thousand names, or rather, He is Nameless. We may worship or pray to Him by whichever name that pleases us. Some call Him Rama, some Krishna, others call Him Rahim, and yet others call Him God. All worship the same spirit, but as all foods do not agree with all, all names do not appeal to all. Each chooses the name according to his associations, and He being the In-Dweller, All-Powerful and Omniscient knows our innermost feelings and responds to us according to our deserts.

Worship or prayer, therefore, is not to be performed with the lips, but with the heart. And the prayers of those whose tongues are endeared but whose hearts are full of poison are never heard.

He, therefore, who would pray to God, must cleanse his heart. Rama was not only on the lips of Hanuman, He was enthroned in his heart. He gave Hanuman exhaustless strength. In His strength he lifted the mountain and crossed the ocean. That faith is nothing but a living, wide awake consciousness of God within. He who has achieved that faith wants nothing. Bodily diseased he is spiritually healthy, physically poor, he rolls in spiritual riches.

The language of the lips is easily taught; but who can teach the language of the heart? Only the bhakta - the true devotee - knows it, can teach it. The Gita has defined the bhakta in three places and talked of him generally everywhere. But a knowledge of the definition of a bhakta is hardly a sufficient guide. They are rare on this earth. I have therefore suggested the Religion of Service as the means. God Himself seeks for His seat the heart of him who serves his fellowmen...

At the morning prayer we first recite the shlokas (verses) printed in Ashram Bhajanavali (hymnal), and then sing one bhajan (hymn) followed by Ramadhun (repetition of the Gita). There is history attached to almost every shloka and every selected bhajan. The Bhajanavali contains, among others, bhajans from Muslim Sufis and fakirs, from Guru Nanak, and from the Christian hymnary. Every religion seems to have found a natural setting in the prayer book. In the evening we have recitation of the last 19 verses of the second chapter of the Gita, one bhajan and Ramadhun and then read a portion of a sacred book.

The shlokas were selected by Shri Kaka Kalelkar who has been in the Ashram since its foundation. Shri Maganlal Gandhi met him in Shantiniketan, when he and the children of the Phoenix Settlement went there from South Africa while I was still in England. Dinabandhu Andrews and the late Mr. Pearson were then in Shantiniketan. I had advised Maganlal to stay at some place selected by Andrews. And Andrews selected Shantiniketan for the party.

Kaka was a teacher there and came into close contact with Maganlal. Maganlal had been feeling the want of a Sanskrit teacher which was supplied by Kaka. Chintamani Shastri assisted him in the work. Kaka taught the children how to recite the verses repeated in prayer. Some of these verses were omitted in the Ashram prayer in order to save time. Such is the history of the verses recited at the morning prayer all these days.

A hymn was sung after the shlokas. Indeed singing hymns was the only item of prayers in South Africa. The shlokas were added in India. Maganlal Gandhi was our leader in song. But we felt that the arrangement was unsatisfactory. We should have an expert singer for the purpose, and that singer should be one who would observe the Ashram rules. One such was found in Naryan Moreshvar Khare, a pupil of Pandit Vishnu Digambar, whom the master kindly sent to the Ashram. Pandit Khare gave us full satisfaction and is now a full member of the Ashram. He made hymn-singing interesting, and the Ashram Bhajanavali (hymnal) which is now read by thousands was in the main compiled by him. He introduced Ramadhun, the third item of our prayers.

The fourth item is recitation of verses from the Gita. The Gita has for years been an authoritative guide to belief and conduct for the Satyagraha Ashram. It has provided us with a test with which to determine the correctness or otherwise of ideas and courses of conduct in question. Therefore we wished that all Ashramites should understand the meaning of the Gita and if possible commit it to memory. If this last was not possible, we wished that they should at least read the original Sanskrit with correct pronunciation. With this end in view we began to recite part of the Gita every day. We would recite a few verses and continue the recitation until we had learnt them by heart. From this we proceeded to the parayan. And the recitation is now so arranged that the whole of the Gita is finished in fourteen days, and everybody knows what verses will be recited on any particular day.

At the evening prayer we recited the last 19 verses of the second chapter of the Gita as well as sing a hymn and repeat Ramanama. These verses describe the characteristics of the sthitaprajna (the man of stable understanding), which a Satyagrahi too must acquire, and are recited in order that he may constantly bear them in mind.

Repeating the same thing at prayer from day to day is objected to on the ground that it thus becomes mechanical. (However) the point is not whether the contents of the prayer are always the same or differ from day to day. Even if they are full of variety, it is possible that they will become ineffective. The Gayatri verse among Hindus, the confession of faith (kalma) among Musalmans, the typical Christian prayer in the Sermon on the Mount have been recited by millions for centuries every day; and yet their power has not diminished but is ever on the increase. It all depends upon the spirit behind the recitation. If an unbeliever or a parrot utters these potent words, they will fall quite flat. On the other hand when a believer utters them always, their influence grows from day to day."

Religion Vs. No Religion: "In the Harijanbandhu of the 5th May you have written that your non-violence contemplates destruction of animals dangerous to mankind, such as leopards, wolves, snakes, scorpions etc.

"You do not believe in giving food to dogs etc. Several other people besides the Gujaratis look upon the feeding of dogs as a meritorious act. Such a belief may not be justifiable in times of food shortage like the present. Yet we must remember that these animals can be very useful to man. One can feed them and take work out of them.

"You had put 27 questions to Shri Raichandbhai from Durban. One of these questions was: What should a seeker do when a snake attacks him? His answer was: He should not kill the snake and, if it bites, he should let to do so. How is it that you speak differently now?"

I have written a lot on this subject in the past. At that time the topic vas the killing of rabid dogs. There was much discussion on the subject but all that seems to have been forgotten.

My non-violence is not merely kindness to all living creatures. The emphasis laid on the sacredness of sub-human life in Jainism is Understandable. But that can never mean that one is to be kind to this life in preference to human life. While writing about the sacredness of such life, I take it that the sacredness of human life has been taken for granted. The former has been overemphasized. And, while putting it into practice, the idea has undergone distortion. For instance, there are many who derive complete satisfaction in feeding ants. It would appear that the theory has become a wooden, lifeless dogma. Hypocrisy and distortion re passing current under the name of religion.

Ahimsa is the highest ideal. It is meant for the brave, never for the cowardly. To benefit by others' killing and delude oneself into the belief that one is being very religious and non-violent is sheer self-deception.

A so-called votary of non-violence will not stay in a village which is visited by a leopard everyday. He will run away and, when someone has killed the leopard, will return to take charge of his hearth and home. This is not non-violence. This is a coward's violence. The man who has killed the leopard has at least given proof of some bravery. The man who takes advantage of the killing is a coward. He can never expect to know true non-violence.

In life it is impossible to eschew violence completely. The question arises, where is one to draw the line? The line cannot be the same for everyone. Although essentially the principle is the same, yet, everyone applies it in his or her own way. What is one man's food can be another's poison. Meat-eating is a sin for me. Yet, for another person, who has always lived on meat and never seen anything wrong in it, to give it up simply in order to copy me will be a sin.

If I wish to be an agriculturist and stay in the jungle, I will have to use the minimum unavoidable violence in order to protect my fields. I will have to kill monkeys, birds and insects which eat up my crops. If I do not wish to do so myself, I will have to engage someone to do it for me. There is not much difference between the two. To allow crops to be eaten up by animals in the name of ahimsa while there is a famine in the land is certainly a sin. Evil and good are relative terms. What is good under certain conditions can become an evil or a sin under a different set of conditions.

Man is not to drown himself in the well of Shastras but he is to dive in their broad ocean and bring out pearls. At every step he has to use his discrimination as to what is ahimsa and what is himsa. In this there is no room for shame or cowardice. The poet has said that the road leading up to God is for the brave, never for the cowardly. Finally, Raichandbhai's advice to me was that if I had courage, if I wanted to see God face to face, I should let myself be bitten by a snake instead of killing it. I have never killed a snake before or after receiving that letter. That is no matter of credit for me. My ideal is to be able to play with snakes and scorpions fearlessly. But it is merely a wish so far. Whether and when it will be realized I do not know. Everywhere I have let my people kill both. I could have prevented them if I had wished. But how could I? I did not have the courage to take them up with my own hands and teach my companions a lesson in fearlessness. I am ashamed that I could not do so. But my shame could not benefit them or me.

If Ramanama favours me I might still attain that courage some day. In the meantime, I consider it my duty to act as I have stated above. Religion is a thing to be lived. It is not mere sophistry.

Gandhi's Views on Satyagraha: Events were so shaping themselves in Johannesburg as to make this self-purification on my part a preliminary as it were to Satyagraha. I can now see that all the principal events of my life, culminating in the vow of brahmacharya, were secretly preparing me for it. The principle called Satyagraha came into being before that name was invented. Indeed when it was born, I myself could not say what it was. In Gujarati also we used the English phrase 'passive resistance' to describe it. When in a meeting of Europeans I found that the term 'passive resistance' was too narrowly construed, that it was supposed to be a weapon of the weak, that it could be characterized by hatred, and that it could finally manifest itself as violence, I had to damur to all these statements and explain the real nature of the Indian movement. It was clear that a new word must be coined by the Indians to designate their struggle.

But I could not for the life of me find out a new name, and therefore offered a nominal prize through Indian Opinion to the reader who made the best suggestion on the subject. As a result Maganlal Gandhi coined the word 'Satyagraha' (Sat=truth, Agraha=firmness) and won the prize. But in order to make it clearer I changed the word to 'Satyagraha' which has since become current in Gujarati as a designation for the struggle.

The history of this struggle is for all practical purposes a history of the remainder of my life in South Africa and especially of my experiments with truth in that sub-continent. I wrote the major portion of this history in Yeravda jail and finished it after I was released. It was published in Navajivan and subsequently issued in book form. Sri Valji Govindji Desai has been translating it into English for Current Thought, but I am now arranging to have the English translation published in book form at an early date, so that those who will may be able to familiarize themselves with my most important experiments in South Africa. I would recommend a perusal of my history of Satyagraha in South Africa to such readers as have not seen it already. I will not repeat what I have put down there, but in the next few chapters will deal only with a few personal incidents of my life in South Africa which have not been covered by that history. And when I have done with these, I will at once proceed to give the reader some idea of my experiments in India. Therefore, anyone who wishes to consider these experiments in their strict chronological order will now do well to keep the history of Satyagraha in South Africa before him.

Truth (Meaning of Truth): I deal with truth first of all, as the Satyagraha Ashram owes its very existence to the pursuit and the attempted practice of truth.

The word satya (Truth) is derived from Sat which means 'being'. Nothing is or exists in reality except Truth. That is why Sat or Truth is perhaps the most important name of God. In fact it is more correct to say that Truth is God than to say God is truth. But as we cannot do without a ruler or a general, such names of God as 'King' or 'Kings' or ' The Almighty' are and will remain generally current. On deeper thinking, however it will be realized that Sat or Satya is the only correct and fully sign fact name for God.

And where there is Truth, there is also is knowledge which is true. Where there is no Truth, there also is knowledge which is true. Where there is no Truth, there can be no true knowledge. That is why the word Chit or knowledge is associated with the name of God. And where there is true knowledge, there is always bliss. (Ananda). There sorrow has no place. And even as Truth is eternal, so is the bliss derived from it. Hence we know God as Sat-Chit-ananda, one who combines in Himself Truth, Knowledge and Bliss.

Devotion to this Truth is the sole justification for our existence. All our activities should be centered in Truth. Truth should be the very breath of our life.

When once this stage in the pilgrim's progress is reached, all other rules of correct living will come without effort, and obedience to them will be instinctive. But without Truth it is impossible to observe any principles or rules in life.

Generally speaking observation of the law of Truth is understood merely to mean that we must speak the Truth. But we in the Ashram should understand the word Satya or Truth in a much wider sense. There should be truth in thought, truth in speech, and truth in action. To the man who has realized this truth in its fullness, nothing else remains to be known , because all knowledge is necessary included in it. What is not included in it is not truth, and so not true knowledge; and there can be no inward peace without true knowledge. If we once learn how to apply this never failing test of Truth, we will at once able to find out what is worth doing, what is worth seeing, what is worth reading.

But how is one to realize this Truth , which may be likened to the philosophers stone or the cow of plenty? By single minded devotion (abhyasa) and indifference to all other interests in life (vairagya) replies the Bhagavadgita. In spite, however of such devotion, what may appear as Truth to one person will often appear as untruth to another person. But that need not worry the seeker. where there is honest effort, it will be realized that what appear to be different truths are like the countless and apparently different leaves of the same tree. Does not God himself appear to different individuals in different aspects? Yet we know that He is one. But Truth is the right designation of God. Hence there is nothing wrong in every man following Truth according to his lights. Indeed it is his duty to do so. Then if there is a mistake on the part of any one so following Truth it will be automatically set right. For the quest of Truth involves tapas self suffering, sometimes even unto death. There can be no place in it even a trace of self interest. In such selfless search for Truth nobody can lose his bearings for long. Directly he takes to the wrong path he stumbles, and is thus redirected to the right path. Therefore the pursuit of Truth is true bhakti (devotion). It is the path that leads to God. There is no place in it for cowardice, no place for defeat. It is the talisman by which death itself becomes the portal to life eternal.

In this connection it will be well to ponder over the lives and examples of Harishchandra , Prahlad, Ramchandra, Imam Hussain, the Christians saints, etc. How beautiful it would be if all of us, young and old, men and women devoted ourselves wholly to Truth in all that we might do in our walking hours, whether working, eating, drinking, or playing till dissolution of the body makes us one with Truth? God as Truth has been for me a treasure beyond price; may He be so to every one of us.

Truth & Beauty: There are two aspects of things-the outward and the inward.... The outward has to meaning except in so far as it helps the inward. All true Art is thus an expression of the soul. The outward forms have value only in so far as they are the expression of the inner spirit of man.

All true Art must help the soul to realize its inner self. In my own case, I find that I can do entirely without external forms in my soul's realization. I can claim, therefore, that there is truly efficient Art in my life, though you might not see what you call works of Art about me.

My room may have blank walls; and I may even dispense with the roof, so that I may gaze out at the starry heavens overhead that stretch in an unending expanse. What conscious Art of man can give me the panoramic scenes that open out before me, when I look up to the sky above with all its shining stars?

This, however, does not mean that I refuse to accept the value of productions of Art, generally accepted as such, but only that I personally feel how inadequate these are compared with the eternal symbols of beauty in Nature. These productions of man's Art have their value only in so far as they help the soul onward towards self-realization.

Truth First: Truth is the first thing to be sought for, and Beauty and Goodness will then be added unto you. Jesus was, to my mind, a supreme artist because he saw and expressed Truth; and so was Muhammad, the Koran being, the most perfect composition in all Arabic literature—at any rate, that is what scholars say. It is because both of them strove first for Truth that the grace of expression naturally came in and yet neither Jesus not Muhammad wrote on Art. That is the Truth and Beauty I crave for, live for, and would die for.

Art for the Millions: Here too, just as elsewhere, I must think in terms of the millions. And to the millions we cannot give that training to acquire a perception of Beauty in such a way as to see Truth in it. Show them Truth first and they will see Beauty afterwards... Whatever can be useful to those starving millions in beautiful to my mind. Let us give today first the vital things of life and all the graces and ornaments of life will follow.

After all, Art can only be expressed not through inanimate power-driven machinery designed for mass-production, but only through the delicate living touch of the hands of men and women.

To a true artist only that face is beautiful which, quite apart from its exterior, shines with the Truth within the soul. There is… no Beauty apart from Truth. On the other hand, Truth may manifest itself in forms, which may not be outwardly beautiful at all. Socrates, we are told, was the most truthful man of his time, and yet his features are said to have been the ugliest in Greece. To my mind he was beautiful, because all his life was a striving after Truth, and you may remember that his outward form did not prevent Phidias from appreciating the beauty of Truth in him, though as an artist he was accustomed to see Beauty in outward forms also.

Truth and Untruth often co-exist; good and evil are often found together. In an artist also not seldom the right perception of things and the wrong co-exist. Truly beautiful creations come when right perception is at work. If these monuments are rare in life, they are also rare in Art.

These beauties are sunset or a crescent moon that shines amid the stars at night'] are truthful, inasmuch as they make me think of the Creator at the back of them. How else could these be beautiful, but for the Truth that is in the center of creation? When I admire the wonder of a sunset or the beauty of the moon, my soul expands in worship of the Creator. I try to see Him and His mercies in all these creations. But even the sunsets and sunrises would be mere hindrances if they did not help me to think of the soul is a delusion and a snare; even like the body, which often does hinder you in the path of salvation.

Why can't you see the beauty of colour in vegetables? And then, there is beauty in the speckless sky. But no, you want the colours of the rainbow, which is a mere optical illusion. We have been taught to believe that what is beautiful need not be useful and what is useful cannot be beautiful. I want to show that what is useful can also be beautiful.

God Through Service: If I did not fee the presence of God within me, I see so much of misery and disappointment every day that I would be a raving maniac and my destination would be the Hooghli.

If I am to identify myself with the grief of the least in India, aye, if I have the power, the least in the world, let me identify myself with the sins of the little ones who are under my care. And so doing in all humility, I hope some day to see God—Truth—face to face.

I am endeavoring to see God through service of humanity, for I know that God is neither in heaven, nor in down below, but in every one.

I am a part and parcel of the whole, and I cannot find Him apart from the rest of humanity. My countrymen are my nearest neighbors. They have become so helpless, so resourceless, so inert that I must concentrate on serving them. If I could persuade myself that I should find Him in a Himalayan cave, I would proceed there immediately. But I know that I cannot find Him apart from humanity.

I claim to know my millions. All the 24 hours of the day I am with them. They are my first care and last because I recognize no God except the God that is to be found in the hearts of the dumb millions. They do not recognize His presence; I do. And I worship the God that is Truth or Truth, which is God through the service of these millions.

Guide and Protector: I must go… with God as my only guide. He is a jealous Lord. He will allow no one to share His authority. One has, therefore, to appear before Him in all one's weakness, empty-handed and in a spirit of full surrender, and then He enables you to stand before a whole world and protects you from all harm.

I have learned this one lesson—that what is impossible with man is child's play with God and if we have faith in that Divinity which presides on the destiny of the meanest of His creation, I have no doubt that all things are possible; and in that final hope, I live and pass my time and endeavor to obey His will.

Even in darkest despair, where there seems to be no helper and no comfort in the wide, wide world, His Name inspires us with strength and puts all doubts and despairs to flight. The sky may be overcast today with clouds, but a fervent prayer to Him is enough to dispel them. It is because of prayer that I have known no disappointment.

…I have known no despair. Why then should you give way to it? Let us pray that He may cleanse our hearts of pettinesses, meannesses and deceit and He will surely answer our prayers. Many I know have always turned to that unfailing source of strength.

I have seen and believe that God never appears to you in person, but in action which can only account for your deliverance in your darkest hour.

Individual worship cannot be described in words. It goes on continuously and even unconsciously. There is not a moment when I do not feel the presence of a Witness whose eye misses nothing and with whom I strive to keep in tune.

I have never found Him lacking in response. I have found Him nearest at hand when the horizon seemed darkest in my ordeals in jails when it was not all-smooth sailing for me. I cannot recall a moment in my life when I had a sense of desertion by God.

Self-realization: I believe it to be possible for every human being to attain to that blessed and indescribable, sinless state in which he feels within himself the presence of God to the exclusion of everything else.

What I want to achieve, -what I have been striving and pining to achieve…,—is self-realization, to see God face to face, to attain moksha. I live and move and have my being in pursuit of this goal. All that I do by way of speaking and writing and all my ventures in the political field are directed to this same end.

For it is an unbroken torture to me that I am still so far from Him, who, as I fully know, governs every breath of my life, and whose offspring I am. I know that it is the evil passions within that keep me so far from Him, and yet I cannot get away from them.

This belief in God has to be based on faith, which transcends reasons. Indeed, even the so-called realization has at bottom an element of faith without which it cannot be sustained. In the very nature of things it must be so. Who can transgress the limitations of his being?

I hold that complete realization is impossible in this embodied life. Nor is it necessary. A living immovable faith is all that is required for reaching the full spiritual height attainable by human beings. God is not outside this earthly case of ours. Therefore, exterior proof is not of much avail, if any at all.

We must ever fail to perceive Him through the senses, because He is beyond them. We can feel Him if we will but withdraw ourselves from the senses. The divine music is incessantly going on within ourselves, but the loud senses drown the delicate music, which is unlike and infinitely superior to anything we can perceive or hear with our senses.

Gandhism (or Gandhi-ism) is an informal reference to the vision, core inspirations, principles, beliefs and philosophy of Mohandas Karamchand Gandhi, who was a major political and spiritual leader of India and the Indian Independence Movement.

It is a body of ideas and principles that best describe not only the inspiration, vision and the life work of Mahatma Gandhi, but what Gandhi's ideas, words and actions meant to common Indians and human beings around the world, and how they used them for guidance in building their own future. Gandhism also permeates into the realm of the individual human being, non-political and non-social.

Under the heading of Gandhism, this article endeavors to discuss the effect of the work and teachings of Gandhi, how it has influenced individuals and nations, and how the interpretation of his words and actions have outlived Gandhi, for better or worse.

Gandhi himself famously stated that *"I have nothing new to teach the World. Truth and Non-violence are as old as the hills."* Certainly no element of Gandhism is entirely Gandhi's original thinking.

Gandhi developed his vision, thought and way of life by his constant experimenting with truth, by making painful errors during his childhood and adolescence, but by having the strength to repent and correct. All 78 years of Gandhi's life, from his childhood and adolescent errors and indulgences, his penances for them, to his adulthood convictions and sacrifices, compose the defining elements of Gandhism.

The goals of different philosophies vary: socialism desires an egalitarian economic and political system; pacifism shall tolerate no war under any circumstances; Buddhism seeks salvation.

Gandhism is thus more the spirit of Gandhi's journey to discover the truth, than what he finally considered to be the truth. It is the foundation of Gandhi's teachings, and the spirit of his whole life to examine and understand for oneself, and not take anybody or any ideology for granted.

The pivotal and defining element of Gandhism is Satya, simply, Truth. Truth to Gandhi, and so to his followers must pervade all considerations of politics, ego, society and convention. Gandhi was neither a pacifist, socialist or on any definable spectrum of politics. He simply adhered to the pure existing facts of life, otherwise known as the true state of things, to make his decisions.

The Truth however is the most difficult value to imbibe and practice for most human beings, and Gandhi's life is evidence and inspiration that it can be done. Gandhi's commitment to non-violence, human freedom, equality and justice arose from the truths of life, after careful personal examination.

Truth is interpreted subjectively. Thus Gandhism as a body does not demand that its adherents agree to Gandhi's own principles to the letter, but essentially in spirit. If one honestly believes that violence is sometimes unavoidable, necessary and cleansing of an immoral situation, it would only be being *truthful* to believe in it. Being *truthful* is the spirit of Gandhism. He found that uncovering the truth was not always popular as many people were resistant to change, preferring instead to maintain the existing status quo because of either inertia, self-interest or misguided beliefs. However he also discovered that once the truth was on the march nothing could stop it. All it took was time to achieve traction and gain momentum. As Gandhi said: *The Truth is far more powerful than any weapon of mass destruction.*

The Indian Independence Movement was not exempt from Gandhi's commitment to Truth. When Gandhi returned to India amidst World War I, he said he would have supported the British in the war. It would have been wrong, according to Gandhi, to demand equal rights for Indians in the Empire, and not contribute to its defence.

Gandhi stopped all nationwide civil resistance in 1922 upon the ugly Chauri Chaura incident. He would forsake political independence for truth the reality here that Indians should not become murderers and commit the very evils they were accusing the British of perpetrating in India.

He said that the most important battle to fight was in overcoming his own demons, fears and insecurities. He thought it was all too easy to blame people, governing powers or enemies for his personal actions and wellbeing. He noted the solution to problems could normally be found just by looking in the mirror.

One of the greatest contributions of Mahatma Gandhi was in the realm of ontology and its association with truth. For Gandhi, "to be" did not mean to exist within the realm of time, as it has in the past with the Greek philosophers. But rather, "to exist" meant to exist within the realm of truth, or to use the term Gandhi did, satya. Gandhi summarized his beliefs first when he said "God is Truth," but as typical of Gandhi, he evolved, later to correct himself and state that "Truth is God." The first statement seemed insufficient to Gandhi, as the mistake could be made that Gandhi was using Truth as a description of God, as opposed to God as an aspect of satya. Satya (Truth) in Gandhi's philosophy is God. It shares all the characteristics of the Hindu concept of God, or Brahman. It lives within us, that little voice that tells us what to do, but also guides the universe.

Brahmacharya and Ahimsa: The concept of nonviolence (ahimsa) and nonresistance has a long history in Indian religious thought and has had many revivals in Hindu, Buddhist, Jain and Christian contexts. Gandhi explains his philosophy and way of life in his autobiography The Story of My Experiments with Truth. He was quoted with saying:

"What difference does it make to the dead, the orphans, and the homeless, whether the mad destruction is wrought under the name of totalitarianism or the holy name of liberty and democracy?"

"An eye for an eye makes the whole world blind".

"It has always been easier to destroy than to create".

"There are many causes that I am prepared to die for but no causes that I am prepared to kill for".

In applying these principles, Gandhi did not balk from taking them to their most logical extremes. In 1940, when invasion of the British Isles by the armed forces of Nazi Germany looked imminent, Gandhi offered the following advice to the British people:

"I would like you to lay down the arms you have as being useless for saving you or humanity. You will invite Herr Hitler and Signor Mussolini to take what they want of the countries you call your possessions.... If these gentlemen choose to occupy your homes, you will vacate them. If they do not give you free passage out, you will allow yourselves, man, woman, and child, to be slaughtered,

but you will refuse to owe allegiance to them". (Non-Violence in Peace and War)

At the age of 36, Gandhi adopted the vow of brahmacharya. He thus committed himself to the control of the senses, thoughts and actions.

Ahimsa rose highly in his mind. Total non-violence rid the person of anger, obsession and destructive impulses. While his vegetarianism was inspired by his rearing in the Hindu-Jain culture of Gujarat, it was just an extension of ahimsa, total non-violence.

Celibacy was important to Gandhi for not only purifying himself of any lust and sexual urges, but also to purify his love for his wife as genuine and not an outlet for any turmoil or aggression within his mind. Celebacy was an extension of ahimsa to him, and the center of his observance of brahmacharya.

Gandhi also adopted the clothing style of most Indians in the early 20th century. His adoption of khadi was to help eradicate the evils of poverty, social and economic discrimination and egotism that exists between most Indians, who were poor and traditional, to the richer classes of the British and educated, liberal-minded Indians who had adopted Western mannerisms, clothing and practices.

The clothing policy was designed to protest the violence of British-imposed economic policies in India, where millions of poor Indian workers were left unemployed and entrenched in poverty, owing to the advent of the machines in Great Britain. If an Indian chose to buy and wear clothes manufacturing in Britain, as many liberal Indians did, scores of Indian workers lost their livelihood.

Gandhi sought to end the destructive impulses and behavior that may poison his marriage and relationships with other human beings, and his personal contribution to society. It was a personal quest which spawned the largest non-violent revolution in human history.

Fasting: To Gandhi, fasting was an important method of exerting mental control over the biological activities. In his autobiography, Gandhi analyzes the need to fast to eradicate the desires for delicious, spicy food, which in turn would diminish the sensual faculties, bringing the body increasingly under the mind's absolute control. Gandhi was opposed to the partaking of meat and most spices, and also eliminated different types of cooking from the food he ate.

Fasting would also put the body through unusual hardship which in turn would cleanse the spirit, by stimulating the courage to withstand all impulses and pain. Gandhi fasted to death on three notable occasions: when he wanted to stop all revolutionary activities after the Chauri Chaura Incident of 1922; when he feared that the 1934 communal award giving separate electorates to Untouchable Hindus would politically divide the Hindu people; and in 1947, when he wanted to stop the bloodshed between Hindus and Muslims in Bengal and Delhi. In all three cases, Gandhi succeeded in achieving his aims: the Poona Pact which ended the separate electorates in turn for voluntary representation and a commitment to abolish untouchability, and in Calcutta and Delhi, where both communities pledged to stop the fighting.

While an effective means of protest, Gandhi also blamed himself for inciting the Chauri Chaura killing of 22 policemen, and the divisive communal politics of both 1934 and 1947, especially blaming himself for the Partition of India. Gandhi sought to purify his soul and expiate his sins, in what he saw as his role in allowing terrible tragedies to happen. It certainly brought him harrowingly close to death's door, and took a heavy toll on his physical health.

Religion: Gandhi questioned religious practices and doctrines regardless of traditions or beliefs. On the subject of Christianity he noted that:

"The only people on earth who do not see Christ and His teachings as nonviolent are Christians".

Although Gandhi was born a Hindu he was critical of most religions, including Hinduism. He wrote in his autobiography:

"Thus if I could not accept Christianity either as a perfect, or the greatest religion, neither was I then convinced of Hinduism being such. Hindu defects were pressingly visible to me. If untouchability could be a part of Hinduism, it could but be a rotten part or an excrescence. I could not understand the raison d'etre of a multitude of sects and castes. What was the meaning of saying that the Vedas were the inspired Word of God? If they were inspired, why not also the Bible and the Koran? As Christian friends were endeavouring to convert me, so were Muslim friends. Abdullah Sheth had kept on inducing me to study Islam, and of course he had always something to say regarding its beauty".

He then went on to say:

"As soon as we lose the moral basis, we cease to be religious. There is no such thing as religion over-riding morality. Man, for instance, cannot be untruthful, cruel or incontinent and claim to have God on his side".

Gandhi was critical of the hypocrisy in organised religion, rather than the principles on which they were based. He also said the following about Hinduism:

"Hinduism as I know it entirely satisfies my soul, fills my whole being ... When doubts haunt me, when disappointments stare me in the face, and when I see not one ray of light on the horizon, I turn to the Bhagavad Gita, and find a verse to comfort me; and I immediately begin to smile in the midst of overwhelming sorrow. My life has been full of tragedies and if they have not left any visible and indelible effect on me, I owe it to the teachings of the Bhagavad Gita".

The concept of Islamic jihad can also be taken to mean a nonviolent struggle or satyagraha, in the way Gandhi practiced it. On Islam he said:

"The sayings of Muhammad are a treasure of wisdom, not only for Muslims but for all of mankind".

Later in his life when he was asked whether he was a Hindu, he replied:

"Yes I am. I am also a Christian, a Muslim, a Buddhist and a Jew".

Gandhi believed that at the core of every religion was Truth (Satya), Love/Nonviolence (Ahimsa) and the Golden Rule. He was deeply influenced by the Christian teaching of nonresistance and "turning the other cheek" once stating that if Christianity practised the Sermon on the Mount, he would indeed be a Christian. Gandhi felt that one should be aware of worshiping the symbols and idols of the religion and not its teachings, such as worshipping the crucifix whilst ignoring its significance as a symbol for self-sacrifice, for example.

In Nehru's India: Gandhi was assassinated in 1948 , but his teachings and philosophy would play a major role in India's economic and social development and foreign relations for decades to come.

Sarvodaya is a term meaning 'universal uplift' or 'progress of all'. It was coined by the Gandhian leader Vinoba Bhave to refer to the struggle of post-independence Gandhians to ensure that self-determination and equality reached the masses and the downtrodden. Sarvodaya workers associated with Vinoba, Jaya Prakash Narayan, Dada Dharmadhikari, undertook various projects aimed at encouraging popular self-organisation during the 1950s and 1960s. Many groups descended from these networks continue to function locally in India today.

While the problem of the desperate poverty of tens of millions of landless farmers across the country had to be addressed, Gandhi did not believe that class warfare was inevitable, as Lenin, Mao Zedong and Stalin did. Bhave and other Gandhi disciples organized the Bhoodan campaign encouraging landlords across the country to award land to their farmers. They were encouraged to acknowledge the desperate poverty and mistreatment of these farmers, to accept them as fellow Indians and their brethren. This peaceful land distribution program was frowned upon by supporters of free-market economics, the Communists and socialists alike, but did enjoy notable successes.

The Prime Minister of India, Jawaharlal Nehru was the protege of Gandhi. Nehru was often considered Gandhi's successor as India's political leader, and used this position to push major ideological policies based on Gandhi's principles.

Nehru's foreign policy was staunch anti-colonialism and neutrality in the Cold War. Nehru backed the independence movement in Tanzania and other African nations, as well as the American Civil Rights Movement led by Martin Luther King Jr. and the anti-apartheid struggle of Nelson Mandela and the African National Congress in South Africa. Nehru refused to align with either the United States or the Soviet Union, and helped found the Non Aligned Movement.

Nehru also pushed through major legislation that granted legal rights and freedoms to Indian women, and outlawed untouchability and many different kinds of social discrimination, much to the opposition of the Indian orthodoxy.

Nehru however, is criticized for hypocrisy for some of his decisions which clearly deviated from the purity of Gandhi's teachings. Nehru refused to condemn the USSR's 1956-57 invasion of Hungary to put down an anti-communist, popular revolt. Some of his economic policies took away the right of property and freedoms from the very landowing peasants of Gujarat for whom Gandhi had fought for in the early 1920s. While Gandhi was never a socialist, Nehru was an avowed fan of the creed.

Where many consider Nehru's biggest failing, the 1962 Sino-Indian War, Gandhi is also criticized for inspiring the pacifism that led to the defeat of the Indian Army against a surprise Chinese invasion. Nehru had neglected the defence budget and disallowed the Army to prepare, which caught the soldiers in India's north eastern frontier woefully off-guard with lack of supplies and reinforcements.

Gandhi's deep commitment and disciplined belief in non-violent civil disobedience as a way to oppose tyranny, oppression and injustice was shared by many contemporary leaders of nations, including Dr. Martin Luther King Jr. of the United States, Julius Nyerere of Tanzania, Nelson Mandela and Steve Biko of South Africa, Lech Wasa of Poland and Aung San Suu Kyi of Myanmar.

Gandhi's early life work in South Africa between the years 1910 and 1915, for the rights of colored peoples oppressed by the racist, white-dominated South African regime inspired the later work of Steve Biko, Nelson Mandela and the African National Congress.

Since the 1950s, the ANC organized non-violent civil disobedience akin to the Indian National

Congress of Gandhi during the Indian Independence Movement. Determined ANC activists braved the sticks and bullets of the police, water-hoses, tear gas and mad dogs to break the back of tyranny, racism and oppression in South Africa, all without retaliating despite the brutality. Many, especially Mandela, languished for decades in jail, while the world outside was divided in its effort to remove apartheid from South Africa. Steve Biko, perhaps the most vocal adherent to non-violent civil resistance, was allegedly murdered in 1977 by agents of the regime.

When Mandela and the ANC finally won in 1994, and when the first universal, free elections were held in South Africa and Mandela became President, he made a special visit to India and publicly honored Gandhi as the man who inspired the freedom struggle of black South Africans. Statues of Gandhi have been erected in Natal, Pretoria and Johannesburg and many South Africans do not hesitate to honor his importance to their revolution.

Dr. Martin Luther King Jr., a young Christian priest and leader of the American Civil Rights Movement seeking the liberation of African Americans from racial segregation in the American South, and also the terrible economic and social injustice and political disenfranchisement, traveled to India in 1962 and Jawaharlal Nehru met him personally. The two discussed Gandhi's teachings, and the methodology of organizing peaceful resistance. The terribly graphic imagery of determined Black protestors being hounded by police, beaten and brutalized, evoked universal admiration for Dr. King and the protestors across America and the world, and precipitated in the 1964 Civil Rights Act. In an unholy coincidence, Dr. King was assassinated by a white fanatic in 1968, even as Gandhi was killed in 1948 by a Hindu extremist.

The non-violent Solidarity movement of Lech Walsa of Poland overthrew a Soviet-backed communist government after two decades of peaceful resistance and strikes, in 1989, beginning the downfall of the Soviet Communist empire. Myanmar's Aung San Suu Kyi, a small young woman, remains under house arrest, and her National League for Democracy suppressed in their non-violent quest for democracy and freedom in military-controlled Myanmar. This struggle was inaugurated when the military dismissed the results of the 1991 democratic elections and imposed harsh military rule.

Criticism, Controversy and the Cult: In post-Gandhi India, adhering to Gandhi's views and teachings became a necessary correctness, thanks primarily to Congress politicians who sought to exploit his independence-era leadership for votes: that only Gandhi's party could be trusted with the nation's affairs, and that Nehru was the successor of Gandhi, anointed by Gandhi himself. The Nehru administration and the Congress party had begun the Gandhi cult.

As a result of what was taught in India's schools, Gandhi became a man who had single-handedly won India its freedom. It was an impression created with India's first post-independence generation that unwittingly undermined the contribution of tens of millions of Indian freedom fighters, and scores of distinguished Indian leaders, both within the Congress and outside it.

Wearing a white khadi kurta and dhoti, or simply khadi pants with a *Gandhi topi (cap)* became the uniform of the members of Parliament, politicians and political activists around India. Wearing a suit became the symbol of elitism and the Western attack on India's culture, and a taboo as far as politics and social work was concerned. For a couple of decades, it became a symbol of the barrier between most Indians, and the privileged few.

Gandhi's rigid ahimsa has been translated as pacifism, thus a source of criticism from across the political spectrum. His view that one should not resist even an armed invasion of one's country, and his comments that the British people should have offered no resistance to Nazi Germany and that the people victimized in the holocaust should have committed mass suicide to prevent Nazis from committing the sin of killing them (see Mohandas Gandhi at wikiquote), and to protest the evil they were committing have been viewed as grossly extreme and impractical, and outrightly insulting to the victims of the holocaust and the peoples subjected to the attacks of Nazi forces. This pacifism was blamed for the lack of readiness of the Indian Army to the Chinese invasion in 1962 due to Nehru's adherence to Gandhi's principles.

Many conservative Hindus blame Gandhi for being too conciliatory and appeasing to India's Muslims and the Untouchable community. Gandhi is faulted for not attempting to *mollycoddle* Muhammad Ali Jinnah, the Muslim separatist leader to drop his demand for Pakistan, for compromising with the divisive, communal politics supposedly espoused by low caste and untouchable Hindus, and for acquiescing to the Partition of India. Gandhi was also angrily viewed when he sought a comprehensive assurance of non-violence and non-intimidation towards Indian Muslims from the Hindus and Sikhs of West Bengal, Punjab and Delhi. It seemed to them he was going overboard in efforts to protect Muslims, while a large number of Hindus and Sikhs had been killed and violently abused while making their migration to India. More than 1 million people were killed in the violence or victims of abuse, rape and incredible hardships.

As a result, a lot of things associated with Gandhi, from quotes to clothing, are a source of a new generation's expression of revolt of the older. The leader of extremist Hindus Vinayak Damodar Savarkar and the Dalit leader B.R. Ambedkar are hailed as heroes by many today for their noted distrust and opposition to Gandhi's leadership. Modern Hindutva politicians such as Narendra Modi, Praveen Togadia and others are noted for their criticisms of Gandhi.

Without Truth, Nothing: Mohandas Gandhi's early life was a series of personal struggles to decipher the truth about life's important issues and discover the true way of living.

As a lad, he was guilty of beating his young wife, for indulging in carnal pleasures out of lust, jealousy and possessiveness, not genuine love. He was guilty of experimenting with meat and smoking a cigarette, and narrowly escaped enjoying a prostitute. It was only after much personal turmoil and repeated failures, did Gandhi finally succeed to become who he was.

His candid confessions in his 1929 autobiography were avoidable had he chosen to conceal these unpleasant facts for fear of loss of respect and support amongst the people. But Gandhi personally disliked having a cult following, and was averse to his being addressed to as *Mahatma*, for he was fully aware he was not a perfect human being.

Gandhism is thus more the spirit of Gandhi's journey to discover the truth, than what he finally considered to be the truth. It is the foundation of Gandhi's teachings, and the spirit of his whole life to examine and understand for oneself, and not taken anybody or any ideology for granted. Furthermore, the Gandhi cult developed in the first decades of independence were directly in violation of the spirit of Gandhism, fcr it arbitrarily imposed his views upon people by political propaganda.

Gandhi had never espoused socialism despite working all his life against the poverty and socioeconomic discrimination of millions of people. It was Nehru who was a committed socialist, and as Prime Minister, responsible for post-independence India's turn to socialism.

Gandhi did believe that the world was one family, and was absolutely committed to the view that non-violent civil resistance was the solution, however unlikely to any act of oppression.

In 1942, while he had already condemned Adolf Hitler, Benito Mussolini and the Japanese militarists, Gandhi took on an offensive in civil resistance, called the Quit India Movement, which was even more dangerous and definitive owing to its direct call for Indian independence. Gandhi was not hypocritical thus - he did not see the British as defenders of freedom giving their continuance of imperialist domination in India. Gandhi did not feel a need to take sides with world powers.

Gandhism is brutal adherence to truth. If it means condemning the practice of untouchability in Hindu society, it means condemning the victimization of Muslim women and coerced conversions to Islam and Christianity in the same breath. Gandhism has no respect for power, especially as the man himself took down the mighty British Empire. No institution or individual is infallible, save God.

And while Gandhi believed that all humans are susceptible to sinful actions and behavior, and the worst of dictators were essentially the same despite the difference in their lives, beliefs and actions, Gandhi firmly believed in humans not having the right to punish any other human beings. Punishment is God's work.

Despite Gandhi's adherence to Hindu cultural and religious values, Gandhism is broad over everything save the truth, which is definite and inviolable. Gandhism is the envelope around the principle of Truth. Truth by itself may be hard and too rigorous to adhere to in very complex period of life, but Gandhism makes truth inviting and redeeming.

A Muslim, a Christian, or an atheist can be a Gandhian without any discrepancy with his or her faith, profession or lifestyle. Gandhism transcends national boundaries, gender, racial and sexual orientation, and is as universal as humanity itself.

To become a Gandhian, one must set upon the same personal journey to seek truth and build one's life around it. It is not necessary to arrive at the same conlusions as Gandhi, or any of Gandhi's disciples did in their time. But undergoing the same personal challenges, travails and the testing of one's spirit, resolve and fundamental values is an important, definitive element.

From personal lifestyle and character, Gandhism extends to the world of politics, human relations and religion. Gandhism yet is very difficult to define just as a religion.

Ram Mohan Roy

Ram Mohan Roy, also written as Rammohan Roy, or Raja Ram Mohun Roy (Bangla: Raja Ram Mohon Ray) (May 22, 1772 – September 27, 1833) was the founder of the Brahmo Samaj, one of the first Indian socio-religious reform movements. His remarkable influence was apparent in the fields of politics, public administration and education as well as religion. He is most known for his efforts to abolish the practice of sati, a Hindu funeral custom in which the widow sacrifices herself on her husband's funeral pyre. Rammohan is regarded as one of the most important figures in the Bengal Renaissance.

Early Life and Education: Roy was born in Radhanagar, Bengal, in 1772. His family background displayed an interesting religious diversity. His father Ramkant, was a Vaishnavite, while his mother,

Tarini, was from a Shakta background. Rammohan learnt successively Bangla, Persian, Arabic and Sanskrit by the age of fifteen.

As a teenager, Roy became dissatisfied with the practices of his family, and travelled widely, before returning to manage his family property. He then worked as a moneylender in Calcutta, and from 1803 to 1814 was employed by the British East India Company.

Social Reformer: In the history of social reform in India, Ram Mohan Roy's name will always be remembered in connection with the abolition of Sati (the immolation of widows, often termed *suttee* in historical works). Ram Mohan Roy also made people aware of the fact that polygamy, which was extremely prevalent in his day, was in fact contrary to law. Challenging the authority of Hindu priesthood he pointed out that it was only under specific circumstances (e.g. if a wife is infertile or has an incurable disease) that a man was permitted to take a second wife while the first was still alive.

Values: In the social, legal and religious reforms that he advocated, Roy was moved primarily by considerations of humanity. He took pains to show that he was not out to destroy the best traditions of the country, but was merely brushing away some of the impurities that had gathered on them in the days of decadence. He respected the Upanishads and studied the Sutras. He condemned idolatry in the strongest terms. He stated that the best means of achieving bliss was through pure spiritual contemplation on and worship of the Supreme Being, and that sacrificial rites were intended only for persons of less subtle intellect.

Roy campaigned for rights for women, including the right for widows to remarry, and the right for women to hold property. As mentioned above, he actively opposed polygamy, a system in which he had grown up.

He also supported education, particularly education of women. He believed that English-language education was superior to the traditional Indian education system, and he opposed the use of government funds to support schools teaching Sanskrit. In 1822, he founded a school based on English education.

Ram Mohan Roy died in Bristol, England, where this statue of him was later erected.

Late Life: In 1831 Ram Mohan Roy travelled to the United Kingdom as an ambassador of the Mughal Empire. He also visited France.

He died at Stapleton near Bristol in 1833 of meningitis and is buried in Arnos Vale Cemetery in Bristol. A statue of him was erected in central Bristol in 1997.

" When Rammohan Roy was born in India, the darkness of a moonless night was reigning. Death was roaming in the skies…When Rammohun Roy awoke and spread his sight on Bengali society it was an abode of the spirits…At that time, only the ghost of the living ancient Hindu religion held its sway in the funeral grounds. It had no life, it had no vitality, it only had its strictures and threats…In the days of Rammohan, the tattered foundations of Hindu society, with thousands of holes filled with creatures, progressively growing from generation to generation, was bulging with the impact of age and immobility. Rammohan proceeded fearlessly to free society from the serpent-like bondage … Today even our youngsters will kick such dead serpents with a smile on the face, we will laugh them off as common field snakes without any poison – we have forgotten their enormous power, the magnetic attraction of their eyes and the dangerous embrace of their long tails. …When the Bengali students came out of Hindu College, imbibed with the new English education, a certain type of intoxication grew in them… They took the blood that oozed from the deeply injured heart of the ancient Hindu society and used it as a plaything… To them nothing was good or sacred in Hindu society, they did not even have that respect for ancient Hindu society that they should pick up its skeletons, scattered hither and thither, cremate them properly and return home with a heavy heart after sprinkling the ashes in the waters of the Ganges… Considering the conditions of the period, they cannot be blamed that much…But the man who scotched the first flames of revolutionary fire in the present Bengali society, that Rammohan Roy was not intoxicated in that manner. He observed everything, good and bad, patiently. He enlightened the dark Hindu society of those days, but did not light the all-consuming fires of cremation. That was the greatness of Rammohun Roy." –Rabindranath Tagore

" The period in which the Raja was born and grew up was, perhaps, the darkest age in modern Indian history. An old society and polity had crumbled down, and a new one had not yet been built in its place. Devastation reigned in the land. All vital limbs of society were paralysed; religious institutions and schools, village and home, agriculture, industry and trade, law and administration, all were in a chaotic condition. An all-round reconstitution and renovation were necessary for the continued existence of social life and order. But what was to be the principle for organisation? For there were three bodies of culture, three bodies of civilisations, which were in conflict, - the Hindu, the Moslem, and the Christian or Occidental; and the question was, - how to find a rapport, of concord, of unity, amongst these heterogeneous, hostile and warring forces. The origin of Modern India lay there. The Raja by his finding of this point of concord and convergence became the Father and Patriarch of Modern India, an India with a composite nationality and a synthetic civilisation; and by the lines of convergence he laid down, as well by the type of personality he developed in and through his own experiences, he pointed the way to the solution of the larger problem of international culture and civilisation in human history, and became a precursor, an archetype, a prophet of coming Humanity." – Brajendra Nath Seal

"Rammohun Roy was to my mind a truly great man, a man who did a truly great work, and whose name, if it is right to prophesy, will be remembered for ever, with some of his fellow-labourers and followers, as one of the great benefactors of mankind…And, therefore, whatever narrow-minded critics may say, I say once more that Rammohun Roy was an unselfish, an honest, a bold man, - a great man in the highest sense of the word." – Friedrich Max Muller

Lokmanya Tilak

Initially the personality and philosophy of Lokmanya Tilak is presented. It is followed by a note on Educational Background in India in the 19th century. Unless this background is known the importance of efforts made by Lokmanya Tilak and his colleagues would not be understood. When Tilak established educational institutions he set a pattern of management of such institutions. The conflict, political versus social reforms is presented next. Lokmanya Tilak as a propounder of nationalistic and political education has been amply described in the next four essays. Tilak was a political leader, a researcher and a scholar too. His work on Indology and Maratha History finds place in the next two essays. Tilak's views on women's education and the medium of instruction are presented in the last two essays.

Lokmanya B.G. Tilak realised that the loss of freedom was not merely a loss of political power but a total destruction of the indigeneous culture, religion and language.

Therefore, to awaken the people towards the goal of freedom became his lifetime pursuit. He was associated with Vishnushastri Chiplunkar in establishing the New English School (1880) to impart National Education in place of British imperialist education to students.

According to him the content of education was an urge for freedom and to prepare the people to fight for the same.

With the help of educational institutions, religious platforms (e.g. Ganeshotsav) and newspapers (Kesari and Maratha) which is quite significant he put an end to mere propagation of knowledge and started an era of actual activities.

His mission of national education and social organisation which he carried with unflinching faith and spiritual strength was the outcome of the life-foundations he secured from the 'Bhagvadgita'. One can know his personality and life philosophy best through his classical book 'Gita-Rahasya'. His views on life and duty rested on the Eternal Law and theistic faith. While propagating, in practical life, the 'Desireless Life of Action' he believed in final emancipationas the ultimate aim of man's action. As his was an integrated personality, this philosophy of life was reflected in his social life which became the philosophy of nationalism which Mahatma Gandhi further strengthened.

Education in India During the period 1800 AD to 1880 AD

To understand Lokmanya Tilak's contribution to philosophy and practice of Education in India, it is necessary to acquaint ourselves with the situation that existed in India during the 19th century.

In the early years of 19th century Tatya Pantoji (one teacher) schools existed in most villages. Reading, writing, arithmetic were the subjects taught. This education was enough to meet everyday needs. Fees were also meagre. However, this education was not open to women and to the scheduled castes. 'Modi' a script similar to Devnagari was also taught.

In 1793 while granting license to the East India Company, the Board of Directors told the company that they would send skilled and suitable persons to India to serve as school masters. Missionaries would also be encouraged. The Board of Directors wanted to educate the natives of India.

In 1813 the British Government asked the Governor General to reserve one lakh rupees every year for the revival and improvement of literature in India and for the introduction and promotion of knowledge of science among the people of India.

Missionaries came to India in the 18th century following the foot-steps of the traders and undertook the responsibility of educating Indians. However, their main aim was to convert the poor and the needy to Christianity. As this was quite clear to upper class Hindus they did not send their children to missionary schools.

In the then Bombay Province, Mount Stuart Elphinstone was appointed as Governor from 1819 to 1827. He had deep interest in the education of Indians. He was in favour of the mother tongue as the medium of instruction. He was of the view that it was the Government's responsibility to educate the people. Due to his encouragement many books were translated into Marathi. English-Marathi Dictionaries were also published.

Educational activity was quite prominent in Mumbai. In 1827 the Bombay Native Education Society was formed. In 1854 a Board of Education was constituted. In 1855, a separate department of Education was also established. During this time there was awakening among the Indians also. Mahatma Phule established his school in 1851-52.

With Wood's Despatch and Macaulay's minutes the upper strata of the society accepted the importance of Western Education with English as the medium. The conflict, Eastern (or Oriental) versus Western was buried and a New Era of Western Education was started by Govt. schools and colleges as also by missionary schools and colleges.

Payments to teachers were low and the percentage of girls and women in schools and colleges was also low.

Tilak, Agarkar and their colleagues started their work against this background.

Lokmanya Tilak on Nature and Management of Educational Institutions

Though education occupied only a few years of his public and social life, his contribution in this field is unique in the sense that the pattern of education he selected and the management style he professed was emulated in the 20th century.

Lokmanya Tilak's contribution to Education is reflected through four important events. They are (i) The establishment of the New English School, Pune, (ii) The formation of the Deccan Education Society, Pune, (iii) The establishment of the Fergusson College, Pune and (iv) Tilak's resignation of life-membership of the Deccan Education society.

The University of Bombay (Mumbai) was established in 1857. The middle class persons and those who had some influence in the Society had accepted Western Education with English as the medium. Tilak, Agarkar and their colleagues had no alternative but to start a school imparting that education. However, there was a vast difference between leaders like Tilak conducting schools and missionaries doing it. Opening of the school proved a new era in the educational and public life of Maharashtra. Following this example many people opened schools in their own towns. People were convinced that Education was a tool towards achieving freedom of the country.

The management style that Tilak and his colleagues formulated while writing the constitution of the Deccan Education Society must be considered unique. They introduced the concept of institutions managed by teachers themselves _ a new concept of Life-Members. This style spread all over western Maharashtra and inspite of all its weaknesses noticed while practicing, it stood the test of time. Life-Membership stood for Service, Sacrifice and Integrity. When there arose differences between Life-Members and particularly between Tilak and Agarkar on how to define sacrifice, Tilak resigned his Life-Membership of the Deccan Education Society.

Fergusson College, Pune, was started on 2nd January 1885. This college was granted affiliation by the University of Bombay. Reputation of this college spread all over the country in later years.

Lala Lajpat Rai, Shrinivas Shastri, Pandit Madan Mohan Malviya and many others have recorded their appreciation of the work done by Tilak and his colleagues.

Educational Thoughts of Tilak's Contemporary : Gopal Ganesh Agarkar

Tilaks' contemporary, Gopal Ganesh Agarkar, was a great reformer of the 19th century. He was also the dearest friend of Tilak. He was one of those great personalities of the time who dedicated themselves to the field of education. These people were influenced by the new rationality of western thought. They believed in the social reforms and boldly advocated the same. Agarkar started his newspaper 'Sudharak' to propagate his new social reforms. His task was very difficult.

Taking into account the conditions then existing, which were mostly dominated by religious sanctions, one can imagine how difficult was the challenge before Agarkar to stand against the existing social order. He had to face humiliation, anger and short-sightedness of people. Many people threatened him with dire consequences but he withstood all such pressures.

As a contemporary social reformer of Tilak, Agarkar repeatedly stressed on people's education through 'Sudharak'. His educational outlook was different from others and was based on a strong belief on rational thinking, scientific approach, individual freedom and moral values.

His main priority was education for all without discrimination of caste, sex, economic strata, etc. He was a true visionary to envisage hundred years ago the difficulties of women's education.

We Can Summarise His Views on Education as Follows :

1. All kinds of reforms though classified as social, political, behavioural and ranked as first, second, etc. for the sake of thinking, are all of equal importance and are interdependent.
2. Necessity of education for all the people in the society to eradicate ignorance and untouchability.
3. Compulsory and primary education should be the responsibility of the Government.
4. Girls' education should be given more importance and equal opportunities must be given to them to learn the same subjects with boys in co-educational system.

Lokmanya Tilak : The pioneer of the Concept of National Education

Lokmanya Bal Gangadhar Tilak was one of the architects of our freedom. He taught people that Swarajya was their birth-right. His teachings had a great impact on the minds of the people because he practiced what he preached. Like many of our political leaders Tilak started his public life as a teacher because he regarded education as a powerful instrument for moulding the impressionable minds of students and for bringing about a change in our society's outlook on life.

Tilak and his colleague Agarkar were idealists who were restless owing to the degenerated conditions of our country. They were greatly impressed by the efforts made by Justice Mahadeo Govind Ranade for enlightening the society. They were also impressed by the writings of the young, powerful writer, Vishnu Shastri Chiplunkar. Agarkar and Tilak were not content with their work as teachers. They decided to undertake the work of educating the people and launched two news papers Kesari and Mahratta. They gave an institutional base to their educational effort by founding educational institutions.

Tilak and his colleagues came from families with a tradition of learning. They perhaps did not realise the aspirations of the masses and put forth the elitist point of view which unintentionally supported social inequality and gave special advantages to the so called higher caste communities.

After leaving the Deccan Education society and Fergusson College Tilak concentrated on Kesari and Mahratha. He mainly appealed to the intellect of the readers rather than striving to arouse their emotions. Tilak taught the people to be conscious of their rights. Through his writings Tilak reached a wide section of the society. As an editor he became an educator.

Tilak wanted to involve the generality of the people in social and political activities. He thought of starting public festivals which would become instruments of public education. He advocated that Ganapati Festival should be celebrated publicly. It should include lectures by eminent persons on different subjects followed by group discussions and group singing. Tilak also launched the Shivaji Festival as Shivaji was a National Hero and a perennial source of inspiration for patriotism. Tilak felt that English education was responsible for destroying the essential bond of relationship between learning, ethics, religious faith and family life. However, he considered Education as an instrument of National Awakening.

Tilak had sown the seeds of the ideal of National Education. After Tilak's demise Gandhiji laid great emphasis on National Education. In Tilak Maharashtra Vidyapeeth in Pune teachers like Acharya Bhagwat, Acharya Jawadekar and others while delivering inspiring lectures on politics, history and literature inculcated in students a national outlook. Almost all of them participated in the Satyagraha movement in 1930. Thus the seed sown by Tilak had grown into a huge banyan tree. In the real sense of the term he was a pioneer of National Education.

Lokmanya Tilak : Propounder of Nationalistic Education

It is the purpose of Education to till the soil of the existing social order and to plant the seeds from which new farms and new social orders grow. When the soil is recalcitrant and unyielding, resistant to the natural forces for change, more radical forces emerge. This applies to the situation that existed in India prior to the Tilak Era. Lokmanya Tilak had to work hard to instil a new spirit in the Indian Society and make the masses understand the importance of freedom. He propounded Nationalistic Education as a path towards Independence or Swaraj.

Nationalism is defined as a state of the mind in which the individual feels that every one owes his supreme secular loyalty to the nation or the state. Nationalistic education instils among the masses the spirit of Nationalism. Tilak's work has to be viewed in the light of these assumptions.

India as a nation is not only a geographical concept or a political entity. It is supposed to be the collective soul of all Indians. In history though India was not geographically a nation there were strong feelings of Nationalism among the Indians even in historical times. As the entire country came under British power and as communication developed in the continent a new wave of Nationalism arose among the Indians.

When Tilak and his colleague Agarkar got their graduation they came to the conclusion that spread of Education was the only method for the country's uplift. Education of the rising generations by the Indians was according to them a sure way to inculcate a National feeling among the youngsters. Keeping this in mind Tilak and his colleagues established the New English School, the Deccan Education Society and the Fergusson College.

Tilak's educational thoughts, especially about nationalistic education evolved out of his own personality as a committed Indian. In his late life Tilak evolved as a public leader. However, it must be noted that the first chapter of his public career opened in the field of education. He had an indomitable spirit, tenacity of purpose and strong determination.

Tilak propounded his concept of Nationalistic Education through the institutions he opened, through his news papers Kesari and Mahratta to which he contributed extensively and through his public speeches.

He was so successful in his mission that he is known as the 'Father of the Indian unrest.'

Political Education by Lokmanya Tilak: Every political system operates in a given society which has its own political culture distinct from that of other countries. The political system, for its maintenance and growth, requires certain knowledge, skills and values on the part of the people. The process of political education gives knowledge, tries to create skills and inculcates values congenial for the working of the political system. As the society consists of divergent groups, the dissatisfied sections in the society can be given political education for the overthrow of the political system. If this attempt gets necessary support from the people there is change in the government and in the political system. The main objective of Lokmanya Tilak was to impart political education to Indian masses and to overthrow the British Rule by peaceful means.

Political Education needs knowledge of the existing society, of the new society that the nation desires to create, the existing government of the country and the basic problems of the country. Skills involve skills of understanding, problem solving, working in groups, skills to understand conflicts and skills to express oneself adequately. Political education also involves education of values some of which are fundamental and absolute.

The Britishers had evolved the policy of divide and rule in India. The British always argued that the Indians did not deserve self-government. Their objective of education was to create a class of people who would act as interpreters between the rulers and the ruled. The British preached superiority of the British over India. Tilak wanted to undo what had happened and therefore undertook a crusade of political education.

Tilak educated masses through social functions like Ganpati Festival and Shivaji Festival, through his writings in Kesari and Mahratta and through his lectures. He became a hero of the masses as he stood like a rock even when persecuted by the British for over two decades. Tilak attempted to promote the concepts of Swadeshi and boycott of foreign goods. He also introduced the concept of National Education. This 'Trisutri' or three devices along with festivals, writings and lectures were his tools of Political Education. Though the British tried to create a wedge between the Hindus and the Muslims, Tilak invited the Muslims to join him in his efforts to gain swaraj. He was mostly successful.

In this way Tilak became the first mass leader of India. He became popular among all castes and religions, equally among the educated and the uneducated as also among the rich and the poor. Tilak was thus the first political educator in India who also got international accredition for the cause for which he fought.

People's Education Through the Editorials of 'Kesari': Lokmanya Tilak was a leader of the down-trodden. He was in a sense a mass-educator. Naturally he used 'Kesari' a newspaper in Marathi as a medium for educating the masses. His editorials in 'Kesari' had a lasting impact on the masses on the subjects like national-education, people's rights, unrest towards British Rule, inculcation of a new idea, i.e. 'Swaraj' as a birth right of every Indian, a mass movement for 'Swadeshi', pride for what is indigenous, etc.

His Indirect Contribution to History: He encouraged other historians to write in Kesari. He gave opportunities to many scholars to publish their researches on controversial issues, in Kesari or Mahratta.

Many people had raised objection against the Shivaji Movement. Tilak stressed that Shivaji is remembered for his nation-building activities and Shivaji gave us the idea that Swarajya was a fundamental right. Biographies of great leaders like Shivaji are sources of inspiration to the younger generation. The purpose of the Shivaji festival was promotion of patriotism and nationalism among the people of this country.

He said, "Research cannot be done by all. It is the privilage of a chosen few. Research should be done for the sake of research only and not for its results or effects. Every activity should not be motivated by material gains. Man works both for his maintenance as well as for satisfying his urge for pure knowledge. It depends on the nature of man, to which he should give priority." One can hardly explain to a common man the ecstasy one gets through research resulting in advancement of knowledge. Tilak knew how to reconcile historical research for political purpose as well as for the advancement of knowledge. His contribution to historical research deserves the attention of scholars and political leaders of modern times.

Lokmanya Bal Gangadhar Tilak's Views on Women's Education: As we enter the new century, it is an appropriate time to look back and take a review of the historical changes that this country has brought in the field of education and especially women's education. Women's education cannot be thought of without its relationship with the other social aspects of women's life such as child marriage, widow remarriage, women's position in the society. In Tilak's time his contemporaries like Gopal Ganesh Agarkar, Mahatma Phule, Vitthal Ramji Shinde, Maharshi Dhondo Keshav Karve, held a different view. It will be interesting to study the reasons for such a different view.

Tilak has written editorials in his newspapers Kesari and Mahratta. Firstly he objected to the curriculum of the girls school because it was just like that of British schools. The cultural and social background of Indian girls is totally different from that of British girls, and so should be the curricula. Secondly he objected the full day school timing i.e. six hours a day for the girls. If necessary they should attend the half-day school, after finishing their duties in the house which according to him was their first moral obligation. His third objection for women's education was that the education given to them would help them become clerks in the British offices. If they start working in these offices they will neglect their first duty which is household work. This is most disgusting and hence should be abandoned. His fourth objection was against hasty reforms. Educating few women would not help the society, but educating the common masses would only help. Spending money hastily on women's education would be a waste if very few women get education.

Tilak in one of his speeches mentioned that English being a strange language one cannot learn it fast. The grammar of English is different than that of vernacular. Learning this language becomes a burden on the learner, and expressing thoughts in that language becomes more difficult. The time spent in learning English is a waste. If the knowledge is imparted through mother-tongue, it can be learnt faster. Thus time and energy can be saved. Therefore, vernacular should be the language of instruction. The knowledge, in other European languages was translated in English and so English became a rich language. We too, can enrich our own language. The educated people from our own land should not forget this and try to enrich vernacular. As saints contributed to enrich our language so should the learned people.

The education given to our children through English, will help them to become clerks in the British offices. This will be harmful to the progress of our society. When University will place vernacular at a higher place in the curricula and judiciary, administration markets start using vernacular for communication then only the society will progress.

□□□

9

MODERN PHILOSOPHERS

Osho

The story of Osho—master, mystic, madman Trying to define Osho is like trying to imprison a rainbow or catch a cloud that's floating through your room. Like sand, he slips through your fingers: like a sparkling drops of dew, his magic vanishes with the rising sun of definition. Samuel Johnson, in his *Preface to Shakespeare*, says that Shakespeare is not a pretty garden, but a great forest, a forest that is wild and wonderful.So is Osho. And it is his wildness that is his greatest flavor. A trip with Osho is no picnic for socialites or fingernail-clicking namby-pambies. Osho's sweep is as vast, as majestic, as diverse, as unpredictable as life itself.There is majesty here, but danger too. Far past the comfortable backwaters of respectability, morality, ethics and so-called sanity, we find ourselves on the high seas of life, with no buffers between us and the elemental powers of the universe and our captain, far from sheltering and consoling us in this our first assay into the world of the uncharted, pushes us into the danger. He removes our props, throws away our crutches, destroys our conditioning, tramples on our most cherished beliefs and abandons us, naked and unprotected, to the gigantic waters of the cosmos. Most of us are too scared to even allow him to take us thus far, and run away, often without even trying to find out what he is really saying. But even amongst those of us who walk some steps with him and encounter the utter nakedness of floating on the high seas of life, almost none of us can deal with the feeling of being unprotected, unguarded, unprepared. We are terrified and rush back, often swearing never to go again. But there is something haunting about the experience. Almost against our will, we wander into this boundless ocean again. An ocean called meditation, where we turn inward to face ourselves. Despite the confusion. Despite the fear. Despite the darkness, the absence of the comfortable, the familiar. Slowly, hesitantly we enter this space. Where, with William Blake, we see "the worlds in a grain of sand, heaven in a wildflower, hold infinity in the eternity in an hour". This is the oceanic world. The world that is Osho...

"BUDDHAM SHARANAM GACCHAMI" Somebody anonymous, somebody who is more a nobody than a somebody; a man who has died long ago as a separate entity. Where does one begin? At the beginning? One wonders. Because this story is as much about time and space as it is about here and now, about eternity. Because this is the story of one who was never born, never died. One who visited plant Earth briefly, and left his gentle imprints on the measureless sands of time. As a child growing up in the grace and openness of total freedom a gift from his wonderful grandparents. As a young adult, exposing the stupidity of a bankrupt educational system with the scalpel of an incisive mind and penetrating insight. As *Acharya* Rajneesh, roaming the vastness of India to encounter people, to enchant them with his incomparable oratory, to help them transform themselves with the Dynamic Meditation he devised for our troubled age. As *Bhagwan Shree* Rajneesh, immobile in Pune, western India, the wanderer in him dissolving into the sage, creating a vibrant "Buddha field', a crucible of the spirit where countless seekers absorbed the energy and used the techniques made available to trigger the process of self-discovery.As *Bhagwan Shree* Rajneesh in the Oregon days, when he and his *sannyasins* transformed the face of a timeless desert into a green and beautiful land before (according to *Bhagwan Shree Rajneesh Poisoned by Ronald Reagan's America* by Sue Appleton) a bigoted government threatened by his extraordinary insight and unparalleled courage, used every foul means at its disposal to poison him with long-acting thallium, depart him and prevent some dozen world governments from entertaining him, in the ugliest way possible. As *Bhagwan Shree* Rajneesh of the World Tour days, when nation after nation passed beneath him like the fleecy clouds beneath the wings of a plane, and his fiery discourses in Greece, in Uruguay startled a shell-shocked world into awareness. As *Bhagwan Shree* Rajneesh, in the days when he returned to his commune in Pune, his discourses were initially as fiery as those he delivered during the Oregon and World Tour days. But they soon mellowed into the most deeply meditative ones he had ever given—they veered towards Zen and, for the first time, began to include group meditation.

A couple of years after he came back home, the *Acharya* who was *Bhagwan* became Osho, the oceanic one. And that's all there was, because soon the thulium administered to him by the US authorities when he had been arrested without a warrant and spirited away to parts unknown (documented by Appleton), began to take effect. His failing health started affecting his work. His regular discourses were interrupted repeatedly. Eventually, he surrendered to the effects of the poisoning; a life rudely cut short, when the world could have benefited from fresh insights and his unique wisdom for many more decades. These details are insignificant trivia. Like looking at the grooves on a gramophone record reveals no mysteries about the music they contain, these biographical benchmarks say little about the spirit, the genius and the effortless ebullience that is Osho. The tense I use is important. His leaving the body has had little effect on his living presence. Whether in the Osho

Commune International in Pune, at other communes and meditation centers around the world or wherever his *sannyasins* and lovers gather in his name, hear him, read him, or talk about him, Osho is tangibly present. What he called the Buddhafield in Pune is the very matrix of the energy field he created around him and has a very powerful and immediately tangible presence even today. His is a presence that pervades the world.Every day, new people take their first hesitant steps towards him and slowly slip into the silence of his presence, the fathomless depths of his insight, the healing aura that emanates around him. Like most enlightened masters, Osho was continuously misunderstood by small minds soaked in prejudice, and fell prey to the gratuitous violence of man—like Jesus and Socrates before him. His truth was too incandescent, his candor too blinding for men who had lived in darkness all their lives. He held the mirror up to us, to reflect our follies, our prejudices, and our superstitions; our implacable and adamantine conditioning that holds us prisoner all our lives. But we were too fainthearted to look. And a vast majority of those who looked, looked briefly, were terrified of their reflection and railed against the mirror.

It is far easier to break the mirror and not have to see our tortured reflection. To look, accept, admit and begin the arduous journey of transforming oneself is difficult, well-nigh impossible. When the mirror that was Jesus reflected us, we crucified him. When the mirror that was Socrates reflected us, we poisoned him. A similar fate was reserved for Osho. We human beings certainly have a strange way of saying 'thank you' to the enlightened beings that make their effulgence available to us. What did Osho do? He told us to give up our phony adherence to an ossified past that haunted us, and live in the moment, use the alchemy of meditation to transform ourselves—to become Christs, not Christians; Krishnas, not Hindus; Buddhas, not Buddhist. His crime was that he spoke the truth.He dared to tell us that sex was the first rung of the ladder to super consciousness; that unless we accept the rung and use it as a stepping stone, we would be stuck forever—the very energy that is sex is transmuted into super consciousness. We continued to sweep sex under the carpet or indulge in it, and called him a Sex Guru. He dared to expose the deep nexus between priests and politicians that has kept humanity enslaved from beginningless time. He showed us how the priest uses the carrot of heaven and the stick of hell in the matrix of a psychologically nonexistent past and future, how he creates guilt and fear and then provides panaceas for it. How the politician divides us into fragments and then speaks of uniting us; creates hatred and ill will, then talks about universal brotherhood; creates and espouses the divisiveness of nation states and then gives it a sanctity that can demand sacrifice. We continued to run like frightened rabbits into the warrens of a bankrupt society and organized religion, and called Osho dangerous, the antichrist, the unbeliever.

Prophets are often ahead of their time, but Osho was centuries ahead of his. When his majestic vision showed us a brave new world, we hung on to the apron strings of society and church, tradition and conditioning, and huddled deeper in the cavern of our own little selves. In his masterpiece, *A Marriage of Heaven and Hell*, William Blake says that if the doors of perception were cleansed, everything would appear to man *as it is*, infinite... But man has closed himself up till he sees all things through the narrow chinks of his cavern. But it is never too late. The italics in "as it is" are mine. That's what Osho said again and again all his life, but our conditioning didn't let us hear. He said we were all Buddhas, gods in exile; that God was not separate from existence, but immanent in existence-only God is an all is God. Osho may not be in the body, but his spirit is ever present, ever available, his Buddha field of transformation a tangible reality. Never born, never died—just visited

Planet Earth. He can still catalyze an unprecedented change in your life today. All you have to do is visit his Buddhafield in Pune, read a book, listen to a tape. And watch the magic unfold within you.

DHAMMAM SHARANAM GACCHAMI".Life is not a problem to be solved, it is a mystery to be lived..." Osho's basic message is no message. His basic teaching is no teaching. He doggedly opposed the creation or following of philosophies and ideologies. Although he spoke on more scriptures than anyone else in the history of human consciousness—and with the greatest authority on subjects and people ranging from subatomic physics to Vincent Van Gogh, Karl Marx and Freud—he warned against following scriptures and underlined the great danger of knowledge; he repeatedly emphasized the importance of one's own experience and the danger of imitating others, no matter how enlightened.This applied as much to him as to anyone else. Although he emphasized the need for a guru, he stressed that it was not the truth, but a necessary evil. That, after crossing the river, the raft becomes a hindrance if still carried. That, when more gross and mundane obstacles have been overcome, the guru becomes the obstacle and has to transcend. He spoke on almost every mystic this world has had the privilege to witness with such insight that they sprang to life; their presence became a living reality while his enlightenment breathed life into them again. And yet he offended more people by criticizing messiahs and prophets than anyone in the history of humanity. He did this with the professed intention of what he used to love calling 'hammering'—a process of deep reconditioning by challenging and uprooting the deepest and most cherished beliefs of a person.

It is only a wholly de-conditioned person, he said, who has the innocence, the fluidity, the effervescence to dissolve into the totality, without leaving a trace. One of Osho's most significant contributions to the seeker of this age, and ages to come, is the breathtaking clarity he brought to the critical, perhaps preeminent, importance of the here-now. Osho was controversial and reviled purely because he lived this insight—he didn't just talk about it. He repeatedly said that there is only one world, one space, the here and now. That it is journeying from one place to another, not this so-called phenomenal world that is the real *sansar*. That being here-now, not journeying at all, is the end of the *sansar*. That ethics and morality and respectability are false coins. That people who give you goals—no matter how laudable—are your enemies, because goals create the future, and trigger the debilitating mechanism of desire. That people who tell you how to become and what to become are the poisoners. Such a person cannot draw lines between the good and the bad, the sacred and the profane. Osho always said that divinity is not separate from existence it is immanent in existence. As Blake said, all that lives is holy. He also continuously emphasized that the divine is not separable from existence, like a painter from his painting.

It is integrally connected with existence, like a dancer with his dance. Which is why he used to say again and again that, if there is such a thing as the divine, it is not a noun but a verb; not a persona but a process; not a creator, but creativity. A person like him has eyes to see. He can see that there is only one energy. It can be blocked or freed. The energy freed from the repression of sex, or indulgence in it can become the ladder to super consciousness. He can see that energy always flows towards the source of the greatest joy—when the window of meditation opens, the energy that was sex, was attachment, was greed, gets absorbed and subsumed by it. That prejudice, no matter how ancient and hallowed, must be destroyed if one wants the authenticity that is the first prerequisite to the unfolding of our hidden splendor. Osho also revealed a great secret to us—do not fight with darkness. It is nonexistent and therefore impervious to struggle. He used to say that when we want light in a room, we do not push the darkness out; we merely light a candle. And the darkness of a million years has no resistance; in just a moment a small candle dispels it. Osho likens all our negative qualities to darkness, and calls all ethics and morality an effort to fight with darkness and therefore doomed to fail. The nature of all ignorance and all unconsciousness is the nature of darkness. The only way to dispel it is by bringing light in—the light of love, the light of meditation. Another very critical contribution from Osho was a strong insistence on change in daily life. He repeatedly said that one should renounce the mind, not the world; that those who renounce the world are nothing but escapists. A monk renounces the world, the crowd for 30 years, but he still remains a Hindu, a Christian, a Buddhist. And to be a Hindu, a Christian, a Buddhist is to be part of a crowd.

The individual can be a Christ, but not a Christian. This is reflected in his notion of *sannyas*, which he called Neo *sannyas*. It is revolutionary. There are no vows. No bindings. The only vow an Osho *sannyasin* takes is a commitment to himself, to meditate. Osho always said that his *sannyasin* is truly like a lotus flower. She lives in the world, but the world does not live in her, just like the lotus rises above the dirty water of the lake it grows in.Osho revolutionized meditation as we know it. He contributed scores of new and innovative meditations to the world. Osho felt that, in the days of old, sitting meditations were beneficial to large numbers of people, because life was less stressful, living simpler. In modern conditions, the mind and body rebel against it. And any force is unnatural and harmful. It leads to what Osho called a state of inner civil war, which dissipates energy and is very destructive. Osho's dynamic meditations begin with activity like jumping or dancing. After some time, when the body is naturally tired and the mind calmed by physical activity, the mediator sits, or lies down, to meditate—in consonance with nature, not struggling against it.

Osho brought laughter back to religion. He used to be very fond of saying that guilt is a state of sickness, that seriousness is pathological. Far from the somnolent and lethargic atmosphere one still associates with religion, his commune and his discourses were distinguished with laughter, ebullience and vivacity. Words like joy, celebration, fun and festivity are key words—not in terms of significance, but in their actualization in the here-now he inhabited. No one used as wide a variety of jokes and anecdotes with consummate skill as Osho, to slip skillfully past conditioning and break down barriers. His discourses, whether on masters and mystics or responses to daily life questions, were filled with vitality and energy—they throbbed with intensity and passion. Osho's discourses, meditations, and the energy he shared with his *sannyasins* and lovers did more than give a delightful freshness, an enticing now-ness to the quest for self-awareness. His words and his life exemplified another unique ability: the ability to simplify, deconstruct and explain some of the most nagging mundane problems that beset humanity. He was also without doubt a psychotherapist par excellence, and took psychotherapy beyond its own frontiers—helping a person adapt to a neurotic society—into the vistas of meditation, freedom from all conditioning, and enlightenment. To me, Osho represents the omega point of the entire spiritual history of mankind. He is the first enlightened master who had the environment and ability to assimilate the million facets of our spiritual heritage into a laser beam-like precision, without losing the flavors, the richness, and the diversity. In a world that had become a global village, Osho had the ability to soak himself in all the religious, social, cultural and intellectual traditions of mankind. And he had the inner depth, breadth, expanse and insight to transmute them into a vision both uniquely his own and man's heritage since eternal time. Some centuries from now, when a more placid humanity views Osho in tranquility, they will see him as he is, always was and will be: a world in a grain of sand. For a grain of sand hides the subatomic dance. And it is a grain of sand that makes our spectacular universe a living reality.

SANGHAM SHARANAM GACCHAMI"I want to sabotage that stupid idea of an ashram: that it should be dead, people should be inactive, dull, uncreative, against life, against love..." One of the most famous tourist hand marks in India is no monument weathered by age, or the ruins of a city made famous by some bloodthirsty army or empire. It is the Osho Commune International in Pune. Located in Koregaon Park, the Osho Commune attracts thousands of *sannyasins* and lovers of Osho who make up a sizeable portion of the floating population in the city. Who are these people? Why are they attracted to Osho? Why are they so controversial? And what exactly happens in the Osho Commune to make people flock there? One of the most significant aspects of Osho's vision was his notion of the New Man, who would be integrated and total. Such a man would be beyond belonging to a religion, a nation, and a caste, even the gender that the phrase implies.

The New Man would also be free of the schism between the inner and the outer. He would, in Osho's words, be Zorba the Buddha. Combining the deep meditative vote of the Buddha with the passion and intensity of Zorba the Greek, he would be a true individual, free of social programming—centered and equanimous, yet full of zest and love of life, with great inner and outer richness.The Osho Commune is a concrete example of this synthesis, this holistic view of life. William Blake says that as the caterpillar lays its eggs on the fairest leaves, so the priest lays his curse on the fairest joys. The commune is a celebration of freedom from the schism between body and spirit, artificially created and exploited by priests and politicians. The New Man says yes to both and no to nothing. Thus, he is wholeness, a totality not torn apart by conflict. And in him, the seed of a new future beings to take birth. The commune is an exemplification of communism with a spiritual base. It is a gathering of individuals, not a crowd of people. Individuals coming from the space of freedom to experiment with freedom. This creates what Osho called a Buddha field, a place where individual seekers can gather with other individual seekers in the voyage of self-discovery. In the commune, distinctions are dissolved. Identities and conditioning slip away.

Religion and race, nationality and caste, gender and status, color and creed disappear in the oneness of meditation and inner exploration. Everyone functions simply as a human being, growing and evolving into the divinity that is their true nature and birthright. The commune is a model, a family of the future. A relationship within the existing family structure is not possible because it is a relationship of mutual possessing and being possessed, with love and freedom sacrifice at the altar of dependence and expectation. People become roles and functions, and relating becomes impossibility. This is a new family structure, free of possessiveness and expectation, based on interdependence, on interconnectedness. The growth of the commune is the growth of individuals, and the growth of individuals is the growth of the commune. This is what makes the difference.

The commune is an authentic space, not a conditioned reflex. One of the most significant aspects of this dissolution is the dissolving of gender. For the first time perhaps in the history of humanity, women can down the yoke of subservience and be truly creative. Osho used to often say that, with the suppression of women, 50 per cent of the world's creativity has not been allowed to blossom. If this hadn't happened, our world would have been a different place. In the commune, a woman can do anything fcrm welding to Japanese gardening, free of role expectations and gender stereotyping.

Being a part of the commune also involves a change in gestalt. We normally look for what we can get, not what we can give. In the commune, two primary principles operate. Contribution. And meditation. Both help the individual and the commune, but in different ways. Contribution allows the seeker to give her time, her energy to the needs of the commune—but this benefits her immensely too because it has a strong therapeutic element. In the easy confluence of the *sangha*, it is easier to empathize, to drop the ego, to surrender totally. Meditation helps the seeker in her own development. But the atmosphere, the energy of meditation permeates the space and contributes in a large measure to the Buddhafield, which nourishes the entire community.

The commune is a laboratory of the spirit, free of respectability, so-called morality and ethics, of meaningless outdated taboos that still torment an unconscious humanity. In the commune, the seeker has access to a wide variety of meditations as well as an incredible range of group therapies to unburden guilt, dissolve age-old fears, obsessions and prejudices. No one was a greater lover of all that is aesthetic than Osho and his Commune reflects it, reveals it, and resonates with it. Interwoven with vegetation and peopled with creatures coexisting with seekers in their natural habitat, the commune is an aesthete's paradise. The Buddha Hall, which can seat as many as 10,000 people used to play witness to Osho's discourses. Today, it is the main center of meditation through the day, followed by an evening celebration called the White Robe Brotherhood, in which seekers, Osho lovers and sannyasins dress in white robes and gather to sway to live music, dance and submerge themselves in the here-now, before they see a video recording of an Osho discourse. Apart from the aesthetic environs, the commune is a nerve center of creative activity. Theater, music, dance, painting are woven into the life of the commune. There is tennis, called zennis, swimming, and the martial arts the commune is buzzing with activity. Everywhere, energies are creating, whether in the silence of meditation or the music of relating and creativity. The commune is perhaps one of the very few places in the world, which are truly modern. Here, the anachronistic baggage of the past that we tend to carry with us is truly forsaken, as are the taboos and conditioning we have too long taken to be ourselves. It is a center of freedom and love, where the individual vibrates in harmony with other individuals and the Buddhafield they create around each other. In an easy and fluid atmosphere, seekers contribute, meditate and grow, in the grace of individuality—in the beautiful environment of their *sangha*.

Rajneesh Chandra Mohan Jain (December 11, 1931-January 19, 1990), better known during the 1970s as Bhagwan Shree Rajneesh and later as Osho was an Indian spiritual teacher. He lived in India and the United States and was the spiritual head of the Osho-Rajneesh movement, a controversial new religious movement.

As is customary with spiritual teachers in India, he received several honorifics over his life. He was known as Acharya Rajneesh (*teacher Rajneesh*) during his early years, later Shree Rajneesh and finally Bhagwan Shree Rajneesh.

Osho was known as Acharya Rajneesh (*teacher Rajneesh*) during his early years as a spiritual teacher. In 1971 he asked his disciples to start calling him "Bhagwan Shree Rajneesh." The Sanskrit word *Bhagwan* means "Blessed one" (historically, it is used to refer to a Hindu god, such as Bhagwan Ram or Bhagwan Krishna or to a spiritually awakened being in Mahayana Buddhism). It is also used to denote individuals who possess a great wealth of spiritual knowledge. *Shree* in Sanskrit means "spiritual wealth" and is thus roughly equivalent to the English word "Lord". It derives this meaning from its use as another name Lakshmi, the Hindu goddess of prosperity.

In February 1989, following a request from Swami Harideva, the well known American disciple who had introduced Rajneeshs' work and meditations to the West in 1971, Rajneesh changed his name to "Osho". 'Osho' is an ancient Japanese term that is used to address a spiritual master in certain Zen traditions. The name "Osho" in this context means "The Friend". It fit how Rajneesh wanted to be known by his followers and lovers.

Unsuccesful attempts have been made by a few lawyers to trademark the name "Osho". All legal attempts by the Canadian lawyers to try and "own" the name Osho have met with failure in the courts. The courts have ruled that it was as outrageous as trying to own the name "God" or "Buddha" or "Jesus".

In the Western world, "Orange People" and *Rajneeshees* were popular terms to designate Rajneesh followers, the former because of the colour of their clothes, which were meant to be the colour of the sky at dawn.

Osho's Philosophy: Osho (Rajneesh) claimed that the greatest values in life are (in no specific order) love, meditation and laughter, and that the highest goal of human life was to reach spiritual enlightenment.

He extracted and expounded philosophies from various spiritual sources. He was a prolific speaker both in Hindi and English on various spiritual traditions including those of Buddha, Krishna, Jesus, Socrates, Zen masters, Hassidism, Sufism and many others. He also took pains to ensure no "system of thought" would define him, since no philosophy can fully express the truth. His was more a "philosophy of no philosophy".

An experienced orator, he used his skills to convey his message, but insisted that the only reason he kept on talking was to convince his listeners to start on a path of meditation.

He was often called the "sex guru" after some speeches in the late 1960s on sexuality which scandalized an orthodox society. These were later compiled under the title *From Sex to Superconsciousness*. According to him, "For Tantra everything is holy, nothing is unholy", and all repressive sexual morality was self-defeating, since one could not transcend sex without experiencing it thoroughly and consciously.

Osho on Meditation: Osho had a different view of meditation than the usual one, at least in the Western world. According to him, meditation is a state beyond mind. It is not concentration. It is not about spiritual thoughts; it is a state of thoughtlessness. It is something that can just happen, it is a state that one can be in, it is not something that one can do. But he said that it is very difficult for modern man to just sit and be in meditation, so he devised some active meditation techniques that naturally take one into meditation. These techniques allow a person to unburden by expressing whatever is repressed in him.

Some of these preparatory exercises can also be found in western psychological therapies (i.e. gestalt therapy), such as altered breathing, gibberish, laughing or crying. His most significant meditation techniques are referred to as *Active Meditations*, such as "Dynamic Meditation", "Kundalini Meditation", "Nadabrahma", "Nataraj", and are quite demanding physically.

He also reintroduced several traditional meditation techniques, reducing them to their most minimal expression, stripping them of ritual and tradition, and retaining the most therapeutic parts. He also supports the theory that, given sufficient practi ce, the meditative state can be achieved and maintained while performing everyday tasks. Furthermore, enlightenment is nothing but being continuously in a meditative state.

Childhood and Awakening: Osho was born at Kuchwada, a small village in Raisen District of Madhya Pradesh state in India. At the time, the astrologer predicted that he might die before he was seven years old according to the birth chart. His parents, who were Jains, chose to send him to be with his maternal grandparents until he was seven years old.

Osho said this was a major influence on his growth because his grandmother gave him the utmost freedom and respect. As a consequence, he was left carefree without an imposed education or restrictions.

Osho explains that children, during their first seven years, have their development negatively affected by being forced to learn and having their dignity ignored. He says ideally it should be the opposite. People can learn from children that which they themselves have forgotten. If a child is allowed freedom during his initial years, he will grow in strength and have enough intelligence to decide and to discuss, and can self-educate with minimal guidance.

This, as he puts it, was what happened to him. When he joined the first school, he was able to discuss with and convince his teacher, who was very strict with children. Osho explains that if the child receives respect, he is more obedient to his parents. If the parents ignore the child's individuality, the child would in turn ignore them.

After Osho was seven, he went back to his parents. Osho explains that he received a similar kind of respect from his paternal grandfather who was staying with them. He was able to be very open with his grandfather. His grandfather used to tell him, "I know you are doing the right thing. Everyone may tell you that you are wrong. But nobody knows which situation you are in. Only you can decide in your situation. Do whatsoever you feel is right. I will support you. I love you and respect you as well."

On 21 March 1953, when Osho was 21 years old, he says that he became spiritually enlightened. He dropped all effort and hope and after an intense seven-day process he went out at night to a garden, where he sat under a maulshree tree.

He did manage to finish his studies and during the 1960s he served as philosophy professor at the University of Jabalpur while touring India, lecturing on his philosophy.

The Commune: In 1969 a group of his disciples established a foundation to support his work and allowed him to drop his university job. They settled in an apartment in Mumbai where he gave daily discourses and received visitors. The number and frequency of visitors soon became too much for the place, overflowing the apartment and bothering the neighbours. A much larger apartment was found on the ground floor (so the visitors would not need to use the elevator, a matter of conflict with the former neighbours).

On September 26, 1970 he initiated his first disciple or sannyasin at an outdoor meditation camp, one of the large gatherings where he lectured and guided group meditations.

Still the new and bigger apartment proved insufficient and the climate of Mumbai was very bad for Osho's health, so a new place had to be found. On the 21st anniversary of his enlightenment a caravan of cars departed from the Mumbai apartment to the newly purchased property in Koregaon

Park, in the city of Pune, a four hour trip from Mumbai. Pune had been the secondary residence of many wealthy families from Mumbai because of the cooler climate (Mumbai lies in a coastal wetland, hot and damp, Pune is inland and much higher so it is drier and cooler).

The two adjoining houses and 6 acres of land had known better times but in little time the nucleus of an Ashram started to grow and those two buildings are still at the heart of the present day Osho International Commune. This stable and ample space allowed for the regular audio and video recording of his discourses and later printing for worldwide distribution, which allowed him to reach far larger audiences internationally.

The U.S. Chapter: In 1981, Rajneesh was taken to the United States in search of better medical care (he suffered from diabetes and severe back problems) and also, allegedly, to escape tax evasion charges in India. His followers, at his request, bought (for US$6 million) a ranch in Wasco County, Oregon, previously known as "The Big Muddy", but later renamed Rajneeshpuram where they settled for the next several years.

Disagreements over zoning rules and building codes in the beginning continued to escalate between not only his followers and the inhabitants of Wasco County, but eventually with the rest of the state. His followers, known as Rajneeshees, settled *en bloc* in Antelope, Oregon, and were able to elect a majority of the town council. They did this after the previously valid legal incorporation of Rajneeshpuram as a city was invalidated by the Oregon Legislature's setting new standards of incorporation and making them retroactive.

Comments by his public spokeswoman, Ma Anand Sheela, only increased tensions. Matters were not helped by Rajneesh's vow of silence, or the 93 Rolls-Royces his followers bought him as gifts-they said that he wanted 365 cars so that he had a new one for each day of the year (technically, he did not have income or own any property). One of his followers explains this in what is called "Face to Faith Parable of the Rolls Royces." When the Rajneeshees subsequently recruited homeless people from across the United States to settle at Rajneeshpuram, it was widely seen as an attempt to use the ballot box to seize control of Wasco County.

At the same time the commune offered an international refuge for his followers to live Osho's teaching; the ideal of meditating, celebrating, and trusting in love. At its largest, Rajneeshpuram consisted of some 7,000 members on a 6.25-square-mile ranch 20 miles from Antelope. It included homes, meditation centers, its own road system, power grid, bus service, schools for children, and even a small airport.

In 1984, a bioterrorist attack involving salmonella typhimurium contamination in the salad bars of the 10 restaurants at The Dalles, Oregon, was traced to the Rajneeshee group. The attack sickened about 750 people and hospitalized forty-five; none died. It was the first known bioterrorist attack of the 20th century in the United States, and is still known as the largest germ warfare attack in the U.S. Eventually Sheela and Ma Anand Puja, one of Sheela's close associates, confessed to the salmonella attack and to attempted poisonings on county officials.

While these controversial events brought much negative publicity to the commune, it is worth noting that Osho himself spoke strongly against these acts, and that it was only a handful of people who were responsible out of the thousands of people who were living in the communce either permanently or temporarily. Osho never apologized to any of the victims of the germ attack, which was orchestrated by his own hand picked disciples. Some of the victims were women and small children.

In May 1985, Sheela called a meeting of Rajneesh's inner circle to plot the assassination of Charles Turner, the U.S. Attorney for Oregon, after the attorney was appointed to head a grand jury investigation into the commune. Catherine Jane Stubbs, known as Ma Shanti Bhadra, volunteered to be the killer. She later bought weapons and scouted Turner's property.

In September 1985, Sheela quit her post as Rajneesh's secretary, and fled to Europe, allegedly with a large piece of the commune's money. After she and twenty of her confederates left, Rajneesh called for an investigation of what she had been doing, during which some of the foregoing came to light.

In late October 1985, Rajneesh was arrested in North Carolina as he was allegedly fleeing the U.S. Though his lawyers had approached the federal grand jury in Portland, Oregon that was about to secretly indict Rajneesh and some of his followers for alleged immigration crimes, and offered for him to be available to them, that offer was refused. Soon after, a Wasco County grand jury returned indictments against Sheela and two others, charging them with the attempted murder of Swami Devaraj, Bhagwan's personal doctor. Rajneesh on advice of his lawyers entered an "Alford plea," or no-contest plea, in regard to the immigration crimes, and was given a suspended sentence on condition that he leave the country.

Back in Pune: On January 19, 1990 four years after his arrest, Osho died, with "heart failure" being the publicly reported cause. Osho claimed that his rapid health decline leading to his death was caused by his poisoning with the element thallium by US authorities while he was in prison. He claimed a plot led by the CIA and Ronald Reagan to assassinate him had been carried out due to their fear of Osho's controversial and counter-cultural teachings combined with his powerful ability to influence people. There has never been any evidence to support this claim, which is contradicted by the fact that thallium poisoning causes dramatic hair loss within one week of exposure. Osho never experienced any abnormal hair loss and he died with a full beard.

Osho was chronically ill most of his adult life and he was exceptionally sensitive to smells and chemicals, a condition known as "multiple chemical sensitivity." Those wishing to meet him were first sniffed by helpers to make sure they were not wearing perfume. It was widely reported that he was addicted to the prescription drug Valium in the 1980s and was a heavy user of nitrous oxide gas. On the CBS television show *60 Minutes*, Ma Anand Sheela claimed that Rajneesh took sixty milligrams of Valium every day. When questioned by journalists about this allegation, however, Osho categorically denied it, adding that Sheela was in no position to know what medication he was given, this being a matter between him and his personal physician.

In a 1998 preface to *Books I Have Loved*, Osho's personal dentist, Swami Devageet, states that Osho dictated three books under the influence of nitrous oxide. They were *Glimpses of a Golden Childhood*, *Notes of a Madman*, and *Books I Have Loved*. Referring to his own nitrous oxide use, Rajneesh himself stated that "Actually oxygen and nitrogen are basic elements of existence. They can be of much use, but for reasons the politicians have been against chemicals of all kinds, all drugs."

After the Rajneeshpuram commune was abandoned, it was discovered that Rajneesh had installed nitrous oxide spigots in his home by his bedside. This was widely reported in newspapers and verified first hand by the FBI and former Oregon Congressman Jim Weaver, who wrote the following in a newspaper article.

> *"A few years later, I went through the abandoned city of Rajneeshpuram and saw things that were almost unbelievable. Ma Anand Sheela's headquarters, a group of mobile homes pieced together, was a hive of secret doors and hidden tunnels, her private room a command post with electronic listening gear tapped into every room in the development. The Bhagwan's parquet-paneled quarters had nitrogen oxide spigots by his bedside, and was surrounded by huge bathrooms with multiple showers." -Jim Weaver*

Osho was 58 years old when he died. His ashes were placed in a reconstructed meditation hall, at his last home place, his Ashram in Pune, India. The epitaph reads, "OSHO. Never Born, Never Died. Only Visited this Planet Earth between Dec 11, 1931-Jan 19, 1990."

Legacy of Rajneesh or Osho: Whatever the posthumous discussion regarding him endevors to establish/contradict about him, he arguably remains the single uncontested, most prolific and intriguing Indian export to date which as a matter of fact is easily observable in the city of Pune (India) where even after sixteen years since his death people untiringy continue flocking his Ashram/commune. The magnitude and extent of his formidable ability to capture popular imagination is also fathomed when one is encountered with a breathtaking fact that all these regular tides of desciples (mostly western)keep trickling in to this abovementioned commune, not due to the magnitism or charm of any of his successor or heir, because there as a matter of fact is/are none, but is solely attributable to the pure undisputed brilliance of the man which through his recorded words/discourses and teachings/philosophies still manages to cast a spell without its most necessary catalyst, his own presence. What is to be explored is not his morality but this rare phenomenon because every person has his own different notions of morality and every version of this subjective analysis would be as moral as much amoral. What is to be explored is the mind-boggling genius of the man.

His marketing strategy also contributed to his exponential popularity as he represented himself as an embodiment of the 'Ancient Indian Mystyiec' with both classical and scientific relevance & applicability. His intrigue not only survives todays Competitive Spiritual Market of India but still retains the tradmark rajneesh ingredient its 'Characteristic Difference' and surprisingly after Sixteen Years of him, without him.

The Philosophy of Jiddu Krishnamurti

Truth is a pathless land "I maintain that truth is a pathless land, and you cannot approach it by any path whatsoever, by any religion, by any sect. That is my point of view, and I adhere to that absolutely and unconditionally. Truth, being limitless, unconditioned, unapproachable by any path whatsoever, cannot be organized; nor should any organization be formed to lead or to coerce people along any particular path. If you first understand that, then you will see how impossible it is to organize a belief. A belief is purely an individual matter, and you cannot and must not organize it. If you do, it becomes dead, crystallized; it becomes a creed, a sect, a religion, to be imposed on others "*J. Krishnamurti at the opening day of the annual Star Camp at Ommen, Holland, on the 3rd August 1929, where he dissolved "The Order of the Star in the East" that was founded by his foster mother Annie Besant in 1911 ,then the President of Theosopy Society*

Love of Truth: J. Krishnamurti uses the term "Philosophy" in its etymological sense of the 'love' of 'truth'. To him, philosophy is not a series of theories about life, man and the world. It is not a bundle of ideas, opinions and conclusions. Nor is it the academic discipline of conceiving, criticizing and interpreting concepts. Philosophy is not the speculative or the intellectual activity of system-building. It is not a logical analysis of language and meaning. On the contrary, philosophy, according to Krishnamurti,, is the love of truth. Love means the instantaneous perception. It is understanding which is beyond the intellect. Truth means the life which is undetermined by thought. It means the mind which is unconditioned. Philosophy is living life independently of systems, images, ideals and beliefs. It is living from moment to moment in the total freedom of the mind. It is living in the 'present'. True life is what is happening this instant. It is not what thought or intellect conceives it to be. Philosophy is living inseparably from what is taking place now. It is the art of living life directly and not through theories and words. Direct living is living holistically without the sense of division, conceptual or psychological. It is not a theoretical exercise of avoiding the actuality of life. "It is exactly what the word philosophy means-the love of truth, the love of life. It is not something that you go to the university to learn. We are learning the art of living in our daily life"', says Krishnamurti He observes that philosophy is the understanding of the truth which is beyond the reality of thought. Philosophy is the ending of the illusion of mistaking reality for truth. It is the realization that reality can never become truth. Philosophy is the actual cessation of the ignorance and the irrationality of approaching truth through reality. It is understanding the finitude of reality and going beyond. Krishnamurti says, "philosophy means love of truth, not love of ideas, not love of speculation... And that means you have to find out for yourself where reality is and that reality cannot become truth. You cannot go through reality to come to truth. You must understand the limitations of reality which is the whole process of thought."

Reality and Truth: Krishnamurti distinguishes between reality and truth. Reality is thought which is the movement of the past. It is a psychological-material process. It is necessarily conditioned by a thing or an idea. Thought is always of something, gross or subtle, physical or psychological. It is never independent. Independent thought is a contradiction in teens. Reality is all that is conceived by thought. Reality, as Krishnamurti puts it, "comes from 'res' and that anything that thought operates on, or fabricates or reflects about, is reality" 3 . According to Krishnamurti, the mind or the consciousness with its thought content is reality. The content comprises the factual as well as the psychological knowledge. The factual content is the knowledge which is reasonable and useful for the biological well-being of humankind. It includes the scientific, the technological, the semantic, the numerical and the historical knowledge or information, whereas the psychological content is a messy conglomeration of the irrational and fictitious knowledge. It consists of the illusions-beliefs, hopes, images, symbols-invented by thought as a means of escape from the inward poverty, the psychological insecurity. The psychological content constitutes the mind which is conditioned, fragmented, self-centred, self-contradictory, conflicting, confused, anxious, insecure, jealous, aggressive, corrupt, violent, war-like, crooked and insane. The psychological content of consciousness is the actuality, the fact of human existence. It is with this content that human being has been living for millions of years. Devoid of self-knowing or awareness, the conditioned consciousness determines itself; it generates its own energy; it adds to its content and perpetuates itself to self-destruction. But Krishnamurti does not condemn human reality to its psychological structure which is superficial and acquired. The psychological content is only the name and form and not the true nature of humanity.

He points out, "The uniqueness of the individual does not lie in the superficial but in the total freedom from the content of consciousness". The task of philosophy is to break the continuity of the conditioned consciousness. It is to end the psychological content of the human mind and regenerate it, like the phoenix. 5 Regeneration is the understanding of the truth which is the emptiness of mind. Truth is the mind which does not contain a 'thing' put together by thought. It is freedom which is totally independent of thought. It is the mind which is devoid of the content of division, contradiction, conflict and so on. It is the mind which is whole and sane. Truth is 'nothing'. It is the mind which is nothing or nothingness.

Truth is a Pathless Land: The core of Krishnamurti's philosophy is contained in his statement that truth is a pathless land. It consists in his concern of setting man unconditionally and absolutely free. To him, the understanding of truth is independent of religious institutions and methods. Conforming to spiritual organisations is an impediment to the understanding of truth. Truth cannot be perceived by professing a particular faith. Truth is not a fixed thing. It does not have a predetermined path. Nor does it have a direction. Truth is neither in the past nor in the future. Truth is in the living 'present', the 'now'. And the understanding of it is immediate and direct. Paths or systems involve time. They only condition the mind according to their pet and patent ideas. They programme and 'industrialise' the individual. They can never liberate the mind completely. Total and ultimate liberation is possible only when the mind is entirely independent of all paths. Krishnamurti says, "I maintain that Truth is a pathless land, and you cannot approach it by any path whatsoever, by any religion, by any sect... If an organisation be created for this purpose, it becomes a crutch, a weakness, a bondage, and must cripple the individual, and prevent him from growing, from establishing his uniqueness, which lies in his discovery for himself of that absolute, unconditioned Truth".

The direct discovery of truth requires freedom not only form the paths and methods but also from the teachers, the leaders of the spiritual organisations. Attachment to 'gurus' is a barrier to the direct perception of truth. Dependence on them keeps the seeker in perpetual ignorance. Following implies faith without understanding. Spiritual teachers are generally regarded as the removers of the ignorance of their followers. The classical meaning of the word 'guru' is the dispeller of darkness. But Krishnamurti holds that a 'guru', however much enlightened he may be, cannot put an end to another's ignorance. Because, basically, one alleviating the ignorance of another is out of the question. The very idea is irrational. Each one has to dispel his or her ignorance by oneself. Krishnamurti declares, "You are all depending for your spirituality on some one else... no man from outside can make you free". Nevertheless, the 'gurus' have a little role to play in the communication of truth. A really enlightened person may point out the truth to others. But his indication has little significance if the seeker is not prepared to 'see' the truth. In understanding truth, the intensity of the seeker's passion for truth is of paramount importance. Mere pointing out is not sufficient. It has as little importance as a signpost pointing the way to a particular destiny. Speaking to a spiritual teacher Krishnamurti said, "You might point out the door and say, 'look, go through the door' but each man has to do the work entirely himself".

Communication of truth is not a matter of one giving to another. The division and the image as the one who knows and the one who does not know preclude communication. Communication of truth is possible only when the speaker and the listener meet on the same level at the same time and with the same intensity. It requires a mind which really says, 'I don't know'. A mind with knowledge-ideas, opinions, conclusion can neither understand nor communicate the truth. Truth cannot be monopolised. It cannot be possessed and bartered. Truth can only be shared. Dialogue is the best means of communication. Krishnamurti says, "I think the idea of the teaching and the taught is basically wrong, at least for me. I think it is a matter of sharing rather than being taught, partaking rather than giving and taking".

Choiceless Observation: Choiceless observation or awareness is the crux of Krishnamurti's philosophy of life. To him, choiceless observation is the only 'way', the direct and 'intelligent' way of understanding the truth of 'what is'. It alone can transform the fact, the actuality by revealing its true nature. It is only 'through' it that consciousness can be emptied of its content. Krishnamurti maintains that excepting choiceless awareness, there is no other way of regenerating the human mind and the world irreversibly and instantaneously. Choiceless observation is the observation of 'what is', the fact or the actuality without the movement of thought which is knowledge or past. It is the observation devoid of the observer, the centre, the censor, the 'me' or the thinker which is thought. It is the awareness without the division as the observer and the observed. It is a holistic observation in which the observer 'is' the observed. In it there in no reaction, resistance, justification and condemnation. It is a pure observation sans remembrance, recollection, recognition and naming. It is free from ideas, ideals and opinions. It is observation without prejudice, likes and dislikes. It is without a motive and an end in view.

Choiceless awareness is an understanding in which the previous experience is totally absent. It is 'experiencing' 'what is' without the experiences. It is a 'negative' approach to the fact. It is an awareness in which the psychological past is totally negated. It is the denial of knowledge in understanding. It is a 'passive' awareness without effort. It is a 'silent' observation without the activity of thought. It is 'silence' with which thought does not interfere in any form. According to Krishnamurti, the negative and the passive approach is the most active and positive one. It alone leads to the absolute certainty which is truth. Scepticism is the basis of true spirituality. Choiceless awareness is not understanding the fact from a particular point of view. It is not moulding it according to a preconceived conclusion. It is not fitting 'what is' into the framework of a system. It does not involve intellectualisation, interpretation, explanation or theorisation. Nor does it warrant analysis or introspection. Choiceless awareness is 'perceiving' the fact without translating it to knowledge. This awareness is not evolutionary. It is not a 'progressive' or a gradual understanding of 'what is' by accumulating knowledge about it. It is not movement from the past to the future, but it is 'seeing' the fact without distorting and dividing it. It is 'remaining with' 'what is' without moving away from it. It is the complete attention of holding the totality of 'what is', like a vessel holding water. Total attention generates the energy that regenerates 'what is'.

Choiceless observation is an experimental approach of allowing 'what is' to reveal itself as it exactly and essentially is. It is an unpremeditated art of 'looking' at 'what is' directly and wholly. It is a non-verbal and non-conceptual understanding. It is an acausal and a timeless 'insight' into 'what is'. Insight is the comprehension of the truth of 'what is', in a 'flash'. "The insight is not analysis, time, remembrance, all that. It is the immediate perception of something". It is an absolute observation of allowing the 'what is' to 'flower' freely and fully. The spontaneous and total flowering of the 'what is' is the ending of its bondage. "Truth is when there is the realisation that the observer is the observed. Then, in that realisation, which is truth, the conditioning disappears".

The Ending of Sorrow: The understanding of the truth, viz., the 'nothingness' of oneself is the ending of sorrow. Human being has been suffering for millions of years. Human consciousness is a stream of sorrow, since it is ridden with division, conflict, fear, anxiety, etc. Suffering is universal and not individualistic. Individual is a part of the humanity which is caught in the net of suffering. Individual consciousness is not different from the consciousness of humanity. Krishnamurti says, "My consciousness is the consciousness of man; it is the consciousness of humanity because man suffers, he is proud, cruel, anxious, unkind, this is the common ground ... That is the psychological structure of man".

Fundamentally, suffering is due to the ignorance of oneself, one's true nature, viz., the 'emptiness'. There are other kinds of suffering which are the outcome of the ignorance of not knowing oneself fundamentally and irrevocably. There is the sorrow of poetry, attachment, detachment, insecurity, responsibility, abandonment, decease and death. Krishnamurti says that sorrow can be ended by being aware of it totally. Sorrow is to be faced without explaining it away by theories. It can be resolved by perceiving the enormous sorrow of the humanity without being caught in one's own little sorrow. Personal sorrow of losing one's kith or kin involves loneliness and self pity. Getting caught in it is an impediment to the awareness of sorrow as such. Observing human sorrow without choice and remaining 'with' it without any movement of thought puts an end to suffering as a whole.

Freedom: Freedom is not choice which is the movement of thought. The free and intelligent mind does not choose. Only the conditioned and confused one chooses. Freedom is not an abstraction. It is action devoid of conditioning and contradiction. Freedom is the same as the truth. It is the nothingness of the mind It is the mind which is empty of its psychological content, the 'known', which is put together by thought. It is the cessation of the messy-and the chaotic consciousness which is self-centred, self-contradictory and the source of sorrow. Freedom is the mind which is the 'Unknown'. The free mind is devoid of the centre, the 'me' and the circumference, the limitation. It is without boundaries. It is infinite, eternal, global and holistic. It is absolutely stable and orderly. Its order and stability are not determined by thought. The free mind is one with the Cosmos. Cosmos means stability and order. The free mind is a meditative mind. Meditation is not the process of thought. It is not a concentration on a fixed goal. It is not a means to an end. Meditation is the movement of the mind in the stability and the order of the Universe. The free mind is truly religious. It is truly secular as well. It does not belong to any religion or nation. Truth is its 'spirit'. World is its home. The free mind is full of love. Love is compassion. Compassion is passion for all. To love is to be 'alone'. Alone means all are one. To be alone is to be one with all.

Love is 'intelligence'. Intelligence means reading between the lines. It uses the physical or the factual knowledge for strictly the biological well-being of humanity. It understands the limitations of thought. It does not allow thought to enter the realm where it has no place. Intelligence guides thought and not vice versa. Thought is essentially a physical and chemical process. Intelligence is truth which is truly spiritual. It is sacred and holy. Intelligence is creative while thought is mechanical. Being limited, thought must inevitably create the problems. And it cannot solve the problems it creates. Intelligence is the freedom which is not the product of time and environment. It alone solves the plight brought about by thought and knowledge-the conditioned consciousness.

The Only Revolution: Regression of the mind is the regeneration of the society. The society we live in is not different from the nature of our mind and the quality of life. It cannot be different from the individuals who constitute it. As is the mind so is the individual. As is the individual so is the society. Society is the relationship of the individuals. Mind is the basis of the relationships. The psychological structure of the individuals constitutes the society. Society is the spectacular manifestation of the mind. It is the outward expression of the individuals' inner being. The mind and the society constitute a single movement, like the ebb and flow of the wave. The actual content of them is one and the same. The crisis in the society is the crisis in consciousness. The separation between the two is an illusion. Because consciousness is divided, the society is ridden with the problems like endless division, conflict, violence and war. Poverty, over-population, environmental degradation, nuclear holocaust are the result of the crisis in the mind. Therefore the real change of the society absolutely requires the change of the mind. Krishnamurti says, "You and the world are not two different entities. You 'are' the world, not as an ideal, but actually... As the world is yourself, in the transformation of yourself you produce a transformation in society".

Radical change in the society cannot be brought about by any other way except by the absolute change in the mind. The mind is the centre of the society. Unless there is change at the centre, there will be no change at the periphery. Social change is not possible through ideologies,-economic, political or religious. It is not possible through the change of the governments. It does not come after a planning or a blueprint. Governmental change is no change at all. Social change cannot be effected through philanthropy either. Neither humanism nor humanitarianism can change the society radically. The timeless transformation of the mind 'through' choiceless awareness is the only way of changing the society. The realisation of the feet that there is no other way of changing the society except by changing oneself, one's mind, brings about the change in the mind. Insight into the fact that "I am the world and the world is 'me' regenerates the mind. Choiceless awareness of the quality of the relationships empties the mind of its psychological content. Freedom of the mind should be the foundation of a sane society. As already mentioned, the free mind is truth. Truth is love. Love alone transforms men and his society. Love is without the 'centre', the 'me'. It is 'nothingness'. For it, far is near. There is no division as mine and shine. Love is the only panacea for all the ills of the society. Krishnamurti says, "There is only one fundamental revolution. This revolution is not of idea; it is not based on any pattern of action. The revolution comes into being when the need for using another ceases. This transformation is not an abstraction, a thing to be wished for, but an actuality which can be experienced as we begin to understand the way of our relationship. This fundamental revolution may be called love; it is the only creative factor in bringing about transformation in ourselves and so in soeicty".

In Listening is Transformation: Krishnamurti does not have philosophical tradition. He does not have a philosophical predecessor. He did not identify himself with any thinker or any school of thought. Just as truth, he was an 'anonymous' and a 'free' thinker. He learned about life by direct observation. He studied the book of life as a whole; 'within' and 'without'-mind, man and Nature. He said, "I am not a Vedantist, a Buddhist, a Muslim. And I watch, I observe what is happening around me. I observe what is happening inside me".

Krishnamurti's teachings are not reactions to any school of philosophy. They are not a modified version of any theory. Nor are they an integrated system of several other religious, philosophical and psychological theories. They are not a propaganda of any idea. They are not meant to convince anybody of anything. Their aim is not to persuade anybody to accept a particular point of view. Krishnamurti's teachings are neither disputatious nor didactic. They are not the intellectual understanding of life. To him intellectual understanding is no understanding. His teachings are the outcome of his direct perception of truth. They are the expressions of the truth he realised independently. They are 'commentaries' on living. Krishnamurti says, "I have merely attempted to put into words that manner of realisation".

Krishnamurti's philosophy is not a consistent system. He has not presented it in the form of a treatise. Truth eludes systems and treatises. Consistency is not its measure. Krishnamurti has offered his philosophy in the form of talks, dialogues and discourses he had with people of all walks of life-intellectuals, scientists, politicians, psychologists, philosophers and the common man. His talks, dialogues and discourses are the inward journeys into the actuality and the truth of oneself and the world. Through them he merely pointed out the truth to others. He never considered himself a 'guru'. He did not act as an authority. He rejected following and devotion from people. Believing truth without understanding leads to misery. He asked those who wanted to understand him or the truth to be free from him. He advised to use him as a 'crutch'. To him, listening is more important than teaching. Attentive listening without the image about oneself and the speaker is necessary for understanding the truth. Listening to Krishnamurti, without choice, brings about a radical change in the mind, in the brain cells. Transformation is possible in the very act of listening. He said, "If you listen to me, that is your transformation. That listening is listening to truth".

Krishnamurti on Solitude: Jiddu Krishnamurti (1895-1986) was a unique figure in twentieth century thought. Born in India and educated in England, Krishnamurti reflects a confluence of Eastern and Western thinking unmatched by any similar contemporary except, perhaps, Gandhi.

Krishnamurti's Western style is evidenced in his tightly organized prose, which relentlessly pursues a given theme or topic. At times he is Socratic in his push for clarity and sometimes he is a rationalist in his Cartesian doubt and his analytical frame of mind.

But Krishnamurti is also, as an Eastern thinker, aware of a tradition of spirituality not dependent on a given system or religion. This perennial thinking underlies much of his work. Krishnamurti's concepts of consciousness, mind, emptiness, and the unmasking of culture and institutions are all strengthened by the insights of the East. The medley of Western methodology and Eastern wisdom is felicitous and rewarding.

Within Krishnamurti's thought, solitude has its place as a methodological tool. Here he anticipates Western psychology while borrowing from Eastern tradition. We know that solitude has little place in the historical philosophy of the West, except among mystics. But Krishnamurti "rescues" solitude from mysticism and makes solitude available to all. Of course, he has seen its efficacy in Eastern traditions, but here there is little trace of solitude as strictly Eastern. This is notable because Krishnamurti is developing these themes as early as the 1930's, before Western audiences, when Westerners still knew little about Eastern thought and even less were they applying it to philosophy.

We can follow Krishnamurti's train of thought concerning solitude by beginning with what he calls "sensitivity." In *Life Ahead*, Krishnamurti explains the context.

Sensitivity means being sensitive to everything around one — to the plants, the animals, the trees, the skies, the waters of the river, the bird on the wing; and also the moods of the people around one, and to the stranger who passes by. This sensitivity brings about the quality of inculcated, unselfish, response, which is true morality and conduct.

Buddhist tradition has identified this virtue as compassion, the origin of which is in mindfulness. Krishnamurti points to it as a methodology for dispelling the arbitrariness of culture and authority. Other traditions will root this virtue in metaphysics or define it as the essence of morality. But from the point of view of Krishnamurti's philosophy and psychology — not Western but not merely Eastern, either — mindfulness or sensitivity is a prerequisite to knowledge of self.

For the total development of the human being, solitude as a means of cultivating sensitivity becomes a necessity. One has to know what it is to be alone, what it is to meditate, what it is to die; and the implications of solitude, of meditation, of death, can be known only by seeking them out.

Krishnamurti points out not only the path of solitude as a necessity to enlightenment but also the necessity of experience rather than ritual or doctrine external to oneself. How much solitude? How much meditation? That is exactly for the individual to discover, not awaiting authority to sanction it or persuade the individual to pursue it.

Solitude cannot be brought about by instruction, or urged by the external authority of tradition, or induced by the influence of those who want to sit quietly but are incapable of being alone. Solitude helps the mind to see itself clearly, as in a mirror, and to free itself from the vain endeavor of ambition with all its complexities, fears, and frustrations, which are the outcome of self-centered activity.

This freedom from personal vanities cultivates a better self, a universal self. One need not be a moralist to witness the fuller humanity that unfolds in such a process. It has great fruits for the individual returning to society.

Solitude gives to the mind a stability, a constancy, which is not to be measured in terms of time. Such clarity of mind is character. The lack of character is the state of self-contradiction.

Krishnamurti is not proposing solitude for hermits and solitaries. He is proposing solitude as a method, for everyone. The result of this process is "character," or integrity, the very heart of the person, especially in a social setting. He is distinguishing solitude from isolation and from what he calls the "cultivation of detachment," (as in, presumably, Stoicism). Instead, Krishnamurti sees solitude as aloneness, but aloneness as that condition distinct from and separate from culture. We may call it alienation in existential terms, but it means separation from the social contrivances and accretions of oppressive culture around us. If we can rid ourselves of all that is merely dependent on culture, says Krishnamurti, we can become alone, yes, but also free.

You are never alone because you are full of all the memories, all the conditioning, all the muttering of yesterday; your mind is never clear of all the rubbish it has accumulated. To be alone you must die to the past. When you are alone, totally alone, not belonging to any family, any nation, any culture, any particular continent, there is the sense of being an outsider.

The word "outsider" is reminiscent of Albert Camus' *L'estranger*, the novel sometimes translated as "outsider" or "stranger." This status is alienation from culture that is not (yet) at a fruitful stage. (This is also reminiscent of Thomas Merton's use of existentialism in his *Notes Towards a Philosophy of Solitude*). For Krishnamurti such a person would achieve "innocence," which is the beginning of a mind "free from sorrow."

We carry about us the burden of what thousands of people have said and the memories of all our misfortunes. To abandon all that is to be alone, and the mind that is alone is not only innocent but young — not in time or age, but young, innocent, alive at whatever age — and only such a mind can see that which is truth and that which is not measurable by words.

Krishnamurti wants the individual to open the mind to the true nature of itself and the universe, and to use solitude to begin to accomplish the task of self-knowledge. While his concept of solitude appears utilitarian, Krishnamurti wisely sees that everyone — hermit or civil servant — has the task of discovering their true nature, and will benefit from the practice of solitude. For in this sense of aloneness, we disclose the essential, and the universe itself discloses it to us at every moment.

❑❑❑

BIBLIOGRAPHY

Women in Buddhism: Images of the Feminine in the Mahayana Tradition: *Berkeley: University of California Press, 1984*

Schools of Indian Philosophical Thought. Calcutta: *Firma K. L. Mukhopadhyay, 1973*

A Source Book in Indian Philosophy: *Princeton: Princeton University Press, 1957*

What the Buddha Taught: *Bedford, England: Gordon Fraser, 1967.*

The Three Jewels: *Anchor Press, New York 1970.*

A Critical Survey of Indian Philosophy: *Rider, London, 1960*

Indian Philosophy of Language: *Dordrecht: Kulwer Academic Press, 1991*

The Vedanta and Modern Thought: *Oxford University Press, 1928*

Walters, John. *The Essence of Buddhism.* New York: Apollo, 1964.

The Bhagavadgita with a Commentary Based on the Original Sources: *Oxford University Press, 1969*

Philosophies of India: *Princeton University Press, Princeton, 1968*

Buddhist Scriptures: A Bibliography: *Lewis Lancaster, New York, Garland, 1982*

Guide to the Buddhist Religion , Boston: G. K. Hall, 1981

The Yogacara School of Buddhism: A Bibliography: *Scarecrow Press, 1991.*

Bibliograpy on Buddhism: *Tokyo, 1961*

Books on Buddhism: An Annotated Subject Guide: *Scarecrow Press, 1976*

The Way of the Buddha: *New Delhi, Government of India, Publications Division, 1956*

The Life ot the Buddha: Murals in the Buddhaisawan Chapel National Museum, Bangkok, Thailand: *Bangkok, Fine Arts Department, 1972*

Amaravati: Buddhist Sculpture from the Great Stupa: *London, British Museum Press, 1992*

Iconographical Dictionary of the Indian Religions: Hinduism, Buddhism, Jainism (Leiden: Brill, 1976).

Buddhism in Translations: *New York: Atheneum, 1963*

Encyclopedia of Buddhism: *Colombo, Government of Sri Lanka, 1961*

Buddhism and Human Rights: *London, Curzon, 1998*

2500 Years of Buddhism: *New Delhi: Government of1*

India, Publications Division, 1956

A Source Book in Indian Philosophy: *Princeton University Press, 1989*

Indian Philosophy: A Very Short Introduction: *Oxford University Press, 2001*

Indian Philosophy: The Concept of Karma: *Dehli/Varanasi: Bharatiya Vidya Prakashan, 1982*

Philosophy in Classical India: The Proper Work of Reason: *London: Routledge, 2001*

The Central Philosophy of Buddhism: *Honolulu: University of Hawaii, 1975*

Reason and Tradition in Indian Thought: an essay on the nature of Indian philosophical thinking: *Clarendon Press; New York: Oxford University Press, 1992*

Hinduism: A Very Short Introduction: *Oxford: Oxford University Press, 1998*

Advaita Vedanta: A Philosophical Introduction: *Honolulu: The University of Hawaii, 1969*

Indian Philosophy: The Concept of Karma: *Dehli/Varanasi: Bharatiya Vidya Prakashan, 1982*

The Heyapaksha of Yoga, or Towards a Constructive Synthesis of Psychological Material in Indian Philosophy: *Ahmedabad 1931*

The Structure of Indian Thought: *Illinois: Charles C. Thomas Publisher, 1970*

Grace of God and Guru :In Sikh Philosophy: *S.P. Sondhi. Delhi, Global Vision, 2002*

Spirit of the Sikh: *Part II Volume Two. Punjabi University, Patiala, 1981*

Guide to the Hindu Religion. Boston: *G.K. Hall, 1981*

Popular Hinduism and Hindu Mythology: An Annotated Bibliography: *Westport, CT: Greenwood, 1979*

Sikhism and the Sikhs: An Annotated Bibliography: *Westport, CT: Greenwood, 1989*

Encyclopedia of Eastern Philosophy and Religion: Buddhism, Hinduism, Taoism, and Zen: *Boston, Shambhala, 1989*

Popular Dictionary of Sikhism: *London: Curzon; Glen Dale, MD: Riverdale, 1990*

Iconographic Dictionary of the Indian Religions: Hinduism - Buddhism - Jainism: *Leiden: Brill, 1976.*

Illustrated Dictionary of Hindu Iconography: *London: Routledge and Kegan Paul, 1985*

Discovering Islam: Making Sense of Muslim History and Society: *New York: Routledge, revised ed., 2002*

The New Encyclopedia of Islam: *Lanham, MD: AltaMira Press, 2003*

Islam: An Introduction: *Albany, NY: State University of New York*

The Spirit of Islam: A History of the Evolution and Ideals of Islam, with a Life of the Prophet: *London: Chatto & Windus, 1978*

Following Muhammad: Rethinking Islam in the Contemporary World: *Chapel Hill, NC: University of North Carolina Press, 2003*

The Traditions of I: lam: An Introduction to the Study of Hadith Literature: *Oxford, UK: Clarendon Press, 1924*

Hinduism, a Cultural Perspective: *Englewood Cliffs, N.J Prentice-Hall, 1982.*

The Christ and the Bodhisattva: *State University of New York Press, 1987.*

How To Know God: The Yoga Sutras of Patanjali: *New York: New American Library, 1953*

The Hindu Temple: An Introduction to Its Meaning and Forms: *Chicago: University of Chicago Press, 1988*

Caste In India: *Oxford: Oxford University Press, 1951.*

Siddhartha: *Hilda Rosner, trans, New Directions, 1951.*

Ethics of India: *New Haven, CT: Yale University Press, 1924.*

Pali Dhamma: vornehmlich in der kanonischen Literature: *Bavarian Academy of Sciences, 1920.*

The Ramayana and the Mhabharata: *J. M. Dent & Sons, 1910*

Hindu Manners, Customs and Ceremonies: *Oxford University Press, 1906*

Gandhi's Religious Thought: *Notre Dame University Press, 1986*

Buddhism, Sexuality, and Gender: *State University of New York Press, 1992*

INDEX

F

G

H

I

J

K

L

M

N

O

P

Q

R

S

T

U

V

W

Z

***